MONEY, BANKING
and the CANADIAN
FINANCIAL SYSTEM

Money, Banking and the Canadian Financial System

H. H. Binhammer

METHUEN

toronto london sydney wellington

Library of Congress Catalogue Card Number 68-8669
SBN 458 94920 5

Printed and Bound in Canada

2 3 4 5 6 7 8 9 74 73 72 71 70 69

to my wife

MARY

my daughter

JANE

and her grandmothers

CONTENTS

PART TWO

COMMERCIAL BANKING

PART FOUR

CENTRAL BANKING AND MONETARY CONTROL

PREFACE

If I were to select one sentence to describe the approach taken in writing this book, I would borrow this sentence from Sir John Hicks: "Money is not a mechanism; it is an institution, one of the most remarkable of human institutions."[1] This book is about Canadian institutions. It is written primarily for students with a background of at least one introductory course in the principles of economics.

Part One is historical and describes the lineage of Canadian monetary and financial institutions and the social framework in which these institutions were conceived and nurtured.

Part Two deals with commercial banks, the tallest among the forest of private financial institutions. However, since non-bank financial intermediaries have grown in number and have undertaken many functions considered the traditional preserve of the banks, they too occupy a distinctive place in this book — Part Three.

Parts Four and Five are concerned with monetary control, its *raison d'être* and its management. Cognizance is taken not only of the role of the central bank, but also of government asset and debt management. The first five parts of the book focus on the money supply. Chapter 18 in Part Five, "The Theory and Determinants of the Money Supply," attempts to synthesize the material discussed in the preceding chapters.

In Part Six, attention is directed from a description of institutions to a discussion on monetary theory. A survey is made of the various theoretical positions that have been taken in describing the role of money in the economy. No attempt is made to deal with all the various aspects of

---

[1] Hicks, Sir John, *Critical Essays in Monetary Theory*, Oxford, Oxford University Press, 1967, p. 59.

macroeconomics since there now are many good texts in this field. Instead, attention is focused on the term structure of interest rates and the effectiveness of monetary policy; these topics are not treated with as much detail in traditional books on money and banking.

In Part Seven, the focus changes from the domestic economy to the international economy, dealing with both historical and theoretical aspects.

Finally, Part Eight presents a brief survey of the use of monetary policy since the founding of the Bank of Canada in 1934.

The book makes a rather broad sweep. Many of the descriptive and historical chapters need not take up much classroom time, but can be assigned as reading for the student. Moreover, some of the more difficult theoretical chapters may be omitted without destroying the continuity of the book. Because money and banking courses now offered at Canadian Universities are very diverse in nature, it is impossible to write a text which presents a menu desired by each and every class.

I owe a great debt of gratitude to Professors David Slater of Queen's University, Craig McIvor of McMaster University and Alasdair Sinclair of Dalhousie University, who read the original manuscript and made valuable suggestions. Also to George Post at the Bank of Canada who read parts of the manuscript.

I wish to thank my colleagues at the Royal Military College of Canada for their perseverance and constant support — J. P. Cairns, M. D. Chaudhry, J. Treddenick, J. D. C. Boulakia, C. W. Newcombe and I. A. Graham. Credit must also be given to John Spurr and his efficient library staff, and to the Gentlemen Cadets who suffered through many drafts of the manuscript in my classes.

Mary, my wife, deserves the greatest share of my gratitude for her unfailing support, encouragement and patience. She and Loro Raymond shared the task of typing the manuscript to the standards demanded by my most helpful publishers. Robert De Clute drew the diagrams.

Alas, while credit must be given to all those who have assisted me, I alone must be held responsible for shortcomings and errors.

The Royal Military College of Canada — H. H. Binhammer
June, 1968

PART ONE

MONEY AND MONETARY STANDARDS

1

THE FUNCTIONS AND EVOLUTION OF MONEY

THE NATURE AND FUNCTIONS OF MONEY

There is probably no subject more talked about than money. But what is money? Anything can serve as money as long as it performs monetary functions. Therefore, to answer the question "what is money?" is to answer the question "what are the functions of money?". Monetary functions include service as a medium of exchange, as a store of value, as a standard of value and as a standard for deferred payment. Money, then, is anything which performs these functions and which is therefore generally accepted in payment of debt or of goods and services rendered.

A STANDARD UNIT OF ACCOUNT

In a barter economy one good is exchanged for another which, in turn, may be exchanged for yet another, and so on. The terms of exchange depend upon the value placed on the goods by those entering into the exchange. The primitive way of establishing values was to compare the sizes of the things to be exchanged. Thus the value of one cow may be expressed as two goats or one hundred bushels of wheat.

The ratios of exchange between goods express their prices. The number of ratios of exchange for any given number of goods can be derived readily by the simple formula

$$\frac{n^2 - n}{2}$$

where *n* is the number of goods. In our example the price of a cow is two goats or one hundred bushels of wheat. With one hundred goods we would have 4,950 different prices in a strictly barter economy. To have an efficient system of exchange it would be necessary for everyone to operate like an electronic computer. Fortunately, there is an alternative: the introduction of a standard unit of account. In a monetary economy money performs this function.

We have said that price is a ratio of exchange. In a barter economy there are as many prices for bread, the numerator of our ratio, as there are items which provide the denominator. If we select just one item to provide a common denominator for all ratios of exchange for bread, we have only one price for bread. Anything can serve as a common denominator or "numeraire" in our equation of exchange.

In a monetary economy money provides us with a common denominator. With it serving as a standard unit of account each good has just one price which is reckoned in terms of money. Money acts as a yardstick or standard value to which everything can be compared.

A unit of account can be a purely abstract phenomenon. For instance, an ounce or a pound, an inch or a foot, are abstract units of account. Historically, however, while the weight and measure of things have been in terms of abstract units of account, the value of things has been reckoned in terms of physical units. In early Canada beaver skins served as the standard measure of value. Today we use the dollar. We can think of the dollar as a purely abstract unit of account, as is usually done by the accountant, or we can think of it in physical or nominal terms as is the case when we hand over a dollar Bank of Canada note (a dollar bill) in settlement of a debt amounting to one dollar.

A MEDIUM OF EXCHANGE

Without money to provide a generally acceptable medium of exchange, the only means of trade available is barter. An example will show that this is a cumbersome and inefficient process. If a farmer wants to exchange his cow for a horse, he must first find someone who wants to sell a horse. Even then he cannot enter into an exchange unless this person also wants to buy a cow. In other words, direct exchange can take place only when there is a **double coincidence of wants.** Without this double coincidence of wants our farmer must engage in a long series of intermediate transactions which will finally lead to the acquisition of a horse for a cow. This very inefficient process of trade is overcome in an economy where money serves as a medium of exchange, and where the farmer with a cow can sell it for money. He is then in a position to exchange the money for a horse even if the seller of the horse does not want to buy a cow.

Money provides generalized purchasing power insofar as it is a "bearer of options". The freedom which a generally accepted medium of exchange provides has been the very foundation of our modern democratic and capitalistic system. Moreover, this kind of freedom has been necessary for the efficient mobilization of all our resources. When the possibilities of trade are limited to barter, each family unit tends to strive for self-sufficiency, with the result that production advantages of occupational specialization and division of labour cannot be effectively exploited. Furthermore, without money a worker must be paid for his services in kind. Waste (the inefficient allocation of resources) is the result of such payment. The worker probably cannot use all the goods he receives and may not be able to exchange them immediately for those he wants; therefore he must store the bulk of them until he is able to use or exchange them.

A STANDARD OF DEFERRED PAYMENT

As soon as money comes into general use as a measure of value and a medium of exchange, it inevitably serves as a measure in terms of which deferred or future payments are stated. A future payment could be reckoned in terms of a cow, a horse or one hundred bushels of wheat, but again this brings us back to all the disadvantages encountered in a society that lacks a standard unit of account and a generally acceptable medium of exchange.

A STORE OF VALUE

Money is but one of the many things which may serve as a store of value. Precious stones, land, buildings, stocks, bonds, to mention only a few, are also stores of value. These things of value which we hold are called assets. But money is a very special kind of asset for it is immediately acceptable in exchange for goods and services. Because of this quality we call money a **liquid asset.** It provides us with a store of value which represents both instant and generalized purchasing power.

When we hold anything as a store of wealth we expect it to have certain qualities. It should be readily exchangeable for other goods and services when the need or desire arises; it should not lose value over time.[1] We also expect a cost or return to result from holding wealth in certain types of assets. If a person carries his wealth in the form of money in his pocket he may receive a return in the form of peace of mind. The cost to him is the interest rate he would receive if he were to hold his money on deposit with a financial institution. In a later part of this book we shall concern ourselves with the community's motives for holding money assets rather than other assets as a store of value.

---

[1] Money has not always maintained this quality. The economist speaks of two kinds of value — **nominal** value and **real** value. Money is a perfect store of nominal value because it retains its original identity. For instance, a dollar is a dollar, tomorrow as well as today. By real value we mean purchasing power and when we say that money has not always served as a good store of value we refer to its real value which has changed over time.

THE EVOLUTION AND KINDS OF MONEY

We cannot speak of the origin of money as an historically unique event because it was not invented once and for all at one time and in one place. The development of money reflects the existence of a social need and the availability and acceptability first of commodities and later of debt instruments to meet that need.

COMMODITY MONEY

Cattle and Articles of Common Use

The first type of money of which we have knowledge is commodity money and its first function was to provide a standard unit of account. In the early pastoral societies everything was valued in terms of cattle which were a symbol of wealth and prestige. It was only after their use as a standard unit of account that they also came to serve as a medium of exchange and a store of value. The use of cattle as money had inherent weaknesses. There was, for instance, no standard cow, bull or ox. Moreover, because cattle are not divisible, small transactions could not be made. On the other hand, for large payments, a herd of oxen constituted a rather difficult method of settlement if payment were to be made some distance away. As a store of value cattle were only as good as their life expectancy. To overcome all these weaknesses cattle were first supplemented and later replaced by articles of common use such as cloth, axes, hoes and fishhooks. The virtual disappearance of the use of cattle as money did not occur without leaving a lasting reminder. The word "pecuniary" is derived from *pecus* the Latin word for cattle, and "fee" comes from the Old English *feoh* (cognate of the German *vieh),* also meaning cattle. Today cattle and goats are still used as a measure of value by the Dinka people of the southern Sudan.

Metals

The transition from cattle to metals was slow. The use of copper, iron, silver and gold can be traced back as far as 5000 B.C. Metals became preferred over other commodities because they contained certain essential characteristics. They were relatively homogeneous, easily recognizable, highly durable, readily portable and divisible into any size. Metals had the additional advantage that a high intrinsic value could be placed upon them. A few ounces of gold or silver could be exchanged for large units of other goods.

At first metals took the form of ordinary implements and adornments and served the dual purpose of being both usable commodities and money.

Only later did their function as money supersede that of useful commodities. But even at this stage of the development of money, its value was related to the shape of objects in common use. For example, the Chinese hoe cast in bronze was first used as an implement and later also as a token of value. In time it was made smaller and thinner and circulated as a "tool coin". The final break in the association between monetary metals and metals in the form of goods came when the value of a metal was determined by its weight. By 2000 B.C. Babylonia had developed a monetary system based on silver. Silver passed by weights known as *sheckels* and *talents* which were used as units of account. These were measures of weight which originated with grain. The British pound,[2] the French *livre*, the German *mark* and the Italian *lira* all date from the time when monetary metals passed by weight.

Coinage

Metals as a medium of exchange had their disadvantages both as to their quality and their quantity. Only persons familiar with the technique of assay using acids could determine the fineness or purity of metals. Moreover, each transaction involved the inconvenience of weighing the metal. For merchants who had to deal in metals continually, determining the purity and weight was cumbersome.

It is believed that in the seventh century B.C. a merchant in Lydia started to punch an identifying mark on each metal ingot after he had assayed it. If the metal again passed through his hands he would recognize his symbol and escape the task of doing another assay. This marked the beginning of rudimentary coinage.

The history of coinage is long and interesting. Coinage originated spontaneously and in many places. At first, as was the case in Lydia, irregular pieces of metal punchmarked to guarantee their purity but not their weight passed from hand to hand. Later, the metal pieces were formed into special identifiable shapes. This was the beginning of the process of minting. Metal was formed into distinctive pieces with distinctive markings recognizable as to both purity and weight and therefore value. It was then an easy step from measure by weight to measure by tale — by count. The essential requirement for this transition was the acceptability of coin for its **face value,** that is, the amount stamped on its face.

Early coin, particularly silver and gold, allowed cheating. The weight of the coins was reduced by **clipping** which involved removing a thin layer of metal from around the edge of the coin. This was prevented in the seven-

---

[2] The conventional symbol for the British pound is a modified L, the initial for the Latin term *librum* corresponding to the French *livre* and the Italian *lira*.

teenth century with the **milling** of the coin. A milled coin has a serrated edge which makes clipping easily noticeable. Milled coins also put a stop to the more difficult and therefore less usual practice of **hollowing** coin. Once clipping and hollowing were prevented **sweating** started. Sweating was the practice of putting coins in a leather bag and shaking them vigorously to collect small amounts of metallic dust in the bag. The only apparent effect this had on the coins was that of normal wear.

As soon as coinage came to play an important role in the economy of the ancient world, the prerogative of minting was assumed by political sovereigns, who viewed it as a source of revenue. The avowed intention was to protect the public interest by providing a uniform readily recognizable and honest system of coins. However, the state frequently used its monopoly on minting to make a profit by debasing the coinage, so that the intention of providing honest coinage was often thwarted. Where the state did not take over the minting of coins completely, private merchants were allowed to mint their own coin; or alternatively the state would mint money and allow a few merchants the exclusive right to distribute it. In either case, the merchants paid a fee or seiniorage to the state for the privilege. In some places where there was free coinage seigniorage was not imposed.[3]

The first coin minted was **full-bodied** insofar as the ingot was intrinsically worth its face value. That is to say, the value written on its face was equal to the value of the metal which composed the coin. With the passage of time, however, society began to think almost entirely in terms of what became the government stamp on the coin rather than of the coin's intrinsic content. This made it possible for the government to issue coins of the same gross value and bearing the same stamp on their faces, but containing a smaller proportion of the precious metal. This is known as **debasement.**

The custom of debasing the coin to provide a source of revenue is almost as old as coinage itself. In Lydia the electrum coins were debased by maintaining their face value while the proportionate amount of gold in them was reduced.[4] Both Greece and Rome had long histories of debasing the coinage. More recently, Henry VIII of England made a personal profit amounting to one quarter of the total value of all the coins minted between 1542 and 1547.

Gresham's Law. With the official debasement of coin and with the depreciation of coin resulting from wear and tear or through the practices of clipping and sweating, much of the coin ceased to be full-bodied and

---

3 For definition of free coinage see Chapter 2, page 13.

4 The electrum coins were composed at first of both gold and silver because the two metals were mined together and no attempt was made to separate them for coinage purposes.

was only **token.** As a result, full-bodied coin or "good money" was hoarded because of its high metallic content while token coin or "bad money" passed from hand to hand. Today this phenomenon is known as Gresham's Law after Sir Thomas Gresham (1519-1579), Queen Elizabeth's Chancellor of the Exchequer, who formulated the theory that "cheap money" drives "dear money" out of circulation.

Coins made from precious metals, particularly gold, presented a difficulty for conducting small transactions. Because of the high value of these metals they could not readily be minted into coin for use in small transactions. To overcome this problem **subsidiary coins** were minted from different metals. An early example of subsidiary coinage may be found in the ancient empires of Persia and Rome where gold coins were the medium of exchange for large transactions, while silver and bronze coins were used for the smaller everyday transactions. Interestingly, a reversed example is to be found in early Roman monetary history where the principal coin was copper. Since this was unsuitable for large transactions the silver *denarius* was introduced in 269 B.C. as a subsidiary coin to facilitate transactions of large value.

A coinage system based on two metals, **bimetallism,** or one based on three metals, **trimetallism,** presents inherent difficulties because the relative values of the various metals tend to change over time. The discussion of these difficulties, which constitutes a further elaboration of Gresham's Law, will be undertaken in our chapter on monetary standards.

PAPER

The final step in the evolution of money is the issuing of paper money which in its later stages of sophistication is associated with the establishment of banks and banking. Paper money, banks and banking as we know them today were predated by a long period of history where the sole purpose of paper instruments was to provide facilities for the transfer of money and credit. Because bullion and coin were difficult to transport and easily stolen, merchants carried with them in their travels written evidences of their command over money. These claims against money were similar to what we know today as warehouse receipts issued by a warehouseman when goods are left in his custody. The ownership of goods can be transferred by simply transferring the ownership of a warehouse receipt. Paper receipts or claims against money were issued by the Chinese emperors from the ninth century A.D. and by the Mongols following the conquests of Genghis Khan.

In the Western world monastic orders during the ninth, tenth and eleventh centuries and the Knights Templar during the following three centuries used paper claims to transfer the ownership of money deposited with the abbeys and temples located in the important centres of the then known world. Although these religious and semi-religious groups concentrated on the safekeeping of money and its transfer from one place to another, they also made loans. Hence they employed money claims to transfer money over time; such claims are now known as credit instruments. The Jews, not subject to canon law prohibiting usury, gradually replaced the monasteries and the religious orders as the chief lenders of money. However, in the thirteenth century they lost favour, partly because of their great financial success, and were plundered and persecuted. Their place was taken by the Lombards, a group of merchant bankers from Venice and Genoa. The Lombards were very successful as money lenders because they enjoyed papal indulgences on the charging of interest. They were the forerunners of the great financiers which included William de la Pole in England, Jacques Coeur in France and the Fuggers and Rothschilds in Germany.

Before the seventeenth century paper claims served the prime purpose of transferring credit and the ownership of money from one place or person to another. Although these claims also served the incidental function of a medium of exchange, it was not until the beginning of the seventeenth century that they became generally accepted as money rather than as a substitute for money. As we shall see in subsequent chapters, the goldsmiths of London issued certificates of deposit and the government of New France "cards" which were accepted as money and served as a medium of exchange. This marked the beginning of paper money and the establishment of banks for its creation.

SELECTED READINGS

Angell, Norman, *The Story of Money,* New York, Garden City Publishing Company, 1929.

Burns, Arthur F., *Money and Monetary Policy in Early Times,* New York, Alfred A. Knopf, 1927.

Cassel, Gustav, *The Theory of Social Economy,* New York, Harcourt, Brace, 1932, Ch. 2, 9 and 10.

Coulborn, W. A. L., *A Discussion of Money* , London, Longmans, Green, 1950, Ch. 1 to 5.

Crowther, Geoffrey, *An Outline of Money,* rev. ed., London, Thomas Nelson and Sons, 1948, Ch. 1.

Einzig, Paul, *Primitive Money,* 2nd ed., Oxford, Pergamon Press, 1966.

James, F. Cyril, *The Economics of Money, Credit and Banking,* 3rd ed., New York, Ronald Press, 1940.

Jevons, W. Stanley, *Money and the Mechanism of Exchange,* New York, D. Appleton, 1896.

Marshall, Alfred, *Money, Credit and Commerce,* London, Macmillan, 1923, Book 1, Ch. 1, and Appendix A.

Quiggin, A. Hingston, *A Survey of Primitive Money,* London, Methuen, 1963.

Robertson, Dennis H., *Money,* London, Nisbet, 1948, Ch. 1.

Von Mises, Ludwig, *The Theory of Money and Credit,* New Haven, Yale University Press, 1953, Part 1, Ch. 1, 3, 4 and 6.

2

MONETARY STANDARDS

All communities or nations, through custom and by legislation, have come to adopt ultimate or basic money in which debts are reckoned and in which final payments can be demanded. When we speak of a country's monetary standard we refer, therefore, to the entire set of laws and practices which have established this ultimate or **standard money.** Non-standard money is credit money which represents promises to pay a designated amount of standard money. Credit money can be issued by the government in the form of paper promises to pay standard money or in the form of subsidiary coin redeemable in standard money. Banks have traditionally been the most important source of credit money. At one time, as we shall see later, they issued bank notes which were promises by the bank to supply standard money on demand. When governments or their agencies took over the issue of notes for circulation the banks' chief form of credit money became their demand deposits.

A country's monetary standard depends upon what is designated as standard money. Although there are many modifications, there are only two basic standards: commodity standards, and credit or inconvertible "managed" paper standards.

COMMODITY STANDARDS

A commodity standard is a monetary system in which the value of the monetary unit is kept equal to the value of a designated quantity of a particular commodity or group of commodities. Of all the commodities that have been used as a base for monetary systems, precious metals, especially gold and silver, have the longest history. Metallic standards based on only one metal are known as **monometallic standards** while those founded on two metals are known as **bimetallic standards.** Monometallic standards using silver (silver standard) were long popular in China and India and in

Central and South America. Gold, on the other hand, has played a more important role in Western nations, particularly Great Britain, France, the United States and Canada. In the latter part of the nineteenth century and the early twentieth century the monometallic gold standard was considered a sign of monetary maturity.

MONOMETALLIC STANDARD

Coin Standard

Monometallic standards achieved their greatest degree of sophistication when gold served as standard money. In its purest form a monometallic standard is also a metallic coin standard. The two major modifications of the metallic coin standard are the **bullion standard** and the **exchange standard** both of which developed while gold was also the standard metal.

A country is said to have a metallic coin standard when its monetary authorities follow certain requisites:

1. The country's money unit of account is defined by statute to contain a specific quantity of the metallic commodity. For example, when Great Britain operated on the gold coin standard before the First World War, the sovereign was declared to be equivalent to 123.2744 grains of fine gold. Before 1933 when the United States was on a gold coin standard, the dollar was defined as containing 25.8 grains of gold nine-tenth fine, or 23.22 grains of fine gold.

2. Under a "full" (also referred to as a "pure" or "free") monometallic coin standard **free coinage** (of metal to coin) and **free convertibility** (of coin to metal) must prevail in an unlimited amount. Free coinage means that the public has the right to take unlimited quantities of the standard metal to the national treasury or its agency and have it minted into coin, at no cost and at a rate fixed by the definition of the unit of account. On the other hand, free convertibility means that the public is free to take metallic coins from its hoards and out of circulation and convert them to industrial use or into bullion.[1] With free coinage and free convertibility and the additional requirement allowing export and import of the standard metal in coin and bullion, equality between the face value of coins and the value of the metal of which they are composed is ensured. For example, when the United States was minting ten dollar gold pieces of 232.2 grains of fine gold, the ten-dollar gold coin had the same value as 232.2 grains of unminted fine gold in the gold commodity market. Only a pure coin standard where coinage is free, or **gratuitous,** will there be complete equality

---

[1] Bullion is uncoined metal in the form of bars.

between the face value of the coin and its metal content. Under the gold coin standard some countries charged a fee called **brassage** to cover the costs of coinage, while others absorbed the cost of operating the mint but charged for the alloys used in hardening coins. Some countries also charged a fee for exchanging coin for unminted metal. By and large, the fees charged produced only slight, if any, discrepancies between the value of the coins and the market value of an equivalent amount of unminted metal. Values did vary, however, where mints were operated to produce **seigniorage,** or profit.

3. Another requisite of a metallic coin standard is that all other types of money are **redeemable** at par into metal coin. In the countries which adopted a silver or gold standard the circulation of full-bodied coins was supplemented with other kinds of money or non-standard money in the form of token coin and credit or paper money. Non-standard money was introduced because full-bodied metal coins could not be minted into small enough denominations for purposes of providing small change. Moreover, non-standard money allowed countries to expand their money supply beyond the limits imposed by the strict amount of the metal available. As long as people were confident that the non-standard money would be redeemed in standard money, and that the value of credit money of various denominations would therefore at all times have value equal to metal coins of the same denominations, they were willing to hold substantial amounts of non-standard money and not exercise their redemption rights. Under normal conditions, the monetary authorities could meet the redemption requirement without holding an amount of the money metal equal to the value of the non-standard money issued. As long as the authorities could gauge public confidence they could issue non-standard money in excess of the standard money available to them, thus expanding the total money supply beyond the limits imposed by the strict amount of the metal available.

Bullion Standard

Public acceptance of non-standard money made possible modifications to the monometallic coin standard. The first of these modifications was the bullion standard. When convenience had made paper money and token coin the day-to-day medium of exchange, coins remained in the vaults of the treasury and the banks, and in the hands of hoarders. As there was no real advantage to the banks or treasury in holding standard money as coin rather than as bullion, minting of coin became an unnecessary expense. The monometallic coin standard was modified therefore to the bullion standard. When unlimited amounts of coin were no longer available to the public, hoarding of the metal declined making it possible to conserve the supply of standard money. With more of the metal left in their hands the monetary authorities were able to maintain a larger money circulation. The production of the monetary metal, especially gold, did not increase at a rate demanded by the expansion of economic activity. Thus, the amount of the metal that the monetary authorities could obtain from the reduction of hoarding became an important factor in the expansion of the total money supply.

The requisites of a monometallic bullion standard are as follows:

1. As under a coin standard, the country's money unit of account is defined by statute to contain a specific quantity of the metallic commodity.

2. The government no longer coins the standard metal. However, it undertakes to buy and sell unlimited quantities of the standard metal at an established price. This provision, along with the free import and export of the metal, ensures an equality between the value of the monetary unit and the domestic and foreign market value of the same quantity of the metal.

3. All kinds of credit money, which provide the only medium of exchange, are redeemable at par in bullion — uncoined metal in the form of bars. However, since gold bars have traditionally been made in minimum sizes containing many hundred ounces of the precious metal, redemption is limited to those who can afford to exchange a relatively large amount of credit money. The gold bullion standard has sometimes been called the rich man's gold standard.

Exchange Standard

The metallic exchange standard, like the bullion standard, was another modification of the metallic standard made by countries in an attempt to remain on a commodity standard at a time when the stock of the standard metal did not increase at a rate required for the desired expansion of economic activity. This was the case after the First World War when the standard metal was gold. The requisites of an exchange standard are as follows:

1. As under both a coin and a bullion standard, the country's money unit of account is defined by statute to contain a specific quantity of the metallic commodity.

2. The country maintains no metallic reserves at home and depends entirely upon the metallic reserves of other countries for its standard money. Or, as is usually the case, the country maintains only partial metallic reserves at home which are supplemented by reserves held in the form of short-term investments in a foreign country. The government or its agency does not

undertake to buy and sell metallic coin or bullion. Instead, it undertakes to buy and sell at an established price unlimited quantities of drafts (or bills of exchange) against the reserves it maintains in foreign financial institutions. These drafts are in turn convertible into metallic coin or bullion in the foreign country. Under an exchange standard a country links its non-standard money indirectly to metal by making it convertible into foreign currency or foreign claims which are directly convertible into metal. For example, when India adopted a gold exchange standard most of its standard money was held in the form of British pounds invested in London. Indian non-standard money was still as good as gold because the Indian monetary authorities could meet the convertibility requirement by selling India's London investments (reserves) for British pounds, which were convertible into gold. For individual Indians convertibility was slow and cumbersone, but for India as a whole there were inherent advantages. Even with few or no metallic reserves of its own, it could remain on a commodity standard. Instead of holding gold which is sterile, pays no interest and involves a storage cost, the country's reserves of standard money were maintained in the form of liquid foreign investments which earned interest and could be converted into metal if necessary.

3. All kinds of credit money, the only medium of exchange, are redeemable at par in metallic drafts convertible into metal abroad. This provision along with a free market of the metallic commodity, including free export and import, ensures that the value of the non-standard money is fixed to the value of the metal serving as standard money.

BIMETALLIC STANDARD

A bimetallic standard differs from a monometallic standard in that two metals (usually gold and silver), instead of one, are used as standard money. Historically, the transition from a monometallic to a bimetallic standard was made as a method of increasing the stock of standard money. In the United States bimetallism was also advocated by the so-called silverites who wanted an assured market for American silver mines. The characteristics of a bimetallic standard are as follows:

1. The country's standard monetary unit is defined by statute to contain a specific quantity of either of two metals. For example, when the United States formally adopted a bimetallic standard for the first time in 1792, the dollar was defined as containing either 24.75 grains of fine gold or 371.25 grains of fine silver. This established a fixed ratio, or **mint ratio,** of 15:1 for the two metals in their use as money.

2. Both metals may be coined in which case they circulate as money, and all other kinds of circulating money are fully and freely convertible to coin

of either metal. If bullion rather than coin is the standard, convertibility is in terms of bullion.

3. If the two metals are coined, coinage must be free. Convertibility of coin to either metal and the free import and export of both metals must be permitted. The convertibility requirement and the free market for both metals must also apply if bullion rather than coin is used for the monetary base.

In order for two metals to coexist in a monetary system their *mint and market ratios must be the same.* We have already noted that the mint ratio is defined by statute. The market ratio is the relative price of the two metals determined in the open market. If these two ratios differ, one of the metals will be drained out of the monetary system. The metal that the mint ratio undervalues in terms of the market ratio will always tend to disappear, leaving only the metal that the mint ratio overvalues in the monetary system. An example will illustrate this phenomenon which, as we noted in Chapter 1, is known as Gresham's Law. Let us assume that the mint ratio is established at 15:1; that is, gold is worth fifteen times as much as silver. Suppose further that the market ratio (or relative free market price) of the metals as commodities is 16:1; gold is worth sixteen times as much as silver. It will now be profitable for speculators and traders to take silver to the mint in exchange for gold, and take the gold thus acquired and exchange it in the free market at the market value of 16:1. The result will be that with gold flowing into the commodity market and silver into the monetary system, the monetary authorities will be left with little or no gold. The country, though still legally on a bimetallic standard, is *de facto* on a monometallic standard. Later chapters will provide various examples of Gresham's Law at work. In our example above we explained the difficulties of maintaining a bimetallic standard when the mint ratio and the domestic market ratio diverge. These divergencies are more acute in terms of the foreign markets of the two metals. In addition, different countries may establish different mint ratios, resulting in the flow of one metal to one country and of the other to another country.

ADVANTAGES AND DISADVANTAGES OF METALLIC STANDARDS

Advocates of commodity standards, particularly metallic standards, have emphasized the importance of the discipline which these standards exact on the monetary authorities of a country. Insofar as these standards operate in an automatic way, the authorities cannot manage the total money supply; they have no discretionary power over changes in the money supply. The money supply changes automatically in some fixed proportion to changes in the stock of the standard monetary metal available to the monetary authorities. The proportion in which the money supply changes as a result of a change in the stock of the standard metal depends upon the public's confidence in the monetary system and the amount of metal reserves held against each unit of non-standard money. Under normal circumstances when the public is confident that the non-standard money it holds can ultimately be converted into the standard metal, a relatively small proportion of metallic reserves will have to be held by the authorities. In other words, non-standard money can be issued without first holding an equal amount of the metal as reserves. For a metallic standard to operate automatically however, metallic reserves must always be held in some designated fixed proportion to the non-standard money. Thus, for example, if the metal reserve ratio is fixed at 50 per cent, an increase of one unit in the metal reserves must be matched by an increase of two monetary units in the total money supply. In this way, a change in the total money supply takes place as the automatic result of a change in the metal reserve.

Expansion and contraction of the metal reserves and therefore of the total money supply can be due to a number of factors: the metal may be imported and exported; there may be new domestic production of the metal; and there may be changes in the amounts hoarded or used for non-monetary purposes. Proponents of a metallic standard argue that the total money supply must bear a fixed relation to some fundamental factors explaining the economy, and that these factors are reflected in the causes for changes in the supply of monetary metal noted previously. However, history has shown that the changes in the money supply that have been produced by the so-called automatic working of metal standards have not always been the changes needed by the economy. The fluctuations in the stock of the monetary reserves due to the factors noted need not be the changes required by the economy. Nor are these fluctuations necessarily related to the nation's capacity to produce and consume. Surely these latter considerations, not the amount of the standard metal available to the monetary authorities, should govern the size of the money stock.

Another virtue claimed for the metallic standard is that it maintains long-run stability in the price level. This argument made by those who favour gold is based on two propositions: the stability of the world's monetary stock, and the inverse relationship between the output of gold and the price level. The gold stocks available for monetary purposes have been relatively stable, since they have been accumulated over the centuries and since the production of any one year has represented only a small fraction of the available stocks. Even in 1940, the year of the greatest output of gold, total production amounted to less than 5 per cent of the existing monetary stocks. The average yearly increment to the total gold stock is around 2 per cent. It is contended, therefore, that a price system based upon a relatively constant metallic foundation, such as gold, ought to be more stable than one based upon a foundation subject to greater variation. The weakness of this argument lies in the fact that while the global stock of gold has shown relatively small annual fluctuation, the supply in an individual country may vary considerably. A country can experience dramatic changes in its stock of the money metal due to its export and import from other countries or to the discovery of gold within its borders. The implications of these flows for an individual country will be considered in a later part of this book where we will deal with the international gold standard.

We have observed that one of the fundamental requisites of all the various kinds of metallic standards is that the standard money of the country is defined by statute to contain a specific quantity of the metallic commodity. This, together with the requirement of convertibility at a fixed price, means that the price at which the metal may be sold is also fixed. As prices in general move up, the output of the monetary metal will decline because its costs of production increase along with the rise in the price level. The decline in the money metal will produce a reduction in the total money supply, which in turn will depress the demand for goods and services and the rise in prices generally. Similarly, if prices in general fall, gold production will become more profitable and will increase; the money supply will then increase preventing any further fall in the price level. This mechanism assumes that there is a direct relationship between the money supply and the price level, and that the production of the monetary metal is turned off and on in response to changes in the cost of its production. We shall discuss the relationship between the money supply and the price level later when we consider the quantity theory of money. Suffice it to say here that a change in the money supply may not produce a change in the price level.

While the output of gold and the price level tend to move in opposite directions, this movement may take a relatively long time. To expand metal production more equipment is needed to mine and process it in less accessible areas and from poorer quality ores. This may delay any immediate increase in gold for monetary purposes. On the other hand, the general rise in prices may not significantly discourage gold production. The producer, having incurred greater fixed costs by installing new machinery, will probably continue his increased output as long as his variable costs are being met, even though the general price rise has reduced his profits.

Finally it is argued that a metallic standard and, here again, one based on gold promotes confidence in a monetary system because gold is almost universally desired for its intrinsic value. That is to say, gold has a value in itself aside from its monetary use. If gold should lose its acceptability as money, it can be fabricated into jewellery, tableware and the like. This is not the case with irredeemable paper money which is worthless once its monetary value is lost.

We have mentioned earlier that variants to the gold coin standard were introduced because of the shortage of gold for monetary purposes. Scarcity of the monetary metal has been one of the more important shortcomings of monometallic standards. Indeed, it has been the scarcity of the metal and the consequent loss of confidence in its availability which has led to "scrambles" for gold and the downfall of the gold standard.

SYMMETALLIC STANDARD AND COMMODITY RESERVE STANDARD

Toward the end of the nineteenth century, a plan known as symmetallism was proposed as a solution to the problem inherent in a bimetallic standard. Because of the difficulty of maintaining a mint ratio that would always correspond to the market ratio, it was proposed that the monetary unit of account be defined as a combination of the two metals in some specific proportion to one another. The monetary unit might be a specified weight of silver plus a specified weight of gold. One can visualize a bar containing a defined amount of grains of the two metals. The market price of silver to that of gold could vary but the price of the particular combination of metals defined as the monetary unit would remain the same.

A natural extension of a symmetallic standard is a commodity reserve standard. This type of standard has been proposed as a means of stabilizing the purchasing power of money. Under such a standard the monetary unit of account would be defined in terms of a fixed combination of storable commodities other than metals. These commodities would be combined into a bundle consisting of a specified quantity of each commodity chosen. Such a bundle would be given a fixed value. If the market price of the aggregate quantity of goods composing the bundle were to fall below this fixed value, the monetary authorities would purchase these commodities in the open market and place them in storage. If the market price of the bundle of commodities were to rise above the fixed value, the authorities would sell some of their reserve of these commodities in the open market. Thus, the price of the bundle of commodities would be stabilized. If basic commodities were chosen to compose the bundle, the general price level would also be stabilized.

INCONVERTIBLE PAPER STANDARDS

Paper money has been referred to as a creature of the state.[2] It has been

[2] There is quite an extensive literature on the so-called State or Chartalist theory of money. See for instance Ludwig von Mises, *The Theory of Money and Credit*, New Haven, Yale University Press, 1953; F. A. Mann, *The Legal Aspect of Money*, md. ed., London, Oxford University Press, 1953, Ch. 1; and J. A. Schumpeter, "Das Sozialprodukt und die Rechenpfennige" translated in *International Economic Papers*, No. 6, New York, Macmillan, 1956, pp. 148-211.

called **fiat money** because it circulates by government decree. However, as we shall see in later chapters, government decree must be accompanied by public acceptability before paper will circulate successfully.

Paper standards first developed out of the breakdowns of convertibility under metallic standards, especially under the pressure of major wars. The government issue of paper to finance wars was an easy solution to the problem of metal shortages. Paper was not employed only as a means of finance for governments or as a method of expanding a money supply restricted by the availability of metal. Sweden and other non-belligerent countries adopted a paper standard during the First World War to avoid inflation resulting from the inflow of gold sent there for safekeeping. Today countries operate under a paper standard mainly because it allows the monetary authorities discretionary power to manage the country's money supply. How the money supply is managed, and to what purpose, will be our chief concerns in the chapters that follow.

Paper standards have the following characteristics:

1. The unit of account is not defined in terms of a commodity. In other words, the unit of account is *abstract*.

2. The commodity value of the circulating media is zero. The various kinds of money in circulation, government notes, bank notes, cheques drawn on deposit accounts, as well as token coin, are usually maintained at parity with each other. The circulating money is always the standard money.

3. The purchasing power of the monetary unit is not kept at par with any commodity.

Proponents of paper money have argued that the quantity of money required by any country depends upon such factors as the organization of business, the volume of business activity, the means of transportation and communication, and the state of development of the banking and financial system. None of these factors is directly related to the volume of commodities used under commodity standards. Only paper money provides the kind of flexibility required to adapt the money supply to the nation's capacity to produce and consume.

Critics of paper money point to the disastrous experience of nearly every country that has adopted it. Later chapters will show that with almost no exception, governments at one time or another have succumbed to the temptation of overissue. As we have noted earlier, one of the strong points of a commodity standard is that it imposes a certain discipline on the monetary authorities. No such discipline exists under a paper standard.

Because paper standards are completely divorced from commodities, they have no direct link with monetary systems of other countries. Under an international commodity standard where each country defines its monetary unit of account in terms of gold, the relationship between the various countries' currencies is fixed. It is argued that this fosters international trade. For example, a Canadian manufacturer is willing to sell his wares in Britain when he knows that for each British pound he receives in payment he can get a specified amount of Canadian dollars. If he were uncertain of what the exchange rate between pounds and dollars would be when payment was made, he would be less willing to deal with Britain.

Today most of the major countries employ a pure paper standard only domestically. These countries, which are members of the International Monetary Fund established after the Second World War define their money in terms of gold or in terms of another country's money so defined. In this way, a fixed relation is maintained between the moneys of the various countries. Countries are prepared to buy all the gold offered either in the free market or by other countries but they will sell it only to foreign governments, sometimes freely, sometimes under restriction. In this way some semblance of a commodity standard is still retained at the international level, although citizens presenting their national money for redemption can get nothing but paper from their governments.

SELECTED READINGS

Breckinridge, S.P., *Legal Tender,* Chicago, University of Chicago Press, 1903.

Carlile, W.W., *The Evolution of Modern Money,* London, Macmillan, 1901, Part 11, Ch. 1 to 3.

Friedman, Milton, "Commodity Reserve Currency", *Essays in Positive Economics,* Chicago, University of Chicago Press, 1953, pp. 204-250.

Graham, Frank D., *World Commodities and World Currency,* New York, McGraw-Hill, 1944.

Hawtrey, R.G., *The Gold Standard in Theory and Practice,* 5th ed., London, Longmans, Green, 1947.

Hawtrey, R.G., *Currency and Credit,* 3rd ed., London, Longmans, Green, 1928.

Helfferich, Karl, *Money,* trans. from the German by Louis Infield, (2 vols.), New York, Adelphi, 1927.

Kemmerer, Edwin W., *Gold and the Gold Standard,* New York, McGraw-Hill, 1944.

Keynes, John Maynard, *A Treatise on Money,* London, Macmillan, 1930, Vol. 1, Ch. 1.

Mann, F.A., *The Legal Aspects of Money,* 2nd ed., London, Oxford, University Press, 1953.

Nussbaum, Arthur, *Money in the Law,* New York, Foundation Press, 1950.

Olivecrona, Karl, *The Problem of the Monetary Unit,* New York, Macmillan, 1957.

Robertson, D.H., *Money,* London, Nisbet, 1948, Ch. 4.

Schumpeter, J.A., "Money and the Social Product" in *International Economic Papers,* No. 6, London, Macmillan, 1956, pp. 148-211.

Walker, Francis A., *International Bimetallism,* New York, Henry Holt, 1896.

Westerfield, Ray B., *Money, Credit and Banking,* rev. ed., New York, Ronald Press, 1947, Ch. 1 to 7.

3

NORTH AMERICAN MONETARY EXPERIENCES

Before the arrival of the white colonists in North America, the Indians had developed a form of money known as **wampum**. Beads or tubes about three quarters of an inch long were made from sea shells in two colours, blue and white. The Indians used wampum to trade with the colonists, who valued the beads at about one *sou* or half a penny for the white and two *sous* or one penny for the blue until the introduction of glass counterfeits made it almost worthless. Wampum enjoyed legal tender status until 1690 but continued to circulate among the colonists until 1704 and among the Indians until about 1825.

CANADA

NEW FRANCE AND THE FRENCH REGIME

Like the English colonies to the south, the French colony in Canada used commodities of various kinds to serve as a unit of account or as a medium of exchange, or both. A list of such commodities would include wheat, moose hides, beaver skins, wild cat skins and even liquor.[1] Also, like the English, colonists in New France employed coin which continually remained scarce. Coin was originally brought to New France by the colonists. The supply was augmented by the funds the French government sent out to maintain its military establishment and the machinery of civil government, and by subscriptions raised throughout France by religious orders to establish and support missionaries. The export trade, mostly in furs, brought coin to the colony but this usually returned to France immediately as payment for essential commodities imported from the mother country.

To overcome the shortage of coin and the chronic shortage of a medium

[1] The soldiers in the garrison at Port Royal were normally paid in liquor.

of exchange in general, the colonial government resorted to two expedients. To prevent the return of coins to France, the colonial officials gave them a legal value above that in France. The higher-valued coins became known as **money of the country** to distinguish them from **money of France.** From 1672 to 1717, for example, a *livre* of money of France contained one quarter more silver than a *livre* of money of the country. This device did not remedy the scarcity of a medium of exchange, for prices in the colony rose in proportion to the increased ratings of the coins.[2]

In 1685, the Intendant Jacques de Meulles turned to another expedient designed to provide a more adequate medium of exchange and to prevent financial embarrassment to the local administration. When funds did not arrive from France to support the colony and all the local resources had been exhausted, he issued **card money.** As there were no printing presses or suitable paper, the seal of the Treasurer and the signature of the Governor and Intendant were affixed to the backs of ordinary playing cards. Although card money began as a short-term financial expedient, it was not long before the cards began to circulate as a medium of common exchange and later issues of cards in whole, halves, quarters and other sizes were provided with this specific purpose in mind.

The issue of card money was backed by the credit of the local administration and the anticipated arrival of coins from France each autumn. It became common to issue card money on the security of bills of exchange drawn on the annual appropriation of the French government to the colony. Since these bills were redeemed in silver coin in France, the colony was really on a silver exchange standard.

One characteristic of card money was that it remained within the colonial territories. This was an advantage in that it relieved the shortage of domestic currency, but card money was of no use in trade with France. Because of the colonies' adverse trade balance the value of card money suffered in comparison with money which could be spent for imports from France. This differential was still further emphasized by the overrated values for French coins in New France.

Another feature of card money which recommended it in the eyes of the colonial authorities was that quantities could be issued on the spot whenever the Intendant was hard pressed for money and was unable to obtain funds from the continental French authorities. The king consistently opposed the issue of card money because it implied a loss of financial control over the colony. Only reluctantly was authorization for issue granted when the need apparently could not be satisfied in other ways.

Card money provided the most important medium of exchange but was supplemented from time to time by other types of paper. In 1690 **treasury**

---

2 Today rating coins higher in the colony than in the mother country would be called devaluation. A rise in prices which offsets the effects of devaluation does not always occur.

notes were issued as a temporary substitute; military commanders sometimes paid with **orders** on the Quebec treasury; and the Quebec administration often used **treasury receipts** as a form of payment. Between 1719 and 1729, when the French government succeeded in withdrawing card money from circulation, merchants issued their own notes in payment of goods and services. Coins were usually hoarded and, because of religious scruples, were not loaned out for interest.

When card money was again issued after 1729 its amount, although increased, was kept within the limits necessary to prevent excessive depreciation and to make it generally acceptable. This was not the case after 1749. With the excessive issue of card money as well as the shortage of bills of exchange and delays in their payment, it depreciated and rapidly disappeared from circulation. The same fate was met by a new kind of paper money, **ordonnances** or promises to pay unauthorized by France and issued by Bigot, the Intendant.

BRITISH NORTH AMERICA

In 1710 British troops raised in New England captured Port Royal and took over the French colony in the Annapolis valley of present day Nova Scotia. The Acadians had engaged in very little trade, up to this time partly because trade between them and the English colonies had been forbidden. The existing currency requirements had been met by a short experiment with card money and by a few coins from outside.

In their dealings with the Acadians the English continued using the French basis of value, the *livre*. Transactions within the garrison at Port Royal (renamed Annapolis Royal) and trade with New England were conducted in terms of **Boston money.** This consisted of drawing sterling bills which were discounted with Boston merchants for colonial currency or Boston bills.[3] On the other hand, accounts with the British government were kept on a sterling basis. Trade was thus carried on with three rather distinct accounting systems and with a heterogenous collection of coin and paper valued in terms of these three units of account. It was therefore only natural that there would be agitation for a standardization of the value of foreign money. This resulted in a system of valuation known as **Halifax money** shortly after the name of Halifax was given to Chebucto in 1749. Halifax money, which was simply a unit of account, became recognized in Boston and New York and exerted an influence on monetary affairs in Canada as late as 1860.

When the British took over Quebec in 1759 they inherited the chaotic paper issues of the French, most of which were all but worthless by this time. While peace was being negotiated, rumours began to circulate that

[3] See discussion on the American colonies p. 31

the British would redeem the outstanding paper and the demand by speculators did add some value to the paper, which the British eventually redeemed at one quarter of its face value.

Under the British regime specie gradually returned to circulation. The odd assortment of gold and silver coins which appeared included many that had previously been hoarded, those sent by Britain to maintain troops and pay for civil administration, and some acquired in trade. The most abundant coins were the Spanish silver dollars which were earned in trade with the American colonies along the Atlantic seaboard. The value of the silver content of the average Spanish dollar was 4 shillings and sixpence but its monetary value depended upon the rating which it was given. East of Quebec it circulated at 5 shillings, being rated in terms of **Halifax currency**; west of Quebec it was rated as 8 shillings and was known as **York currency,** since this was the rating current in New York.

By overvaluing coins used in domestic trade the authorities were attempting to keep them in the country. By establishing official rates of exchange for the various coins, they were endeavouring to bring some order to the confusion created by the heterogeneous nature of the coins. One of the more ambitious attempts at regulating the currency was the Act of 1796 which established the rates shown in Table 3-1.

The disastrous paper issues of the French regime left a lasting prejudice against paper money in Lower and Upper Canada. In 1794 John McGill was appointed by Lord Simcoe to the new office of Agent of Purchases. McGill started to pay for supplies, which he bought directly from the settlers rather than by contract from merchants, with **transferable certificates.** While they were few in number and were not legal tender, they did pass into circulation and marked the beginning of a successful paper issue in Upper Canada. In Lower Canada, especially Montreal, merchants issued their own paper notes or **bons** to their customers. These were redeemed in goods at the store of issue and circulated fairly widely. While both these early issues of paper money helped to break down the prejudice against paper money in the Canadas, the most important influence toward this end was the fortunate experience with **army bills** issued during the War of 1812.

After the United States had declared war on Great Britain, Sir Isaac Brock was instructed to prepare for the attack. To pay for the goods and services which he requisitioned, he issued paper money known as army bills. These had face values of 4, 25, 100 and 400 Spanish dollars. Those of 25 dollars or more bore interest while the smaller units were payable in cash on demand. As the war progressed bills of smaller denominations were added. The exchange value of the Spanish dollar at Halifax was rated at 5 shillings at the time and the army bills were based on this valuation. The complete redemption of all bills outstanding in gold and silver at the end of the war went a long way toward wiping out the unhappy memories of earlier and less satisfactory paper. The new confidence in paper money also helped prepare the way for the establishment of commercial banks soon after the war.

In the Maritimes, where the stigma of the paper issues of New France remained relatively unknown, the government resorted to paper issues quite early to provide a medium of exchange. As early as 1766 Nova Scotia authorized a limited issue of treasury bills against expected customs revenues. Prince Edward Island issued bills in 1790, while New Brunswick issued a small quantity of treasury notes as a financial expedient in 1808. In

TABLE 3-1

Currency in The English Colony, 1796

Coin	*Weight*		*Rates*		
Gold Coins	**Penny Weight**	**Grains Troy**	**£**	**s**	**d**
British guinea	5	6	1	3	4
Johannes of Portugal	18	-	4	0	0
Moidore of Portugal	6	18	1	10	0
Milled dubloon of four	-	-	-	-	-
pistole piece of Spain	17	-	3	14	0
French louis d'or coined	-	-	-	-	-
before 1793	5	4	1	2	6
French pistole coined	-	-	-	-	-
before 1793	4	4	0	18	0
American eagle	11	6	2	10	0
Silver Coins					
British crown				5	6
British shilling				1	1
Spanish milled dollar (at 5 shillings)				4	6
Spanish pistereen				1	0
French crown coined before 1793				5	6
French piece of 4 livres and 10 sols tournois				4	2
French piece of 36 sols tournois				1	8
French piece of 24 sols tournois				1	1
American dollar				5	0

Source: The Provincial Statutes of Lower Canada, 1 Geo. III, Ch. 5, May 27, 1796, reprinted in E.P. Neufeld Money and Banking in Canada, Toronto, McClelland and Stewart, 1964, pp. 24-27.

order to finance its commitments in the War of 1812, Nova Scotia issued treasury notes which circulated successfully. Further issues followed in an attempt to offset the continuing scarcity of specie in the postwar period, but these were not adequately controlled and suffered severe depreciation. In 1834 the government passed legislation which in effect gave it a monopoly of small denomination notes.

The shortage of coins or "hard money" was a continuing problem in British North America. Coins were most urgently needed to provide sufficient standard currency for making change. After 1800 much of the small change in circulation consisted of merchants' tokens. Many were copper penny and half penny tokens of good quality imported from Britain, but these were gradually replaced by lighter tokens of copper or brass. These latter were driven out of circulation in Lower and Upper Canada after 1838 by bank issues of copper tokens. At various times between 1823 and 1871 the provinces of Nova Scotia, New Brunswick, Prince Edward Island and British Columbia produced coinage of various sorts. Prince Edward Island, for example, imported light weight tokens which bore patriotic slogans such as "Success to the Fisheries" and "Speed the Plough". During an earlier period the Spanish silver dollar circulated in Prince Edward Island. However, since it was rated higher in Halifax than on the Island, it tended to move to the mainland. In 1813, in an attempt to retain these coins, Governor Smith had the centres punched out of 1,000 of them to make them unacceptable for circulation elsewhere. The "holey dollar", as it was called circulated on the Island at 5 shillings and the "centre plug" at one shilling. British Columbia established a mint in 1862 for the production of ten- and twenty-dollar gold pieces, but only a few sample pieces were ever issued.

In 1854 the Hudson's Bay Company introduced a metallic token called a **made-beaver** which continued to be used in the north until as late as 1910. It originated as a unit of account introduced by the company for its trade with the Indians and early trappers. A made-beaver was equal to the value of an adult male beaver in prime condition. Before the company issued tokens its unit of account was at various times represented by sticks, porcupine quills, ivory discs and musket balls. In the eastern Arctic, fox tokens served the same purpose. With the arrival of settlers the company issued its own one- and five-pound notes which were generally used in the west until about the 1840's.

After the union of Upper and Lower Canada, the question of providing a common national currency became an issue of high priority. The British government had resisted for a long time all suggestions for a distinctive Canadian coinage based on the United States decimal system. It feared that such a decimal system would increase the dangers for Canada of political annexation by the United States. Moreover, there was still a hope, although faint, that the British sterling currency standard of value and medium of exchange might be introduced throughout the Empire.

The Currency Act of 1841 passed by the new Union Parliament of Upper and Lower Canada retained the Halifax standard but there were still no coins corresponding to it. The American eagle and the British sovereign, both gold coins, were given the status of full legal tender. Silver coins given the same status were the American dollar and half dollar, and the new French five-franc piece. Other coins, including British silver coins, were accorded a limited legal tender status. An act passed in 1850 authorizing the issue of Canadian silver coins, denominated in pounds sterling but corresponding to the value of the United States' coinage, was immediately disallowed by the British government.

Finally in 1853 after agreement among the provinces, the British authorities accepted the idea of a distinctive currency common to the British North American colonies. No further objections were made to the decimal system, although it was still felt in Britain that the unit of account should be pound currency. The proposal that the pound be represented by an actual gold coin to be called a **royal** with subsidiary gold and copper coins in decimal ratios was turned down by the Union Parliament.

The Provinces of Canada Currency Act of 1853 legalized transactions in decimal currency for the first time. Gold coin was made unlimited legal tender and the adoption of the gold standard dates from this time. The move to a decimal system was completed in 1858 when the Currency Act of that year required all government accounts to be kept in decimal currency. Toward mid-year the first shipment of coins in denominations of one, 5, 10 and 20 cents was received for circulation from the Royal Mint in Britain. Thus, Canada came to have decimal coinage and for the first time the measure of value and the medium of exchange really corresponded.

CONFEDERATION

With Confederation in 1867, the British North America Act allocated to the new federal government exclusive jurisdiction over currency and coinage as well as over banking, the incorporation of banks and the issue of paper money, Under the Dominion Notes Act, passed as a temporary currency measure, the federal government took over all provincial notes. [4] Another Dominion Notes Act passed two years later restricted the chartered banks to issuing notes of a minimum denomination of $5 whereupon the government began to issue Dominion notes of 25 cents, and $1 and $2. The government was required to hold a gold reserve of 20 per cent against

[4] See Chapter 6.

the first $9 million of notes issued, with each additional dollar printed above this amount to be covered dollar for dollar by gold.

The Uniform Currency Act of 1871 extended decimal currency throughout the Dominion. The act authorized the issue of a five-dollar Canadian gold coin, but none was struck before the establishment of the mint in Ottawa in 1908. At that time sovereigns were struck ($4.866). In 1910 the Canadian dollar was defined in terms of a specified weight and fineness of gold bullion rather than in terms of the British sovereign. The gold weight and fineness of the Canadian dollar was made the same as that of the American dollar.

When the Bank of Canada was established in 1934 as the central bank, provision was made to transfer to it eventually the sole responsibility for the issue of paper money.

THE UNITED STATES

THE AMERICAN COLONIES

Like their neighbours to the north, the American colonies along the eastern seaboard suffered a chronic shortage of coins to meet the needs of trade. To fill this need the colonists early resorted to the use of various commodities as money. Corn, tobacco and rice were common substitutes for coin.

The American colonies acquired specie from immigrants and pirates and as a result of trade. It consisted largely of Spanish coins, some English coins, French *louis d'ors,* Dutch coins, Venetian *sequins* and gold coins from Portugese Brazil. Because much of American trade was with the Spanish colonies, the greater part of early colonial coinage consisted of Spanish "pieces of eight", containing 8 *reals* and known by the colonists as Spanish milled dollars. Because of the dearth of small coins for making change, the Spanish milled dollar was often cut into pieces. Thus, a quarter piece consisting of 2 *reals* became known as **two bits.** Since it was the traditional practice of the colonists to reckon in pounds, shilling and pence, legal ratios were established between the dollar and the English units. In the early days the parity of the dollar on the basis of its silver content was 4 shillings and sixpence.

In 1652 Massachusetts set up its own mint. There other coins, particularly the Spanish dollars gained in trade with the West Indies, were melted down and coined into "pine tree shillings" which circulated in the New England colonies. In 1684 King Charles II closed the mint because it violated the royal prerogative of coinage.

The first issue of paper money in the American colonies was made by the government of Massachusetts in 1690. An expedition had been sent against Quebec, and when the soldiers returned home the government was unable to pay them. As an immediate expedient the men were given **bills of exchange,** which were promises of payment backed by the credit of the government. Further issues were made and in 1692 they became legal tender.

The shortage of coin led other colonies to experiment with paper issues. Some of these were bills without backing issued by governments to meet expenses; others were notes issued by governments, private individuals or institutions against the security of land or commodities. Early institutions which issued paper against land collateral were known as **land banks.** These should not be confused with modern banks, since their only purpose was to make loans by paying out their own currency against land collateral. While some were successful, most of them ended in financial disaster owing to the overissue of paper and to falling land values, or to land values that were fictitious.

A somewhat novel type of paper issuing institution was established in Virginia in 1730. The legislature authorized tobacco warehouses to issue transferable tobacco notes. This practice was later followed in Maryland. After 1750 the British parliament attempted unsuccessfully to prohibit the circulation of paper in the form of bills and notes.

MONEY DURING THE AMERICAN REVOLUTION

With the outbreak of the Revolutionary War in 1775, one of the first tasks of the Continental Congress as the central authority of the belligerent colonists was to finance the mobilization for war. Since the Congress had little or no authority to tax, and since its credit was too weak to permit borrowing, its only alternative was to issue bills of credit. This proceeded at such a rate that within a year sellers refused to accept the bills or would do so only at a discount. With every issue of "continentals" prices rose higher; as prices rose more money was needed to meet expenses; and the more money was needed the more it was printed. By 1781 this money was literally worthless and had passed almost completely out of circulation.

THE CONFEDERACY

In 1781 the Articles of Confederation were ratified by the states and two years later peace was made with England, bringing to an end the war of the American Revolution. The period between 1781 and 1789, when the federal institution became effective, marked the beginning of a monetary controversy in the United States which was to make a lasting impression on its monetary system.

At the end of the Revolution, continental currency had ceased to circulate as money. Only about half of the amount outstanding had been converted into new notes. With the limited circulation of the paper money of the Confederacy, state banks which had all but discontinued their issues after 1777 resumed circulation of their paper at the request of the Continental Congress. The urban areas, which in particular had been hurt by the inflationary consequences of previous overissues, wanted either the complete abolition of paper issues or very strict control of them. The rural areas, on the other hand, desired additional issues of paper. In Massachusetts the failure to issue paper money was one of the grievances which resulted in Shay's Rebellion. In Rhode Island, by contrast, much ill will was created over the establishment of a land bank. In the midst of all these controversies over state issues, the first commercial banks were established in the United States.

After the Revolution specie again began to circulate. It was an odd assortment of coin, including some which had been hoarded, some from British colonies and some obtained in trade with France, Spain and the Spanish colonies.[5]

MONEY AND THE CONSTITUTION

In adopting a monetary system, the first Congress of the United States followed very closely the proposals of the first Secretary of the Treasury, Alexander Hamilton. He proposed separating government financing from note issuing, which was to be left in the hands of banks. Toward this end, in 1791, Congress granted a charter to the First Bank of the United States, and in the following year passed the Coinage Act which among other things defined America's monetary base and provided for the establishment of the mint.

Under the Coinage Act of 1792, the Spanish dollar was adopted as the American dollar. Since the Spanish dollar was estimated to contain an average of 371.25 grains of silver, the official silver weight of the United States dollar was set at this amount. Moreover, since the United States was to have a bimetallic standard the dollar was also defined in terms of gold. This was to create difficulties later.

Hamilton, familiar with Gresham's Law, realized that the official or mint ratio of gold to silver had to correspond to the market ratio, which was estimated to be 15 to 1. Therefore, the gold content of the United States dollar was defined as 24.75 grains of gold. The United States mint was subsequently authorized to mint the full bodied coins shown in Table 3-2.

[5] These were the same coins included in Table 3-1. There were also some private issues consisting of brass, copper and tin.

When the Treasury defined the pure metal content of the dollar as 371.25 grains of silver or 24.75 grains of gold, it overvalued silver. In other leading nations the prevailing ratios were 16:1 or 15.5:1. Consequently silver flowed to the mint where 15 ounces could secure one ounce of gold, and gold flowed to the market where it could be sold for 15.5 to 16 ounces of silver. With silver flowing into the mint and gold flowing out, the United States, although on a *de jure* bimetallic standard, was actually on a *de facto* silver standard.

TABLE 3-2

United States Coins, 1792

Gold	
Eagle	$10.00
Half eagle	5.00
Quarter eagle	2.50
Silver	
Dollar	$ 1.00
Half dollar	.50
Quarter dollar	.25
Dime	.10
Half dime	.05
Copper	
Cent	$ .01
Half cent	.0½

Source: A. Barton Hepburn, A History of Currency in the United States, New York, Macmillan, 1915, p. 43

By legislation in 1834 and 1837 which established a new mint ratio between gold and silver, Congress expected to attract gold back to the mint. The new mint ratio of 16:1 left the pure silver content of the dollar at 371.25 grains but reduced its gold content from 24.75 to 23.22 grains of gold, so that every ounce of gold brought to the mint fetched $20.67 instead of $19.39 and every ounce of silver, $1.29.

With the new ratio, gold was now overvalued and silver undervalued.

This made it profitable to export silver coin or melt it down and sell bullion as a commodity. The few silver coins that still remained in circulation quickly disappeared, leaving the country without a supply of currency of small denominations. To remedy this situation, in 1853 Congress reduced the silver content and stopped free coinage of the half dollar, quarter, dime and half dime. In their place the mint produced new lightweight token subsidiary coins. In 1857 all acts making foreign coins legal tender were repealed, and the United States at last had a national coinage system with uniform coins of relatively stable value.

PAPER MONEY DURING THE WAR OF 1812 AND THE CIVIL WAR

The federal government was reluctant to issue paper money, mainly because the constitution did not appear to define explicitly who had the right to do so. Under these circumstances, commercial banks chartered by both the federal and the state governments provided notes for circulation.

Necessity forced the federal Treasury to print paper during the War of 1812. This paper was not made legal tender nor was it considered money. Instead of selling bonds to finance the war, the Treasury sold short-term notes. Later issues, which were in small denominations and bore no maturity date and paid no interest, had a small circulation. The notes that were outstanding at the end of the war were converted into long-term bonds, and the federal government stopped printing notes.

Financial necessity again put the government into the money printing business during the Civil War. No national tax collecting system had as yet been established. Even if there had been one, it was politically impracticable to exact heavy taxes, and there was probably not enough good money to pay the taxes on the scale required.

A few months after the beginning of the Civil War, the Treasury issued non-interest bearing treasury notes similar to those issued during the War of 1812. Many Americans foresaw the fate of the paper issues and hurried to the banks to demand specie before it was too late. Specie again disappeared from circulation, and by the end of 1861 the Treasury,

---

[6] After 1792 the United States government found itself in the embarrassing position of operating a mint supplying coins to other countries while foreign coins continued to circulate at home. Although Spanish dollars contained an average of three or four more grains of gold, natives in the West Indies preferred the shiny fresh United States dollars. A profit could therefore be made by exchanging American dollars for Spanish dollars which were melted down and sold by weight. The export of American coins stopped in 1806 when President Jefferson suspended the coinage of United States dollars.

following the banks, suspended specie payments. The United States was thus on an inconvertible paper standard.[7]

As the Treasury's printing presses rolled on, the government's notes, or **greenbacks** as they were known, depreciated. To provide change, since all coins except the one cent copper had disappeared from circulation, a variety of practices came into use. Notes were cut into a number of pieces; merchants circulated script known as **shin-plasters;** and some cities and towns issued their own fractional currency. The government also issued special postage stamps, ungummed and oversized, which were later replaced by fractional notes.

When the war ended the government started to retire the greenbacks, but it was forced to change its policy in the face of political opposition. The general fall in prices aroused strong inflationary sentiments and people agitated for an increase in greenbacks rather than a withdrawal. When the country returned to a gold base with the Specie-Resumption Act of 1879, persons holding United States notes could redeem them in gold and the Treasury then reissued the notes. About $347 million in greenbacks remain outstanding to this day, but are no longer redeemable in gold.

THE GOLD STANDARD AND THE SILVER QUESTION

With the resumption of specie payments in 1879, the United States again returned to a metallic monetary base. During this period Europe was turning from bimetallism to monometallism on a gold base. The consequent decrease in the demand for silver together with the discovery of rich silver lodes in the western United States depressed the price of silver. The silver interests were quick to respond by demanding that the government resume the free coinage of silver discontinued in 1873. One of their arguments was that the scarcity of gold had caused the depressed prices of the time. The so-called "Crime of '73" was a rallying point as the price of silver fell below the $1.29 per ounce paid by the Treasury before the Coinage Act of 1873.

The silverites' push for legislation resulted in the Bland-Allison Act of 1878. The act restored the legal tender status of silver and required the Treasury to purchase silver in quantities of between $2 and $4 million per month to be coined into dollars. Provision was made also for the issuance of silver certificates upon the deposit of silver dollars. In 1890 the Sherman Silver Purchases Act replaced the Bland-Allison Act. The Treasury was required to increase its monthly purchases of silver and pay market prices for it. Moreover, the silver was to be paid for with legal

[7] See Chapter 2, Monetary Standards.

tender Treasury notes redeemable in either gold or silver at the will of the Secretary of the Treasury.

With the falling silver prices, and the relatively small gold holdings of the Treasury, both American citizens and foreigners feared that their dollars might not be convertible into gold for very long. A rush for gold ensued. Even after the repeal of the Sherman Act in 1893, the United States held on to a narrow gold base only after an extraordinary loan from a syndicate of bankers headed by J. P. Morgan.

The era of the silverites all but culminated in the presidential election of 1896. William Jennings Bryan, the Democratic nominee, became the leader of the silver movement. It was during one of his campaign speeches that he said, "You shall not press down upon the brow of labor this crown of thorns, you shall not crucify mankind upon a cross of gold."[8] William McKinley, the Republican nominee, was elected president.

In the dying years of the century, through new gold discoveries and a favourable balance of trade the United States was able to return to a steadier gold base. The Gold Standard Act of 1900 unequivocally placed the United States on a legal gold standard. The gold dollar consisting of 25.8 grains of gold nine-tenth fine was to be the standard unit of account, and all other forms of money issued by the United States were to be maintained at parity with it. In 1934 the weight of the gold dollar was reduced to 15.238 grains of gold nine-tenth fine, changing the mint price of gold from $20.67 to $35 per fine ounce troy weight, where it remains to this day.

SELECTED READINGS

Bank of Canada, *The Story of Canada's Currency*, Ottawa, 1955.

Leavens, Dickson H., *Silver Money*, Bloomington, Ind., Principia Press, 1939.

Linderman, H.R., *Money and Legal Tender in the United States*, New York, G.P. Putman's Sons, 1877.

McIvor, R. Craig, *Canadian Monetary, Banking and Fiscal Development*, Toronto, Macmillan, 1961, Ch. 1 and 2.

Newfeld, E.P. (ed), *Money and Banking in Canada*, Toronto, McClelland and Stewart, 1964.

Nussbaum, Arthur, *A History of the Dollar*, New York, Columbia University Press, 1957.

[8] *Speeches of William Jennings Bryan* (revised and arranged by himself), New York, Funk and Wagnalls, 1909, Vol. 1, p. 249.

PART TWO

COMMERCIAL BANKING

4 THE ORIGIN OF MODERN BANKING

THE GOLDSMITHS

The origin of modern banking can be traced to the operations of the goldsmiths of seventeenth century England. The goldsmiths had strongrooms for the safekeeping of the materials of their trade. Extra space in these rooms was often rented to merchants and others to safekeep valuables, including large sums of money. At first the money was accepted in locked and sealed boxes which were returned to their owners in the same condition in which they had been left for safekeeping. Later, it became common for customers to deposit coin in return for a receipt or certificate of deposit. In time the goldsmiths observed that their depositors did not demand the identical coin initially left with them but only coin equal to the value shown on the certificates of deposit. In practice, if not in law, the goldsmiths assumed ownership of the coin deposited with them and employed the coin as required, being careful that they always held an amount sufficient to convert certificates of deposit into coin on demand. This marked the beginning of **deposit taking,** a characteristic of commercial banking as distinct from the functions of safekeeping.

The goldsmiths also observed that a predictable quantity of coin was always left with them. They could gauge the quantity by observing the activities of the merchants, many of whom deposited their coin with the same goldsmith. When one merchant wished to make payment to another, he would simply write an order to his goldsmith requesting the transfer of coin from his own account to that of his creditor without converting his deposit certificate into coin. This was the beginning of **chequing** or **clearing,** another characteristic of commercial banking.

To facilitate more efficient clearing services, the goldsmiths, instead of issuing one certificate of deposit to cover a customer's entire deposit of coin, started to issue **notes** in small denominations, usually of standard value. The total amount of these notes added up to the value of all deposits. When these notes became generally accepted for payment the goldsmiths made them payable to bearer. This marked the beginning of **note issue,** a characteristic of early commercial banking which later became the prerogative of central banks.

As a rule, the goldsmiths were men of wealth. It had therefore been not uncommon for them to lend to customers from their own resources. When it became a common practice for their notes to circulate as a medium of exchange, the goldsmiths began to make loans by using not their own coin or coin deposited with them, but their notes. These notes were the same as the notes given to the depositors of coin, with one important exception. They were not issued in return for a deposit of coin, but in return for a promissory note left by the borrower with the goldsmith. The distinction is important. As long as all the notes issued by the goldsmiths were not turned in at one time for conversion into coin, the goldsmiths could issue notes to a greater value than the value of the coin which they held. This marked the beginning of **fractional reserve banking.** The goldsmith assumed the role of a commercial banker who, through his lending operations, *creates money* out of his customers' promises to pay.

The total quantity of notes that the goldsmiths could issue against a given reserve base of coin depended upon the note holders' propensity to redeem them in coin. The goldsmiths soon learned from experience how much coin would remain with them during any given period and that this amount fluctuated with the temper of the times. When they miscalculated, as was the case when the British fleet was destroyed by the Dutch at Chatham (1667), they met certain doom. On hearing of the disaster at Chatham, Englishmen did what people were to do again and again during periods of social or political uncertainty: they hurried to convert their paper money holdings into as intrinsic a form as possible. They ran to the goldsmiths and demanded coin for their notes precipitating what we now call a **run on the bank.** Since the goldsmiths' notes were only partially secured by specie (gold and silver coin and bullion), not all note holders could be satisfied and the goldsmiths had to declare bankruptcy.

THE CHARTERED BANKS

Although fractional reserve banking is usually traced to the operations of the goldsmiths, it was by no means confined to them. Soon after the goldsmiths began the practice, if not simultaneously, merchants began to issue notes which were only fractionally secured by specie and which served as a medium of exchange. Moreover, governments started to grant charters incorporating companies authorized to conduct banking operations which included accepting deposits, clearing or transferring money, and issuing notes only fractionally secured by reserves of specie. Among the first chartered banks were the Bank of Sweden, the Bank of England, and the Banque Générale (John Law's Bank) in France.

THE BANK OF SWEDEN

The first modern bank was probably the Bank of Sweden. In 1656 John Palmstruck, head of the Swedish Merchants' Guild, obtained a government charter for a bank which would take deposits, effect transfers, make loans and issue notes. The Bank, like many of its successors in other countries, issued notes considerably in excess of its specie reserves. The result was inflationary pressures on the economy which led to a loss of confidence in the bank notes. A run on the Bank followed and the Bank was forced to suspend payment of its notes. Although this experience was to be repeated even after several reorganizations, the Bank of Sweden survived and is today Sweden's central bank.

THE BANK OF ENGLAND

The Bank of England, which also survived to become a central bank, was established as a result of a proposal by William Patterson to provide funds to the British government to finance its wars with France. In 1694 the Bank of England was granted a charter on condition that it would lend £1.2 million to the government at 8 per cent interest. At the time the government was accustomed to paying 40 per cent interest for its loans from the goldsmiths. From the sale of its stock the Bank provided the government with the requisite funds. However, since the Bank's capital was equal to its loans to the government, it began operations with a portfolio of government obligations but with little cash. The Bank's charter allowed it to accept deposits, make loans, deal in bills of exchange and issue bank notes against its portfolio of government loans. From the beginning it was plagued by a shortage of cash, and as a result of a run on the Bank within its first two years of operation, it was forced to suspend the conversion of its notes into specie (cash). The Bank survived and in 1697 its authorized capital was increased, allowing it to obtain additional cash from the sale of shares. At the same time the Bank was granted a partial monopoly on joint-stock banking insofar as no other company of more than six persons was allowed to issue bank notes. Despite this monopoly the Bank of England did only a small part of the commercial banking business in the city of London and almost none in the rest of the country. The bulk of English banking was carried on by private bankers, the descendants of goldsmiths and merchants who had started a banking business as a sideline but had come to regard it as their main enterprise. The Bank of England was able to survive the growing competition from other bankers because of its superior legal position and its connection with government finance.

THE BANQUE GENERALE

John Law, a Scot who gambled away his father's fortune, attempted to convince the English and Scottish financial authorities that paper money was of inestimable value for economic growth. He argued that it could never cause price inflation as long as it was issued to meet the needs of both business and trade. His proposals for paper money based solely on assets other than specie were welcomed in France after being turned down in Britain.

France was in dire financial straits at the turn of the eighteenth century. As a last resort to pay its debts, the Crown had issued paper currency, or *billets d'état* which circulated at a large discount from their face value. John Law promised to restore prosperity and in 1716 was granted letters patent for an incorporated bank with a monopoly of note issue. As was the case with the Bank of England, the French Banque Générale started with a weak financial structure. One quarter of its initial share capital was subscribed in coin and the remainder in *billets d'état* at face value. However, unlike the Bank of England, it was immediately successful. Its notes were only fractionally secured but fully convertible into specie (silver). It loaned its notes on good security at 6 per cent, a rate which at the time was extraordinarily low.

With sound currency and available credit confidence was restored almost miraculously. If Law's career had ended at this point, he would probably have remained a national hero of France for creating a sound banking system where none had ever existed.

The Bank was so successful that in 1718 the king took it over with the purchase of all the stock from private stockholders. He renamed it the Banque Royale and its notes were made legal tender and were redeemed in the old *billets d'état* instead of silver.

Although Law remained head of the Bank, he turned his attention to more grandiose schemes. He established the Compagnie d'Occident whose alleged purpose was the colonization of the Mississippi Valley, but which in practice bought government bonds. Next he added the Compagnie des Indes which eventually, together with the Compagnie d'Occident, gathered in the monopoly of the tobacco trade, the African slave trade, the operations of the mint, the collection of taxes and the entire public debt for which it received 3 per cent interest. The operations of these companies and the sale of their stock were financed with the expansion of bank notes.

By 1720 the shares of the Compagnie des Indes were selling at more than thirty-five times their face value. As the price rose, the bank allowed larger and larger loans against the shares driving up their price on the bourse. Finally some speculators realized that the speculation in shares and the inflation of share prices and prices generally due to the overissue of bank notes could not last and they began to sell. The selling fever was soon caught by all and the whole financial structure came tumbling down. The Banque Royale, which was holding as security against its note issue less than 2 per cent in specie (gold and silver) and less than 10 per cent in all assets combined, collapsed with such a crash that no other bank was chartered in France for over fifty years.

THE SOUTH SEA COMPANY

In England the cost of Marlborough's wars had increased the government's floating debt to the point where further financial support for its wars could be obtained only after funding part of this debt.[1] In 1711, in an attempt to reorganize its financial affairs, the government granted a charter to the "Governor and Company of the Merchants of Great Britain trading to the South Seas and other parts of America". The South Sea Company, as it came to be known, received what was only a fictional monopoly of trade in the Spanish dominions in Central and South America. In return for this it agreed to take over a large part of the government's debt. The financial success which the company experienced in the first few years of operation was due almost entirely to the interest it received on the government debt and not to its few trading ventures.

With the news of the apparent success of John Law's schemes, the directors of the South Sea Company proposed to pay £3.5 million for the privilege of taking over the entire national debt of some £30 million. The Bank of England, fearful for its competitive position, offered the government a premium of £5 million. The government accepted the South Sea Company's counter offer of £7.5 million, a blessing in disguise for the Bank. To raise the necessary funds the company offered its own stock, which with the speculative fever of the times rose in three months to thirteen times its face value.

In 1720, the bubble year, the magic of making huge profits from the sale of stock encouraged the promotion of all sorts of schemes. One, for example, was the "Insurance from Death by drinking Geneva" (Holland gin). Concerned about competition, the South Sea Company prevailed upon the government to warn those who issued stock illegally that they

---

[1] When a government borrows money for short periods of time, the debt incurred is referred to as a floating debt. When, on the other hand, it borrows money for a longer period by issuing bonds or similar security we say its debt is funded.

would be prosecuted. The warning frightened investors who began to suspect they were the victims of unscrupulous promoters. In the ensuing general scramble to dump stock, several banks failed. Although the Bank of England called in some of its loans, it was not deeply involved in either the speculative boom or the liquidation after the bubble burst. In the end it loaned money to prevent the South Sea Company from collapsing.

THE DEVELOPMENT OF BRITISH BANKING[2]

By the end of the eighteenth century, an integrated banking system was beginning to emerge in Britain with the Bank of England becoming the centrepiece of this system. Outside the city of London there were approximately fifty merchant or country banks. Within the city there were about three hundred private banks and the Bank of England. The country banks issued their own notes and held a large proportion of their cash reserves with the private city banks where they earned interest. The city banks, in turn, were able to earn interest on reserves which they deposited with the Bank of England. The Bank of England had become the main depository of the nation's specie reserves. Moreover, its notes enjoyed a virtual monopoly in the city since the city banks had all but ceased issuing their own notes.

London, the financial centre, and the country were linked through **inland bills of exchange.** These were orders for payment drawn by farmers and merchant-manufacturers on the London merchants who purchased their produce. These bills were usually sold (discounted) through London bill brokers. A large part of the proceeds from the sale of bills was left on deposit with the city banks. In this way the city banks reached out to gather in savings from the country districts. However, as industrial development in England quickened, the need for working capital in the expanding manufacturing districts of the Midlands and the North could not be satisfied with the proceeds from sales to the city. The inland bill of exchange then became the means for obtaining credit. Merchants or manufacturers with good credit reputations could meet their needs for funds by drawing bills of exchange on London banks. As this method of financing was not open to relatively unknown newcomers, they arranged

2 "A large part of all monetary and banking theory, modern as well as classical, derives from the public discussion of English conditions and the disputes concerning English policy. Bankers, economists, and statesmen throughout the world have turned to England for the models of their banks, banking theories and national policies. Whether or not English institutions and policies were the best that could have been designed given the times, and, much less, whether or not they were suitable models for other nations, are entirely separate questions. But that they have been used as such is a fact". Rondo Cameron, *Banking in the Early Stages of Industrialization,* New York, Oxford University Press, 1967, p. 15.

with established merchants whose names were known in London to draw bills for them on city banks. Many of these merchants became full-fledged commercial bankers — the merchant or country banker.

When a country bank found itself in difficulty because of a large demand for metallic money (a run on the bank), it would repatriate its reserves from the city banks in the form of specie. The city banks, in turn, would draw on their reserves held with the Bank of England. The Bank of England could also make additional specie available for circulation by discounting bills for its own notes which were convertible into specie. Before 1797 the Bank discounted bills only for London merchants, but after that date it extended its discounting privileges to other bankers. The Bank's willingness to supply specie by discounting bills during emergencies prevented such crises as those of 1763, 1772 and 1783 from ending in monetary collapse.[3]

THE BANK RESTRICTION PERIOD

A continuous drain on the metallic reserves of the Bank of England started after the beginning of England's wars with France in 1793. While most of the loss of the Bank's reserves was due to an external drain to the continent, there was also an internal drain due to public hoarding against a possible French invasion. The flow of metallic currency to the continent was the result of England's expenditures for maintaining troops there and of the loans made by Parliament to the Hapsburg Emperor of Germany to bring about a coalition of power against Napoleon. The private export of gold to France was forbidden. However, much gold left England at a profit when French currency was restored to a metallic basis, following the disastrous experiment with paper currency *(assignats)*.[4]

On February 21, 1797 the metallic reserves of the Bank of England stood at an all time low of no more than £1 million. On Saturday, February 25 the *London Gazette Extraordinary* reported the landing in Wales of a force from a French frigate. As this news was likely to cause a violent run on the Bank on the following Monday, the government responded with

3 In 1763 there was a financial crisis following the end of the Seven Years War; in 1772 the stock market speculation that followed the war was climaxed by the failure of the Ayr Bank in Scotland; and in 1783 a crisis developed with the conclusion of the American War of Independence.

4 The *assignat* experiment is a classic example of paper money made worthless by overissue. See R. G. Hawtrey, *Currency and Credit*, London, Longmans, Green. 1934, Ch. 17; and S. E. Harris, *The Assignats*, Cambridge, Harvard University Press, 1930.

an order-in-council stating, "It is indispensably necessary for the public service that the directors of the Bank of England should forebear issuing any cash in payment until the sense of Parliament can be taken on that subject." This order introduced the period of the **paper pound** or **bank restriction.**

Before the restriction of specie payment, the amount of notes issued by the Bank of England was closely tied to the specie flows in and out of its vaults. With an outflow of specie it contracted its issue of notes by discounting fewer bills of exchange. Alternatively, with an inflow of specie it would usually increase its note issue by discounting more bills. The Bank's role in controlling the financial system was passive insofar as its note issue followed generally the ebb and flow of specie. However, after bank restriction the Bank of England managed its note issue according to the "real bills" doctrine. It discounted bills of exchange only if it considered them of good quality. The Bank assumed that its responsibility was to meet the legitimate demands for loans and that as long as the money it supplied (paper pounds) was used in trade and not for speculation, an overissue was impossible.

With economic expansion in Britain during the Napoleonic Wars and the consequent increase in the amount of bills presented for discount, the Bank of England expanded its note issue. Added to this was the note issue resulting from the Bank's reluctant purchase of government bonds.

Between 1797 and 1810 domestic prices rose by about 50 per cent. Higher prices led to an increase in imports and an adverse balance in England's foreign trade. This in turn increased the demand for, and consequently the price of, specie required to settle foreign accounts. In other words, the value of the pound depreciated in terms of specie on the foreign exchange markets. The exact relationship of the increase in note circulation and the rise in prices to the fall of the pound in the foreign exchange market does not appear to have been understood by the majority of people, including the directors of the Bank of England.

In the fall of 1809 David Ricardo, who was to become England's leading economist, wrote a series of articles in the *Morning Chronicle* in which he emphasized that an excessive issue of inconvertible paper would inevitably reduce the value of the paper currency below that of the gold coin it was supposed to represent. That is to say, an excessive issue of paper money would lead to an increase in prices generally.

Ricardo's observation led to questions being asked in the House of Commons and ultimately to the appointment of the Bullion Committee in 1810 "to inquire into the Cause of the High Price of Gold Bullion, and to take into consideration the state of the Circulating Medium and of the Exchanges between Great Britain and Foreign Parts; and to report the same, with their Observations thereupon ... to the House (of Commons)".

THE BULLION REPORT

The Bullion Committee made its report in June of 1810. The report blamed the rise in prices in general, and the high price of bullion in particular, on the overissue of paper money. It noted that the Bank of England had made a bad job of managing paper currency, and that managing the currency was too great a responsibility to be left in the hands of "any man or set of men". It recommended that the law suspending cash payments be repealed within two years.

Although the Bullion Report was rejected by Parliament, it evoked public debate on the relationship of the activities of the Bank of England, the money supply and domestic prices to the value of the paper pound on the foreign exchange market (the high price of bullion), a debate which lasted for more than thirty years. In 1810 and 1811 alone the report inspired some ninety pamphlets on monetary and banking problems.

THE BULLION CONTROVERSY

The bullion controversy focused on the high price of bullion, or what we would call today the low price of the paper pound, on the foreign exchange markets. The bullionists supported the Bullion Report. They argued that if the Bank of England had had to convert its notes into specie on demand, overissue would have been checked and the high price of bullion (specie) prevented. As the Bank increased its discounting of commercial paper (bills of exchange and promissory notes), it increased the amount of money in public circulation outside London as well. Since the large amount of Bank of England notes made more plentiful the reserves of cash in which the country banks were required to redeem their notes, they were encouraged to expand their own note issues. An increase in the overall amount of notes in public circulation was seen as the cause of high domestic prices and the expansion of foreign imports. The consequent unfavourable balance of foreign payments increased the demand for and the price of foreign exchange and bullion. The high price of bullion therefore was proof, although not an exact measure, of the depreciation of bank notes.

The anti-bullionists defended the Bank of England. They contended that the high price of bullion was not the result of overissue by the Bank but could be directly traced to non-monetary causes such as poor harvests and the scale of the government's remittances to its continental allies. Wars had caused an increase in the demand for specie at a time when its supply was reduced by increased hoarding. Moreover, the anti-bullionists argued that an overissue of bank notes was impossible because the Bank managed its note issue according to the real bills doctrine. This doctrine was to play an important role in the development of banking, not only in Britain but also in Canada, the United States and other countries.

According to the real bills doctrine, the Bank of England discounted only "real" bills. These were bills drawn by merchants to finance inventories of goods. Hence the expansion of bank notes resulting from the Bank's discounting of bills was accompanied by an equivalent increase in the amount of goods held by the merchants. Alternatively a reduction in bank notes from a reduction in the real bills held by the Bank was accompanied by an equivalent decrease in the amount of goods held by the merchants. Insofar as the amount of money and the quantity of goods in trade were assumed to move together, changes in the money supply were considered to have no effect on prices and therefore had none on the foreign exchanges. There is a basic flaw in this theory. Goods produced for inventories result in an increase in income. As long as these goods remain unsold, and as long as there is no expansion in money hoarding, additional expenditures resulting from the high income will affect prices.

SPECIE RESUMPTION AND THE PALMER RULE

In 1819 Parliament passed legislation for the complete redemption of bank notes after May 1, 1821. The new metallic standard was not to be the one abandoned in 1797. Silver was dropped as a standard metal and England became the first country to adopt a complete gold standard, a step not followed by any other country for nearly fifty years.

The first test for the gold standard came with the crisis of 1825-1826. Prices in England had started to rise about 1822 as foreign investment in South America touched off a speculative boom. With an external drain of gold accompanied by internal drains, many country banks were unable to withstand runs and failed. The Bank of England, after some prodding by the government, probably averted complete financial collapse by increasing its own note issue. This introduced an important new concept to banking — panics can be cured by being "fed". This concept has one important corollary: there must be an institution which can do the "feeding". The Bank of England was able to feed the panic of 1825-1826 because the public was willing to accept its notes. However, under the gold standard the note issue could be increased only if the dwindling gold reserves could be replenished. The Bank through the good offices of the Rothschilds was able to obtain gold from Paris for this purpose.

In the aftermath of the crisis demands for banking reform became more intense. The private country banks had long been held responsible for the periodic financial crises that shook the country. Legislation enacted in 1826 restricted note issue by prohibiting circulation of notes of less than

£5 after 1829.[5] Joint-stock banks (with unlimited liability and any number of stockholders) were authorized beyond a sixty-five mile radius of London, and the Bank of England was allowed to open branches in any part of England. Parliament intended to strengthen country banking by the competitive elimination of unsound small banks; leaving only the larger and sounder joint-stock banks. The Bank of England by the discipline it imposed upon the country banks after 1826 did much to assist the government in achieving its goal of sounder country banks.

The Bank extended its branches, especially into the industrial areas of the Midlands and Lancashire. At these branches the Bank of England would accept on deposit the notes of a country bank only if that bank had a reserve with the particular branch that equalled or exceeded the amount of the notes being offered for deposit. Many of the new joint-stock banks did not issue their own notes because the Bank of England granted special facilities to those banks that handled its notes instead of their own and because it refused to rediscount bills for joint-stock banks of issue. In 1833 the Bank Charter Act allowed joint-stock banks to be established in London if they did not issue their own notes, and the notes of the Bank of England were made legal tender.

After the crisis of 1825 the London private banks stopped paying interest on money deposited with them by the country banks. These banks then cut their deposits with London bankers to a minimum and left the surplus with bill brokers at low call money rates. The London bankers gave up their reliance on rediscounting with the Bank of England in periods of stringency and relied instead on higher cash reserves of their own and larger deposits with the Bank of England. They also left surplus funds with bill brokers, particularly after 1830 when the Bank of England extended rediscount privileges to the brokers.

With the specie redemption of its notes, the Bank of England attempted to follow a new policy which became known as the **currency principle** or the **Palmer Rule.**[6] According to the rule, variations in the Bank's note circulation were to occur only as a result of changes in the public's deposits or withdrawals of specie at the Bank, and not from the Bank's discounting activities. Toward this end the Bank rate (the rate at which the Bank discounted commercial paper) was maintained above market rates. Thus borrowing from the Bank of England was discouraged while at the same time the Bank stood prepared to accommodate the market during periods of financial emergency. The Bank of England became a "bank of last resort".

---

5 While it remained uncertain as to whether the Bank of England was included under the Bank Notes Act, it also discontinued circulation of notes of less than £5.

6 This was first made public in 1832 by J. Horsely Palmer, Governor of the Bank of England.

The Palmer rule, which attempted to fix the amount of note circulation to specie drains, did not work out in practice because the Bank of England did not follow a consistent Bank rate policy and because bank deposits now played a new role. Bullion dealers were able to get gold from the Bank of England by drawing cheques on their deposit accounts with the Bank instead of by turning in bank notes. During the economic expansion after 1834 the Bank rate was maintained at 4 per cent even after the market rate moved to higher levels. It was not until after the expansion had reached its climax and economic conditions had collapsed in mid-1836 that the Bank finally started to increase its rate. Again in 1839 with an external drain of gold resulting largely from poor harvests and loans to the United States, the Bank rate was raised only after the Bank's specie reserves had dropped to a dangerously low level. Suspension of specie was averted probably only because the Bank was able to borrow gold in Paris and Hamburg. The behaviour of the Bank of England in 1836 and 1839 came under close scrutiny both by the public and by various parliamentary committees. It was generally agreed that the note issue should be so regulated as to diminish the possibility of changes in the price level and fluctuations in business activity. How this was to be accomplished sparked the now famous controversy between the **currency school** on the one hand, and the **banking school** on the other.

THE CURRENCY AND BANKING CONTROVERSY

The currency school insisted that only bank notes and coin could be included under the definition of money and that it was variations in this money that produced fluctuations in the general level of commodity prices. Bank deposits, on the other hand, were not money but a form of capital. Since they were not a medium of exchange they could not affect the volume of money. The currency school advocated the strict adherence to the currency principle according to which paper currency should be backed 100 per cent with gold. What the currency school wanted was an automatic gold standard where the amount of note circulation would be free from the control of either the government or the Bank of England. They concluded that the note issue privilege should be vested in a single authority which would be closely scrutinized by the state.

The banking school insisted that no simple separation of monetary and banking operations was possible. This argument was based on the contention that cheques and circulating bills of exchange were just as much media of payment as bank notes. It was absurd to try to regulate prices by controlling the issue of notes since they were merely a part — and a diminishing part — of total paper circulation. Moreover, the quantity of notes in circulation was the direct result of price changes and not the cause of them. Thomas Tooke, one of the banking school's most vocal proponents rationalized this conclusion as follows: borrowing by merchants during economic expansion increased their deposits and cheque payments; the increase in payments tended to create higher prices which induced the public to withdraw bank notes from the banks, increasing the amount of paper in circulation; if prices fell, notes again returned to the banks.[7] The banking school concluded that the most important monetary influence was not the volume of bank notes outstanding but the volume of lending and discounting undertaken by the banks. They were not sure what control, if any, was necessary over bank lending. They believed that as long as the banks confined their lending to self-liquidating loans and discounted only real bills, overissue of notes would be prevented.

THE BANK CHARTER ACT OF 1844

In 1844 Parliament revised the charter of the Bank of England according to recommendations of the Directors of the Bank who adhered to the principles of the currency school. The Bank Charter Act separated the Bank into two parts, the *issue* department and the *banking* department. The sole responsibility for the issuance of bank notes was given to the issue department. It was allowed to issue up to £14 million in notes backed only by government securities. Above this so-called "uncovered" issue, additional notes could be issued only against a 100 per cent specie reserve.[8] The banking department was allowed to function as any other commercial bank of the time using as its cash reserves Bank of England notes which it earned from its business activity.

The Bank Charter Act of 1844 also effectively ended the expansionary powers of other banks. No bank could issue its own notes in excess of the amount it had in circulation in 1844. If any bank gave up its note issue, the Bank of England was allowed to add two thirds of the amount given up to its uncovered circulation. Not until 1923 did the Bank of England get the monopoly of note issue.

THE ACCEPTANCE OF CENTRAL BANKING

The Bank Charter Act was an anachronism from the time it was enacted. It attempted to regulate the money supply by regulating bank notes at a time when bank deposits were becoming an important medium of ex-

7 See Thomas Tooke, *An Inquiry into the Currency Principle, the Connexion of the Currency with Prices, and the Expediency of a Separation of Issue from Banking*. London, 1844.

8 Gold coin and gold and silver bullion. However, the value of silver held could not exceed one fourth that of gold.

change. The act itself encouraged the increased use of bank deposits and chequing as a means of avoiding the use of currency.

The Act of 1844 both failed to limit effectively expansion of the total money supply (and therefore of economic activity), and made it more difficult to avert financial panics. We noted earlier that financial panics must be fed and that there must be an institution that can do the feeding. During the financial crises in 1847 and 1857,[9] gold flowed out of the country and the Bank, having reached the limit of its uncovered issue was unable to satisfy the public's demand for currency. On both occasions complete financial collapse was prevented by the government authorizing the Bank to exceed the limit of its uncovered issue. The Bank's note expansion in both cases was made conditional on a higher Bank rate to discourage further borrowing from the Bank.

After the 1850's the Bank of England gradually developed the attitudes and instruments of policy which have become the common possession of central banking. During periods of rapid economic expansion and gold drains it increased the Bank rate to discourage borrowing. This was the case in 1863 when the American Civil War precipitated a gold drain. On the other hand, during periods of market uncertainty or financial crises as was the case in 1866 with the failure of a long established and highly respected banking house, the Bank made advances to bankers, bill brokers and merchants in sufficient amounts to prevent financial panic. The Bank had come to accept the responsibility of a bank of last resort and of a watchdog over financial markets. It was not until Walter Bagehot's *Lombard Street* was published in 1873, however, that the special position of the Bank of England as a central bank and the principles of central banking became generally understood and taken for granted.

---

9 The 1847 crisis was precipated by successive potato crop failures in Ireland and the 1857 crisis by the sudden depreciation of American railway securities.

SELECTED READINGS

Ashton, T.S., and R. S. Sayers, *Papers in English Monetary History*, 2nd ed., Oxford, Clarendon Press, 1954.

Cannon, E., *The Paper Pound of 1797-1821*, London, Staples Press, Ltd., 1919.

Clapham, Sir John Harold, *The Bank of England*, 2 vols., New York, Macmillan, 1944.

Feavearyear, Sir Albert, *The Pound Sterling: A History of English Money*, 2nd ed., revised by E. Victor Morgan, Oxford, Clarendon Press, 1963.

Fetter, Frank Whitson, *Development of British Monetary Orthodoxy, 1797-1875*, Cambridge, Mass., Harvard University Press, 1965.

James, F. Cyril, *The Economics of Money, Credit and Banking*, New York, Ronald Press, 1940, Ch. 7 and 8.

Law, John, *Money and Trade considered, with a Proposal for Supplying the Nation with Money*, 2nd ed., London, 1720.

Lawson, William John, *The History of Banking*, 1st U.S. ed., Boston, Gould and Lincoln, 1852.

Mints, Lloyd W., *A History of Banking Theory*, Chicago, University of Chicago Press, 1945.

Oudard, George, *John Law: A Fantastic Financier, 1671-1729*, London, Jonathan Cape, 1928.

Viner, Jacob, *Studies in the Theory of International Trade*, New York, Harper and Brothers, 1937, Ch. 3-5.

5

THE DEVELOPMENT OF UNITED STATES BANKING

We noted in Chapter 3 the shortage of currency in the American colonies and the attempts by the colonial assemblies to overcome this problem by issuing bills of exchange. The British Parliament strongly objected to the issue of paper in the colonies and made many attempts, especially in 1764, to prohibit it. The British were afraid that inflationary tendencies in the colonies would encourage trade rather than agriculture, a situation which conflicted with their mercantilist philosophy. Moreover, British creditors who were net creditors objected to the depreciation of their claims against American debtors. The Americans, on the other hand, tended to favour paper money and inflation because they thought this would encourage trade and lead to rapid economic growth.

Before the Revolution there were some "banks" which were nothing more than "batches of paper money". These were the land banks, some private and some public. Their bills of credit circulated on the security of mortgages on real estate.

The Pennsylvania Bank, the first to be incorporated on the American continent, had as its sole purpose the collection from its shareholders of funds to lend to the government to finance the Revolutionary War. This bank was liquidated soon after the war, its purpose fulfilled.

The first bank incorporated to carry out the essential functions of commercial banking was the Bank of North America established by the Continental Congress in 1781. Its capital was initially subscribed by the Congress, but because of the inability of Congress to obtain adequate specie, the stock was shortly transferred to the public. The bank, by careful management of its note issuing privileges, was able to avoid the excesses of previous colonial money issuing schemes. It was able to redeem its notes in silver on demand at all times. As a result its notes circulated at par with coin at a time when the continental currency was depreciating into oblivion.[1] Since there was confusion over whether the Continental Congress had the power to incorporate a bank, the Bank of North America obtained a charter from the state of Pennsylvania under which it operated until it joined the National Banking System in 1864. The success of the bank led to the establishment of the Bank of Massachusetts and the Bank of New York in 1784, and others soon followed.

THE FIRST BANK OF THE UNITED STATES

When Alexander Hamilton became Secretary of the Treasury in George Washington's first cabinet, he proposed the reorganization of the Bank of North America. He wished to make it a national bank that would undertake central banking functions similar to those performed by the Bank of England. However, the directors of the bank preferred to retain their state charter and to operate as an ordinary commercial bank.

Hamilton then turned his attention to the establishment of a new bank to serve as the national bank. In 1791 Congress granted a twenty-year charter to the First Bank of the United States. It was a private bank, although the federal government was obliged to subscribe to 20 per cent of the stock because of the shortage of private funds. Most of the remaining stock was purchased by foreigners, a fact which made the Bank suspect from the start.

The Bank was allowed to issue its own notes which, in order to prevent overissue, had to be redeemed in specie on demand and were limited to the amount of the paid-up capital of the bank. The notes were not given legal tender status but became government tender insofar as they were used to pay all obligations of the federal government as long as the Bank continued to redeem them at par in specie.

From the beginning the Bank was soundly managed. It transacted most of the fiscal business of the federal government and loaned money to the Treasury in anticipation of tax revenue. It was the custodian of public funds and transmitted these funds through its branches in the major cities. However, the Bank was from its very inception under continual attack. We have already mentioned the fear of foreign control. Many also thought the federal government had no power to charter a bank and that it was unconstitutional. The most potent attack on the Bank resulted from its success in providing a sound and national currency. The Bank did not accept the notes of any bank that refused to redeem them in specie. This policy made it difficult for many commercial banks to expand their loans. Hardest hit were the state chartered banks in the rural areas. Banks making loans commonly gave their customers their own

[1] See Chapter 3, page 32.

notes, rather than deposit balances for chequing purposes. Therefore, any restriction on their own note issue also restricted their lending ability and growth, a situation which created resentment in the state legislatures and the banking fraternity.

Although the First Bank of the United States was a success, its charter was not renewed in 1811. Congress refused the Bank's application as a result of a controversy which was to leave a lasting impression on American banking. On one side were the federalists who advocated a strong federal government with close control over money and banking. On the other side were the anti-federalists who wanted a weak federal government, allowing the states to control banking. While the federalists were concerned with the establishment of sound and conservative monetary policies, the anti-federalists saw great benefit in paper issues ("easy money") and called for a multitude of state banks.

THE SECOND BANK OF THE UNITED STATES

When the First Bank of the United States left the scene any restraint on unsound bank note issues disappeared and a rapid growth of state banks followed. Their proliferation was encouraged by the War of 1812 when the government, finding itself in financial difficulties, used the depreciated notes of state banks to pay its debt. The new state chartered banks overissued their notes and fed the war-induced inflation to such an extent that by 1814 specie payments had been discontinued and most notes were all but worthless. In 1816, after a long and acrimonious debate Congress issued a twenty-year charter for a second Bank of the United States.

In chartering a second bank Congress hoped to quickly restore specie payments and to receive assistance in its own financial operations. The charter provisions of the Second Bank of the United States followed almost exactly those of its predecessor. The government reserved the right to subscribe to 20 per cent of the Bank's stock, as well as to appoint five of its twenty-five directors. The Bank was the government's fiscal agent and like its predecessor established a branch system. However, unlike the First Bank it came under much closer inspection and supervisory regulation by both the Secretary of the Treasury and Congress.

The Second Bank of the United States had an even stormier history than the First Bank. At the start it was badly managed. It made loans to its own stockholders who used their Bank stock as collateral. It added to the already inflationary conditions by expanding its own loans and notes too rapidly. Late in 1818 when its own specie reserve was in danger it instituted a restrictive policy by curtailing its own lending policy and by refusing to accept the notes of state banks that did not redeem their notes in specie. Unfortunately, this restrictive policy came at a time when the American economy was declining as a result of a drop in the foreign demand for agricultural products. The Bank received much of the blame for the depression of 1818-1820 to which it probably contributed.

When Nicholas Biddle took over the management of the Bank in 1823 the "War on the Bank" started. Biddle concentrated his efforts on expanding the Bank's business, especially in the southern and western states where good banks were few. He also attempted to improve the quality of bank notes in circulation by forcing state banks to redeem any of their notes which came into the hands of the Second Bank. The Second Bank grew large enough to influence the monetary system of the entire nation. Biddle seems to have recognized its power and to have felt it the Bank's responsibility to control the money supply. Under his direction the Bank did not expand or contract credit on the basis of the profit motive alone but rather with a view to the condition of the national economy. In the process this Bank, too, gained the enmity of the state banks.

The Second Bank encountered serious opposition after 1828 when General Andrew Jackson was elected President of the United States. Jackson was sympathetic to the southern and western interests, who thought the main cure for economic ills was the creation of more money. He was also suspicious of the power wielded by the Second Bank and in particular by Biddle.

In 1831 a bill to recharter the Bank was passed by Congress but vetoed by President Jackson. In the following year when Jackson won the presidential election mainly over the bank issue, the Bank was doomed. In 1833 he transferred federal government deposits from the Second Bank to various state **pet banks.** Biddle, who had openly opposed Jackson's re-election, immediately countered by contracting the Second Bank's assets and liabilities. The result was nation-wide economic contraction, and when the Second Bank's charter expired in 1836 it was not renewed.[2] The bank war had been so painful and the political controversy so acrimonious that the federal government abstained from any formal attempt to regulate the American banking system until 1863 and did not authorize a central bank until 1914.

In the absence of a central body to assume regulation of the banking system some attempts were made to reform bank practices, at least regionally. These reforms had two main purposes: the security of bank notes, and the prevention of speculative fevers based on their overissue. Some of these reforms had been introduced before the demise of the Second Bank.

---

2 The Bank carried on with a Pennsylvania charter until it failed in 1841.

THE SUFFOLK BANKING SYSTEM

The Suffolk System was established in Boston as early as 1824. Most of the notes of country banks in the Boston area found their way to Boston, the centre of trade and commerce. Since these notes were redeemable only at their place of issue in the country, they circulated below par in Boston. Because the notes of the Boston banks circulated at par, these "good" notes were hoarded and driven out of circulation by the "poor" notes of the country banks which were used to transact day-to-day business.[3] The Boston banks tried to increase their own note circulation and consequently their earnings by a rather ingenious device, the Suffolk Banking System.

The Suffolk Bank of Boston, acting for the other city banks and for itself, redeemed the notes of the country banks at par if these banks maintained a redemption fund with it. The country banks were persuaded to join because of the Suffolk Bank's practice of accumulating the notes of a recalcitrant bank and presenting them for redemption in substantial volume. The possibility of a sudden drain on their reserves induced the country banks to cooperate with the Suffolk Bank and to maintain satisfactory banking standards.

THE SAFETY FUND SYSTEM

The legislature of the state of New York set up the Safety Fund System in 1829. It was concerned not only with excessive note issue but also with the protection of depositors in the event of bank failure. The legislation required all chartered banks of the state to limit their maximum note issue to twice their capital stock, to limit their loans and discounts to two and a half times their paid-up capital, and to pay to the state an amount equal to 3 per cent of their capital stock to provide a fund out of which the public liabilities (notes and deposits) of insolvent banks could be paid.

The fund worked suceessfully until the rash of bank failures after 1836 following the decline of the Second Bank of the United States. To meet the crisis the fund was obliged to obtain a loan from the state. Subsequently payment was limited to the claims of note holders only. Bank notes were given a prior claim on the assets of a bank and stock holders were made subject to a double liability. This meant that a stock holder on record at the time of the bank failure could be assessed an amount equal to the par value of the shares he held, so that he stood to lose both his original investment and an equivalent sum. Because the Safety Fund System applied only to banks with special charters from the state, it expired in 1866 when all charters were cancelled by the free banking legislation.

---

3 This is another example of Gresham's Law at work. See Chapter 1.

Three features of the New York Safety Fund legislation subsequently became part of the Canadian bank act: prior lien of bank notes, double liability of bank stock holders and a guarantee fund. The deposit insurance system, long a part of American banking and introduced into Canadian banking in 1967, is based on the same principle as the early New York experiment.

WILDCAT BANKING

The period between the fall of the Second Bank and the introduction of the National Banking System is generally referred to as the era of wildcat banking. The term was originally applied to banks located "where only wildcats could find them". Inaccessibility made presenting their worthless paper for redemption all but impossible.

The mushroom growth of state banks was stimulated by the economic conditions of the 1840's and 1850's and by the institution of free banking. During these decades there was a great demand for capital to finance the building of railroads and the westward push of settlement. As more agricultural areas were opened up and agricultural production increased, farm prices fell. The remedy for both the shortage of capital and low agricultural prices was thought to be the creation of more money by more banks. The establishment of new banks was made easier by the adoption of free banking. In many states, the reserve requirements for note issue were so low that the banks were merely "paper mills" operating with very little financial backing.

FREE BANKING

The move to free banking was made on political as well as on economic grounds. Because of their earnest wish to create a new democracy where no privileged order of wealth could exist, Americans tended to be suspicious of all incorporations, especially those of banks, since a special act of the legislature was required to establish each new bank. Opponents of the system charged that it concentrated bank ownership in the hands of a small group whose vested interests it protected. They also claimed that those seeking a charter were often obliged to resort to graft and corruption. Free banking was to make entry into banking more democratic.

The New York Free Banking Act of 1838 provided a blueprint followed by other states. [4] It established the principle that a bank charter could be obtained by anyone who fulfilled uniform conditions specified in a general banking law. These conditions were concerned with the issuance

4 A similar law was enacted in Michigan a year earlier, but was actually based on the New York plan.

of bank notes rather than with the capitalization of a bank. Under the legislation bank notes were issued to a bank by the state comptroller's office upon the bank's depositing with him an equivalent amount of specified securities as collateral. While the notes were issued by the state, they carried the individual bank's name and circulated after being signed by the officers of the bank. The collateral, equivalent to the full amount of notes issued, could be sold to redeem the notes in case of bank failure. It was assumed that a note issued secured by an equivalent volume of securities not only provided safety for the individual note holder but also safeguarded against inflation. The advocates of free banking believed, as did the English currency school, that if the issue of notes were closely regulated in terms of the security behind it, the banking system could be safely left to take care of itself without further regulation.

At first the New York Bank Act also imposed a 12½ per cent specie reserve requirement on notes but this was repealed in 1844. Most of the early state banking laws did not require banks to hold specie reserves against their notes or deposits. Because payment in specie was required to purchase the bank's capital stock, it was felt that obtaining adequate cash reserves was merely a matter of setting capital requirements at a suitably high level. Moreover, the limitation of the maximum amount of note issue to a multiple of the bank's capital stock, as was widely done, created the impression that note issue was in fact regulated by specie. However, when banks were established in the western states their capitalization was small and specie subscriptions were few. It was common practice for directors to borrow notes from a new bank with which to pay later instalments on their capital subscriptions. With the failure of more and more banks, legally required minimum cash reserves made their appearance in state bank legislation. By 1860 the wisdom of a specie reserve against notes as well as against deposits was generally recognized even by those states where both legislation and enforcement still tended to be lax.

THE INDEPENDENT TREASURY SYSTEM

We noted earlier that in 1833 President Jackson transferred federal funds to various state pet banks. These banks were supposed to maintain separate specie reserves to cover Treasury deposits. During the period of wildcat and free banking many of the banks holding such deposits failed. In many cases the banks had used the Treasury deposits as a basis for expanding their own loans and note issues. Thus, when they failed or were in difficulty the Treasury lost its deposits. Such losses prompted the government to establish banking offices of its own to take care of its receipts and disbursements.

An independent treasury system was established in 1840, but because of a change of the administration its operations were suspended in the following year. In 1846 the system was established on a permanent basis. The federal government undertook to be its own banker by collecting public revenue in the Treasury in Washington and in sub-treasuries located in important cities throughout the country, and by making disbursements directly from these offices.

While the Independent Treasury System safeguarded federal deposits it produced problems for the banking system and credit needs generally. Payments to the government had to be made in the form of specie or the government's own obligations. When the federal Treasury had a surplus, funds would accumulate in the sub-treasuries. This reduced the specie reserves available to the banks so that their ability to expand their loans and in some cases to redeem their notes was reduced. On the other hand, when the federal Treasury experienced deficits, funds would flow out of the sub-treasuries and provide a basis for expansion by the banks. Thus, note issue often depended upon the federal government's financial needs which did not necessarilty coincide with the needs of business. After 1863 the Treasury was again permitted to hold funds with the commerical banks, but the Independent Treasury System was not abolished until 1920. In 1913, banks which were members of the newly established Federal Reserve System became the principal fiscal agents of the federal government.

THE NATIONAL BANKING SYSTEM

With the exception of a few states, banking conditions in the United States were chaotic in the years after the Second Bank of the United States passed from the scene. Although there was continual agitation for reform it did not come until the Civil War when the federal government again began chartering banks under the National Banking Acts of 1863 and 1864.[5] By introducing the National Banking Acts the government hoped to fulfill three objectives: to assist the Treasury in financing the Civil War, to organize a safer and sounder banking system, and to provide a safe and uniform currency. The legislation provided for the establishment of new national banks which constituted the National Banking System. The office of the Comptroller of the Currency under the Treasury Department was organized to grant charters to new national banks and to examine and supervise their operations. The principles of free banking were followed insofar as any group (of more than five persons) which met the conditions specified in the legislation was granted a

5 The Act of 1863 was so poorly framed that it was replaced by a new act in the following year.

charter. To provide funds for the government, each new bank was obliged to purchase a specified amount of government bonds prior to its establishment, a requirement which was to remain in force until the First World War. To provide sounder banks, larger capital subscriptions were required to set up a national bank than were commonly required for the establishment of banks under state laws.[6]

By way of reforming bank note circulation, national bank notes could be issued only against United States bonds deposited with the Comptroller of the Currency, the amount of notes not to exceed 90 per cent of the face or the market value of the bonds, whichever should be smaller. Subsequently, the rule was modified to 100 per cent of the par value of the bonds. The amount of notes any bank could issue was limited to the total of its paid-up capital, and the bank was required to maintain with the Comptroller a redemption fund of 5 per cent of its notes outstanding. Notes had a first lien against the assets of the issuing bank. Although the notes were accepted at par in payment of federal taxes they were not legal tender until 1933. In 1874 the initial regulation limiting total note issue by all banks to $300 million was dropped and notes were exempted from reserve requirements which had originally applied to both notes and deposits.

For purposes of defining minimum reserve requirements national banks were designated as **central reserve city, reserve city** and **country banks.** National banks in central reserve cities were required to hold reserves of 25 per cent in vault cash consisting of legal tender specie and Treasury currency. Banks in reserve cities also had to keep reserves of 25 per cent, but half could be in the form of deposits with national banks in central reserve cities. The country banks were required to keep reserves of 15 per cent, but three fifths could be in the form of deposits with national banks in reserve and central reserve cities. At first only New York was a central reserve city. Later, in 1887, Chicago and St. Louis were included in this category.

Banker response to the national banking law was disappointing. State banks were reluctant to join the National Banking System because of the loss of freedom that was generally implied. To induce more banks to join the system a 10 per cent tax was imposed in 1866 on the notes issued by non-member state banks.

Although the National Banking System accomplished its purpose of providing a safe, uniform bank note issue and established banking standards, it failed to solve some problems and created still others. Under the

[6] The minimum capital requirements for establishing national banks were as follows: $50,000 for banks in cities under 6,000 inhabitants, $100,000 for banks in cities from 6,000 to 50,000 inhabitants and $200,000 for banks in cities with still larger populations. These requirements which still apply today to banks established under federal legislation are lower than those required for the establishment of banks in Canada.

system the volume of bank notes remained inelastic because it was tied to the volume of eligible securities that could be used as collateral. The availability of these securities was determined by federal surpluses and deficits which did not necessarily reflect needed seasonal, cyclical or secular variations in bank notes.

Both reserve city and central reserve city banks used the reserves left with them by other banks to expand their own loans and deposits. A sudden increase in the demand for cash often found the banks unable to convert their loans and deposits into cash to satisfy public demand. The financial panics of 1873, 1884, 1893 and 1907 were in large part the result of currency demands by the public at a time when the banking system was fully loaned up. The National Banking System could not avert a crisis because there was no central bank which could feed panics with its own liabilities.

SUBSTITUTES FOR A CENTRAL BANK

With the passage of time the Treasury began to assume some responsibility for the proper operation of the banking system. It could do this by transferring funds between the Treasury vaults established under the Independent Treasury System and the commercial banks. By withdrawing cash from the Treasury vaults and depositing it with the banks the Treasury increased the banks' reserves. On the other hand, by drawing cash from the banks and depositing it in its vaults the Treasury reduced the banks' cash reserves and thus their ability to expand. Unfortunately this form of monetary management was not powerful enough to prevent liquidity crises.

The commercial banks as a group also began to assume central banking functions through the establishment of **clearing houses.** In crises they issued clearing house certificates which took the place of reserve cash in the settlement of the claim of one bank against another bank. These certificates were, in effect, a loan by the banks as a group to one of their number, who, though solvent, required temporary accommodation. The borrowing bank provided assets as collateral and paid interest on the certificates. Under this arrangement the clearing house associations assumed the role of a bank of last resort.

THE CRISIS OF 1907 AND THE ALDRICH COMMISSION

The monetary panic of 1907, although no different from earlier panics, finally led to a re-examination of the American monetary system. In 1908 Congress passed the Aldrich Vreeland Act authorizing the issue of emergency currency subject to a tax to encourage its early retirement as soon as the emergency was past. For the first time, commercial paper, bonds of state and city governments, and certain other classes of securities could be accepted by the Comptroller of the Currency as collateral for bank note issues.[7] The act also provided for the appointment of a National Monetary Commission to recommend a more effective monetary organization for the nation. Early in 1912 the commission submitted its report which proposed the creation of a National Reserve Association, a voluntary affiliation of banks which would issue notes, hold deposits of member banks and make loans to them against acceptable collateral. The so-called Aldrich Plan was introduced in Congress but because of strong opposition was never brought to a vote. However, the work of the commission was by no means fruitless. In the following year in a more favourable political climate Congress passed the Federal Reserve Act which introduced central banking on a permanent basis.

THE FEDERAL RESERVE SYSTEM

The Federal Reserve Act of 1913 established the Federal Reserve System which now acts as a central bank for the United States. Instead of one bank to provide central bank functions, the act provided for the establishment of the present twelve regional central banks known as Federal Reserve Banks. These Banks, while owned by their members, are controlled by a Board of Governors (initially the Federal Reserve Board). From the outset all national banks had to become members by holding reserves with and by purchasing stock of the Federal Reserve Bank in their region. State chartered banks could join but, as is still the case today, many chose not to because the Federal Reserve requirements are more stringent than those of state banking laws. Today member banks of the Federal Reserve System hold about 85 per cent of all commercial bank assets, but their number is still significantly smaller than that of state banks outside the system.

The main purpose for establishing the Federal Reserve System was to introduce a mechanism for correcting inelasticity in the currency system. The Federal Reserve Banks were authorized to issue a new type of bank note — Federal Reserve notes secured by gold and by commercial and agricultural paper. It was not until 1968 that Congress removed the requirement that gold reserves be held (in the form of gold certificates) against Federal Reserve notes. At a much earlier date government securities had replaced commercial and agricultural paper as security for note issue.

[7] Only "national currency associations" (groups of ten or more national banks with combined capital stock and surplus of at least $5 million) and individual banks when permitted by the Secretary of the Treasury, could issue emergency currency.

— The principles of the gold standard mechanism and the commercial loan theory (the real bills doctrine) provided the philosophical basis of the new system. It was held that the supply of money could be regulated by an adherence to automatic controls without conscious management by a centralized authority. Although the system was to be coordinated by the Federal Reserve Board, its early function was confined to examination and supervision. Monetary policy was limited to changing the rate of interest at which Federal Reserve Banks purchased discounted paper for member banks. This rate, in turn, was to be dictated by the supply of gold held by the Federal Reserve Banks.

It was not until after the financial crises of 1929 and the deperssion years that followed that the Federal Reserve Act of 1913 was amended to allow the system to actively manage the money supply and to control credit conditions. An important step in this direction was the establishment of the Federal Open-Market Committee to centralize the control of Federal Reserve open-market operations.

SELECTED READINGS

Board of Governors of the Federal Reserve System, *The Federal Reserve System: Purposes and Functions*, Washington, D. C., 1963.

Friedman, Milton, and Anna Schwartz, *A Monetary History of the United States, 1867-1960*, Princeton, N.J., Princeton University Press, 1963.

Hammond, Bray, *Banks and Politics in America, from the Revolution to the Civil War*, Princeton, N.J., Princeton University Press, 1957.

Smith, Walter Buckingham, *Economic Aspects of the Second Bank of the United States*, Cambridge, Mass., Harvard University Press, 1953.

Sprague, O.M.W., *History of Crises under the National Banking System*, Washington, D.C., Publications of the National Monetary Commission, 1910.

Taus, E. R., *Central Banking Functions of the United States Treasury, 1789-1941*, New York, Columbia University Press, 1943.

6 THE DEVELOPMENT OF CANADIAN BANKING

Early banking developments in the colonies that were to become the Dominion of Canada were determined by three main evolutionary forces: The strongest of these was the British connection. The British government made its views known through memoranda, minutes, circulars and letters issued by the colonial office in London, and by disallowing bills passed by the colonial legislatures. The British influence was further emphasized by the early bankers themselves, most of whom had come from the United Kingdom, particularly Scotland, and who stressed heavily the virtues of prudent banking.

The second of these forces was the American experience. Because of the later development of the Canadian money and banking system, its founders had the opportunity to observe and avoid many of the difficulties encountered by their neighbours to the south.

Finally, the actual experience of operating in Canada gave to Canadian banking characteristics which were neither American nor British. Overbanking did not become a problem in Canada partly because Canadians, not having the intense individualism of their American cousins, were not so concerned with "democratic" banking and were prepared to accept branch banking rather than a unit bank in every community. Charters were very difficult to obtain in Canada because of the close connection between the legislatures and the early banking interests. Both government and banking in the two Canadas were controlled by select groups — in Lower Canada by the Rouge and in Upper Canada by the Family Compact.

EARLY ATTEMPTS TO ESTABLISH BANKS

The initiative toward establishing a bank in Lower Canada was taken by merchants in Montreal in 1792. They proposed to form the Canadian Banking Company to receive deposits in cash, to issue notes for circulation and to discount bills. Their proposals resulted in a private bank which took deposits but did not issue notes. In 1808 another attempt was made to establish a bank, this time in Quebec City, but the legislature of Lower Canada refused to grant it a charter.

Further efforts to establish banks were interrupted by the War of 1812, but after the war the situation was favourable for the promotion of banking. Early redemption of the war-time army bills did much to create confidence in paper issues, a precondition for successful banking. The genuine shortage of currency, the nuisance created by the circulating paper originated by merchants and others, and the shortage of capital, all served to point out the urgent need for a sound paper circulation. The successful operation of the First Bank of the United States provided an example of how sound banking could furnish such paper.

THE FIRST CHARTERED BANKS

In 1817 nine Montreal merchants signed Articles of Association to establish the Bank of Montreal without statutory authority. Their second petition for a charter was approved by the legislature of Lower Canada but it was not until 1822 that the charter was finally confirmed by royal assent. In rank of precedence, the Bank of New Brunswick is the first chartered bank in British North America. Its act of incorporation both passed the legislature of New Brunswick and received royal assent in 1820.

Although there are many similarities between the charters of these two banks, there are differences which reflect their independent evolution. The twenty-year charter of the Bank of New Brunswick followed the banking traditions of New England, partly because its founders included a Loyalist from Virginia and a Harvard graduate, and partly because most of the commerce of the Maritimes was carried on with the New England states. The terms of the ten-year Bank of Montreal charter, on the other hand, duplicated almost exactly the terms governing Alexander Hamilton's First Bank of the United States.

The charter of the Bank of New Brunswick reflected the traditionally conservative banking practices of New England. The debts of the bank were limited to twice its paid-up capital. By contrast, the Bank of Montreal's charter limited its total debts to three times the amount of its paid-up capital stock, plus an amount equal to moneys deposited for safekeeping. The New Brunswick bank was also more restricted in its note issue. While both banks were allowed to issue notes up to the amount of their paid-up capital plus holdings of gold and silver and debentures or other securities issued or guaranteed by the respective legislatures, the directors of the New Brunswick bank were held personally liable for an overissue of notes. Arrangements for paying capital were also stricter. The capital of

£50,000 of the Bank of New Brunswick had to be fully paid "in current Gold and Silver coins of the Province" a year and a half after incorporation. The charter of the Bank of Montreal authorized capital of £250,000 which had to be paid in by instalments of 10 per cent within nine years in the money then current in Lower Canada. While the Bank of New Brunswick had to make regular yearly statements to the government, the Bank of Montreal had to provide statements only upon request. Finally, the former was not allowed to open branches while the latter was permitted to establish branches in any part of Upper or Lower Canada.

There were some similarities in the two charters. Both limited the number of votes any one stockholder might cast; a Bank of New Brunswick stockholder was limited to a maximum of ten votes and a Bank of Montreal stockholder to twenty votes, regardless of the number of shares held. Neither bank was allowed to lend money on mortgages, land or real property. Both banks were permitted to receive deposits, to deal in gold and silver bullion, to issue notes which were redeemable in specie on demand, and to discount bills.[1]

The return of prosperity in the early 1820's and the economic expansion in the 1830's up to the crisis of 1837 encouraged the establishment of a few more banks. Their number remained small, however, because of the monopoly position held by a few banks and because of restraining rules issued in 1830 by the British government governing colonial bank charters.

The legislature of Upper Canada granted its first charter in 1817 to the Bank of Upper Canada in Kingston, but since royal assent was delayed for about two years, the charter lapsed and the bank failed almost immediately. Its place was taken by the Chartered Bank of Upper Canada established in York (Toronto). This bank was chartered by the legislature in 1819 and received royal assent in 1821. Its charter differed from others of the time in that the government of Upper Canada was authorized to subscribe to the bank's stock.

Because of the close political alliances of those associated with these banks, the Chartered Bank of Upper Canada and the Bank of Montreal in Lower Canada were able to exert an effective restricting influence on the number of banks their respective legislatures chartered. The same was true in Nova Scotia where the Halifax Banking Company (organized in 1825), although a private bank, was able to maintain its monopoly position until the formation of the Bank of Nova Scotia in 1832. Another reason for the

[1] The discount procedure of the Bank of New Brunswick followed by other banks is recounted in *The Bank of Nova Scotia, Monthly Review*, Toronto, May 1956. "The Directors were to vote by ballot on the discounts, three negative votes being sufficient to reject a note or bill. Voting was by black beans and white beans. According to evidence later produced in a public inquiry, a Director interested in a particular discount would sometimes threaten his brother Directors with the Black Beans on discounts in which *they* were interested' ."

relatively late chartering of banks in Nova Scotia was that most of the applications stipulated a franchise of monopoly which the legislature was unwilling to grant.

THE COMMERCIAL CRISIS OF 1837-1838

The period of rapid economic expansion after the mid-1820's came to an end with a commercial crisis which started in the United Kingdom. In Lower Canada the banks, following the trend in the United States, suspended specie payments on their notes. This action was given legal sanction in 1838, but at the same time each bank was required to restrict the total amount of notes issued during the period of suspension to its paid-up capital. In Upper Canada the Lieutenant-Governor was opposed to suspension primarily on the grounds that it meant copying the Americans. At first he promised assistance to the Bank of Upper Canada from the military chest, but when other banks demanded equal treatment the government announced that it would receive at par the notes of all banks. In a special session of the legislature specie suspension was finally authorized, but the banks' note issue was limited at first to twice and later to three times their paid-up capital. Maritime banks also suspended specie redemption during this period.

As a result of the suspensions between 1837 and 1840, private individuals and institutions, including the Toronto city council, issued paper money payable at some future date. While the principle that financial crisis must be fed rather than starved appears to have been understood at the time, the method of providing paper money during such periods remained unsolved.

The provision of sufficient notes in times of stress became a public issue following the crisis of 1837. Bank notes tended to increase in number during the prosperous times as discounting by the banks increased, and to decline during the depressed times when the public reduced its bank borrowing. Low prices, therefore, were blamed on an insufficiency of circulating money. This situation could be remedied, it was felt, by allowing the banks to issue their notes against government bonds rather than against a fluctuating amount of commercial paper.

BOND BACKED NOTES

Following the union of Upper and Lower Canada in 1841 the first Governor-General, Lord Sydenham, exerted his influence to have legislation passed which would provide for a more stable money supply. Lord Sydenham had been an active participant in the English currency school; therefore it is not surprising that the new Union Government's proposals for reform followed closely those in England. All the existing banks were to forfeit their privilege of note issue. A new government bank of issue was to be created. This new bank, to be named the Bank of the Province of Canada, was to be allowed to issue notes to a maximum amount of £1 million redeemable in specie, and against gold equal to 25 per cent and government securities equal to 75 per cent of the notes issued. Any amount of notes in excess of £1 million was to be backed by a 100 per cent specie reserve.

To put these notes into circulation, the government used them to pay its expenses and issued them to the chartered banks in return for gold or government securities. The banks were to be requested to buy government securities and exchange them for notes, but unlike legislation current in the United States the banks were to receive no interest on the bonds turned over to the government bank for new notes.

The government's proposed scheme was designed to kill two birds with one stone. On the one hand it would provide a market for the bonds of the government, which was in financial difficulty, and on the other it would provide a money supply which could be controlled during both prosperity and depression. The chartered banks openly opposed the government's proposals. Since deposit banking was as yet little developed, the banks would deprive themselves of their single most important source of revenue by giving up their right to issue notes. Moreover, as was later pointed out, the government's plan would have stabilized the money supply by sacrificing its essential elasticity. The plan was never enacted and the government sought an alternative way to control the note issue. The new bank charters imposed double liability on shareholders and limited note issue to an amount equal to a bank's paid-up capital. An annual tax of one per cent was levied on the amount of circulating bank notes in excess of the amount of specie, legal tender and government securities held by a bank. In this way the government intended to compensate itself for the interest it would have received had its earlier proposal been accepted. Moreover, when the charter of the Bank of Montreal came up for renewal in 1841, the government assured a market for its own bonds by amending the charter to require the bank, by this time the largest, to hold a certain percentage of its assets in government bonds. This was made a general provision of all chartered banks in 1854.

THE FREE BANKING ACT, 1850

Depressed economic conditions returned in 1847 and remained until 1850. Although no banks failed, their capital was substantially impaired by business failures. As a result of reduced bank capital and the reduced demand for credit, bank notes tended to become scarce. At first the Canadian government issued government debentures in the form of ordinary notes payable one year after date of issue with interest at 6 per cent. Later, debentures were issued payable either on demand or at some future date, and either with or without interest. This, as one commentator of the times has noted, "laid the foundation for a permanent element of government paper in the currency of the country." [2]

With the return of prosperous conditions in 1850, the government ended its paper note issues. However, the apparent success of these issues at a time when the banks were unable to meet the demand for notes revived interest in establishing a government bank of issue. The system of free banking which had developed in New York State attracted considerable attention since it appeared to contain the principles, earlier advocated by Lord Sydenham, of a sound basis for note issue and a market for government securities.

The Free Banking Act, modelled on a New York law, was passed in 1850. The act provided that individuals, general partners or joint stock companies could organize a bank with a minimum capital of £25,000. This was a small amount by chartered bank standards; the intent was to encourage the formation of unit banks similar to those in the United States and to avoid application to the legislature for a charter. Bank notes were to be printed by the government and could be obtained by the banks from the Inspector General of the province upon depositing with him public securities of an equivalent amount. The banks were to redeem these notes in gold but should they fail to do so, the government would assume the responsibility. The chartered banks were allowed to continue issuing their own notes if they so desired, but the one per cent government tax imposed in 1841 on the unsecured portion of their notes would remain in force.

The Free Banking Act, which was the first general act to apply to all banks, had little success. Only five relatively unimportant banks were formed under its provisions before it was repealed in 1880. The capital requirement, although small compared to those for chartered banks, was high for a unit bank operating in a smaller town. Also, the note provision which required the banks to turn over securities to the government made banking less profitable than it was for the chartered banks which issued bank notes as a consequence of bank lending.

BANK EXPANSION

Except for a short period after 1857, the Canadian provinces experienced an economic boom which lasted from 1850 until Confederation in 1867. The Reciprocity Treaty with the United States in 1854 assured Canadians a market for their growing extractive industries, while the Crimean War created a demand for agricultural products. Railroad construction opened

[2] Shortt, Adam, "Currency and Banking, 1840-1867", reprinted in E. P. Neufeld, *Money and Banking in Canada*, Toronto, McClelland and Stewart, 1964, p. 134.

the frontiers, providing the opportunity for land speculation. During these years the number of banks in Canada increased rapidly, an experience that was to recur only in the early 1870's.[3]

In this era of economic expansion the banks held one tenth of their funds in government securities, with the rest almost entirely committed to loans. Very little was held in the form of coin or bullion. Consequently the banks were in a vulnerable position when caught by the crisis of 1857, which originated in England as had the crisis of a decade before. In Canada, the crisis of 1857 coincided with poor harvests and the collapse of the real estate boom. The banks, which had invested heavily in real estate and depreciated railroad stock, were unable to feed the crisis by meeting the demands for credit.

In 1859 the government appointed a committee to investigate the banking and currency system. An Act Granting Additional Facilities in Commercial Transactions, passed in the same year, incorporated provisions that became a distinctive feature of Canadian banking. The act and subsequent amendments in 1861 and 1865 allowed the banks to make loans secured by bills of lading or warehouse receipts. Thus, a farmer could have a warehouse receipt issued for grain stored in his granary and could use this receipt as collateral for a bank loan. This principle, modified and expanded, is distinctive to Canadian banking in that it transgresses the strict definition of commercial banking based on commercial or self-liquidating loans. As a result of this feature the banks have played an important role in the development of the nation's agriculture and mineral resources.

THE PROVINCIAL NOTE ACT, 1866

Notes issued by the provincial governments had been in circulation in Nova Scotia from 1812. Although provincial notes circulated from time to time in the central provinces, all proposals for a permanent issue were turned down. Both Lord Sydenham's proposal in 1841 and its revival by Alexander Galt in 1860 were rejected. In 1866, however, the proponents of a government currency finally achieved the enactment of the Provincial Notes Act. Three factors contributed to their success: the government's financial requirements; the final collapse of the Bank of Upper Canada, the first big bank failure in Canadian history; and, following the suspension of specie payments by the American banks during the Civil War, the recognition of the need for greater soundness in the currency.

[3] Included in the number of banks that made an appearance during the 1850's were the following: the Bank of Toronto, St. Francis Bank, the Eastern Township Bank, the Bank of Brantford, the Bank of Western Canada, the Bank of the County of Elgin, the Ontario Bank; La Banque Nationale, the International Bank and the Chartered Bank of Canada, which later became the Canadian Bank of Commerce.

The act of 1866 authorized a provincial note issue of $8 million redeemable in gold. The first $5 million of this issue was to be secured by 20 per cent specie and the next $3 million by 25 per cent specie with government bonds providing the remaining security. By way of compromise, the government agreed that if $5 million could be obtained from the banks as a government loan, it would not use the note issue powers provided in the act. The banks failed to provide the government with the loan and it proceeded to issue its own notes. To discourage the banks from issuing their own notes the act further authorized the provincial government to pay a subsidy of 5 per cent per annum on the value of any notes the banks should retire before their charters expired, and to pay them a commission of one quarter of one per cent for handling and servicing provincial notes. The banks, except the Bank of Montreal, continued to issue notes in spite of the provisions of the act.[4] However, they began gradually to hold small quantities of the new currency which, because of its legal reserve status, could be substituted for specie. Thus began the shift from the banks to the government of the responsibility of maintaining the national specie reserves.

BANKING AFTER CONFEDERATION

The British North America Act gave the new federal government exclusive jurisdiction over all matters pertaining to currency and coinage, banking, the incorporation of banks and the issue of paper money. In the first session of the new parliament an interim Act Respecting Banking extended the existing charters of all banks until a general revision of the banking legislation could be made.

The failure in 1867 of the second large Canadian bank, the Commerce Bank, raised the matter of the need for a sound currency. Alexander Galt, the first Minister of Finance, introduced a bill for a bond secured currency similar to the United States National Bank notes, but this bill was later withdrawn. It was replaced by a temporary currency measure, the Dominion Notes Act of 1868, extending to all the provinces the provisions contained in the Provincial Notes Act of 1866. Two years later the Dominion Notes Act of 1870 was passed as the first step toward a strictly government issue. The act restricted the chartered banks to issuing notes of a minimum denomination of $5, giving the federal government a monopoly of $1 and $2 issues. The act also authorized the government to increase its note issue to $9 million against which it had to hold 20 per cent specie reserve. Any issue in excess of this amount had to be covered dollar for dollar by gold. The Dominion Notes Act was amended frequently between

[4] The Bank of Montreal had become the government's banker in 1864 and was therefore in a position to benefit by following the government's wishes.

1870 and the beginning of the First World War to allow the government to expand its note issue. By the last amendment of 1903 a 25 per cent gold reserve was required against the first $30 million of Dominion notes issued, with a 100 per cent gold reserve for any excess issue. By 1914 the issue had grown to the point where, with the number of notes in circulation above $30 million, the gold reserve held against the total issue was 85 per cent. Dominion notes had practically become gold certificates.

THE BANK ACT, 1871

The Bank Act of 1871 was preceded in 1870 by a temporary act which included the provisions of the Dominion Notes Act of that year and which required the banks to hold from one third to one half of their cash reserves in the form of Dominion notes. The act also repealed the earlier provisions that banks pay a one per cent annual tax on their notes and invest 10 per cent of their paid-up capital in government securities.

The Bank Act of 1871 was the first permanent legislation governing banking passed by the new federal government. It consolidated into a general statute the provisions contained in the charters of the individual banks granted before Confederation. The act, the more important features of which are outlined below, served as a blueprint not only for all future banking legislation, but for the development of Canadian banking practices generally.

New Banks. All new banks were to be chartered by a special act of parliament. All new charters were to conform to the general provisions of the Bank Act, and all existing charters were extended until July 1, 1881. This common date for the expiry of all charters became a feature of the Canadian system. Since charters are granted for a ten-year period, a periodic revision of the Bank Act is automatic while annual tinkering is minimized.

The capital requirement for new banks remained large. Subscribed capital was set at $500,000 of which $100,000 had to be paid up before a bank could open for business, and a further sum of $100,000 had to be paid within two years. The high capital requirement, together with permission to open branches, preserved the Canadian branch banking structure.

Note Issue. The banks were to restrict their circulation to notes of $4 and upward, the government being given a monopoly of small note issues. The banks' note issue was limited to the amount of their paid-up capital. Bank notes were made redeemable at certain designated places and suspension of payment by a bank for ninety days would result in the forfeiture of its charter.

Reserves. The banks were required to hold at least one third of whatever cash reserves they chose to carry in the form of Dominion notes.

Dividends. Dividends or bonuses by a bank were to be limited to 8 per cent until it accumulated a rest or surplus fund, after allowing for all bad or doubtful debts, equal to 20 per cent of its paid-up capital stock.

Liability. Directors were individually liable for the impairment of paid-up capital. Shareholders, on the other hand, were liable for the amount of their subscription and to an equal amount in addition; in other words, stockholders were subject to double liability.

Accountability. Each bank was required to make a monthly statement to the government.

Bank Lending. Loans against real estate or with a bank's own stock as security were prohibited. The so-called "pledge" provision allowing banks to make loans on certain bills of lading and warehouse receipts was continued and extended.

Revisions Strengthening Bank Note Issue.

The revisions made to the Bank Act in the period before the First World War were intended to provide greater safety for holders of bank notes, to ensure that these notes would circulate at par throughout the country, and to provide a means whereby they could be increased beyond the limits set in the act.

Six years of prosperity following Confederation came to an end with a depression that lasted from 1873 to 1879. The banks were hard hit for during the preceding years of prosperity and optimism they had become involved to an undesirable degree in the financing of the lumber industry and shipbuilding. As the depression had its origin in Canada's main export markets, these industries together with agriculture suffered. Many of the small and weaker banks were doomed to failure. The consequent loss to note holders created a public demand for greater security of bank notes.

In the Bank Act revisions of 1880 bank notes were made a first charge against a bank's assets in the event of liquidation. It was argued at the time that, in contrast to depositors, note holders were involuntary creditors of the banks and should therefore be given preferential treatment. The revisions to the act also gave the government a further monopoly of the note issue from \$4 to \$5 and multiples thereof. Moreover, the cash reserves which the banks were required to hold in the form of Dominion notes were raised to 40 per cent.

Because bank notes could be redeemed only at the head offices of the issuing banks, they did not circulate at par throughout the country. To overcome this fault, the Bank Act revision of 1890 required the banks to maintain a redemption office in each province. A Bank Circulation Redemption Fund was established to provide a mutual guarantee of bank notes in circulation into which the banks had to deposit 5 per cent of their average annual circulation. The fund was supervised by the Minister of Finance whose Department paid 3 per cent interest on such deposits. To protect the fund, notes were made a first lien on the assets of a failed bank. In addition, to ensure that note holders would not lose after a bank was liquidated, its notes were to bear interest at 6 per cent (later reduced to 5 per cent) until paid, and the Bank Circulation Redemption Fund was to redeem the notes of a failed bank within sixty days of suspension if the liquidator was unable to do so.

Revisions Increasing Bank Note Issues.

The period after mid-1890 was one of unprecedented economic development in which the banks played an important role. The expansion, especially after 1900, caused bank notes issues to hit the ceiling which the Bank Act had fixed at paid-up capital. The demand for additional credit was especially strong in the autumn as farmers were paid for their crops. In 1907 a low-quality wheat crop which had to be moved to market quickly lest it deteriorate precipitated an unprecedented demand for extra notes. As the banks showed no intention of increasing their capital stock (and thus their note issues), the government provided for an emergency issue by lending Dominion notes to the banks. In the following year, a special amendment to the Bank Act permitted the banks to exceed their capital stock limit of note issue during the months of October, November, December, and January. By a further revision in 1912 the period of permitted excess issue was extended to six months beginning in September of each year. In both cases the permitted excess was limited to 15 per cent of a bank's paid-up capital and surplus, and a penalty tax of 5 per cent per annum was imposed to ensure withdrawal of the excess issue as quickly as possible.

In 1913, the decennial revision of the Bank Act (postponed since 1911) provided for a more elastic note issue system. Being subject to a special 5 per cent tax, the excess issue provided for in 1908 and 1912 was not very profitable to the banks. They therefore generally paid out cash in the form of Dominion notes rather than avail themselves of the excess issue privilege. The amendment of 1913 permitted the banks to issue notes beyond the capital stock limit without tax after depositing dollar for dollar gold or Dominion notes in a fund known as the Central Gold Reserve. This was not in fact a central reserve but only a depository for a certain form of collateral against excess bank note issues.

THE FINANCE ACT AND THE MONEY SUPPLY

With the approach of war the future of the Canadian dollar became uncertain. Some depositors began converting their funds to gold for hoarding, whereupon the banks became anxious about their gold reserves. Customarily relatively small cash reserves were retained in the banks' vaults, most of their cash being held in the form of secondary reserves invested in New York. With war looming, the banks feared that it might become impossible to repatriate their reserves, particularly in gold. They consulted the Minister of Finance, and the government responded by passing an order-in-council on August 3, 1914 ending the convertibility of Dominion notes and bank notes into gold. In addition, the Department of Finance was authorized to make loans of Dominion notes to chartered banks on the promissory notes of the banks bearing such a rate of discount as the Department might determine and backed by their full value in Dominion government securities.

The abandonment of gold payments and advances from the Department of Finance became the essential features of the Finance Act passed at a special autumn session of Parliament in 1914. This legislation which was to be a temporary wartime expedient was re-enacted each year until 1923 when it was made a permanent feature of the Canadian financial system. Under the terms of the Finance Act the Department of Finance was allowed to function as a pseudo central bank until the establishment of the Bank of Canada in 1935.

TOWARD A CENTRAL BANK

During the war the expansion of bank notes and deposits became the prime source of government and business borrowing. The government borrowed from the banks through the sale of its Treasury bills, floated war loans to repay these bills at maturity and immediately began to borrow from the banks again to finance current expenditures. The banks used their holdings of government securities to obtain advances of Dominion notes from the Department of Finance. These notes in turn were deposited with the Central Gold Reserve to allow the banks to expand their own note issue. The banks were able to expand their cash positions not only as a result of the advances of Dominion notes from the Department of Finance, but also as a result of the direct issues by the government of unsecured Dominion notes and of an increase in their foreign balances which could be repatriated in the form of gold.

Toward the end of the war the first serious attempt was made to establish a central bank in Canada. The Canadian Bankers Association at the instigation of its president, E.L. Pease, formed a committee to investigate the possibilities of founding a "bank of rediscount". Pease himself proposed the establishment of such a bank which would take over the Dominion note issue, the Central Gold Reserves and the operations under the Finance Act. At the same time the chartered banks were to retain their note issue. While the bank was to be controlled directly by the government, its capitalization was to be shared between it and the chartered banks. The banking community, which was quite satisfied with the operations of the Finance Act, considered a bank of rediscount quite unnecessary and therefore turned down the proposals by Pease. Instead they recommended that the Finance Act be renewed.

War-time monetary expansion carried over into the postwar period. Except for a short down-turn in economic activity after the latter part of 1920, Canada experienced almost unprecedented boom conditions until the end of 1929. Although the banks continued to take advances from the Department of Finance, during most of this period they were able to reduce their dependence on such advances for cash and rely on Canada's favourable balance of payments to provide cash resources from abroad.

On July 1, 1926, Dominion notes were again made convertible into gold at a specified price and Canada was back on the gold standard. [5] However, about this time imports began to rise sharply and by 1928, with the decrease in the inflow of long-term investment capital, large deficits in the balance of payments occurred. The country's gold and foreign exchange reserves had to be called upon to finance this imbalance. The banks were able to meet the demands made on them for gold and foreign exchange and at the same time maintain their cash reserves at a level which permitted monetary expansion. They accomplished this by taking advances of Dominion notes from the Department of Finance which, in turn, was obliged to redeem these notes in gold as requested. Hence, the gold drain was transferred from the banks to the government. Because the Department of Finance was not prepared to exercise discretionary powers in limiting its advances to the banks, the government, at the beginning of 1929, terminated the unrestricted convertibility of Dominion notes in order to avoid a depletion in its gold holdings. This *de facto* departure from the gold standard was not officially recognized by the government until 1931.

By late 1929 Canada was in the midst of the world wide depression. While other countries responded by depreciating their currencies and by putting up tariff barriers, the Canadian government continued what it considered to be a sound monetary policy. It refused to depreciate the Canadian dollar, largely because of the extra burden this would have placed on Canada as a result of its large external debt. For a short time at least, it was aided in maintaining the external value of the dollar by the inflow of capital as the confidence of foreign investors in the Cana-

---

[5] Dominion notes were unofficially convertible into gold before 1926. After 1922, in its transactions with the chartered banks the government accepted gold in exchange for Dominion notes and redeemed Dominion notes in gold.

dian economy persisted. However, as the depression deepened the Canadian dollar began to slide and assumed an intermediate position above sterling and below the American dollar. Despite this depreciation, Canada suffered an adverse balance of payments which had to be financed by a reduction in the banks' monetary gold and their external assets. The banks, however, did not have to secure additional cash by taking advances of Dominion notes, because with the depressed economic conditions there was an internal flow of cash into the banks from businesses retiring their bank loans. The banks, not cognizant of the connection between monetary contraction and business conditions, used the extra cash to reduce their advances from the Department of Finance, rather than to encourage bank lending.

As economic conditions deteriorated and the money supply contracted, more and more voices were heard on the subject of monetary reform. In November 1932, in an attempt to increase the money supply and ease credit conditions, the government forced the banks to borrow $35 million in Dominion notes under the Finance Act. At the same time the banks loaned an equal amount to the government by purchasing a two-year issue of Treasury bills. The banks took advantage of these bills to obtain advances of Dominion notes. However, instead of expanding their loans with this cash they used it to reduce their indebtedness to the government. In 1934, in another attempt to achieve monetary expansion the government made a direct issue of Dominion notes to finance public works.

As none of these attempts improved economic conditions rising criticism of monetary policy at last led the government to appoint a Royal Commission on Banking and Finance. In 1934 the recommendations of the Commission were written into the Bank of Canada Act giving Canada a central bank.[6]

SELECTED READINGS

Breckenridge, R. M., *The History of Banking in Canada*, Washington, National Monetary Commission, 1910.

McIvor, R. Craig, *Canadian Monetary, Banking and Fiscal Development*, Toronto, Macmillan of Canada, 1961.

Neufeld, E. P., *Money and Banking in Canada*, Toronto, McClelland and Stewart, 1964.

Shortt, Adam, "The Early History of Canadian Banking", *Journal of the Canadian Bankers' Association*, 4, 5, 7; and "Founders of Canadian Banking", *Journal of the Canadian Bankers' Association*, 29, 30, 33.

[6] The Bank of Canada is discussed in Chapter 14.

7 COMMERCIAL BANKS AS CREATORS OF MONEY

DEBT MONETIZATION AND THE MONEY SUPPLY

Commercial banks were traditionally considered unique among financial institutions in that they are able to create money. Other financial institutions were assumed not to have this ability but shared with the banks the function of transferring funds. As we shall see later, the traditional dichotomy of banking functions between the banks and non-bank financial intermediaries is no longer valid.

Financial institutions create money by monetizing debt. In order to understand what is meant by monetizing debt, we must be sure of our definition of the money supply. The money supply consists of the currency holdings of the public (currency outside the banks) and commercial bank deposits. This definition of the money supply excludes the near banks, at least officially, from performing the function of monetizing debt.

Currency consists of subsidiary coin and paper notes or bills issued by a government or by an agent of government such as a central bank. Paper notes or bills which circulate as money are nothing more than government debt instruments. In Canada, they are the circulating debt of the Bank of Canada. As we shall see in later chapters, this debt is the result of the Bank's purchases of government securities for which it has paid by issuing its own promissory notes, Bank of Canada notes. Insofar, as government debt in the form of securities is exchanged for Bank of Canada notes, it can be said that government debt is monetized. In other words, *Bank of Canada notes are the result of government debt monetization by the central bank.*

The other component of the money supply, and indeed the more important, consists of commercial bank deposits. As we shall see, the banks create money when they exchange their debt for that of the public. The public enters into such an exchange because the banks' debt has the special quality of being accepted by others in payment of personal debt. This acceptability puts the commercial banks along with some of the non-bank financial intermediaries (near-banks) in a position to monetize the public's debt.

Debt monetization is, of course, easier for a government than for banking institutions. A government can pass legislation making its debt legal tender so that by law certain kinds of government debt have to be accepted as payment. Commercial banks, on the other hand, are essentially private institutions and must depend upon the public's acceptance of their debt as money. Over the years, the banks have gained public confidence, and the deposits of the banks have become the most important component of the money supply. This same confidence is being shared increasingly by the near-banks but as yet their circulating debt is not officially recognized as money.

The commercial banks have traditionally been singled out for special attention by government officials, economists and others, not only because some of their debt is monetized but also because of their ability to vary the amount of their debt outstanding. Insofar as the banks can vary their debt which is considered part of the money supply, they can create and destroy money. This chapter outlines just how, and by how much, the banks can change the total volume of money. First, however, let us again point out that today the debt of some financial intermediaries (i.e. credit unions, loan and trust companies) is circulating as money, although it is not recognized as such in the official money supply statistics. Economists are giving increased attention to the growth and the activities of the near-banks in order to assess their influence as "creators of money" on the overall performance of our economy.

BANK DEPOSITS AND THE MONEY SUPPLY

A commercial bank's deposits are shown on its balance sheet as a liability because they represent an amount which is owed by the bank and which it must ultimately pay or transfer to someone else. Deposits which must be paid or transferred on demand by a bank are commonly referred to as its demand liabilities. For analytical purposes they are classified as **primary deposits** and **derivative** or **secondary deposits.** The essential difference between the two is that only derivative or secondary deposits add to or subtract from the total money supply.

Primary Deposits. Let us assume that an individual deposits currency with a commercial bank which credits his account accordingly. In the following example $100 in the form of currency has been deposited with Bank A. The bank's demand deposits have increased by $100 and at the same time its assets in the form of currency have increased by a corresponding amount. Currency is a speical kind of asset to a commercial bank for it also acts as a reserve since individuals, business firms and governments who hold demand deposits with a bank have the prerogative to demand currency from the bank. An increase in a bank's deposits which increases its currency holdings, or reserves, by a corresponding amount is called a primary deposit.

BALANCE SHEET CHANGES FOR COMMERCIAL BANK A

Assets		Liabilities	
Reserves (currency)	+$100	Primary deposit	+$100

Primary deposits may result not only from the deposit of currency (cash) but also from the deposit of cheques drawn on other banks. These cheques will increase the reserves of the receiving bank, since cheques may be converted into currency on demand through the clearing house operations which will be discussed later.

While a demand deposit is part of the official money supply, changes in a bank's primary deposits do not result in a net addition to or subtraction from the money supply. All that occurs is a change in the composition of the money supply. In the case where currency is deposited in Bank A and the depositor chooses to hold money in the form of bank deposits rather than currency, the decrease in the amount of currency in the hands of the public equals the increase in bank deposits. Therefore, the total money supply remains unaffected.

In the next example where the depositor chooses to transfer a bank deposit by means of a cheque from one bank to another the total money supply also remains unaffected. The only change, as shown in the balance sheets of the two banks, is a transfer of deposits (and reserves) from one commercial bank to another.

BALANCE SHEET CHANGES FOR COMMERCIAL BANK A

Assets		Liabilities	
Reserves	+$100	Primary Deposits	+$100

BALANCE SHEET CHANGES FOR COMMERCIAL BANK B

Assets		Liabilities	
Reserves	−$100	Primary Deposits	−$100

Derivative Deposits. When an individual obtains a loan from a commercial bank he usually receives the proceeds of the loan in the form of a demand deposit. The bank's balance sheet will show an increase in deposits and a corresponding increase in loans.

BALANCE SHEET CHANGES FOR COMMERCIAL BANK A

Assets		Liabilities	
Loans	+$100	Derived Deposits	+$100

The newly created deposits are called derivative or secondary deposits. They differ from primary deposits in that they do not increase the reserves of the lending bank. In return for a borrower's promissory note — debt which is not money — the bank creates a deposit — its own debt which is money. Thus, when a bank extends a loan it makes a net addition to the money supply; the borrower's debt is monetized. The money supply is also increased when a bank buys a bond or other financial security in the market.

Assume Bank A buys a security for $1,000 and pays for it by writing a cashier's cheque.[1] The seller deposits this cheque in his account in Bank A. The following change will be recorded in Bank A's balance sheet.

BALANCE SHEET CHANGES FOR COMMERCIAL BANK A

Assets		Liabilities	
Securities	+$1,000	Derived Deposit	+$1,000

In return for the public's debt in the form of a security, the bank has created its own debt in the form of a derivative deposit. The significant difference between these two types of debts is that only the bank's debt is money.

In the above case we assumed that the seller of the financial security deposited the proceeds (the cashier's cheque) in the bank which purchased the security from him. Let us now assume that the seller of the security has no account in Bank A but has one in Bank B where he deposits the proceeds of his sale. This will transfer reserves from Bank A to Bank B as shown on the next page.

[1] A cheque drawn by a bank on itself is referred to as a cashier's cheque. In the early history of banking a bank's cashier was the only employee who could transfer funds on behalf of a bank. It is more usual today for the bank manager or the chief accountant to sign such cheques. However, they are still called cashier's cheques.

BALANCE SHEET CHANGES FOR COMMERCIAL BANK A

Assets		Liabilities	
Reserves	−$1,000		
Securities	+$1,000		

BALANCE SHEET CHANGES FOR COMMERCIAL BANK B

Assets		Liabilities	
Reserves	+$1,000	Deposits	+$1,000

For the banking system as a whole deposits and security holdings have increased, but reserves have remained unchanged. From the point of view of Bank B the new deposits are primary because the bank's reserves have been increased by an amount equal to the increase of deposit liabilities. In terms of the whole banking system, however, they are derivative deposits since there has been no corresponding change in the total volume of the banking system's reserves.

We have shown that a commercial bank can increase the money supply by *creating credit*. Credit is created when a bank extends loans and when it buys securities. Similarily, when a bank sells securities or retires loans without extending new ones, credit is destroyed and the money supply decreased.

We must now answer a very critical question. Is there a limit to the amount of credit a bank or a banking system can create or destroy? In answering we must beware of what is called the "fallacy of composition". We must remember that what is true for the individual bank in a banking system is not true for the banking system as a whole, nor is it true for a monopoly bank which also constitutes a banking system.

DEPOSIT CREATING BY AN INDIVIDUAL BANK IN A BANKING SYSTEM

RESERVE REQUIREMENTS

The public will regularly use bank deposits as money if it is confident that the banks can convert these deposits on demand into currency and that cheques written against these deposits will be generally accepted in payment of debt. The ability of a bank to convert its deposits to currency does not require it to hold against each deposit an equivalent amount of currency. From experience the banks know what amount of their deposits will be converted into currency under normal circumstances. They know, therefore how much currency must be held in their vaults and cash tills against a given amount of deposits. The absolute amount of currency held by a bank is called the **bank's cash reserves** and the percentage of deposits held in the form of currency is known as the **bank's cash reserve ratio.**[2] During the early history of banking a bank determined the reserve ratio through custom and experience. Later, in order to ensure a sound monetary and banking system, and to protect the interests of depositors, governments imposed a **legal minimum cash reserve ratio.**

We noted earlier that a bank has two types of deposits — primary and derivative. Primary deposits can increase without limit because with each change in such deposits the bank's currency and reserves change by a corresponding amount. But as this is not the case with a change in derivative deposits, the ability of an individual bank to create deposits is not unlimited. Let us illustrate this proposition.

Assume that a bank is required by law to hold an amount of currency in its vaults and cash tills equal to 5 per cent of its deposits. [3] This amount is sufficient to meet all of the bank's normal demands to convert deposits into currency.

Now an individual deposits $1,000 in the form of currency in Commercial Bank A which makes the following entry in its books.

Balance Sheet Changes for Commercial Bank A

Assets		Liabilities	
Reserves (currency)	+$1,000	Primary Deposits	+$1,000

The bank's balance sheet shows that its currency holdings have increased by an amount equal to the increase in its deposits. As a result, its reserves are equal to 100 per cent of the increase in deposits. With a legal minimum reserve ratio of 5 per cent its required reserves against the increase in deposits are only $50.

Commercial banks are in business to make profits. They have to produce a reasonable return to their shareholders; otherwise, the shareholders will employ their funds elsewhere. The banks do not earn a penny on currency which sits idle in their vaults and cash tills. It is, therefore, in

2 At this stage of our discussion we assume that the bank's cash reserves consist of currency. At a later stage we shall learn that in practice the cash reserves of the banks consist of their currency holdings and their deposits with the central bank. Insofar as the banks can draw down these deposits at any time they may be considered as currency.

3 We assume here and in the discussion that follows that all of the banks' deposits are demand deposits. Later we will consider time or notice deposits.

the best interests of a bank to hold only sufficient currency to meet the day-to-day demands of its customers and the legal reserve requirements. The legal minimum reserve requirement is usually set at a level which also meets day-to-day demands under normal conditions. There may be times, especially in periods of economic depression, when the banks hold more currency than is needed to meet the normal demands of their customers or than is required by law. This may be the result of the banks' inability to put their currency holdings into earning assets or their desire to avoid the risks of lending and purchasing securities at low prevailing interest rates by holding more currency and therefore larger reserves.

In our example, under normal conditions, Commercial Bank A holds only $50 of the $1,000 in currency as required reserves. The remaining $950 which is not required for cash reserve purposes can be considered as **excess reserves** (excess reserves = actual reserves less required reserves). In order to maximize its profit potential the bank will put its excess reserves to work earning returns for its shareholders, by using them to extend loans and to buy securities.

When a bank makes a loan or purchases a security it can make payment by paying out currency directly from its vaults and cash tills, by issuing a cashier's cheque, or by establishing a deposit account. If the bank employs the first method of settlement, it will immediately lose currency in an amount equal to its loans or purchases of securities. The amount of currency paid out must not exceed its excess reserves. *As a first approximation, we can therefore conclude that an individual bank must restrict any net increase in its loans and purchase of securities to an amount equal to its excess reserves.*

More usually a bank will make settlement by issuing a cashier's cheque or by creating a deposit account. If a cheque is issued, the bank can lose cash through the clearing house operations to be discussed. On the other hand, if settlement is made by creation of a deposit, currency will be lost only if the holder of the deposit writes a cheque against it or withdraws it in cash. In the event that the deposit were held indefinitely, the bank would lose no currency. Then the only restriction on a bank's ability to expand its loans and security holdings would be its reserve requirements against its deposits. In practice such a situation is conceivable for an individual bank only if it is a monopoly bank and if bank deposits are the only form of currency.

A borrower of funds will not usually leave them in his account indefinitely. He will probably withdraw currency from his account in the lending bank or write cheques against it to meet his obligations to individuals, businesses or governments. His cheques may be taken to other banks which will then demand currency from the lending bank. As a result, borrowed funds in the form of demand deposits will be lost by the lending bank to other banks and to non-bank currency holdings. The individual bank, therefore, cannot assume that any of the funds transferred when it makes loans will remain with it. This is also true when it transfers funds in payment of security purchases. Our initial conclusion remains: an individual bank cannot safely expand its loans and investments beyond its excess reserves.

CLEARING HOUSE OPERATIONS AND THE CLEARING DRAIN

The loss of currency by one bank to another is called a **clearing drain.** It can be illustrated by the clearing house operations. Every day regular customers of a bank will write cheques against their deposits in payment for goods and services and financial assets. Many of the recipients of these cheques will take them to other banks where they will demand currency or place them on deposit. Other banks will now hold claims on the deposits in the bank against which the cheques were originally issued. The banks holding these claims or cheques may send a messenger with them to the bank holding the respective deposits and demand an amount of currency shown on the face of the cheques. Since currency is also reserve money, reserves are transferred from one bank to others when a bank redeems cheques drawn on its deposits and presented by other banks. Moreover, if one bank in a banking system expands its net investments and its deposits faster than the other banks in the system, it can expect a net outflow of reserves. Even if expansion is in line with the other banks in the system, a small net outflow may take place as the public, for one reason or another, decides to transfer its deposits from one bank to another.

In our example, sending a messenger from one bank to another every time a bank received a cheque drawn on a deposit in another bank, or even at the end of each business day, would be a cumbersome procedure if not a physical impossibility. In eighteenth century London, the banks did employ messengers to deliver daily to each other cheques drawn on their deposits. In time, however, messengers using a little bit of initiative developed the habit of meeting at a coffee house in the financial district where in one "foot-saving" operation they settled their entire business. For example, let us assume that there were four banks whose messengers gathered for coffee. One of the more enterprising messengers would gather up all the cheques and make a tabulation (see Table 7-1). Clearing operations are much more sophisticated today. Although the basic principles remain the same, most of the work that was formerly done by messengers is now done electronically.

The table shows the clearing drains among four banks in a banking system. Bank A experiences no drain since the claims by it are equal to the claims on it. Both banks C and D, however, lose currency and therefore reserves. Their loss is a net gain to Bank B.

TABLE 7-1

Clearing Operations
(*thousands of pounds*)

Claims by	Cheques drawn against deposits in				Total Claims by
	A	B	C	D	
A	–	5	6	7	18
B	6	–	7	9	22
C	8	4	–	2	14
D	4	6	4	–	14
Total Claims Against	18	15	17	18	68

Bank	Total Claims by	Total Claims Against	Net
A	18	18	0
B	22	15	+7
C	14	17	–3
D	14	18	–4

To guard itself against adverse clearing drains the individual bank will not lend beyond its excess reserves. Returning to our earlier example, Commercial Bank A will maximize its earning potential and at the same time remain in a position to meet all its clearing obligations when its balance sheet reads as follows.

BALANCE SHEET CHANGES FOR COMMERCIAL BANK A

Assets		Liabilities	
Reserves (currency)	+ $50	Deposits	+$1.000
Investments (securities and loans)	+ $950		
	+$1,000		+$1,000

The time required for Commercial Bank A to arrive at the position shown in the balance sheet above will depend upon the structure of the banking system. If the system consists of many banks in close proximity to each other, Commercial Bank A can expect cash drains following its creations of deposits. If the banks are some distance apart the time required for a cheque to travel from one bank to another will delay the clearing drain of the individual bank for some time. If there are only a few banks in a banking system, it is likely that cheques drawn on an account will be redeposited in other accounts in the same bank.[4]

The prudent banker will follow as a general rule of thumb the policy of lending no more in a day than the bank's excess reserves at the beginning of the day. If, however, in granting a loan he requires the customer to maintain a specific minimum balance in his account (a practice becoming more common today), he may want to expand his loans somewhat beyond his initial excess reserves. This may also be the case if the bank experiences a favourable clearing balance over a period of time.[5] On the other hand, if a bank regularly has an adverse clearing balance, expansion of investments and deposits must be limited to an amount less than the volume of excess reserves.

Table 7-2 shows the net effect on the balance sheet of Commercial Bank A following an increase in primary deposits of $1,000. The table is divided into two parts. In Part I our bank maintains a 5 per cent reserve ratio and expands its loans and deposits by $950. All of these deposits and an equivalent amount of reserves are lost by the bank in subsequent clearing house operations. Therefore, the net effect of the initial increase in primary deposits is a net increase of $1,000 in deposits, of $950 in loans and of $50 in reserves.

In Part II we assume that Commercial Bank A has a consistently fa-

---

4 For an analysis of the effects of different structures of the banking system on the individual bank's ability to expand its earning assets and deposits see E.S. Shaw, *Money, Income and Monetary Policy*, Chicago, Richard D. Irwin, 1950, pp. 129-142.

5 Looked at somewhat differently, a favourable clearing balance over a period of time provides a bank with excess reserves. Thus, while during any given day a banker may expand his investments and deposits beyond the bank's excess reserves, in the long run the expansion must be equal to the increase in reserves (to its excess reserves).

TABLE 7-2

I

Balance Sheet Changes for Commercial Bank A
(5 per cent Reserve ratio)
(in dollars)

	Assets			Liabilities		
STAGE 1 Primary Deposit	Reserves:	+	1,000	Deposits:	+	1,000
STAGE 2 Credit Expansion	Loans:	+	950	Deposits:	+	950
STAGE 3 Clearing Drain	Reserves:	–	950	Deposits:	–	950
NET EFFECT	Reserves:	+	50	Deposits:	+	1,000
	Loans:	+	950			
		+	1,000		+	1,000

II

Balance Sheet Changes for Commercial Bank A
(5 per cent reserve ratio and favourable clearing drain)
(in dollars)

	Assets			Liabilities		
STAGE 1 Primary Deposit	Reserves:	+	1,000.00	Deposits:	+	1,000.00
STAGE 2 Credit Expansion	Loans:	+	968.40	Deposits:	+	968.40
STAGE 3 Clearing Drain	Reserves:	–	949.04	Deposits:	–	949.04
NET EFFECT	Reserves:	+	50.96	Deposits:	+	1,019.36
	Loans:	+	968.40			
		+	1,019.36		+	1,019.36

vourable clearing balance equal to 2 per cent of its newly created deposits. With a clearing balance of zero, our bank can create $950 in loans and deposits, the amount of its excess reserves. With a favourable clearing balance, the bank can create more than $950 in deposits and still meet all the demands on it for cash. It can create deposits of 1/.981 times the volume of its excess reserves.[6] With excess reserves equal to $950 following an initial increase in primary deposits of $1,000 and a reserve ratio of 5 per cent, the bank can create deposits equal to $968.40. The cheques presented by other banks for collection are 2 per cent less than the amount of these newly created deposits. The banks' reserves therefore decline by only $949.04. The net effect as shown in the table is a $1,019.36 increase in deposits, a $50.96 increase in reserves and a $968.40 increase in loans. A favourable clearing balance equal in value to 2 per cent of its newly created deposits allowed our bank to expand its loans and deposits by $19.36 more than it did without such a favourable clearing balance.

If one bank in a banking system has a favourable clearing balance, other banks in the system must have unfavourable balances. The bank or banks in the system that have adverse clearing balances cannot expand their investments and deposits to the full extent of their excess reserves. [7] But for the banking system as a whole there can be neither a favourable nor an unfavourable clearing position.

THE CURRENCY DRAIN

We have seen that the ability of an individual commercial bank to create deposit money depends principally on its reserve position. A proportion of its reserves, which we have defined as **required reserves,** specified by custom, by experience and usually by law, has to be held in the bank's vaults and cash tills, and usually also with an agency of the government such as a central bank. The remainder, which we have called **excess reserves,** is available for the creation of deposits. However, the amount of excess reserves, and therefore a bank's *potential* ability to expand its deposits, is subject to fluctuation resulting from favourable or adverse

---

[6] The ratio 1/.981 is based on the following formula: $x = \dfrac{1}{(1\text{-}q) + (r)(q)}$

where *r* is the reserve ratio, *q* the percentage of new deposits which return to the bank and *x* that multiple of its excess reserves by which the bank may expand its deposits. In the formula *r* acts as the contractionary force while *q* has the opposite effect.

[7] The formula for a bank with an adverse clearing balance is: $x = \dfrac{1}{\{1 - (-q)\} + (r)(-q)}$

where *r* is the reserve requirement and *q* is the percentage by which the clearing drain exceeds the volume of newly created deposits. Therefore *q* has a negative value and reduces deposit creation while *r* helps to maintain it.

clearing balances. There are other factors which affect a bank's excess reserves. Some of the more important of these are the non-bank public's propensity to change its holdings of currency, the relative preferences of the non-bank public for time and demand deposits, the willingness of a bank to lend and of borrowers to borrow, and government economic policy. The latter will be considered in later chapters dealing with central banking and the policies of the federal Treasury.

The total money holdings of the non-bank public consists of currency and commercial bank deposits. When people decide to hold more currency as part of their given money holdings, they exchange bank deposits for currency. The cash reserves and deposits of the individual bank and of the entire banking system are reduced by an amount equal to the withdrawal of currency into public circulation. In Table 7-3 we present three examples of currency withdrawal from Commercial Bank A. In the first example the bank supplies $100 of currency demanded for circulation by reducing its deposits by this amount, and by reducing its required reserves by $5 and its excess reserves by $95. In the second example the bank does not initially hold any excess reserves. As in the first case it supplies $5 in currency to the public by reducing its reserves by this amount. In order to supply the remaining $95 of currency it liquidates $95 in loans for cash which it pays out to the public.

In the third example the bank's initial deposits are $10,000 against which it holds reserves of $500. It meets the demand for currency by reducing its deposits and reserves by the $100 the public withdraws. With a 5 per cent reserve requirement, $400 of reserves will support only $8,000 of deposits so that $1,900 in loans must be liquidated. In the second example the loans are repaid in cash. In the third example they are paid with the reduction in customers' deposit accounts.

The three examples in the table show how the withdrawal of currency from a bank may affect its potential money creating ability. We refer to the withdrawal of currency from the banking system into public circulation as the **currency drain.**

In recent years the non-bank public has held currency equal, on the average, to about 14 per cent of its commercial bank deposits.[8] This percentage is referred to as the **coefficient of the average currency drain.**[9]

---

8 If the average currency holdings are equal to 14 per cent of deposits it follows that currency as a percentage of the money supply (currency and deposits) is equal to 12.3 per cent.

9 The coefficient of the marginal currency drain expresses the rate of change of currency held outside the banks with respect to a change in bank deposits. For example, if this coefficient is .25, a $1.00 change in demand deposits alters currency holdings by 25 cents. For analytical purposes it makes no difference whether one uses the marginal or average coefficient if the latter is constant. When there is a constant average coefficient of the currency drain and a change in the money supply occurs, the percentage change in currency must be the same as the percentage change in deposits.

TABLE 7-3

Balance Sheet Changes for Commercial Bank A

(5 per cent Reserve ratio)
(in dollars)

I

	Assets			**Liabilities**		
STAGE 1 Initial position with excess	Reserves:			Deposits:	+	1,000
	(Required)	+	50			
	(Excess)	+	95			
	Loans:	+	855			
		+	1,000		+	1,000
STAGE 2 Currency withdrawal	Reserves:			Deposits:		100
	(Required)	−	5			
	(Excess)	−	95			
NET EFFECT	Reserves:	+	45	Deposits:	+	900
	Loans:	+	855			
		+	900		+	900

II

	Assets			**Liabilities**		
STAGE 1 Initial position no excess reserves	Reserves:			Deposits:	+	1,000
	(Required)	+	50			
	Loans:	+	950			
		+	1,000		+	1,000
STAGE 2 Currency withdrawal	Reserves:	−	5	Deposits:	−	100
	Loans:	−	95			
NET EFFECT	Reserves:	+	45	Deposits:	+	900
	Loans:	+	855			
		+	900		+	900

III

	Assets			**Liabilities**		
STAGE 1 Initial position no excess reserves	Reserves:			Deposits:	+	10,000
	(Required)		500			
	Loans:	+	9,500			
			10,000		+	10,000
STAGE 2 Currency withdrawal	Reserves:	−	100	Deposits:	−	100
STAGE 3 Reduction in loans and deposits	Loans:	−	1,900	Deposits:	−	1,900
NET EFFECT	Reserves:	+	400	Deposits:	+	8,000
	Loans:	+	7,600			
		+	8,000		+	8,000

While this coefficient remains relatively stable over long periods of time, it can fluctuate over shorter periods. For instance, during the Christmas season when people make more cash purchases than usual its value ordinarily increases. Central banks normally provide commercial banks with the needed reserves during seasonal fluctuations in the value of the coefficient.

There are also times when the public reduces its currency holdings relative to its bank deposits, thereby increasing excess reserves and deposits in the banks. This often happens following holiday seasons. The banks as a rule do not respond with an immediate increase in their loans. If they do, central banks can prevent such an increase by reducing the reserves of commercial banks. However, since the demand for loans tends to fall off when there is a sudden seasonal influx of currency, central bank restrictions are generally unnecessary.

THE DEMAND FOR TIME DEPOSITS

Up to this point we have considered the deposits of the banks as if they were all the same and all demand deposits. In reality, the commercial banks hold two major types of deposits: demand or chequing deposits, and savings or time deposits. While the banks can require holders of savings accounts to give prior notice of a withdrawal, the accounts are in practice treated the same as demand deposits. The banks allow cheques to be drawn on them and currency withdrawals to be made from them without notice. In Canada, unlike the United States, the close affinity between demand and time deposits is recognized by the treatment of both as part of the money supply. Moreover, prior to 1967 Canadian chartered banks were required to hold the same percentage of reserves against their time deposits as against their demand deposits. Since then the banking regulations have been altered. Similar to United States banking practices, Canadian banks may now hold a smaller percentage of reserves against time deposits than against demand deposits. The difference in reserve requirements weakens the reserve position of a bank when the public shifts its bank accounts from time to demand deposits. Table 7-4 illustrates this point. Commercial Bank A initially holds $20,000 in deposits divided equally between time and demand deposits. The reserve requirement for demand deposits is 12 per cent (or $1,200) and for time deposits, 4 per cent (or $400). The public now shifts $5,000 from time deposits to demand deposits. As a result the reserve requirement for time deposits is reduced by $200 while that for demand deposits is increased by $600. The total reserve requirement has increased by $400 to $2,000, so that with no change in its total reserves Commercial Bank A now has a reserve deficiency of $400 and will have to decrease its loans and deposits accordingly. If the shift had been from demand deposits to time deposits,

TABLE 7-4

Balance Sheet Changes for Commercial Bank A

(in dollars)

	Assets		**Liabilities**	
INITIAL POSITION	Reserves (12%)	+1,200	Demand Deposits	+10,000
	Reserves (4%)	+ 400	Time Deposits	+10,000
		+1,600		+20,000
SHIFT IN DEPOSITS AND CHANGE IN REQUIRED RESERVES	Required Reserves	+ 600	Demand Deposits	+ 5,000
	Required Reserves	− 200	Time Deposits	− 5,000
NET EFFECT	Required Reserves:			
	Demand Deposits	1,800	Demand Deposits	15,000
	Time Deposits	200	Time Deposits	5,000
		2,000		20,000
	Actual Reserves	1,600		
	RESERVE DEFICIENCY	400		

the bank would have acquired excess reserves allowing it to expand loans and deposits.

THE WILLINGNESS TO LEND AND BORROW

A bank's ability to expand its deposits and therefore to create money is in no way automatic. A bank must be willing to extend loans and purchase securities. On the other hand, even if a bank wishes to expand, it cannot do so unless the non-banking public is willing to sell securities or to seek loans. Thus while excess reserves are a necessary condition for bank expansion, they are not the only condition.

DEPOSIT CREATING BY A BANKING SYSTEM

The ability of an entire banking system to create (and destroy) deposits, and therefore money, depends — like that of an individual bank — upon reserve positions. However, unlike an individual bank whose potential to create deposits is limited by the volume of its own excess reserves, a banking system has the potential to expand deposits by a multiple of the entire system's excess reserves.

To illustrate the multiple money creating ability of a commercial banking system let us begin by assuming that each bank's required reserve ratio is 12 per cent. Let us further assume that a primary deposit of $1,000 is made in Commercial Bank A which allocates $120 of this to its required reserves leaving $880 in excess reserves.

It is important to keep in mind just how the banking system initially receives excess reserves. In our example we assume that $1,000 in currency from *outside the banking system* is deposited in Bank A. Later we shall see that an increase in the reserves of a banking system can take place without a change in primary deposits, and that the way in which a banking system gains reserves has important implications for the expansionary potential of the system.

Now let us return to Bank A. On the basis of its excess reserves of $880, it attempts to maximize its profits by extending its loans and secondary deposits by this amount. Since bank borrowers do not usually borrow funds to let them sit idle in a bank, we shall assume that all of the secondary deposits are withdrawn in cash and by cheque. The recipients are all customers of another bank, say Bank B, where the funds are placed on deposit. After all the cheques have been cleared through the clearing house process, Bank A will have lost secondary deposits and reserves equal to $880 and Bank B will have new primary deposits and a net addition to its reserves of an equal amount.

When it has allowed for its 12 per cent required reserve ratio against the new primary deposits of $880, Bank B will have $774.40 (88 per cent of $880) in new excess reserves and will be in a position to expand its loans and purchases of securities. Suppose Bank B lends the whole $774.40. Again, as was the case with Bank A, borrowers pay debts to individuals and firms who deposit this money with yet another bank in the banking system, Bank C.

Now Bank C will hold the required reserve of $92.93 (12 per cent of $774.40) and put its excess reserves of $681.47 ($774.40 less $92.93) to work by extending its loans and its purchases of securities. Bank C, therefore, has created secondary deposits of $681.47. The expansion of loans and secondary deposits is outlined in Table 7-5.

As a result of an initial deposit of $1,000 in currency in Bank A, Banks A, B and C are able, on the basis of a 12 per cent reserve ratio and with no cash drains, to expand their loans and create secondary deposits in the total amount of $2,335.87 ($880 + $774.40 + $681.47). In addition Banks D,E,F,G (the rest of the banking system) increase their secondary deposits by an aggregate of $4,997.46, so that the total increase in secondary deposits for all the banks in the banking system is $7,333.33. *The banking system must stop expanding its deposits when all the reserves that were excess at the beginning ($880 in our example) have come to be required to support existing deposits.* With a 12 per cent required reserve ratio and with no cash drains, this point is reached when the banking system has created secondary deposits in the amount of $7,333.33. Total additional deposits of all the banks are then equal to $8,333.33 against which a required reserve of $1,000 is held.

An alternative way of showing the process of deposit expansion by the banking system is presented in Table 7-6. Here, too, it is assumed that each bank holds a required reserve of 12 per cent and that each bank ex-

TABLE 7-5

Multiple Expansion of Lending and Deposits Through the Banking System
(Required reserves 12 per cent, no other drains)
(in dollars)

Assets			Liabilities	
BANK A				
Reserves:		+1,000.00	Deposits:	
Required Reserves	+120.00		Initial Primary Deposit	+1,000.00
Excess reserves	+880.00		Secondary Deposits	+ 880.00
Loans		+ 880.00		
Total Assets		+1,880.00	Total Liabilities	+1,880.00
BANK B				
Reserves:		+ 880.00	Deposits:	
Required Reserves	+105.60		Primary Deposit	+ 880.00
Excess Reserves	+774.40		Secondary Deposits	+ 774.40
Loans		+ 774.40		
Total Assets		+1,654.40	Total Liabilities	+1,654.40
BANK C				
Reserves:		+ 774.40	Deposits:	
Required Reserves	+ 92.93		Primary Deposits	+ 774.40
Excess Reserves	+681.47		Secondary Deposits	+ 681.47
Loans		+ 681.47		
Total Assets		+1,455.87	Total Liabilities	+1,455.87
ADDITIONAL BANKS D, E, F, G . . .				
Reserves:		+ 681.47	Deposits:	
Required Reserves	+681.47		Primary Deposits	+ 681.47
Excess Reserves	0		Secondary Deposits	+4,997.46
Loans		+4,997.46		
Total Assets		+5,678.93	Total Liabilities	+5,678.93
ALL BANKS				
Reserves:		+1,000.00	Deposits:	
			Initial Primary Deposit	+1,000.00
Required Reserves	1,000.00		Secondary Deposits	+7,333.33
Excess Reserves	0			
Loans		+7,333.33		
Total Assets		+8,333.33	Total Liabilities	+8,333.33

TABLE 7-6

Multiple Expansion of Lending and Deposits through the Banking System

Banks	Primary Deposits	Required Reserves	Excess Reserves	Loans	Secondary Deposits
Bank A	$ 1,000.00	$ 120.00	$ 880.00	$ 880.00	$ 880.00
Bank B	880.00	105.60	774.40	774.40	774.40
Bank C	774.40	92.93	681.47	681.47	681.47
Bank D	681.47	81.78	599.69	599.69	599.69
Bank E	599.69	71.96	527.73	527.73	527.73
Bank F	527.73	63.33	464.40	464.40	464.40
Bank G	464.40	55.73	408.67	408.67	408.67
Bank H	408.67	49.04	359.58	359.58	359.58
Bank I	359.59	43.15	316.43	316.43	316.43
Bank J	316.43	37.97	278.46	278.46	278.46
Still other banks	2,320.96	278.51	1,320.96	1,320.96	1,320.96
Total, all banks	$ 8,333.33	$ 1,000.00	$ 7,333.33	$ 7,333.33	$ 7,333.33

pands its deposits to the full potential of its excess reserves. The expansionary process follows an initial deposit of currency in Bank A which is fully loaned up before it receives this deposit. Again we assume that not a penny of the initial deposit of currency is drained out of the banking system.

We must now take into account factors which were omitted from our oversimplified example. Up to this point in our explanation of the deposit expansion potential of the banking system, we have assumed that any initial excess reserves of the banking system remain within the system and are ultimately employed as required reserves defined by the minimum required reserve ratio. In our earlier discussion of the individual bank we observed that it is subject to two drains which use up its reserves: the clearing drain and the currency drain. The difference in behaviour between individual banks and the whole banking system is caused by the fact that while the clearing drain is internal to the system it is external to the individual bank. The banking system as a whole does not experience a clearing house drain.[10] On the other hand, the currency drain is external to both the system and the individual bank.

Table 7-7 illustrates the effects of a currency drain on the banking system's potential to expand. As in our previous example, the banks hold currency reserves equal to 12 per cent of their total deposits. The currency drain is expressed as the coefficient of the marginal currency drain with a value of 0.10. As in our previous example, an initial deposit of currency in

[10] The exception to this would be an international clearing drain among banking systems.

TABLE 7-7

Multiple Expansion of Lending and Deposits through the Banking System
(*Reserve ratio = 0.12, Coefficient of marginal currency drain = 0.10*)
(*in dollars*)

	Assets			**Liabilities**		
			BANK A			
Reserve Loss	Reserves:		+ 1,000.00	Deposits:		Currency Drain
	Required	+ 120.00		Initial Primary Deposit	+ 1,000.00	
	Excess	+ 880.00		Secondary Deposit	+ 880.00	
88.00	Loans		+ 880.00			88.00
			BANK B			
	Reserves:		+ 792.00	Deposits:		
	Required	+ 95.04		Primary Deposit	+ 792.00	
	Excess	+ 696.96		Secondary Deposit	+ 696.96	
69.70	Loans		+ 696.96			69.70
			BANK C			
	Reserves:		+ 627.26	Deposits:		
	Required	+ 75.27		Primary Deposit	+ 627.26	
	Excess	+ 551.99		Secondary Deposit	+ 551.99	
55.20	Loans		+ 551.99			55.20
			ADDITIONAL BANKS D, E, F, G . . .			
	Reserves:			Deposits:		
187.10	Required	+ 309.69		Primary Deposits	+ 309.69	
	Excess	0		Secondary Deposits	+ 2,271.05	
	Loans		+ 2,271.08			187.10

ALL BANKS

Total Reserve Drain						Currency Outside Banks
	Reserves:		+ 600.00	Deposits:		
	Required	+ 600.00		Initial Primary Deposit	+ 1,000.00	
400.00	Excess	0		Secondary Deposits	4,000.00	400.00
	Loans		+ 4,400.00			
			+ 5,000.00		+ 5,000.00	

the amount of $1,000 is made in Bank A. The bank holds a 12 per cent cash reserve equal to $120 and in the process of lending out its excess reserves of $880 creates secondary deposits of an equal amount. Unlike our previous example which had no currency drain, primary deposits in Bank B are not increased by the full $880 because the public decides to hold 10 cents of each additional dollar of secondary deposits in the form of currency outside the banking system. This currency drain reduces reserves by an equal amount. In other words, the currency drain absorbs the system's reserves by 100 per cent of the amount of the drain, as compared with deposits which absorb reserves only in the amount of the reserve ratio.

As other banks increase their loans and secondary deposits, the initial currency deposited in Bank A will be absorbed as required reserves for the banking system and as currency holdings by the non-bank public. In our example, the expansionary process in the banking system halts when required reserves are equal to $600 and the currency drain is equal to $400. The two together ($1,000) absorb all of the reserves available for potential deposit expansion. A quick look at our two examples of multiple expansion of lending and deposits through the banking system will reveal that the expansionary potential of the system is dampened by the presence of a currency drain.

ACTUAL AND POTENTIAL EXPANSION IN THE BANKING SYSTEM

For both the individual bank in a banking system and the banking system as a whole, the potential expansion of earning assets and the potential creation of deposit money depends principally on the volume of reserves and the reserve requirements of the banks. Under normal circumstances an individual bank in a banking system has the potential to safely increase its deposits through the extension of its loans and the purchase of securities in an amount equal to its excess reserves. The banking system, on the other hand, has the potential to expand its earning assets in the form of loans and securities by some multiple of the excess reserves in the system. This is also true for the individual bank which enjoys a monopoly position and therefore constitutes a banking system in itself.[11]

When all the banks are fully loaned up and are holding reserves just equal to some specified proportion of their deposits, expansion is possible only if new reserves can be acquired or if deposits with a high reserve ratio are shifted to deposits with a lower reserve ratio.

We have demonstrated the expansionary potential of the banks when

---

[11] A bank with a favourable clearing drain as is shown in Table 7-2, Part II, also has the potential to expand its earning assets by some multiple of its initial excess reserves.

new reserves are acquired by a deposit of currency. Banks can also obtain reserves by borrowing from a central bank. As is demonstrated in the appendix to this chapter, reserves originated in this way give the banks a larger potential to expand than is the case when the initial increase in reserves is accompanied by a corresponding increase in primary deposits.

A certain proportion of the new reserves determined by the reserve ratio has to be held by the banks as required reserves. In our discussion we assumed that the required reserves were held in the banks' vaults and cash tills and that this amount was sufficient to meet not only the banks' minimum reserve ratio required by law but also their day-to-day needs. When these needs are larger the actual reserve ratio of the banks is larger than the minimum legal reserve ratio. When banks have to hold part of their reserves on deposit with a central bank, and when these reserves are not as readily available to the banks as those held in their vaults and cash tills, the banks will be inclined to hold reserves in excess of those required by law. Extra reserves will also be held when the banks are uncertain of the future economic climate and the consequent unpredictability of currency drains.

For the most part we have assumed that all bank deposits are demand deposits and that only one legal minimum reserve ratio applies. In practice banks hold savings or time deposits as well as demand deposits. If a different legal minimum reserve ratio is held against each type of deposit, a shift from one to the other will affect the banks' expansionary potential. The implications of such a shift are developed further in the appendix to this chapter.

In the process of expansion part or all of the banks' reserves may be drained away and will therefore no longer be available as required reserves against deposits. The individual bank in a banking system of more than one bank experiences two kinds of drains: a clearing drain and a currency drain. The clearing drain is a cash drain from one bank to another bank within the system while the currency drain is a drain out of the banks into the hands of the public. We have shown that the clearing drain which is restricted to the individual bank results from the clearing house operations. The currency drain on the other hand, is external to all banks and results from the public's propensity to hold currency in an amount relative to bank deposits. The ratio of currency holdings to bank deposits depends upon such factors as prices, the level of income and the rate of interest. A significant amount of currency is also held outside the banking system in the vaults and cash tills of a growing number of non-bank financial institutions.

A currency drain may be external in nature if the drain of currency out of the banking system is also a drain out of the country. External drains were particularly common when the banks' reserves included specie, but they still occur when foreigners decide to hold Canadian dollars outside the country.

We cannot be sure that the banks will or can reach the limits of potential expansion. In our discussion and in our examples we have assumed that because of the profit motive the banks will at all times attempt to increase their earning assets and deposits to the limit. While a good case can be made that this is their long-run objective, it need not follow in the short run. There are times when banks may want to hold excess reserves rather than assume the risks involved in increasing their earning assets at current interest rates. Even if the banks are willing to commit all their excess reserves to the market, they must be able to find borrowers. During recessionary periods these may be scarce. For all these reasons actual expansion by the banks may fall short of potential expansion.

THE CONTRACTION OF DEPOSITS

So far we have discussed only the expansion of bank deposits resulting from an increase in bank reserves and the consequent increase in the banks' earning assets. Bank deposits can also contract or be destroyed. Essentially the processes we have described for bank expansion are reversible. Just as excess reserves in a banking system may result in the multiple creation of deposits, the loss of reserves when a banking system is loaned up (total reserves are required reserves) *may* result in a multiple contraction of deposits. A description of the process by which a reduction in reserves affects bank deposits and therefore the money supply is left as a useful exercise for the student.

APPENDIX

MONEY AND CREDIT MULTIPLIERS

The results of our analysis in Chapter 7 can be readily obtained by a system of equations from which multipliers are derived.[12]

Let us assume that the following seven equations contain the important variables and their relationships in a banking and monetary system.

[12] The system of equations employed here follows that of William J. Frazer, Jr. and William Yohe, *Introduction to the Analytics and Institutions of Money and Banking*, Princeton, N.J., Van Nostrand, 1966.

$$\begin{aligned}
\triangle M &= \triangle D_0 + \triangle D_1 + \triangle C && (1)\\
\triangle C &= c\triangle D_1 && (2)\\
\triangle R &= rD_0 + r\triangle D_1 && (3)\\
\triangle R_0 &= \triangle C + \triangle R && (4)\\
\triangle A &= \triangle D_1 + \triangle C && (5)\\
\triangle D_0 &= \triangle R_0 && (6)\\
\triangle R_0 &= \text{Given amount} && (7)
\end{aligned}$$

The seven variables are:

$\triangle M$ = the change in the money supply
$\triangle D_0$ = an initial primary deposit
$\triangle D_1$ = the bank-induced deposits
$\triangle C$ = the change in the public's currency holdings outside the banks
$\triangle R_0$ = an initial change in reserves
$\triangle R$ = the change in required reserves
$\triangle A$ = the change in the banks' earning assets

There are two parameters in the system: the currency drain or behavioural parameter, and the minimum reserve ratio or institutional parameter. They have the following specifications:

c = the currency drain expressed as a ratio of the change in the currency holdings of the public outside the banks to a change in bank-induced deposits; i.e.

$$\frac{\triangle C}{\triangle D_1}$$

r = the minimum reserve ratio expressed as required reserves to total deposits; i.e.,

$$\frac{\triangle R}{\triangle D_0 + \triangle D_1}$$

Furthermore, $0 < c < 1$ *and* $0 < r < 1$.

Equation *(1)* defines the money supply as consisting of all bank deposits plus currency holdings of the public outside the banks. Equation *(2)* is a behavioural equation indicating the public's preference to hold additional currency outside the banking system with each addition to bank-induced or secondary deposits. The amount of reserves which the banks must hold against their deposits is specified by equation *(3)*. Equations *(4)* and *(5)* are identities. Equation *(4)* tells us that the banks are fully loaned up and can therefore no longer continue an expansionary process, after any increase in reserves is fully used to meet the banks' reserve requirement and the public's preference for currency. Equation *(5)* expresses the equality between the increase in bank earning assets and the induced increases in currency and demand deposits. In other words, the banks when changing their earning assets make settlement in the form of bank deposits and currency the total of which must be equal to the total change in the banks' earning assets. Equation *(6)* informs us that the banks initially receive additional reserves through a deposit of currency. Later we shall modify this assumption.

We have a linear system of seven equations and seven variables of which six are unknown *(R_o* is a known amount). We can now find the effect of a change in reserves, or in one of the parameters of the system, on the equilibrium values of M, D_l and A. Equations *(I)*, *(II)*, *(III)*, derived through a series of cumbersome substitutions, do just this.[13]

$$\triangle D_1 = \frac{1}{r+c}\ 1-r\ \triangle R_0 \qquad (I)$$

$$\triangle M = \underbrace{\triangle D_0}_{\textit{primary deposit}} + \underbrace{\frac{1+c}{r+c}\ \underbrace{(1-r)\ \triangle R_0}_{\textit{initial excess reserves}}}_{\triangle D_1 + \triangle C} \qquad (II)$$

$$= R_0 \qquad \triangle D_1 + \triangle C$$

$$\triangle A = \frac{1+c}{r+c}\ (1-r)\ \triangle R_0 \qquad (III)$$

---

[13] Equations (*I*) and (*II*) can be derived in the following way:

From equations (*4*) and (*6*)	$\Delta D_0 =$	$\Delta C + \Delta R$	
Substituting from (*2*) and (*3*)	$=$	$c\,\Delta D_1 + r\,\Delta D_0 + r\,\Delta D_1$	
	or $\Delta D_0 - r\,\Delta D_0 =$	$c\,\Delta D_1 + r\,\Delta D_1$	
	or $\Delta D_0\ (1-r) =$	$\Delta D_1\ (r+c)$	
Substituting from (*6*)	$\Delta R_0\ (1-r) =$	$\Delta D_1\ (r+c)$	
	or $\Delta D_1 =$	$\frac{1-r}{r+c}\ \Delta R_0$	(*I*)
But, from (*1*)	$\Delta M =$	$\Delta D_0 + \Delta D_1 + \Delta C$	
Substitution from (*2*)	$\Delta M =$	$\Delta D_0 + \Delta D_1 + c\,\Delta D_1$	
	or $\Delta M =$	$\Delta D_0 + (1+c)\ \Delta D_1$	
and substituting from (*I*)	$\Delta M =$	$\Delta D_0 + \frac{1+c}{r+c}(1-r)\,\Delta R_0$	(*II*)

The coefficients in equations *(I)* and *(II)* which express the multiple by which bank deposits and the total money supply, respectively, change as a result of a change in bank reserves are called **money multipliers.** The coefficient in equation *(III)* which tells us by what multiple the banks' earning assets change as a result of a change in their reserves is called the **credit multiplier.**

If we now substitute the values for the variables and the parameters used in Table 7-7 in equations *(I)*, *(II)* and *(III)* we obtain the results shown in the table.

$$\triangle D_1 = \frac{1}{0.12 + 0.10} (1\text{-}0.12) \quad \$1{,}000 = \$4{,}000.00$$

$$\triangle M = \$1{,}000 + \frac{1 + 0.10}{0.12 + 0.10} (1\text{-}0.12) \quad \$1{,}000 = \$5{,}000.00$$

$$\triangle A = \frac{1 + 0.10}{0.12 + 0.10} (1\text{-}0.12) \quad \$1{,}000 = \$4{,}400.00$$

When the initial increase in the banks' reserves is not accompanied by a corresponding initial primary deposit equation (*6*) has to be rewritten as follows:

$$\triangle D_0 = 0 \qquad (6a)$$

This will be the case when the banks obtain additional reserves by borrowing from a central bank. If we substitute equation (*6a*) for (*6*) in our system of seven equations the multipliers take the following form:

$$\triangle D_1 = \frac{1}{r + c} \triangle R_0 \qquad (Ia)$$

$$\triangle M = \frac{1 + c}{r + c} \triangle R_0 \qquad (IIa)$$

$$\triangle A = \frac{1 + c}{r + c} \triangle R_0 \qquad (IIIa)$$

Where the initial increase in reserves is not accompanied by a corresponding initial increase in primary deposits, all of the initial increase of equation *(IIa)* is the same as the credit multiplier of equation *(IIIa)*. Furthermore, if equations *(Ia)*, *(IIa)* and *(IIIa)* are compared with equations *(I)*, *(II)* and *(III)* it will be noticed that the corresponding multipliers are larger when the initial increase in reserves is not accompanied by an initial increase in primary deposits. This is so because with an initial primary deposit (D_o), excess reserves are equal to the primary deposit less the required amount of reserves that have to be held against this deposit.

Instead of assuming that all bank deposits are demand deposits, let us now suppose that the banks hold both demand and time deposits. Furthermore, let us assume that the minimum reserve ratio for time deposits is different from that for demand deposits. We will for the moment continue to assume that both demand and time deposits constitute part of the money supply. We now have to add an additional equation to our original system of seven. This we can specify as:

$$\triangle Dt = t\triangle D_1 \qquad (8)$$

D_t represents the change in the public's time deposits held at the banks. We also have to modify the reserve ratio parameter and add two more parameters. Our new set of parameters is now:

c = the currency drain expressed as a ratio of the change in currency holdings of the public outside the banks to a change in bank-induced demand deposits; i.e.,

$$\frac{\triangle C}{\triangle D_1}$$

r = the minimum reserve ratio for demand deposits expressed as required reserves to demand deposits; *i.e.*,

$$\frac{\triangle R}{\triangle D_1}$$

r′ = the minimum reserve ratio for time deposits expressed as required reserves to time deposits; i.e.,

$$\frac{\triangle R}{\triangle Dt}$$

t = the ratio of the desired change in time deposits to a change in demand deposits; i.e.,

$$\frac{\triangle Dt}{\triangle D_1}$$

From our system of eight equations and eight variables (seven unknown) we derive the following multipliers:

Money multiplier $$\frac{1 + c}{r + c + tr'} \qquad (IIb)$$

Credit multiplier $$\frac{1 + c + t}{r + c + tr'} \qquad (IIIb)$$

If we use the same set of equations and parameters, but assume that both demand and time deposits are part of the money supply the credit multiplier in *(IIIb)* is also the corresponding money multiplier.

Finally, let us again point out that credit and money multipliers show the *potential* expansion by the banking system. Actual expansion will depend upon the underlying assumptions which were noted in the text of the chapter.

SELECTED READINGS

Angell, J.W., and Ficek, K., "Expansion of Bank Credit", *Journal of Political Economy,* 1933, pp. 1-32, 152-193.

Crick, W.F., "The Genesis of Bank Deposits", *Economica,* Vol. 7, 1927, pp. 191-202. Reprinted in American Economic Association, *Readings in Monetary Theory,* Philadelphia, Blakiston Co., 1951, pp. 41-53.

Keynes, J.M., *A Treatise on Money,* Vol. 2, New York, Harcourt Brace, 1930, Ch. 25.

Orr, Daniel and W.J. Mellon, "Stochastic Reserve Losses and Bank Credit", *American Economic Review,* Vol. 51, September, 1961, pp. 614-623.

Phillips, C.A., *Bank Credit,* New York, Macmillan, 1921, Ch. 1-4.

Shaw, E.S., *Money, Income, and Monetary Policy,* Chicago, Richard D. Irwin, 1950.

Thomson, P., "Variations on a Theme by Phillips", *American Economic Review,* Vol. 46, December, 1956, pp. 965-970.

Vining, R., "A Process Analysis of Bank Credit Expansion", *Quarterly Journal of Economics,* Vol. 54, August, 1940, pp. 599-623.

8

COMMERCIAL BANKING OPERATIONS

The name **commercial bank** derived from the belief that banks should make only short-term "commercial loans".[1] These were defined as loans no longer than a year in duration which were made to traders and merchants to finance the transportation of goods from producers to wholesalers and to finance the holding of inventories during the relatively short time required for their sale. While the term commercial banking is in general use today in the United Kingdom, the United States and Canada, banks are often referred to in more specific ways in each of these countries. In England they are known as **joint-stock banks,** a term which dates from their early formation as incorporated institutions with limited liability. They are also called **clearing banks,** as the few remaining commercial banks which have absorbed all of the banking business in England are still members of the London Bankers' Clearing House.

In the United States commercial banks are sometimes known by the body which incorporates or charters them or by the agency which regulates them. Thus a **national bank** is a bank incorporated under federal law while a **state bank** is one incorporated by state legislatures. A **member bank** is a member of the Federal Reserve System. National banks are also member banks since they are obliged to belong to the System. State banks may or may not be member banks; their membership is voluntary.

In Canada banks are known as **chartered banks** because of the Canadian tradition of establishing commercial banks only through government charter. Today commercial banks in Canada operate under the authority

[1] The word "bank" is of German origin but came into English usage from French and Italian. At first it referred to the bench or counter used by money changers and dealers. Later it assumed its more general meaning of the place of business of money dealers. Akin to the early English use of the word bank is the use of the French word *banque* and the Italian word *banca*.

vested in them by the Parliament of Canada through the Bank Act — "An Act Respecting Banks and Banking". The word bank is restricted by law to commercial banks operating under the Bank Act and to the Quebec savings banks operating under "An Act Respecting Savings Banks in the Province of Quebec".

COMMERCIAL BANK FUNCTIONS

Canadian commercial banks have traditionally fulfilled two functions: **saving and banking.** The saving function involves gathering in the savings of the community to make them available for consumer spending and the financing of capital projects. Many other financial institutions also perform this function. They, along with the banks, are intermediaries between those in the community who have excess funds (lenders) and those who have a deficiency of funds (borrowers). All financial institutions which provide a savings function are financial intermediaries.

The banking function involves the creation, destruction and transfer of deposit money, and the provision of commercial credits. Traditionally the commercial banks alone among all private institutions were considered to perform a banking function because they could create and destroy deposit money. Now, however, other financial institutions perform a quasi banking function. As is the case with the banks, some of the liabilities of these institutions serve as a means of payment and, therefore, as a medium of exchange. In its report in 1964, the Royal Commission on Banking and Finance, known as the Porter Commission, observed that "the liabilities of a group of private financial institutions are now the most common means of payment in Canada and that these institutions provide the payments mechanism essential to the efficient functioning of our modern economy".[2] In the larger urban areas cheques drawn on some deposit accounts with trust and mortgage loan companies are now accepted as means of payment. The same is true for cheques drawn against the caisses populaires in the province of Quebec and credit unions in the western provinces. Because these institutions are now performing a quasi banking function they are referred to as **near-banks.** While it is now generally accepted that they can create and destroy deposits. their influence on the money supply is not considered to be as great as that of the banks.

The deposit creating ability of the near-banks differs from that of the banks in two significant ways. We noted in Chapter 7 that the banking system's ability to create deposits results from a predictable proportion

---

2 *Report of the Royal Commission on Banking and Finance,* Ottawa, Queen's Printer, 1964, p. 93.

of the loaned funds flowing back as deposits into the banking system. Since the circulation of the liabilities of near-banks is still relatively small, their return flow is similarly small and unpredictable. They do not as yet have the same money creating potential as do the banks.

The money creating ability of the near-banks is restricted further by law. Banks can create deposits against non-negotiable promissory notes (see Chapter 7). Under most legal jurisdictions the near-banks can make loans and thus create deposits only against negotiable financial instruments. This excludes many would-be borrowers from borrowing at near-banks and restricts the banking activity of these institutions.

We have included the transfer of funds as a feature of the banking function. In Canada, as in the United Kingdom, the clearing of cheques drawn on the banks has traditionally been the function of the chartered banks. The right to operate a clearing system, the heart of a modern payment mechanism, was assumed by the banks under the Canadian Banker's Association Act of 1890. Recently the right of the banks to exercise control of the Canadian clearing mechanism has been questioned. With the growth of near-banks that allow cheques to be written against their deposits, an increasing number of cheques other than those drawn against commercial banks require clearing. The banks have extended clearing privileges to the near-banks whereby cheques or orders drawn on them by their customers and cheques negotiated by them for their customers are cleared through the facilities maintained by the banks. For this service the near-banks pay an annual fee and hold balances with the chartered banks for settlement purposes. It can be argued that the near-banks should have the right rather than the privilege of access to the clearing system. Under the existing system the chartered banks could manage the clearing system so as to discriminate against their competitors in the payment mechanism. The Porter Commission, recognizing this possibility, recommended that control over the clearing system should be exercised by all the institutions performing a banking function, including the near-banks.[3]

Clearing operations are handled in another way in the United States, where most of the operations are performed by the Federal Reserve System and only to a limited extent by the banks themselves. The Federal Reserve System assumed this responsibility to facilitate the efficient handling of cheque clearing in a banking system composed of thousands of individual banks, and also to establish **par clearing.** Par clearing prohibits the charging of "exchange" by a bank for the out-of-town cheques which it negotiates. These charges when imposed by one bank on another are usually passed on to the customer cashing the cheque. In Canada, the

---

[3] *Ibid.*, p. 182.

chartered banks still charge exchange on some cheques which are drawn on out-of-town banks.[4]

In the United States, unlike Canada, a large proportion of the commercial banks also provide a **trust function.** Before the 1840's trust functions were combined with insurance, but after the rise of mutual life insurance companies the two were separated. About 1870 trust companies started to invade the traditional domain of commercial banking. At the same time commercial banks added trust departments. Today it is difficult to differentiate between the activities of trust companies and those of commercial banks in the United States. In Canada commercial banks have not entered the trust field directly, but trust companies moved into the banking field in the 1950's.

In the 1920's American commercial banks again ventured beyond usual banking practice and began to underwrite and distribute securities. Although the Banking Act of 1933 forced them to give up this function, numerous exceptions have been made.

In Canada the banks frequently participate in the underwriting of high grade security issues, particularly provincial and municipal issues, with experienced and reputable partners in an underwriting syndicate. In both Canada and the United States the banks also act as brokers in buying and selling bonds.

OBJECTIVES AND RESPONSIBILITY OF COMMERCIAL BANKING

The *raison d'être* of commercial banking is to make profit for the banks' shareholders. However, as we have already noted, the prosperity of banking institutions cannot be separated from that of the community which they serve. They cannot operate as strictly private institutions. Indeed, commercial banks have become quasi public institutions. Although traditionally the banks have of their own volition accepted this role, to ensure that the public interest will be served at all times, governments have superimposed regulations and supervision on prudent banking practices and customs. Initially government regulation and supervision concerned itself with the safety of bank notes and deposits. the payment of notes and deposits on par at demand, and the adequacy of bank lending. To this has been added concern over the banks' operations as money creating

4 See Canadian Banker's Association, *Submissions to the Royal Commission on Banking and Finance*, Supplement to the Canadian Banker, Spring 1963, pp. 91-93 and Appendix.

institutions and the control of these operations for the overall conduct of the economy.

Because the banks no longer issue their own notes, the safety of their deposits is of prime importance for the soundness of the monetary system. Banks are considered solvent when the value of their assets exceeds the value of their liabilities. Since the total value of the banks' liabilities is fixed, while that of their assets fluctuates, their solvency and therefore the safety of their deposits depends upon the type of assets which they hold. As we shall see later, aside from the type of assets which the banks may hold to guarantee their solvency, their capital funds are also considered an important cushion of safety for depositors.

So far then, we have noted that one responsibility of banks is to provide a return to their owners, the shareholders. Bankers are therefore concerned with making profits. In addition banks are responsible for the safety of their deposits. Toward this end their objective is to remain solvent.

Another responsibility of banks is to pay on demand. For this purpose their assets include a relatively high proportion of **liquid assets** in the form of cash or near-cash. Banks achieve liquidity by holding assets which can be readily converted to cash with little or no loss. Liquidity, then, must be an objective of commercial banks. Liquidity also enables banks to meet promptly the legitimate credit demands of business. But since commercial banks can extend credit only if the public is willing to hold deposits with them, they must maintain solvency as well as liquidity.

The first defence of a bank against a demand for cash is its primary reserves, which are themselves cash. Part of these are held in the form of coin and Bank of Canada notes in the cash tills and vaults of the banks, and part as deposits with the Bank of Canada and other banks. The deposits with the Bank of Canada serve mainly to perform clearing operations between banks and to meet seasonal and cyclical fluctuations in the demand for cash. Experience has shown that a bank's immediate cash requirement is a fairly consistent ratio of its deposits.

Traditionally it was held that a bank's funds which were not employed as primary reserves should be put out in short-term self-liquidating loans. When commercial bank notes provided the most important medium of exchange, many thought that as long as the banks met the legitimate credit needs of commerce and industry, they would provide the country with an adequate amount of money for circulation in the form of their own notes. Moreover, since commercial loans are self-liquidating and of short maturity, the liquidity requirements of the banks would be satisfied. This theory, known in England as the real bills doctrine (in North America, the commercial loans theory), proved inadequate as a basis for providing an elastic money supply and for maintaining the liquidity requirements of banks.

Creating money only for the needs of business resulted at times in a scarcity of the medium of exchange, since money is required for many needs aside from those of business. On the other hand, allowing businesses to expand without limit on the basis of commercial loans for goods and services led to inflation and the depreciation of the currency. Thus the commercial loan theory failed to provide the "proper" amount of the medium of exchange.

Furthermore, commercial loans did not provide the banks with sufficient liquidity to meet the demands for cash at all times, especially during periods of financial crisis. Commercial loans were, as a rule, repaid out of the income resulting from transactions financed by the loan. However, in many cases the ability to purchase the goods produced by a firm which was financed by a bank depended upon bank loans to the purchasers of such goods. In other words, the repayment of one bank loan depended upon the acquisition of yet another.

The liquidity of any one bank loan depends upon the ability of the banking system to extend loans. When the banking system lacks this ability, the banks' commercial loans are no longer liquid.

After the First World War when a market for government securities was developed in the United States, and later in Canada, the commercial loan theory gave way to a new **shiftability doctrine of liquidity.** The gist of this theory is that the banks can protect themselves better against large deposit withdrawals by holding assets for which there is a highly organized and ready market. Such a market makes it easier to find someone who is willing to give up cash for securities. Moreover, with an established market, there exists a much greater possibility that securities can be shifted into cash without incurring a heavy loss. The shiftability doctrine assumes that the security market is sufficiently large that those wishing to shift will constitute a relatively small proportion of the total security holdings and that therefore any losses will be relatively small.

The business of commercial banking is to make profits for the shareholders, satisfy the credit needs of business, and at the same time hold assets that are liquid and safe to protect the interests of both bank depositors and the financial community. The banks must therefore manage their funds to meet four major requirements — **profits, credit, liquidity and safety.** These represent conflicting goals. In order to satisfy the safety and liquidity requirements assets must be held in cash or near-cash, bringing small financial rewards to the banks. On the other hand, to maximize potential profits the banks must put their funds into long-term loans and securities, or other financial instruments, which pay a risk premium. The way banks attempt to resolve this conflict is the story of how they manage their funds: the cash they hold, the loans they take and the investments they make.

BANK DEPOSITS

Canadian Dollar Deposits

Deposits of money accepted by the chartered banks have been their chief source of funds. The only other source is the banks' capital fund which we shall discuss later. About 75 per cent of the banks' deposits are denominated in Canadian dollars, the remainder being in foreign currencies. Table 8-1 shows the composition of the banks' Canadian dollar deposits.

Demand Deposits

Government of Canada. Deposits of the federal government are allocated among the banks on an agreed ratio according to each bank's share of the unrecovered costs of handling federal government business. Until 1953 the banks paid no interest on these deposits. This was intended to compensate them for handling the clearing operation of government cheques for which they are not allowed to charge a fee. By a 1953 agreement the banks now pay interest to the government on some portion of these funds.[5]

Provincial Government Deposits. Although these are shown separately by the banks, they are essentially the same as corporate current accounts discussed below.

Deposits of Other Banks. These represent primarily accounts maintained by foreign banks in Canada. They are used to cover the drawings of foreign banks on Canada and also to facilitate the cashing of Canadian cheques in other countries. For example, cheques of Canadian drawers cashed in Florida would be cleared by the American bank to the Canadian correspondent, who would credit the deposit account of the American bank with the proceeds. Canadian banks for similar reason maintain reciprocal deposits with foreign banks. The growth of Canadian dollar deposits in Canadian banks by foreign banks reflects the increase in Canada's international transactions.

Other Demand Deposits These are essentially current accounts held by businesses, used by them for all their normal payment needs and maintained to a limited extent as a reserve of liquid assets. Although banks are not specifically prohibited from paying interest on demand deposits, as has been the case in the United States since 1933, it is their practice not to except in the case of the federal government deposits noted previously. Current account holders are usually required to pay a service

---

[5] Legal status for such agreements was introduced in the Bank Act revisions of 1967.

TABLE 8-1

Deposits in Canadian Chartered Banks
Selected Years

Canadian Dollar Deposits
(millions of dollars)

At Dec. 31	1930	1935	1940	1945	1950	1955	1960	1965
Demand Deposits								
Government of Canada	27	12	66	922	339	517	510	797
Provincial governments	21	41	67	91	161	181	119	344
Other banks	13	14	13	19	117	139	201	198
Other current	642	641	1,031	2,063	2,770	3,915	4,301	5,486
Total Repayable on demand	703	708	1,177	3,095	3,387	4,752	5,131	6,825
Notice Deposits								
Personal savings*	1,426	1,486	1,641	2,865	4,558	5,633	7,215	9,725
Other Notice*						464	576	2,044
Total	2,128	2,194	2,818	5,960	7,945	10,848	12,922	18,594
Foreign Currency Deposits								
	372	379	405	901	835	1,056	2,654	5,083

* Before 1954 Personal savings and Other Notice were shown together as "Other Notice".

Source: M. C. Urquhart (ed.), Historical Statistics of Canada, Toronto, Macmillan, 1965, p. 240. Bank of Canada, Statistical Summary, 1966 Supplement pp. 36-37.

charge calculated on specified average minimum balances and on the number of cheques written.

Notice Deposits

Personal Savings Deposits. The chartered banks are probably still the most important savings institutions in Canada. Personal savings deposits in banks are used by individuals both as a savings instrument and as working accounts through which pass the regular flow of their income and spending. In Canada, unlike the United States and the United Kingdom, customers are allowed full chequing privileges against these accounts. While the banks reserve the right to demand notice of withdrawal, it has been the practice not to enforce it. Furthermore, unlike the United States, Canada has placed no legal restrictions on the amount of interest that banks are allowed to pay on these deposits.

The wide-spread use of chequing privileges has increased the banks' costs of operating their savings departments. They have attempted to offset some of these costs by charging a fee for each withdrawal or for withdrawals above a specified number per minimum balance held. In 1957 the banks introduced personal chequing accounts on which they pay no interest but provide the customer with regular statements and charge him less per cheque.

Other Notice Deposits. At one time these included only the savings deposits of corporations and religious, educational and welfare institutions, and were similar to personal savings deposits. Before the mid-1950's corporations with excess funds for short periods usually held them in savings deposits. Then with the development of a money market in Canada and with the rise in levels of market interest rates, corporations started to switch from savings accounts to money market paper. To meet this competition, the banks introduced short-term interest bearing deposit instruments of their own. These now include fixed term **deposit receipts** of specified amounts, which are not negotiable and which may be withdrawn before the agreed term of from thirty to 364 days subject to an interest penalty. They also include **certificates of deposit** or CD's as they have come to be known which are bearer time deposits negotiable in the money market. They are available only in specified minimum amounts with maturities from one to six years.

The chartered banks also sell **bearer deposit notes** and **savings certificates.** The notes, from twenty-eight days to one year duration, are transferable but non-redeemable prior to maturity. They are issued only in multiples of $100,000 and are sold at a discount.[6] Savings certificates, also sold at a discount, are issued in multiples of $10. They are redeemable at any time at graduated rates printed on the certificates.

Foreign Currency Deposits [7]

Deposits with the chartered banks denominated in foreign currencies now comprise almost 25 per cent of their total deposits. This relatively large proportion reflects the considerable volume of business conducted by Canadian banks in foreign countries and the size of Canada's overall foreign transactions. Foreign currency deposits are made by Canadian exporters, by Canadian companies operating plants abroad and by bank customers who require a depository for investment capital awaiting exchange into Canadian dollars or for the repatriation of funds to foreign

---

[6] For example, if the rate of interest on these notes is 6 per cent, a note paying $100,000 at maturity can be purchased for $94,000.

[7] See also foreign currency swapped deposits discussed in Chapter 10, page 152.

countries. In recent years the banks have actively sought foreign currency deposits in the international markets. International interest rate differentials and foreign exchange rate movements play an important part in the banks' success in attracting these deposits.

DEPOSIT INSURANCE

The safety of deposits accepted from the public by the chartered banks and by the trust and loan companies outside the Province of Quebec are protected by the Canada Deposit Insurance Corporation. In Quebec deposits accepted from the public by all financial institutions other than the chartered banks are guaranteed by the Quebec Deposit Insurance Board.

The Canada Deposit Insurance Corporation (CDIC) was established in 1967. It protects the safety of deposits in institutions insured with it in three ways: it examines and supervises the financial affairs and management of these institutions; it pays each depositor's claim on a failed institution up to a maximum of $20,000; and it may prevent an institution from failing by providing financial and management assistance.

When an institution fails, the CDIC settles a depositor's claim either with a cash payment or by way of a transferred deposit with another insured institution. In practice, deposits are insured 100 per cent because of the financial assistance provided by the CDIC to prevent failure. The CDIC is authorized, for the purpose of "reducing a risk" to itself or of "reducing and averting a threatened loss" to itself, to acquire assets from an insured institution and to make secured loans or advances or guarantee loans to or deposits with an insured institution.

The resources available to the CDIC to meet its obligations include: $10 million in share capital subscribed by the federal government; the annual payment of premiums by insured institutions accumulated in the Deposit Insurance Fund; and accumulated net earnings. In addition by way of standby credit, the CDIC can borrow from the federal government through the sale of its bonds and debentures issued for this purpose. The aggregate amount of money the government is authorized to have outstanding with the CDIC at any one time is $500 million.

MANAGEMENT AND REGULATION OF BANK FUNDS

THE BANKS' "MORE LIQUID ASSETS"

The Bank Act requires the banks to maintain cash reserves in the form of Bank of Canada notes, and deposits in Canadian currency with the Bank of Canada. The reserves must be equal to 12 per cent of the banks' demand deposits (in Canadian currency) and 4 per cent of their notice deposits (also in Canadian currency).

Before the revisions of the Bank Act of 1967 there was no legal requirement for the banks to hold secondary reserves. However, the banks held such reserves in the form of Government of Canada treasury bills and bonds maturing within two years, day-to-day loans, and call loans. Treasury bills are short-term obligations of the federal government, usually with a ninety-one day maturity. Day-to-day loans (or simply day loans) are made by the banks to investment dealers and are callable before noon on any day by either party. These loans are liquid, even if all the banks decide to call them at the same time, because the dealers have lines of credit with the Bank of Canada to which they can turn to meet the banks' call. Call loans made to stock brokers were at one time payable on demand (upon call), but with interbank competition for such loans, repayment is usually required at the earliest convenience of the brokers after call.

In November 1955 the banks agreed to a request by the Governor of the Bank of Canada that after June 1956 in addition to the legal cash reserve, each bank would hold day-to-day loans and Government of Canada Treasury bills in such amounts that the total of cash, day loans and bills would average no less than 15 per cent of deposit liabilities in each month. This arrangement was voluntary on the part of the banks. In the revisions to the Bank Act in 1967, however, the Bank of Canada was given power to require the banks to maintain secondary reserves as specified from time to time in the form of Bank of Canada notes and deposits with the Bank, Treasury bills and day loans to investment dealers who have lines of credit with the Bank. Table 8-2 shows the composition of the bank's more liquid assets.

BANK LENDING

Bankers, following prudent banking practices, make loans on the basis of the **credit worthiness** of the borrowers. They determine credit worthiness by the character of the borrower and his financial capacities as revealed by his past record and future prospects. They may require collateral in the form of marketable securities, but this is not generally the determining factor in making business loans.

Short-Term Business Loans

The Canadian chartered banks still consider short-term business lending their most important lending responsibility. Lending to business is usually facilitated by **loan agreements.** Business credit needs are essentially recurrent and at the same time unpredictable. As a result businesses arrange with their bankers for a **line of credit.** This is an expression of willingness

TABLE 8-2

Chartered Banks Canadian Cash Reserves and Liquid Assets
Daily Averages
(millions of dollars)

Year	Cash Reserves: Bank of Canada Deposits	Cash Reserves: Bank of Canada Notes	Cash Reserves: Total	Canadian Dollar Deposit Liabilities	Average Cash Reserve Ratio %	Day-to-Day Loans	Treasury Bills	Canadian Liquid Assets	Average Liquid Asset Ratio %
1957	535	335	870	10,601	8.21	113	802	1,786	16.85
1958	607	336	943	11,452	8.24	116	908	1,968	17.18
1959	648	351	999	12,187	8.20	64	939	2,002	16.43
1960	625	360	985	12,052	8.17	111	985	2,081	17.27
1961	673	367	1,040	12,804	8.12	150	1,154	2,345	18.31
1962	748	376	1,124	13,812	8.14	145	1,092	2,362	17.10
1963	775	394	1,169	14,400	8.12	155	1,262	2,586	17.96
1964	857	407	1,263	15,598	8.10	193	1,226	2,682	17.20
1965	965	427	1,392	17,186	8.10	205	1,307	2,903	16.89
1966	1,057	449	1,506	18,607	8.10	221	1,477	3,205	17.22

Note: Figures for Day-to-day loans, Treasury bills, Canadian liquid assets and average liquid asset ratio not available on daily average basis prior to June 1956.

Source: Bank of Canada Statistical Summary, 1966 Supplement, p. 18.

by the banks to lend up to a specified maximum for agreed purposes. Under normal circumstances lines of credit are extended for a period of one year and renewed from year to year. To avoid the necessity of annual renegotiation, and as a means of obtaining more formal assurance of the availability of credit, many businesses arrange **revolving credits** which are normally for more than a year and are used to obtain longer term working capital. Under a revolving credit, which is usually expressed in a formal contractual agreement, the borrower may pay a small commitment fee on the unused portion of his line of credit in addition to the agreed upon rate of interest on the amount actually used.

Term Loans

In the 1950's term lending by the banks started to assume increasing importance. Term loans usually have an original maturity of more than one year.[8] They are made to businesses wishing to acquire capital assets

[8] The direct purchase by the banks of corporate securities with similar maturities are usually also referred to as term loans.

such as plants and equipment, and are repaid over a considerable period of time from the net cash income of businesses. They are particularly important to small businesses for whom the costs of market issue, in terms both of interest and cost of underwriting, would be disproportionately high.

Government Guaranteed Loans

From time to time the federal government has introduced legislation to inducc the banks to make loans to essential sectors of the economy without incurring unnecessary risks, and without charging higher interest rates to compensate for their higher than ordinary risks. For instance, the Farm Improvements Loans Act was passed in 1944 to induce freer bank lending on a term basis for the purchase of equipment and livestock, and for the construction or repair of farm buildings. Each bank's losses up to 10 per cent are guaranteed by the government subject to a maximum amount outstanding for all banks at any one time. The maximum of any one Farm Improvement Loan is established by the legislation, as are the maximum maturity period allowed for such loans and the maximum lending rate. The Home Improvement Loans Act, the Fisheries Improvement Loans Act, the Small Business Loans Act, the Canada Student Loans Act, and the various acts assisting veterans and prairie grain producers also sponsor lending along the same lines as the Farm Improvements Loans Act.[9] Bank Loans to farmers are extended also under certain provincial farm credit acts, such as the Junior Farmer Establishment Act of Ontario, the Quebec Farm Improvement Act and the Farm Loans Act of New Brunswick.

One of the most distinctive features of bank lending in Canada is the section of the Bank Act which has come to be known as the **pledge provisions.** As we noted earlier, such loans date from the Act Granting Additional Facilities to Commercial Transactions in 1859. While these provisions are designed to assist businesses and farmers who do not have paper collateral to obtain short-term banking accommodation, they make short-term lending more attractive to the banks by enabling them to acquire a prior claim on the goods which may be pledged.

The pledge provisions of the Bank Act set out the procedures by which a bank may lend on the security of goods in the process of being prepared for market or on the security of a warehouse receipt or bill of lad-

[9] The Porter Commission recommended that the interest rates on guaranteed loans should be made flexible and that all such loan guarantee programmes should be temporary measures to open up new credit channels. Moreover, they should not be restricted to the banks but also should be made available to other lending institutions with suitable facilties. *Report of Royal Commission on Banking and Finance, 1964*, p. 125 and Ch. 12.

ing. Under these provisions a bank is able to make loans on the security of natural products and goods, wares and merchandise which remain in the borrower's possession. For example, Section 82 of the Bank Act allows banks to lend money upon the security of "hydrocarbons in, under or upon the ground, in place or in storage", while Section 88 allows the banks to make loans "to any farmer, upon the security of crops growing or produced upon the farm ... to any fisherman upon the security of fishing vessels, fishing equipment and supplies or products of the sea ...". Without the pledge provisions of the Bank Act prudent banking practices probably would have prevented the banks from assisting in the development of primary products.

Loans to Governments

In addition to loans already mentioned banks also make personal loans, mortgage loans and loans to government. The latter are usually used to finance current expenses pending receipt of revenue and to finance capital expenditures pending the sale of a public issue. These loans are commonly made to provincial governments, municipalities and school boards.

Consumer Credit Loans

While banks are still the main source of short-term business finance, the development of the Canadian money market after 1954 has made it possible for businesses, particularly the larger ones, to finance themselves increasingly through the commercial paper market. In response to this competition the banks have cultivated the consumer instalment credit field long dominated by consumer finance companies. This move, which was especially pronounced after 1957, was facilitated by the 1954 revision of the Bank Act allowing the banks to take chattel mortgages as security. Canadian banks were encouraged by the fact that banks in the United Kingdom were entering the field on a large scale in the late 1950's and that banks in the United States had been successful in the consumer credit field since the end of the Second World War.

Consumer instalment loans, also known as personal loans, are intended to be repaid out of the future income of the borrower and are usually repaid in equal monthly instalments on an amortized basis. They are insured so that the balance of the loan will be repaid in case of the death of the borrower. Consumer loans are made to individuals to provide assistance in the purchase of durable goods, to finance larger expenditures, or to consolidate the borrower's debts.

The banks' share of the consumer loans market has now increased to the point where they are the largest lenders in this field. Although consumer loans were long looked upon with suspicion by bankers, many of whom felt that it was somewhat immoral for a person to buy something before he had earned and saved the money, consumer credit has become an important way of life.

Mortgage Lending

The early disastrous experiences, particularly in the United States, of banks lending on the security of real estate induced governments, almost without exception, to prohibit banks from making loans with mortgage security save as subsequent security. Following the revisions to the National Housing Act (NHA) and the Bank Act in 1954, Canadian banks were allowed to acquire mortgages to secure loans made under the terms of the National Housing Act. After some initial reluctance the banks became major mortgage lenders for a short period, until the maximum rates permitted on NHA mortgages were raised above the rates the banks were allowed to charge under the Bank Act. The banks could have taken mortgages at less than the maximum rate set under the National Housing Act, but this would have created such a rush for loans that they would have been unable to ration their funds equitably. As a result they virtually withdrew from the direct financing of residential construction.

Following the recommendation of the Porter Commission the Bank Act revisions of 1967 extended the banks' lending on the security of mortgages to include **conventional mortgages.** Conventional mortgages, unlike NHA mortgages, are not guaranteed or insured by the government. Conventional mortgage loans made by the banks must be first mortgages (having a prior claim) and are limited to 75 per cent of the value of property. The total amount of residential mortgage loans that any bank may have outstanding at the end of any one year is limited to 10 per cent of its deposit liabilities in Canadian currency and its outstanding bank debentures.[10]

It might be argued that since most of the liabilities of the banks have a very short life, it is impossible for the banks to remain sufficiently liquid if they invest in long-term mortgages. This argument appears to be no longer valid. As for NHA mortgages a secondary market has developed giving these instruments marketability. This will probably also be the case with conventional mortgages as they become more standardized. Moreover, present day practices as pioneered by NHA mortgages requiring insurance and the regular amortization of mortgage contracts, not only reduce the risk of loss to the banks prevalent with earlier mortgage lending but also provide the banks with a steady flow of funds as these contracts are repaid.

---

[10] See Chapter 9.

BANK INVESTMENTS

The banks consider it their primary function to make loans. Their investment activities are, therefore, normally subsidiary to their lending activities. Their investments in short-term government securities included in their "more liquid assets" are made to provide them with liquidity and at the same time with a return, although comparatively small, on their funds. Their investments, other than those made for liquidity purposes, are mostly in the form of medium-term Government of Canada direct and guaranteed bonds.[11] Their holdings of provincial, municipal and corporate bonds constitute a relatively small proportion of their total assets. These securities are usually acquired to obtain good yields and to assist in their underwriting and marketing.

In Canada, the banks are the prime dealers in foreign exchange. When their foreign currency holdings exceed those required immediately or in the near future to meet customer demands, they are invested in short-term foreign securities. These investments have increased significantly in the past few years as Canada's international transactions have grown.

The banks do not purchase equities to any great extent because they consider these to be "foreign to the main purpose and nature of a commercial bank".[12] The corporate shares held by the banks are usually in subsidiary companies. Since the revisions to the Bank Act in 1967 a bank is not allowed to hold more than 10 per cent of the voting stock of any one trust or loan corporation or of any other Canadian corporation if its total investment in any such corporation is more than $5 million. Where the cost of acquisition of the voting stock by a bank of a corporation other than a trust or loan corporation is less than $5 million, it may hold up to 50 per cent of the voting shares.[13]

AN OVERALL VIEW OF BANK PORTFOLIO MANAGEMENT

As we have seen, the banks manage their funds to satisfy four major requirements — profits, credit, liquidity and safety. To ensure that the last three requirements are met the Bank Act specifies the type, and in some cases the amount, of certain assets that the banks must or may

[11] An example of guaranteed bonds are those issued by the Canadian National Railways which are guaranteed by the Government of Canada.

[12] The Canadian Bankers' Association, *Submission to the Royal Commission on Banking and Finance*, Supplement to the Canadian Banker, Spring 1963, p. 18.

[13] These restrictions do not apply in the case of a bank service corporation (a corporation providing to a bank a service other than financial) and the Export Finance Corporation of Canada Ltd.

hold. Before 1967 the Bank Act also specified the maximum rate of interest that the banks were allowed to charge on their loans.

Not all government legislation has been confined to restricting the activities of the banks in managing their assets. By guaranteeing to reimburse the banks for certain losses on loans, the government has attempted to induce them to make loans to essential sectors of the economy.

Table 8-2 shows the total assets of the chartered banks as at December 31 for each year from 1956 to 1966. Many of the legislative restrictions on the banks' ability to manage their assets during this ten-year period were removed by the amendments to the Bank Act in 1967. Hence, a statement of the banks' assets today is significantly different from that shown in the table.

THE BANKS' CAPITAL FUNDS

If the safety of bank deposits is to be assured a bank must remain solvent. It will be remembered that a bank is said to be solvent when the value of its assets is equal to or exceeds the value of its liabilities. The excess of assets over liabilities is called the **net worth** of a bank and represents the ownership claim or equity in a bank. The net worth is also the **book value** of the stockholders property and, as shown in a bank's balance sheet, includes the paid-up capital, the rest account and undivided profits. The above relationships are commonly expressed as

$$\text{Assets} = \text{Liabilities} + \text{Net Worth}$$
$$\text{Net Worth} = \text{Assets} - \text{Liabilities}$$

The book value of a share is found by dividing the net worth of a bank by the number of shares of stock.[14] The **par value** of a share is the value at which stock is brought on the books at the time of issue. If the book value of shares is below their par value, a bank's capital is said to be impaired. That is, the net worth of a bank is less than the par value of its stock outstanding.

The net worth of a bank has traditionally been considered to provide a cushion of safety for depositors (the bank's creditors) in case of losses resulting from a decrease in the value of its assets. When a bank is first formed this cushion of safety consists entirely of its paid-up capital. For this reason successive Bank Acts have specified the minimum amount of capital that must be paid by shareholders before a bank can open its doors for business. At present the authorized capital stock of a bank cannot be less than $1 million of which $500,000 must be paid by the

---

[14] This assumes, as is usual, that there is only one class of stock outstanding. During the depression of the 1930's banks in the United States sold preferred shares, most of which were taken by the Reconstruction Finance Company. These were subsequently retired.

subscribers before the bank can open. While a minimum capital requirement has served to keep out of the banking business "fly by night" bankers, it may also have discouraged an adequate degree of competition. It is also argued that a relatively high capital requirement causes the shareholders to take a more personal interest in the affairs of the bank to make sure that their investment is protected. Before the revision of the Bank Act in 1967 directors of a bank were required to hold a substantial proportion of a bank's total shares outstanding. The Porter Commission pointed out that this was a deterrent to drawing directors from a broader spectrum.[15]

At one time stockholders of banks in both Canada and the United States were subject to **double liability.**[16] If a bank failed, a stockholder might be assessed as much as the par value of the stock he held to assist in payment of creditors. He could, therefore, lose his initial payment for the stock plus an amount equal to its par value. This provision was supposed to encourage more careful management and to serve as an added safeguard for creditors. In fact it restricted the banks' operations by making it very difficult to raise additional capital, especially during the 1930's. Furthermore, American experience had proved that this regulation could not be enforced; in the United States, collecting from stockholders had proved extremely difficult if not impossible.

The adequacy of bank capital and the solvency of the banks are assured and protected by legislative prohibitions on the payment of dividends. In Canada, the banks are not allowed to pay dividends if by so doing they will impair their paid-up capital or if their paid-up capital is already impaired. Moreover, dividends cannot exceed 8 per cent per annum on the paid-up capital stock of a bank unless its rest account equals at least 30 per cent of its paid-up capital. The latter requirement and similar requirements in the United States are equivalent in nature to the former double liability but are more efficient.

The banks' two main sources of capital funds have been new stock financing and retained earnings including appropriations to reserves. During the 1930's some American banks issued preferred stock in addition to common, but most of the preferred shares were subsequently redeemed. Traditionally Canadian chartered banks have had to issue new stock with pre-emptive rights and with a specified par value, which in 1944 was reduced from $100 to $10 a share. Before 1954 the banks were reluctant to offer new shares because this meant offering them to non-resident holders

---

[15] *Report of the Royal Commission on Banking and Finance, 1964*, p. 114. Another provision to ensure active participation in a bank by its directors is an age limit of 75 which was included in the revisions of the Bank Act in 1954.

[16] The double liability provision expired in January 1950.

in countries, particularly the United States, where securities exchange regulations required public disclosure of information which in Canada was given only to the government. The Bank Act revisions of 1954 gave the banks permission to exclude from share offers non-residents whose countries require banks to make public more information than is required under Canadian law. In 1967 another obstacle to the issue of new bank stock was removed when the banks were allowed to divide their authorized capital into shares having a par value of one dollar or multiples thereof not exceeding $10. The banks were quick to take advantage of splitting their stock and offering it at more attractive prices.

The sale of debentures by banks was for a long time considered inappropriate. However, in 1962 some American banks started issuing their own debentures and in 1967 the revisions to the Bank Act allowed Canadian banks to do the same. Bank debentures have to be issued with maturities of at least five years and are not callable during the first five years after issue. Moreover, they are subordinate in right of payment to the prior payment in full of a bank's deposit liabilities and such other liabilities as may be mentioned in the debenture instruments. The aggregate principal amount of debentures that a bank may have outstanding after 1970 is limited to an amount equal to 50 per cent of the total of its paid-up capital and rest account.[17] The sale of debentures has provided chartered banks with an important new source of capital funds.

THE BANKS' CAPITAL RESERVES

The value of the banks' assets can erode because of market changes in interest rates, and it can disappear because of default by borrowers. From experience the banks can calculate normal losses fairly accurately, but they cannot calculate random losses. Just like any other business, the banks provide against bad debts by retaining revenue in the form of capital reserves. However, unlike other businesses, they set aside reserves not only for specified losses but also for contingency losses (losses on existing assets which are likely to appear but are not yet specific).

Banks hold two kinds of capital reserves, **inner reserves** and **outer reserves.** Before the Bank Act revisions of 1967 inner reserves remained secret from the public and hence were often referred to as hidden reserves. These reserves include the accounts held by banks to reduce the book values of their assets.

The justification for the holding of hidden inner reserves has long been

[17] Banks chartered either five years before or five years after October 31, 1965 must determine their maximum debenture issue on the basis of a formula specified in the Bank Act which allows them a smaller proportionate amount of debentures depending upon the number of financial years since their charter was issued.

debated.[18] In the United Kingdom the banks are still allowed to conceal certain of their reserves. While this is also still the case in some American legislation, some banks have felt it in their interest to reveal them. In Canada, despite the defence made by the banking fraternity, the 1967 revisions to the Bank Act for the first time required the banks to reveal the amount of all the funds accumulated as reserves.

The secrecy of inner reserves has been defended on the grounds that it is not possible for the public to assess the adequacy of such reserves without at the same time assessing the quality of each of the banks' assets. This would require revealing individual loan accounts and confidential information from customers which would adversely affect the banks' business. Unless this information were supplied annual fluctuations of inner reserves would be misleading to the general public and could create a lack of confidence in the banks. It has also been argued that the secrecy of reserves induces banks to put aside additional capital funds in good times when they might otherwise be less concerned about their capital ratios. Moreover, it is said to encourage traditional conservative bankers to be more venturesome in their lending policy. The Porter Commission was of the opinion that the existence of secret reserves had contributed to the soundness of the Canadian banking system and that banks should therefore be allowed to continue to accumulate such reserves. In spite of this recommendation the Bank Act was revised in 1967 to require the banks to make an annual public accounting of their inner reserves, although they are still permitted to accumulate such reserves from pre-tax revenue.

Retained revenues not distributed to inner reserves are alloted to undivided profits, and to outer reserves shown on the bank's balance sheet as a **rest fund.** Outer reserves are accumulated from after-tax earnings.

Before 1944, there was no statutory limit to the amount of inner and outer reserves that the banks could appropriate. The Inspector General of Banks, however, had the responsibility of seeing that bank assets were neither overvalued nor undervalued. In the revisions to the Bank Act in 1944 the Minister of Finance was made responsible for determing the amount which he thought was a reasonable appropriation for a bank to make each year to its inner reserves. Subsequently he allowed banks to accumulate inner reserves based on a specified percentage of certain issues.[19] In 1955 percentage limits were set to apply to the sum of outer

---

[18] See for instance the *Jenkins Committee Report*, London, HMSO, Cmnd. 1749; Canada Standing Committee on Banking and Commerce, *Proceedings*, 1954; *National Banks and the Future*, the Report of the Advisory Committee on the Comptroller of the Currency, 1962.

[19] Inner reserves were limited to 2 per cent of Government of Canada, United States and United Kingdom issues with maturities of one year or more, 3 per cent of provincial securi-

and inner reserves, and two years later reserves against Government of Canada and provincial securities were disallowed. In 1960, the fixed percentage was replaced by a single variable percentage to change each year in proportion to changes in the average loss experience of all banks over the preceding twenty-five years. Bankers have been critical of this procedure because "by definition, reserves are a cushion against the contingencies of the future rather than those of the past and any allowance based solely on historical experience may often be inappropriate to current circumstances".[20]

THE ADEQUACY OF BANK CAPITAL FUNDS

The amount of capital that banks should hold to provide adequate safety for depositors has been a much debated question. **Capital-deposit ratios** have been suggested as a measure of the capital required to protect creditors. **Capital-asset ratios** have also been suggested and are perhaps more meaningful as they indicate the percentage by which assets of a bank may decline in value before losses will be incurred by depositors. For instance, a bank with total assets of $50 million and total capital of $4 million will be able to pay its creditors in full as long as its assets do not decline by more than $4 million or 8 per cent. However, because the asset composition among banks may vary widely, a better measure may be a **ratio of capital to risk assets.** The principle that the quality of bank assets should be considered in judging capital adequacy has received growing acceptance among American bank supervisory and regulatory bodies.

Capital ratios of the type discussed above can be used only as a guide, and no more, for judging capital adequacy. They neglect many other important factors, such as the age and size of banks and the experience of their management, the diversification of assets and the nature of the collateral held against loans.

---

ties and 5 per cent of other investments of loans and letters of credit and of long foreign exchange positions.

20 Canadian Bankers' Association, *Submission to the Royal Commission on Banking and Finance*, Supplement to the Canadian Banker, Spring 1963, p. 79.

SELECTED READINGS

Binhammer, H. H., and J. D.C. Bonlakia, "Deposit Insurance in Canada", *Canadian Banker,* Spring 1968, pp. 38-47.

Crosse, H. D., *Management Policies for Commercial Banks,* Englewood Cliffs, N.J., Prentice-Hall, 1962.

Galbraith, J.A., *The Economics of Banking Operations, A Canadian Study,* Montreal, McGill University Press, 1963.

Hodgman, Donald R., *Commercial Bank Loan and Investment Policy,* Champaign, Ill., University of Illinois, Bureau of Economic and Business Research, 1963.

Reed, E.W., *Commercial Bank Management,* New York, Harper and Row, 1963.

Robinson, R.I., *The Management of Bank Funds,* 2nd ed., New York, McGraw-Hill, 1962.

The Canadian Bankers' Association, *Submission to the Royal Commission on Banking and Finance,* Supplement to the Canadian Banker, Spring 1963.

9 BANKING STRUCTURE AND COMPETITION

THE STRUCTURE OF COMMERCIAL BANKING

There are two general types of banking systems. England and Canada have a **branch banking system** characterized by a few large banking organizations or banks with a multitude of country-wide branches. In 1965 in Canada there were eight chartered banks with over 5,000 branches, while in England the eleven banks, members of the London Bankers' Clearing House, had about 10,000 branches in England and Wales.

Although the United States started with branch banking it has had for most of its history a **unit banking system** where each bank office represents an independent bank serving primarily its local community. Only in recent years has there been a tendency to return to branch banking, but this has been confined to regional rather than national boundaries. In 1920 there were 30,921 banks in the United States and 1,281 branches. In 1961 the total number of banks was 13,432 and the total number of branches 11,105. One of the controversial policies adopted by James Saxon when he became Comptroller of the Currency in 1961 was to increase the ease with which national bank charters could be obtained. This put pressure on state authorities to ease their regulations. As a result the decline in the number of banks in the United States was halted. In 1964 the total number of banks had increased to 13,760 and the total number of branches to 14,338.

The early rejection of branch banking in the United States stemmed from the fear that all the banks would fall into the "Money Trusts" and come under the dominance of New York financiers. Moreover, the emphasis in the United States on free enterprise and rugged individualism supported the concept that everyone has the right to become a banker.

While American unit banks concentrate their activities locally, they do reach out beyond their respective communities through **correspondent**

bank relationships. These are informal arrangements whereby the small banks in towns and villages maintain deposit balances with larger banks in nearby cities and look to them for a wide variety of services and assistance. The city banks in turn keep correspondent balances with the still larger banks in the principal money centres.

American bankers have devised arrangements permitting them to operate on a large scale while still observing the legal prohibitions against branch banking. For instance, **chain banking** and **group banking** are not uncommon. Chain banking links banks through the medium of interlocking directorships. Usually two or more banks are controlled by a single individual who owns the majority of stock in both or all the banks. Group banking operates similarly, but the major part of the stock is held by a holding company.[1] Both chain and group banking have provided a degree of centralization of management, and have made possible the specialization of certain services such as foreign exchange operations and the management of investment portfolios, either in one bank of the group or in a service organization. While chain and group banking may not realize the economies of scale open to branch banking, they have served the important purpose of providing a means whereby banks may cross state lines.

The relative merits of unit and branch banking form one of the oldest banking controversies, especially in the United States. The proponents of unit banking believe that such a system is essential to the maintenance of competition and the preservation of small banks. The proponents of branch banking, on the other hand, insist that efficiency and stability require large multi-office institutions. There is considerable evidence that large banks are able to introduce economies of scale not possible for small banks. For example, electronic equipment may be introduced to handle routine tasks. While the smaller banks may be able to rent much of this equipment and thereby economize, in the long run large banks tend to incur proportionately lower costs.

[1] In 1956 Congress passed the Bank Holding Company Act to control the expansion of bank holding companies. Under the act approval to establish bank holding companies has to be received from the various regulatory bodies. To the extent that the act gave bankers certain ground rules, it probably increased concentration through holding companies. The uncertainty of Congress's intent before 1956 probably restrained many banks which might otherwise have considered concentration.

The largest holding company at the end of 1965 was Firstamerica formed in 1958 to take over the banking interests of Transamerica Corporation, which under the Bank Holding Act had been required to separate its banking from its non-banking activities. In 1959 Firstamerica with the approval of the Board of Governors of the Federal Reserve System attempted to acquire a large California bank, but the Department of Justice filed suit to prevent such an expansion as a violation of the anti-trust laws.

Other large holding companies are the Midland Marine Corporation of New York, and the Northwest Bank Corporation and the First Bank Stock Corporation, both with head offices in Minneapolis.

Many of the arguments in support of branch banking are no longer relevant because they apply only to a financial system which lacks well organized money and capital markets. These markets are discussed separately in Chapter 10.

It has been claimed that under a branch banking system the large banking organization is able to minimize the risks incurred in making loans. It can readily diversify its loans by lending to a variety of industries and by placing loans in different parts of the country. Thus it avoids the risk of severe losses when financial disaster strikes a single industry or one particular region. Moreover, where diversification in lending is possible, losses in one sector of the economy can be offset by gains in another. A unit bank, on the other hand, cannot diversify its loans to the same extent unless it has access to well organized national money and capital markets. Without such markets its risks can be large. This explains why there were many more bank failures in the early banking history of the United States than there were in Canada.

In addition to the limited opportunity for diversification of its loans, a local unit bank may also be persuaded to make unwise loans through the "friendly pressures" of small town loyalties.

The proponents of branch banking have argued further that this system can more easily employ cash reserves and prevent excess reserves from accumulating than can a unit system.[2] This again depends upon the existence and development of the money and capital markets. With no such markets or with imperfect markets, local bank loans are the only outlet for employing excess reserves. Unit banks which find it difficult to place loans will find it difficult to employ their excess reserves. The branch bank, on the other hand, can employ the facilities of its head office to make any excess reserves available to banks which are experiencing a deficiency of reserves.

Under present conditions banks can buy and sell securities and money market instruments in well organized markets; therefore, the effective utilization of their reserves need not be affected by banking structure. Moreover, in the American system there is a **federal funds market** where a unit bank can buy and sell excess reserves from other unit banks and does not have to depend on the open market.

---

[2] John Galbraith has pointed out that the contention that a branch banking system mobilizes deposits (excess savings) at some branches for use at branches with excess loans and elsewhere is based on a false premise. He suggests that the public rather than the banking system initiates the interregional movement of funds. The type of banking structure affects only the smoothness and ease with which these movements are accommodated. The movement of savings and capital is related to the interregional payments of the regions concerned and not to the status of excess deposits and excess loans which reflect only the net effect of interregional payment.

See J. A. Galbraith, *The Economics of Banking Operations, A Canadian Study*, Montreal, McGill University Press, 1963, Ch. 4.

The cost of remaining fully loaned up may be higher in a unit system than in a branch system. For instance, unit banks may find it difficult to expand their loans locally and therefore may be obliged to employ their funds in lower yielding market securities. Insofar as unit banks may earn less on their investments and therefore incur higher costs in keeping loaned up, their lending rates may reflect these higher costs. In the early banking history of this continent one finds evidence that interest rates were much more uniform in Canada under a branch system than in the United States with its unit system.

It has long been held that if unit banking is more costly branch banks are likely to be established in new communities some time before unit banks are able to enter.[3] John Chant and Allen Green of Queen's University have challenged this traditional hypothesis.[4] In their examination of banking in Manitoba and North Dakota in 1880 and 1890 they found evidence suggesting that the unit banking system in North Dakota provided banking facilities in smaller communities than did the branch banking system in Manitoba. There are four possible explanations. A unit bank may have an information advantage: "local businessmen may become aware of the possible profitability of banking in a community before such knowledge would be available to established branch bankers at some distant point."[5] Moreover, because a unit bank usually has a greater familiarity with its environment, it can more accurately assess credit risks and therefore realize a higher return on its lending than a branch bank. Third, a unit bank may be established in a smaller community before a branch bank because of "a lack of interdependence among banking offices".[6] Since a branch bank may divert business away from previously established branches in adjacent communities, head office may be reluctant to open a new branch. Finally, in the early frontier communities unit banks may have pre-dated branch banks because they could quite often reduce their costs by combining banking with other commercial activity.

Many of the arguments presented in favour of branch banking no longer appear to apply. The most important advantage that a branch banking system still retains is its ability to introduce economies of scale

---

3 It can also be argued that a branch will pre-date a unit bank because it can operate mainly as a collector of deposits or an extender of credit without being overly concerned with the balance between deposits and loans.

4 "Financial Structure and Patterns of Population Distribution; A Hypothesis", an unpublished paper by J. F. Chant and A. G. Green.

5 *Ibid.*

6 *Ibid.*

more readily than unit banks. In terms of monetary control, the concentration of bank management permits more personal contact between the central banking authorities and the chief officers of the banks. Because of the limited number of commercial banking institutions in Canada moral suasion has been employed frequently and with considerable success by the Bank of Canada.

BANKING COMPETITION

The question of banking structure and its relation to banking competition has never been as contentious an issue in Canada as in the United States, and it has therefore generated little public debate. Canadians seem to have early accepted that a few large banking institutions with a multitude of branches can provide the necessary competitive climate without an undue concentration of banking power. In both countries because banking competition is tied up with the problems of safety and the efficient operation of the payment mechanism, banking has never been allowed to rely on free market forces. Limited entry into banking is justified on the grounds of monetary stability. Because the banks hold a large fraction of the community's savings and means of payment, they must be shielded against the vigorous competition that characterizes some other industries in which failure is considered part of the game. The social costs of bank failures, in most instances, outweigh whatever inefficiencies result from restricted bank entry.

In Canada the establishment of banking institutions has been restricted to those who can meet the statutory capital requirement and the public scrutiny of good faith implicit in receiving a charter by a special act of the federal Parliament. Neither appears to be any longer a serious barrier.[7] In the United States minimum capital requirements were never imposed to the same extent as in Canada. The critical restraint to entry has always been the requirements of respective regulatory or supervisory bodies. While these usually include capital adequacy, others such as future earning prospects, character of management, and the convenience and needs of the community have played an important role.

To remain in business the banks must provide a reasonable return to their shareholders, otherwise they will invest their money elsewhere. The earning potential of a bank depends upon the amount of funds it can attract and the return it can receive from investing these funds, as well as upon the costs of accomplishing both. In meeting these ends a bank is in competition not only with other banks but with a host of non-bank financial institutions and money market instruments.

---

[7] The capital requirement to establish a bank was set at $500,000 in 1870 and raised to $1 million in 1954.

Interbank competition can be in terms of price and of services rendered. Because the banks' deposit services are relatively homogeneous, price competition among the banks has never been significant in attracting funds. In lending, competition has been reflected in the amount and length of credit, and to some extent in the rate of interest charged by the banks. On good risks of standard quality the banks usually charge the same rate, the **banks' prime rate.** However, borrowers who cannot qualify for this rate can shop for and usually find a certain amount of price competition among the banks. The 1967 revisions of the Bank Act explicitly prohibit agreements among banks on interest rates both on loans and on deposits. Non-price competition in the form of the accessibility of branch offices has been important, not only in attracting funds but also in lending.

In Canada, as elsewhere, competition for the individual bank has developed not so much from other commercial banks as from non-bank institutions. Banking functions have been undertaken at an increasing rate by institutions other than the chartered banks, and financial claims other than the notes of the central bank and the deposits of the chartered banks are significant elements in the payment mechanism. In reviewing Canada's financial development the Porter Commission welcomed such competition for the banks but pointed out that in many respects the banks were unable to compete successfully because of the restrictions placed upon them by the Bank Act. The Porter Commission recommended that in certain areas the banks be given greater freedom while at the same time all institutions which wished to continue to perform a banking function be subject to the controls and regulations of the Bank Act.[8] Although the Bank Act revisions of 1967 did grant the banks greater freedom of competition, they did not restrict the near-banks as the Commission had recommended.

Prior to the Bank Act revisions and amendments of 1967 the major restrictions which prevented the banks from competing effectively with the near-banks included their primary and secondary reserve requirements, the legal maximum rate of interest they were allowed to charge on their loans, the limitations on mortgage lending, and the prohibition on issuing bank debentures.

These restrictions affected the banks' earning ability and consequently their ability to compete for funds. For instance, primary and secondary reserve requirements which apply only to the banks put them at a competitive disadvantage with the near-banks which do not have legal reserve requirements. Legal cash reserve requirements do not appear to be as important for insuring the safety of bank deposits as in former times.

[8] See *The Report of the Royal Commission on Banking and Finance*, 1964, Ch. 18.

Moreover, a large proportion of the banks' liabilities are in the form of notice deposits and cash reserve requirements against these deposits are not as important as those against demand deposits. The Bank Act revisions of 1967 reflected this distinction by allowing the banks to hold lower cash reserves against savings deposits than against demand deposits. Although the legal reserve ratio was increased at the same time from 8 to 12 per cent on demand deposits, the overall reserve ratio for banks was lowered to 6.6 per cent by a reduction of 4 per cent in the reserves against notice deposits. The banks' competitive position vis-a-vis the near-banks was thus improved.

A more severe restriction for the banks, particularly during the post-war period of tight money and high market rates of interest, was the legal maximum rate of interest which they were allowed to charge on their loans. It was extremely difficult for the banks to compete in the market for funds because the rate they could pay to attract deposits was held down by the maximum rate they were allowed to charge on a major proportion of their loans.[9]

The 1967 revisions of the Bank Act allowed for the removal in three stages of the fixed maximum interest rate ceiling for banks. During stage one, from the passing of the act until December 31, 1967, the ceiling was lifted from 6 per cent to 7¼ per cent. In stage two, the fixed ceiling was to be replaced by a floating ceiling, calculated by adding 1¾ per cent to the average yield on short-term government bonds. Finally, in stage three, the ceiling was to be lifted when the yield on these bonds dropped below 5 per cent. However, when the yields on short-term Canada bonds fell below 5 per cent during the first three months of 1967 the transition period which the government had anticipated as stage two was eliminated and the ceiling was lifted on December 31, 1967.

The decennial revision of the Bank Act in 1954 had permitted the banks to make insured residential mortgage loans under the National Housing Act. The principal reason for allowing the banks to take hither-to forbidden mortgage security against their loans was to alleviate a shortage of residential mortgage funds. However, when the interest rate for these loans rose above the banks' 6 per cent ceiling, they withdrew from NHA lending. To overcome this difficulty the 1967 revisions of the Bank Act not only removed the interest rate ceiling on the banks' mortgage loans but also allowed them to make conventional mortgage loans.[10]

---

9 Some banks attempted to circumvent the restriction by persuading customers to hold increased deposit balances with them. In their consumer lending the banks were able to obtain more than 6 per cent per annum by placing repayments of such loans in a deposit account which was credited against the outstanding amount of a loan when it accumulated to the whole principal of the loan. While this device was considered by many to be illegal it was never contested in the courts.

10 See Chapter 8.

To avoid creating difficulties for the traditional lenders in the conventional mortgage market caused by the sudden entry of banks into this field, a bank's holdings of all types of residential mortgage loans was restricted initially to an amount equal to 3 per cent of its deposit liabilities plus its debentures. Provision was made for this percentage to increase by one point with each financial year completed by a bank until the maximum limit of 10 per cent is reached.

While all the changes mentioned above allow the banks to compete more effectively with the near-banks, the exemption from banking regulations is bound to give the near-banks certain competitive advantages. From the point of view of both safety and monetary control, certain restrictions must apply to the banks' assets. These restrictions prevent the banks from competing in terms of price for deposit funds. This competitive disadvantage is compensated to a degree by the provision in the 1967 Bank Act which allows the banks to obtain additional funds by issuing debentures.

The prohibitions which applied to the banks before 1967 encouraged them to seek interlocking directorates with and/or effective control of, non-bank financial institutions which were exempt from such prohibitions. It followed that when the banks were given new freedoms these relationships should be abandoned in order to create a desirable competitive environment.

After 1969 a director of a chartered bank may not be also a director of a Quebec savings bank, or of a trust or loan corporation, or of another company which holds more than 10 per cent of the voting shares of a Quebec savings bank or a trust or loan corporation. Furthermore, after July 1, 1971, with only a few minor exceptions,[11] the directors of a bank may not constitute more than one fifth of the board of directors of any other corporation.

The new spirit of bank independence is reflected in the provisions introduced in 1967 concerning bank ownership. Traditionally, ownership of one bank by another was prohibited among Canadian chartered banks. Since 1967 no shareholder, alone or in association with others, is allowed to hold more than 10 per cent of the voting shares of a bank. However, when this legislative change was made, the government thought that a large shareholding by one interest was desirable, and therefore provided that new banks be allowed, with the prior approval of the government, to issue more than 10 percent of their stock to any one resident shareholder.

Governments as well as officials or corporations administering, managing or investing any fund established to provide hospitalization, medical

[11] Excluded are corporations controlled by a bank, a bank service corporation as defined in the Bank Act and religious, educational, cultural, social, welfare, philanthropic and charitable corporations.

care, annuity, pension or similar benefits to particular classes of individuals are excluded from owning voting shares of a bank. If more than 25 per cent of a bank's shares are held by any one shareholder and his associates, resident or non-resident, the size of the bank is limited insofar as its total liabilities (including paid-up capital, rest account and undivided profits) cannot exceed 20 times its authorized capital stock.

Not only is the ownership of a bank restricted but a bank's holding of the voting shares of other corporations is also limited. A bank is not allowed to hold more than 10 per cent of the voting stock of any one Canadian trust or loan corporation or of any other Canadian corporation if its total investment in any such corporation is more than $5 million. Where the cost of acquisition of the voting stock by a bank of a corporation other than a trust or loan corporation is less than $5 million it may hold up to 50 per cent of the voting shares. Excluded from the above provisions is the Export Finance Corporation of Canada established by the banks in 1961 to provide medium-term export credit to Canadian companies. Also excluded is a bank's shareholding of a service corporation such as a real estate company which owns a bank's premises. To ensure that the strict spirit of the Bank Act is respected, if in the opinion of the government a bank, while meeting the stockholding requirements specified in the act, still is able to exercise directly or indirectly effective control of a trust or loan corporation, the government may order it to reduce its stockholdings below the percentage requirements set out in the act.

The Bank Act also prohibits agreements among the banks on interest rates for both bank loans and deposits. It also requires the banks to disclose the cost of borrowing from them expressed both as a rate per annum and an amount in dollars. Similar provincial legislation requires non-bank financial intermediaries to disclose their lending rates.

In the United States many of the state governments allow foreign banks to compete on a limited basis for domestic business and for foreign business conducted by American banks. Competition is facilitated through representative offices or through the establishment of foreign branches, foreign subsidiaries and foreign agencies.

The Porter Commission recommended that foreign banks should be allowed to compete with Canadian banks and to apply for a licence to open agencies which would be free to conduct all phases of their business, other than the acceptance of deposits in Canada.[12] The Commission suggested that a licence should be issued if the applying foreign bank can

12 Because of the restrictions on the establishment of foreign bank agencies, some American banks have acquired ownership in Canadian financial institutions other than banks, in order to promote their business interests in Canada.

demonstrate to the Inspector General of Banks the need for such banking services. Although the 1967 revisions of the Bank Act did not include these suggestions, the government at that time noted that further study should be made of the problems and benefits involved.

SELECTED READINGS

Binhammer, H.H., "Canada's Revised Banking Legislation," *The National Banking Review,* Vol. 4, No. 4, June, 1967, pp. 493-501.

The Canadian Bankers' Association, *Submission to the Royal Commission on Banking and Finance,* Supplement to the Canadian Banker, Spring 1963, pp. 81-102.

Carson, Dean, *Banking and Monetary Studies,* Homewood, Ill., Richard D. Irwin, 1963, Ch. 15, 16, 17.

Galbraith, J.A., *The Economics of Banking Operations, A Canadian Study,* Montreal, McGill University Press, 1963, Ch. 4.

Report of the Royal Commission on Banking and Finance, Ottawa, Queen's Printer, 1964, especially Ch. 18.

United States Treasury, The Administration of National Banks, *Studies in Banking Competition and the Banking Structure,* Washington, D. C., 1966.

Zwick, Jack, "Foreign Banking in the United States", *Joint Economic Committee Print,* Washington, D.C., July, 1966.

Zwick, Jack, "The Regulation of Foreign Banks in the United States", *The National Banking Review,* Vol. 4, No. 1, 1966, pp. 1-19.

PART THREE

FINANCIAL MARKETS AND NON-BANK FINANCIAL INSTITUTIONS

10 FINANCIAL ASSETS AND FINANCIAL MARKETS

FINANCIAL ASSETS

Financial assets may be viewed as financial debts for the assets of one party consist of the debts of others. So far we have considered a very special kind of financial asset or debt — that of the banking system. It is different from all other kinds of financial debt in that it serves as our most important medium of exchange. We call it money, and as we have seen, it is created when the banking system acquires the debts of others. Since the debts of the chartered banks are mainly in the form of demand liabilities payable on demand or after short notice, the banks exchange their own debts for other debt which is also short-term. Moreover, as we shall observe later, central banks have a preference to exchange their own debts for other debt which is short-term in nature.

The exchange of the banking system's debts (its monetary liabilities) for other short-term debts takes place in what is known as the **money market.** There are no specified places where buyers and sellers of short-term debts regularly meet to conduct their exchange. The money market consists of financial institutions and specialized dealers in short-term securities who are in almost constant touch with each other by telephone. In a separate section we shall consider the money market in some detail.

The money market is one segment of the financial market. It relates to highly marketable and liquid debt instruments which may mature within three years and usually mature within one year. The other segment of the financial market, which we call the capital market, relates to longer-term, less marketable and less liquid debt instruments. Quite often, the financial market is referred to as the capital market, the money market being considered part of the capital market. We will refer to the overall market for financial debts as the financial market and subdivide it into the money market and the capital market.

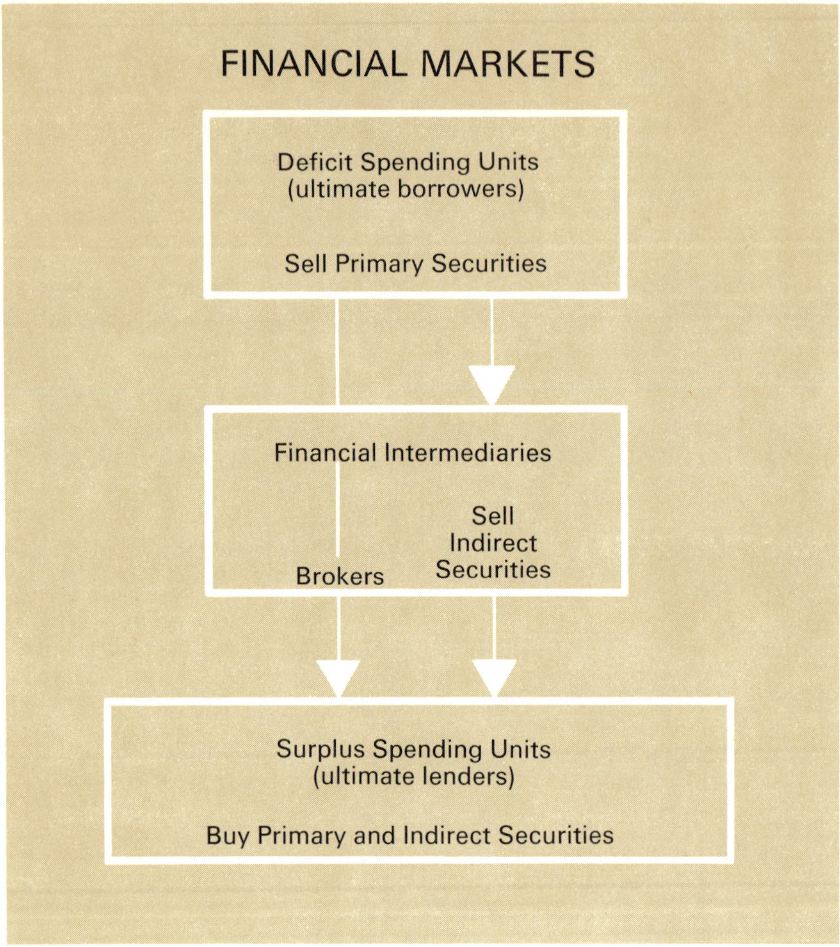

Figure 10-1

Debt instruments (financial assets) include both **primary securities** and **indirect securities.** Deficit spending units borrow funds by creating and selling bonds, equities, mortgages and so on. These debt instruments created by ultimate borrowers are called primary securities. They may be sold to ultimate lenders or to financial institutions including dealers in debt. Financial institutions may act merely as **brokers,** in which case they sell primary securities acquired from ultimate borrowers directly to ultimate lenders or to other financial institutions. Financial institutions today, however, do more than merely perform a **brokerage function.** They also perform what has come to be known as an **intermediation function,** and hence are now generally referred to as financial intermediaries.

When the financial intermediaries acquire the primary securities of ultimate borrowers they usually do not sell these directly to ultimate lenders. Instead they issue their own securities, indirect securities, which they sell to ultimate lenders. The banking system, of course, and to some degree the other financial institutions, because of the type of indirect security which they issue can also assume the role of ultimate lender. They can do so because the indirect securities which they issue circulate as a medium of exchange. If these securities cannot circulate, the financial intermediaries must acquire indirect securities which will circulate in order to purchase the primary debts of deficit spending units. The simplest way of acquiring circulating securities would appear to be for the financial intermediaries to act as brokers and to find a surplus spending unit willing to purchase the primary security of a deficit spending unit. However, finding the appropriate surplus spending unit (lender) may be difficult since these units usually want to acquire the kind of debts that best satisfy their own needs. Bringing the two together can be accomplished by the intermediation function. Financial intermediaries purchase the primary debts of deficit spending units with the money they receive from the sale of their own indirect securities. These indirect securities can be fashioned so as to meet all the various needs of deficit spending units. Life insurance companies, for instance, sell indirect securities in the form of life insurance contracts which provide retirement annuities and death benefits. Moreover, as we shall see later, the advantage for surplus units in acquiring the indirect securities of financial intermediaries rather than the primary securities of deficit spending units is that these are usually less risky and can be sold in case the lender requires his funds before the time initially anticipated.

THE FUNCTIONS OF THE FINANCIAL MARKET

The financial market can be regarded as fulfilling four major functions; regulating the amount of money outstanding; facilitating the transfer of funds from surplus spending units to deficit spending units; providing for the liquidity of non-monetary financial assets; and providing a financial structure which will allow an efficient allocation of resources.

Changes in the money supply are brought about by the banking system, the chartered banks and the central bank exchanging their monetary liabilities for non-monetary financial assets and vice versa. Hence the monetary system is directly influenced by the conditions existing in the market for non-monetary financial assets of the type acquired and disposed of by the banking system. We have mentioned that the type of assets traded by the banking system is found in the money market. If this market is well organized and operates efficiently, the monetary authorities can produce changes in the money supply and credit conditions appropriate to the economy's overall performance without creating unwanted disturbances in the financial markets generally.

The second function of the financial market is to facilitate the transfer of funds from surplus spending units to deficit spending units. The direct flow of money between savers and borrowers is hindered by risk, and the inconvenience and cost of transfer, as well as by desire on the part of savers (lenders) to avoid illiquidity. Because individual lenders are unfamiliar with ultimate borrowers, they would have to assume additional risk if they were obliged to deal directly with ultimate borrowers to employ their surplus funds. Moreover, much time and money would have to be expended to locate borrowers willing to offer debt instruments of just the right terms, maturity and amount to satisfy the individual needs of lenders. In the absence of a financial market and financial intermediaries, borrowers would have to expend both time and effort to find individual savers willing to meet *their* exact needs. With a financial market, dominated by financial institutions, the barriers hindering the flow of funds from savers to borrowers are all but eliminated.

The third function of the financial market is to provide liquidity to non-monetary financial assets. A prospective lender is reluctant to transfer his idle funds to a borrower if he thinks he may require them before the borrower can make repayment. Financial intermediaries provide a substitute for direct financing and, by substituting their own indirect debt for the primary securities of borrowers, provide the lenders with more readily marketable securities. Lenders are able, therefore, to receive cash before the borrowers' contracts mature. Because it is less risky, the indirect debt of the financial institutions is as a rule more marketable than that of individual borrowers. Financial institutions when purchasing primary securities from deficit spending units have the specialized skills not available to most lenders to investigate the credit-worthiness of borrowers. In this way, they are able to minimize their risks. Furthermore, although they must assume a certain amount of risk they can minimize it with the assistance of the law of averages. Because of their size, financial institutions are able to lend funds to many borrowers in different circumstances. By diversifying their loans, financial intermediaries accept the possibility of small losses but avoid the danger of heavy losses. For this reason the indirect debts of financial intermediaries are more acceptable to lenders than those of ultimate borrowers. Financial intermediaries provide the community with liquidity by substituting their own less risky debt for the relatively risky debts of many individual borrowers. Through their brokerage function they also provide an organized market where the investor can find a buyer for his debt or ownership claims. For example, there are organized stock exchanges in Toronto, Montreal and Vancouver.

Finally, insofar as it provides the country with an appropriate financial structure, the financial market makes possible the efficient and equitable allocation of resources, and provides for real growth in the economy. Financial intermediation tends to raise the levels of saving and investment and to allocate scarce savings more efficiently among alternative investment opportunities. Moreover, the financial market allows consumers and lenders to achieve an optimum consumption pattern with respect to time, and an efficient ordering of investment. Without an adequate financial market there is a greater possibility that relatively inferior investment projects will be undertaken while many superior ones will be neglected because of the inadequate distribution of funds.

THE MONEY MARKET

The money market requires our special attention since, as we have seen, it is an inherent part of our monetary mechanism. We shall first consider the various financial instruments traded in the money market. Then we shall present a survey of the formation and growth of the Canadian money market, and finally we shall consider the implications of this market for monetary policy.

FINANCIAL INSTRUMENTS IN THE MONEY MARKET

Treasury Bills Treasury bills are promissory notes issued by the Government of Canada. They are offered weekly, through a competitive tender, by the Bank of Canada on behalf of the government.[1] There are no restrictions on who may tender, but the chartered banks, money market dealers and the Bank of Canada are the principal bidders. Financial intermediaries other than banks, as well as non-financial corporations, usually purchase Treasury bills from money market dealers or from chartered banks.

A week before each tender the Bank of Canada announces the amounts and maturities of the bills to be offered. The bills usually mature in ninety-one days, but 182-day bills and occasionally longer issues have been offered. Sealed tenders are submitted to the Bank of Canada and are opened at 12:00 noon on Thursdays (except where holidays intervene). The highest bidder is allotted all the bills for which he bid. Succeeding high bids also are allotted bills in full, and bids at the lowest successful price are allotted pro rata. Frequently bidders will submit bids at various prices in the hope that at least one of them will be successful.

[1] From time to time some of the provincial governments have also sold treasury bills.

The Bank of Canada usually submits one bid for bills it desires for its own portfolio and another as a reserve bid for the entire issue. The latter bid is to guarantee that the entire issue will be sold and embarrassment for the Government avoided, and to prevent bidders from forming an agreement to submit a low bid in an attempt to lower the price of the minimum successful bids. Such agreements could bring about a sudden collapse in the price of bills and allow bidders to manipulate prices.[2] Treasury bills have no coupon rate, and because they are sold at auction below their par or face value, the yield is determined on a discount basis. In other words, the yield comes from the difference between the price at which they were purchased and their value at maturity.

At approximately 2:00 p.m. on the day of the tender each participant in the auction receives a telephone call from the Bank of Canada telling him the number of bills he has succeeded in obtaining, if any, the high, low and average tender price of each maturity offered, and usually the amount and maturity of bills to be auctioned on the following Thursday. After he receives this information the successful bidder has until 4:00 p.m. of the same day to inform the Bank as to the denominations required and at which agency office of the Bank delivery will be taken. Bills are issued in denominations of $1,000, $5,000, $25,000, $100,000 and $1 million. Delivery of bills must be taken by 3:00 p.m. of the day following the auction and payment must be made at the same time by certified cheque, bank draft or clearing house settlement.

Short-Term and Short-Dated Government Bonds. In recent years the Government of Canada has substantially increased its issue of bonds with maturities of less than three years. In part this has been done as a means of influencing short-term rates and thereby the flow of foreign short-term funds and the level of the government's foreign exchange reserves. These bonds have become an important part of the money market. Long-term bonds which are close to maturity, known as short-dated bonds, are also traded in the money market. Before the change in the tax laws, corporations were especially attracted to short-dated bonds because they could claim as a tax-free capital gain the full amount of the difference between their purchase price and the face value realized upon maturity.[3]

Day-to-Day Loans. These are loans made by the chartered banks to jobbers, a group of fifteen investment dealers with purchase and resale

---

2 In England commercial banks do not tender directly for Treasury bills. Instead they purchase their bills from the discount houses. The discount houses which are members of the London Discount Market Association submit one tender, a "syndicated bid," which covers the total of each week's bill offering.

3 See Hansard, December 20, 1960, p. 1,011.

agreement privileges with the Bank of Canada. Such loans are callable any day by either party, providing notice is given before noon. The only securities acceptable as collateral for day loans are Government of Canada direct and guaranteed short-term bonds maturing in three years or less, Government of Canada Treasury bills and bankers' acceptances drawn on another bank. The rates on day loans may be adjusted by the lender each day. Loans in amounts of less than $100,000 are not common.

Repurchase Agreements or "Buy-Backs". There are times when an investor wishes to invest his funds for a particular period for which no adequate short-term government security exists. A repurchase agreement is an arrangement which allows tailoring investments in debt maturities to lender's requirements. For example, an investor wishes to invest his funds for a minimum period of 100 days but there are no securities presently trading on the market with such a maturity. He is therefore obliged to commit his funds for a period longer or shorter than the desired 100 days. There is, however, an alternative available to him in the form of a repurchase agreement or buy-back. He can buy from a dealer a government bond which matures, say, within two years. At the same time he can enter into an agreement with the dealer whereby the dealer contracts to repurchase the bond at a specified price at the end of 100 days. The spread between the selling and repurchase price provides the lender with a return. Repurchase agreements are used by the Bank of Canada as a method of making short-term advances to approved money market dealers.

Finance Company Paper. Sales finance companies have raised a substantial proportion of their borrowing requirements in both the domestic and foreign money markets. They usually purchase instalment debt contracts — notes signed by purchasers of consumer durable goods — from the dealers involved. They then "package" these contracts according to maturity usually, and use them as collateral to borrow funds from the financial intermediaries. Sales finance companies issue notes or certificates against each package of contracts which serves as collateral, and sell them in the money market. These notes or certificates are called finance paper. While finance paper is negotiable and transferable it is usually not as readily marketable as most other money market instruments. Until the early 1960's the chartered banks were the main purchasers of these notes and they usually held them until maturity. During the 1950's and early 1960's finance paper became an important part of the money market. However, after the collapse of a large finance company in 1965 lenders became reluctant to purchase finance paper and turned to other money market instruments. A larger market for finance paper is gradually being re-established and the financial intermediaries have become frequent purchasers.

Corporate Paper. Corporate paper first made its appearance in Canada in substantial amounts after mid-1950 when the cost of corporate borrowing from the chartered banks became relatively high compared with the availability of other sources of short-term funds. Large corporations began the practice of obtaining funds temporarily by selling their own notes in the money market. These notes are secured by the corporations' general credit standing and usually by their lines of credit at the chartered banks. With the growth of a market for corporate paper, corporations with temporarily excess funds have been induced to make these available to the money market rather than to hold them as bank deposits. Financial management by non-financial companies, especially the larger ones, has become an important part of their overall operations.

Bankers' Acceptances. In June 1962, the Canadian Bankers' Association announced that its members were introducing bankers' acceptances into the Canadian money market. These are negotiable drafts which mature in up to ninety days and which have been endorsed or accepted by a bank. For example, a producer has shipped a large order to a buyer. He draws a draft which is an order for the buyer to pay within a certain time. After the buyer accepts the draft he returns it to the producer. The producer may want cash immediately in which case he takes the draft to a bank which, for a fee, will accept it. When accepting it the bank guarantees that it will pay the draft at maturity in case the firm on which it is drawn defaults. Once the bank has accepted the draft it can be sold in the money market. The minimum denomination of bankers' acceptances is $100,000. Since they qualify for rediscounting by the Bank of Canada they are highly liquid, although as yet they are not a very important instrument in the Canadian money market.

Bank Certificates of Deposit. Bank certificates of deposit, known as CD's are also a relatively new money market instrument. They were first introduced by New York City banks in early 1961 and by Canadian banks in 1964. With the growth of financial intermediaries and money markets, many of the larger non-financial firms transferred their temporary balances held on deposit with the banks to higher yielding money market instruments. In order to meet this competition the banks introduced CD's. At first these were time deposits which were registered and transferable. To develop a market in Canada for the certificates the banks assisted holders to sell (transfer) them prior to maturity. Later the banks issued CD's in the form of bearer time deposits negotiable in the money market.

Foreign Currency Swapped Deposits. Swapped deposits are another recent addition to the Canadian money market. They are chartered bank term deposits converted into foreign currency, usually United States dollars, which the banks undertake through a forward contract to convert back into Canadian dollars at maturity. The return to the depositor on the investment in Canadian dollars is made up of the yield on his foreign currency deposit and the profit or loss on the exchange risk. Since August 4, 1960 a Toronto investment firm has published weekly quotations on thirty-, sixty-, ninety- and 180-day swapped deposits. These quotations include the interest on the foreign dollar deposit and the forward exchange premium or discount. Swapped deposits provide a link between the Canadian money market and foreign money markets.

FORMATION AND GROWTH OF THE CANADIAN MONEY MARKET

The Canadian money market may be said to have had its beginnings in 1934 when the Government of Canada started to sell Treasury bills. These were sold on an irregular basis until 1937 when a fortnightly tender was introduced.[4] Until 1954 Treasury bills were not an important method of government finance. From July 1945 to January 1953, for instance, there was a constant $450 million in Treasuries outstanding so that each issue came to $75 million in ninety-one-day bills. Between July 1942 and October 1947, to help finance war spending, the federal government obtained temporary financing through the direct sale of deposit certificates to the chartered banks. These certificates usually matured in six months and their price was negotiated. Although the banks were not required to purchase them, they bought them out of "patriotism to war finance". The certificates were not negotiable in the money market and the banks bought them with the understanding that they would be held to maturity. Because they were illiquid they served to control both the banks' liquidity and war inflation. After 1947 the government continued to sell deposit certificates to the banks but on a much more irregular basis than during the war years. Between 1947 and 1952 there were only four such issues.

Before 1954 trading in Treasury bills took place almost entirely between the chartered banks and the Bank of Canada.[5] The Bank, in order to assure their liquidity, was always prepared to buy all the Treasuries

---

[4] There were seven issues in 1934, fourteen in 1935 and twenty-two in 1936.

[5] During this period the price of Treasury bills was maintained at a relatively high level and their yields were correspondingly low. This was the result partly of the limited amount of bills issued by the government and partly of the Bank of Canada's practice of not selling bills immediately after an issue and of occasionally selling them between issues. During this period the Treasury bill rate in Canada was held at a level lower than that on Treasuries in the United States, while the opposite was true for longer-term government securities.

offered to it by the chartered banks. From the chartered banks' point of view, they preferred selling Treasuries to the Bank of Canada rather than on the market because they could thus adjust their reserve positions very quickly and could also conceal such adjustments from their competitors. As the Bank of Canada was committed to maintaining a market for Treasuries, its freedom to use open market operations effectively as a policy variable was restricted.

Beginning in 1953, upon the initiative of the Bank of Canada with the cooperation of the chartered banks and the money market dealers, attempts were made to develop an organized money market in Canada, a market that would have depth (a large number of different financial instruments) and breadth (a large amount of securities outstanding at any one time).

The first step was the introduction of a weekly Treasury bill auction on January 30, 1953. At the time, in addition to offering the usual ninety-one-day bills, 273-day bills were also offered. Later in the same year, in order to encourage dealers to hold inventories of Treasury bills and to trade more regularly in them, the Bank of Canada instituted purchase and resale agreements with approved dealers. Initially only thirteen dealers were allowed this privilege, but the number has increased slightly since then. Purchase and resale agreements encourage dealers to hold inventories of Treasuries and other short-term government securities. If dealers are at any time caught short of cash, they can sell these securities for cash to the Bank of Canada, on condition that they agree to repurchase them at a specified price. Repurchase usually must take place within thirty days.

The opportunity to borrow at the Bank of Canada is granted to a certain number of dealers as a privilege and not as a matter of right. Dealers are expected to make every effort to secure accommodation in the market before coming to the Bank. Each approved dealer is granted a line of credit at the Bank which must be renewed each month. Since June 24, 1962 the rate the Bank charges when a line of credit is used through a purchase and resale agreement has been fixed at one quarter of one per cent above the rate on three-month Treasury bills during the preceding weekly tender, or at the Bank rate, whichever is lower.[6]

In 1954 the Bank of Canada also started to allow the approved dealers to borrow securities of a certain term from the Bank on the guarantee of securities of a different term. This has encouraged more active trading in government securities insofar as the dealers are better able to satisfy the particular needs of their clients.

---

[6] If a dealer borrows more than once in any one month, he is usually charged a progressively higher rate.

The chartered banks' active participation in the establishment of the money market began in 1954 with the introduction of day-to-day loans to market dealers. These loans have encouraged the dealers to hold inventories of securities, since the rates they pay on such loans are generally below the rates they earn on their security holdings. The introduction by the banks of bankers' acceptances, certificates of deposit and swapped deposits has further assisted the development of an active money market in Canada. The chartered banks' opportunity to participate in the money market has also been widened; the Bank Act revision of 1954 provided them with a more flexible method for calculating their required cash reserves, and the Bank Act revision of 1967 allowed them to hold smaller cash reserves.

From its beginnings in the early 1950's, the Canadian money market has grown and matured. It has deepened with the periodic sale of new issues of short-term government securities, with the diversity of corporate paper, and with the introduction of bankers' acceptances, certificates of deposits and swapped deposits. At the same time it has acquired breadth. For example, at the end of 1954, Treasury bills outstanding amounted to $180 million; at the end of 1966 this figure was over $2 billion. Government of Canada securities, other than Treasury bills outstanding and maturing in two years or less, amounted to $1.7 billion at the end of 1954 and $2.6 billion at the end of 1966.[7] The chartered banks' day-to-day loans have grown from zero in 1953 to a daily average of over $275 million. Bankers' acceptances introduced in 1962 have grown somewhat more modestly to a daily average of around $185 million during 1967. Foreign currency swapped deposits on the other hand have fluctuated between approximately $425 million and $800 million. Finance paper, which amounted to $1.3 billion early in 1965, declined dramatically at the end of that year but has grown again to its earlier level.

MONETARY POLICY AND THE MONEY MARKET

In a well organized money market that is characterized by both depth and breadth, most of the cash in the monetary system is employed in some form of earning asset. When this is the case, the central bank can effectively control credit conditions. For example, suppose the Bank of Canada uses the techniques available to it to reduce chartered bank cash.

[7] The Bank of Canada now publishes the amount of Government of Canada securities maturing within three years. At the end of 1963 these amounted to $3.8 billion, excluding Treasury bills.

The chartered banks will respond by calling in their loans from money market dealers and or by taking advances from the Bank of Canada. If the banks call in their loans, then the money market dealers will be forced to take advances from the Bank of Canada through purchase and resale agreements. If there is no place to turn for cash except to the Bank of Canada, the Bank is in a position to dictate the terms on which it will make cash available. In other words, the Bank of Canada, can effectively control credit conditions. The process, however, is by no means as direct as implied above.

SELECTED READINGS

See list following Chapter 12.

11 PRIVATE FINANCIAL INTERMEDIARIES IN CANADA

Canada now has a relatively highly developed and centralized financial system. Most lending and borrowing is done through the intermediation of financial institutions rather than directly between ultimate lenders and ultimate borrowers. Although the chartered banks constitute by far the largest single group of financial intermediaries in terms of total assets, an important part is also played by other financial institutions, as well as by government institutions and agencies of one kind or another. This is illustrated in Table 11-1.

Although most types of financial institutions provide specialized services, there is a great deal of overlapping. This is important because it ensures that a variety of financial services are available in communities lacking specialized institutions and that the financial system displays a fair amount of competition. For example, the chartered banks provide the economy with the bulk of its means of payment through their deposit liabilities. However, similar services are provided by savings banks, trust and mortgage loan companies, caisses populaires and credit unions, and certain government savings institutions. The trust companies specialize in providing fiduciary trust services but at the same time they accept deposits and make long-term investments. The mortgage loan companies which traditionally have concentrated on making long-term mortgage loans also compete with other financial institutions in accepting short-term deposits, the majority of which are in the form of debentures. Life insurance, a more complex type of financial liability, is handled almost exclusively by life insurance companies; however, they too compete with other financial institutions in acquiring their investment portfolios. The finance companies specialize in the financing of consumer durables but they share such lending activities with the chartered banks, the caisses populaires and the credit unions. The Canadian financial system is by no means compart-

TABLE 11-1

Total Assets of Selected Financial Institutions, 1965
(millions of dollars)

BANK AND OTHER DEPOSIT ACCEPTING INSTITUTIONS	
Bank of Canada	3,956
Chartered banks	20,792
Quebec savings banks	430
Government savings institutions	226
Credit Unions and caisses populaires	2,542
Trust companies	3,439
Mortgage loan companies	2,426
Total	33,811
INSURANCE AND PENSIONS	
Life insurance	11,424
Trusteed pension funds	6,600
Fire and casualty insurance	1,830
Total	19,854
OTHER FINANCIAL INSTITUTIONS	
Sales finance and consumer loan companies	4,228
Mutual funds	1,574
Closed-end funds	509
Investment dealers	534
Central Mortgage and Housing Corporation	2,574
Alberta Municipal Financing Corporation	377
Export Credits Insurance Corporation	281
Farm Credit Corporation	608
Industrial Development Bank	271
Total	10,956

Source: Financial Statistics Branch, Dominion Bureau of Statistics.

mentalized; there is an overlapping of services provided by most institutions.

The financial intermediaries are in business to make profits. Most of their profits result from "trading on the yield curve". They sell their liabilities at a cost which is lower than the return they receive from holding the liabilities of others. This is possible because their own liabilities usually have shorter maturity periods and are more liquid than their investments in the liabilities of others.

Although the financial intermediaries sell most of their own liabilities directly to the public, they usually acquire those of others through investment dealers and stockbrokers. The investment dealers perform two important functions in marketing securities: that of underwriting and that of trading. Underwriting is the acquisition of primary securities from ultimate borrowers for distribution to lenders. The dealers acquire the security issues of borrowers either by negotiation or through auction. For large issues, dealers combine their efforts in syndicates of which chartered banks are often members. A few provinces have underwritten their own issues and in the case of federal government issues the Bank of Canada acting as the government's fiscal agent assumes a large part of the underwriting functions. The return received by investment dealers is either a commission, or the difference between the price paid to the borrower for the securities and the price at which they are sold to the public. When a dealer acquires securities through underwriting, the entire issue is not always available for sale to the public. The dealer may want to hold securities for his own account or he may have arranged previously to sell the issue directly to a financial intermediary.

Securities, once underwritten and distributed, are traded in the secondary market which is maintained by the dealers. Dealers service their customers by buying for and selling from their inventories. For example, large investment dealers have direct telephone communications with as many as forty other dealers. With a flick of a switch they can respond instantly to bids and offers.

Investment dealers finance their inventories of securities with funds borrowed from banks and near-banks, by issuing promissory notes and accepting short-term deposits from corporations, and by using customer credit balances. The larger investment dealers in federal government securities also have lines of credit with the Bank of Canada.

Aside from making a market for bonds, the investment dealers make a market for the money market instruments discussed in the previous chapter. The investment dealers together with the chartered banks and the Bank of Canada are the important traders in the money market.

While the market for bonds and money market securities is centred in the investment dealers, that for stocks is centred in organized stock exchanges formed by stock brokers. In Canada there are stock exchanges in Montreal, Toronto, Winnipeg, Calgary and Vancouver. The members of an exchange are individuals who have bought a seat which gives them the right to deal on the floor of the exchange. A member may be an individual trading on his own account or for other brokers, or a partner or director of a brokerage firm. The stock exchange is a non-profit organization which meets its expenses from the subscription paid by its members and by the companies whose shares are listed. Although the main function of stock exchanges is to provide a secondary market for stocks, some Canadian exchanges permit the primary distribution of stock.

Usually, jobbers or broker-dealers underwrite and distribute stock issues. Stocks may be offered directly to the public either in the "over-the-counter market"[1] or through the stock exchanges.

THE QUEBEC SAVINGS BANKS

Government legislation "to encourage the establishment of and regulate Savings Banks" was passed in 1841. Of the various savings banks founded by the colonial government and by private interests only two remain today — La Banque d'Epargne de la Cité et du District de Montréal (The Montreal City and District Savings Bank) founded in 1846, and La Banque d'Economie de Québec (The Quebec Savings Bank) founded in 1848. The banks were mutuals before they were brought under Dominion legislation in 1871. Both are now federally chartered and operate under the Quebec Savings Banks Act which applies specifically to them. In recent years amendments made to the act have liberalized the traditional strict limits imposed on the savings banks' investment powers. These limits were designed to exclude them from commercial banking and to ensure the safety of their deposits. In earlier years they were obliged to use most of their funds to purchase government securities, a restriction intended to protect their depositors and to assure a market for government debt. The act allows the two Quebec savings banks to open branches in the districts in which their head offices are situated. As their main function is collecting individual savings from persons residing within their respective districts, their most important source of funds is deposits. A small proportion of these deposits is made by the Government of Canada and provincial governments. Their deposit accounts are similar to chartered bank personal savings deposits. Although nominally subject to notice, they are transferable by cheque. The Quebec savings banks are required to hold a cash reserve equal to 5 per cent of deposits in Bank of Canada notes or deposits, or chartered bank deposits. In addition they must hold secondary reserves equal to 15 per cent of their deposit liabilities in Bank of Canada notes or deposits, or chartered bank deposits, or securities issued or guaranteed by the federal or provincial governments. Both the cash and secondary reserves are calculated on a monthly basis.

Other sources of funds for the Quebec savings banks include the sale of their stock, and secured advances from the Bank of Canada and the chartered banks.

Before 1948 the Quebec savings banks employed most of their funds to purchase federal and provincial securities. However, with the amend-

---

1 "Over-the-counter market" is an expression which refers to all buying and selling of financial assets other than on the stock exchange.

TABLE 11-2

Quebec Savings Banks, Assets and Liabilities
End of Year, 1965
(millions of dollars)

Assets	Cash: Bank of Canada notes and deposits with the chartered banks and the Bank of Canada		28.1
	Government of Canada securities	21.3	
	Provincial securities	67.0	
	Municipal securities	29.7	
	Other securities	29.9	147.8
	Mortgages		203.7
	Loans		26.5
	All other assets		24.1
	Total		430.2
Liabilities	Deposits		408.4
	Secured advances from chartered banks and Bank of Canada		1.4
	All other liabilities		1.4
	Shareholders' equity		19.0
	Total		430.2

Note: Errors due to rounding
Source: Bank of Canada, Statistical Summary, 1966 Supplement.

ments to the Quebec Savings Banks Act in that year and subsequently, they have shifted the largest proportion of their assets into higher yielding mortgage loans. Government securities comprise their second largest asset. However, here there has been a shift from Government of Canada securities to provincial and municipal securities. Aggregate mortgage loans made by a savings bank cannot exceed an amount equal to 60 per cent of its deposit liabilities. Since 1967 the banks have no longer been restricted in the amount of shares of Canadian corporations which they may hold. They have shown, however, a strong preference not to purchase many such shares.

The Quebec Savings Banks were not permitted to grant unsecured loans except to governments, school boards and religious bodies before 1948. They are now allowed to make unsecured loans to both business and individuals. However, such loans can be made only to business corporations which have unimpaired paid-up capital and earned surplus in excess of $500,000 and which have a five year dividend payment record. Personal unsecured loans are not allowed to exceed $10,000 per loan.

The total unsecured loans made by a savings bank, excluding those made to federal and provincial governments, may not exceed 15 per cent of the bank's deposit liabilities. Even with the broader powers allowed them the Quebec savings banks continue to concentrate their attention on personal savings and family businesses. The restrictions on their operations other than those we have mentioned are similar to those of the commercial banks.

CAISSES POPULAIRES AND CREDIT UNIONS

Caisses populaires and credit unions are savings and credit cooperatives which trace their origin to the mutual savings bank movement in Europe during the eighteenth century and the People's Bank movement during the nineteenth century. The first of these movements stressed the virtues of mutuality and thrift, and the second those of cooperation, self-help and the democratic structure of management. Moreover, in contrast to the savings banks which were oriented toward inducing the habit of saving, the people's banks emphasized the provision of credit facilities for the little man. In Canada the early formation of caisses populaires followed closely the concept of European savings banks, while credit unions were modelled on the European people's banks.

Caisses populaires were founded in 1900 in the Province of Quebec by Alfonse Desjardins. Although they are still largely concentrated in Quebec, they have been established in French speaking communities of other provinces. Following the intent of their founder, caisses populaires have emphasized the virtues of thrift and have considered the provision of credit to their members as a necessary evil. They have been organized on a territorial basis, usually consisting of a Roman Catholic parish. Each local society is a cooperative organization and its members are both owners and consumers of its services. Local societies are affiliated with regional unions which in turn are affiliated with a **centrale.** The regional unions concern themselves mainly with organization and education while the centrales provide financial services to local societies and regional unions. The main purpose for the formation of centrales was to provide a better system of supervision over the financial welfare of local societies. The government of the Province of Quebec has given centrales an annual subsidy to assist them in carrying out their supervisory functions. Centrales also serve as intermediaries for local societies by clearing their cheques, managing their liquid reserves when requested to do so and providing loans to them when necessary.

Because of their different origins credit unions display a greater diversity than caisses populaires. The Antigonish type of credit union was started as part of the cooperative movement fostered by St. Francis Xavier

University in Antigonish, Nova Scotia in the late 1920's. They were organized on a community basis in farming and fishing communities in much the same way as caisses polpulaires were organized in parishes. However, unlike the caisses populaires, they emphasize the provision of more adequate credit facilities for their members rather than the virtues of thrift. Although Antigonish credit unions closely associated with the cooperative movement are found mainly in the Maritime provinces, they have been established in the prairies also, particularly in the province of Saskatchewan.

In Ontario most of the credit unions have been modelled on their American counterparts. These differ from Antigonish unions in that they are generally not organized on a territorial basis but on an occupational basis or according to some other common bond of association. They have a consumer oriented lending tradition which stems from their early purposes — to allow members to escape usury by providing a convenient source of low-cost credit.

Most credit unions are bound loosely together into provincial leagues which in turn may be members of a central union. The centrals function in much the same was as those of the caisses populaires. Credit union leagues may also be members of the Credit Union National Association

TABLE 11-3

Credit Unions and Caisses Populaires, Assets and Liabilities
Year end 1955 and 1965
(*millions of dollars*)

	1955	**1965**
Assets		
Loans	174	987
Mortgages	211	695
Investments	163	486
Cash	87	283
Other Assets	18	90
Total	653	2,542
Liabilities		
Shares	194	979
Deposits	409	1,296
Other liabilities	11	107
Surplus funds	39	160
Total	653	2,542

Note: Errors due to rounding

Source: Bank of Canada. Statistical Summary, November 1966 and 1966 Supplement.

(CUNA), an international organization which promotes the credit union movement.

Caisses populaires and credit unions derive funds from their members through the sale of shares and by accepting deposits. Membership is gained usually by the payment of a nominal entrance fee and by a pledge to purchase at least one share, the value of which is normally $5. Shares are redeemed on demand but are nominally subject to notice of sixty to ninety days. Caisses populaires deliberately discourage the purchase of shares by charging a fee. As a result, they rely on member deposits as their main source of funds. Although withdrawal of deposits from the caisses populaires is nominally subject to notice as is a withdrawal from a bank savings account, cheques can generally be written on these accounts; in some rural communities this has now become the most important means of payment. Credit unions, on the other hand, obtain most of their funds from the sale of their shares. Members may obtain life insurance coverage on their share holdings.

Caisses populaires and credit unions also differ in the use of their funds. Because of their traditional emphasis on thrift, and in order to protect their depositors, caisses populaires usually do not hold more than 50 per cent of their assets as loans to the members. Credit unions have up to 80 per cent of their assets in loans to their members. Moreover, while the caisses populaires have concentrated their member loans in the form of residential first mortgage loans, credit unions have engaged primarily in consumer loans. The relatively few consumer loans made by caisses populaires are guaranteed only by the signature of the endorser. Such loans are usually insured upon payment of a premium in addition to the regular interest charge. In contrast, credit union loans, also usually insured, are guaranteed either by the borrower's share in the union, or by real estate or chattel liens. Caisses populaires consider it a moral obligation to assist with the financing of local institutions. As a result a large proportion of their security assets are bonds issued by minicipalities and school boards.

Caisses populaires and credit unions come under provincial legislation which sets out the amount of reserves they are required to hold and the type of investments they are allowed to make. Because small, local institutions are not able to diversify their risks as well as large financial intermediaries, there has been a tendency to establish mutual aid funds to meet liquidity difficulties when they arise. In some provinces legislation requires all local societies to join mutual aid funds. In its report the Porter Commission recommended that all local societies belong to provincial and regional centrals and that these take a more active role in supervising and regulating the movement of liquid reserves among locals. The Commission also recommended that centrals be brought into a national system of regulation and that they be required to maintain adequate reserves in relation to their own liabilities and the liabilities of their member societies. "Moreover, in order to integrate them more fully into the financial system and give them access to central bank credit when need arises, they should hold these cash reserves at the Bank of Canada."[2] In 1953, the federal government passed the Co-operative Credit Associations Act, the only federal law respecting credit unions. The act established the Canadian Co-operative Credit Society Limited, a "super-central" for central cooperative associations. The Society has not proved very successful, mainly because of the high cash reserves which centrals belonging to it are required to maintain. The Porter Commission recommended that the act should be replaced with "legislation more attuned to the character and needs of the credit union movement and the public it serves".[3]

The sources and uses of funds by credit unions and caisses populaires for the years 1955 and 1965 are shown in Table 11-3.

Ancillary to the operations of the caisses populaires has been the establishment of their own general insurance company (La Société d'Assurance des Caisses Populaires, 1946), a life insurance company (L'Assurance — Vie Desjardins, 1950) and a trust company (La Société de Fiducie du Québec, 1963). In 1962 an important life insurance company, La Sauvegarde, was acquired by them. Caisses populaires also participated as shareholders in the establishment in 1962 of the General Investment Corporation in the Province of Quebec.

MORTGAGE LOAN COMPANIES

Mortgage loan companies, which were first established in the 1840's, were patterned on the building societies that had developed in the United Kingdom during the early part of the nineteenth century. The objective of building societies was to enable their members to acquire land, build houses or develop farms. In the early phase, each member would contribute a certain amount of money on a regular basis to a building society. When the accumulated funds were large enough to, say, build a house, they were auctioned off to the highest bidder or made available to a member chosen by lot. A member receiving the funds assumed a mortgage which he paid back over a period of years while continuing his regular contributions to the society.

In the second phase, persons joined building societies without the intention of eventually borrowing money from them. It was usual for these societies to sell two kinds of shares. Persons who did not want to avail

---

2 *Report of the Royal Commission on Banking and Finance*, 1964, p. 170

3 *Ibid*, p. 167.

themselves of the privilege of borrowing from a society purchased investing shares and participated in the profits of the society. For many, these shares were an attractive investment because they provided a means of escaping the early usury laws. On the other hand, persons whose prime interest was to build a house made regular contributions to a society by purchasing advance shares which did not allow them to participate directly in a society's profits.

The early building societies were "terminating" in that they ceased to exist when each member in turn had taken out and repaid his building loan. In the third phase of their development, in the 1850's, "permanent" societies were established. Permanent societies or companies began to

TABLE 11-4

Mortgage Loan Companies, Assets and Liabilities
Fourth Quarter estimates, 1955 and 1965
(*millions of dollars*)

Assets	**1955**	**1965**
Cash	20	54
Government of Canada securities	60	117
Provincial and Municipal government debt	20	49
Short-term notes }	12	2
Corporate and institutional bonds }		31
Mortgages	450	1,827
Collateral loans	3	20
Canadian stocks	18	55
Foreign securities }		4
Investment in affiliated companies }	15	201
Other assets }		65
Total	599	2,426
Liabilities		
Deposits: chequable }	124	162
non-chequable }		203
Certificates, debentures, term deposits	321	1,372
Bank loans }	1	63
Short-term loans and notes payable }		125
Owing parent and affiliated companies }	153	207
Shareholders' equity }		295
Total	599	2,426

Note: Errors due to estimation and rounding

Source: Dominion Bureau of Statistics, "Business Financial Statistics" Bank of Canada, Statistical Summary, 1966 Supplement

accept deposits from the public to raise mortgage money. Legislation, however, generally restricted the amount of deposits they were allowed to accept to 75 per cent of the amount paid up on unadvanced shares plus the company's investment in securities (excluding mortgages). In the 1870's mortgage loan companies were allowed for the first time to raise money by the issue of debentures.

The main source of the funds used by mortgage loan companies is the sale of their debentures. Although the companies have different preferences as to the maturity of their debenture issues, they are usually concentrated in the five-year and under range. The companies have their debentures continuously on sale over the counter. The majority of debentures are purchased by individual savers, but there has been a tendency for corporations to hold them as short-term investments. More and more of the mortgage loan companies have been invading the banking field by accepting deposits, both chequable and non-chequable. Since 1967 these deposits have been insured by either the federal or the provincial deposit insurance systems. In recent years mortgage loan companies, particularly the large ones, have sold their short-term notes in the money market to acquire funds and have borrowed more on short term from the banks. In addition to their short-term borrowing they acquire funds from the sale of long-term bonds and mortgages and from other funded debt.

In the use of their funds, as well as in the way they acquire these funds, mortgage loan companies are controlled by government legislation. They may be incorporated by either the federal government or the provincial government. Most of them have provincial charters and hence come directly under provincial jurisdiction. The bulk of their lending is on conventional residential mortgages with terms of five years.[4] Under federal legislation they are now allowed to lend up to 75 per cent of the value of real estate.

Mortgage loan companies are not allowed to make unsecured commercial and personal loans. Collateral loans have made up a small proportion of their assets. The larger companies have participated in the money market through the purchase as well as the sale of short-term notes. The remainder of their funds after mortgage loans is invested in Government of Canada, provincial and municipal securities. Under federal legislation mortgage loan companies are allowed to invest 25 per cent of their assets in common shares of companies having a five-year dividend record.

---

4 This dates from the Orton Act of 1880 which provided that a mortgagor must be allowed to repay his mortgage loan at any time after five years, no matter how long the terms in the mortgage contract, upon payment of a bonus of three months' interest. This was to protect a borrower against being committed to a high interest rate payment in the future when rates might be significantly lower. Short maturities, on the other hand, protect the mortgage loan companies from being committed to lower rates in the future.

Many of the provincial acts now have "basket clauses" which allow mortgage loan companies complete freedom in investing a specified proportion of their assets.

TRUST COMPANIES

Trust companies were originally organized because under common law corporations were not allowed to act as trustees. The execution of a trust was considered to require a conscience not possessed by corporations which by their very nature are artificial beings. The concept of trust companies, first organized in the United States in the 1820's, probably came from the agency houses in India which carried on the business of receiving money on deposit and administering estates. Most of the first companies in the United States that were granted trust or fiduciary powers were life insurance companies. Gradually giving up life insurance and other functions, they began to concentrate on the fiduciary business. However, after the early 1900's trust companies started to invade the banking field and today most of the fiduciary business is carried on by the banks. Canadian trust companies are the sole survivors of the earlier movement of establishing companies whose prime function is to conduct fiduciary business. But even in Canada, this may be a passing phase as more and more trust companies are invading other financial fields.

Funds administered by trust companies are generally grouped into one of three categories: estates, trust and agency funds; guaranteed funds; and company funds. The basic function of trust companies has been the professional management and employment of funds entrusted to them. Estate funds are set up under wills. The companies administer such funds according to the instructions contained in wills and the legislation of all jurisdictions in which the assets and claims exist. Trust funds may be set up under "living trusts", in which case the companies assume a responsibility during the life time of the trustor. For example, a person may turn over funds to a company to provide a life income for an invalid relative. Trust funds may also be set up to provide a perpetual income for a university or charitable organization. In recent years the most important source of trust funds to be administered by trust companies has been the pension plans of businesses and institutions.

Agency funds of trust companies differ from estate and trust funds in that the companies do not assume a direct responsibility for their management. Under agency agreements companies take only custody of assets and carry out the instructions of the owner for their administration. This may involve property management, the collection of dividends and interest, and a variety of other duties.

Estates, trusts and agency business of trust companies, being a matter

TABLE 11-5

Trust Companies, Assets and Liabilities
Fourth Quarter Estimates for 1955 and 1965
(*millions of dollars*)

Assets	**1955**	**1965**
Cash	35	99
Government of Canada securities	151	387
Provincial and municipal government debt	137	321
Money market paper, term deposits etc.	72	208
Corporate and institutional bonds		219
Mortgage loans and sales agreements	228	1,927
Collateral loans	36	108
Canadian stocks	23	75
Foreign securities	4	5
Investments in affiliated companies	23	19
Other assets		73
Total	709	3,439
Liabilities		
Deposits: chequable	268	559
non-chequable		556
Deposit receipts and certificates	329	2,006
Bank loans	7	4
Short-term loans and loans payable	2	37
Owing parent and affiliated companies		3
Reserves and equity	107	274
Total	709	3,439

Note: Errors due to estimation and rounding. (Bracketed 1955 figures cover the grouped items.)

Source: Dominion Bureau of Statistics, "Business Financial Statistics" and Bank of Canada, Statistical Summary, 1966 Supplement.

of property and civil rights, is entirely subject to provincial jurisdiction. All provinces have trustee acts which specify the type of investments trust companies can make with funds entrusted to them where such instructions are not given in trust agreements. As a rule investments are allowed in Government of Canada bonds, provincial bonds, municipal bonds, school and hospital bonds, and first mortgages on residential property.

Trusts have to be administered separately according to each trust deed. This makes it difficult for a trustee to sufficiently diversify individual trust portfolios in order to provide a high return without assuming an undue risk. The provincial governments have begun to change their trust legislation to allow companies to invest a small proportion of trust money in common funds which are in effect mutual funds operated by the companies for the benefit of the account administered.

Guaranteed funds result from the acceptance of deposits and the sale of guaranteed investment certificates. These funds are called guaranteed because they cannot exceed the limits specified in both provincial and federal legislation. Federal law since 1965 has restricted borrowing by a trust company to fifteen times its capital, reserves and surplus. Moreover, some provincial trustee acts restrict the type of assets trust companies may purchase with borrowed funds, and require that such funds be backed not only by a general claim on a company's assets, as is the case with most other financial institutions, but by specifically segregated and ear-marked assets.

Trust companies offer both chequable and non-chequable demand accounts as well as term deposits. They have successfully expanded their demand deposits by extending branches into suburban areas, by maintaining flexible branch hours to meet the needs of potential customers, and by offering a variety of gifts and bonuses to attract new customers. Since 1967 their demand deposits have been insured by either provincial or federal deposit insurance systems.

Trust company demand deposits and guaranteed investment certificates over one year are held mainly by individual savers, while their term deposits and some investment certificates are sold to corporations and money market dealers. The companies have been willing to tailor the amounts and maturities of their term deposits and investment certificates to meet market demands.

Company funds consist of capital stock sold to the public, retained earnings and funds borrowed from the banks. The largest proportion of company funds and guaranteed funds is invested in conventional residential mortgage loans. Federally chartered trust companies and most provincially chartered companies are now allowed to lend up to 75 per cent of the value of real estate. The second most important use of their funds is the financing of provincial and municipal government through the purchase of their bonds. Trust companies invest a small proportion of their funds in corporate stock. Since 1965 federal legislation has allowed them to invest an amount equal to 25 per cent of their assets in the stock of companies which have a five-year dividend record.

Trust companies are not allowed to make unsecured commercial and personal loans. Although collateral loans have represented a small proportion of their assets, this proportion has steadily increased. The companies which have become important borrowers in the money market have also become important lenders to this market. They often supply a substantial part of investment dealers' requirements for inventory finance. As such they have become known as "country bankers".

LIFE INSURANCE COMPANIES

Life insurance companies provide two basic services: they offer protection, and they provide a means of accumulating savings. Over the past decade saving through life insurance companies has averaged about 25 per cent of total personal savings. [5]

The three basic types of life insurance are term, whole life and endowment insurance. Term insurance provides the policyholder with nothing more than protection: a contracted insurance payment is made to a beneficiary at the death of the insured person provided death occurs within a specified period of time, or before a certain age. Under a regular term insurance contract the insured person pays a higher insurance premium for subsequent contract periods because the probability of death increases as he grows older. With decreasing term insurance, the amount of insurance protection decreases each year until the insurance expires, usually in fifteen, twenty or twenty-five years, or at a certain age such as sixty-five. Regardless of the type of term insurance no benefits are paid by the insurance company if death does not occur within the contract period. Group insurance, covering a collection of people under a master contract, is a form of term insurance which is now commonly employed.

In the case of a whole life insurance contract, insurance benefits are paid at death and protection is provided for the whole life of the insured. In contrast to regular term insurance, whole life policies carry a level premium. Premiums on straight life contracts are paid until death; premiums on limited payment life contracts are paid for a specified number of years, or until death if death occurs within the specified period. Whole life policies can also be purchased by making a lump sum payment. With fixed or level premiums the insured makes excess payments with regard to mortality expectations in early years. The excess payments accumulate as savings of the policyholders and provide insurance companies with a pool of funds for investment purposes. These savings are available to policy-holders as the cash surrender value of policies if they are cancelled or as funds that may be borrowed by policyholders.

Endowment contracts also combine savings with protection but their main purpose is saving. The policyholder pays a lump sum or makes regular payments to an insurance company for a specified number of years. At the end of the period (usually at age sixty-five) the company pays a definite sum of money (the face amount of the policy plus any dividends)

---

5 In the National Income and Expenditure Accounts insurance companies are considered to be the agents of the policyholders. The companies' investment income is considered as consumer income, and their expenses and profits are regarded as expenses for the consumer. Cash premiums, investment income, and profits less expenses and cash claims paid out are equal to the item in the Accounts called policyholders' saving. This represents savings consumers make through life insurance companies.

to the policyholder if he is still living. If he dies during the endowment period, payment of the same sum is made to a beneficiary.

Life insurance companies also sell annuity contracts. Under a fixed or conventional annuity contract a company receives a lump sum or regular payments with the obligation to pay the annuitant a stipulated sum of money periodically (usually monthly) beginning at a specified time and extending for a designated period of years or for the remainder of the annuitant's life. The usual term is for the life of the annuitant with a fixed number of years guaranteed. For example, under an annuity payable for life with ten years guaranteed, payment is made to the annuitant's estate for ten years even if he dies the day the payments are to start. While life insurance protects the insured against the financial difficulties resulting from dying too soon, an annuity contract protects the annuitant against financial difficulties consequent upon living too long.

For the annuitant, fixed contracts do not meet his needs if prices have risen substantially by the time he receives his fixed dollar annuity. To deal with this problem insurance companies in the United States began offering in the early 1950's variable annuity contracts in those states where legislation permitted them to do so. Variable annuity contracts are designed to make annuity payments reflect the changes in the cost of living. Insurance companies which offer such contracts invest part of the funds in common stocks whose prices move in general sympathy with overall prices. The amount received by the annuitant varies with the success of the company's investment policy.

In recent years with the growth of both corporate and institutional pension plans, life insurance companies have expanded their activities by providing insured pension plans. The two general types of such plans offered on a group basis are permanent life insurance with cash values providing the required funds to finance retirement payments, and deferred group annuities with paid-up insurance purchased in each year and income payments deferred until retirement. Life insurance companies also administer pension funds left with them in much the same way as trust companies.

Life insurance companies, when channelling funds from policyholders, annuitants and past investments to seekers of funds in the capital market, must operate within a legal framework set out in statutory regulations. Most companies are both registered with the federal government and licenced by provincial authorities. As a general rule, all companies must be licenced in each province in which they do business. Canadian insurance company legislation protects the policyholder by restricting company investments to certain types of assets and by subjecting the companies to government supervision. In recent years the investment powers of life insurance companies have been substantially broadened. Since 1965 federal legislation which applies to most companies has allowed them to invest in common shares an amount equal to 25 per cent of their assets. In addition 7 per cent of their assets may be invested relatively free of any restriction. Prior to 1965 life insurance companies could hold common stock only of companies which had paid at least a 4 per cent dividend for seven years. They are now allowed to hold the common stock of any corporation with a five-year record of earnings sufficient to pay a divident of at least 4 per cent (whether paid or not) of the average value at which shares are carried in capital stock accounts. Moreover, in 1965 valuation rules were modified to allow insurance companies to spread the impact of market price changes over a three-year period instead of obliging them to record full declines in the year in which they occur. Most life

TABLE 11-6

Life Insurance Companies: Assets Held in Canada, 1965*
(millions of dollars)

Canadian Securities	
Government of Canada	525
Provincial	1,048
Municipal	722
Corporate and other bonds	2,388
Preferred and common stocks	407
Own stock purchased for mutualization	7
Foreign securities	
Bonds	163
Preferred and common stocks	89
Mortgage loans and sale agreements	4,984
Real estate	386
Policy loans	411
Cash	66
Other assets	228
Total	11,424

*Life branch assets of all companies registered under the federal Insurance Acts. Comprises all assets at book value, physically held in Canada by Canadian companies and British and foreign companies; excludes Canadian dollar assets held outside Canada.

Source: Bank of Canada, Statistical Summary, 1966 Supplement.

insurance companies have followed a traditionally conservative approach to investing in common shares and have taken advantage of the more liberal powers to invest in common shares only reluctantly. They have preferred to concentrate most of their investments in mortgage loans and long-term government and corporate bonds. Since the liabilities of life insurance companies are relatively long-term in nature these companies are able to invest a high proportion of their funds in long-term assets. Moreover, well established insurance companies need retain only a comparatively modest liquidity position since they can count on a net cash inflow from contracts already in force. These companies are the principal buyers of mortgages in Canada and the largest group of investors in corporate bonds. At the end of 1965, 44 per cent of their funds were in mortgages and 21 per cent in corporate bonds. Many of these bonds are acquired through "direct placement", negotiated directly with the borrower or with the assistance of financial intermediaries. Where this is the case bond issues do not come to the market in the traditional fashion.

Life insurance companies are either stock companies owned by their shareholders, or mutual companies belonging to their policyholders. The profits of mutual companies are distributed to policyholders in the form of rebates on premiums or as additional insurance. Some stock companies sell participating contracts which allow policyholders a share of the profits. Since 1957 the stock companies have been permitted to convert themselves into mutual companies by the purchase of their outstanding shares. About 60 per cent of all companies are now mutuals. About half of all insurance companies in Canada are foreign companies. At the same time the operations of most Canadian companies are international in scope.

NON-LIFE INSURANCE COMPANIES

Property and casualty insurance is sold by general insurance companies. They specialize in such types as fire, hail, automobile and health insurance, as well as insurance against loss, damage or liability. Like life insurance companies the main source of revenue for fire and casualty companies is premium income collected on a contractual basis. However, unlike life insurance companies, capital accounts provide a substantial source of funds for general insurance companies. Although they do not collect savings, they do accumulate pools of funds from premium and investment income out of which to meet claims under their policies. Since their liabilities are normally short-term in nature (contracts are usually written for no more than three-year periods) and since claims against them are unpredictable, their assets are held in relatively liquid form. They invest very little in mortgages and concentrate their long-term investments in Government of Canada and provincial issues which can be readily liquidated if the need arises. For immediate liquidity they hold deposits with other financial intermediaries and invest in short-term market securities and paper. A small proportion of their assets is held in preferred and common stocks.

FINANCE COMPANIES

There are two main types of finance companies: consumer loan companies, and sales finance companies. Consumer loan companies deal almost exclusively with consumers, making cash loans usually on the security of a promissory note. Most of their customers are borrowers who because of low income or the amount of their debts are unable to obtain credit elsewhere. All loan companies making personal loans of $1,500 or less and charging more than one per cent per month on any loan must apply to the Minister of Finance for a licence which is renewable annually under the federal Small Loans Act. This act was first passed in 1939 to control the total charges on small personal loans. The act stipulates the maximum amount of interest which can be charged on personal loans of $1,500 or less.[6]

Many of the consumer loan companies are subsidiaries or affiliates of sales finance companies, or are owned by foreign consumer loan companies. The larger ones rely on parent or associated companies for the main source of their funds. The smaller companies obtain most of their funds from their own shareholders and from the chartered banks. In recent years the larger companies have also obtained a substantial amount of their funds from the sale of short-term market paper.

Sales finance companies differ from most other financial intermediaries in that they usually do not deal directly with the public. These companies developed with the introduction of the automobile after the turn of the century. Although their major function is still to provide credit for the financing of automobile purchases, they have extended their operations to include the financing of most durable goods. In practice, a dealer or retailer sells a durable good to a customer who signs a conditional sales contract. The customer does not assume ownership of the product until through regular instalment payments he has paid fully for the product. Included in his regular instalment payments is the interest charge on borrowed funds. Conditional sales contracts accepted from

---

6 The Small Loans Act states that the maximum rates on a loan, including all charges, cannot exceed 2 per cent per month on the unpaid balance of a loan under $300, one per cent per month on the portion of the balance between $300 and $1,000 and one half of one per cent of the balance between $1,000 and $1,500. No interest rate regulations exist on loans over $1,500. Unlicenced lenders must charge less than one per cent per month or deal in amounts of more than $1,500.

TABLE 11-7

Sales Finance and Consumer Loan Companies Assets and Liabilities
Fourth Quarter Estimates, 1965
(*millions of dollars*)

Assets	
Cash and money market paper and bills	62
Accounts and notes receivable by sales finance companies	2,248
Instalment credit and cash loans by small loan companies	1,043
Other receivables (net)	447
Investment in subsidiary and associated companies	277
Securities	73
Other assets	79
Total	4,228
Liabilities	
Owing parent and associated companies	686
Bank loans	534
Demand and short-term securities	911
Long-term debt	1,178
Unearned income and other liabilities	412
Paid-in capital and retained income	506
Total	4,228

Note: Errors due to estimation and rounding.

Source: Dominion Bureau of Statistics, "Business Financial Statistics" and Bank of Canada, Statistical Summary, 1966 Supplement.

their customers by dealers are purchased (discounted) by sales finance companies which take over the rights to the product and collection of payments. They may assume all or none of the risks or share them with the dealer. The larger companies, most of which are affiliates of manufacturers, also provide wholesale financing. The General Motors Acceptance Corporation, for example, provides credit to General Motors' dealers to carry their inventory of automobiles. The larger sales finance corporations also make capital loans to dealers to improve their facilities. In recent years competition by the chartered banks for consumer instalment loans has forced the sales finance companies into new fields of lending. Many of them now finance the purchase of machinery and equipment. Some provide interim finance on real estate and construction and make mortgage loans. Some are engaging in commercial financing — financing business receivables by lending against them; and in factoring — purchasing business receivables outright.

Sales finance companies do not operate under specific legislation, chiefly because they do not deal directly with the public. In their early history their main sources of funds were the sale of their stock, retained earnings and bank borrowing. However, with the large demand for consumer instalment finance after the Second World War these traditional sources of funds were supplemented by the issue of a wide variety of notes, bonds and debentures sold to other financial institutions and corporations. Sales finance companies are among the most important participants in the money and capital markets. When funds are not readily available in these markets some of the companies turn to their foreign affiliates for assistance and directly or indirectly to foreign financial markets.

INVESTMENT COMPANIES

There are two basic types of investment companies: closed-end companies and open-end companies, now commonly referred to as mutual funds. Closed-end investment companies trace their origins to the investment trusts developed in Europe during the nineteenth century. They first became popular in the United States and Canada in the 1920's when they were established as a vehicle to gain control of other companies and to take advantage of "leverage" on a given amount of equity investment.[7] For example, a typical company might be formed by the sale of shares in the amount of $100,000. After formation the company raises $900,000 in the market from an issue of bonds. The $1 million then available to the company is used to purchase the common shares of other companies. If at the end of the year these shares have appreciated by 10 per cent, the original investors in the equity of the investment trust company have doubled their investment of $100,000. Most of the early companies were nothing more than speculative ventures. Today's closed-end investment companies operate in a much more conservative way and concentrate their investments in companies whose development potential looks promising. The shares of these companies are sold to the public as any other shares which are traded in the open market. Closed-end investment companies differ from most other financial intermediaries in that they stress gain rather than safety for the investor.

The first open-end investment company or mutual fund was probably the Massachusetts Investors Trust founded in 1924. The first such company in Canada was founded in the early 1930's. However, the growth and expansion of open-end companies dates only from the mid-1950's.

[7] In England this is more commonly known as "gearing".

TABLE 11-8

Investment Companies, Assets and Liabilities
Fourth Quarter Estimates, 1965
(*millions of dollars*)

	Mutual Funds	Closed-End Funds
Assets		
Cash	45	8
Money market notes and bills	34	13
Government of Canada bonds	70	6
Provincial and municipal government debt	58	1
Corporate bonds and debentures	67	9
Mortgages and sales agreements	13	1
Shares	918	429
Foreign securities	320	38
Other assets	49	4
Total	1,574	509
Liabilities		
Short-term loans: bank	–	14
other	–	2
Long-term debt	1	30
Other liabilities	11	4
Paid-in capital	1,423	238
Retained earnings	139	221
Total	1,574	509

Note: Errors due to estimation and rounding.

Source: Dominion Bureau of Statistics, "Business Financial Statistics and Bank of Canada, Statistical Summary, 1966 Supplement

Open-end investment companies obtain funds by selling their stock directly to the public through brokers or through their own sales offices and agents. New stock is issued to meet the demands of the public. When a stockholder of an open-end investment company wishes to redeem his shares he does so by selling his stock back to the company. Companies sell their shares and redeem them at all times at prices based on the current value of their assets. A person purchasing a share pays an acquisition fee. If he contracts to buy a certain number of shares, the acquisition fee for the total purchase may be deducted from his early payments. This is called a front-end loading and may result in a loss to the shareholder because the fee is deducted from the redemption price of the shares.

Various types of mutual funds are sold according to the investment policies of companies. With so-called "balanced" funds the companies' assets consist of bonds, preferred stocks and common stocks. With so-called "fully managed" funds, the companies shift their investments according to the state of markets and yields. However, all companies hold the majority of their shares in common stocks, usually of well established companies. Their investment policies have been influenced by the provisions of the Income Tax Act. Income tax rates vary with the main sources of income and how it is distributed.

Mutual funds have grown in popularity because of the affluence of our society and because of the features they provide for many individual savers. The modest saver is provided with professional management of his savings and diversity of investment. Moreover, in that his shares can be redeemed at any time his assets are kept relatively liquid.

PENSION FUNDS

Pension funds are accumulated to provide income for people after retirement. There are two types of pension plans: insured and non-insured plans. Insured plans, as we have already seen, are administered by life insurance companies. Funds collected by life insurance companies are used to purchase a collective annuity with pension payments guaranteed in the form of annuities. Uninsured pension plans are administered by trust companies, by pension fund societies or by independent trustees.

TABLE 11-9

Distribution of Assets of Trusteed Pension Plans, 1965
(millions of dollars)

Government of Canada bonds	513	
Provincial bonds	2,022	
Municipal bonds	656	
Other bonds	1,036	4,227
Stocks		997
Mortgage loans		626
Cash		107
Investment in pooled and mutual funds		459
Other assets		184
Total		6,600

Source: Bank of Canada, Statistical Summary, 1966 Supplement.

Since 1908 the federal government also has sold annuities of limited size, and in 1965 it and the Province of Quebec initiated compulsory government pension plans.

Pension plans may be funded or non-funded. In the case of non-funded plans, pension payments are made out of current income; the federal government's annuity plan is non-funded. Funded plans collect and invest funds to provide future benefit payments.

Investment policies of trusteed pension plans vary widely. In Canada trusteed pension funds have been invested rather conservatively. About 70 per cent of their assets have been invested in government bonds. The predominant proportion are bonds of provincial governments.

The Canada and Quebec Pension Plans are coordinated, thereby providing one nation-wide system of contributory pensions. The contribution rate of the Canada Pension Plan is 1.8 per cent of earnings each from employer and employee and a combined rate of 3.6 per cent from self-employed persons. Initially the upper limit for contributory earnings is set at $5,000 a year and earnings up to $600 a year are exempt. The pool of funds accumulated under the Canada Pension Plan and not needed for benefit and administrative expenses is credited to an investment fund and invested in provincial securities.

OTHER PRIVATE FINANCIAL INSTITUTIONS

Existing financial institutions are almost continuously changing the pattern of their business to meet the demands of changing circumstances, and new institutions are being created for this purpose also. Several examples of new institutions created to meet new demands are given here.

Because of the restrictions on chartered bank lending, many of which were removed in 1967, the banks traditionally were unable to meet adequately the demands of small businesses for medium and long-term credit. The banks, in association with other private financial institutions, established separate corporations to meet these demands. Some of these newer corporations, aside from providing longer-term credits by taking mortgage security, also provide equity capital to establish companies with growth potential, and provide technical and business advice to companies in which they invest. Many of the newer financial institutions are essentially private development companies.

Another financial institution established to fill a gap in the Canadian financial system is the Export Finance Corporation of Canada. This company, taken over by the banks in 1961, was formed in 1959 to rediscount medium-term export loans insured by the Export Credits Insurance

Corporation.[8] Funds available to the company include $10 million of capital provided by the banks, and funds borrowed from both the Canadian and foreign money markets. Its operations have been quite modest; at the end of its fiscal year in April 1965 it had discounted a total of some $328 million in bills.

SELECTED READINGS

See list following Chapter 12

8 The Export Credits Insurance Corporation is discussed in the next chapter.

12 GOVERNMENTS AND CANADIAN FINANCIAL MARKETS

The role of governments in financial markets is both large and diverse. Governments are the most important issuers of financial assets. They are also important lenders — with two major goals: to stimulate and promote certain sectors or activities such as agriculture, housing, exports and education; and to fill "credit gaps" by making credit available to borrowers who cannot obtain it from private sources. Governments regulate the operations of financial intermediaries and insure and guarantee certain private financial liabilities. Under the British North America Act provincial governments have jurisdiction over financial institutions other than banks and banking operations.

In this chapter we will examine the more important government financial institutions, and some of the operations of government agencies and departments which assist savers, borrowers and lenders. Insofar as government activities in financial markets improve the allocation of credit they also provide greater efficiency in the allocation of resources generally.

GOVERNMENT SAVINGS BANKS

The federal government established the Post Office Savings Bank in 1867 "to enlarge the facilities (now) available for the deposit of small savings ... and to give the direct security of the nation to every depositor for repayment of all money deposited by him together with interest due thereon". Post Office savings accounts are not chequable nor can more than $100 be withdrawn from an account in any one day. Moreover, individual accounts are limited to a maximum of $10,000 plus interest due thereon. Deposit facilities are available at any Post Office which sells money orders. Total deposits with the Post Office Savings Bank have steadily declined. In 1955, for example, they were $37 million; in 1965, only $23 million.

The Newfoundland Savings Bank was established in 1834 and Province of Ontario Savings Offices in 1921. The Newfoundland Savings Bank ceased operations in 1962 when it was purchased by the Bank of Montreal. Unlike deposits with the Post Office Savings Bank those of the Province of Ontario Savings Office have grown; in 1955 they were $72 million, in 1965, $81 million.

Treasury Branches, established in 1938 by the government of the province of Alberta, provide financial services similar to those offered by chartered banks. The branches extend loans, and accept both current and savings deposits from the public and deposits from the Alberta government. Since 1962 they have also issued term deposit receipts.

THE INDUSTRIAL DEVELOPMENT BANK

In 1944 the federal government established the Industrial Development Bank (IDB) to provide a source of medium- and long-term finance for businesses unable to raise funds from other sources on reasonable terms and conditions. Particular consideration is given to the financing problems of small enterprises. Initially its lending was limited to manufacturing concerns but since 1961 it has been allowed to lend to virtually every kind of enterprise.

Most of the loans granted by the IDB have been for amounts of less than $25,000, indicating its orientation toward assisting relatively small businesses. It acts as a lender of last resort. Before granting a loan the IDB must be satisfied that a borrower seeking assistance cannot get alternative financing on "reasonable terms and conditions" elsewhere. Aside from this restriction,

TABLE 12-1

Deposits with Government Savings Institutions
End of 1965
(*millions of dollars*)

Post Office Savings Bank		23
Province of Ontario Savings Bank		81
Alberta Treasury Branches		
Public Deposits:		
Not bearing interest	32	
Bearing interest	57	
Provincial Government Deposits	14	
Term Deposit Receipts	19	122
Total Deposits		226

Source: Bank of Canada, Statistical Summary, 1966 Supplement.

the IDB will grant credit to provide fixed capital if the business requesting such credit shows a reasonable profit earning potential.

The Industrial Development Bank obtains its funds from its capital, from its reserves and from the issue of bonds. All its capital has been provided by the Bank of Canada which also purchases all its bonds. Borrowing by the IDB may not exceed ten times the aggregate amount of its paid-up capital and reserve fund. Its maximum allowable liability is $200 million. The authorized capital of the IDB is $75 million. As of September 30, 1966 its paid-up capital was $41 million.

With the emergence of new financial institutions and the extension of activities of other intermediaries, the Industrial Development Bank may have to change its lending policies in the future. Many loans once made only by the IDB are now granted by private financial intermediaries. If it is to survive, the IDB may have to become more venturesome and make loans with a high degree of risk. It may then run into opposition from those who do not consider this the proper role for a government institution.

PROVINCIAL GOVERNMENT DEVELOPMENT ORGANIZATIONS

Provincial governments have set up corporations, agencies and funds to provide assistance to local businessmen and to stimulate economic development generally within their boundaries. These include the New Brunswick Development Corporation (1963), the Industrial Estates Limited in

TABLE 12-2

Industrial Development Bank, Sources and Uses of Funds
Year end, 1965
(*millions of dollars*)

Liabilities (sources of funds)	
Capital and reserves	62.7
Bonds and debentures	205.1
Other liabilities	3.1
	270.9
Assets (uses of funds)	
Loans outstanding	264.3
All other	6.6
	270.9

Source: Bank of Canada, Statistical Summary, 1966 Supplement.

Nova Scotia (1958), the Industrial Enterprises in Prince Edward Island (1965), the General Investment Corporation in Quebec (1962), the Ontario Development Agency (1963), the Manitoba Development Fund (1959), the Saskatchewan Economic Development Fund (1966), and the Alberta Investment Fund (1966). The financial activities of these provincial organizations are generally much more diverse than those of the IDB. While some of them grant medium- and long-term credits with or without guarantees to a large variety of projects, others confine themselves to guaranteeing loans made by private financial institutions. Still others provide management advice or, as is the case with the General Investment Corporation in Quebec, participate in the management of corporations by purchasing the majority of their common shares.

CENTRAL MORTGAGE AND HOUSING CORPORATION

The Central Mortgage and Housing Corporation (CMHC) was established by the federal government in December 1945 to administer the National Housing Acts.[1] Its original purpose was to assist individuals to obtain financing for home construction and home improvement and to improve housing standards generally. With successive amendments to the legislation its functions and its operations have been expanded. Today the CMHC has eight main functions:

1. to insure mortgage loans made by financial institutions for the construction of new housing, the purchase of existing housing and to guarantee loans for home improvement and extension;

2. to make direct loans to individuals and at times to builders;

3. to make loans to non-profit organizations to assist in financing low rental housing projects for individuals and families of low income;

4. to provide student housing accommodation by making loans to a province or its agency, to a hospital, a school board, a university or college, to a cooperative association or a charitable corporation;

5. to make loans to municipalities for sewage treatment projects;

6. to acquire and improve land and construct and manage housing on its own account, or in cooperation with the federal government, the municipalities or the provinces.

---

[1] The first federal housing legislation was the Dominion Housing Act of 1935. In 1937 the Home Improvement Loans Guarantee Act was added and in the following year the original 1935 legislation was replaced by the National Housing Act. In 1944 this act was revised to include the Home Improvement Loans guarantee legislation. Another major revision followed in 1954.

7. to buy and sell insured mortgages and make short-term advances to financial institutions holding NHA mortgages;

8. to promote improvement and progress in housing standards and community planning and to engage in research necessary to achieve this.

Loans made under the National Housing Acts have been an important method of financing residential construction. For example, mortgage debt outstanding under the National Housing Acts at the end of 1965 amounted to $6 billion or approximately 35 per cent of all mortgage debt in Canada. About 75 per cent of the total mortgage debt is related to housing and the remainder to commercial or industrial buildings and to institutions. The characteristic feature of NHA loans is that they are insured by CMHC; so-called conventional loans are not insured. The insurance fee for NHA loans is paid by the borrower at a cost of about 2 per cent of the amount of the loan and is accumulated in a mortgage insurance fund established by CMHC. The National Housing Act specifies a maximum limit for each loan, a maximum maturity date and the maximum amount of interest that may be charged. NHA mortgage loans are made by the private financial intermediaries and, from time to time, directly by CMHC.

The quantity of mortgage credit supplied by the non-government institutional lenders is determined by the legal restraints on their portfolio practices, their attitudes toward liquidity and solvency, the size and growth of their assets, and their behaviour in response to changes in the yield differentials of different kinds of assets. The life insurance companies and the mortgage loan and trust companies, because of the long-term nature of their liabilities, have traditionally been the most important source of mortgage credit. They make mortgage loans by acquiring mortgages either directly from borrowers or indirectly from mortgage brokers. Moreover, because of the portfolio composition they desire and because of the difficulty of selling them in the financial markets, in most cases they hold these mortgages in their portfolios until they mature. Mortgages are secured by many different kinds and types of property with the result that they lack the homogeneity essential for the existence of a developed market. National Housing Act mortgages are more readily negotiable than conventional mortgages because they are insured and guaranteed by the government. It has been the desire of the government to develop a market where mortgages are regularly bought and sold before maturity — a so-called secondary mortgage market. Some progress in this direction has been made in recent years. In 1961, CMHC began to sell mortgages out of its own portfolio at auctions open to approved NHA lenders and members of the Investment Dealers Association. This encouraged the establishment of new financial institutions whose prime purpose is to purchase NHA mort-

TABLE 12-3

Central Mortgage and Housing Corporation, Assets and Liabilities
End of year, 1965
(*millions of dollars*)

Liabilities	
Capital—authorized and fully paid by Government of Canada	25
Borrowings from Government of Canada	2,328
Reserve Fund	5
Reserves of Insurance and Guarantee Funds*	157
Other liabilities	59
	2,574
Assets	
Cash	4
Loans	2,136
Investments under Federal - Provincial agreements	117
Assets of Insurance and Guarantee Funds	157
Other Assets	160
	2,574

* These assets consist essentially of Government of Canada securities, real estate and mortgages arising from the sale of real estate.

Source: Central Mortgage and Housing Corporation, Twentieth Annual Report, 1965.

gages in the secondary market with funds borrowed from the banks and from the sale of short-term paper and debentures in the securities markets. Future expansion of these companies, as well as the secondary mortgage market, will depend in large part upon the policies followed by CMHC. Its auctions, which have not been entirely successful, might be replaced by a policy whereby it continually stands prepared to sell mortgages at posted prices, a policy once used by the Bank of Canada to develop a government securities market. Moreover, CMHC might become more willing to discount NHA mortgages for dealers and institutions specializing in such mortgages. CMHC has the legal authority to provide short-term credit to holders of NHA mortgages but has been reluctant to establish a "discount window" on a basis similar to that of the Bank of Canada.

Direct loans made by CMHC from its own funds are made on a residual basis as part of the government's Winter House Building Incentive Programme and when funds are not generally available from non-government lenders. As a result of the government's desire to reduce its direct participation in the mortgage loan business, the chartered banks were allowed for the first time to enter the mortgage market on a restricted basis in 1954; the restrictions were largely removed with the amendments to the Bank Act in 1967. Bank participation in the mortgage market before 1967 did little to provide a more even flow of mortlage credit with the result that CMHC was often called upon to be the principal supplier of NHA loans. The maximum rates that institutional lenders were allowed to charge for NHA loans were usually changed by the government only after other market rates had already changed. During inflationary periods when other market rates moved up and the differential between these rates and those allowed on NHA loans narrowed, the institutional lenders turned away from NHA lending. In some periods the banks virtually stopped extending such loans. Two changes in the legislation were made after 1965 to provide a more even flow of residential credit from non-government sources. The first, made in November 1966, provided for a quarterly adjustment of the maximum rate permitted on NHA mortgages to allow this rate to fluctuate in relation to changing yields on long-term Government of Canada bonds. The second, made in the Bank Act revisions in 1967, removed most of the restrictions of bank mortgage lending. These changes, if supplemented by those we suggested for CMHC policy, would make possible the establishment of a well developed mortgage market in Canada: funds would then flow in a more orderly fashion into residential mortgage financing.

EXPORT CREDIT INSURANCE CORPORATION

The financing of export sales involves sellers in credit risks not usually associated with domestic trade. While some of these are strictly of a commercial nature, most are political risks over which neither the seller nor the buyer has any control. Foreign buyers may fail to meet their obligations due to war, changes in foreign exchange regulations and import quotas, or other political events. Because of these uncertainties and in order to encourage foreign sales, many governments have provided assistance to finance export trade originating within their jurisdictions. In Canada the Export Credits Insurance Act of 1944 provided for the establishment of the Export Credits Insurance Corporation (ECIC). This is a Crown agency which assists the financing of exports by insuring export credits (credit provided by Canadian exporters to foreign buyers) and by providing long-term export financing.

Credit insurance is an essential condition for obtaining export credit. The duration of such credit normally ranges from six months to five years, although more recently longer periods have been granted. The Export Credits Insurance Corporation sells insurance covering 90 per cent of losses from commercial and political risks; exporters assume the remaining risk. Since the government does not want to subsidize exporters, insurance rates are set at a level that allows ECIC to meet its operating expenses and net claims over the long run.

The ECIC sells three types of insurance policies. A **general commodities policy** covers consumer goods and other exports sold on short-term credit. The exporter can be issued such a policy from the time he receives an order until it is paid for (a contracts policy) or from the date of shipment only (a shipments policy). Exporters are generally required to insure their exports to all countries. Excluded are sales made against irrevocable letters of credit or paid for in advance, and those made to buyers in the United States. The wide variety of sales which must be insured allows ECIC to spread its risks; sales to the United States are excluded because insurance and credit is available through regular commercial channels.

A **capital goods policy** is issued to cover *individual* sales of capital goods such as plant equipment, locomotives, ships and heavy machinery sold on terms of payment which may extend to a maximum of five years.

A **service policy** is sold either on an individual basis or on a whole-turnover basis to cover engineering, construction, technical or similar services provided to foreigners on credit.

The total amount of insurance liability which ECIC may have outstanding at any one time is specified in the legislation. ECIC may be authorized by an order-in-council to provide insurance in excess of the specified maximum and for a longer than normal period, if the Minister of Trade and Commerce considers the export contract in question to be in the national interest. Such contracts are issued at the direct risk of the government and not ECIC.

In October 1965, ECIC extended its insurance facilities by undertaking to provide unconditional guarantees to the banks. This enables exporters to obtain non-recourse financing for sales of capital equipment sold on medium-term credit (180 days to five years).

Aside from its major function of providing insurance for export credits, ECIC has also provided since 1961 long-term financing for export sales of capital goods and related engineering and technical services. The long-term export financing program is intended to assist Canadian exporters in undertaking substantial projects in foreign countries on internationally accepted terms. Such financing can be obtained only if the foreign buyer and the country of purchase have a satisfactory credit standing and if the Canadian content of each sale is at least 80 per cent. The transaction must also give rise to significant employment and industrial benefits in Canada, as well as promising a continuing export trade.

GUARANTEED GOVERNMENT LOAN PLANS

Agriculture has long been an important sector of the Canadian economy, and governments recognized early the problem of providing farmers with a continuing source of funds to meet their requirements. In 1929 the federal government established the Canadian Farm Loan Board to make mortgage loans to farmers. This board was replaced in 1959 by the Farm Credits Corporation. The activities of the corporation were greatly expanded from those of its predecessor to include direct government lending to finance the purchase of farm land, as well as loans for the repayment of existing farm debts, the improvement of farms and the purchase of livestock and equipment.

In order to help farmers modernize and improve their productive facilities after the Second World War, the Farm Improvement Loans Act was introduced in 1944. The provisions of this act extend to farmers medium-term credit which is provided not from government funds but by the banks. Farm Improvement Loans are made by the banks; the federal government guarantees them against loss up to an amount equal to 10 per cent of the aggregate principal amount of the loans made by each bank, during each lending period of about three years.[2] The maximum amount of each loan, the purposes for which loans may be made, and the maximum term and rate of interest are specified in the act.

Most provincial governments also have agencies to provide financial assistance to farmers. For example, the Province of Quebec introduced a loan guarantee program in 1961. Its distinguishing features are the inclusion of the caisses populaires as lenders and the reimbursement of half the interest cost to the borrower. The Ontario Junior Farmer Establishment Loan Corporation makes direct loans to assist young Ontario farmers and provides partial guarantees for loans extended by the banks.

The Veterans' Business and Professional Loans Act was passed in 1946 to meet the special problems of re-establishing veterans in civilian life after the Second World War. Subsequently the benefits under this legislation were extended to cover veterans of the Korean War as well. The act authorizes the Minister of Finance to guarantee a bank against losses up to 25 per cent of the first $1 million of its approved loans to veterans and

---

2 The concept of providing partial guarantees for bank loans for specified purposes was introduced by the Home Improvement Loans Act of 1937. In 1945 the Home Improvement Loan program became part of the National Housing Act administered by the Central Mortgage and Housing Corporation. The Corporation guarantees each bank up to 5 per cent of the aggregate of all loans made by it under the Home Improvement Loans program.

15 per cent of the aggregate of loans in excess of $1 million. Guaranteed loans may be made to veterans in amounts specified in the act for the purchase of businesses of equipment for use in business, the purchase or repair of machinery, construction, repair and alteration or extension of buildings, and the purchase of land associated with business enterprise. Aside from these guaranteed loans, veterans may receive direct government loans and grants under other government legislation.[3]

With the success of its loan guarantee program to farmers, the federal government provided a similar program for fishermen. In 1955 the Fisheries Improvement Loans Act extended to fishermen the same type of medium-term credit available to farmers under the Farm Improvement Loans Act. Under the provisions of the act the banks and credit unions make the loans to fishermen. The government guarantee covers an amount equal to 15 per cent of the total loans made by an individual lender up to $500,000, and 10 per cent of the total over this amount. Loans may be made for the purchase or construction of fishing vessels, fishing equipment and shore installations; the major repair or overhaul of vessels; and the construction, repair or alteration of buildings required by a primary fishing enterprise and other prescribed improvements. The act specifies the maximum amount and terms of each loan, the minimum down payment required and the maximum rate of interest. Guaranteed loans to fishermen have been modest compared with those to farmers. Fishermen prefer to rely on fish processors and merchants who lend on the basis of commercial considerations as distinct from financial institutions which apply different and more rigorous criteria.

In 1961, the Small Businesses Loans Act further extended the federal government's loan guarantee program.[4] This act makes term credit available to small businesses engaged in manufacturing, wholesaling, retailing and services for the purpose of making a wide range of capital improvements. The federal government guarantees each bank against a loss of up to 10 per cent on the total of such loans. Specified conditions are similar to those of other government guaranteed loans.

Finally, in 1964 the government guaranteed loan program included bank loans to students. Under the Canada Student Loans Plan provincial authorities determine the eligibility of the individual student and the amount each student shall be allowed to borrow. The student does not have to provide security for such loans and the federal government guarantees them to the full amount.

---

[3] Re-establishment credits are available to discharged veterans for the purchase, repair or furnishing of a home or business and miscellaneous other purposes. Loans are also available under the Veterans' Land Act.

[4] A small business is considered to be one whose estimated gross fiscal yearly revenue is less than $250,000.

SELECTED READINGS

Brewis, T. N., *et. al., Canadian Economic Policy,* rev. ed., Toronto, Macmillan, 1965, Ch. 4 and 5.

Carr, D. W., and associates, *Farm Credit in Canada,* working paper prepared for the Royal Commission on Banking and Finance, Ottawa, 1962.

Dowsley, J. J., and Buck Hart, "The Short-Term Money Market and Instruments", *The Canadian Banker,* Vol. 73, Autumn, 1966, pp. 79-90.

Fullerton, D. G., *The Bond Market in Canada,* Toronto, Carswell, 1962.

Goldsmith, R. W., *Financial Intermediaries in the American Economy Since 1900,* Princeton, Princeton University Press, 1958.

Graham, J. F., *et. al., The Role of the Trust and Loan Companies in the Canadian Economy,* London, School of Business Administration, University of Western Ontario, 1965.

Gurley, John C., and Edward S. Shaw, *Money in a Theory of Finance,* Washington, Brookings Institution, 1960.

Helleiner, G. K., "Connections between United States and Canadian Capital Markets, 1952-1960", *Yale Economic Essays,* Vol. 2, Fall, 1962.

Hood, W. C., *Financing of Economic Acitivity in Canada,* study for the Royal Commission on Canada's Economic Prospects, Ottawa, Queen's Printer, 1958.

Horvitz, Paul M., *et. al., Private Financial Institutions,* Commission on Money and Credit, Englewood Cliffs, N.J. Prentice-Hall, 1963.

Johnson, A. W., and J. M. Andrews, *Provincial and Municipal Governments and the Capital Markets,* working paper prepared for the Royal Commission on Banking and Finance, Ottawa, 1962.

Mercure, Gilles, *Credit Unions and Caisses Populaires,* working paper prepared for the Royal Commission on Banking and Finance, Ottawa, 1962.

Pedoe, Arthur, *Life Insurance, Annuities and Pensions,* Toronto, University of Toronto Press, 1964.

Poapst, J. V., *The Residential Mortgage Market,* working paper for the Royal Commission on Banking and Finance, Ottawa, 1962.

Report of the Royal Commission on Banking Finance, Ottawa, Queen's Printer, 1964.

Wilson, J. G. L., "The Canadian Money Market Experiment", *Banca Nazionale del Lavoro Quarterly Review,* March, 1958.

Woodworth, G. Walter, *The Money Market and Monetary Management,* New York, Harper and Row, 1965.

PART FOUR

CENTRAL BANKING AND MONETARY CONTROL

13

THE NATURE AND CHARACTERISTICS OF CENTRAL BANKS

The essence of central banking is the control of the monetary system to serve the interests of the general public. These interests, as we shall see in the next chapter, have been translated into specific objectives which have evolved with the changing social and economic demands of society. In most countries the instruments of monetary control have been entrusted to institutions called central banks. For this reason the instruments of monetary control have come to be known as **central banking operations.** The prerogative for central banking operations has not always been that of central banks. For example, the Department of Finance in Canada carried on such operations before the establishment of a central bank, as did the United States Treasury before the establishment of the Federal Reserve System. With the growth of government economic activities which exert a significant influence on a country's monetary system, national government treasuries, as we shall see in Chapter 17, again undertake important central banking operations. However, in most instances these are closely related to the activities of central banks, which are entrusted with the overall responsibility of day-to-day monetary management.

While there is diversity among central banks, they have certain general characteristics. As their name implies, they occupy a pivotal position in the monetary and banking structure of the country in which they operate. In most cases central banking operations are entrusted to a single institution, such as the Bank of Canada. The exception to this rule is found in the United States where central banking operations are split among twelve regional banks whose activities are unified by a board created for this purpose.

The major characteristics of central banks include the authority to issue notes for circulation and to manage commercial bank reserves; their position as an organ of government; their role as a banker's bank; and their operations as a non-profit seeking institution.

Note Issue. In almost all countries commercial banks have been deprived of their right to issue notes for circulation. This authority has been given to central banks, either alone or in cooperation with national treasuries. Where a central bank does not have a complete monopoly, the preponderant amount of its notes in circulation gives it control of the volume of hand-to-hand money.

The Management of Bank Reserves. The note issue powers of a central bank are usually combined with powers to control the volume of the reserves of commercial banks. We observed in an earlier chapter that the credit creating ability of commercial banks and their ability to create deposits is determined by the cash reserves available to them. Therefore, where the central bank controls the note issue as well as the reserves of the commercial banks, it controls the two most important components of the money supply.

Because the central bank can provide the commercial banks with additional reserves, it is referred to as the **bank of last resort** or **lender of last resort.** In most countries today the central bank is the ultimate source of credit. Its ability to issue legal tender notes and to provide reserves to the commercial banks makes it responsible for feeding the demands for cash made by the public on the commercial bank and thereby for preventing monetary panics. The methods by which the central bank controls the community's cash — the monetary stock — is the topic of a subsequent chapter.

An Organ of Government. Although it has not always been the case, most central banks today are an arm of the government but enjoy some semblance of independence to prevent political tinkering. Usually central banks are either owned or operated, or both, by national governments. Many began, however, as private companies. The Bank of Canada, for instance, started as an institution wholly privately owned. In 1936 its stock was increased and the government by purchasing the additional stock gained a controlling interest. Two years later the government acquired all the stock held by private shareholders and became the sole owner. Other central banks which have been nationalized include those of England, France, Norway and the Netherlands.[1] In the United States, Italy and South Africa the central banks are owned privately. In the United States, for example, the twelve regional central banks are owned by the commercial banks who are members of the Federal Reserve System. Ownership, however, need not imply control. In the United States, the Board of Governors of the Federal Reserve System is appointed by

[1] These have all been nationalized since 1945.

the President with the advice and consent of the Senate. In other countries, including Chile, Venezuela, Pakistan, Japan, Belgium and Turkey, the stock of the central banks is owned jointly by the national government and by private interests. The management of these banks is either directly or indirectly controlled or supervised by their respective governments. The management of the Bank of Japan is chosen by the government which holds a little over 50 per cent of its stock.

In recent years the degree of independence of the central bank has been questioned in Canada, the United States and the United Kingdom. In all cases where there has been conflict, a closer relationship between the central bank and the government, particularly its treasury, has been recommended. In these countries it is now generally recognized that the government must be ultimately responsible for establishing the country's overall monetary policy but that the central bank must be able to determine how the policy goals are to be achieved.

While overall policy decisions must be made by the government, the central bank is usually its chief financial advisor and as such can influence policy. A governor of the Bank of England once said that the central bank has "the unique right to offer advice and to press such advice even to the point of nagging; but always of course subject to the supreme authority of the Government". [2]

Usually, the central bank is also the government's principal fiscal agent. As such it holds the government's deposit accounts, collects and transfers government funds, manages its foreign exchange holdings, pays the interest on the government debt, and manages the national debt. As the government's fiscal agent, and in cooperation with the national treasury, the central bank must ensure that the fiscal activities of the government do not unduly disrupt financial markets. As we shall see in later chapters, there are times when the central bank must take compensatory monetary action to cushion the impact of government fiscal activities.

The Banker's Bank. The central bank is often called a "banker's bank" because of the special relations it has with commercial banks and because the major part of its business is with commercial banks. As we have already noted, the central bank seeks to control the volume of commercial bank reserves. Part or all of these reserves are usually held on deposit with the central bank.

In Canada, as in many other countries, the central bank is restricted from direct participation in business transactions with the non-banking public. The Bank of Canada, for instance, does not hold deposits of the general public. The deposits it holds are those of the federal government, the chartered banks and the Quebec savings banks, and also those of for-

2 Quoted by R. S. Sayers, *Modern Banking*, 6th ed., Oxford, Clarendon Press, 1964, p. 67.

eign banks and governments. The only contact the Bank of Canada has with the non-bank public is the arrangement it has with a small group of investment dealers who can take advances from it.

Some central banks do deal directly with the general public. The Bank of England still looks after a few customers who patronized it when it was an important commercial bank. The Bank of France, the National Bank of Belgium, the Bank of Italy and the Bank of Finland are more or less commercial banks as well as central banks. The tendency today, however, is for central banks to reduce or eliminate their direct transactions with the general public. It is felt that a central bank cannot effectively solicit the cooperation of the commercial banks if it is in active competition with them for public business.

The Profit Motive. The prime function of a central bank is to control the monetary system under the guidelines of the government's monetary policy to serve the interests of the general public. While the *raison d'être* of a central bank cannot be to make profits they result nevertheless from the type of operations the bank conducts. Most of a central bank's funds consist of cash deposited with it by the commercial banks on which it usually pays no interest. These funds are invested in interest-bearing securities. The losses that a central bank may incur from time to time result from the sale of these securities at less than their original purchase price. Moreover, at times a central bank, for reasons to be explained later, must purchase securities with short maturities and low rates of interest and must forego opportunities for more profitable investments.

Where central banks are wholly owned by governments, the profits are turned over to the governments after provision is made for sufficient reserves. The Bank of Canada, having accumulated a rest fund of $25 million, pays its annual profits to the Receiver General of Canada. In 1964 the profits so paid amounted to $128 million.

In those countries where the central bank is not wholly owned by the national government, the dividends that the central bank may pay to its stockholders are limited in order to reduce the influence of the profit motive.

SELECTED READINGS

Aufricht, Hans, *Comparative Survey of Central Bank Law,* New York, Frederick A. Praeger, 1965.

Bagehot, Walter, *Lombard Street,* Homewood, Ill., Richard D. Irwin, 1962, reprinted from Scribner, Armstrong edition, New York, 1873.

Beckhart, Benjamin H. (ed.) *Banking Systems,* New York, Columbia University Press, 1954.

Dacey, W. Manning, *The British Banking Mechanism,* 5th ed., London, Hutchinson, 1964.

De Kock, M. H., *Central Banking,* 3rd ed., London, Staples Press, 1954.

Fousek, Peter G., *Foreign Central Banking: The Instruments of Monetary Policy,* Federal Reserve Bank of New York, 1957.

Hawtrey, R. G., *The Art of Central Banking,* London, Longmans, Green, 1932.

Sayers, R. S., *Banking in Western Europe,* Fair Lawn, N.J., Oxford University Press, 1962.

Sayers, R. S., and W. F. Crick (eds.), *Commonwealth Banking Systems,* Fair Lawn, N.J., Oxford University Press, 1965.

Sayers, R. S., *Modern Banking,* 6th ed., London, Oxford University Press, 1964.

Sayers, R. S., *Central Banking After Bagehot,* Oxford, Clarendon Press, 1957.

14

THE BANK OF CANADA

FOUNDING THE BANK

In 1933 in response to mounting criticism of monetary leadership and demands for monetary reform, the government appointed the Royal Commission on Banking and Finance with Lord Macmillan as chairman. The main terms of reference of the Macmillan Commission were to explore the desirability of establishing a central bank in Canada.

After touring the country and listening to the evidence and the various briefs presented to it, the Commission submitted its report on September 22, 1933. The report recommended, against the wishes of the chartered banks, the establishment of a central bank. However, it cautioned that such a bank "could not cure all the economic ills of Canada". The real root of the chartered banks opposition was their reluctance to give up their own note issues which were a source of both profit and prestige.

Unlike most royal commission reports, the Macmillan report was acted upon almost immediately and most of its recommendations were adopted. In 1934 Parliament passed the Bank of Canada Act establishing the country's central bank. The structure and the powers of the Bank as defined in the act were intended to make it immune to both excessive private interference and political pressures. Since all the stock of the Bank was sold to the public, it was at the start a privately owned bank. However, private interference was considered to have been minimized by the provisions of the act. Individual holdings of stock were limited and no one directly connected with chartered banks was permitted to hold Bank of Canada stock. Officers and employees of banks and financial institutions were not eligible for appointment as Governor, Deputy Governor or Assistant Deputy Governor of the Bank. Dividends paid to stockholders were limited to 4½ per cent; any excess profits accrued to the government. There were also provisions to establish a link with the government but at the same time to prevent undue political pressures. The first Governor and directors of the Bank were to be appointed by the government and all subsequent directors were to be elected by the shareholders; all future appointments of Governor and Deputy Governor were to be approved by the government. The Deputy Minister of Finance was made a non-voting member of the Board of Directors and its Executive Committee. To be effective the decisions of these two bodies required the approval of the Governor of the Bank.

In 1936, the Liberal government which had assumed office in the fall of 1935 fulfilled one of its election promises by bringing the Bank of Canada under closer government control. In an amendment to the Bank of Canada Act the Bank was required to issue additional shares which were purchased by the government thus giving it 51 per cent ownership. The extra directors that the government added to the Bank's board confirmed its control of the Bank. In 1938 the government acquired all of the shares of the Bank completing its nationalization.

MANAGEMENT OF THE BANK

The Bank of Canada is managed by a Board of Directors composed of the Governor, the Deputy Governor and twelve directors. The directors are appointed for three-year terms by the Minister of Finance with the approval of the Cabinet (the Governor in Council). They must be selected from diversified occupations and no person is eligible who is a director, partner, officer or employee of a firm or organization with whom the Bank has direct dealings.[1] In practice, the basis for appointments has been regional rather than occupational. The directors appoint the Governor and Deputy Governor, also with Cabinet approval, for seven-year terms. In the transaction of the business of the Bank each of the fourteen members of the Board has one vote. The Deputy Minister of Finance is also a member of the Board but does not have the right to vote. The Board normally meets eight times a year. Between meetings the Executive Committee acts for the Board with all the powers of the Board. The Committee is composed of the Governor, the Deputy Governor, two directors selected by the Board and the Deputy Minister of Finance (without a vote). Its decisions must be submitted to the next meeting of the Board. The Committee, for example, determines "the minimum rate at which the Bank is prepared to discount or rediscount bills or to make advances ...". A by-law of the Bank specifies that the Executive Committee shall meet at least once every week and in practice meetings are attended by any director who is in Ottawa (where the Bank's head office is located) on the day of the meeting.

---

[1] Under the Bank of Canada Act this includes a chartered bank, a bank to which the Quebec Savings Banks Act applies or an investment dealer who acts as a primary distributor of new Government of Canada securities.

In order to permit more frequent meetings of the Board, an amendment to the Bank of Canada Act in 1967 increased the aggregate of fees that may be paid to all directors exclusive of expenses from $30,000 a year to $60,000 a year. In recent years, to acquaint the Board with the country's regional problems, some of its regular meetings have been held in centres other than Ottawa. This new policy is probably a response to a suggestion made by the Porter Commission that the Board establish regional advisory committees.[2]

RESPONSIBILITY FOR MONETARY POLICY

From the beginning the Bank's function was assumed to be that of an independent body carrying out national policy in the public interest. The Bank's duty was thought to be the formulation and implementation of the day-to-day money management policy that would realize the government's long-run monetary policy. It was assumed that ultimate responsibility for overall monetary policy was the government's alone, but that execution of it should be left to the Bank's management. This was broadly the consensus of opinion as enunciated from time to time before 1956 by both Graham Towers and James Coyne, the first and second Governors of the Bank, and by all Ministers of Finance up to that time. Both the Bank and the government agreed that a Governor who found himself in fundamental conflict with government policy should resign.

In 1956, however, a difference of opinion arose between James Coyne, Governor of the Bank, and Walter Harris, Minister of Finance. The Bank, at a time when unemployment was high and economic growth had slowed, was pursuing a tight money policy. Harris declared that the Bank was responsible for the restrictive monetary policy, not the government. In 1959, Donald Fleming, then Minister of Finance, reaffirmed that the Bank and not the government was responsible for the monetary policy being followed. By 1960 it was evident that the Bank's monetary policy was conflicting directly with the government's fiscal measures. James Coyne refused to resign even after the government had asked him to do so. The government was obliged to introduce legislation declaring vacant the office of the Governor of the Bank of Canada. Coyne finally resigned while this legislation was being considered in the Senate and it never became law.

Louis Rasminsky became the third Governor of the Bank of Canada on July 24, 1961. Upon assuming office he issued a statement making public his views of the relationship between the Bank and the government. He presented two main principles: "(1) in the ordinary course of

[2] *The Report of the Royal Commission on Banking and Finance*, 1964, p. 548.

events, the Bank has the responsibility for monetary policy, and (2) if the Government disapproves of the monetary policy being carried out by the Bank it has the right and the responsibility to direct the Bank as to the policy which the Bank is to carry out.... If this policy, as communicated to the Bank, was one which the Governor felt he could not in good conscience carry out, his duty would be to resign and to make way for someone who took a different view".[3] On the same day that Rasminsky issued his statement the Minister of Finance, Donald Fleming, issued a concurrent one. The Porter Commission, whose appointment was in part initiated by the so-called "Coyne Affair" accepted Rasminsky's views and recommended "... a dual system of responsibility under which the Bank formulates monetary policy and executes it from day-to-day but under which the government must accept full and continuous responsibility for the policy being followed, although not in the normal course for the details of its execution". Moreover, in order to avoid another bitter controversy between the Governor of the Bank and the government, the Commission recommended that the Bank of Canada Act be amended to provide the Minister of Finance with the authority to issue a directive to the Bank if the government disapproves of its policy.[4] Subsequently in the 1967 amendments to the Bank of Canada Act the relationship between the government and the Bank in regard to monetary policy was defined. The act now makes clear that there be continuous consultation between the government and the Bank. In the event of a disagreement over monetary policy between the Minister of Finance and the Bank, the Minister may, after consultation with the Governor of the Bank and with the approval of the Cabinet, give the Governor a written directive on the policy to be followed. Such a directive, with which the Bank must comply, must be in specific terms and applicable for a specified period. It must also be immediately published in the *Canada Gazette* and laid before Parliament within fifteen days after it is issued, or, if Parliament is not sitting, during the first fifteen days after Parliament resumes sitting.[5]

The 1967 amendment to the Bank of Canada Act gives the Bank of Canada sufficient independence to be an institution oriented to financial markets, and at the same time through the process of directives, insures that the Bank's monetary policy is also government policy. Moreover, as

3 Bank of Canada, *Annual Report of the Governor to the Minister of Finance*, 1961, pp. 1-2.

4 *Report of the Royal Commission on Banking and Finance*, 1964, p. 543.

5 The amendment to the Bank of Canada Act which provides for government directives also removed the previous power of the Governor to veto any action or decision of the Board of Directors or the Executive Committee, subject to informing the Minister in writing of the circumstances within seven days. The Cabinet was then required to confirm or disallow the veto. This provision was originally put into the Act when the directors were elected by private shareholders and had long since become an anachronism.

directives have to be made public and presented to Parliament there is the additional assurance that government policy is also public policy.

It has been suggested that the central bank should be a department of government or little more than a technical arm of the Treasury. This view is held by those who feel that central bank independence cannot be reconciled with the democratic process since the electorate must be able to hold the government responsible for all details of public economic policy, including monetary policy.[6] The traditional consensus of opinion in Canada has been that the Bank of Canada should be independent enough to be immune from the gusts of political fancy. The very nature of central banking requires the Bank of Canada to operate continuously in financial markets. It can do so effectively only it if is free of all suspicion of government interference. Moreover, in its day-to-day market operation the bank must be allowed complete flexibility unencumbered by the need to seek prior approval from a minister of government for its every action. Monetary management can be effectively directed toward meeting the objectives of public policy within the traditional framework of central bank independence in Canada counterbalanced by the 1967 revisions of the Bank of Canada Act which call for continuous consultation between the Bank and the government, for government directives and for public debate of monetary issues. In the final analysis, the degree of independence which the Bank of Canada can command depends upon "the objectivity and cogency of its views as judged in the light of experience and on the proven degree of competence it displays in performing its own specialized role. It depends, too, on the contribution that it is able to make to the public understanding of economic and financial issues ... and in elucidating the basic rationale underlying the policies it has followed."[7]

FUNCTIONS OF THE BANK

The functions of the Bank of Canada are outlined in the preamble to the Bank of Canada Act which states that the Bank is to "regulate credit and currency in the best interests of the economic life of the nation, to control and protect the external value of the national monetary unit and to mitigate by its influence fluctuations in the general level of production, trade, prices and employment so far as may be possible within the scope

---

[6] See H.S. Gordon, "The Bank of Canada in a System of Responsible Government", *Canadian Journal of Economics and Political Science*, Vol. 27, No. 1, February 1961, pp 13-22, reprinted in James P. Cairns and H.H. Binhammer, *Canadian Banking and Monetary Policy*, Toronto, McGraw-Hill, 1965, pp. 105-116.

[7] Louis Rasminsky, "The Role of the Central Banker Today", Per Jacobsson Memorial Lecture, Rome, November 9, 1966, reprinted in *The Canadian Banker*, Vol, 74, Spring, 1967, pp. 25-44

of monetary action, and generally to promote the economic and financial welfare of the Dominion". As we shall see in the following chapter, the best interests of the economic life of the nation are concerned with high levels of employment, domestic and external monetary stability, appropriate economic growth to provide rising standards of living, and an acceptable degree of economic freedom. The burden of achieving these broad goals does not fall on the Bank alone; it is shared with the government in its fiscal policy, debt management policy and other financial policies. The success of the Bank's monetary policies can be no greater than that of other public policies used to achieve the economic goals of the nation.

One of the more immediate concerns of the Bank of Canada is to provide the nation with an acceptable medium of exchange. On the day it began operations, the Bank took over the note issuing function of the federal government and provision was made for the gradual curtailment of the note issuing privileges of the chartered banks.[8] It was not until 1945, when the chartered banks were no longer permitted to issue any notes for circulation in Canada, that the Bank of Canada received the monopoly on note issue.[9] Bank of Canada notes are legal tender and, except for gold coin and subsidiary coin in very small amounts, are the only form of legal tender in Canada.

The Bank of Canada Act of 1934 required the Bank to redeem its notes in gold "in the form of bars containing approximately four hundred ounces of gold". Although this provision remained in the act until 1967, it had been suspended from the beginning. Initially the Bank was also required to maintain a gold reserve of at least 25 per cent against its outstanding notes and deposit liability. This requirement was suspended in 1940 when, following the outbreak of the Second World War, the Bank's holdings of gold and foreign exchange were transferred to the Foreign Exchange Control Board and after its abandonment to the Foreign Exchange Fund Account. In 1967 the gold reserve requirements specified in the Bank of Canada Act were repealed.[10]

---

8 When the Bank of Canada assumed the responsibility for the redemption of Dominion notes, the government gave the Bank $69 million in gold, $1 million in silver and $115 million in Dominion securities to offset this liability.

9 After 1934 the note issue of a chartered bank was limited to the amount of its paid-up capital. However, beginning in 1936 this limit was reduced by 5 per cent per annum and beginning in 1940 by 10 per cent per annum, so that by the end of 1945 it was 25 per cent of a bank's paid-up capital. The 1944 revisions to the Bank Act prohibited any further issue or reissue of chartered bank notes. This gave the Bank of Canada the sole privilege of issuing notes for circulation in Canada. In 1950 after the chartered banks made a cash payment to the Bank of Canada the Bank assumed the liability for all chartered bank notes still outstanding.

10 When the Bank began operations it actually held gold in excess of the 25 per cent re-

In managing the country's monetary system the Bank of Canada has the authority to employ the techniques usually associated with central banking. These are considered in the next chapter.

The Bank of Canada is an important arm of government insofar as it is the government's fiscal agent, a function it performs without charge. As fiscal agent the Bank operates the government's deposit account, handles debt management and foreign exchange transactions for the government, and acts as an advisor. Debt management involves the Bank in arranging for the sale of new government security issues, for the retirement of securities and for the payment of interest. Aside from looking after the foreign exchange business of the government the Bank also manages the Foreign Exchange Fund Account on the instructions of the Minister of Finance.

In addition to the accounts of the Government of Canada and the chartered banks, the Bank of Canada operates deposit accounts for the banks to which the Quebec Savings Banks Act applies and for foreign central banks and international financial institutions. The Bank may enter into an agreement with a provincial government to act as its banker and fiscal agent. No arrangements of this nature have been made to date.

Although the Bank carries out all its duties without the profit motive in mind, its operations produce an annual surplus. Before 1956 surpluses were allowed to accumulate at a specified rate in the Bank's surplus or rest fund with the remainder being turned over to the government (the Receiver General). In 1956 the total amount of the Bank's rest fund reached $25 million. As this is the maximum specified in the Bank Act, all of the Bank's annual surpluses have been paid to the government since that time.

serve requirement. In addition to the $69 million in gold received from the government for taking over the redemption of Dominion notes, the Bank also received $37 million in gold which the chartered banks had to surrender as part of their cash reserves. In 1935 when gold was revalued from $20.67 (U. S.) to $35.00 (U. S.) an ounce the profit realized by the Bank was turned over to the chartered banks and the Exchange Fund. This was provided for in the original legislation.

SELECTED READINGS

Bank of Canada, *Evidence of the Governor Before the Royal Commission on Banking and Finance,* Ottawa, May, 1964, pp. 113-115.

Cairns, James P., and H.H. Binhammer, *Canadian Banking and Monetary Policy,* Toronto, McGraw-Hill, 1965, Part 3.

Jamieson, A.B., *Chartered Banking in Canada,* Toronto, Ryerson Press, 1966.

McIvor, R. Craig, *Canadian Monetary, Banking and Fiscal Development,* Toronto, Macmillan, 1961.

Neufeld, E.P., *Bank of Canada Operations and Policy,* Toronto, University of Toronto Press, 1958.

15

MONETARY POLICY AND ITS OBJECTIVES

While the term "monetary policy" is of comparatively recent origin, monetary policy has been pursued since time immemorial. In its broadest sense, monetary policy has been defined as "the attitude of the political authority towards the monetary system of the community under its control".[1] In ancient and early medieval times, the choice and maintenance of the monetary standard, the determination of the value of the monetary unit and the enforcement of the state prerogative of coinage were all part and parcel of monetary policy. The attempts, at first of the medieval bullionists and later the mercantilists, to attract and maintain bullion and coin "within the realm" are further examples of early monetary policy.

Today monetary policy is more narrowly defined and is commonly considered to be *the management of the monetary system toward the achievement of certain objectives.* These objectives should serve to enhance public welfare. Unfortunately this has not always been the case, in either early or more recent times. For example, Cleopatra debased the coinage to finance her life of luxury; Hitler pursued inflationary monetary policies after 1933 to prepare for and wage his imperialistic wars; and the communist controlled regime in Hungary after the Second World War depreciated the currency to wipe out all "bourgeois" wealth and income.

EARLY CONCEPTS

When banking institutions developed or were established to conduct central banking operations their prime objectives were to finance the government, to establish and maintain a sound and stable currency system, to

[1] Einzig, Paul, *Monetary Policy: Ends and Means*, Baltimore, Penguin Books, 1964, p. 48.

provide an elastic money supply and to provide effective supervision of banking activities.

As we have already seen, both the United States and the United Kingdom provide excellent examples of the early intention to establish institutions as a method to finance government activity. During the First and Second World Wars the central banks in both these countries and in Canada played an important role in facilitating their respective governments' war expenditures.

The early commercial banks were established to furnish an identifiable currency and a sound monetary system. However, a relatively long time passed before it was recognized that a commercial banking system's ability to supply money in the form of bank notes and deposits rested on a rather vulnerable foundation. The Bank of England, long before it was recognized as performing central banking operations, rescued the English banks and the English monetary system from disaster. It was able to play this role not because its notes were legal tender but because they had general acceptability. When other countries developed or established their central banking institutions, they gave them the power to issue legal tender. The central banks thus became bankers' banks which could supply reserves to the banking system. A central bank which can supply reserves is a prerequisite of a sound monetary system.

At first central banking institutions were not intended to use discretionary power to change the stock of money in circulation. It was thought that an automatic mechanism existed which would, over the long run, provide the proper amount of money. The commercial loan theory explained how the commercial banks supplied their liabilities (notes and deposits) to meet the needs of society at large. Central banking institutions existed to provide the commercial banks with adequate reserves to allow them to go about their business. The monetary system was regulated only by the fact that the amount of reserves central banking institutions could supply to commercial banks was limited by the specie reserves of the central banks. The amount of specie reserves at any one time depended upon past accumulation, current production and international flows. The discovery of gold in California and Australia toward the middle of the nineteenth century, and in South Africa, the Klondike and Alaska toward the end of the century resulted in rising trends in the volume of money and in prices. This was due not to discretionary monetary policy but to the automatic working of the gold standard. Moreover the lack of discretionary policy allowed deflationary conditions to occur between these two periods of gold rushes when the world's monetary gold supply did not keep up with the growing demands of business.

After the First World War the concept of a managed gold standard was introduced. It aimed at maintaining stability by neutralizing the effects on the price level of unwanted increases or decreases of the gold reserves. During the early 1920's the return to the gold standard remained the major concern of monetary policy in many countries. However, there began to appear a growing tendency to focus more attention on internal economic conditions and the need for greater business and price stability. The newly created Federal Reserve System in the United States, for instance, considered that its main purpose was to meet the legitimate needs of business.

In most countries during the 1920's monetary stability was interpreted to mean monetary expansion, while price stability, a widely accepted objective of policy, was interpreted as the prevention of falling prices. Monetary expansion was hailed by many as the major reason for the prosperity of that time. Few realized that it was encouraging the speculative boom which was soon to end in collapse.

Economic collapse in the early thirties ushered in a long period of stagnation and unemployment. Largely as a result of the new economic philosophy of John Maynard Keynes, monetary policy as a means to recovery was abandoned in favour of fiscal policy.

During the Second World War monetary policy was directed toward facilitating government financial requirements while direct controls were used to maintain price stability. Monetary policy was generally expansionary in order to make a sufficient amount of credit available and to hold interest rates at a level which would minimize the government's borrowing costs.

Monetary expansion was continued after the war in Britain, the United States and Canada. The primary reason for this was the fear of a postwar recession. Moreover since all three governments had sold their debts during the war to a wide cross-section of their citizens, they considered it their moral obligation to allow the holders of this debt to cash it without loss. An expansionary monetary policy was one way of holding interest rates down and bond prices up.[2] For some years after the war, monetary expansion and rising prices were a way of life. Indeed, many thought this was necessary to ensure an increase in output, and at the same time to secure a market for the larger output. Perhaps one reason why a policy of moderate inflation gained wide acceptance in the Anglo-Saxon countries was that none of these countries had experienced runaway inflation for over a generation.

When monetary policy again returned to its former respectability in the early 1950's, its attempts first to halt inflation and later to stop recurring conditions of deflation proved disappointing. Some thought that monetary policy had become an inadequate tool when used alone for

[2] The relationship between bond prices and interest rates is explained in Chapter 22.

short-run stabilization. Others felt that its failures were due not so much to its ineffectiveness as to its inappropriate use. Wide criticism prompted a reassessment of monetary policy in Britain, the United States and Canada. A reappraisal of objectives followed.

NATIONAL ECONOMIC GOALS

Today the broad objectives of monetary policy are considered to be those of economic policy generally. Monetary policy must be conducted so as to assist a country in meeting its economic as well as its political and social goals. These goals include a high and stable level of employment; reasonable price stability; a high rate of economic growth; a sound external financial position; the equitable sharing of economic benefits and burdens; and an acceptable degree of economic freedom.

A HIGH AND STABLE LEVEL OF EMPLOYMENT

When an economy fails to utilize fully its labour resources, as well as its other resources, it does not achieve its economic potential and produces at a level which usually creates economic and social hardships for a wide cross-section of the population. Unemployed labour services result in a loss of production which can never be recovered. National output does not realize its full potential and certain sectors of the population are unable to share in what is being produced.

Full employment exists when all the owners of productive services, including labour services, are successful in voluntarily selling the desired amount of services at the prevailing market price. In a modern society where demands and technology are continually changing one hundred per cent full employment is impossible. This is why we now speak of a high level of employment distinct from full employment as an economic objective. Progress and change require readjustments. For instance, with automation many machines that were formerly operated by persons with particular skills are now run by electronic gadgetry which in turn is operated by persons with entirely different and new training. The machinist remains unemployed until he is retrained or until he succeeds somehow in finding a job still requiring his traditional skills. It is impossible to eliminate this type of unemployment in the short run if we are to reap the fruits of change. However, it should be society's concern to ensure that the required readjustments are made as easily and as quickly as possible. A high and stable level of employment, therefore, requires a growing and expanding economy which will enable a growing labour force to find *useful* employment and which will make readjustments less difficult.

REASONABLE PRICE STABILITY

Reasonable price stability as a goal of economic policy is taken to mean the minimizing of upward movement of the general level of prices. It implies that individual (or relative) prices are allowed to adjust to changes in underlying demand and supply conditions, thereby acting as allocators of resources.

When we speak of price stability we are referring to the general level of prices and not to relative prices. Relative prices refer to the price of one good as compared with that of another. These prices must remain flexible in order to play their role as allocators of resources in the economy. For example, an increase in the price of a particular good may signal the existence of serious bottlenecks or shortages which may be eliminated by the attraction of additional resources in response to the price signal. However, changes in relative prices are not always the perfect allocator of resources because they may occur due to the exercise of market power and various discretionary processes employed in setting prices.

The case for reasonable price stability as a goal for economic policy rests upon the charges that can be made against inflation. These include the inequitable distribution of income, the impairment of international competitiveness, the destabilizing effects on the economy and the reduced usefulness of money.

Inflation produces an arbitrary and often capricious redistribution of income causing hardships to many people. With a general increase in prices some prices and money rates of return rise faster than others. As a result, persons or groups whose money incomes remain fixed or rise more slowly than prices are rising lose command over goods and services. Most severely affected by inflation are persons whose money incomes are absolutely fixed such as some pension recipients and persons whose wealth is held in a form that is fixed in dollar terms such as bonds and most life insurance. Insofar as these people are unable to defend themselves against erosion in the real purchasing power of their incomes, inequity and hardship accompany inflation.

Canada depends upon selling a large proportion of its total output to foreigners. Exporting has been necessary to keep resources employed and to provide the means for paying for the goods and services that Canadians are required to purchase from foreigners. In order for Canadian exports to sell competitively in world markets, costs and prices in Canada cannot rise significantly more than they do in other countries, particularly in the United States. If they do the consequences are serious for Canadian export industries, the import-competing industries and the economy generally.

Businessmen may come to consider continuous price increases as the normal course of events. They will add to their inventories and plant with the intention of escaping higher costs and prices in the future. Moreover, they will be inclined to proceed with less caution in the hope that mistakes can be compensated by higher prices in the future. As a result inflation leads to the misdirected use of resources, inefficiency and waste, which have destabilizing effects on the economy and eventually may end in economic recession or depression.

Finally, as prices continue to rise, the public will try to protect itself against anticipated further increases. People will make every attempt to move out of money into goods; this will only push prices still higher. Inflation becomes self-generating, ending in hyperinflation where the value of money and its usefulness as a standard unit of account, a store of value and a medium of exchange is destroyed. Hyperinflation inevitably leads to economic collapse.

ECONOMIC GROWTH

For a long time it was thought by many that in the long run material progress, in the form of a rising standard of living and an increase of accumulated wealth, was a natural automatic process. Whenever this secular process was interrupted by wars and crises, it resumed its course automatically. Before the Second World War totalitarian states introduced plans for stimulating secular growth. Others relied on the maintenance of full employment as necessarily serving the cause of growth. It was not until after the mid-1950's that it became generally understood that policies aiming at full employment and those aiming at growth are not necessarily identical. Indeed there are some today who would give policies directed toward long-term growth precedence over those directed at cyclical stabilization. They base their conclusions on the inability of western economies to stabilize cyclical disturbances in the postwar period. Inappropriate decisions resulting in misdirected and ill-timed policies may have accentuated rather than stabilized cyclical fluctuations.

A high and sustained rate of economic growth is desirable because it facilitates a higher standard of living and achievement of overall economic and social objectives. For example, with a high rate of growth, desirable public services can be expanded without curtailing private consumption.

Long-term expansion of the potential output or productive capacity of the economy requires an increase in the quantity of productive resources which can be put to use and an increase in their productivity. Productive resources include both labour resources and physical resources such as stocks of machinery, equipment, buildings and structures, land and natural resources. When, during any period, resources (or productive inputs) are fully employed any increase in total output will depend upon the availability of additional resources from other countries and an increase in the productivity of the resources being employed.

The Economic Council of Canada has stressed that productivity gains are the real source of improvement in the living standards of a nation.[3] Furthermore, a rapid and sustained increase in productivity may dampen price increases and improve international competitiveness. Productivity is defined as the increase in output yielded by each quantitative unit of resources available in the economy. It is usually expressed as the ratio of the physical volume of output to the manpower required to produce it. Increases in productivity result from improvement in the quality of factors of production (such as a more educated and skilled labour force and improved technology) and improvements in the efficiency with which the productive factors are combined (such as more efficient organization and production processes). More specialization, larger scale output and shifts of resources to more productive lines of employment also lead to increased productivity.

Economic growth requires not only the availability of an appropriate amount of resources and an increase in their productivity, but also a high level of employment of resources on a sustained basis. Hence economic policy must be oriented not only to maintain the supply capabilities of the economy, but also to maintain stable and sustained expansion of final demand for goods and services. Canada's success in pursuing appropriate policies to facilitate steady and balanced economic growth depends upon the rate of growth being maintained in the world economy.

A SOUND EXTERNAL POSITION

Under the international gold standard the maintenance of the standard became the over-riding objective of most countries even if it meant an increase in unemployment and price fluctuations. Although we are no longer on the gold standard those countries who are members of the International Monetary Fund have agreed to hold the external value of their currencies within relatively narrow limits. Toward this end it has become important for nations to pursue policies, especially monetary policy, which will maintain either large and liquid foreign exchange reserves, or an economic and financial position to make possible the securing of international credit when required. When international payments are facilitated international trade is encouraged. This is important for a country such as Canada. In 1966, for example, the value of exports of goods and

3 The Economic Council of Canada, *Towards Sustained and Balanced Economic Growth*, Second Annual Review, Ottawa, Queen's Printer, 1965.

services was 22 per cent and the value of imports of goods and services was 24 per cent of Canadian gross national product. Overvaluation of the dollar could close foreign markets to Canadian exporters. On the other hand, undervaluation of the dollar could raise the cost of importing, promote inflation and impair growth.

The strength of Canada's external position depends not only on her own domestic policies but also on those followed in other countries. It is in Canada's best interests to bring about a strong world monetary, trade and economic system.

OTHER OBJECTIVES

Economic objectives are not ends in themselves; they cannot be defined in a vacuum. For instance, economic growth is undesirable if as a result the poor become poorer while the rich grow richer. This is why we include as an objective the equitable sharing of economic benefits and burdens in a country. Moreover, economic benefits are undesirable, and probably not attainable, if a society's economic freedoms are taken away. The definition of "equitable" and the degree of economic and social freedom considered desirable varies from country to country. However, once these decisions are made it becomes the objective of the society to see that they are preserved in the attainment of its other goals.

COMPROMISE AND TRADE-OFFS

In principle, high levels of employment, price stability, economic growth and a sound external position are mutually consistent. In practice, however, inconsistencies or conflicts may at times develop. There is now fairly general agreement that the objectives of price stability and a high level of employment are independent of the long-run rate of economic growth. The important determinants of the latter are educational improvement and long-run capital accumulation. Because capital accumulation has been closely associated with Canada's external position, conflict between secular growth and a strong external position could arise if such a position implies less dependence on foreign capital for Canadian development.

It is now generally conceded that too much emphasis on full employment will usually prevent restraint necessary to maintain price stability. The relationship between the annual average percentage increase in prices and the average percentage rate of unemployment is depicted by the trade-off zone shown in Figure 15-1. This gives a rough approximation of the menu of choice that the Canadian policy makers had between

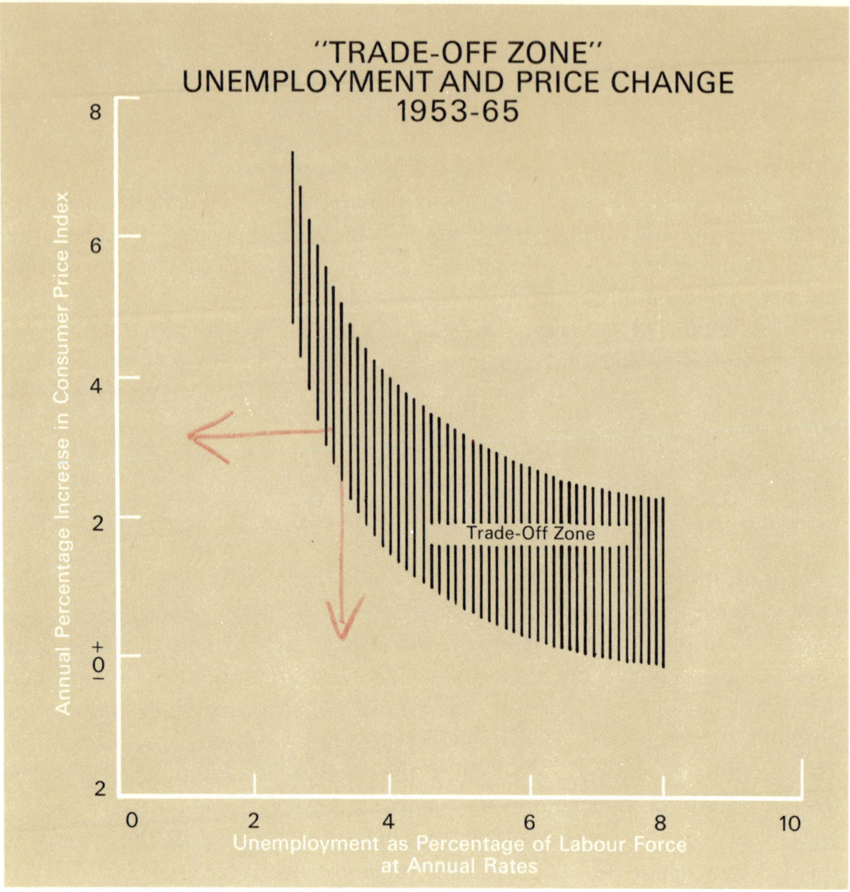

Figure 15-1

different degrees of unemployment and price stability in the period 1953-1965. [4]

If we interpret price stability in terms of an annual percentage increase in the consumer price index between zero and 2½ per cent, we have had to trade off a little over 8 per cent of unemployment, the social cost of price stability. On the other hand, if we consider as desirable an annual rate of unemployment equal to 2¼ per cent we would have had to trade off an annual rate of rise in the consumer price index of between 5 and 7 per cent. Presented with such choice, the essential task in the short run is to use the various policy instruments to keep the economy away from the upper and lower extremities of the trade-off zone. That is to say, both relatively high annual percentage increases in price and high rates of unemployment must be avoided.

---

[4] Our discussion as well as Figure 15-1 is based on the Economic Council of Canada, "Prices, Productivity and Employment", *Third Annual Review*, Queen's Printer, Ottawa, 1966.

In the longer run, new policy instruments should be introduced, and an optimal mix of policy instruments should be sought to improve the trade-offs. In terms of Figure 15-1 we must seek ways to shift the whole trade-off zone downward and to the left.[5] This may be difficult if foreign prices, particularly those in the United States, rise appreciably faster than Canadian prices. Under these circumstances the tendency will be for the trade-off zone to shift upward and to the right increasing the social cost of price stability in terms of unemployment. To prevent the trade-off zone from shifting upward and, further, to induce it to shift downward the choice of policies and their use must be kept under constant surveillance.

MONETARY POLICY AND ULTIMATE GOALS

Monetary policy must be directed toward the ultimate goals defined previously. The day-to-day role of monetary policy, however, must concern itself more directly with the attainment of an intermediate target — that of providing appropriate money and credit conditions. The intermediate target of monetary policy can be viewed as a policy instrument used to achieve society's ultimate goals.

The management of the monetary system is only one of many instruments required to attain society's ultimate objectives. Jan Tinbergen of the Netherlands School of Economics has shown that the minimum requirement for organizing economic policy is the use of at least as many distinct instruments or strategies of policy as there are economic objectives and constraints.[6] Even if these minimum conditions are met, the instruments must be mixed and blended properly. For example, assume that a deficit in the country's international balance of payments is to be corrected at the same time that internal economic expansion is to be promoted. If monetary policy is the only instrument available, easy money and credit conditions would improve internal economic conditions but worsen the balance of payments deficits. If, however, fiscal policy is available as an additional instrument, an appropriate mix of two distinct strategies can be employed. Depending on the country's exchange rate system fiscal ease might be introduced to improve internal economic conditions while at the same time monetary tightness might be employed to assist the country's external position.

[5] The Economic Council of Canada in its *Third Annual Review* emphasized the use of policies "designed to improve the mobility and adapability of manpower, to strengthen productivity gains, to maintain effective competition, to facilitate adjustments to change, and to deal with pressure points and bottlenecks". *Ibid.* p. 145.

[6] Tinbergen, Jan, *On The Theory of Economic Policy*, Amsterdam, North-Holland Publishing Co., 1952.

Monetary management as an instrument must be judiciously administered with an eye to encompassing all the ultimate goals. Canadian experience has proven that an overconcentration of one instrument on one particular objective can produce gross errors. Unfortunately we do not always learn through experience.

SELECTED READINGS

Alexander, Sidney S., *et. al., Economics and the Policy Maker,* Brookings Lectures, 1958-1959, Washington, Brookings Institution, 1959.

Boulding, Kenneth, *Principles of Economic Policy,* Englewood Cliffs, N.J., Prentice-Hall, 1958.

Cairns, James P., and H. H. Binhammer, *Canadian Banking and Monetary Policy,* Toronto, McGraw-Hill, 1965, Part I.

Commission on Money and Credit, *Inflation, Growth and Employment,* Englewood Cliffs, N.J., Prentice-Hall, 1964.

Economic Council of Canada, "Economic Goals for Canada to 1970", *First Annual Review,* Ottawa, Queen's Printer, December, 1964.

Economic Council of Canada, "Towards Sustained and Balanced Economic Growth", *Second Annual Review,* Ottawa, Queen's Printer, December, 1965.

Economic Council of Canada, "Prices, Productivity and Employment", *Third Annual Review,* Ottawa, Queen's Printer, November, 1966.

Economic Council of Canada, "The Canadian Economy from the 1960's to the 1970's", *Fourth Annual Review,* Ottawa, Queen's Printer, September, 1967.

Economic Council of Canada, *Conference on Stabilization Policies, Report of the Conference at University of Western Ontario,* August, 1965, Ottawa, Queen's Printer, 1966.

Economic Council of Canada, *Price Stability and High Employment; The Options for Canadian Economic Policy: An Econometric Study,* special study by R. G. Bodkin, E. P. Bond, G. L. Reuber and T. R. Robinson, Ottawa, Queen's Printer, 1967.

Edwards, Edgar D. (ed.), *The Nation's Economic Objectives,* Chicago, University of Chicago Press, 1964.

Einzig, Paul, *Monetary Policy: Ends and Means,* 2nd ed., Penguin, Baltimore, 1964.

Johnson, H. G., "Objectives, Monetary Standards and Potentialities", *Review of Economics and Statistics,* Supplement, Vol. 45, February, 1963.

Reuber, G. L., *The Objectives of Monetary Policy,* Royal Commission on Banking and Finance, Ottawa, Queen's Printer, 1962.

Tinbergen, Jan, *Economic Policy: Principles and Design,* Amsterdam, North-Holland Publishing Co. Ltd., 1956.

16 MONETARY CONTROL: CENTRAL BANK INSTRUMENTS

THE MONETARY BASE

Under a commodity standard some particular item such as gold serves as the monetary base. Gold is the ultimate source of cash, and all monetary instruments are based on the amount of gold available for monetary purposes. Under a pure paper standard the ultimate source of cash is paper in the form of liabilities of the government and/or the central bank. Subsidiary coin is quite often also a part of the monetary base, but as a rule provides a relatively small and therefore insignificant proportion of the total. In Canada today the monetary base consists of the liabilities of the Bank of Canada in the form of Bank of Canada notes, and chartered bank deposits with the Bank of Canada.

As we have noted earlier, the cash reserves of the commercial banks are comprised of till and vault cash in the form of coin and Bank of Canada notes, and deposits with the Bank of Canada.[1] Moreover, the cash reserves of the banks are the principal determinant of their ability to expand credit and deposit money. A single bank in a banking system has the potential to create credit and deposits equal to its excess cash reserves. A banking system, on the other hand, has the potential to create credit and deposits equal to some multiple of excess cash reserves depending upon the minimum cash reserve ratio maintained by the banks (see Chapter 7). Control of excess reserves, therefore, means control over the capacity of the banking system to create credit and deposit money. If excess reserves are eliminated, expansion can be stopped; if excess reserves are created, expansion can proceed. Since excess reserves represent the difference between total reserves and required minimum reserves,

[1] In Canada coin cannot be included as part of the chartered bank's legal reserve requirements and therefore it is not included in our definition of the monetary base.

they can be increased by increasing total reserves or by reducing minimum required reserves. Similarly they can be reduced by reducing total reserves or by increasing minimum required reserves.

The main purpose of central banking is to influence credit and monetary conditions within a country so that the country can achieve the ultimate goals which we outlined in the preceding chapter. Central bank influence over credit and monetary conditions involves essentially the management of cash in the monetary system. By managing the cash base (the monetary base) of the system it can effectively manage the total monetary stock (currency plus commercial bank deposits); and by managing the monetary stock it can effectively manage credit conditions. Central bank techniques designed to control the total monetary stock are generally referred to as **quantitative controls.**

By employing quantitative controls the central bank attempts to manage credit conditions indirectly and impersonally. For example, let us assume that the central bank places the banking system in a position where it has to acquire additional cash. The banks will respond by selling some of their assets (usually short-term securities) for cash and by reducing or halting their acquisition of other assets (usually loans). The sale of securities and the consequent increase in the supply of securities in the market can depress the market price and increase the market yields of securities. This will lead to higher interest rates on new security offerings in the market. The reduction in loans by the banks will be accomplished by charging higher interest rates and by resorting to non-price rationing. Thus the central bank sets in motion a chain of events resulting in a change in credit conditions — the cost and availability of credit. If the central bank feels that the effects of its initial action will be delayed for too long a time, it can try to affect credit conditions in a direct way. As the central bank is as a rule an important participant in security markets, its own activities in the market may be of such a magnitude as to influence security prices directly.

In some countries such as the United States central banks can exert **qualitative** or **selective controls** which change the amount of money flowing to selected areas of economic activity (for example, stock, consumer and capital markets, and real estate). These may be used to influence not only the supply of but also the demand for credit in certain sectors of the economy. The Bank of Canada has no such powers. However, as we shall see, it has attempted to influence the flow of funds to designated sectors of the economy by persuading certain financial institutions to alter their lending activity. Normally the Bank prefers only to change the banks' cash positions and allow them a free hand in determining which types of loans and investments they will make.

The three most common techniques at the disposal of central banks for manipulating commercial bank reserve positions are setting reserve requirements, employing open market operations and the Bank rate policy. These are all quantitative controls since they are employed to bring about changes in the quantity of money. Moral suasion, another control technique, may be used for the same purpose. However, it has also been used to bring about changes in the composition of credit. When it is used for this purpose it falls into the category of qualitative controls.

COMMERCIAL BANK RESERVES AND RESERVE REQUIREMENTS

LEGAL CASH RESERVE REQUIREMENTS

Historically, cash reserve requirements were imposed upon commercial banks to ensure sound management by them and to protect the public. These reasons are now considered secondary to their role in monetary management and control. Reserve requirements are the fulcrum for commercial bank expansion (or contraction) and, therefore, the fulcrum around which monetary policy is made effective.

When the Bank of Canada commenced operations in 1935 each chartered bank was required to maintain a daily cash reserve in the form of Bank of Canada notes and deposits equal to 5 per cent of its Canadian deposit liabilities. Because of the difficulty of meeting the daily 5 per cent ratio at all times, the banks generally held reserves equal to 10 per cent of their deposits. In 1954 the required reserve ratio was increased to 8 per cent and the basis of its calculation changed from a daily to a monthly average. At the same time the Bank of Canada was given power to vary the cash reserve ratio of the chartered banks between 8 and 12 per cent. The Bank never used this power and it was withdrawn in 1967.

It has become general practice for central banks to specify minimum cash reserve requirements for commercial banks, although this is not necessary for monetary control as long as the banks work toward some average cash ratio known to the central bank. Central bankers prefer not only to specify legal reserve requirements but also to set these requirements at a level above that which the banks would ordinarily consider prudent. Doing so assures the central bank that the banks will work close to the specified minimum and respond quickly to the availability of reserves. However, care is usually taken not to set reserve requirements so high as to discriminate against the banks' earning ability.[2]

[2] It can be argued that if the banks were required to hold larger reserves than they need, they could contribute to the expenses incurred by the central bank in maintaining the currency. However, the banks would then be taxed while other financial institutions performing banking functions would not.

The revisions to the banking legislation in 1967 authorized the Bank of Canada to calculate reserve requirements in the following way:

$$\left.\begin{array}{c}\text{Average cash}\\ \text{reserve ratio}\\ \text{during first}\\ \text{15 days of}\\ \text{any month or}\\ \text{the remaining}\\ \text{days of}\\ \text{any month}\end{array}\right\} = \left\{\frac{\begin{array}{c}\text{Average holding of}\\ \text{Bank of Canada notes}\\ \text{on the four Wednesdays}\\ \text{of the previous month}\end{array} + \begin{array}{c}\text{Average of daily deposits}\\ \text{with the Bank of}\\ \text{Canada during the}\\ \text{current averaging period}\end{array}}{\begin{array}{c}\text{Average of deposit liabilities (demand or notice)}\\ \text{in Canadian currency held on the}\\ \text{four Wednesdays of the previous month}\end{array}}\right.$$

The banks know at the beginning of each two week period the amount of Bank of Canada deposits they must hold on the average during the period. Since they are required to observe only the minimum on an average of business days they are given a little manoeuvrability, as they can allow their Bank of Canada deposits to run low on some days and recoup them on other days. However, they must keep a constant eye on these deposits because the Bank of Canada has the power to alter the total of such deposits to influence the expansionary and contractionary activities of the commercial banks.

Although the Bank of Canada announced that beginning in May 1968 it would replace the monthly averaging system for reserves introduced in 1954 with the half-monthly system, it informed the banks in early March 1968 that it was deferring this requirement until after mid-year.

Since February 1968 the chartered banks have been required to maintain a different cash reserve ratio for notice deposits and demand deposits. Following the revisions to the Bank Act in 1967 the legal minimum ratio for notice deposits was reduced in steps to 4 per cent and that for demand deposits was increased in steps to 12 per cent. Split reserve requirements have long been used in the United States where they have been criticized for their possible weakening of monetary control. Insofar as the banks are successful in persuading the public to shift its funds from demand to notice accounts, their overall legal cash reserve requirement may be decreased while earning assets and deposits may be expanded. In the United States the Federal Reserve imposes ceilings on the interest rates banks are allowed to pay on notice deposits to discourage such a shift. In Canada the lagged calculation of the reserve ratio gives the Bank of Canada effective control of reserve alterations caused by any shifts in deposits which the banks may try to induce. Moreover, the Bank of Canada by increasing the liquid asset requirements can restrict the banks' earning ability and therefore the rate of interest they are prepared to pay on notice deposits.

VARIABLE CASH RESERVE REQUIREMENTS

In 1954 the Bank of Canada was given the power to vary the chartered banks, cash reserves from 8 to 12 per cent subject to a month's notice for each change and a limit of one per cent a month on increases in the ratio. This power was replaced in 1967 by the variable liquid asset ratio. The Federal Reserve Banks in the United States were given the power in 1935 to change member bank reserve requirements.[3] The Bank of England has no such authority.

Control of cash reserve requirements is probably the most powerful tool a central bank can possess. Changes in reserve requirements affect not only excess reserves but also the deposit-creation multiplier of the banking system. A simple example will illustrate the powerful nature of changes in reserve requirements.

Let us assume that the banking system holds $20 billion in the form of public deposits and $5 billion in reserves. With a 10 per cent legal minimum reserve ratio, and on the basis of the deposits which they hold, the banks have to consider $2 billion of their reserves as required reserves. The remaining $3 billion are excess reserves which will support a tenfold increase, or $30 billion, in additional deposits.[4] If the reserve requirements are doubled while the total reserves of the banks remain at $5 billion, required reserves increase to $4 billion leaving only $1 billion as excess reserves. With the new 20 per cent reserve requirement the expansion multiplier is halved to 5 and the potential expansion of deposits with $1 billion of excess reserves is only $5 billion.

Varying reserve requirements has been considered too powerful and therefore too blunt an instrument for monetary control. Even small increases in reserve requirements can produce undesirable "shock effects" leading to disturbances and instability in money markets.[5] On the other

3 In the Thomas Amendment to the Agricultural Adjustment Act of 1933, the Federal Reserve System was granted as an emergency measure the power to vary reserve requirements. This power could be exercised only with the permission of the President of the United States. In 1935 the Federal Reserve Act made the provision permanent and independent of Presidential permission. The initial use of the measure in 1936-1937 to double reserve requirements in three steps had rather unfortunate results. The System regarded the large excess reserves held by the banks at that time as unintentional accumulations due to shortages of loans and suitable investments. However, due to bitter experiences between 1929 and 1933 the banks had shifted their liquidity preference and were holding these reserves deliberately. When the System increased reserve requirements the banks immediately took drastic steps to regain their former liquidity with the result that the economy contracted even further.

4 This is based on Equation *(I)* in the Appendix of Chapter 7. Here, we assume r given as 0.10 and c as zero.

5 Some of the bluntness of an increase in required reserves could probably be eliminated by applying the higher ratios only to deposits above some pre-determined level.

hand, if the banks prefer to hold larger reserves, a reduction in reserve requirements will have no effect on the money supply and credit conditions. Varying reserve requirements has also the disadvantage of affecting at the same time and to the same extent all commercial banks regardless of their individual reserve needs.

In countries where there is not a well organized money market for the central bank to adjust the cash position of the banks by its open market operations, varying reserve requirements may have to be relied upon as an important tool for cash management.[6] In countries with well defined money markets, and where the central banks have the power to vary cash reserve ratios, the technique is used only in emergencies. For example, the results of a sudden and large flow of short-term international capital can usually be effectively neutralized by changing the banks' reserve requirements.

MINIMUM AND VARIABLE LIQUID ASSET RATIO

In Chapter 7 where we discussed the portfolio management of commercial banks we observed that the banks hold some proportion of their assets in relatively liquid form as protection against unexpected cash withdrawals. A cushion of liquid assets also gives them sufficient flexibility to take advantage of attractive lending opportunities when they arise. Moreover, in a well developed money market when the government upholds a policy limiting fluctuations in market rates, banks will hold liquid assets as a substitute for cash to increase their earnings. With little or no fluctuations in the market value of these assets they are as good as cash.

Large holdings of liquid assets by the banks can present difficulties for monetary control. If the central bank is committed to maintaining a certain level and pattern of interest rates, restricting the banks' cash reserves may not curtail their lending policies because they can sell their liquid assets with little or no loss to themselves and obtain the cash for expanding their loans. If, however, the central bank has no commitment to maintain market rates, and there are no market imperfections, there will be a limit to the amount of switching from liquid assets to cash, and in turn to loans, that the banks will want to do. The sale of liquid assets by the banks will tend to depress their price and make it unprofitable for the banks to continue their switching operations.

During postwar expansionary periods the chartered banks often responded slowly to the Bank of Canada's restrictive action; they were pre-

---

[6] This was the case in New Zealand where even today with a developing money market, varying the reserve ratio is still the most important means of manipulating the excess cash of the banking system.

pared to allow their holdings of liquid assets to run low in order to continue expanding their loans. To make restrictive measures effective, the Governor of the Bank of Canada requested the chartered banks in 1955 to maintain a minimum liquid asset ratio of 15 per cent. The banks agreed to hold a combination of cash, Treasury bills and day-to-day loans equal to 15 per cent of their deposit liabilities after July 1956. This meant that in future the banks would not expand their loans by selling liquid assets if the total of such assets held by them was less than 15 per cent of their deposit liabilities. The banks could of course still switch any liquid assets above the 15 per cent minimum. However, the Bank of Canada had set the minimum high enough that the banks' profit motive induced them to work fairly closely to the minimum.

In 1967 the Bank of Canada received statutory power to impose on the chartered banks a minimum secondary reserve requirement and to vary this requirement within limits. The liquid assets which may be included as secondary reserves are holdings of Treasury bills, day-to-day loans to investment dealers, and that part of a bank's holdings of notes of, or deposits with, the Bank of Canada which is in excess of the minimum cash reserve requirement. The Bank cannot require the banks to hold secondary reserves against their Canadian dollar deposit liabilities in excess of 12 per cent on the average during any month. The Bank must also give a month's notice of its intention to impose or vary a requirement. Moreover, when no requirement is in effect the announced percentage cannot be greater than 6 and when a percentage is in effect it cannot be increased by more than one per cent for the following month. The Bank first used its new power in January 1968 when it announced that the ratio would be 6 per cent in March and would rise to 7 per cent in April.

When the Bank was given statutory power to set and vary secondary reserve requirements its previous authority to vary cash reserve requirements was withdrawn. The two techniques for monetary control are very similar. In the one case the central bank can impound some of the excess cash of the banking system, and in the other, some of the excess liquidity of the system. The advantage of working with liquid assets rather than cash is that the effects are not as blunt and therefore do not lead as readily to severe disturbances and instability in money markets. There is also a direct advantage for the banks in that they can earn interest on their holdings of securites even if their use is restricted, whereas increased cash reserves earn no interest. These techniques should be used only in emergencies and not in the day-to-day management of cash reserves. The use of either technique usually requires the banks to make portfolio adjustments which create money market disturbances of a magnitude undesirable and unnecessary for monetary control under normal circumstances.

In some countries, such as Britain, the central bank requires the commercial banks from time to time to deposit funds with it over and above the normal requirements.[7] These funds are released when economic conditions change. The British system of "special deposits" is essentially the same as the use of a variable cash reserve requirement. However, insofar as the banks have also been requested to invest in special non-marketable government securities, the special deposits scheme is similar to the technique of varying the banks' liquid asset requirements.

Liquid asset reserve requirements can be used for purposes other than monetary control. They may be used to assure the solvency of the commercial banking system, or to provide a market for government debt at rates pegged by the government. In the latter case the government can hold down the cost of servicing the national debt without committing the central bank to peg the market rate on government securities.

OPEN MARKET OPERATIONS

The Bank of Canada, like the Bank of England and the Federal Reserve Banks in the United States, relies on open market operations as the main instrument for the management of the monetary system. We have seen that commercial banks create deposit liabilities when they acquire financial assets and extinguish them when they dispose of financial assets. The same principle also applies to central banks. However, there is an important difference. Most of the liabilities which a central bank creates when it acquires financial assets become cash reserves for the chartered banks and provide bank notes for circulation.

Central bank open market operations involve the acquisition and liquidation of marketable financial assets. In the nineteenth century the Bank of England initiated such operations to adjust its own gold reserve position. It was not until the 1920's that the Bank employed open market transactions to manage the cash reserve position of the commercial banks; this is the essential purpose of their use today. In fact, the use of open market operations for this purpose on a continuing basis was pioneered in the United States after 1923. The Bank of Canada traded in government securities from the time of its establishment in 1935. However, its early activities were not concerned so much with managing the cash position of the chartered banks as with the development of a market for government securities. After 1938, for instance, the Bank of Canada attempted to make a market for these securities by adopting the practice of submitting to the market a daily list of the bids it would accept and the offers it was prepared to make. During the war and in the immediate

[7] The banks in Britain are paid interest on their special deposits.

postwar period, the Bank's open market operations were directed toward stabilizing interest rates. The Bank began altering the purpose of its open market operations in 1948 when it stopped issuing daily lists of bids and offers. In 1950 the Bank ceased to support the government bond market on a continuing basis. However, effective and flexible use of open market operations as a means of controlling commercial bank reserves did not occur until after 1953 when, with the help of the Bank of Canada, a mature money market was developed. Since then the Bank has been relieved of much of its earlier responsibility for the day-to-day development and maintenance of the money market and is free to concentrate its open market operations on managing the cash reserves of the chartered banks.

OPEN MARKET OPERATIONS AND BANK RESERVES

Central bank purchases of securities supply reserves to the banking system and central bank sales withdraw reserves from the system. When the central bank buys securities — let us say $10 million of Government of Canada Treasury bills from money market dealers — it pays for these bills with cheques drawn on itself. The dealers deposit these cheques in their accounts with the banks. In the clearing house operations the chartered banks acquire $10 million in additional deposits with the Bank of Canada and a corresponding increase in their cash reserves. The following changes will be observed in the balance sheets of the Bank of Canada and of the chartered banks:

BANK OF CANADA

Assets		Liabilities	
Treasury bills	+$10,000,000	Deposits of the chartered banks	+$10,000,000

CHARTERED BANKS

Assets		Liabilities	
Reserves:		Deposits:	
Deposits with the Bank of Canada	+$10,000,000	Deposits	+$10,000,000

Instead of purchasing Treasury bills from the investment dealers, the Bank of Canada may purchase them directly from the chartered banks.

In this case the balance sheet of the Bank of Canada remains as shown in the above example but that of the chartered banks takes the following form:

CHARTERED BANKS

Assets		**Liabilities**
Reserves:		
Deposits with the Bank of Canada	+$10,000,000	
Securities:		
Treasury bills	−$10,000,000	

It makes no difference to the total cash reserves of the banks whether the Bank of Canada buys securities directly from the banks or from investment dealers and other non-bank sources. It does, however, make a difference to the banks' excess reserves. When the central bank purchases securities from non-bank sources the chartered banks receive primary deposits against which they have to hold cash reserves. If, in our example, the chartered banks' legal minimum cash reserve ratio is 12 per cent they will have to hold $120,000 as required reserves. With no currency drains out of the banking system $880,000 remain as excess reserves to support a multiple expansion of credit and deposits by the banking system (see Chapter 7).

When the central bank purchases securities directly from the banks the entire amount becomes excess reserves since there is no initial primary deposit against which required reserves must be held.

In the same way that open market purchases of securities by the central bank create chartered bank reserves, open market sales extinguish chartered bank reserves.

THE CHOICE OF OPEN MARKET OPERATIONS

With the growth in size of government debt central banks in most countries now conduct the major part of their open market operations in government securities. Although the Bank of Canada may deal in certain private financial paper, securities issued and guaranteed by a province, and certain securities of the governments of the United States and the United Kingdom, it has preferred to conduct open market operations almost exclusively in Government of Canada securities. This policy has a number of advantages. Government of Canada securities are available in a broad range of maturities and their value at maturity is guaranteed by the government. They are widely held and traded by all of the financial institutions, investment dealers and the general public. Moreover, by dealing in these securities the Bank of Canada can coordinate its own market operation with the management of government debt.

In Canada, as in the United States,[8] the open market operations of the central bank are conducted with a relatively small number of security dealers (about forty) and with the banks. The Bank of England does not trade itself but conducts its open market operations through established brokers who transact business on its behalf.

The central bank conducts its open market operations primarily in either short-term or long-term securities, or a combination of both. The choice will depend upon what the bank considers to be its role in influencing security prices and yields. In Canada, as in the United Kingdom and the United States, the normal preference of the central bank open market operations is to change the cash reserves of the banking system thereby allowing the market to produce the subsequent change in security prices and yields. As we have seen earlier, any addition to or subtraction from commercial bank reserves has a multiple expansive or contractive effect on the banking system's lending and investing ability. When the central bank's open market operations cause a change in the banks' reserves, a change several times as large may be made in their portfolios of loans and investments. This leads to the change in credit conditions anticipated by the central bank's open market operations.

When the central bank trades securities it affects the market supply and demand relationship of these securities and this in turn affects their price and yields. The central bank can usually minimize the direct effects of its open market operations on market rates by confining its activities to the short end of the market. The shorter the term of a security, the closer it is to cash for which it is being exchanged, and the smaller the impact will be on its price and yield when traded.

We have said that the Bank of Canada normally prefers to influence the level of interest rates indirectly by conducting open market operations to affect the reserve position of the banking system without directly affecting interest rates. To this end, its operations are concentrated in the short end of the market of Government of Canada securities. Likewise, the larger commercial and industrial firms now make it a practice to invest excess balances in short-term government securities. They accumulate excess balances against large payments such as taxes and dividends. With a relatively broad and active market in short-term Government of

[8] Open market operations for the Federal Reserve Banks are conducted by the Open Market Investment Committee. Transactions on its behalf are conducted by the Federal Reserve Bank of New York which deals with six banks designated as dealer banks and with a select group of non-bank dealers whose business is dealing in United States Government securities.

Canada securities the Bank of Canada can minimize, under normal circumstances, any direct effects of its market transactions by responding to day-to-day bids and offers on the market. Moreover, insofar as the Bank of Canada's activities at any one time may be small relative to the total transactions in the market, their role in determining directly the price and yields of securities is insignificant.

Whether or not the central bank should confine its activities exclusively to the short end of the market became a controversial issue in the United States after 1953. In that year the Federal Open Market Investment Committee of the Federal Reserve System announced that its operations would henceforth be confined to the short end of the securities market. Moreover, support of the market during Treasury refinancing was to be discontinued. In effect, the Federal Reserve System intended to use open market operations solely to regulate the reserve position of the banking system and not to support any pattern of prices and yields on the market.[9] The proponents of the "bills only" policy defended it on several grounds. They argued that Federal Reserve intervention in all sectors of the market inhibited the development of the market and created artificial conditions in it. Moreover continuous central bank activity in long-term securities was thought to encourage bullish or bearish expectations resulting in unstable prices and yields which did not reflect basic demand and supply forces. They asserted, for example, that Federal Reserve activities in the long end of the market could produce mistaken expectations and result in higher security prices than those justified by actual supply and demand conditions. With higher security prices, offerings would have to be rationed producing congestion and disorderly market conditions at a later date.[10] The critics of the "bills only" policy felt that the Federal Reserve was neglecting its responsibility of leadership by assuming a submissive role in the market.[11]

[9] The Federal Reserve authorities in the United States spoke in terms of "leaning against the wind", implying that the central bank simply modifies the basic private forces for expansion and contraction of credit and changes in the level of interest rates. This policy is in direct opposition to those who want the central bank to establish rates of interest and their structure.

[10] When the market considers that the central bank's action is producing artificially high prices, expectations in the market can weaken rather than strengthen market prices.

[11] Early in 1961 the "bills only" policy was changed to a more flexible one permitting operations in all maturity ranges of the United States Government securities market. The primary reason for the 1961 change in policy was the emergence of serious balance of payments deficits caused partly by large outflows of short-term capital at a time when the American economy was suffering from substantial unemployment and underutilization of productive capacity. After 1961 open market operations in all maturity ranges, assisted by debt management and other policy actions, were used to "twist" the interest rate structure, *i.e.*, to raise short-term rates while exerting as much downward pressure as possible on long-term rates.

Although the Bank of Canada usually prefers to exert indirect influence on the market through the management of cash reserves, it can and does apply direct influence when circumstances call for such action. On these occasions the Bank trades in certain types of securities to such an extent that the level and structure of market yields is directly influenced. Purposes for which the Bank might exert direct pressure include correcting disorderly market conditions, halting disruptive international capital flows and facilitating government debt management operations.

Disorderly market conditions can arise from unexpected shocks such as substantial shifts of assets caused by large-scale private or public debt operations or sudden changes in the public's expectations of future market yields. During the Cuban Crisis in October 1962 there was a sudden shift out of Government of Canada bonds and their prices began to fall sharply. The Bank of Canada intervened to steady the market by making cash purchases of $111 million of these bonds in three days, $73 million of which were bought in a single day.[12]

In June 1965 Atlantic Acceptance Corporation, a medium-sized sales finance company, failed and there were rumours that a trust company which had large investments in Atlantic might also fail. The Bank of Canada staved off disorderly money market conditions which could have adversely affected other financial institutions by using its open market operations to increase the cash reserves of the chartered banks, thereby easing the liquidity position of the financial markets generally. The Bank's market operations on this occasion differed from those mentioned previously in that liquidity in the market rather than prices of securities was the primary concern.

In 1962 the Canadian government fixed the external value of the Canadian dollar at 92.5 U.S. cents. At the same time it assumed the full responsibility as a member of the International Monetary Fund to prevent fluctuations of more than one per cent in this fixed parity. The value of the dollar is maintained primarily by the Exchange Fund Account which buys and sells Canadian dollars on the foreign exchange market. These transactions will be discussed in detail in Chapter 30.

The central bank helps the government to prevent fluctuations in the external value of the dollar by providing interest rate levels that will assure appropriate international capital flows. The close affinity of Canadian and American money and capital markets makes international money and capital flows extremely sensitive to interest rate differentials

---

[12] In order to prevent a large increase in the banks' reserves resulting from the Bank of Canada operations, the Department of Finance made temporary changes in the level of government balances with the Bank and conducted certain transactions between the Bank and the government's Securities Investment Account. See Chapter 17.

between the two countries. For instance, in the autumn of 1965 when credit conditions in Canada were tightening, Canadian borrowers turned to the United States for funds. Upward pressure was placed on the external value of the Canadian dollar as Canadians purchased Canadian dollars with borrowed American dollars. The Bank of Canada increased its open market purchases of securities in order to counter the rising trend in interest rates and thereby shift borrowing back to the Canadian money and capital markets.

An outflow of capital from a country at a time when there is also domestic unemployment may create difficulties for the monetary authorities. This was the case in the United States and Canada in the early 1960's. To stop an external drain of capital and thereby prevent downward pressure on the external value of its currency, a country generally must establish higher domestic interest rates to provide an appropriate differential between domestic and foreign rates. However, to expand domestic investment and aggregate demand, interest rates should be depressed. Insofar as foreign capital movements are primarily sensitive to changes in short-term interest rates, while domestic investment is influenced more by long-term rates, the monetary authorities may be able to find a way out of their dilemma. For instance, the central bank can sell short-term securities to increase short-term rates and thereby hold or reverse foreign capital flows. At the same time it can buy long-term securities to depress long-term rates and stimulate domestic investment. Such actions by the central bank are undertaken to change the shape of the interest-yield curve — that is, to change the *relative* yields of securities with different terms to maturity. The central bank's success in bending the interest-yield curve depends upon the factors which determine the yield structure of interest rates. This rather complex story is discussed further in Chapter 26.

The responsibility for managing the federal government's debt lies with the government itself. However, this does not mean that the Bank of Canada plays a passive role, for it is the government's fiscal agent and advisor.

During and after the Second World War the central banks in Canada, the United States and the United Kingdom considered it government policy to peg the yield structure of government securities. This was done so that the public which had purchased large quantities of government bonds during the war could cash them without loss, and so that interest rates could be held at a level which would make peacetime transition easier. Pegging interest rates led to some unwarranted inflation. It is now generally agreed that the central bank should not be made a slave to government debt management policies.

The central bank's role in debt management is essentially two-fold. It prepares the financial market for large government debt operations; and it assists the market in preventing disorderly conditions while such operations are being undertaken. In 1958, for example, in order to restore confidence and allay uncertainties in the government bond market, the government decided to engage in the largest refinancing operation in Canadian history. Uneasiness had developed as a result of heavy government borrowing in the market during the year, and because of the approaching maturity of an extremely large proportion of government "Victory Bonds" issued during the war. The government decided to offer issues of a new long-term Conversion Loan in exchange for Victory Bonds. Because of the magnitude of the conversion program disruptions in the market could be anticipated. In order to minimize these, and to assure the success of the conversion, the Bank of Canada played an active role in the market. Since the prices of Victory Bonds offered by the government were raised and fixed at very attractive levels to induce the public to convert, throughout the operation and for some weeks thereafter the Bank of Canada had to support bond prices in the face of a rapid upward adjustment of interest rates in the United States.

While government debt management operations are not usually of such a magnitude as the 1958 conversion loan, the Bank of Canada engages in similar though more moderate open market activities whenever the government borrows.

OPEN MARKET OPERATIONS IN 1965: A CASE STUDY

Table 16-1 shows the bank of Canada's net transactions in government securities on a monthly basis during 1965. All the transactions with banks and investment dealers shown at the left of the table, except for advances to the dealers under purchase and resale agreements, represent the Bank's open market operations.[13] The transactions shown at the right of the table, except for those in which the Bank purchases Treasury bills by tender, are not open market operations since they are negotiated between the Bank and the government. These transactions are discussed in the next chapter.

The Bank of Canada's open market operations during 1965 demonstrate that while the Bank's normal preference is to trade mainly in the short end of the market, it is prepared to deal in all maturities whenever a more direct influence on market prices is required. During February

[13] When the rate at which the Bank of Canada enters into purchase and resale agreements with investment dealers is established by competitive tender these transactions are similar to open market operations. Usually the interest rate on purchase and resale agreements (PRA's) is set by the Bank's so-called Money Market Rate, in which case these transactions take the form of central bank advances.

Table 16-1

Bank of Canada Net Transactions in Government Securities in 1965

(delivered basis par value in millions of dollars)

	Net purchases from (+) or net sales to (−) investment dealers and banks							*Net transactions with Government and other accounts*								
1965	**Treasury Bills**	**Bonds* 2 and under**	**Bonds* 2 to 5**	**Bonds* 5 to 10**	**Bonds* Over 10**	**Sub-Total Bills and Bonds**	**Securities under PRA**	**Purchases (+) of new issues less matured holdings**		**Net sales (−) to Securities Invest. Acct.**		**Net sales (−) to other Gov. and Client Accounts**		**Net change in holdings of Gov. Securities**		
								Bills	*Bonds*	*Bills*	*Bonds*	*Bills*	*Bonds*	*Bills*	*Bonds*	*Total*
Jan.	+19	+ 75	− 71	−14	——	+ 9	−100**	− 11	——	——	+ 5	− 46	——	− 41	−102	−143
Feb.	+15	+ 67	+ 3	−46	+ 8	+ 46	——	+ 26	+ 3	——	− 60	+ 6	——	+ 47	− 26	+ 21
Mar.	−18	+ 51	+ 4	+ 7	+ 17	+ 61	——	+ 37	——	+10	− 30	− 31	−26	− 2	+ 23	+ 21
Apr.	−51	+ 82	+ 31	+15	+ 10	+ 87	——	+ 16	+ 27	——	− 80	+ 12	+10	− 23	+ 96	+ 73
May	+69	+ 8	+ 10	+ 7	+ 12	+106	+ 3	− 42	——	——	+105	− 23	+ 9	+ 6	+152	+158
June	−54	+ 2	+ 2	+ 5	+ 37	− 7	− 3	+ 76	——	——	− 75	− 17	+ 5	+ 4	− 25	− 20
July	−13	− 9	+ 15	——	+ 2	− 5	——	+ 12	+ 44	——	——	− 36	——	− 36	+ 52	+ 16
Aug.	− 9	− 4	− 18	——	− 18	− 48	——	+ 14	——	——	——	− 16	——	− 10	− 40	− 50
Sept.	−21	− 30	− 70	——	+ 1	−119	——	+ 45	+122	——	——	− 22	+ 5	+ 3	+ 29	+ 31
Oct.	+27	+ 2	——	——	——	+ 29	——	+140	——	——	——	− 15	− 2	+152	——	+153
Nov.	+ 4	+ 8	——	+ 5	+ 31	+ 48	——	+ 17	——	——	——	− 20	− 1	——	+ 43	+ 44
Dec.	+39	− 12	− 7	− 1	+ 5	+ 24	——	+ 5	+ 43	——	——	− 14	− 4	+ 30	+ 24	+ 54
Total	+ 7	+239	−101	−22	+105	+229	−100	+337	+239	+10	−135	−219	− 3	+131	+226	+357

* Classified by years to maturity at time of transaction.

** Special PRA's includes $97 million in bonds and $3 million in Treasury bills.

Note: errors due to estimation and rounding.

Source: Bank of Canada, Annual Report of the Governor to the Minister of Finance, 1965, pp. 42-43.

1965, uncertainty was created in the Canadian bond market and prices weakened as a result of the announcement in the United States of a new program to improve American balance of payments. The Bank of Canada resisted this downward pressure with its net purchases of government securities in all maturity ranges over the next few months.

In May the Bank apparently foresaw the impending default of the Atlantic Acceptance Corporation in early June, and was a large net purchaser of government securities which provided the banks with sufficient cash reserves to ease credit conditions and guard against the possibility of other financial institutions falling into liquidity difficulties.

After August, when the government announced a large sale of wheat to the Soviet Union, a shift in market expectations resulted in a tendency for bond prices to rise. The Bank of Canada countered by selling securities in the market. As was reflected by its activities in the long end of the market, at that time it was concerned with market prices rather than with the cash position of the banks. This was also the case during the latter part of the year when, in order to lower the level of interest rates and discourage borrowing in the United States, it became a large net purchaser of government securities.

DISCOUNTS, ADVANCES AND THE BANK RATE

Because a central bank is the ultimate source of cash for the financial system, one of its most important functions is to act as a lender of last resort. In the early nineteenth century the banks in the city of London made loans by discounting (purchasing) commercial bills in the London discount market. When the banks required additional cash to discount all the good quality bills presented to them, they sold bills they had previously discounted for their customers to the Bank of England. This gave the banks deposits with the Bank of England which could be drawn down in gold and Bank of England notes. However since the notes were also redeemable in gold, any increase in the Bank of England's purchase of bills was a potential threat to its gold reserves. The Bank was usually requested to (re)discount bills for the commercial banks during periods of economic expansion when there was an increased demand for gold for domestic circulation and for export abroad. The bank was therefore guided in the amount of discounting it was prepared to do at any given time by the adequacy of its gold reserves. The volume of its discounts was controlled by the rate it charged and the quality of bills it was prepared to accept. Its discount rate became known as the **Bank rate.**

A rise in the Bank rate usually served as a signal for other lending rates to follow and the subsequent increase in interest rates generally dampened economic activity. The opposite was true when the Bank rate was lowered. Thus by changing the Bank rate the Bank of England attempted to control the inward and outward flow of gold from its vaults.

Early in its development as a central bank the Bank of England began the practice of discounting bills for the London discount houses instead of for the banks. When the city banks required additional cash they called their loans to the discount houses, who could always meet these demands because to them the Bank of England acted as lender of last resort. To prevent the discount houses from abusing this privilege the Bank rate was ordinarily set above the money market rates but at the same time within reach of the discount dealers. The twelve London discount houses that form the London Discount Market are still the main borrowers from the Bank of England and as such serve as a buffer between the commercial banking system and the Bank.

THE BANK RATE

It has been British tradition (also followed in Canada) to make the Bank rate a penalty rate but at the same time to keep it low enough to maintain the central bank's function of lender of last resort during credit crises. In the United States the Federal Reserve Banks' discount rate (the term still commonly used) is not a penalty rate. Contrary to British and Canadian practice, borrowing from the Federal Reserve Banks is considered a privilege rather than a right. While the central banks in all three systems define the type of paper eligible for discounting, and the conditions under which discounting is allowed, only the Federal Reserve Banks consistently practise non-price rationing by scrutinizing the reason and purpose for which they are requested to act as lenders of last resort. Member-bank borrowing from the Federal Reserve Banks is subject to "the principles of prudent discounting".[14]

CENTRAL BANK ADVANCES AND COMMERCIAL BANK CASH RESERVES

Discounting of bills and other paper by central banks has been replaced by central bank advances. These loans are made by a central bank upon the promissory note of the borrower secured by government obligations (usually Treasury bills) or eligible paper. In Canada, purchase and resale agreements have become the Bank of Canada's main method of lending.

---

[14] Board of Governors of the Federal Reserve System, *Annual Report for 1957*, Washington, D. C., 1958, p.11. In practice, where the borrowing privilege seems to be in danger of being abused, the Federal Reserve officials use moral suasion to discourage borrowing from the Federal Reserve Banks.

Traditionally the commercial banks have been reluctant to borrow from the central bank; and the central banks usually discourage such borrowing. At one time commercial bankers believed that acquiring a loan from another bank might be interpreted as a sign of financial weakness. As we have mentioned, the banks in Britain fill their needs for cash by calling loans from discount houses so that they borrow only indirectly from the Bank of England. Central banks consider that as a lender of last resort they should make loans to commercial banks only in exceptional circumstances. Under normal conditions the comercial banks are expected to adjust their cash reserves by selling securities in the market.

The Bank of Canada makes advances to the chartered banks for a minimum period of seven days against the hypothecation of suitable securities.[15] The first advance made to a bank in any calendar month bears interest at the Bank rate. The total amount of such an advance is specified in the terms of the bank's line of credit with the Bank of Canada. A second advance to a bank in the same calendar month or a renewal of an advance, or an advance in excess of the specified amount bears interest at a rate higher than the Bank rate. The banks are encouraged therefore to look upon central bank advances as truly a last resort.

The initial impact of advances made by the Bank of Canada to the chartered banks is an increase in the banks' cash reserves. The example below shows the changes in the balance sheets of the Bank of Canada and the chartered banks as a result of advances totalling $10 million. An advance of $10 million from the Bank of Canada immediately makes available to the banking system a corresponding amount of excess cash reserves in the form of Bank of Canada deposits. We observed earlier in our discussion of central bank open market operations that when the Bank of Canada purchases $10 million in bonds in the market not all of

BANK OF CANADA

Assets		**Liabilities**	
Advances to the chartered banks	+$10,000,000	Deposits Chartered banks	+$10,000,000

CHARTERED BANKS

Assets		**Liabilities**	
Reserves:			
Deposits with the Bank of Canada	+$10,000,000	Advances from the Bank of Canada	+$10,000,000

[15] Advances made by the Bank of England and the Federal Reserve Banks are for a minimum period of seven and fifteen days respectively.

the $10 million is available as excess reserves because part must be held as reserves against the deposits created by open market purchases. Therefore an advance from the central bank to a chartered bank has a potentially larger expansionary effect on the banking system than central bank open market purchases of equal magnitude.[16]

If central banks were prepared to allow commercial banks to remain continuously in debt to them, central bank advances could serve as a continuing reserve base for the multiple expansion of credit and deposits by the banking system. The Federal Reserve Banks in the United States make advances to the commercial banks with some reluctance and only on a temporary basis; but because of the large number of banks the banking system as a whole is normally indebted to the Federal Reserve System at any given time. Therefore, central bank advances serve indirectly as a continuing reserve base for the American banking system. This is not the case in Canada. For example, Bank of Canada advances to the banks were outstanding on forty-eight business days in 1965 and on only fifteen business days in 1964. If the banks were continuously and substantially in debt to the central bank, discretionary changes in the Bank rate by the central bank could serve as an important technique for managing the cash reserves of the banks.

The fact that the banks have access to the central bank's "discount window" (they can borrow at the central bank), even if it is used only sparingly, probably encourages them under normal circumstances to lend more freely because they can remedy a deficiency of reserves if they are caught short. However, their willingness to risk being caught short is determined by the costs involved. If the level of the Bank rate in relation to other interest rates is high, banks will be inclined to reduce lending and investing activity to avoid the possibility of having to pay the costs involved in borrowing from the central bank. Market interest rates will then move up toward the level of the Bank rate.[17] On the other hand, if the differential between the Bank rate and money market rates is small, the banks may consider the cost of having to turn to the central bank for assistance worth the risk of being caught short. As a result they will be more liberal in their lending activity. After mid-1956 when the Bank of Canada increased the Bank rate on six successive occasions and the banks began to announce corresponding increases in their own lending

---

[16] If the securities are purchased from the banks the full $10 million becomes *excess* reserves.

[17] If the central bank wishes to maintain restrictive credit conditions it will have to make successive upward adjustments in the Bank rate as market interest rates rise in order to preserve an appropriate differential in rates.

rates, the Bank rate appears to have been considered an important cost factor by the chartered banks.

In Britain the commercial banks automatically change their own rates, particularly in an upward direction, with each change in the Bank rate. The banks react to the changes in the Bank rate in Britain because the Bank of England usually coordinates its open market operations with its Bank rate policy. For example, the Bank of England sells Treasury bills in the open market to reduce the cash reserves of the commercial banks. To replenish their cash reserves the banks call some of their loans to the discount houses. The discount houses, in turn, are forced to borrow from the Bank of England at the (penalty) Bank rate, and as a result of consequent adjustments, bill rates are forced up. Thus open market operations are used to "force the market into the Bank" and to "make the Bank rate effective".

A certain amount of "leakage" in monetary control occurs when the commercial banks increase their borrowing from the central bank at a time when the central bank is pursuing a restrictive policy. Insofar as the central bank can adjust the Bank rate it can regulate the amount of "leakage" it allows. On the other hand, the central bank may be inclined to use open market operations more vigorously if it knows that there is an "overflow" in case it overshoots the mark.[18]

THE SIGNAL EFFECT OF THE BANK RATE

Historically, the Bank rate has also served as a signal of the intentions of the monetary authorities. An increase in the Bank rate has usually been interpreted to mean that the "informed" central banking authorities feel the pace of bank credit and monetary expansion is in danger of becoming too rapid.

The response by the banks and other financial institutions, as well as the public, to changes in the Bank rate depends upon their expectations as to the ensuing economic climate. If the announcement of an increase in the Bank rate leads to the anticipation of further interest rate increases, there may be an increased demand for loans by borrowers who expect future Bank rate and market interest rate increases. Borrowers,

18 Paul Samuelson compares the discount window with a brake on an automobile. The brake allows one to drive at a higher speed than would otherwise be possible. See P. A. Samuelson, "Reflections on Monetary Policy", *Review of Economics and Statistics,* Vol. 42, August 1960, p. 266. Warren Smith, however, feels that this is not a proper analogy. He contends that the discount window is more like a defective clutch than a brake, and that a slipping clutch makes it more difficult to drive at a higher rate of speed. See Warren L. Smith, "The Instruments of General Monetary Control", *National Banking Review,* Vol. 1, September 1963, pp. 47-76.

however, may be frustrated in their attempts to seek additional funds if lenders foreseeing high rates in the future refuse to lend.[19] In this case, the announcement of a Bank rate increase may have the desired effect.

Where the central bank attempts to maintain a penalty Bank rate, as is done in Canada and Britain, frequent changes in the rate may have to be made to retain a penalty level. Such technical adjustments can be misinterpreted by the public as having policy implications not intended by the monetary authorities. Because of the possibility of misinterpretation, Bank rate changes are now usually accompanied by a statement of intent.

REFORMS IN BANK RATE POLICY

Milton Friedman of the University of Chicago has suggested that the discount window of the Federal Reserve System in the United States should be abolished.[20] He argues that the legitimate function of the central bank is to control the stock of money and that the discount rate (the Bank rate in the United States) is an ineffective instrument for this purpose. The complete abolition of the discount mechanism would also mean abandoning its useful function as a safety valve by which banks are able to make adjustments in their cash reserve positions and the central bank is able to come to their aid in case of a liquidity crisis. Friedman would still allow the banks to make short-term adjustments in their reserve ratio by permitting them to run their reserves below the legal level. However, in order to discourage the banks from abusing this privilege he suggests levying a fixed fine on reserve deficiencies at a penalty level. Friedman believes that the success of deposit insurance has made liquidity crises in the United States a thing of the past and that the Federal Reserve's lender of last resort function is therefore obsolete.

An alternative to the complete abolition of borrowing at the central bank is replacing the **discretionary** Bank rate, which is changed from time to time, with a **floating** Bank rate, which varies automatically with market rates. A floating rate was employed in Canada from November 1956 to June 1962 during which time it remained at one quarter of one per cent above the average rate on Treasury bills. When the floating rate was introduced, James Coyne, then the Governor of the Bank of Canada stated that the change was being made because a floating rate was the simplest method of keeping the Bank rate at a penalty level.[21] Frequent

---

19 See Chapter 22 for a detailed discussion of expectational effects on lenders, borrowers, and spenders.

20 Friedman, Milton, *A Program for Monetary Stability*, New York, Fordham University Press, 1960, pp. 35-45.

21 See Bank of Canada, *Annual Report of the Governor to the Minister of Finance*, 1956, pp. 45-46.

adjustments are necessary in order to keep a fixed rate at a penalty level. These adjustments are subject to misinterpretation by the public. Moreover, as Coyne noted, Bank rate changes can be made only with undesirable lags. Frequent changes and their lags have disturbing effects on money markets and the business community generally. He also justified the move to a floating rate on the grounds that the policy of the Bank of Canada was not to lead market rates but rather to follow them.[22] This view of the role of central bank policy is difficult to accept. It suggests that the central bank should play a submissive role, an idea which is incompatible with the bank's duty of discretionary monetary control.

Instead of abolishing the discount window of the central bank, or allowing the Bank rate to become an even less useful technique for monetary control, James Tobin of Yale University[23] has suggested that the central bank pay interest at the Bank rate on commercial bank cash reserves in excess of legal requirements. Then the opportunity cost to a bank of increasing its loans and its investments (whether it were in debt to the central bank or not) would be the return it could earn by holding excess reserves, a cost under the control of the central bank. Moreover, the interest rates that the banks would be prepared to pay on their customer deposit accounts would be linked rather closely to the rate paid on excess reserves — the Bank rate.[24] Thus, to restrict credit conditions, the central bank would merely raise the Bank rate. The banks' opportunity cost of lending would be increased and they would then be willing to lend only at higher interest rates. At the same time the banks would be inclined to raise the rates on their customer deposits encouraging the public to hold deposits rather than other assets. Prices of these other assets would tend to fall and their yields to increase. This change would be reflected in a general upward movement of market rates. Although Tobin's proposal for reforming the discount window of the central bank is

22 During the period that the Bank rate was allowed to float with the Treasury bill rate the monetary authorities retained control of the rate insofar as they were able to influence the Treasury bill rate by controlling the amount of bills the Department of Finance was willing to offer each week and by setting the amount of bills the Bank of Canada was prepared to take up. However, since it was the Bank of Canada's policy to allow the Bank rate to follow rather than lead market trends, the authorities generally refrained from interfering with the normal course of the Treasury bill market.

23 Tobin, James, "Towards Improving the Efficiency of the Monetary Mechanism", *Review of Economics and Statistics*, Vol. 42, August 1960, pp. 276-279.

24 A bank could always earn a return on its deposits equal to one minus its reserve requirement times the discount rate. Since Tobin's proposal was made for reforming the discount mechanism of the Federal Reserve in the United States where prohibitions have been placed on the payment of interest on demand deposits, and interest rate ceilings on time and savings deposits, he also proposed that all such prohibitions and ceilings be repealed.

attractive for purposes of monetary control, it is probably unacceptable because paying interest on excess reserves held with the central bank could be interpreted as subsidy payments to commercial banks by the central bank.

HISTORY OF BANK RATE IN CANADA

When the Bank of Canada began operations in 1935, the Bank rate was set at 2½ per cent where it remained until 1944 when it was decreased to 1½ per cent. The decrease was announced to indicate the Bank's desire to maintain a low level of interest rates during the postwar reconstruction period. In 1950 with the threat of inflation caused by the Korean War, the rate was raised to announce to the market what level the Bank considered appropriate for market rates.

Early in 1955 the Bank rate was again reduced to 1½ per cent. This reduction was made not to signal a shift in the direction of monetary policy but to bring the Bank rate into closer relation with the rates in the developing money market in order to facilitate its more flexible use in the future. From August 1955 to November 1956 the Bank rate was increased on six separate occasions. Although most of these increases were of a technical nature to keep the rate at a penalty level, the upward movement came at a time when the Bank of Canada wished to impose monetary restraint. During this period, the banks for the first time made frequent use of the central bank as a lender of last resort. Moreover, the Bank rate probably became a cost factor and not merely a psychological factor in the market. The chartered banks adjusted their rates in line with changes in the Bank rate and announced these changes with reference to changes in the Bank rate. As the Bank rate had become an important factor in influencing market rates it is difficult to explain why the Bank of Canada abandoned the fixed Bank rate for a floating rate in November 1956. After that date, until June 1962, the Bank rate was set at one quarter of one per cent above the weekly Treasury bill rate and was allowed to float with this rate.

In June 1962, as part of a program for dealing with the country's foreign exchange crisis, the Bank rate was again fixed and was raised to 6 per cent as a signal to the rest of the world of Canada's determination to defend the external value of the Canadian dollar.[25] When this objective had been achieved and Canada's official foreign exchange holdings had been rebuilt, the Bank rate was reduced; after three separate reductions it was set at 3½ per cent in 1963.

---

25 See Bank of Canada, *Annual Report of the Governor to the Minister of Finance*, 1962, pp. 3-4 and 72-73.

TABLE 16-2

History of the Bank Rate in Canada

Date of Change	Rate Set (per cent)
1935	2½
1944, February	1½
1950, October	2
1955, February	1½
1955, August	2
1955, October	2¼
1955, November	2¾
1956, April	3
1956, August	3¼
1956, October	3½
1956, November	Floating Rate
1962, June	6
1962, September	5½
1962, October	5
1962, November	4
1963, May	3½
1963, August	4
1964, November	4¼
1965, December	4¾
1966, March	5¼
1967, January	5
1967, April	4½
1967, September	5
1967, November	6
1968, January	7

From August 1964 to early 1966 there were four increases in the Bank rate. Each of these was made to achieve an appropriate differential in market interest rates between Canada and foreign countries, particularly the United States. International short-term capital flows have become fairly sensitive to interest rate differentials between countries. These flows, insofar as they affect a country's holdings of foreign exchange, may put pressure on the external value of a country's currency. Most countries are members of the International Monetary Fund and as such agree to prevent the external value of their currency from fluctuating more than one per cent on either side of an agreed parity. Therefore, as we shall see later, a close watch must be kept on their holdings of foreign exchange. The amount of these holdings can be influenced by short-term international capital flows, which are induced by interest rate differentials between countries.

The use of the Bank rate to protect the external value of the currency, while still relatively new to Canada and the United States, has a long history in Britain. As we noted earlier, changes in the Bank of England's rate were first introduced primarily to protect its gold reserves which also constituted most of the reserves of the country. In the heyday of the gold standard it was believed that the Bank of England by setting the Bank rate at 7 per cent could produce an inflow of foreign capital sufficient "to bring gold from the moon" [26]

THE BANK'S MONEY MARKET RATE

In 1954, in its attempt to develop a money market in Canada, the Bank of Canada began extending its lender of last resort privileges to a small group of investment dealers. Since then, a select group of dealers have availed themselves of this opportunity. Borrowing is usually facilitated through purchase and resale agreements. When in 1962 the Bank returned to a fixed rate for lending to the banks, it retained the floating rate for its transactions with the investment dealers. This rate subsequently became known as the Bank's Money Market rate.

In 1963 the Bank of Canada for the first time made special one-month purchase and resale agreements with the money market by entering into contracts with approved dealers at a special interest charge lower than the Bank's Money Market rate. In the following year, the same technique was employed but the rate was established by competitive tender. Later the rate was set at one quarter of one per cent above the Treasury bill rate or at the Bank rate, whichever is lower. These purchase and resale agreements with the money market dealers have been employed to handle the sharp seasonal rise and fall in note circulation over Christmas. [27] Advances to money market dealers in the form of purchase and resale agreements at rates arrived at competitively rather than determined by the Bank of Canada are in effect a special type of open market operation similar to the Bank of England's practice of accommodating directly discount houses and commercial banks at the so-called open back door. When the Bank of England offers accommodation through the **back door**

[26] For instance, in November 1907, the Bank of England raised its rate to 7 per cent attracting gold from no fewer than twenty-four countries in a matter of weeks and permitting the Bank rate to drop back to 4 per cent by January 1908. It was the willingness of the British authorities to use high Bank rates when necessary that bulwarked confidence in the pound. Seven per cent generally did the trick, though in some crises the Bank rate was put up briefly to 8, 9 or even 10 per cent.

[27] See Bank of Canada, *Annual Report of the Governor to the Minister of Finance*, 1963, p. 62, and 1964, pp. 36-37.

it charges rates that do not disturb the market level of interest rates. In practice the Bank buys Treasury bills at the rate it considers to represent the market rate. When the Bank provides accommodation at or above the penalty Bank rate it is said to be operating through the **front door.**

MORAL SUASION AND SELECTIVE CONTROLS

The control measures which we have discussed so far — reserve requirements and their variation, open market operations and changes in the Bank rate — are concerned primarily with overall money and credit conditions. They are quantitative controls which operate in an impersonal way by influencing the cost, volume and availability of bank reserves. Allocation of credit is left to market forces for quantitative controls cannot be used effectively to serve this purpose.

Qualitative or selective controls, on the other hand, seek to regulate the supply of credit available to, and the amount of credit demanded by, *particular* areas and sectors of the economy. Although some central banks have the power to impose qualitative and selective controls from time to time, they usually rely on quantitative controls and allow the market forces to allocate credit. When however, they have considered the market to be working inefficiently or inequitably, they have attempted to correct these deficiencies by persuading financial institutions to change their lending, investing and other policies.

MORAL SUASION

The central bank may use moral suasion to persuade financial institutions to "voluntarily" pursue some objective of financial policy. The resulting agreements may be formal or informal. The object of moral suasion is usually to restrict or expand the terms and availability of credit to certain areas or sectors of the economy. On some occasions, as in 1953 when the Bank of Canada was endeavouring to develop a money market, the intention is to modify or improve market practices.

The cooperation which the central bank (the persuader) receives from the financial community depends particularly upon the success or failure of the bank's leadership in the past. The prestige gained from a history of success will make it easier for the central bank to solicit cooperation. A poor record, on the other hand, will make the task of the persuader more difficult. Under most circumstances it is probably easier to gain support through persuasion from a small group of financial institutions than from a large one. This probably explains why the Bank of Canada has relied more on moral suasion than has the Federal Reserve System in the United States. Moreover, when a large group is persuaded to follow a certain course of action the possibility of side-stepping is increased since individual institutions may consider their deviations to have insignificant effects on the total.

The support which the central bank can expect from financial institutions will also depend upon the nature, frequency and duration of its requests. For instance, the central bank may request the chartered banks to restrict a certain type of profitable lending. If the central bank can persuade the banks that this is in the national interest or is for a relatively short period, the banks will probably comply. However, even if the requests call for only temporary compliance, frequent requests of this nature may be coolly received.

In general, commercial banks usually respond to moral suasion by the central bank because they know that it can employ those techniques which we have already explained to restrict their ability to increase their total lending and investing and thereby their ability to increase their profits.

THE USE OF MORAL SUASION IN CANADA

When the Bank of Canada opened its doors in 1935 there were only ten chartered banks. The small number of chartered banks throughout the Canadian history of central banking has made possible an intimate relationship between the Bank of Canada and the banks. Although the chartered banks accepted the establishment of the Bank of Canada in 1934 with much suspicion, Graham Towers, the first Governor of the Bank, early gained the respect of his fellow bankers and the Bank soon established a favourable reputation.[28]

The Bank of Canada first used moral suasion in 1936. In that year the Governor of the Bank held meetings with committees of the stock exchanges and the banks to request them to raise margin requirements for loans intended for speculation.[29] Ten years later the Bank of Canada requested that the banks restrict their holdings of Government of Canada bonds to an amount not exceeding 90 per cent of their Canadian personal savings deposits and that they restrict their net earnings on such securities to a specified maximum.

In February 1948 the banks agreed to a request by the Bank of Canada to refrain from making term loans to or purchasing directly bonds

---

28 The appointment of Graham Towers, who at the age of thirty-seven was the assistant general manager of one of Canada's largest chartered banks, was probably the single most important reason for allaying early suspicions of a central bank.

29 For an explanation of margin requirements see p. 250.

and debentures from corporate customers in amounts exceeding a certain limit.[30] This request was withdrawn a year later.

A more detailed and extensive agreement by the banks was reached following the Bank of Canada's request in 1951 to limit credit expansion. The banks agreed to a "credit ceiling" by not allowing further expansion in their loans under existing inflationary conditions, to stop making term loans or purchasing corporate securities in amounts in excess of a certain sum, to request at least a 50 per cent margin in the case of loans to carry corporate stock, and to allow no further increases in total loans to finance companies. This agreement was extended in January of 1952 and was suspended later in the year.

Although the Bank of Canada has used moral suasion primarily to influence the lending policies of the banks, it has been used for other purposes. In 1956, as in 1936, the Bank had discussions with members of the governing bodies of the stock exchanges to request them to limit any further increases in the volume of credit used in stock market trading. During the same year the Bank also met with representatives of the major instalment finance companies, and the major department and chain stores to seek voluntary agreement to prevent significant increases in the volume of consumer credit extended by them. On this occasion no general agreement was reached. The Bank was not entirely unsuccessful, however, as the banks were persuaded to curtail the credit extended to finance companies and retail stores providing instalment finance facilities. Companies which were subsidiaries of large foreign corporations had access to funds through them, and could still escape monetary restraint.

Up to the end of 1956 the use of moral suasion in Canada was concerned primarily with the restriction of credit. The only exception to this was the persuasion, more in the form of advice than request, used by the Bank after 1953 to encourage the development of a money market in Canada.

In 1957 moral suasion by the Bank of Canada was used for the first time as a qualitative control to encourage the flow of credit to a certain sector of the economy. In March of that year the Bank of Canada requested the banks to resume their residential mortgage lending activity under the National Housing Act on the same scale as in 1956. In the early months of 1957 the chartered banks had virtually withdrawn from the insured residential mortgage market as other market yields became more attractive. The Bank of Canada indicated that if the banks increased their NHA lending on the 1956 scale it would provide extra reserves to

[30] Term loans were defined as loans to business corporations for fixed rather than working capital purposes.

the banking system. The banks would then be able to maintain a flow of funds for insured mortgages without having to dispose of other assets.

In 1965, after the failure of Atlantic Acceptance Corporation, the Governor of the Bank of Canada consulted with the chartered banks. He indicated that the Bank was prepared to provide the necessary reserves so that the banking system could accommodate any credit-worthy finance company which might find itself in a difficult liquidity position. The banks responded by making additional credit available and at least some of the uneasiness in the market was relieved. In this case, the Bank used moral suasion in an attempt to maintain confidence in the financial system.

The last use of moral suasion we shall consider here also took place in 1965 and was concerned with the possible effects of a change in the flow of international capital on Canada's domestic financial market. In an attempt to solve its continuing balance of payments problems the American government introduced a "guideline program" to stem the flow of capital from the United States and to encourage the repatriation of funds earned in foreign countries. The Bank of Canada foresaw that subsidiaries of American companies might seek to raise substantially larger amounts of capital in Canada from the banks or securities markets. It therefore requested the banks to meet in full the normal demands for business loans from their credit-worthy customers and to give priority to customers who had relied on them in the past for credit needs.

The Bank of Canada has employed persuasion, suggestion and advice as an important technique for monetary control. It has perhaps relied too much on moral suasion at times when more forceful techniques would have been more appropriate.

SELECTIVE CREDIT CONTROLS

Selective credit controls are directed to types of lending rather than to the lending of particular institutions. Because they involve the direct interference with the free play of market forces they have been used reluctantly and only during time of war and periods of postwar readjustment. The authority to impose such controls was granted to the Bank of Canada during the Second World War by order-in-council under the War Measures Act.

The more common types of selective credit controls that have been employed include those on margin requirements, consumer credit, real estate credit and new capital issues.

Margin requirements are that part of the purchase price of securities listed on stock exchanges that must be paid directly by the purchaser. When the margin requirement is 60 per cent, a buyer of a listed stock with a current value of $1,000 has to put up at least $600 of his own funds and may borrow no more than $400 using the stock as collateral. By increasing margin requirements the authorities make it more difficult for those who must borrow funds to speculate on the stock market. The authority to set margin requirements was given to the Board of Governors of the Federal Reserve System in the United States in the Securities Exchange Act of 1934 and has been used continuously since then. The Bank of Canada has no such authority but, as we have seen, has used moral suasion to this end.

Consumer credit controls were employed in Canada during the Second World War and the Korean War. The Bank of Canada issued regulations which set minimum required down payments for the purchase of consumer goods and the maximum number of months allowed to pay the balance. Consumer credit controls have been used to decrease the demand for consumer goods, to restrain inflationary pressures during periods of scarcity and to make resources available for such purposes as essential war industries. Because they postpone the demand for consumer durables during war periods, they also help to prevent recessionary tendencies which usually follow the sudden decline of government demand for war materials when war is over.

Real estate credit controls are similar to controls on consumer credit discussed above. They are intended to restrict the purchase of real estate and thereby to restrict construction and speculation by prescribing minimum down payments for the purchase of real estate and maximum maturity dates for loans.

The National Housing Act in Canada has had effects similar to those resulting from selective credit controls. Under the act the government guarantees loans made by the Central Mortgage and Housing Corporation and approved institutional lenders for the construction of new houses. By setting down payment requirements, the minimum maturity of the loans and the maximum interest chargeable, the government has influenced the demand for and the supply of funds for residential construction.

In Britain direct control was exercised over new capital issues in the 1950's to limit overseas borrowing in that country and also to allocate domestic funds for capital investment purposes. Because direct controls that attempt to affect the allocation of credit are usually difficult to administer, they are used only in emergency situations.

SELECTED READINGS

Aschheim, Joseph, *Techniques of Monetary Control,* Baltimore, Johns Hopkins Press, 1961.

Aschheim, Joseph, "Open-Market Operations Versus Reserve-Requirement Increases: A Reformation", *Economic Journal*, Vol. 73, pp. 254-266.

Bagehot, Walter, *Lombard Street*, New York, Scribner, Armstrong, 1873, Ch. 7, 12, 13.

Cairns, James P., and H. H. Binhammer, *Canadian Banking and Monetary Policy*, Toronto, McGraw-Hill, 1965, Part 4.

Carson, Deane, "The Bills Only Doctrine in Retrospect", in M. J. Brennan, (ed.), *Patterns of Market Behaviour: Essays in Honor of Philip Taft*, Providence, Brown University Press, 1965, pp. 155-172, reprinted in Deane Carson, *Money and Finance: Readings in Theory, Policy and Institutions*, New York, John Wiley, 1966, pp. 309-326.

Committee on the Working of the Monetary System, *Report*, London, Her Majesty's Stationery Office, 1959.

Eckstein, Otto, and John Kareken, "The 'Bills Only' Policy: A Summary of the Issues", *Employment, Growth and Price Levels, Hearings before the Joint Economic Committee*, U. S. Congress, July 1959, pp. 1248-1251, reprinted in Lawrence S. Ritter (ed.), *Money and Economic Activity*, 2nd ed., Boston, Houghton Mifflin, 1961, pp. 274-277.

Friedman, Milton, *A Program for Monetary Stability*, New York, Fordham University Press, 1960.

Galbraith, John A., *The Economics of Banking Operations: A Canadian Study*, Montreal, McGill University Press, 1963, Ch. 7.

Gibson, N. J., "Special Deposits as an Instrument of Monetary Policy", *The Manchester School of Economics and Social Studies*, Vol. 23, September 1964, pp. 239-259.

Guttentag, J., "The Strategy of Open-Market Operations", *Quarterly Journal of Economics*, Vol. 80, 1966, pp. 1-30.

Hawtrey, R. G., *A Century of Bank Rate*, 2nd ed., London, Frank Cass, 1962.

Jacoby, Neil, "The Structure and Use of Variable Bank Reserve Requirements", in Deane Carson (ed.), *Banking and Monetary Studies*, Homewood, Ill., Richard D. Irwin, 1963, pp. 213-233.

Johnston, Robert A., "The Canadian Experience with the Floating Discount Rate", *Yale Economic Essays*, Vol. 6, Spring 1966, pp. 3-46.

Polakoff, Murray E., "Federal Reserve Discount Policy and Its Critics", in Deane Carson (ed.), *Banking and Monetary Studies*, Homewood, Ill., Richard D. Irwin, 1963, pp. 190-212.

Rasminsky, Louis, "Central Banking in the Canadian Financial System", in *Challenges and Trends in Modern Banking*, Toronto, Canadian Bankers' Association, 1967.

Riefler, Winfield W., "Open Market Operations in Long-Term Securities", *Federal Reserve Bulletin*, Vol. 44, No. 11, Nov. 1958, pp. 1260-1274, reprinted in Deane Carson, *Money and Finance: Readings in Theory, Policy and Institutions*, New York, John Wiley & Sons, 1966, pp. 291-308.

Rowan, David C. "The Techniques of Monetary Control: A Review Article", *Banca Nazionale Del Lavoro, Quarterly Review*, No. 65, June 1963, pp. 192-215.

Samuelson, Paul A., "Recent Monetary Controversy", The *Three Banks Review*, No. 29, March 1956, pp. 3-21, reprinted in Lawrence S. Ritter (ed.), *Money and Economic Activity*, 2nd ed., Boston, Houghton Mifflin, 1961, pp. 252-261.

Sayers, R. S., *Modern Banking*, 6th ed., Oxford, Clarendon Press, 1964, Ch. 5.

Sayers, R. S., *Central Banking After Bagehot*, London, Oxford University Press, 1957.

Smith, Warren L., "The Instruments of General Monetary Control", *National Banking Review*, Vol. 1, September 1963, pp. 47-76.

Smith, Warren L., "The Discount Rate as a Credit-Control Weapon", *Journal of Political Economy*, Vol. 46, 1958, pp. 171-177.

Smithies, Arthur, "Uses of Selective Credit Controls", in Neil H. Jacoby (ed.), *United States Monetary Policy*, New York, American Assembly, 1968, Ch. 3.

Tamagna, F. M., *et. al.*, *Monetary Management*, prepared for the Commission on Money and Credit, Englewood Cliffs, N. J., Prentice-Hall, 1963.

United States, Board of Governors of the Federal Reserve System, *The Federal Reserve System: Its Purposes and Functions*, Washington, D. C., 1964.

Young, Ralph A., "Tools and Processes of Monetary Policy", in Neil H. Jacoby (ed.), *United States Monetary Policy*, New York, American Assembly, 1958, Ch. 1.

17 GOVERNMENT OPERATIONS AND MONETARY CONTROL

The financial transactions of the central government influence the monetary system and credit conditions to almost as great a degree as do the activities of the central bank. Management of the government's cash deposits brings indirect influence to bear on credit conditions by affecting the cash reserves of the banking system. Direct influence on credit conditions may be exerted by the management of government assets (other than cash deposits) and of government debt.

THE NATURE OF GOVERNMENT FINANCIAL TRANSACTIONS

During any given period the federal government requires cash to meet its budgetary and non-budgetary obligations. These cash requirements can be met by increasing debt (borrowing), by running down cash balances or by liquidating assets held in the investment account and sinking funds. When, however, its overall transactions result in cash surpluses rather than deficits, the government is able to reduce its overall debt or increase its cash balances, or add to the security holdings of the investment account and sinking funds. Table 17-1 shows the overall cash requirements of the Government of Canada during recent years and how these have been financed.

The financial budget[1] of the Government of Canada refers to the federal government's general financial operations. The financial budget together with non-budgetary receipts and disbursements shows the government's overall cash surplus or cash needs.

[1] Since 1946 federal government's revenue and expenditures have also been shown on a national accounts basis. The so-called national accounts budget includes only income and expenditure transactions which have a direct and immediate impact on the flow of incomes on the economy. See Canadian Tax Foundation, *The National Finances 1966-67*, Toronto, 1966, pp. 23-26.

Budgetary revenue is derived from taxes, duties and other assessments, and from the sale of government goods and services.[2] Also included in budgetary revenue are the return from the government's investments in Crown corporations, the profits earned by the Bank of Canada, revenue from the operations of the Royal Canadian Mint and the Post Office, and earnings of the Exchange Fund and sinking funds.

Budgetary expenditures include those for the purchase of goods and services and for subsidies, grants and other transfers. Interest on the public debt, salaries and wages to civil servants, grants to the Canadian National Railway and to other governments are only a few of the many other items included in budgetary expenditures.

Budgetary transactions do not reflect the government's total cash surpluses or cash needs. In addition to these transactions there are non-budgetary disbursements in the form of government loans, and investments in and advances to Crown corporations, government funds, foreign governments and international organizations. When these are repaid they become non-budgetary receipts. Also included as non-budgetary receipts and disbursements are the transactions of the government's annuity, insurance and pension accounts as well as receipts and credits from such items as accounts payable, accrued interest and outstanding cheques.

During the federal government's fiscal year ending on March 31, 1965 its budgetary expenditures were $7,218 million and its budgetary revenue was $7,180 million. Therefore, there was a budgetary deficit, as shown in the table, of $38 million. During the same fiscal year the non-budgetary receipts and credits amounted to $685 million and non-budgetary disbursements and charges totalled $1,069 million, for a deficit of $384.2 million on non-budgetary items. The total cash needs of the government made up of the budgetary and non-budgetary deficits amounted to $422.2 million. These were financed by an increase of $238.1 million in unmatured debt outstanding, a $146.7 million decrease in the government's cash balances and the use of $37.4 million from the security investment account and sinking funds.

MANAGEMENT OF GOVERNMENT DEPOSITS

The Government of Canada maintains cash balances, in the name of the **Receiver General,** with the Bank of Canada, the chartered banks, two Quebec savings banks and banks in a few foreign countries. By statutory definition, the total of these deposits constitutes the **Consolidated Revenue**

[2] The Old Age Security taxes on personal and corporate income and on sales are not included in budgetary revenue but are placed into the Old Age Security Fund which is separate from the budgetary accounts. Surpluses or deficits in this Fund are non-budgetary transactions.

Fund of the Government of Canada. The Bank of Canada is the main government banker and as such holds its operating account.

The day-to-day receipts and disbursements of the federal government are handled through its account with the Bank of Canada. Daily Canadian dollar receipts, whether in the form of cash receipts or cheques to be cleared are received by the Bank of Canada's agencies throughout the country and are deposited directly to the credit of the Receiver General's account with the Bank.

Payments to the public by the government are made from its account with the Bank of Canada. The value of government cheques cashed by the chartered banks and presented by them to the Bank of Canada agencies for payment during the day-to-day clearing house operations are charged to the account of the Receiver General. In practice, when these cheques are received by the Bank of Canada, the government's account is debited upon receipt of a cheque drawn on the Receiver General's account and signed on behalf of the Minister of Finance.

Payments by the public to the government are normally made with cheques drawn on deposit accounts with the chartered banks and other financial institutions. After these cheques are settled through the clearing house operations and credited to the government's account with the central bank, the latter has a claim on the chartered banks. This claim is settled by drawing down the banks' deposits with the central bank. As a result the cash reserves of the banks are reduced. When the government's cheques made out to the public are settled through the clearing house operations, the banks acquire a net claim on the central bank and their cash reserves are increased.

If the government were to maintain a deposit account with the central bank alone, the cash reserves of the chartered banks would fluctuate with the daily ebb and flow of government transactions. If on balance, the government's payments to the public exceeded its receipts from the public, the banks' deposits with the central bank and therefore their cash reserves would increase. Conversely, if on balance the government's receipts from the public were to exceed its payments to the public, the cash reserves of the banks would decline as their deposits with the central bank were reduced. To eliminate or reduce frequent changes in the cash reserves of the banks caused by government funds flowing in and out of its account with the central bank, the government maintains deposit accounts with the chartered banks.

Transfers between the government's account with the central bank and its accounts with the chartered banks may be made daily in order to maintain a relatively constant balance with the central bank, or infrequently to produce changes in the cash reserves of the banks consistent with the central bank's current monetary policy. Transferring balances

TABLE 17-1

Government of Canada: Overall Financial Statement

(*millions of dollars*)

	1961-62	1962-63	1963-64	1964-65	1965-66
Budgetary Revenue	5,729.6	5,878.7	6,253.2	7,180.3	7,695.8
Budgetary Expenditures	6,520.6	6,570.3	6,872.4	7,218.3	7,734.8
Budgetary Surplus (+) or Deficit (−)	−791.0	− 691.6	−619.2	− 38.0	− 39.0
Non-Budgetary Surplus (+) or Deficit (−)	+313.4	− 772.3	+336.7	−384.2	−120.9
Overall Cash Requirements (−)	−477.6	−1,463.9	−282.5	−422.2	−159.9
Financed by:					
Decrease (+) in cash balances	−416.9	+ 400.2	−451.7	+146.7	+ 47.3
Decrease (+) in securities investment account holdings	+ 19.1	+ 50.5	− 66.4	+ 42.8	− 19.0
Decrease (+) in sinking fund holdings	− 2.4	− 2.9	+ 22.3	− 5.4	—
Increase (+) in unmatured debt outstanding	+887.8	+1,016.1	+778.3	+238.1	+131.6
Total Overall Cash Requirement	+477.6	+1,463.9	+282.5	+422.2	+159.9

Source: Bank of Canada Statistical Summary Supplement 1966, pp. 122-123.

between deposit accounts in the central bank and the commercial banks can be used as a technique of monetary control. For example, let us assume that the government wishes to follow an expansionary policy and increases its expenditures so that these exceed its receipts. If the excess of government expenditures over receipts is $5 million and if the government finances all of this deficit by allowing its cash balances with the central bank to run down by this amount, the following changes are observed in the balance sheets of the central bank and the chartered banks.

CENTRAL BANK

Assets		Liabilities	
		Deposits:	
		Government	−$5,000,000
		Chartered Banks	+$5,000,000

CHARTERED BANKS

Assets		Liabilities	
Reserves:		Deposits:	
Deposits with the		Government	0
Central Bank	+$5,000,000	Public	+$5,000,000
NET EFFECT			
Reserves:			
Required	+$ 600,000		
Excess	+$4,400,000	Deposits	+$5,000,000

The total cash reserves of the banks are increased by $5 million and their excess reserves by an amount determined by their cash reserve ratio. If the reserve ratio is 12 per cent and if the banks were already fully loaned, $4,400,000 in excess reserves would be available to support an expansion in their loans and deposits.

The cash reserves of the banks can be increased also in a period when the government's revenue exceeds its expenditures, if an amount greater than its excess receipts is transferred from its deposit account with the central bank to its accounts with the chartered banks. This is shown in the next illustration where we assume that government revenue exceeds its expenditures by $5 million and the government transfers $7 million from its central bank account to those with the chartered banks. The net result is an increase of $2 million in the banks' cash reserves and, assuming a 12 per cent cash reserve ratio, an increase of $1,760,000 in their excess reserves. If the government were to transfer only $5 million from

CENTRAL BANK

	Assets		Liabilities	
STAGE I			Deposits:	
	Net Government Receipts		Government	+$5,000,000
			Chartered banks	−$5,000,000
STAGE II			Deposits:	
	Transfer from Government Account		Government	−$7,000,000
			Chartered banks	+$7,000,000
NET EFFECT			Deposits:	
			Government	−$2,000,000
			Chartered banks	+$2,000,000

CHARTERED BANKS

	Assets		Liabilities	
STAGE I	Reserves:		Deposits:	
	Deposits with the Central Bank	−$5,000,000	Government	0
			Public	−$5,000,000
STAGE II	Reserves:		Deposits:	
	Deposits with the Central Bank	+$7,000,000	Government	+$7,000,000
			Public	0
NET EFFECT	Reserves:		Deposits:	
	Required	+$ 240,000	Deposits	+$2,000,000
	Excess	+$1,760,000		

its account with the central bank to the chartered banks, the net effect on the banks' cash reserves would be zero; if it transferred less than $5 million, the net effect would be a reduction in the banks' cash reserves. Managing the bank's cash reserves by transferring government funds from the central bank to the commercial banks has the advantage over open market operations of not disturbing the money market. Only if such transfers were large enough to require major portfolio shifts by the banks would their effects create market disturbances.

The degree to which government deposit transfers may be used as a technique for discretionary monetary policy depends upon the amount of available government balances and the distribution of these balances between the central bank and the chartered banks. Governments generally are reluctant to hold large deposit balances and therefore the management of government deposits is confined to the relatively passive role of minimizing the impact on the banks' cash reserves of the government's day-to-day financial operations.

We have already mentioned that in Canada the federal government holds cash balances with the chartered banks. Cash balances redeposited from the government's account with the Bank of Canada to its accounts in the chartered banks are allocated on the basis of a percentage formula established by agreement among the banks and communicated to the Department of Finance by the Canadian Banker's Association. This formula is based on the percentage of the total work done by each bank in handling government cheques, money orders, government bond coupons and other government business. [3]

On minimum monthly Receiver General balances in excess of an aggregate of $100 million, the chartered banks have paid interest equal to the weekly average Treasury bill tender rate for three-month Treasury bills less 10 per cent.

---

[3] The government is not required to keep minimum balances with the chartered banks. However, it seems to have held substantial balances with them as compensation for the banking services they provide to the government, especially for cashing government cheques without charge as required in the Bank Act.

In November 1962 the percentage allocation among the banks was as follows:

Montreal	21.73%	Nationale	6.96%
Royal	21.55%	Toronto-Dominion	9.92%
Imperial Commerce	25.03%	Provinciale	3.92%
Nova Scotia	10.80%	Mercantile	0.09%
			100.00%

Not all of the government's cash balances redeposited with the chartered banks are subject to the percentage allocation formula. Excluded are accounts which concern departmental banking, imprest and revenue trust accounts and accounts in respect of the issue of warrants and letters-of-credit. Moreover, in the case of Canada Savings Bond issues, redeposit takes place on the basis of the bank against which funds were originally drawn.

Although the Bank of Canada requires the concurrence of the Minister of Finance to transfer government deposits between the Bank and the chartered banks, permission is extended on a continuing basis to allow the Bank to make daily transfers. The Bank of Canada manages the government's deposits to prevent severe fluctuations in the cash reserves of the banks which could result from the uneven flow of government receipts and expenditures and from the sudden withdrawal of cash into public circulation. [4] For example, the Bank of Canada has turned over its annual profits to the government in instalments during the latter part of the year. After being credited to the government's account with the Bank of Canada, these moneys have been redeposited in the government's deposit accounts with the chartered banks to offset the effects on the cash reserves of the banks of the sharp rise in note circulation during the Christmas period. [5] As a rule, transfers in the government's deposit accounts are made only to maintain and not to change the level of the banks' cash reserves. An exception to this normal practice was made in 1962 when, during the country's foreign exchange crisis, transfers in government deposits were made deliberately to effect changes in the chartered banks' reserves.

ASSET MANAGEMENT

The government maintains non-deposit financial accounts in accordance with the special financial purposes for which the accounts are established. These are general investment accounts, such as the Government Securities Investment Account and the Government Purchase Fund, and special investment accounts. The latter are mainly annuity, pension and insurance accounts and include the Unemployment Insurance Fund and the Old Age Security Fund.

The Securities Investment Account of the Government of Canada was originally established to facilitate the investment of the government's

[4] In Britain the issues and maturities of Treasury bills are manipulated so as to stabilize government deposits with the Bank of England.

In the United States as the flow of cash to the Treasury for tax payments or the proceeds of borrowing come in, they are first deposited in the Treasury's Tax and Loan Accounts with commercial banks. Although the principal objective of the Treasury's deposit policy is to minimize the effects of its operation on the commercial banks, it has at times shifted deposits to its working balance with the Federal Reserve with a lead or a lag.

[5] In more recent years the Bank of Canada's net earnings have been transferred to the Receiver General at various times during the year. To offset seasonal currency movements during December and January the Bank of Canada has employed the technique of entering into special one-month purchase and resale agreements with money market dealers, or regular open market transactions in addition to variations in the level of the government's deposit at the Bank of Canada.

temporary excess cash balances in its own securities. Since the chartered banks began paying interest on Government of Canada cash balances over a certain minimum amount, the Account has been directed to other purposes. During the Second World War and in the immediate postwar period, the Account was used to purchase and sell Government of Canada bonds to stabilize their prices. In more recent years it has been used to offset the effect on the cash reserves of the banks of seasonal changes in statutory till money in February and March. The Bank of Canada usually sells government bonds to the Securities Investment Account for delivery on February 1 and repurchase on March 1. The Account has also been used on other occasions for managing the cash reserves of the banks. For example, in 1964 and 1965 when the government had relatively large cash balances available for short-term investment, the Account purchased securities from the Bank of Canada.

The Government Purchase Fund was established in 1961 to provide for the orderly retirement of government debt and at the same time to contribute to the stability of the long-term bond market.[6] The Securities Investment Account has also been used to assist the government in its debt management by purchasing Government securities nearing maturity.

— Special investment accounts are usually less subject to manipulation for monetary and debt management policies than the general funds discussed above. When these accounts run a surplus, it is invested in government securities. The financial aspect of such purchases is similar to that of government debt retirement considered below.

The degree to which government funds are used for monetary management is reflected in Table 16-1 which shows the net transactions of these funds with the Bank of Canada.

DEBT MANAGEMENT AND THE MONEY SUPPLY

We have said that during any period the government meets its cash needs by running down its cash deposits, by borrowing, or by both. There are three sources from which the government may borrow: the public, the commercial banking system and the central bank. The monetary effects of government borrowing depend upon the source of such borrowing.

BORROWING FROM THE PUBLIC

Let us assume that the government, anticipating a cash deficit in its total transactions, sells new bonds to the non-bank public. The public pays for these bonds by writing cheques against its accounts in the chartered banks (see Stage I in the following illustration). In settlement of these

[6] To March 31, 1962, cancellations of securities held by the Purchase Fund amounted to $166 million, valued at par.

cheques the government's account with the central bank is increased and the chartered banks' deposits with the central bank and their cash reserves are reduced by an equivalent amount (see Stage II). If the government writes cheques drawn on its increased deposits with the central

EFFECTS OF GOVERNMENT BORROWING FROM THE NON-BANK PUBLIC

CENTRAL BANK

	Assets		Liabilities	
Stage I				
Stage II			Deposits: Government Chartered Banks	 + –
Stage III			Deposits: Government Chartered Banks	 – +

CHARTERED BANKS

	Assets		Liabilities	
Stage I			Deposits: Government Public	 0 –
Stage II	Reserves: Deposits with the Central Bank	 –		
Stage III	Reserves: Deposits with the Central Bank	 +	Deposits: Government Public	 0 +
NET EFFECT	Reserves: Deposits with the Central Bank	 0	Deposits: Government Public	 0 0

bank to cover its excess expenditures, the public's deposits and the banks' cash reserves are built back (see Stage III).

When an increase in the government's expenditures in the non-bank public sector is matched by a sale of government bonds to this sector, the final effect on the cash reserves of the chartered banks and the money supply is neutral. It is possible, however, to introduce temporary changes because leads and lags occur between the three stages we have defined.

Although the money supply is not altered by government borrowing from the non-bank public, the total effect on the community is by no means neutral. The public, holding more government bonds, has increased its financial assets. The **wealth effect** of this increase may induce spending, affecting prices and income in a manner similar to an increase in the money supply. The monetary effect, therefore, will be in the form of an increase in the velocity of circulation of money.

BORROWING FROM CHARTERED BANKS

When the government sells new bonds to the chartered banks their assets increase by an amount equal to the purchase price of the bonds (see Stage I in the following illustration). Settlement for these bonds is made by crediting the government's account and debiting the chartered banks' accounts with the central bank by an equivalent amount (see Stage II). As the government writes cheques against its increased deposits with the central bank, these decline and the public's deposits at the chartered banks, together with the banks' cash reserves, increase by a corresponding amount (see Stage III). The net result of government borrowing from the chartered banks matched by a corresponding increase in its purchases of goods and services from the public is that no change occurs in the cash reserves of the banks while the money supply increases. However, since the public's deposits with the chartered banks have increased, the banks' required reserves have also increased by an amount determined by the legal cash reserve ratio. Unless the banks can obtain the required amount of cash reserves the increase in the public's deposits with them is not maintainable.

BORROWING FROM THE CENTRAL BANK

Because of the pronounced monetary effects of direct borrowing by the government from the central bank, most of its borrowing is from the banks and the non-bank public. The central bank normally provides the banking system with any reserves necessary to absorb government security issues.

When the central bank buys bonds from the government it pays for them by crediting the government's deposit account (see Stage I in the following illustration). As the government writes cheques against this account the public's deposits in the banking system increase. The banks' cash reserves also increase by the same amount (Stage II). Since the banks' cash reserves increase by the same amount as their deposits, they will have excess reserves and may expand credit. Thus, without any offsetting action by the central bank, direct borrowing by the government

Effects of Government Borrowing from the Chartered Banks

Central Bank

	Assets		Liabilities	
Stage I				
Stage II			Deposits: Government Chartered Banks	 + –
Stage III			Deposits: Government Chartered Banks	 – +

Chartered Banks

	Assets		Liabilities	
Stage I	Securities: Government Bonds	 +		
Stage III	Reserves: Deposits with the Central Bank	 –		
Stage III	Reserves: Deposits with the Central Bank	 +	Deposits: Government Public	 0 +
Net Effect	Reserves: Deposits with the Central Bank Securities: Government Bonds	 0 +	Deposits: Government Public	 0 +

from the central bank makes possible the multiple expansion of deposits by the banking system, and therefore has an expansionary effect on the money supply.

SUMMARY OF MONETARY EFFECTS OF GOVERNMENT BORROWING

When the government finances its expenditures by borrowing from the public there is no effect on the public's money supply and bank reserves. However, the public's financial wealth holdings are increased and this may influence its level and pattern of spending much as would an increase in the monetary stock.

If the government borrows from the chartered banks the public's money supply is increased, total bank reserves are unchanged, but required reserves rise. The net change is an increase in the money supply but this is maintainable only if the chartered banks obtain the required cash reserves.

EFFECTS OF GOVERNMENT BORROWING FROM THE CENTRAL BANK

CENTRAL BANK

	Assets		Liabilities	
Stage I	Securities:		Deposits:	
	Government Bonds	+	Government	+
Stage II			Deposits:	
			Government	−
			Chartered Banks	+

CHARTERED BANKS

	Assets		Liabilities	
Stage I				
Stage II	Reserves:		Deposits:	
	Deposits with the Central Bank	+	Government	0
			Public	+
NET EFFECT	Reserves:		Deposits:	
	Deposits with the Central Bank	+	Government	0
			Public	+

When the government borrows directly from the central bank the monetary effects are most pronounced. Both the money supply and the reserves of the chartered banks are increased. With excess reserves there exists the potential for still more expansion in the money supply.

We have considered above only government deficits and the issue of new debt. The government may also have surpluses and retire debt. What we have said about the issue of new debt holds true for debt retirement but in reverse. The illustration below shows the net effects on the chartered banks of debt retirement.

CHARTERED BANKS
NET EFFECT OF DEBT RETIREMENT

	Assets		Liabilities	
HELD BY NON-BANK PUBLIC	Reserves: Deposits with the Central Bank	0	Deposits: Government	0
			Public	0
HELD BY CHARTERED BANKS	Reserves: Deposits with the Central Bank	0	Deposits: Government	0
	Securities: Government Bonds	–	Public	–
HELD BY CENTRAL BANK	Reserves: Deposits with the Central Bank	–	Deposits: Government	0
			Public	–

FURTHER EFFECTS OF DEBT MANAGEMENT

SIZE OF THE FEDERAL GOVERNMENT DEBT

At the end of 1965 the direct and guaranteed debt of the Government of Canada outstanding (shown in Table 17-2) was $20.7 billion. This debt represents the net cumulation of the government's total cash deficits and cash surpluses since Confederation. After allowing for changes in cash balances, changes in the debt in any period represent the net balance between the government's cash receipts and its outlays of all kinds.

The rate at which the debt changes over time depends upon the government's **fiscal policy.** There are times when the government deliberately unbalances its cash budget in order to directly affect aggregate demand. Students who remember the theory of the income multiplier will know that the higher government expenditures are in relation to receipts, the greater is aggregate demand. We shall deal separately with fiscal policy in a later chapter.

Aside from the direct fiscal effect on aggregate demand, changes in the size of federal government debt may also have an indirect effect in that they may influence credit conditions. For example, when the government has large cash requirements which must be met by borrowing, credit conditions may become tighter than would otherwise be the case. Because of the implications for credit conditions, fiscal policy should be closely coordinated with monetary policy. When the government attempts to expand aggregate demand by increasing its own expenditures, its increased borrowing may create tighter credit conditions discouraging consumer and business demands and frustrating the government's intent. To prevent restrictive credit conditions the central bank can coordinate its own policy with the government's fiscal and debt management operations and increase the cash reserves of the banks. Insofar as this is accomplished by open market purchases, central bank action may also directly help to stabilize interest rates.

As the federal government's debt has grown, it has come to constitute an important proportion of the wealth holdings of the various spending units. To the extent that the public's wealth holdings in the form of federal government debt is a determinant of the public's spending habits, changes in the market value of the debt may influence aggregate demand.

TABLE 17-2

THE FEDERAL GOVERNMENT DEBT

Government of Canada Direct and Guaranteed Securities

(millions of dollars)

As at Dec. 31	Bank of Canada	Chartered Banks	Government of Canada Accounts	General Public	Total*	Non Marketable
1955	2,416	3,124	1,491	8,969	16,000	2,433
1956	2,426	2,524	1,518	8,766	15,234	2,541
1957	2,463	2,641	1,367	8,693	15,165	2,649
1958	2,670	3,521	1,258	8,968	16,416	2,895
1959	2,677	2,811	923	10,725	17,135	3,212
1960	2,744	3,057	866	11,080	17,747	3,594
1961	2,876	3,792	644	11,323	18,636	4,237
1962	2,936	3,371	670	12,472	19,448	4,720
1963	3,091	3,933	516	12,736	20,276	5,199
1964	3,115	3,705	769	13,144	20,733	5,701
1965	3,472	3,723	557	12,929	20,681	6,034

*Resident and non-resident.

Source: Bank of Canada Statistical Summary, November 1966; Bank of Canada Statistical Summary Supplement 1965, p. 46.

For example, if interest rates rise and the market value of the debt declines, spending units may feel poorer and consequently spend less. This so-called wealth effect, which is probably very small, tends to expand aggregate demand in periods of falling interest rates and rising market values. Non-marketable government debt, which at the end of 1965 represented 29 per cent of the public's total holdings of federal government debt, has a fixed value and therefore has no real wealth effect, although spending units may feel wealthier by holding this type of asset rather than another.

THE COMPOSITION OF THE FEDERAL GOVERNMENT DEBT

Two important features of the debt are its **marketability** and its **liquidity** or time to maturity. The largest part of the total debt outstanding is marketable. By this we mean that it can be offered for sale at any time on the market, and that its price (and therefore its yield) fluctuates with market demand and supply conditions. Nearly all of the non-marketable debt is now in the form of Canada Savings Bonds held by the general public. Although these bonds cannot be sold on the market, the government will redeem them at any time at their face value plus accrued interest. That part of the non-marketable debt not in the form of Canada Savings Bonds consists of special issues sold to the government's investment funds. At times special non-marketable issues have also been sold to the chartered banks.

TABLE 17-3

Composition of the Direct and Guaranteed Securities of the Government of Canada as at December 31, 1965

(millions of dollars, par value)

Market fixed-term securities	
Treasury bills, notes and CD's	2,150
Bonds 2 years and under to maturity	3,388
over 2 years to 5 years to maturity	2,410
over 5 years to 10 years to maturity	2,796
over 10 years to maturity	4,830
Market Perpetual bonds	55
Market Issues matured and outstanding	18
Non-market securities	
Canada Savings Bonds	5,866
Bonds issued to the Unemployment Insurance Fund	168
	$20,681

Source: Bank of Canada Statistical Summary Supplement, 1965, p. 48.

The liquidity of the debt is associated with its term to maturity. As a rule, when a security is close to maturity its market value is close to its face value. Moreover, any fluctuation in the market value of a security with a short term to maturity, or close to maturity, is usually relatively small. If a security can be sold at or near its face value at any time or in the very near future it is "close to money" and therefore liquid. Canada Savings Bonds, for example, are very close to money since, as we have already mentioned, they are redeemed by the government at their face value at any time. However, the liquidity of these bonds is not associated with their term to maturity but with their redeemability.

Just as a security with a short term to maturity is usually liquid, the opposite is true for a security with a long term to maturity. Fluctuations in the market price of securities tend to increase with their terms to maturity. Therefore, as a rule, the longer the term to maturity, the less liquid a security.

Since short-term securities are closer substitutes for money than securities of longer term, a reduction in the average term of the government debt outstanding increases the liquidity of the debt and therefore of the economy. The liquidity of the economy also increases as a larger proportion of the debt takes the form of redeemable non-market issues.

Given its ability to shift the term of its debt the government may have an influence not only upon the supply of liquid spendable assets in the economy, but also upon the supply of credit available to other borrowers. The decisions of the debt manager as to the timing and character of the government's financing affect the availability of funds at various maturities to borrowers and therefore, in combination with monetary policy, may guide credit conditions.

The characteristics of the government's debt outstanding at the end of 1965 are shown in Table 17-3. As is shown in the table, the government's outstanding securities differ widely in their term to maturity, ranging from Treasury bills, some of which fall due for repayment each week, to perpetual bonds with no specified final maturity date.

PRINCIPLES OF DEBT MANAGEMENT

In deciding upon the kind of refunding[7] operation to undertake and the type of new offering to be made, the government's debt manager may be guided by four general considerations:

(1) the financial requirements of the government;
(2) the cost of the overall debt to the government;
(3) the effect of debt management operations on market conditions;
(4) changes in the composition of the debt for the purposes of economic stabilization.

[7] Refunding is the replacement of a maturing security issue with another issue.

The essential consideration of the government's debt manager is the borrowing of funds required by the government to finance its operations. The debt manager must therefore keep a constant eye on investor preferences for securities, including the preferences of the central bank. If he wants to be sure of acquiring the funds needed by the government, he must offer securities with terms to maturity, yield and other characteristics desired by investors.

Probably the oldest principle of government debt management is that of minimizing at all times the interest and other costs of the debt. Closely associated is another old concept that most of the government's debt should be funded (long-term) rather than floating (short-term). Cost minimization, it is argued, can be accomplished by issuing long-term securities during recessionary periods when long-term rates are near their cyclical lows and gradually shifting to the short-term market as interest rates rise during periods of expansion. Long-term debt, whose market rate fluctuates with shifting interest rates, may act as a built-in stabilizer. However, there is no assurance that following a policy to minimize the costs of the debt will result in its lengthening. In extended periods of high and rising interest rates issuing short-term debt in anticipation of refunding it into longer-term debt when interest rates decline may result in an actual shortening of the debt. The government may then have to undertake frequent refunding operations with the result that the overall cost of the debt may increase. Moreover, frequent refunding will increase the likelihood of conflict between monetary policy and debt management operations. During periods of debt refunding the central bank usually maintains credit conditions at a level which makes the terms of the government's offerings attractive and ensures that they will not be substantially undersubscribed. If the central bank must concentrate its activities on ensuring the success of frequent debt management operations, it may be hampered in carrying out its overall monetary policy objectives.

Another principle of debt management which has been put forward from time to time is that the government's debt operations should have, at best, a neutral effect on security market conditions. Toward this end the government should try to avoid participating in the market by concentrating its activities in long-term securities. This policy would result in fewer government debt operations, but they would be much larger and could lead to relatively large market disturbances, thereby increasing the government's influence on market conditions rather than lessening it.

A better approach to achieving neutrality of government debt operations might be for the debt manager to tailor security offerings to the particular needs of the market. However, since investors' preferences are continually changing, this approach might imply that the debt manager is unconcerned with the composition of the debt at any given time.

A neutral effect might be obtained if the debt manager followed a regular pattern of debt issue and management, offering and refunding issues at regular intervals in order to maintain a uniform maturity structure of the debt. Insofar as the market could anticipate the government's refunding activity, market stability would be more certain. This could also serve to lower the government's average borrowing costs.

A more recent principle for managing government debt dating from the work of John Maynard Keynes is that of changing the composition of the debt for purposes of economic stabilization. The proponents of a counter-cyclical debt policy argue that during periods of economic boom the public's debt holdings should be lengthened and during recessionary periods it should be shortened. Thus during periods calling for economic restraint the government should meet its new borrowing by selling long-term securities, should refund maturing securities with longer ones and should sell existing long-term debt from official accounts. The increased supply of long-term issues on the market will tend to depress their price and raise long-term rates generally. Since a large proportion of expenditures is thought to be very sensitive to long-term interest rates, aggregate demand will be depressed. On the other hand, during periods of credit ease the debt manager should pursue policies which shorten the debt and put a downward pressure on interest rates.

Aside from the possible direct effect on interest rates, the usefulness of debt management as an instrument for economic stabilization rests on the proposition that changes in the liquidity of the debt influence aggregate demand. As we noted earlier, if liquidity is a significant determinant of demand, then lengthening the maturity of the debt will tend to restrain private expenditures and shortening it will tend to stimulate private expenditures.

If the debt is managed in a counter-cyclical fashion, it will be difficult to follow the principles of cost minimization and the principle of neutrality.

DEBT MANAGEMENT IN CANADA SINCE 1945

Following the war government policy consisted of maintaining fixed bond prices and repaying debt from cash surpluses. It was feared that if the public cashed large quantities of bonds in order to make expenditures postponed during the war, unstable security market conditions would result destroying confidence in the government's credit and undermining investment incentives. Moreover, uncertain about postwar economic conditions, the government wished to maintain interest rates at a level that would stimulate aggregate demand. As a result of the support given to government bonds through debt management and central bank operations, excessively easy credit conditions were produced and spending was stimulated when, as it proved later, restraint would have been more appropriate.

In 1950 the government abandoned its policy of continuous pegging of bond prices, but no real effort was made to dampen inflationary conditions through the management of the public debt which had shortened progressively since the end of the war. Shortening continued until 1958, except for a brief period in 1954 when the debt was lengthened even though the central bank was pursuing a policy of credit ease. On the other hand, in 1955 and 1956, despite other measures to restrict investment, the term of the debt held by the public was again allowed to shorten. One abortive attempt to lengthen the debt was made in September 1956. However, at the time the government seemed reluctant to allow long-term interest rates to rise above 4 per cent and the bond issue was priced too high for successful distribution, so that the Bank of Canada and the government accounts were obliged to take up a substantial part of it. In the recession after 1957, when an expansionary monetary policy was followed, the debt was again lengthened. Thus in the postwar period up to 1958, debt management was generally conducted in a cyclical rather than a counter-cyclical fashion.

The maturing after 1958 of substantial amounts of Victory Bonds created instability in the bond market. The government, therefore, converted these maturing issues into long-term bonds. Between July and September 1958, the government's conversion loan operations lengthened the maturity date of over 40 per cent of the outstanding marketable debt by raising the average maturity of the public's holdings from almost seven years to fourteen years and nine months. Unfortunately the magnitude of the conversion operation caused further instability in the market.[8] Moreover, the conversion loan put upward pressure on interest rates at a time when credit ease was appropriate.

From 1958 to the end of 1966 the debt was again allowed to shorten with no attempt to manage it for economic stabilization purposes. However, in August 1962, as part of its overall policy to halt the outflow of foreign capital and restore foreign confidence in the Canadian dollar, the government issued long-term securities to place upward pressure on long-term interest rates. This direct method was used to force up interest rates rather than the indirect method of manipulating the money supply by decreasing the cash reserve of the banks, which would have required them to restrict lending at a time when economic expansion was desirable.

Debt management plays an increasingly important role in assisting

---

[8] At least part of the instability in Canadian markets was the result of rising interest rates in the United States.

government authorities to meet their external economic objectives. In 1962 to rebuild its foreign exchange reserves the Canadian government not only sold government bonds in the United States but also employed debt management policy to put upward pressure on interest rates to reverse the outflow of capital funds from Canada.

Since 1961 in the United States, the Treasury has combined its debt management policy with the Federal Reserve's monetary policy to alter the structure of interest rates through "operations nudge" or "operations twist". In order to stem the outflow of short-term funds the Treasury has at times concentrated its financing in shorter-term securities to force short-term rates of interest upward to levels competitive with rates abroad. When at the same time domestic expansionary policies were called for, the Federal Reserve has purchased long-term securities in order to force down long-term rates to which domestic investment expenditures are considered sensitive.

The history of Canadian debt management policy shows that the authorities have been reluctant to exploit the full potential of debt management as a policy instrument to supplement fiscal, monetary and other government policies. The only exception, as noted above, has been the use of debt management to assist the government in meeting its objectives regarding its external financial position. By and large, debt management appears to have been overly concerned with keeping security markets orderly. For instance, after the conversion loan in 1958 almost all of the few long-term maturities issued by the government were sold to the Bank of Canada for resale to the public. The Bank in turn fed these long issues to the market when it thought the market could digest them without influencing credit conditions.[9] In recent years the Bank of Canada and the government's accounts have undertaken advance refunding operations. By exchanging issues which are approaching maturity for longer-term securities, the instability created in the market by a large overhang of securities about to mature at any one time is avoided.

[9] This technique is common in the United Kingdom where the Bank of England buys long-term securities from the government and feeds them to the market through what is called "the tap".

SELECTED READINGS

Committee on the Working of the Monetary System, *Report,* Cmnd. 827, London, Her Majesty's Stationery Office, August 1959, Ch. 8.

Culbertson, J. M., "A Positive Debt Management Program", *Review of Economics and Statistics,* Vol. 41, No. 2, Part I, May 1959.

Fellner, W., *et. al., Fiscal and Debt Management Policies,* prepared for the Commission on Money and Credit, Englewood Cliffs, N.J., Prentice-Hall, 1963.

Gaines, T. C., *Techniques of Treasury Debt Management,* New York, Free Press of Glencoe, 1962.

Gaines, Tilford, "The Economics of Treasury Debt Management", *Banking,* May 1964, pp. 42-44; reprinted in James A. Crutchfield, *et. al.,* (eds.), *Money, Financial Institutions and the Economy,* Englewood Cliffs, N.J., Prentice-Hall, 1965, pp. 395-403.

Galbraith, John A., *The Economics of Banking Operations, A Canadian Study,* Montreal, McGill University Press, 1963, Ch. 6.

Laird, William E., "The Changing Views on Debt Management", *Quarterly Review of Economics and Business,* Autumn 1963, pp. 7-17; reprinted in Alan D. Entine, *Monetary Economics: Readings,* Belmont, Cal., Wadsworth Publishing, 1968, pp. 465-479.

Report of the Royal Commission on Banking and Finance, Ottawa, Queen's Printer, 1964, Ch. 22; reprinted in part in James P. Cairnes and H. H. Binhammer, *Canadian Banking and Monetary Policy,* Toronto, McGraw-Hill, 1965, pp. 170-183.

Smith, Warren L., *Debt Management in the United States,* Joint Economic Committee, Study of Employment, Growth and Price Levels, Study Paper No. 19, Washington, Government Printing Office, 1960.

18

DETERMINANTS AND THEORY OF THE MONEY SUPPLY

DETERMINANTS OF THE MONEY SUPPLY

In previous chapters we have dealt separately with the operations of the chartered banks, the Bank of Canada and the federal government. We have explained how the operations of each may affect the reserves of the chartered banks, the money supply and credit conditions. In this chapter we shall consolidate the previous discussion to gain an overall view of the determinants of the money supply.

To recapitulate, the total monetary stock in Canada is, by definition, equal to the total deposits of the chartered banks plus currency (coin and Bank of Canada notes) in public circulation outside the banking system. The most important determinants of the total money stock are the monetary base consisting of Bank of Canada notes and chartered bank deposits with the Bank of Canada; the level of the chartered banks' legal reserve requirements; and the asset preference of the public.

The largest component of the money stock is the deposits of the chartered banks. We include all of the chartered banks' deposits in our definition of money. The Bank of Canada publishes two money supply series. One includes all of the banks' deposits; the other excludes the deposits of the Government of Canada with the chartered banks. We shall use the money supply series which includes government deposits. [1] The total volume of chartered bank deposits is determined by the size of the monetary base, the amount of the monetary base the banks are required to hold or may want to hold as reserves against their deposits, the banks' ability and desire to lend and invest, and the public's preference in holding currency and chartered bank deposits.

---

[1] Although the banks also accept foreign currency deposits, only Canadian dollar deposits are part of the money supply.

Changes in the total volume of chartered bank deposits depend on the banks' excess reserves. These reserves are equal to the total amount of the monetary base in their possession less the amount they must or may hold as reserves. As we have seen in previous chapters, variations in the size of the monetary base are controlled by the Bank of Canada and the federal government. The Bank of Canada increases the base by acquiring assets and decreases it by disposing of assets. The federal government increases the base by transferring its deposit balances with the central bank to the chartered banks and decreases it by transferring its balances in the opposite direction.

The techniques employed by the Bank of Canada to change or induce changes in the monetary base are open market operations and Bank rate manipulation. These two techniques, as well as that of varying the reserve requirements of the chartered banks, may be used by the Bank of Canada to produce changes in the excess reserves of the banks and therefore their deposits. Of these techniques open market operations are employed most frequently. They are used to manage the chartered banks reserves for **dynamic** counter-cyclical purposes and also for **defensive** purposes to prevent changes in the chartered banks' reserves resulting from seasonal and unanticipated shifts of currency by the public.

QUANTITATIVE DETERMINATION OF CHARTERED BANK RESERVES

Table 18-1 lists all the various factors that tend to increase or decrease chartered bank reserves. We say that each individual factor shown in the table *tends* to increase or decrease the reserves of the banks because the overall change in the banks' reserves depends upon the changes in the other factors as well. While an individual factor moves the reserves of the banks in a certain direction, the net effect of all factors may be zero or opposite.

In Table 18-2 we have rearranged the items in Table 18-1 and shown them in terms of factors supplying reserves and factors absorbing reserves. In Table 18-2 where we also show the net changes in the various factors between December 31, 1964 and December 31, 1965 some of the items of Table 18-1 have been consolidated. In order to compare the two tables more readily letter notations to Table 18-2 have been made in the right hand margin in Table 18-1.

Factors supplying reserve funds are all assets of the Bank of Canada. Thus changes in the *source* of reserve funds (the monetary base) result from changes in the various asset items of the Bank of Canada. The principal factor supplying reserves to the banking system is the Bank of Canada's holdings of Government of Canada direct and guaranteed securities (Table 18-2,A). These securities, which are manipulated to change the

TABLE 18-1

Factors which tend to Increase or Decrease Chartered Bank Reserves

Factors which Tend to Increase the Volume of Chartered Bank Cash Reserves	*Factors which Tend to Decrease the Volume of Chartered Bank Cash Reserves*	*Reference to Table 18-2*
1. Bank of Canada open market purchases of securities.	1. Bank of Canada open market sales of securities.	A and B
2. Bank of Canada investments and purchases of securities other than in the open market.	2. Bank of Canada sale of securities other than in the open market.	
3. Increase in chartered bank and dealer borrowing at the Bank of Canada.	3. Decrease in chartered bank and dealer borrowing at the Bank of Canada.	
4. Increase in foreign currency assets by Bank of Canada.	4. Increase in foreign currency liabilities by Bank of Canada.	C and I
5. Reduction in government deposits at the Bank of Canada.	5. Increase in government deposits at the Bank of Canada.	G
6. Decrease in other deposits at the Bank of Canada.	6. Increase in other deposits at the Bank of Canada.	H
7. Decrease in other Bank of Canada accounts.	7. Increase in other Bank of Canada accounts.	E and K
8. Increase in Bank of Canada float (cheques on other banks).	8. Decrease in Bank of Canada float (Bank of Canada cheques outstanding).	D and J
9. Decrease in the public's demand for currency.	9. Increase in the public's demand for currency.	F
10. Downward revision in chartered bank legal reserve requirements.*	10. Upward revision in chartered bank legal reserve requirements.*	

* These do not affect the total volume of reserves but do affect the distribution of the total volume as between reserves and excess reserves. They can therefore be considered as the equivalent of a change in the total volume of reserves.

TABLE 18-2

Factors tending to Increase or Decrease Chartered Bank Reserves
(*millions of dollars*)
December 1964 and December 1965

	December 31, 1964	December 31, 1965	Expansive Factors	Contractive Factors
Factors Supplying Reserve Funds				
A Government of Canada direct and guaranteed securities	3,064.3	3,416.6	+352.3	
B Investments in Industrial Development Bank	212.5	239.7	+ 27.2	
C Foreign currency assets	111.0	42.3		− 68.7
D Float	201.5	199.6		− 1.9
E Other	52.5	57.5	+ 5.0	
	3,641.9	3,955.8		
Factors Absorbing Reserve Funds				
F Bank of Canada notes in circulation	2,025.5	2,153.0		−127.5
G Government of Canada deposits at the Bank of Canada	68.9	116.2		− 47.3
H Other deposits at the Bank of Canada	35.6	34.5	+ 1.1	
I Foreign currency liabilities of Bank of Canada	44.9	30.8	+ 14.1	
J Float	197.9	172.4	− 25.5	
K Other	31.9	32.0		− 0.1
	2,404.7	2,538.9		
Chartered Bank Reserves (*The Monetary Base*)				
Bank of Canada notes	355.1	382.7		
Deposits with the Bank of Canada	882.1	1,034.2		
	1,237.2	1,416.9		
Total Changes Increasing Reserves			+452.2	
Total Changes Decreasing Reserves				−245.5
Net Increase in Chartered Bank Reserves			+206.7	

Source: Bank of Canada Statistical Summary Supplement, 1965

supply of reserve funds, are purchased and sold in the open market, in transactions with government funds and accounts, and through purchase and resale agreements with money market dealers. They may also be purchased directly from the government at time of issue. The Bank holds securities other than those of the Government of Canada as well as market paper such as bankers' acceptances. These are included in item 2 in Table 18-1 but are not shown in Table 18-2 because of the Bank had no such holdings at the end of 1964 and 1965. Chartered bank borrowing from the Bank of Canada shown as item 3 in Table 18-1 does not appear in Table 18-2 as there were no loans outstanding on these two occasions.

The second largest source of chartered bank reserve funds has been the Bank of Canada's purchase of the capital stock, bonds and debentures of the Industrial Development Corporation (Table 18-2, B). The Bank appears to acquire these investments to meet the needs of the Corporation rather than to manage the reserves of the banks. The Bank of Canada also holds foreign government securities and foreign exchange (Table 18-2, C) but these, too, are not used to manage the banks' reserve positions. In recent years the Bank of Canada has actively assisted the government in maintaining the country's official foreign exchange reserves and in holding fluctuations in the external value of the Canadian dollar within agreed limits. Toward these ends the Bank purchases foreign securities and currencies. However, to prevent large fluctuations in the banks' reserves resulting from its purchase of foreign securities and currencies, the Bank at the same time changes other items supplying or absorbing reserve funds.

The last two items listed in Table 18-2 as supplying reserve funds are Float (D) and "Other" (E). Float includes cheques drawn on other banks and held by the Bank of Canada, and net balances of Government of Canada collections and payments in the process of settlement. The item shown as "Other" is made up of accrued interest on the Bank of Canada's investments, the book value of its premises and some miscellaneous items.

Only part of the total reserve funds supplied by the factors noted is available to the chartered banks. Factors (F) to (K) in Table 18-2 compete with the banks for these funds. The principal factors absorbing reserve funds are Bank of Canada notes held by the public outside the banks (F), and Government of Canada and other deposits with the Bank of Canada (G and H). Government of Canada enterprises, foreign central banks, and government institutions and international organizations hold deposits with the Bank of Canada.

In the same way that the Bank of Canada's holdings of foreign currency assets are a factor supplying reserve funds, its foreign currency liabilities (I) is a factor absorbing reserve funds. Float shown as a source of reserve funds also has its counterpart absorbing funds. Float which absorbs reserve funds consists of Bank of Canada cheques outstanding (J). Other factors are essentially the capital accounts including the rest fund of the Bank which has amounted to $30 million since December 31, 1955.

Finally, when all the factors absorbing funds are subtracted from those supplying funds, the net balance represents the chartered banks' reserves. The interrelationship among the basic determinants of chartered bank reserves can be summed up in a reserve equation:

$$\left.\begin{array}{c}\text{Chartered}\\ \text{Bank}\\ \text{Reserves}\end{array}\right\} = \left\{\begin{array}{c}\text{The}\\ \text{Monetary}\\ \text{Base}\\ \text{(central bank}\\ \text{credit)}\end{array}\right\} - \left\{\begin{array}{c}\text{Bank of Canada notes}\\ \text{in public circulation}\\ +\\ \text{Government, foreign and}\\ \text{other deposits with the}\\ \text{Bank of Canada}\\ +\\ \text{other Bank of}\\ \text{Canada accounts}\end{array}\right.$$

QUANTITATIVE DETERMINATION OF THE MONEY STOCK

Now that we have described the quantitative determination of the chartered banks' reserves, we can proceed one step further and describe the quantitative determination of the stock of money. Two institutions have the power to vary the money supply: the chartered banking system and the Bank of Canada. The two most important components of our money supply — chartered bank deposits and Bank of Canada notes — are liabilities of these two institutions, and as such are monetary liabilities. The other component of our money supply is coin in public circulation. It is the only component of the money stock which is not a monetary liability of either the chartered banks or the Bank of Canada. Coin is treated as a commodity produced and sold by the federal government, and from the balance sheet point of view considered on the next page it is not somebody's liability as is the case with the other components of the money stock.[2]

A basic principle of accounting is that assets must equal liabilities plus capital accounts. Unlike the liabilities of other institutions which are all non-monetary, those of the Bank of Canada and the chartered banks

---

[2] Coin is considered an asset to the person or institution holding it. There is no corresponding liability.

include monetary liabilities. Thus the basic asset-liability identity for these two institutions is shown as:

$$\begin{aligned} \text{Assets} = & \ \text{Monetary liabilities} \\ & + \text{non-monetary liabilities} \\ & + \text{capital accounts} \end{aligned}$$

By rearranging the terms of this identity we have:

$$\begin{aligned} \text{Monetary liabilities} = & \ \text{Assets} \\ & - \text{non-monetary liabilities} \\ & - \text{capital accounts} \end{aligned}$$

The quantity of the money stock exclusive of coin in public circulation is determined by subtracting the non-monetary liabilities and capital accounts from the assets of the two institutions that create monetary liabilities. This is shown in Table 18-3. The table illustrates how the money stock varies directly with changes in the assets of the Bank of Canada and the chartered banks and inversely with changes in their non-monetary liabilities and capital accounts.

Chartered bank loans and investments are the largest source of money. When the chartered banks make loans or investments they either create deposits or put currency into circulation. When they reduce their loans and investments they reduce their deposits. In addition, since some people repay their bank loans with currency, currency outside the banks is reduced.

The other source of money is Bank of Canada loans and investments.[3] When the Bank of Canada purchases financial assets as well as goods and services from the non-bank public, the stock of money directly increases, and the reserves of the chartered banks increase by a corresponding amount. When, however, the Bank of Canada purchases securities directly from the chartered banks it is the banks' reserves that are initially affected and not the currency and demand deposit holdings of the non-bank public. This is also the case when the Bank of Canada extends discounts and advances to the chartered banks. When the Bank of Canada, the government, and government funds and accounts increase or decrease their transactions with the chartered banks, it is non-monetary rather than monetary liabilities which are affected. Only subsequently, when as a result of these transactions the chartered banks increase or contract their loans and investments or when the government, govern-

[3] At one time the Treasury issued currency secured by gold and government bonds. Then the gold and government bonds securing the Treasury's currency was also a source of money.

TABLE 18-3

Factors tending to Increase the Stock of Money
December 31, 1964 and December 31, 1965
(*in millions of dollars*)

	December 1964	December 1965	Change in Factors from Dec. 1964 to Dec. 1965
Factors Supplying Money (Assets)			
Bank of Canada Loans and Investments	3,642	3,956	+ 314
Chartered Bank Loans and Investments	18,661	20,792	+ 2,131
Total	22,303	24,748	+ 2,445
Factors Absorbing Funds Supplying Money (Liabilities and Capital Accounts)			
Non-Monetary Liabilities			
Chartered Bank Deposits at Bank of Canada and Holdings of Bank of Canada notes	1,237	1,417	+ 180
Government and other Deposits at Bank of Canada	1,045	1,507	+ 462
Other Non-monetary Liabilities and Capital Account	1,299	1,077	− 222
Total	3,581	4,001	+ 420
Monetary Liabilities			
Bank of Canada Notes Outside the Banks	2,025	2,153	+ 128
Chartered Bank Deposits	16,697	18,594	+ 1,897
Total	18,722	20,747	+ 2,025
Total	22,303	24,748	+ 2,445
Total Monetary Stock			
Monetary Liabilities	18,722	20,747	+ 2,025
Monetary Assets - Coin in Public Circulation*	225	262	+ 37
	18,947	21,009	+ 2,062

*1964 figure is as of December 30 and 1965 as of December 29.
Source: Bank of Canada Statistical Summary 1965.

ment funds and accounts deal directly with the non-bank public, are monetary liabilities also affected.

The distribution of monetary liabilities between chartered bank deposits and Bank of Canada notes in public circulation is determined by the public's preference for holding notes. If the public desires to hold more Bank of Canada notes, it obtains them from the banks. If the notes are paid for with cheques written on deposits with the banks, no change in the total money supply occurs. If, however, the Bank of Canada notes are borrowed from the chartered banks, the banks' assets increase by an amount equal to the public's holdings of notes and the total money stock increases.

The total monetary stock consists of monetary liabilities in the form of Bank of Canada notes outside the banks and chartered bank deposits and monetary assets in the form of coin in public circulation. From December 31, 1964 to December 31, 1965, all the factors that tend to increase monetary liabilities expanded by $2.4 billion but the amount of monetary liabilities increased by only $2 billion. The smaller increase in monetary liabilities was due to the $420 million rise in non-monetary liabilities. During the same period monetary assets increased by $37 million. The change in monetary assets is entirely due to the public's demand for coin. When the public increases its holdings of coin the net effect on the balance sheets of the Bank of Canada and the chartered banks is zero. In the final analysis all that happens is a decrease in the public's holdings of the metal from which the coin is made and an increase in its holdings of coin. Table 18-4 illustrates this point.

Coins are produced by the Royal Canadian Mint. All revenues of the Mint are paid into the Consolidated Revenue Fund of the federal government, and the Fund covers all expenses for metals and other inputs. The Bank of Canada buys coin from the Mint at its full face value and distributes it to the chartered banks who in turn distribute it to the public. In Table 18-4, Stage 1 represents an initial increase in the public's demand for coin; the effects are traced through to Stage 4. The illustration assumes that the Bank of Canada and the chartered banks hold an inventory of coin at all times. If they did not, we would have to start our analysis at Stage 4 and proceed backwards to Stage 1. The final result would be the same.

THEORY OF THE MONEY SUPPLY

The traditional theory of money supply determination assumes that the central bank has virtually complete control and that the commercial banks play a relatively passive role. In other words, the central bank decides upon the specific amount of money it considers appropriate for the

TABLE 18-4

An Increase in Coin in Public Circulation

CHARTERED BANKS

		Assets		Liabilities	
STAGE 1:	Public purchases coin from banks	Coin	–	Deposits: public	–
STAGE 2:	Banks replenish coin from Bank of Canada	Coin Deposits with Bank of Canada	+ –		
STAGE 3:					
STAGE 4:	Government (the Mint) purchases metals from public	Deposits with Bank of Canada	+	Deposits: Public	+
NET EFFECT			0		0

BANK OF CANADA

		Assets		Liabilities	
STAGE 1:					
STAGE 2:	Banks replenish coin from Bank of Canada	Coin	–	Deposits: Chartered Banks	–
STAGE 3:	Bank of Canada purchases coin from Mint	Coin	+	Deposits: Gov't.	+
STAGE 4:	Mint purchases metals for coinage from public			Deposits: Gov't. Chartered Banks	 – +
NET EFFECT			0		0

PUBLIC

		Assets		Liabilities
STAGE 1:	Public obtains coin from Chartered Banks	Coin Bank Deposits	+ –	
STAGE 4:	Public sells metals to the Mint (Government)	Metals Bank Deposits	– +	
NET EFFECT	Public exchanges metals for monetary assets (coin)			

economy and supplies the banking system with an appropriate amount of reserve funds. The banking system in turn responds automatically to the change in its reserves and, given its reserve requirements, automatically increases deposits by some multiple of its excess reserves. This simple theory gives rise to two questions.

1. Does the central bank indeed have a specific amount of money in mind when it varies the supply of reserve funds, or does it consider credit conditions as a more appropriate economic indicator?
2. Do the banks react automatically to changes in the supply of reserve funds (the monetary base) or are there behavioural factors which explain their reaction?

In recent years some economists, departing from the traditional approach, have assumed that the central bank's principal concern is with credit conditions and that the commercial banks do not react automatically to changes in the supply of reserve funds. During periods of economic upturn the banks economize on their reserves, expand their loans and investments, and increase the rate of the turnover of money and the money stock so as to maximize their earnings. The implication is that the banking system's response to changes in the monetary base is determined by the movement in interest rates. During periods of rising interest rates the banks expand and absorb their excess reserves; during periods of falling interest rates they contract and accumulate excess reserves in preparation for the next period of rising interest rates.[4]

As a first approximation of a theory of money supply determination we can say that, other things being given, the money supply is a function of the reserve base (the monetary base) and the return the commercial banks can earn on loans and investments. This function can be expressed in terms of the following equation:

$$M_s = f(R,i,Z)$$

where M_s denotes the money supply, R the reserve base of the banking system, i the rate of interest, and Z all other factors affecting the money supply. M_s is assumed to be an increasing function of R and i; that is, the money supply expands as the reserve base and the rate of interest increase and contracts as the reserve base and the rate of interest decline.

The relationship between i and M_s given R is shown in Figure 18-1. Assuming the reserve base to be fixed by the central bank, and other factors affecting the money supply to remain unchanged, MM is the money

[4] Insofar as the chartered banks' liquidity ratios fluctuate more widely and may be more sensitive to interest rate changes than their cash ratios, a theory of the money supply as applied to Canada should probably focus on liquidity ratios rather than cash ratios.

supply schedule. The schedule slopes upward and to the right indicating that larger amounts of money accompany higher interest rates. As shown, the money supply is not very responsive to interest rate changes at very high levels. Given *R* and *Z*, this is the result of the banks' diminishing margins of excess reserves as their loans and investments increase. At some point, i_l in Figure 18-1, the banks with a given reserve base have no excess reserves left and cannot expand the money supply by creating deposits. Therefore, at interest rates above i_l the *MM* schedule is perfectly vertical. Given *R* the money supply cannot expand beyond $(M_s)_1$. If, however, the central bank increases the monetary base, an expansion beyond $(M_s)_l$ is possible. If we assume that *R* increases as a result of central bank open market purchases, the *MM* curve in Figure 18-1 shifts to the right. With the larger monetary base the maximum amount of monetary expansion, all other things remaining equal, is $(M_s)_2$.

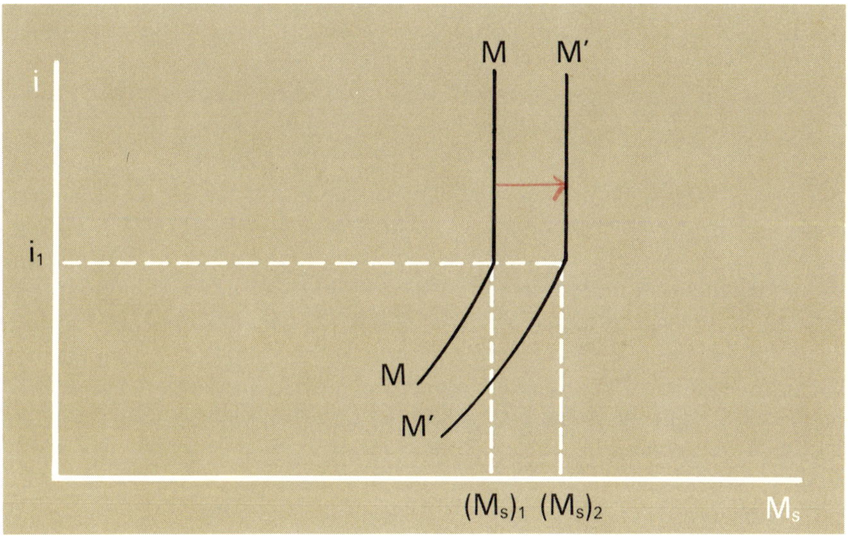

Figure 18-1 The Money Supply Schedule

As a second approximation of a theory of money supply determination, we include explicitly into our equation some of the factors which are included in *Z*. Our equation becomes:

$$M_s = f(R, i, r_d, r_t, B, D_d/D_t, c)$$

where *R* denotes the reserve base, *i* the rate of interest, r_d the reserve requirement for demand deposits, r_t the reserve requirement for time deposits, *B* the Bank rate, D_d/D_t the ratio of demand deposits to time deposits, and c the ratio of currency held outside the banks to total commercial bank deposits.

The central bank has control over changes in R, r_d, r_t and B. We have already considered the effect on the money supply of an increase in R resulting from open market purchases by the central bank. If the central bank decreases the banks' reserve requirements (r_d and r_t), at any given rate of interest the banks have more excess reserves and can therefore create additional deposit money. This is shown by a rightward shift of the MM curve in Figure 18-1. A decrease in the total reserve requirement enlarges the money expansion multiplier. If, however, the central bank decreases R through open market sales to absorb the banks excess reserves resulting from reduction in r_d and r_t, no shift in the MM curve will be possible; nor does the MM curve shift when an increase in R is offset by an increase in r_d and r_t. An increase in R accompanied by a decrease in r_d and r_t will produce a shift in the MM curve beyond $M'M'$ and increase the maximum money supply beyond $(M_s)_2$, the limit allowed by a given change in R, all other things remaining the same.

Now let us consider B, the Bank rate. Assume that the banking system follows the practice of regularly borrowing from the central bank in order to expand its loans and investments. With a decrease in the Bank rate the spread widens between the return to be earned by the banks on loans and investments and the cost of borrowing reserves. As a result the banks may be induced to lend more money. If the other factors remain the same, the maximum amount of money that can be created is not enlarged. However, the banks will create a larger amount of money at any given rate of interest up to the maximum money supply as determined by the other factors. The result of a reduction in the Bank rate is shown in Figure 18-2. The MM curve shifts to MM'. Conversely, an increase in the Bank rate would cause a shift to the left without changing the maximum money supply $(M_s)_3$. For example, if the market rate of interest is i_1, a reduction in the Bank rate will expand the money supply from $(M_s)_1$ to $(M_s)_2$; a Bank rate increase of the same magnitude will reduce the money supply from $(M_s)_2$ to $(M_s)_1$. If, however, the rate of interest is i_2, a change in the Bank rate will have no effect on the money supply.

The two remaining factors which determine the money supply are D_d/D_t, the ratio of demand deposits to time deposits and c, the ratio of currency in circulation to total deposits. Neither of these factors is controlled by the monetary authorities. When the public shifts from demand to time deposits (the D_d/D_t ratio decreases) the required reserves of the banks decline as they are permitted to hold a lower ratio of reserves against their time deposits than against their demand deposits. Other factors remaining the same, at any given rate of interest the banks then have more excess reserves and can therefore create additional deposits. Under these circumstances the *MM* curve in Figure 18-1 shifts to the right. Conversely, if the D_d/D_t ratio increases, the money supply schedule shifts to the left.

When the public increases its holdings of currency outside the bank it also decreases initially its bank deposits by a corresponding amount. However, the withdrawal of currency from the banks also reduces their total reserves (a reduction in *R*) and the money supply schedule therefore shifts to the left. A rightward shift would result if the public decided to decrease its holdings of currency relative to bank deposits (an increase in *c*).

As a third approximation of a theory of money supply determination we can introduce behavioural equations explaining the monetary authorities' use of policy instruments (R, r_d, r_t and B). We mentioned earlier that the traditional approach considers movements in the policy instruments as reflecting the central bank's judgment of an appropriate *quantity of money* for given economic conditions. A more recent approach is to consider movements in the policy instruments as reflecting the central

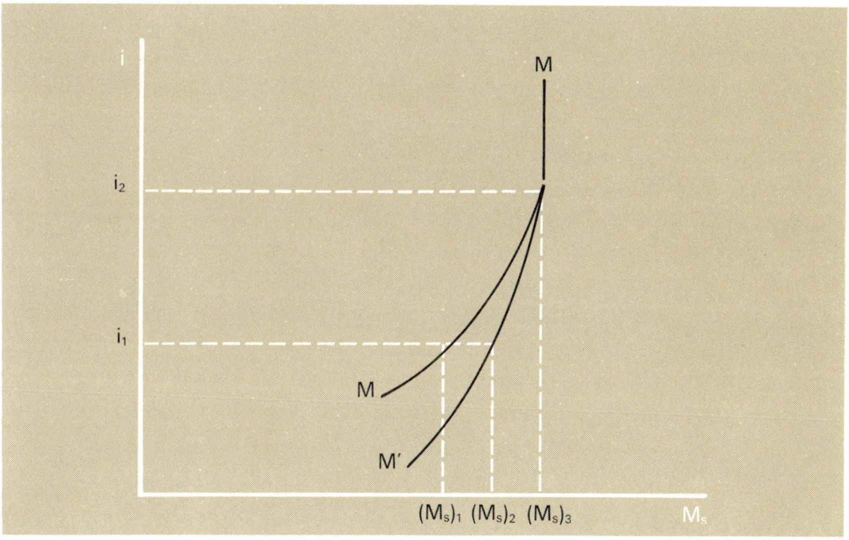

Figure 18-2
Changes in the Money Supply Schedule as a result of Bank Rate Changes

bank's judgment of appropriate *credit conditions* for given economic circumstances. A further step is the introduction of behavioural equations explaining the reaction of the central bank to the changing emphasis in society's objectives relating to output (or real income), unemployment, price levels and the balance of payments, as well as non-policy forces which influence these objectives. The frontier of monetary theory is moving along these lines.[5]

A complete theory of the money supply would tell us not only the potential quantity of money that the monetary system can generate but also the actual amount of money in the economy at any one time. To determine the amount of money in the economy at a specific time we must consider not only the determinants of the money supply but also the determinants of the demand for money. Moreover, if we know both the supply of and the demand for money, we can estimate the equilibrium amount of money in the economy — the amount the institutions wish to supply and the amount economic units desire to hold. The determinants of the demand for money will be one of the main topics of succeeding chapters.

SOME EMPIRICAL STUDIES OF MONEY SUPPLY DETERMINANTS

In recent years economists in the United States have turned their attention to identifying the determinants of the money supply and to measuring the impact of each on the money supply. A greater understanding of the forces influencing the money supply will enable monetary managers to operate with more precision insofar as they are able to forecast with greater accuracy changes in the factors affecting the money supply.

Most of the studies to date have included asset ratios to represent behaviour relationships. Friedman and Schwartz[6] have concentrated on three variables: high-powered money (bank reserves plus currency outstanding); a deposit-currency ratio to explain the public's asset behaviour; and a deposit-reserve ratio to show the banks' behaviour. Phillip Cagan[7] followed similar lines but replaced the deposit-currency ratio with a currency-money ratio. Cagan defines the total money supply *(M)* as consisting of commercial bank deposits *(D)* including time and demand deposits, plus currency in circulation outside the banks *(C)*.

$$M = C + D \qquad (1)$$

The assets which the banks may use as reserves for their monetary liabilities are called high-powered money *(H)* and consist of currency held by

---

[5] See for instance John H. Wood, " A Model of Federal Reserve Behaviour", *Staff Economic Studies,* No. 17, Board of Governors of the Federal Reserve System, Washington, D.C., 1966.

[6] Friedman, Milton and Anna J. Schwartz, *A Monetary History of the United States, 1867-1960*, Princeton, Princeton University Press, 1963.

[7] Cagan, Phillip, *Determinants and Effects of Changes in the Stock of Money 1875-1960*, Princeton, Princeton University Press, 1965.

the public *(C)* and reserves (currency and central bank deposits) held by the commercial banks *(R)*.

$$H = C + R \tag{2}$$

Both sides of this identity are divided by *M*.

$$\frac{H}{M} = \frac{C}{M} + \frac{R}{M} \tag{3}$$

Cagan studies the money supply in relation to these three ratios which express the behaviour of three economic units regarding the disposition of high-powered money, *H/M* reflects the behaviour of the government, *C/M* that of the public and *R/M* that of the commercial banks.

R/M is explained more explicitly as:

$$\frac{R}{M} = \frac{R}{D} \bullet \frac{D}{M} \tag{4}$$

Since

$$\frac{D}{M} = 1 - \frac{C}{M} \tag{4a}$$ [8]

$$\frac{R}{M} = \left(\frac{R}{D}\right)\left(1 - \frac{C}{M}\right) \tag{5}$$

Substituting for $\frac{R}{M}$ from (*5*) in (*3*)

$$\frac{H}{M} = \frac{C}{M} + \frac{R}{D}\left(1 - \frac{C}{M}\right) \tag{6}$$

or

$$\frac{H}{M} = \frac{C}{M} + \frac{R}{D} - \frac{C}{M}\,\frac{R}{D} \tag{6a}$$

or

$$M = \frac{H}{C/M + R/D - C/M\ R/D} \tag{6b}$$

8 M = D + C; Dividing both sides by M; $\frac{M}{M} = \frac{D}{M} + \frac{C}{M}$; $\frac{D}{M} = \frac{M}{M} - \frac{C}{M}$; $\frac{D}{M} = 1 - \frac{C}{M}$

This identity expresses the total money supply in terms of the three variables — high-powered money, currency-money ratio (currency ratio) and reserve-deposit ratio (reserve ratio). From his analysis of the movements in these three variables in relation to the money stock Cagan concludes that nine tenths of the secular growth of the money stock in the United States from 1875 to 1955 is accounted for by the expansion of high-powered money, and the remaining one tenth resulted from declines in the currency and reserve ratio. He also notes that while the dependence of the money stock on prices, business activity and other variables is strong, it is not rigid, uniform or immediate.[9] On the other hand, he lends support to the quantity theory of money by suggesting that there is evidence that money stock changes produced the changes in prices.[10]

While Friedman and Schwartz and Cagan have been concerned with explaining the secular changes of the money supply, others have concentrated on short-run explanations and on the behaviour of individual banks instead of the banking system. Some of these studies are listed in the bibliography at the end of this chapter.

SELECTED READINGS

Andersen, Leonall C., "A Study of Factors Affecting the Money Stock: Phase One", Board of Governors of the Federal Reserve System, *Staff Economic Studies,* October 1965.

Argy, V., "Money Supply Theory and the Money Multiplier", *Australian Economic Journal,* June-December 1965.

Bell, G. L., and L. S. Berman, "Changes in the Money Supply in the United Kingdom, 1954 to 1964", *Economica,* Vol. 33, May 1966, pp. 148-165.

Black, R. P., "The Impact of Member Banks Reserves Upon the Money Supply", *Southern Economic Journal,* Vol. 29, January 1963, pp. 199-210.

Brunner, Karl, "A Schema for the Supply Theory of Money", *International Economic Review Papers,* Vol. 2, January 1961, pp. 79-100.

Brunner, Karl, and Allan H. Metzler, "Some Further Investigations of Demand and Supply Functions for Money", *The Journal of Finance,* Vol. 19, No. 2, May 1964, pp. 240-283.

Cagan Phillip, *Determinants and Effects of Changes in the Stock of Money 1875-1960.* Princeton, Princeton University Press, 1965.

9 *Ibid.,* p. 14.

10 *Ibid.,* p. 284.

Cagan, Phillip, "The Demand for Currency Relative to Total Money Supply", *The Journal of Political Economy,* (1958), pp. 303-328.

Fand, David I., "Some Implications of Money Supply Analysis", *American Economic Review,* Vol. 57, May 1967, pp. 380-400.

Fand, David I., and John E. Tower, "An Analysis of the Money Supply Process in Canada", a paper presented to the Canadian Political Science Association, Ottawa, June 1967.

Friedman, Milton and Anna J. Schwartz, *A Monetary History of the United States, 1867-1960,* Princeton, Princeton University Press, 1963.

Goldfeld, Stephen M., and Edward J. Kane, "The Determinants of Member-Bank Borrowing: An Econometric Study", *The Journal of Finance,* Vol. 21, September 1966, pp. 499-514.

Meigs, A. James, *Free Reserves and the Money Supply,* Chicago, University of Chicago Press, 1962.

Orr, D., and W. J. Mellon, "Stochastic Reserve Losses and Expansion of Bank Credit", *American Economic Review,* Vol. 51, September 1961, pp. 614-623.

Polak, J. J., and W. H. White, "The Effect of Income Expansion on the Quantity of Money", *International Monetary Fund Staff Papers IV,* August 1955, pp. 398-433.

Rangarajan, C., and K. Severn, "The Response of Banks to Changes in Aggregate Reserves", *The Journal of Finance,* Vol. 20, December 1965, pp. 651-664; "Bank Responses to Reserve Changes: Comment", William R. Bryan, *The Journal of Finance,* Vol. 21, September 1966, pp. 539-541 and "Reply", pp. 542-543.

Smith, Warren L., "Time Deposits, Free Reserves, and Monetary Policy" in Giulio Pontecorvo, *et. al.* (eds.), *Issues in Banking and Monetary Analysis,* New York, Holt, Rinehart and Winston, 1967, Ch. 3.

Royal Bank of Canada, *How the Canadian Money Supply is Affected by Various Banking and Financial Transactions and Developments,* Montreal, 1967.

Tiegen, Ronald L., "The Demand for and Supply of Money" in Warren Smith and Ronald L. Tiegen, *Readings in Money, National Income and Stabilization Policy,* Homewood, Ill., Richard D. Irwin, 1965, pp. 44-76.

Wood, John H., "A Model of Federal Reserve Behaviour", Board of Governors of the Federal Reserve System, *Staff Economic Studies,* No. 17, Washington, D.C., 1966.

PART FIVE

MONETARY THEORY AND POLICY

19

THE DEVELOPMENT OF MONETARY THEORY

COMMODITY THEORY OF MONEY

Not surprisingly, those who first concerned themselves with the nature of money turned their attention to the value of the money unit. Since the first kind of money to serve as a medium of exchange consisted of articles of common use, the value of money was considered to be determined by the same laws that determine the value of ordinary commodities. This concept of the value of money carried over to the period when money no longer consisted of immediately useful articles but of metals. The concept was still prevalent when money had come to consist of a paper claim on a specified amount of metal. Those who adhered to this school of thought were known as the commodity theorists or metallists. The commodity theory of money, probably the oldest explanation of the value of money, was valid as long as the non-monetary use of the commodity overshadowed its monetary use. The theory was no longer tenable when gold became the most important commodity associated with the monetary unit. Throughout history, the amount of gold has been limited in relation to the demand for it — an important reason for its continued association with the monetary unit. When the monetary demand for gold exceeded the commodity demand its value ceased to bear a close relationship to its usefulness as an ordinary commodity. Obviously, the time had come to revise the commodity theory. Although the up-dated interpretation no longer held that the demand for gold was just like the demand for any other commodity, the idea that money was essentially gold lingered on. Even when money was no longer redeemable in gold, its "ghost" remained. Commodities were thought to have **gold prices** which were translated into money prices.

Under the gold standard the value of the monetary unit was defined as consisting of a certain amount of gold. The commodity theorists thought therefore that the money prices of commodities were nothing more than the reflection of their gold prices. From this it followed that money prices could be altered by a simple stroke of the pen which redefined the value of the monetary unit in terms of its gold content. It is hard to believe that such a naive concept played an important role in persuading the American government to redefine the gold content of the United States dollar in 1933-1934. When the gold content of the American dollar was lowered and the price of gold was raised from $20.67 to $35 an ounce, commodity theorists, particularly George Warren, persuaded President Roosevelt that commodity prices in the United States would immediately rise by about 75 per cent. However, as was only natural, the public no longer associated the value of the dollar with its gold content, and for this reason alone, prices did not rise.

EARLY QUANTITY THEORY OF MONEY

As we have seen, the commodity theorists believed that money was accepted because it actually consisted of or could be freely converted into a valuable commodity. With the transition from basically barter to money economies this idea slowly gave way to the new idea that people desired money because it was a generally acceptable medium of exchange. Regardless of the size of the monetary stock, people desired money because it could be passed along sooner or later to purchase other things. While this concept of the nature of money reflected its changing social role, the idea that money might also be held as a store of value was still a long way off. However, the belief that money was held strictly for the purchase of other things remained a fundamental concept until modern times and became the foundation for the quantity theory of money.

In its earliest and crudest form, the quantity theory stated that the value of money — its purchasing power — depended upon the quantities of money relative to the quantities of things to be purchased with it. Although the early developments of the quantity theory came during the price revolution of the sixteenth century, crude statements of it go as far back as Roman times. The early sixteenth century enunciations of the quantity theory of money came during the period known as **mercantilism.** It is difficult to summarize all the issues which are embodied in mercantilism. However, among the more important were the principles that wealth consisted of gold and silver and that the prudent nation would either mine these metals if it could, or regulate its trade with foreign countries so as to attract the metals.

The question arose as to what would happen to the domestic purchasing power of money when a country succeeded in increasing its wealth, which was synonomous with its money supply. In the sixteenth century

Jean Bodin (1530-1596) discussed the effect of the influx of gold and silver on prices in France.[1] "I find that the high prices we see to-day are due to some four or five causes. The principal & almost the only one (which no one has referred to until now) is the abundance of gold & silver, which is to-day much greater in this Kingdom than it was four hundred years ago, to go no further back."

John Locke (1632-1704) writing a century later noted:

> The change of this marketable value of any commodity, in respect of another commodity, or in respect of a standing, common measure, is not the altering of any intrinsic value ... but the alteration of some proportion, which that commodity bears to something else .... Money, whilst the same quantity of it is passing up and down the kingdom in trade, is really a standing measure of the falling and rising value of other things, in reference to one another . . . But if you increase, or lessen, the quantity of money, current in traffic, in any place, then the alteration of value is in the money. . . . But the value or price of all commodities, amongst which money passing in trade is truly one, consisting in proportion, you alter this, as you do all other proportions, whether you increase one, or lessen the other.[2]

In this statement Locke directly refuted the commodity theory of money and placed the determination of the value of money squarely on its quantity. However, he also recognized the role played by its velocity of circulation. In considering the proportion of money that was needed to the amount of trade to be conducted, he said:

> ...what proportion that is, is hard to determine; because it depends not barely on the quantity of money, but the quickness of its circulation. The very same shilling may, at one time, pay twenty men in twenty days: at another, rest in the same hands one hundred days together.[3]

In relating the quantity of money and its velocity to "trade", Locke was among the first to look beyond its relationship to prices alone and to theorize its effect on economic activity. He also held a fairly advanced notion of the rate of interest, believing that the quantity of money influenced the rate of interest on loans as well as the price level.

John Law (1671-1729), whom we met in an earlier chapter, also made a contribution to monetary theory aside from his financial scheming. In

1 Jean Bodin, "La Réponse de Jean Bodin aux paradoxes de Malestroit touchant l'encherissement de toutes choses et le moyen d'y remedier", reprinted in Arthur E. Monroe (ed.), *Early Economic Thought*, Cambridge, Mass., Harvard University Press, 1924, p. 127.

2 *The Works of John Locke*, 10th ed., London, 1801, Vol. 5, pp. 43-45.

3 *Ibid.*, p. 23.

his *Money and Trade Consider'd; with a Proposal for Supplying the Nation with Money* published in 1705, he argued for an increase in the money supply, especially the "credit money" created by his Banque Générale in France. He proposed the issue of notes secured by the value of land. Although the maximum amount of notes that could be issued would be limited by the total value of land, this would still provide the quantity of money required to satisfy the needs of trade. Law argued for an increase in the money supply because there were positive relationships among employment, trade and the amount of metallic and bank money in the economy.

Richard Cantillon (1680-1734) was an investment banker who lived most of his years in Holland and England. His *Essai sur la nature du commerce en général* ("Essay on the Nature of Commerce in General"), published posthumously in 1755 almost two decades after it was written, remained virtually unnoticed until Stanley Jevons rediscovered it in the latter half of the nineteenth century. Jevons said that it was "more than any other book I know, *the first treatise on economics*" and "more emphatically than any other single work 'the Cradle of Political Economy' ".[4] This opinion is being shared by more and more economists today.

In his *Essai* Cantillon made a significant contribution to the quantity theory of money. He appears to have been one of the first to offer an explanation of how an increase in the supply of money (specie) affects the price level. His explanation was: "I hold that in general an increase in the monetary stock causes in a State a proportional increase in consumption, which by degrees produces the rise of prices." [5] Cantillon recognized that an increase in the quantity of money stimulates demand which in turn gradually leads to price increases. He presented several explanations as to how this could happen. For example, if the increase in the monetary stock came from an expansion in mining the money metal, the mineowners, smelters and refiners would be the first to increase their expenditures on food, clothing and shelter. This would provide additional employment to artisans, who in turn would increase their own spending, and so the increase in spending would spiral upwards. The prices of meat, wine and wool would rise, encouraging the production of these goods. Farmers would gain and increase their expenditures. However, the

---

4 "Richard Cantillon and the Nationality of Political Economy", reprinted from *Contemporary Review*, 1881, in Richard Cantillon, *Essai sur la nature du commerce en général*, trans. H. Higgs, London, Macmillan, for the Royal Economic Society, 1931, p. 342. Reprinted by Augustus M. Kelley, New York, 1964.

5 Richard, Cantillon, "On the Nature of Commerce in General" as reprinted in Arthur E. Monroe, *op. cit.*, p. 264.

landlords with existing leases would lose, as would their servants, many of whom would be dismissed. Only when the landlords' leases expired would they be able to raise their rents and return to their former standard of living. The general rise in prices would cause more goods to be imported from abroad and the money metal would begin to leave the country. A smaller stock of money, a lower money circulation, lower prices and even misery would follow.

Another of Cantillon's examples explains the rise in expenditures and prices caused by the inflow of money from abroad as a result of an export surplus. Cantillon recognized that a rise in the price level need not be proportionate to the increase in the quantity of money, because "an acceleration, or a greater speed, in the circulation of money in trade amounts to the same thing as an increase in standard money, up to a certain point."[6]

David Hume (1711-1776) is probably the most quoted of the early quantity theorists. Although he had adopted Locke's theory of money, he developed some aspects of the quantity theory more fully than Locke had done. In "Of Money", one of his many essays, Hume commented, "It seems a maxim almost self-evident, that the prices of everything depend on the proportion between commodities and money".[7] In his essay "Of the Balance of Trade", he reasoned:

> Suppose four-fifths of all the money in BRITAIN to be annihilated in one night ... Must not the price of all labour and commodities sink in proportion ...? What nation could then dispute with us in any foreign market ...? In how little time, therefore, must this bring back the money we had lost, and raise us to the level of all the neighboring nations? Where, after we have arrived, we immediately lose the advantage of the cheapness of labour and commodities; and the further flowing in of money is stopped by our fullness and repletion.[8]

Hume recognized a proportionate relationship between money and the level of prices. He also saw a relationship between the level of prices and the volume of a country's imports and exports, and in turn between the balance of a country's imports and exports and the international flow of money. These connecting links were later to become known as the price-specie-flow mechanism used to explain adjustments in a country's balance of payments.

---

6 *Ibid.*

7 Hume, David, *Essays and Treatises on Several Subjects*, 2 vols., London, 1772, Vol. 1. p.149. Hume's essays are available in *Essays: Moral, Political and Literary*, Oxford University Press, 1963.

8 *Ibid.*, Vol. 1, pp. 323-324.

Hume, and as mentioned earlier, Cantillon, explained how the increase in the price level followed an increase in the money supply. He wrote in his essay "Of Money":

> . . . we find that, in every Kingdom, into which money begins to flow in greater abundance than formerly, everything takes a new face; labour and industry gain life; the merchant becomes more enterprising, the manufacturer more diligent and skilful, and even the farmer follows the plough with greater alacrity and attention . . .[9]

Hume's explanation of how changes in the quantity of money lead to a proportional change in the level of prices is now referred to as the crude quantity theory of money or the transactions approach of the quantity theory. This approach certainly did not originate with him as can be seen from our discussion of his predecessors. However, since Hume was one of the more widely-read writers, his name is most often associated with this theory. According to Hume, the increase in spending followed directly from an increase in the *quantity* of money. The quantity of money did not determine the rate of interest which in turn might stimulate investment expenditures. On the contrary the interest rate was determined by industry and frugality, that is, productivity and thrift. As we shall see, Hume's proposition long remained a basic tenet of economic theory.

We have traced the lineage of the quantity theory of money through the sixteenth, seventeenth and eighteenth centuries. As first enunciated in the writings of Jean Bodin, it was purely a theory of quantity. Locke and his successors in the following two centuries took into account the velocity of money as well as the volume of trade. Both Cantillon and Hume recognized that the increase in trade and in the velocity of money following an expansion of the money supply produced a rise in prices and usually also expanded employment.

CLASSICAL SCHOOL OF ECONOMICS

The classical school of economics is the school of Adam Smith (1723-1790).[10] It includes the English economists David Ricardo (1772-1823), Thomas Robert Malthus (1766-1834), Nassau William Senior (1790-1864, John Stuart Mill (1806-1873) and the French economist Jean Baptiste Say (1767-1832). These men did not, as is commonly assumed, make up a homogeneous group. However, most of them were adherents of the *laissez faire* policy which marks the break from mercantilism, and

---

[9] *Ibid.*, p. 297.

[10] The term "classical economists" was used by Karl Marx to cover the period from Adam Smith to James Mill. Marx had Ricardo in mind primarily as the true representative of the classical school. Keynes broadened the definition of classical economists to include the neo-classical economists discussed in the following section.

were concerned essentially with developing a theory to explain commodity pricing and resource allocation. In addition, the majority, excluding notably Malthus, accepted Say's law of the markets according to which effective demand always tends to be sufficient for capacity production.

Say's law was fundamental to classical economists. It was enunciated by Say as the *théorie des debouchés* (theory of the markets) in his *Traite d'économie politique* ("Treatise on Political Economy") first published in 1803.

> . . . a product is no sooner created, than it, from that instant, affords a market for other products to the full extent of its own value. When the producer has put the finishing hand to his product, he is most anxious to sell it immediately, lest its value should diminish in his hands. Nor is he less anxious to dispose of the money he may get for it; for the value of money is also perishable. But the only way of getting rid of money is in the purchase of some product or other. Thus the mere circumstance of the creation of one product immediately opens a vent for other products.[11]

In its most general terms Say's law was regarded by the classical economists as meaning that for the economy as a whole, supply necessarily creates its own demand of equivalent magnitude. Sellers sell goods and services merely to buy other goods and services. However, all products will not always find a market for it is possible to produce too much of one good and not enough of another. This situation was considered to represent both an oversupply and a scarcity. Total production has not been too great — it has been mis-directed creating an oversupply of some commodities and an undersupply of others.

The classical economists were interested mainly in developing a theory to explain commodity pricing and resource allocation. They felt that money played a neutral role in the pricing process; it was a medium of exchange and did nothing more than facilitate trade. It was assumed by the classical school that all money immediately finds its way into the expenditure stream. Although individuals save part of their money income, this is immediately available for investment expenditures. In fact, savers were assumed to make investment expenditures possible because by saving and not consuming they released factors of production required to produce capital goods. In classical economics, as we shall see in Chapter 21, saving is always equal to investment; the rate of interest attends to this. The amount of each good exchanged depends upon its relative price, which is determined by production costs, essentially labour costs, which are in turn determined by the scarcity of resources and the efficiency of the factors of production. John Stuart Mill summarized the role of money in

[11] Say, Jean Baptiste, *A Treatise on Political Economy*, trans. from the 4th ed. of the French by C. R. Prinsep, New American Edition, Philadelphia, Claxton, Remsen and Haffelfinger, 1880. Reprinted by Augustus M. Kelley, New York 1964, pp. 134-135.

the classical theory: "There cannot, in short, be intrinsically a more insignificant thing, in the economy of a society, than money; except in the character of a contrivance for sparing time and labour."[12]

The classical economists accepted the quantity theory as developed by their predecessors adding little, if anything, to it. Any change in the money supply was assumed to affect only absolute prices (the price level) leaving relative prices unchanged. Hence, there came to be two distinct theories of economics. The pricing process of goods and resources used in their production was explained in terms of the "real" forces in the economy such as productivity and thrift, while the price level was explained in terms of the monetary forces. The separation of the two is known as the **classical dichotomy.**

During the Napoleonic wars, when the Bank of England no longer converted its notes into specie, concern was expressed over the relation between prices and the amount of notes issued by the Bank. Two of the leading writers who took part in the debate at the time, Henry Thornton (1760-1815) and David Ricardo (1772-1823) expressed the quantity theory of money in the same way as their predecessors.

According to Thornton, prices rise as the result of an increase in aggregate demand following an increase in Bank notes, but they do not necessarily rise proportionately to the increase in money. An increase in money could lead to employment of idle factors of production and an increase in output without an increase in prices. However, as this theory would hold good only until all the unemployed persons had been put to work, he considered the cause of high prices to be an overissue of notes by the Bank of England.

David Ricardo also held that the value of money could be maintained by limiting its quantity. However, he recognized that even if the stock of money is held constant with no changes in productivity, an increase in the "rapidity of circulation" (velocity) will lead to an increase in the price level. In "The High Price of Bullion", for example, he wrote:

> The value of the circulating medium of every country bears some proportion to the value of the commodities which it circulates. In some countries this proportion is much greater than in others, and varies, on some occasions, in the same country. It depends upon the rapidity of circulation, upon the degree of confidence and credit existing between traders, and, above all, on the judicious operations of banking.[13]

---

12 Mill, John Stuart, *Principles of Political Economy*, in J. M. Robson (ed.), *Collected Works of John Stuart Mill*, Vol. 3, Toronto, University of Toronto Press, 1965, p. 506.

13 Ricardo, David, "The High Price of Bullion, A Proof of the Depreciation of Bank Notes 1810-1811", in Piero Straffa, *The Works and Correspondence of David Ricardo*, Cambridge, England, Cambridge University Press, 1951, Vol. 3, p. 90.

Both Thornton and Ricardo concluded that in general there was a proportional relationship between money and prices. Thornton was led to this belief because he thought that the number of unemployed persons was limited. Ricardo arrived at the same conclusion because he thought the velocity of money was as high as possible in Great Britain and therefore constant.

HISTORICAL SCHOOL AND STATE THEORY OF MONEY

During the mid-nineteenth century some German writers led a general movement away from the classical approach to economics which was considered unrealistic because of its inductive approach. The new school replaced what it called the "abstractions" of the classical economists, particularly Ricardo, with a more realistic or historical approach. The so-called historical school was centred in the German universities but had many adherents in Great Britain. The historical approach was accompanied by an increasing attention to social problems and socialism in general. The main contributor, and there were many, was Karl Marx (1818-1883).

The German historical school's concept of money is known as the **state theory of money.** This theory can be traced to Aristotle who says in his *Politics* and *Nichomachean Ethics* that the value of money is derived "not from nature but from law". A German philosopher, J. G. Fichte (1762-1814), accepting this concept of the nature of money noted that:

> . . . by the issuing of money the state guarantees that it will furnish to the holder of money at any time, for his money, those articles whereof the state has guaranteed the enjoyment to every one: for each piece of money in the hands of a private person is a sign of an indebtedness on the part of the state.[14]

The idea that money has no value except that given to it by the state (also known as chartalism) was further explored by Georg Friedrich Knapp, (1842-1926). He wrote that "the soul of currency is not in the material of the pieces, but in the legal ordinances which regulate their use".[15] During the First World War the state theory of money popularized by Knapp and his followers was employed by those who wanted to show that the expansion of the currency had nothing to do with soaring prices.

---

[14] *Grundlage des Naturrechts,*1796, translated as *The Science of Rights,* by A. E. Kroeger, London, Trubner, 1889, p. 319.

[15] Knapp, Georg Friedrich, *Die Staatleche Theorie des Geldes,* ("State Theory of Money", 1905), abridged ed., trans. by H. M. Lucas and J. Bonar, London, Macmillan, 1924, p. 2.

NEO-CLASSICAL SCHOOL

The neo-classical period of economics, characterized by a resurgence of classical economics, was centred on the work of Alfred Marshall (1842-1924). In England Stanley Jevons (1835-1882) and in Austria Karl Menger (1840-1921) were among the early leaders. The mainstream of neo-classical economists includes Alfred Marshall and his followers at Cambridge University as well as Eugen von Böhm Bawerk (1851-1914) and Friedrich von Wieser (1851-1926) in Vienna, Léon Walras (1834-1910) and Vilfredo Pareto (1848-1923) in Lausanne, Knut Wicksell (1851-1926) in Sweden, and John Bates Clark (1847-1938) in the United States.

The neo-classical economists developed a two-fold theory of value. One part was the theory of marginal productivity and profit maximization which applied to the producer, and the other the theory of marginal utility and utility maximization which applied to the individual. Within their framework of marginal analysis these economists explained the volume of output and employment in terms of the relative prices of commodities. As long as relative prices were flexible, and Say's law of the markets applied, output would always tend toward full employment, at least in the long run. Absolute prices were still explained by the quantity theory of money which had become more sophisticated. In the United States Irving Fisher (1867-1947) developed a mathematical formula for the quantity theory — his now famous equation of exchange, or transactions equation, which will be discussed in Chapter 20. Fisher, however, followed traditional lines. He himself acknowledged the earlier work of Francis Edgeworth (1845-1926) and Simon Newcomb (1835-1909) who had presented mathematical formulations of the quantity theory of money.

In England, following the earlier work of Walras on the continent, the Cambridge school, especially Arthur Pigou (1877-1959) and D. H. Robertson (1890-1963), developed a cash balance equation to explain the relation between money and the price level. The central concept of Walras' monetary analysis was his **encaisse desirée;** that is, the amount of cash that people individually desire to hold at any moment.[16] The Cambridge tradition expressed this principle in terms of the cash balance equation. As we shall see in Chapter 20 the difference between this equation and Fisher's transactions equation is important. Whereas the Cambridge cash balance equation is concerned with why money is held, the Fisher transactions equation is concerned with why cash is not spent as yet. D. H. Robertson has expressed this distinction as money "sitting" and money

---

[16] Walras, Léon, *Elements of Pure Economics*, trans. by William Jaffé, published for the American Economic Association and the Royal Economic Society, Homewood, Ill., Richard D. Irwin, 1954, p. 326.

"on the wing".[17] The Cambridge approach marked an important step forward in monetary theory as it introduced motivation and volition into the theory. Unfortunately, the quantity theory of money which neo-classical economists generally propounded did not fully exploit the potential of the cash balance approach. They continued to believe that the prime motive for holding money was to facilitate transactions: they neglected or paid only cursory attention to the possibility that money may also be held as an asset.

TOWARD A GENERAL THEORY OF ECONOMICS

The neo-classical economists perpetuated the classical dichotomy mentioned previously. The first step toward integrating monetary theory and price theory was the recognition of the money side of the rate of interest. In both classical and neo-classical economics the rate of interest was generally considered to be determined by the real forces in the economy. There were of course exceptions. For example, Henry Thornton whom we included in the classical period showed the rate of interest to be a link between the money and commodity market.[18] Such observations, however, received little attention until a century later when Knut Wicksell produced his theory of two rates of interest — the natural rate and the money or market rate. Theories to explain the business cycle grew up around Wicksell's concept of the two rates of interest. They were known as over-investment theories which attempted to explain how changes in investment resulting from changes in the money supply and the rate of interest produced short-run economic fluctuations. As for the long run, Say's law was still relied upon to explain effective demand and the tendency toward full employment. Hence the classical dichotomy remained.

THE KEYNESIAN REVOLUTION

The cornerstone of the Keynesian revolution is *The General Theory of Employment, Interest and Money*.[19] As the title implies, John Maynard Keynes wanted to derive a general theory which would resolve the traditional dichotomy between monetary theory and price theory. He wanted to show among other things that money by way of its influence on the

[17] Robertson, D. H., *Money*, University of Chicago Press, 1959 Ch. 2.

[18] Thornton, Henry, *An Enquiry Into the Nature of the Proper Credit of Great Britain*, London, J. Hatchard, 1802.

[19] Keynes, John Maynard, *The General Theory of Employment, Interest and Money*, London, Macmillan, 1936.

rate of interest could play an important role in the determination of income and employment.

Keynes launched his attack on both classical and neo-classical theory with a new explanation of savings. He considered the level of income to be the most important determinant of saving, and not the rate of interest as the classical economists had held. What the rate of interest determines is the proportion of their savings that individuals are prepared to release to the capital market for investment purposes. During any given period an individual's total income does not immediately flow back into the expenditure stream in the form of either consumer or investment spending because it is quite rational for an individual to prefer to keep some part of his assets liquid — to hold cash as an asset. This behaviour was considered irrational by the classical economists who assumed that money served essentially as a medium of exchange. Keynes, unlike most of his predecessors, held that investors do not automatically increase their investment expenditures as individuals increase their thrift and the rate of interest falls. The rate of interest is only one of many determinants of the level of investment. Hence Keynes detached the decision to invest from the decision to save and showed that the equality between the two is not determined by the rate of interest. According to Keynes, during any past period saving is equal to investment, but this equality is achieved because saving is determined by the level of income. For example, if business decides to spend more, say with bank funds, income expands. As income increases so does the level of saving and ultimately saving and investment are again equal.

In Keynesian theory, as opposed to classical theory, national income or national production is not a given quantity determined by productive capacity. The latter serves only as a ceiling to production and there is no assurance that at any time the economy will operate at full capacity. Hence Say's law of the markets is denied. In the simple Keynesian model aggregate demand is composed of consumer, investment and government expenditures. In the extended model presented in Chapter 24 we have included exports — the demand for goods and services by foreigners. The total of these demands need not be sufficient to absorb full capacity output which will therefore not be attained. The classical economists would argue that full employment is the necessary consequence of a situation in which all prices including wages and the rate of interest are flexible downward. Keynes countered that in the real world such flexibility does not exist and even if it did, it would not assure aggregate demand sufficient to induce full employment output. With flexible prices (Keynes was concerned essentially with flexible wages) full employment equilibrium may not be reached where spending is not responsive to changes in the rate of interest. Nor will full employment occur where the demand for money is infinitely elastic with respect to the rate of interest so that interest rates are not allowed to fall as the quantity of money increases.

A. C. Pigou and, more recently, D. Patinkin [20] have refuted Keynes' underemployment equilibrium proposition. They base their argument on what has become known as the "Pigou effect" or the "real balances effect". According to this doctrine, as the price level falls the real value of the community's money balances increases, people become wealthier and consumption increases. The rate of interest may remain completely unchanged. However, as Patinkin has pointed out, if the rate of interest declines, the market value of the community's security holdings increases and support is lent to the real balances effect insofar as a wealth effect comes into play. The wealth effect depends, of course, upon what proportion of the community's security holdings is represented by government securities. An increase in the price of private securities makes creditors feel richer but makes debtors feel poorer; so that while creditors may increase their spending, debtors may reduce theirs by an equal amount. Thus, if the community holds large amounts of private securities, the wealth effect may be washed out. On the other hand, the government remains unconcerned about fluctuations in the market value of its liabilities and neither increases nor decreases its expenditures on this basis. Critics of the Pigou or real balances effect point out that expectations may be such that a change in the price level leaves aggregate demand unaffected. Patinkin has also argued that the introduction of the real balances effect disposes of the classical dichotomy. Moreover, the concept preserves the classical proposition that only the level of prices and not the real equilibrium of the system will be affected by the amount of money.

Although Keynes provided all the building blocks to show the interdependent relationship between the money and the goods markets it was left to J. R. Hicks and Alvin Hansen to show explicitly how Say's law of the markets and the classical dichotomy have no place in a general theory of economics.[21] Their now-famous *IS* and *LM* curves will be discussed in Chapters 23, 24 and 25.

20 Pigou, A. C. "The Classical Stationary State", *Economic Journal,* 1943 and "Economic Progress in a Stable Environment", *Economica,* 1947; Don Patinkin, *Money, Interest and Prices,* New York , Harper and Row, 1965.

21 Hicks, J. R., "Mr. Keynes and the Classics: A Suggested Interpretation", *Econometrica,* April 1937, pp. 147-159; Alvin H. Hansen, *A Guide to Keynes,* New York, McGraw-Hill, 1953. See also F. Modligiani, "Liquidity Preference and the Theory of Interest and Money", in F. A. Lutz and L. W. Mints, (eds.), *Readings in Monetary Theory,* Homewood, Ill., Richard D. Irwin, 1951.

The way money influences the real sector of the economy is still an issue for debate. Some economists, notably Milton Friedman of the University of Chicago, believe that the real sector is directly affected by changes in the money supply. The Keynesians believe that the effect is indirect, occurring only via the rate of interest. The approach which one takes to explain the relationship between money and prices, output and employment has important implications for monetary policy as we shall see in Chapter 27.

SELECTED READINGS

American Economic Association, *Readings in Monetary Theory*, New York, McGraw-Hill, 1951.

Blaug, M., *Economic Theory in Retrospect*, Homewood, Ill., Richard D. Irwin, 1962.

Eshag, Eprime, *From Marshall to Keynes*, Oxford, Basil Blackwell, 1963.

Hansen, Alvin H., *A Guide to Keynes*, New York, McGraw-Hill, 1953.

Hutchison, T. W., *A Review of Economic Doctrines, 1870-1929*, Oxford, Clarendon Press, 1953.

Johnson, Harry G., "Monetary Theory and Policy", *American Economic Review*, Vol. 52, June 1962, pp. 335-384.

Keynes, John Maynard, *A Treatise on Money*, 2 vols., London, Macmillan, 1930.

Keynes, John Maynard, *The General Theory of Employment, Interest and Money*, London, Macmillan, 1936.

Klein, L. R. *The Keynesian Revolution*, New York, Macmillan, 1950.

Kuhn, W. F., *The Evolution of Economic Thought*, Cincinnati, Ohio, South-Western Publishing, 1963.

Kurihara, Kenneth K., *Monetary Theory and Public Policy*, New York, W. W. Norton, 1950.

Lekachman, Robert (ed.), *Keynes and the Classics*, Boston, D. C. Heath, 1964.

Marget, Arthur W., *The Theory of Prices*, 2 vols., New York, Prentice-Hall, 1938.

Monroe, Arthur Eli (ed.), *Early Economic Thought*, Cambridge, Mass., Harvard University Press, 1951.

Niebyl, Karl H., *Studies in the Classical Theories of Money*, New York, Columbia University Press, 1946.

Patinkin, Don, *Money, Interest and Prices,* 2nd ed., New York, Harper and Row, 1965.

Rist, Charles, *History of Monetary and Credit Theory,* London, George Allen & Unwin, 1940.

Samuelson, Paul A., "What Classical and Neo-Classical Monetary Theory Really Was", *Canadian Journal of Economics,* Vol. 1, February, 1968, pp. 1-15.

Schumpeter, Joseph A., *History of Economic Analysis,* New York, Oxford University Press, 1963.

Vickers, Douglas, *Studies in the Theory of Money 1690-1776,* Philadelphia, Chilton Company, 1959.

Warren, George F. and Frank A. Pearson, *Gold and Prices,* New York, John Wiley & Sons, 1935.

Wicksell, Knut, *Interesi and Prices* (Geldzins und Guterpreise) trans. by R. F. Kahn for Royal Economic Society, London, Macmillan, 1936.

20

THE QUANTITY THEORY OF MONEY

In the last chapter we traced the lineage of the quantity theory of money. In this chapter we shall concentrate on its development during the early parts of the twentieth century. We shall return to it in later chapters to show its modern rehabilitation at the hands of Milton Friedman and Don Patinkin.

VELOCITY APPROACHES TO THE QUANTITY THEORY OF MONEY

TRANSACTIONS-VELOCITY APPROACH

As developed by Irving Fisher this approach uses the framework of the **equation of exchange** to show the relationship between money and prices. The equation of exchange is an algebraic statement of the total transactions involving money effected over a specified period of time in a given community. It is the sum of the equations of exchange for all individual transactions in the given period.

Suppose a person makes a transaction *(t)* consisting of the purchase from a grocer of five loaves of bread at a price *(p)* of 20 cents per loaf and turns over *(v)* to the grocer a one-dollar bill *(m)* in exchange for the bread. This exchange transaction can be summarized in the following way:

$$p \cdot t \equiv m \cdot v \quad \text{or} \quad \$0.20 \times 5 \equiv \$1.00 \times 1 \tag{1}$$

Every individual sale or purchase can be expressed in a similar way. An equation of exchange for a particular community is obtained by adding together all of these transactions involving money over a certain period of time.

Let us assume an economy where during the period of a year only three transactions take place each having a value of $1. The total value of all business transactions is equal to \$3. Three separate dollar bills are not required to transact this amount of business because the same dollar bill can be used to facilitate all three transactions. For example, when I give the grocer a dollar bill for the bread I purchase from him he can exchange the same dollar bill for a dollar's worth of milk and the milkman in turn can use this same bill to buy a dollar's worth of meat. Thus by employing the same dollar bill on three separate occasions it is possible to transact business amounting to \$3. In an individual transaction the amount of money exchanged is shown as $m \times v$ where m is the dollar bill referred to above and v its rate of turnover which is once for each transaction. If we add together all three transactions the value of m remains the same while the value of v corresponds to the total number of times m is employed — in our example, three. In order to differentiate between the amount of money paid for all transactions in an economy during the year and the money spent on each individual transaction a large M and V are used for the former and a small m and v for the latter. MV is now the total amount of money spent for all transactions in the economy during the year. M is the total amount of money in circulation and V its transactions-velocity of circulation (the number of times an average dollar changes hands during the year).

All the individual small p's and t's must also be totalled. Since the t's usually comprise a diverse group of commodities plus services and property rights, simply adding them together is meaningless. Therefore an index number is used, weighted to reflect the importance of each transaction in a total index number. Similarly, instead of adding together all the individual small p's, an average weighted price index number is employed. If we call T our index number of the physical volume of transactions (sales) during the year, and P an index number representing the general price level, then PT is the value of all transactions which by definition must also be equal to MV, the amount of money paid for PT. We can therefore write the equation of exchange for an entire community over a certain period as

$$MV \equiv PT \qquad (2)$$

This equation is a tautology or a truism. It tells us simply that the dollar value of everything bought equals the dollar value of everything sold. Each side of the equation is merely a different way of describing the same phenomenon — expenditures. The left side of the equation *(MV)* tells us that the money spent on purchases is equal to the volume of money in circulation (the money supply) multiplied by the number of times it is used to complete the transactions *(PT)* specified on the right side of the equation. Therefore we can learn nothing from the equation that is not self evident. However, once we make certain assumptions about the behaviour of the four variables which make up the equation, we can say something about the relation between changes in the quantity of money and changes in the general price level. In other words, we can turn the definitional identity into a monetary theory by the assumptions we make about the behaviour of M, V, P and T. Traditionally, the following assumptions were usually made by *most* of the quantity theorists of money:

1. The average amount of money (M) in the economy during any given period is determined solely by the monetary authorities. The velocity of money (V), the general price level (P), and the physical volume of transactions (T) in no way influence M either as to size or as to changes of it.
2. Changes in M will not produce inverse changes in V. While V can change in the same direction as M, V is usually assumed to remain relatively constant.
3. Changes in M will not produce parallel changes in T. Like V, T is usually assumed to remain relatively constant.
4. The price level (P) is a passive variable in the equation of exchange. While it exerts no influence over the other variables in the equation, it is influenced by them. However, since both V and T are assumed to remain relatively constant, only M can produce changes in P. This is also true if V and T are allowed to change so that a change in one will be offset by a change in the other.

If all these assumptions can be shown to be valid then it follows that changes in the money supply lead to changes in the price level. Moreover, if V and T remain constant over the period under consideration or if a change in one is offset by an equal change in the other, it can be shown that changes in the money supply generate equiproportionate changes in the price level.

This can be expressed in the following way:

$$M = P\frac{T}{V} \qquad (3)$$

and assuming T/V to remain constant, then by doubling the money supply

$$2M = 2P \qquad (4)$$

This conclusion depends upon the behaviour of V and T. Fisher listed the influences that determine the volume of trade (transaction) as follows:[1]

[1] Fisher, Irving, *The Purchasing Power of Money*, New York, Macmillan, 1911, pp. 74-75.

1. *Conditions affecting producers*
   - (a) Geographical differences in natural resources.
   - (b) The division of labour.
   - (c) Knowledge of the technique of production.
   - (d) The accumulation of capital.

2. *Conditions affecting consumers*
   - (a) The extent and variety of human wants.

3. *Conditions connecting producers and consumers*
   - (a) Facilities for transportation.
   - (b) Relative freedom of trade.
   - (c) Character of monetary and banking systems.
   - (d) Business confidence.

Because the factors which determine the real volume of all market transactions change only slowly over time, Fisher and his followers generally assumed that T remained relatively constant. This was also considered to be the case for the transactions velocity of money which according to Fisher was determined by the following factors.[2]

1. *Habits of the individual*
   - (a) As to thrift and hoarding.
   - (b) As to book credit.
   - (c) As to the use of checks.

2. *Systems of payments in the community*
   - (a) As to frequency of receipt and disbursements.
   - (b) As to regularity of receipts and disbursements.
   - (c) As to correspondence between times and amounts of receipts and disbursements.

3. *General Causes*
   - (a) Density of population.
   - (b) Rapidity of transportation.

Although Fisher assumed that under long-run normal conditions T and V remained relatively constant he recognized that in the short run fluctuations could occur. In what he referred to as "transition periods" (the short run), temporary changes in T and V could take place. Moreover, he admitted the existence of a lagged relationship between the rate of interest and the price level which allowed T to influence V and M. Fisher's theory of the relationship between money and the price level has been generally interpreted as a strictly long-run explanation when all the components in the equation of exchange except M and P are assumed to remain relatively constant.

---

[2] *Ibid.*, p. 79.

When he presented his equation of exchange, Fisher divided the total money supply into its two basic components: coin and bank notes (M), and demand deposits (M') with V and V' their respective velocity of circulation. The equation of exchange was presented as:

$$MV + M'V' \equiv PT \tag{5}$$

Fisher noted that normally M' was a fixed proportion of the total money supply and that the determinants that explained V also explained V'. If so, it makes little difference whether the equation of exchange includes only one term representing the total money supply or two.

INCOME-VELOCITY APPROACH

In the 1930's following the work of the Swedish economists and John Maynard Keynes, attention shifted away from the concept of total expenditures and turned to that of expenditures on **final goods currently produced.** The change was reflected in what has become known as the income-velocity equation of exchange, expressed as:

$$MV_y = P_y T_y \text{ or } MV_y = Y \tag{6}$$

In contrast to the transactions-velocity equation, the income-velocity equation includes only the physical volume of final goods currently produced, T_y. The average price of this output is P_y. The total value of final output currently produced during a designated period is shown as $P_y T_y$ or, the more commonly used symbol, Y. We can think of Y as the gross national production (GNP). As in the transactions-velocity equation, M is the average supply of money during the period and V_y its income velocity, here defined as the turnover of the average money supply required to transact final output. Since the physical volume of final goods currently produced is smaller than the physical volume of all transactions taking place in an economy over a specified period of time, with a given money supply, the income-velocity of money (V_y) is smaller than its transaction's velocity (V). If we assume that the total real output in an economy during any given period is determined by the population, technological knowledge and capital accumulation, all of which change slowly and over time, T_y can be considered to remain relatively constant as was the case with T. Moreover, if we assume that the income velocity of money depends essentially upon institutional factors which also change only slowly and over extended periods, V_y, too, can be considered to remain relatively constant. These assumptions bring us back to the conclusions of the transactions-velocity approach to the quantity theory: the price level is determined by the money supply and changes in the money supply lead to equiproportionate changes in the price level in the same direction.

CASH-BALANCE APPROACH TO THE QUANTITY THEORY OF MONEY

While Irving Fisher was formulating the velocity approach to the quantity theory of money in the United States, A. C. Pigou, J. M. Keynes and D. H. Robertson at Cambridge University in England were developing the cash-balance approach along the earlier lines of Alfred Marshall and Léon Walras. As we have seen, Fisher showed the relationship between money and the price level in terms of the equation of exchange which focuses on the relationship among M, V, P and T. The Cambridge economists used the cash-balance equation which places emphasis on the demand for money, or the so-called "Marshallian K", to show the connection between money the price level. While there are various versions of the cash-balance equation, the more usual one is:

$$M \equiv KRP \tag{7}$$

Here M is the amount of money in circulation at a moment of time and R the real national output of goods and services currently produced over a particular period, say a year. The average price of a unit of this output is P, and the value of total output RP. This is identical to the expression $P_y T_y$ in the income-velocity equation. If we were to define R as the total of all transactions in an economy over a specified period of time, RP would be synonomous with PT in the transactions-velocity equation. K is that proportion of the national output (RP or R) over which the community desires to exercise control at any given moment of time by holding cash balances. The community is assumed to want to retain a certain amount of purchasing power in the form of money to enable it to purchase a certain proportion of the total national output, or to participate in a certain proportion of the total transactions involving final goods and services during a specified period.

In the cash-balance equation, as in the equation of exchange, M is the total amount of money in circulation at a *moment* of time. The economist refers to this as a **stock concept.** Money remains a stock concept whether we define it as the absolute amount in existence in any one day, or the average amount in existence in any one month or in any one year. In both equations, on the other hand, RP and $P_y T_y$ are **flow concepts** in that they refer to the value of the final output produced over a *period* of time. The basic difference between the equation of exchange and the cash-balance equation is that the former is transformed entirely into a flow concept while the latter is transformed entirely into a stock concept. These two transformations are accomplished by including V_y (or V) on the left side of the equation of exchange and K on the right side of the cash-balance equation.

In the exchange equation multiplying the money stock M by its income velocity V_y produces MV_y, the total money expenditures on final output over a period of time. The inclusion of V_y transforms the left side of the equation of exchange into a flow concept and equates it to the right side of the equation, P_yT_y, also a flow concept.

In the cash-balance equation the left side of the equation, the money stock, remains a stock concept while the right side of the equation, RP, undergoes a transformation from a flow to a stock concept when RP is multiplied by K. The product KRP tells us that the total amount of money held by the community is equal to a fraction, K, of the value of the national output. The total amount of money held by the community at any moment of time must be equal to the total money stock in existence at the same moment of time because by definition the money supply is the total amount of money in circulation outside the banking system. The cash-balance equation, therefore, like the equation of exchange is nothing more than a truism where KRP is a different way of expressing M just as MV_y is a different way of expressing P_yT_y (or MV is a different way of expressing PT). In the equation of exchange we note that *over any period of time* money expenditures are equal to the value of goods and services sold (or purchased). In the cash-balance equation we note that *at any moment of time* the total amount of money in existence is equal to the total amount of money held by the community.

What more can we say about V and K? The relationship between them can be illustrated in the following way:

$$MV \equiv P_yT_y \tag{8}$$

$$V \equiv \frac{P_yT_y}{M} \tag{9}$$

$$M \equiv KRP \text{ or } KP_yT_y \tag{10}$$

By substituting for M in *(9)* from *(10)* we derive

$$V \equiv \frac{P_yT_y}{KP_yT_y} \equiv \frac{1}{K} \tag{11}$$

Algebraically, therefore, V and K are simply the reciprocal of one another. If, for example, a unit of money passes from hand to hand four times a year, each unit of money must remain in someone's hands for an average time of three months or one quarter of the year. Does it really matter if we concern ourselves with how many times during a year a given amount of money is spent — the velocity approach — or with how long on the average a given amount of money is held between spending periods — the cash-balance approach? The two approaches are really only two different observations of the same phenomena. We mentioned in the previous chapter that D. H. Robertson has identified the cash-balance approach as "money sitting" and the velocity approach as "money on the wing". For analytical purposes, the cash-balance approach is more meaningful than the velocity approach. Money takes flight because it is required to meet expenditures. But why does money sit? In answering this question we introduce human motivation and behaviour. Moreover, we can include in a theory of money such factors as uncertainty, expectations and the rate of interest. Unfortunately the Cambridge economists did not exploit the possibilities inherent in the cash-balance equation for formulating a **dynamic** theory of the relationship between money and prices. Robertson called K "the Prince of Denmark in the Hamlet of the Cambridge equation" but he gave it only the status of a duke. His list of the factors that determine K is not much different from Fisher's list of the factors determining V. The five determinants of K as outlined by Robertson are [3]

> (1) Factors connected with business habits — the frequency and regularity with which payments are made, and so forth;
>
> (2) Factors connected with the structure of industry — in particular how far the production and sale of output are split up into stages in the hands of different firms between whom payments have to be made for the transfer of goods in process or in store;
>
> (3) The general conditions of social and business life and hence the degree of certainty and confidence with which consumers and producers are making their plans ...;
>
> (4) The state of development of the market for existing capital goods — land, houses, etc., and of paper titles thereto: this works both ways, — such things need money to exchange them with, but some of them are also partial substitutes for money;
>
> (5) The rate of return obtainable by employing resources otherwise than by tying them up in the form of money ....

The first four factors in this list can be considered in the same light as Fisher's list which determined V as institutional. Like most of his colleagues at Cambridge, Robertson was led to believe that individuals hold money essentially because given institutional structures they must. Moreover, since institutional patterns change slowly and over extended time

[3] Roberston, D.H., *Lectures on Economic Principles*, Vol. 3, London, Staples Press, 1959, pp. 20-21.

periods, K remains relatively constant in much the same way as Fisher's V. Only the fifth factor in Robertson's list hints that the individual may have a choice as to the amount of money he holds at any given time. The incorporation of choice and uncertainty as an integral part of a theory of the demand for money, however, was not fully exploited until Keynes.

Along with K, the total output R was assumed to be constant. The Cambridge economists believed that changes in output could come about only as a result of changes in population, technology and capital accumulation, all of which change slowly and over time. Because of these assumptions about K and T, the cash-balance equation became another dress for the quantity theory of money. Suppose, for instance, that given K and R, the money supply is equal to the amount of money the community *desires* to hold. Now suppose the money supply is doubled. Since by assumption people hold money only as a convenience to make anticipated purchases, or to make certain that they can participate in the purchase of output in the future, they now hold more money than they desire or find necessary. They will rid themselves of this excess cash by spending it on goods and services. The additional expenditure raises aggregate demand. However, output cannot be increased to meet this demand because all the resources in the community are fully employed. Therefore, prices will rise. When the price level has doubled the total money supply will again be required for transactions balances, the desired demand for money will be equal to its supply, and the economy will again be in equilibrium. This same story can be told using our algebra.

$$M = KRP \qquad (12)$$

Dividing both sides of this equation by KR

$$\frac{M}{KR} = P \qquad (13)$$

Assuming KR to remain constant, and doubling the money supply

$$2M = 2P \qquad (14)$$

ATTACK ON THE QUANTITY THEORY OF MONEY

PROPORTIONALITY CONCEPT

The quantity theory of money as formulated by Fisher within the framework of the equation of exchange is based on the assumption that changes in the money supply produce changes in the price level without affecting the velocity of money and total transactions or output. Although Fisher considered the possibility of a change in the money stock leading to changes in its velocity and in the volume of transactions, he rejected such effects because he considered them to occur only during short-term periods of transition. He was led to conclude "that the strictly proportional effect on prices of an increase in M is only the *normal* or *ultimate* effect after transition periods are over".[4] His conclusion was oversimplified. The four variables, M, V, P and T in the transactions-velocity equation, as is also the case for the variables in the income-velocity equation, are not independent of one another regardless of the time period one chooses. A change in M is likely to bring about a change in V which need not be in the same direction. As later economists have attempted to show, it makes more sense to regard MV as a single entity rather than to give V independent status. T, too, does not deserve independent treatment because an increase in M or MV usually tends to stimulate an increase in T. If we allow both V and T to change it is still possible to conclude that a change in M will lead to a proportional change in P as long as any change in V is at the same time offset by a change in T in the same direction. However, this is probably the exception rather than the rule. Money is by no means the sole explanation of price level changes. Such changes can come about both in the short and the long run by movements in V and T which do not offset each other. Moreover, if we assume a change in M leading to a change in P with V remaining constant, movements in P may produce changes in T. The classical and neo-classical economists were able to disregard this effect of a change in money on T by assuming that production was determined entirely independently of the price level.

ERRORS AND OMISSIONS

One of the more serious shortcomings of the velocity approach to the quantity theory of money is its mechanistic nature. It tells us how fast money is spent but not why it is spent as fast as it is. The cash-balance approach seeks a remedy by asking why money is held. Unfortunately, as we have mentioned, the Cambridge economists before Keynes did not exploit the potential inherent in the cash-balance equation. They continued to assume that the role of money was that of a medium of exchange and that it was held essentially to facilitate transactions. Moreover, in that the factors they used to determine K were not much different from those used by Fisher to explain V, the cash-balance approach assumed the same mechanistic interpretation as the velocity approach. In Keynes' hands the cash-balance approach was transformed into a theory of money which finally included the motivations for holding money other than to facilitate transactions.

[4] Fisher, Irving, *op. cit.*, p. 159.

The quantity theory as developed in the early part of the twentieth century cannot be regarded as an adequate theory of money because by neglecting to consider the role of money as a store of value it also took no account of the rate of interest. "Changes in the quantity of money," says Joan Robinson, "are of the utmost importance, but their importance lies in their influence upon the rate of interest, and a theory of money which does not mention the rate of interest is not a theory of money at all." [5]

Fisher and the Cambridge economists neglected to consider the rate of interest in their monetary theory because they assumed that the immediate impact of any change in the money stock was felt in the goods market. They argued that even where an increase in money was used to purchase bonds this money was automatically transferred to investors who in turn purchased capital goods. Insofar as money was not held as a store of value, and was therefore not hoarded, changes in the stock of money did not influence the rate of interest. The rate of interest, as we shall see in the following chapter, was assumed to be determined only by the real forces of supply and demand for real capital. Moreover, since people were assumed to hold money either directly or indirectly for transactions purposes, the rate of interest was not considered a motive for holding money.

The neglect of the rate of interest as an important motive for holding money was closely associated with the neglect of the short-run influences of a change in the money stock. The comparatively static theory which resulted was concerned with looking at the price level at one point of equilibrium and again at a subsequent point of equilibrium following a change in the money supply. Concern with the short run and the incorporation of the interest rate effect would have led Fisher and the early Cambridge economists toward the development of a dynamic theory explaining the path from one equilibrium situation to another. Keynes, the Swedish economists, and others achieved this when they developed a monetary theory which included such factors as the rate of interest, uncertainty and expectations.

CONCEPT OF A GENERAL PRICE LEVEL

The quantity theory focuses undue attention on general price levels. The effect of a change in money on the *relative structure* of prices is assumed away. In the classical and neo-classical economic analysis relative prices are considered to be determined by the relative strength of the demand for

---

[5] Robinson, J., *Introduction to the Theory of Employment*, London, Macmillan, 1956, p. 77.

and supply of commodities with money playing a neutral role except for facilitating exchange. This proved to be an oversimplification of how the economic system actually works. When the money supply changes all prices do not move proportionately. For them to do so, the elasticity of demand and of supply of all commodities and services would have to be the same. As it is not, a change in the money supply changes prices disproportionately and a change in relative prices will produce changes in output. The heroic assumptions necessary to separate the monetary sector from the goods sector, and to deny the effects of changes in the money supply on relative prices cannot be justified except as strictly academic exercises. If the classical and neo-classical economists had concerned themselves more with the dynamic forces which bring about a new equilibrium situation following a change in the money supply, they would have seen that one cannot isolate absolute prices (the general price level) from relative prices and that one cannot assume a direct relationship between money and the price level.

SELECTED READINGS

Chandler, Lester V., *An Introduction to Monetary Theory,* New York, Harper & Row, 1940.

Dean, Edwin (ed.), *The Controversy Over the Quantity Theory of Money,* Boston, D. C. Heath, 1965.

Fisher, Irving, *The Purchasing Power of Money,* New York, Macmillan, 1911.

Hansen, Alvin, *Monetary Theory and Fiscal Policy,* New York, McGraw-Hill, 1949.

Hegeland, Hugo, *The Quantity Theory of Money: A Critical History of Its Historical Development and Interpretation and a Restatement,* Goteborg, Sweden, Elanders Boktryckeri Aktiebolag, 1951.

Laughlin, J. Laurence, *The Principles of Money,* New York, Charles Scribner's Sons, 1903, Ch. 7 and 8.

Marshall, Alfred, *Money, Credit and Commerce,* London, Macmillan, 1923.

Patinkin, Don, "Keynesian Economics and the Quantity Theory", in K. K. Kurihara (ed.), *Post-Keynesian Economics,* New Brunswick, N.J., Rutgers University Press, 1954, pp. 123-152.

Patinkin, Don, *Money, Interest and Prices,* 2nd ed., New York, Harper & Row, 1965.

Robertson, D. H., *Money,* Cambridge University Press, 1948, Ch. 2 and 3.

Robertson D.H., *Lectures on Economic Principles,* Vol. 3, London, Staples Press, 1959.

Wicksell, Knut, *Lectures on Political Economy,* trans. by E. Classen, *Money,* Vol. 2, London, Macmillan, 1934.

21

THE RATE OF INTEREST

In many respects the nature of the rate of interest and its role in the economy are still unsettled issues of economic analysis. One of the more important controversial questions is whether interest is a "real" or a "monetary" phenomenon: is it determined by real factors such as the marginal productivity of capital and marginal time preference, or is it determined by monetary factors such as the supply of and demand for money? As we shall show in this chapter classical economics which was carried over into the mainstream of neo-classical economics focused on real factors as the determinants of the rate of interest. In the loanable-funds theory developed by Robertson and by Wicksell and his Swedish colleagues, both real and monetary factors are given a role to play in interest rate determination. Knut Wicksell in his analysis of the "cumulative process" showed how monetary factors, particularly changes in the money supply, through their effect on what he calls the "money rate" of interest, influence the level of aggregate economic activity. This marked a dramatic departure from traditional economic thought where the only role assigned to money was its influence on absolute prices. Keynes also emphasized the importance of monetary factors in determining the rate of interest; however, as we shall show in the next chapter, he by no means neglected the role played by real factors.

Whether one relies on real or on monetary factors to explain the rate of interest depends to a large extent on whether one is concerned with short-run or long-run analysis. The classical and most of the neo-classical economists were concerned with long-run tendencies and were therefore not unnaturally led to a real theory of interest. Keynes took the opposite route because he was concerned with the short run.

Today it is generally agreed that the equilibrium rate of interest is simultaneously determined by both real and monetary factors. Moreover, the rate of interest exerts its influence in all markets and operates simultaneously on what Robertson has called a "three-fold margin".[1] This consists of the marginal time preference (consumption decisions), the marginal productivity of capital (investment decisions) and the liquidity preference (the margin of choice between money and holding bonds). Here and in subsequent chapters it will be our task first to identify these "margins" and then to show their role in determining both the rate of interest and aggregate economic activity.

THE CLASSICAL REAL THEORY

Economists writing in the classical tradition regarded the rate of interest as the price at which the supply of saving is equated with the demand for saving to purchase capital goods. In other words, the interest rate was considered a reward for saving. This reward was paid to overcome a person's time preference. Individuals were assumed to have a positive time preference — to prefer present goods to future goods.[2] But why would people on the average prefer present to future goods? One reason offered was that people generally have a "defective telescopic vision of the future". This myopia may reflect their lack of imagination, foresight and self-control, and their uncertainty about their length of life. Their myopia as an explanation of their desire to consume now rather than later has been called **pure time preference.** Another explanation of time preference concentrates on the size, certainty and time shape of an individual's income stream. If an individual assumes no change in his income or needs in the future, he may consider that the satisfaction (or utility) foregone by reducing his present consumption (that is, by saving) will be greater than the satisfaction to be gained from the larger consumption he could have made in the future had he continued to save. In this case, interest will have to be paid to the individual to induce him to exchange present for future consumption and to offset the diminishing marginal utility of his income. Even if his pure time preference is zero, interest will have to be paid. If, however, the individual believes his income will decrease in the future, he may be willing to reduce his present consumption in order to increase his future consumption even without a reward or a payment of interest. If the individual expects his income to increase in the future

---

[1] Robertson , D. H., *Essays in Monetary Theory*, London, Staples Press, 1940, p. 17.

[2] For a good discussion of the theory of time preference see J. W. Conard, *An Introduction to the Theory of Interest*, Berkeley and Los Angeles, University of California Press, 1959, Ch. 4 and 5. For the early presentation see Boehm-Bowerk, *Positive Theory of Capital*, translated by William Smart, New York, Stechert, 1923; Irving Fisher, *The Positive Theory of Interest*, New York, Macmillan, 1930.

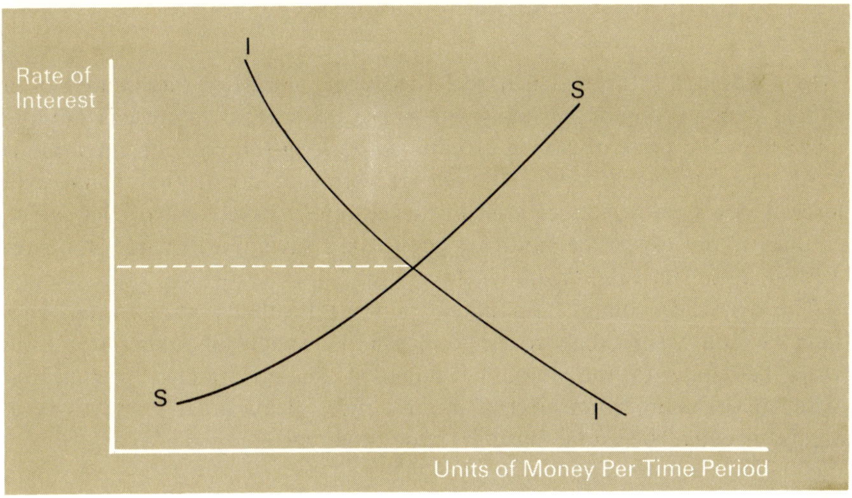

Figure 21-1 The Classical Rate of Interest

and his needs to remain static, he may maximize his present satisfaction (or utility) by borrowing to increase his present consumption and then wipe out this debt in the future by consuming less. Under these circumstances an extremely high reward would have to be offered to induce the individual to consume less and save in the present.

The classical economists assumed that time preference is positive — that individuals on the average prefer present to future consumption — and that individuals can be induced to postpone present consumption (to save) if they are offered sufficient reward in terms of an interest payment. Saving was therefore assumed to be an increasing function of the rate of interest. This is shown by the saving curve (*SS*) in Figure 21-1; the higher the rate of interest the larger the amount of saving.

From the investor's point of view the factor governing the payment of interest is the marginal productivity of capital (in the technological sense). He pays savers a rate of interest to induce them to reduce their present consumption and make resources available for investment in capital goods. As long as the rate of interest that he must pay to savers is no larger than his marginal return from adding to his capital stock, he will continue to invest. Since the classical economists assumed full employment and a constant level of output, they concluded that marginal return (or productivity) declines with each addition to capital stock. Even if allowance is made for growth in the full employment level of output, the marginal return of capital may still decline with increases in its stock since the most remunerative opportunities are usually exploited first. As the marginal productivity of capital declines investors offer correspondingly declining rates of interest to savers. This behaviour is represented by the investment schedule (*II*) in Figure 21-1.

In Figure 21-1 the classical real theory of interest is represented by a simple demand and supply diagram where the rate of interest is nothing more than the price of saving or capital. Its long-run equilibrium value is *i*. At any rate higher than *i* the excess supply of saving (or capital) will force it down toward its equilibrium level. Alternatively, at any level lower than *i*, the excess demand for capital (or saving) will force it up toward its long-run equilibrium level.

The classical economists assumed that the flexibility of the rate of interest would assure that in the long run the supply of saving would always be equal to the amount demanded for investment expenditures. Also, at the equilibrium level of interest the real marginal productivity of capital is equal to savers' marginal time preference.

THE NORMAL RATE OF INTEREST

Knut Wicksell in his *Geldzins und Guterpreise*[3] was among the first to show how the rate of interest serves as a link between the monetary and real sectors of an economy. Wicksell conceived a normal rate of interest whose long-run equilibrium level was determined by real factors but whose attainment depended upon monetary factors. He assumed that there exist two rates of interest: a **real or natural rate of interest** and a **market or money rate of interest.** When these two rates are equal the equilibrium normal rate is achieved.[4]

The natural rate of interest refers to the physical productivity of capital in conjunction with the demand for and supply of the goods which are produced by using capital. Changes in the natural rate of interest depend upon such real factors as population growth, tastes and technological innovations. Since these change only slowly and over time, the natural rate of interest can be considered to remain relatively stable, especially in the short run.

Wicksell assumed the existence of pure gold standard conditions where the quantity of money is the metallic currency which serves as legal tender and as the ultimate reserves of the banking system. He treated changes in demand deposits as changes in the velocity of metallic bank reserves. In Wicksell's model the banking system is initially in equilibrium in that the amount of metallic currency in the vaults of the banks is

---

[3] Knut Wicksell, *Geldzins und Guterpreise*, Jena, Gustav Fischer, 1898; Trans. by R. F. Kahn, *Interest and Prices*, London, Macmillan, 1936.

[4] Wicksell's natural rate is often considered to be the same as what Keynes called the marginal efficiency of capital. However, the two are identical only at a given period of time. The marginal efficiency of capital is a schedule and the marginal productivity of capital (the natural rate of interest) is only a point on this schedule.

equal to their legal or conventional reserve requirement. The banks then acquire excess reserves, say from the inflow of foreign gold. Being profit motivated institutions they will want to employ these excess reserves to expand their loans. To attract borrowers they will lower the rate charged on their loans. This rate, the bank rate, is what Wicksell calls the money or market rate of interest. A reduction in the money rate of interest, with no change in the natural rate of interest, gives entrepreneurs new profit opportunities and they respond by borrowing funds from the banks for capital goods production.

Assuming, as did Wicksell, that the economy is fully employed, entrepreneurs must bid resources away from other sectors of the economy in order to expand their production of capital goods. The higher prices paid for factors of production are reflected in higher money incomes. However, there is a lag between the time that higher incomes are earned and the time that they are available for spending. During this interval prices rise but, with no immediate increase in spendable income, income receivers will have to reduce the amount of goods they previously purchased. They are temporarily forced to save in real terms. The reduction in the amount of consumer goods that can be purchased resulting from the increase in prices releases resources necessary for capital goods production. After a time the higher earned incomes become available and are spent, forcing prices to still higher levels. Entrepreneurs, believing that present high prices will persist into the future, continue to borrow from the banks as long as the discrepancy between the money rate of interest and the natural rate of interest remains. The cumulative price rise is not self generating; it does not continue by itself but depends primarily on the availability of bank credit, and there is a limit to the banking system's ability to provide loans.

As prices rise the banks experience drains on their reserves. An **external drain** occurs in the form of gold flowing abroad as higher domestic prices encourage an increase in foreign imports. An **internal drain** on the metallic reserves of the banks also takes place. Because of higher prices the community will want more currency for hand-to-hand circulation. In order to protect their reserves from falling below their legal or conventional levels, the banks increase the rate of interest on loans. When this rate, the market rate of interest, rises to the level of the natural rate of interest entrepreneurs will cease to expand their capital expenditures. When the market rate is equal to the natural rate the price level is stabilized. The funds available for capital expenditures in the loan market will be supplied out of savings only, and the normal equilibrium rate of interest will be exactly equal to the marginal yield of capital.

A similar cumulative process, but in a downward direction, would result if the banks were to artificially set the market rate of interest above the natural rate of interest. In this case falling prices would cause reserves to flow into the banks' vaults. The banks would respond by lowering the market rate and when this rate were again equal to the natural rate, the cumulative process would halt.

Wicksell concluded that monetary equilibrium would exist if three conditions were fulfilled: equality between the money and the natural rate of interest, equality between the volume of saving and the demand for real capital, and price stability. He showed that monetary equilibrium is achieved only as a result of the interplay of both real and monetary factors which combine to produce the normal rate of interest. Although the level of this rate is determined by real factors, it is maintained by monetary factors. Wicksell went on to argue that the monetary authorities should conduct their affairs with the sole objective of keeping the money rate of interest equal to the natural rate of interest. If this were possible, money would play a neutral role in that only real factors such as technological change and population growth would determine the level of economic activity. Unfortunately for Wicksell's policy conclusions it is difficult to derive an adequate measure of the marginal productivity of capital and hence a natural rate of interest. Moreover, as David Davidson, a colleague of Wicksell, pointed out, economic growth involves continually increasing productivity, reducing costs of production and lowering the level of prices.[5] To maintain price stability the monetary authorities would have to increase the money supply continuously. As a result the money rate of interest would remain below both the natural rate and the level at which the demand for investment funds equals the supply of savings. Thus, Wicksell's criteria for monetary equilibrium would be unattainable.

THE LOANABLE FUNDS THEORY

We saw earlier that the classical economists assumed a market for saving or capital in which the rate of interest is determined. Although this theory of interest carried over into the mainstream of neo-classical economics, important modifications were made following the work of Knut Wicksell and his colleagues in Sweden and by D. H. Robertson in England.[6] These modifications which resulted in the so-called loanable funds

[5] Thomas, Y. B., "The Monetary Doctrines of Professor Davidson", *The Economic Journal,* 1935, pp. 36-50.

[6] The main difference between the Swedish economists and Robertson in the approach to the loanable funds theory is their definition of saving. Robertson considered economic units to save out of previous levels of income; today's behaviour is described in terms of yesterday's income rather than today's. This approach is referred to as "period analysis". Swedish economists, on the other hand, defined saving as depending upon expectations regarding current income.

theory consisted of the introduction of financial considerations into the classical theory of interest rate determination.

Unlike the classical economists who considered that all of current saving was available for investment expenditures, the neo-classical economists who presented the loanable funds theory of interest rate determination assumed that only part of current saving may be available for investment expenditures but that this part could be supplemented by the part of past saving still held idle. The relationship between saving and the supply of and demand for loanable funds is illustrated in Figure 21-2.

In the figure, *OQ* represents that amount of their current income which individuals plan to save. This amount of saving is not automatically available as part of the total supply of loanable funds in the credit market. Individuals will lend their saving only if the reward paid to them is high enough to overcome their desire for liquidity and to compensate them for the costs involved in lending and the risk of loss of principal. Insofar as the reward for lending is the rate of interest, curve F_s in the figure shows the amount of savings individuals are prepared to supply to the loan market at various rates of interest. The curve is drawn to show that as the interest rate increases individuals are induced to supply more of their saving to the loan market. When, for example, the rate of interest is at level *i*, out of total current saving *OQ*, an amount equal to *OU* will be supplied to the loan market. The remaining portion, *UQ*, will be held idle. We refer to the amount *UQ* as being **hoarded.** If the rate of interest rises high enough, to level i_1 in the figure, all current saving will

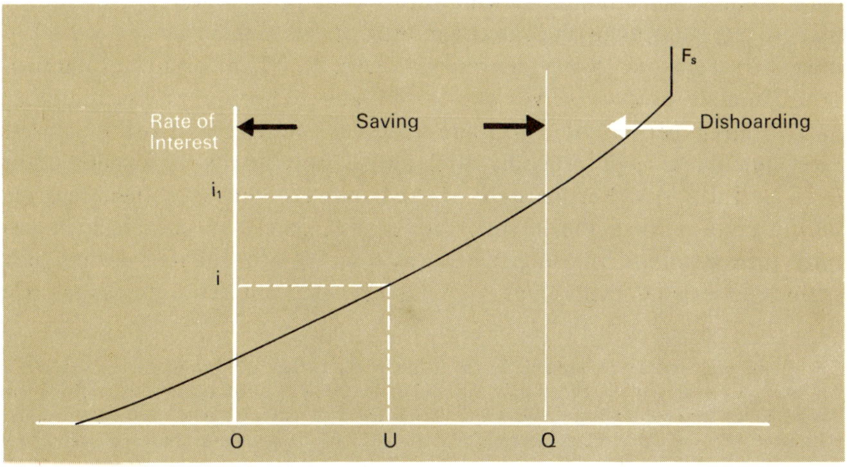

Figure 21-2 The Supply of Loanable Funds Out of Savings

flow into the loan market and none will be hoarded. Moreover, when the rate of interest rises above i_l, individuals will supply not only all of their current saving to the loan market but also some of their past savings still held idle (hoarded). When individuals supply past savings to the loan market they are said to be **dishoarding.** The amount by which dishoarding may supplement the supply of loanable funds from current saving is limited by the amount of past savings that has been hoarded. This limit is shown by the vertical upper portion of the F_s curve in Figure 21-2.

In addition to the amount of funds flowing into the loan market from current saving and dishoarding out of past savings the loanable funds theory includes the role played by the monetary authorities. They are able to augment or to diminish the flow of money into the loan market.[7]

On the demand side of the loan market the classical economists included only the demand for funds for investment expenditures. The loanable funds theory makes an important addition by recognizing that funds may be demanded to satisfy demands of individuals for idle balances or hoards.

Figure 21-3 summarizes the loanable funds theory of interest. The rate of interest is measured on the vertical axis and the quantities of loanable funds on the horizontal axis. The ΔM curve shows the net new money flowing over a given period of time into the loan or credit market from the banking system. It is drawn to the right of the vertical axis indicating that net new money is a positive amount. During any period it could be a negative amount in which case the net decrease in the amount of money would be shown by drawing the ΔM curve to the left of vertical axis. In Figure 21-3 the ΔM curve is also drawn perfectly vertical indicating that the amount of new money flowing into the market is interest inelastic — that is, independent of the rate of interest. New money is not necessarily interest inelastic. At lower interest rate levels the banks may involuntarily accumulate excess reserves due to the lack of borrowers. On the other hand, during periods of expanding economic activity and rising interest rates the banks will probably find ample opportunity to expand their loans and deposits. Furthermore, if the banks economize on their reserves during periods when the interest rate is low, they may be able to maximize their earnings by using the excess reserves accumulated during such periods to expand their loans even further when interest rates again rise

[7] Various refinements can be made to the loanable funds theory presented here. Robertson, for example, included on the supply side what he called "disentanglements". These are funds made available, at least temporarily, from the liquidation of inventory and the liquidation of fixed assets through depreciation charges. When including disentanglements one also has to add their opposite, "reintanglements", to the demand side of the loanable funds market. See Dennis H. Robertson, "Mr. Keynes and the Interest Rate", in *Essays in Monetary Theory*, London, Staples Press, 1940, p. 3.

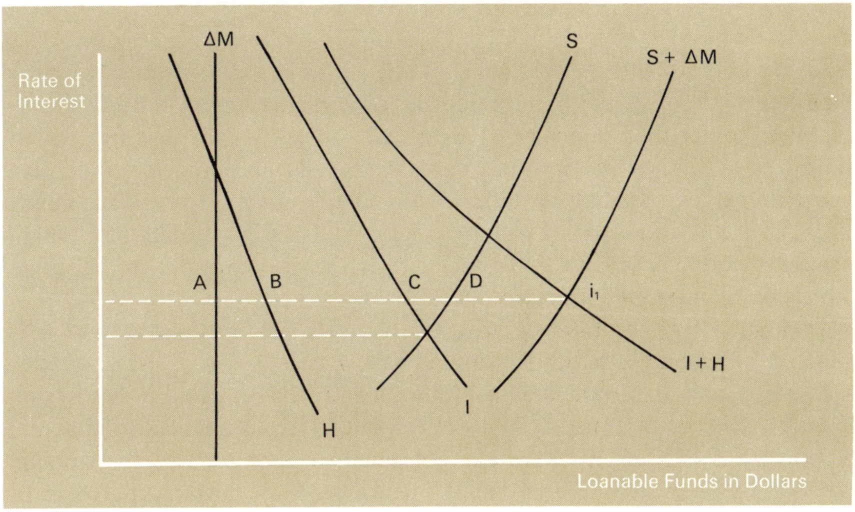

Figure 21-3 The Loanable Funds Theory of Interest

to higher levels. Where the changes in the money supply are related to the rate of interest, the ΔM curve is drawn sloping upward to the right until the banking system has absorbed all of its excess reserves at which stage it becomes vertical. We have not included these refinements in drawing the ΔM curve in Figure 21-3.

The S curve in Figure 21-3 is a saving schedule which is no different from that included in the classical theory of interest and shown in Figure 21-1. It slopes upward from left to right indicating that individuals will be induced to save more as the interest rate rises.[8] The total amount of loanable funds flowing into the market during any given periods is shown by the $(S+\Delta M)$ curve. It is derived by adding the ΔM and the S curves together horizontally.

The demand for loanable funds for investment expenditures is shown by the I curve which is similar to the curve shown in Figure 21-1 explaining the classical theory of interest. But now we make an important addition. We explained earlier that because of hoarding not all of current saving is necessarily available for loans. Individuals may hoard not only part of their current saving but also part of the new funds flowing into the market from the banking system. Hoarding can therefore be considered as a demand for loanable funds. However, while during any given period some individuals may want to hoard, others may want to dishoard. In Figure 21-3 we combine hoarding and dishoarding into one schedule, H,

---

8 If individuals save in order to have a specified lump sum sometime in the future, an increase in the rate of interest will enable them to accumulate this before it is required. In this case individuals may save less rather than more as interest rates rise.

which we may call net hoarding. The curve is drawn to show net hoarding as being a positive amount at each rate of interest. If dishoarding were larger than hoarding at each rate of interest, the *H* curve would lie to the left of the vertical axis denoting net dishoarding. We could also consider net dishoarding as an addition to the supply of loanable funds and show it as a separate supply schedule. Then we would have three separate supply schedules to be added horizontally to derive the schedule for the total supply of loanable funds.[9]

In Figure 21-3 the total demand for loanable funds shown as $I + H$ is derived by adding together horizontally the *I* and *H* schedules. The interest rate is now determined at the intersection of the loanable funds supply $(S+\Delta M)$ and demand $(I + H)$ curves. It is not an equilibrium rate because at this level investment is not equal to saving nor is the demand for hoards equal to the amount of money available for this purpose. In the figure saving exceeds investment by *CD*. The excess of saving over investment expenditures is absorbed by additional hoarding. In Figure 21-3 this is equal to *AB* (which is equal to *CD*), the difference between net hoarding and net new money at the interest rate level i_1.

Implicit in the loanable funds theory was the belief that in the long run the rate of interest would adjust to the level which equates investment and saving. One can rationalize this in several ways. When saving exceeds investment a deflationary situation occurs. If we assume real income to remain constant and prices to fall, the demand for hoards at each rate of interest may decline. The *H* schedule, and with it the $(I + H)$ schedule, will shift to the left and an equilibrium position will be attained where $\Delta M = H$, $S = I$ and $(\Delta M + H) = (S + I)$. The three sets of schedules intersect at a level of interest which ordinarily equates saving and investment.

Alternatively, we could assume that a shift in the *H* function is accompanied by a shift in the same direction in the *S* function. In this case a full equilibrium situation would be attained, but at a level of interest higher than that which initially equated saving and investment.

The classical and most of the neo-classical economists who presented the loanable funds theory of interest believed that the rate of interest would always fall far enough to call forth an amount of investment equal to the amount of saving at a full employment level of income. It was this proposition which Keynes questioned, and which more than anything else, led to the "Keynesian departure".

---

[9]One can make all sorts of refinements to the loanable funds theory as mentioned in footnote 7. On the demand side, for example, one should show separately the demand by consumers to finance durable consumer goods.

THE CRUDE LIQUIDITY PREFERENCE THEORY

We call the theory of interest which J. M. Keynes presented in his *General Theory of Interest, Employment and Money,* the crude liquidity preference theory to differentiate it from the liquidity preference theory which developed from it. In his attack on what he called the "classical" theory of interest Keynes said, "The rate of interest is not the price which brings into equilibrium the demand for resources to invest with the readiness to abstain from present consumption. It is the price which equilibrates the desire to hold wealth in the form of cash with the available quantity of cash ..." [10]

Keynes rejected theories of interest rate determination based on savings and investment on two main grounds. He believed that saving was primarily dependent upon income and not on the rate of interest. Moreover, he contended that his predecessors were mistaken in assuming that saving and investment were independent of each other. He pointed out that since the level of saving depends largely upon the level of income which in turn depends upon investment expenditures, saving also depends, at least indirectly, upon investment. It is therefore incorrect to consider saving and investment as being independent of each other.

Keynes noted that individuals have two decisions to make. They must first decide how much of their income they will save and then how to employ their new saving. The amount that individuals wish to save depends upon their income and is part and parcel of the Keynesian theory of income determination to be discussed in Chapter 24. Individuals' decisions as to how to hold their saving is the heart of Keynes' interest rate theory. Savings can be held in two forms: in interest bearing securities or other evidences of debt, and in cash (currency and bank deposits). For convenience Keynes regarded the holding of bonds as the alternative to holding money. But why do individuals as well as businesses want to hold money? Keynes distinguished three motives for holding money: the transactions motive, the precautionary motive, and the speculative motive. He defined the transactions motive as "the need of cash for the current transactions of personal and business exchanges" [11] and split this need into an "income motive" and a "business motive". [12] The income motive refers to the need for individuals to hold cash to bridge the interval between receipt of income and its disbursement. The business motive refers

---

[10] Keynes, J. M., *The General Theory of Employment, Interest and Money,* London, Macmillan, 1936, p. 167.

[11] *Ibid.*, p. 170.

[12] *Ibid.*, p. 195.

to the demand for money holdings by businesses to bridge the gap between the time of incurring business costs and that of receiving the proceeds from the sale of goods. The amount of transactions balances held by individuals and businesses at any given time depends upon the level of income and upon such institutional factors as the quantity theorists consider to explain the constancy of the velocity of money (as discussed in the previous chapter).

Keynes described the precautionary motive as the desire to hold cash "to provide for contingencies requiring sudden expenditures and for unforeseen opportunities of advantageous purchases".[13] In other words, the precautionary demand for money arises primarily because of the uncertainty of future receipts and expenditures. Keynes lumped together the transactions and precautionary demand for money balances into what he called the active demand for money balances. This is identical to the classical concept that money serves as a medium of exchange and is held for transaction purposes only.

Probably the most important departure that Keynes made from classical economics was the introduction of speculation as a motive for holding money. By the speculation motive Keynes meant the inducement to hold money for the purpose "of securing profit from knowing better than the market what the future will bring forth".[14] If, for instance, an individual expects the rate of interest to decline (the price of bonds to rise), he will want to exchange his money holdings for bonds. If, on the other hand, an individual expects the rate of interest to rise (the price of bonds to fall) he will want to change from holding bonds to holding money. Keynes noted that "experience indicates that the aggregate demand for money to satisfy the speculative motive usually shows a continuous response to gradual changes in the rate of interest — *i.e.* there is a continuous curve relating to changes in the demand for money to satisfy the speculative motive and changes in the rate of interest as given by changes in the price of bonds and debts of various maturities."[15]

Individuals prefer to hold money rather than bonds because of their *uncertainty* as to the future rate of interest. If the future rate of interest (the price of bonds) were known with certainty, and if there were no change in the assessment of the credit risk on bonds, there would be no speculative demand for money. The only reason for holding money would then be for transactions purposes. It is because of the uncertainty about

---

[13] *Ibid.*, p. 196.

[14] *Ibid.*, p. 170.

[15] *Ibid.*, p. 197.

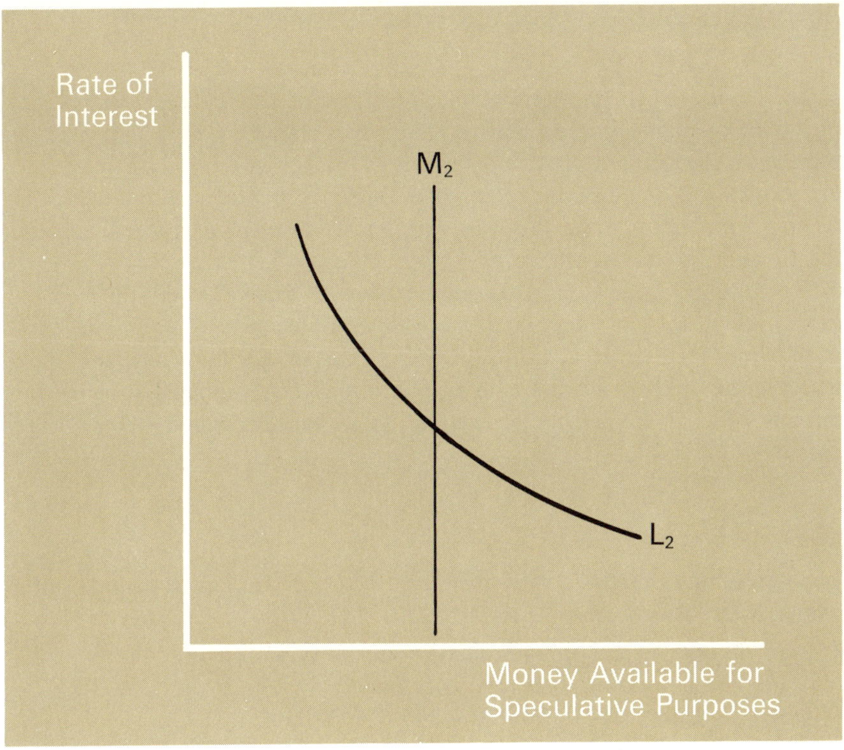

Figure 21-4 **The Crude Keynesian Theory of Interest**

future events, particularly changes in the rate of interest, that money is held as an asset.[16]

Keynes divided the total stock of money M into two parts, M_1 and M_2. The amount M_1 is held to satisfy total transactions motives and M_2 to satisfy the speculative motive or what is now more generally called the asset motive. At any given moment in time the level of income can be considered to remain constant; since the demand for total transactions balances is assumed to depend essentially on the level of income, the amount of these balances is also given. That portion of the money supply not held for transactions balances is therefore available for speculative balances. The money held for speculative purposes may be referred to as idle or inactive money balances.

According to Keynes, the rate of interest is uniquely determined by the speculative demand for money and the amount of the money supply available to satisfy this demand. This is illustrated in Figure 21-4. The demand for speculative money balances is represented by the liquidity preference proper schedule L_2. As we shall show in the next chapter, Keynes made

16 A more detailed discussion of the demand for money is given in the next chapter.

some important assumptions about the slope of this curve. The amount of money available for speculative balances is shown as M_2. This amount represents the total money supply autonomously given by the monetary authorities less the amount required to satisfy total transactions demands. At any moment in time the rate of interest is given at the point where the L_2 and M_2 curves intersect.

The rate of interest as determined by the crude liquidity preference theory which we have discussed is not an equilibrium rate unless the level of income is also in equilibrium. The analysis so far does not show whether the level of income is in equilibrium. Keynes himself supplied the missing links in his theory of income determination which we shall discuss in Chapter 24.

SUMMARY AND CONCLUSIONS

The determination of the rate of interest has been explained in terms of a combination of two or more of the following factors:

(1) I, investment (the marginal productivity of capital)
(2) S, saving (marginal time preference)
(3) H, net hoarding (hoarding and dishoarding)
(4) ΔM_l, changes in the money supply
(5) L_2, the speculative demand for money (liquidity preference proper)
(6) M_2, the supply of money available to satisfy the demand for speculative balances.

In the classical theory the rate of interest i is determined by the marginal productivity of capital or demand price for capital and by the marginal rate of time preference or supply price of capital (saving):

$$i = f(S, I)$$

The classical economists were able to neglect the role of money in determining the rate of interest because they were concerned only with the long-run equilibrium rate of interest and because they assumed that it was irrational for persons and firms to hold money idle. People held money only for transactions purposes. Due to institutional arrangements money had to be held unwillingly to bridge the gap between its receipt and expenditure. In the long run the money held for transactions purposes would be used to purchase goods and services. Money did not affect the amount of saving or investment but served only as a medium of exchange. Its role in the economy was therefore considered to be neutral. Adjustments in relative prices, including the rate of interest, would provide full employment levels of income. As long as interest rates were flexible saving would always be equal to investment in the long run.

The loanable funds theory of interest attempted to correct the classical assumption that all money saved is available to borrowers and the only money available to borrowers is that supplied by savers. In the loanable funds theory of interest net hoarding and changes in the money supply are introduced as two additional determinants of the rate of interest:

$$i = f(S, I, H, \Delta M)$$

The loanable funds theory was an improvement over the classical theory insofar as it pointed out that, at least in the short run, the rate of interest is not always at a level which equates saving and investment. This proposition was especially clarified by Knut Wicksell in his concept of a market rate of interest and a natural rate of interest. Only in the long run and with proper behaviour on the part of the monetary authorities, does a normal equilibrium rate of interest exist which makes saving equal to investment.

In the crude Keynesian version of interest rate determination, monetary factors — the demand for and supply of money for speculative purposes — are given centre stage:

$$i = f(L_2, M_2)$$

Although this theory was at first criticized because it neglected the real factors of productivity and thrift, it was subsequently shown that they can be included "through the back door". Insofar as investment and saving (or consumption) can affect income, they can also offset the transactions demand for money. With a given money supply, any change in the transactions demand for money will automatically mean a change in the amount of money available to satisfy the speculative demand for money. This, as we have seen, will produce changes in the rate of interest. The role of the real factors, however, depends upon the time period considered. Since Keynes was dealing with very short periods, he considered real factors to play an insignificant role in determining the level of the rate of interest.

Economists have made various attempts to prove the equivalence of the loanable funds and the liquidity preference theories of interest.[17] None of these attempts has as yet provided an answer which has found general acceptance. The loanable funds theory is expressed in terms of a

---

17 For a discussion of the literature dealing with the questions of stock versus flow analysis and liquidity preference versus loanable funds theories see: Harry G. Johnson, "Monetary Theory and Policy", *American Economic Review*, Vol. 52, June, 1962, pp. 359-365; G.L. S. Shackle, "Recent Theories Concerning the Nature and Role of Interest", *Economic Journal*, Vol. 71, June, 1961, pp. 209-254; Friedrich A. Lutz, *The Theory of Interest*, Chicago, Aldine Publishing, 1968, Ch. 13. Lutz notes "that the entire debate about the equivalence of liquidity preference theory and loanable funds theory seems to be one of those intensive discussions on a problem of formal logic, not rare in theoretical economics, which

flow of funds over a period of time and focuses on the demand for and supply of securities as the determinants of the rate of interest. The liquidity preference theory is expressed in terms of the *stocks* of money and securities and focuses on the stock of money available at a moment in time to satisfy speculative motives. Economists have preferred to use the liquidity preference theory as it lends itself more readily for inclusion in models specifying conditions of full equilibrium. The loanable funds theory, on the other hand, has received attention from those concerned with changes in the market rate of interest. This has been encouraged in recent years as more regular data on sources and uses of funds have become available.

Neither the loanable funds theory nor the Keynesian theory of interest are complete explanations of how the rate of interest is determined. A complete equilibrium theory of interest must include explicitly the level of income (output) and the price level. Toward this end the Keynesian theory has been modified and included in a full equilibrium analysis of the economy which we shall discuss in the chapters that follow.

SELECTED READINGS

Baumol, W.J., "Stocks, Flows and Monetary Theory", *Quarterly Journal of Economics*, Vol. 74, February, 1962, pp. 46-56.

Conard, Joseph W., *An Introduction to the Theory of Interest*, Berkeley and Los Angeles, University of California Press, 1959.

Ellis, H. S. (ed.), *A Survey of Contemporary Economics*, American Economic Association, Philadelphia, Blakiston Company, 1948, pp. 39-44.

Fellner, William, and Harold M. Somers, "Alternative Monetary Approaches in Interest Theory", *Review of Economics and Statistics*, Vol. 23, February, 1941, pp. 43-48, reprinted in Richard S. Thorn (ed.), *Monetary Theory and Policy*, New York, Random House, 1966, pp. 469-481.

Fisher, Irving, *The Positive Theory of Interest*, New York, Macmillan, 1930.

Hahn, F. H., and F. P. R, Brechling (eds.), *The Theory of Interest Rates*, London, Macmillan, 1965.

---

does not really deserve the efforts devoted to it since it does not, and cannot, give any material new insights into the problem of the interest rate. One can only hope (and perhaps even expect) that this topic ceases to fill the columns of our periodicals...", p. 208.

Hicks, J. R., "Mr. Keynes and the Classics: A Suggested Interpretation", *Econometrica,* Vol. 5, April, 1937, reprinted in the American Economic Association, *Readings in the Theory of Income Determination,* Philadelphia, Blakiston Company, 1951, pp. 461-476.

Johnson, Harry G., "Some Cambridge Controversies in Monetary Theory", *The Review of Economic Studies,* Vol. 19, 1951-1952, pp. 90-104.

Keynes, J. M., *The General Theory of Employment, Interest and Money,* London, Macmillan, 1936.

Klein, L. R., W. Fellner, H. M. Somers, and K. Brunner, discussion on "Stock and Flow Analysis in Economics", *Econometrica,* Vol. 18, July, 1950, pp. 236-252.

Lerner, A.P., "Alternative Formulations of the Theory of Interest", *Economic Journal,* Vol. 48, 1938, pp. 211-230.

Lerner, A.P., "Interest Theory—Supply and Demand for Loans or Supply and Demand for Cash", *Review of Economics and Statistics,* Vol. 26, May, 1944, pp. 88-91

Lutz, Friedrich, *The Theory of Interest,* Chicago, Aldine Publishing, 1968.

Moore, Basil J., *An Introduction to the Theory of Finance,* New York, The Free Press, 1968.

Patinkin, Don, *Money, Interest and Prices,* New York, Harper & Row, 1965, Ch. 15.

Robertson, Dennis H., "Mr. Keynes and the Rate of Interest", in *Essays in Monetary Theory,* London, Staples Press, 1940, Ch. 1.

Robinson, Joan, *The Rate of Interest and Other Essays,* London, Macmillan, 1952.

Shackle, G.L.S., "Recent Theories Concerning the Nature and Role of Interest", *Economic Journal,* Vol. 71, June, 1961, pp. 209-254, reprinted in Richard S. Thorn, *Monetary Theory and Policy,* New York, Random House, 1966, pp. 419-468.

Smith, W.L., "Monetary Theories of the Rate of Interest: A Dynamic Analysis", *Review of Economics and Statistics,* Vol. 40, February, 1958, pp. 15-21.

Wicksell, Knut, *Interest and Prices,* London, Macmillan, 1936.

Wicksell, Knut, *Lectures on Political Economy,* trans. by E. Classen, *Money,* Vol. 2, London, Macmillan, 1934.

22

THE DEMAND FOR MONEY

The theory of the demand for money traces its lineage to classical and neo-classical economics which, as we have already seen, assumed that money has no utility *per se* and that the only reason for holding it is to facilitate transactions. This concept was an integral part of the quantity theory of money.

Keynes defined three motives for holding money. His transactions motive was identical to the classical explanation for holding money. His precautionary motive, based on the possibility of cash being held because of unforeseen contingencies or opportunities, could be readily incorporated into the classical notion for holding money. It was with his third reason for holding money — the speculative motive — that Keynes made an important departure from his predecessors. In fact, his suggestion that it was quite rational for people to hold money as an asset (a store of value) was somewhat heretical.

In this chapter we shall consider first the demand for money within the framework of the three Keynesian motives for holding it. We will then have the background required to formulate the theory of the demand for money which follows. Finally we shall discuss some of the divergent views as to the determinants of the demand for money and the issues which remain unsettled in a general theory of the demand for money.

THE TRANSACTIONS DEMAND

All of us hold money balances to carry on ordinary day-to-day exchanges. Money held in the form of cash temporarily to meet day-to-day expenditures for goods and services between the intervals when money income is paid has already been referred to as transactions balances. What determines how much money the community will want to hold to satisfy what we call its transactions demand? As a first approximation we can define five determinants of the transactions demand for money:

(1) the community's payment habits
(2) the degree of vertical integration of production
(3) the development of the financial system
(4) the level of income
(5) the rate of interest

By the community's payments habits we mean the time pattern of its expenditures and the payment interval — that is, the frequency with which income payments are made. An individual who regularly receives his income on the first day of each week has a payment interval of one week or seven days. If, for example, an individual receives \$140 per week on the beginning of the first day of each week and spends \$20 on each of the seven days during the week, he holds from the beginning of the first day to the end of the last day of the week an average balance of \$70. This is illustrated by the solid lines in Figure 22-1. Our assumption of a time pattern of expenditures where the individual spends his weekly money income at a constant rate ending with a zero money balance at the end of the last day of the week is an oversimplification. Under normal circumstances rents and utilities are paid at the beginning of each payment interval with the result that money balances decrease rapidly

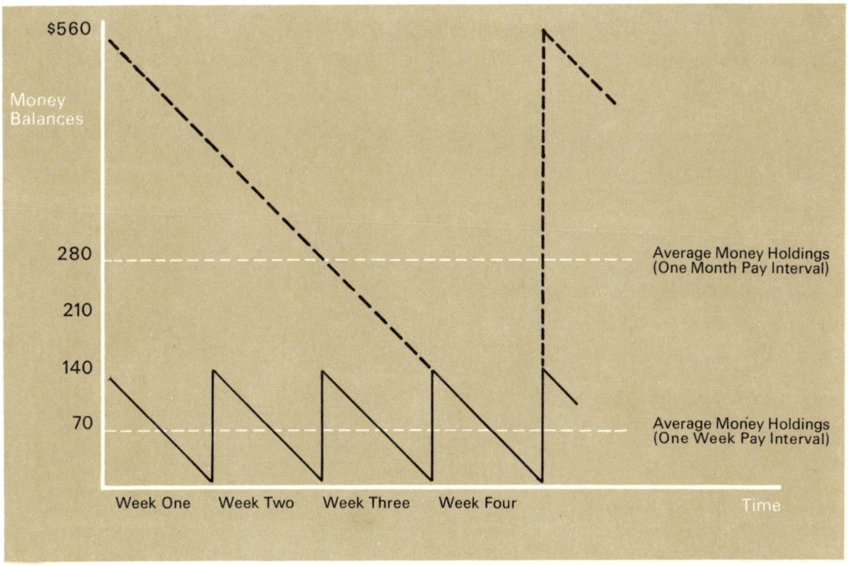

Figure 22-1

immediately after receipt of income and more slowly thereafter until they are exhausted just before the next receipt of income. Under these circumstances our straight-line curve in Figure 22-1 showing the time pattern of expenditures would be curvilinear.

Now let us assume that with no change in his income, the individual is paid on the first day of each month rather than each week. What effect will this have on his average money holdings if he spends his income at a constant rate throughout the month? This is represented in Figure 22-1 by the broken straight-line curve. We have divided the month into four weeks. With a constant expenditures pattern but a monthly instead of a weekly payment interval his average money holdings increase from $70 to $280. Thus, all other things remaining the same, a simple lengthening of an individual's payment interval will result in larger average money holdings. The opposite, of course, is true for a shortening of the pay interval.

The individual's average money balances are also affected by changes in his expenditure pattern as we have already noted. In Figure 22-2 we assume that the pay interval remains at one month (four weeks) but the time pattern of expenditures changes. The solid line shows income being spent at a constant rate over a four week period and the broken line the same income being spent over only a two week period. In the first case the individual's average money holdings over the month are $280. In the second they are only $140 since during each day of the last two weeks in the month his actual money holdings are zero. Thus if the individual spends his income so as to run out of money before the next payment

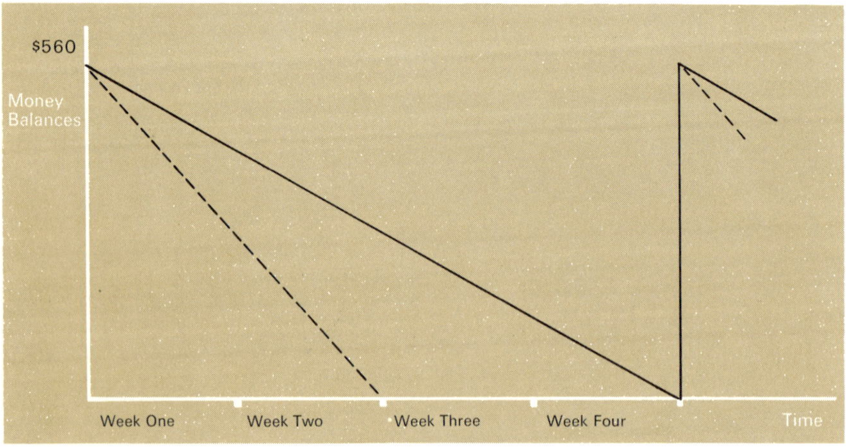

Figure 22-2

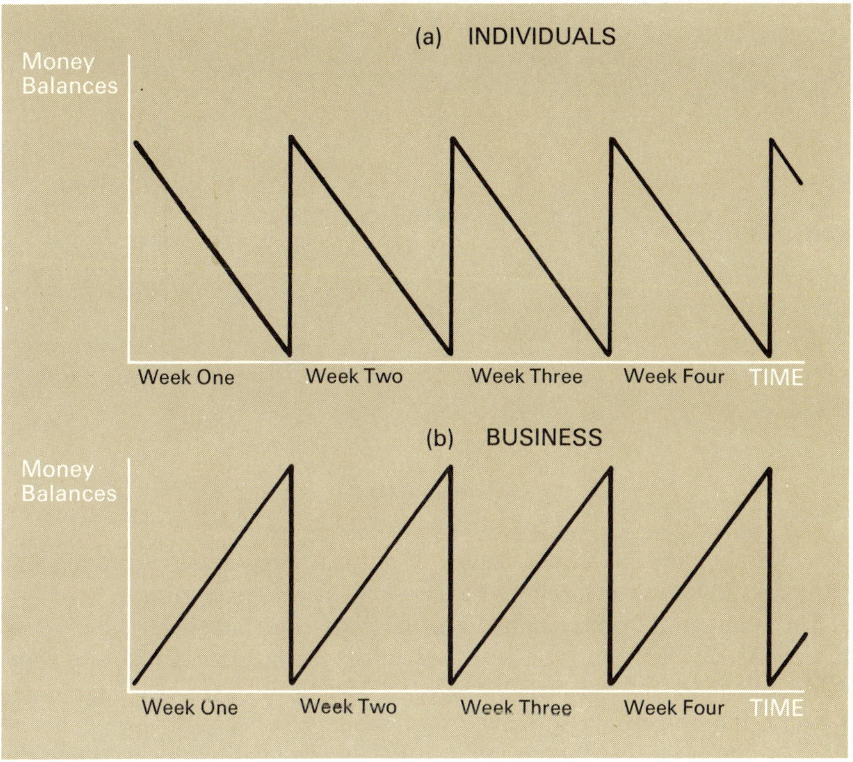

Figure 22-3

receipt his average money holdings during the month are smaller than they would be if they were equally distributed throughout the month.

So far we have considered only the average money holdings of an individual. Let us now go back to Figure 22-1 and assume that it represents the total cash holdings of all individual income recipients in an economy. Moreover, let us go one step further and assume that all businesses are organized into one giant firm and that there is no government. In other words, on the first of each week, our giant business firm pays out wages, salaries, interest and profits which are received by individuals during the same day. During the week as individuals spend their income this money flows back to the giant firm. Thus while individuals run down their cash balances those of business are increased by exactly the same amount. This is shown in Figure 22-3. The pattern of business cash balance is shown as the mirror image of cash balances held by all individuals.

Of course, it would have been more realistic to assume that the productive process is carried out by many firms each of which hold transactions cash balances rather than by one huge firm. It is reasonable to

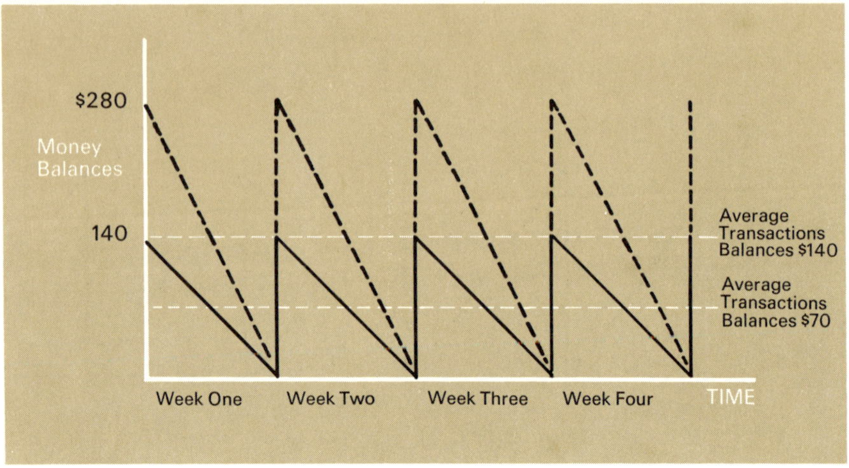

Figure 22-4

assume that the smaller the degree of vertical integration of production, the larger the total transactions balance held at any given time.

The amount of transactions cash balances that individuals and firms are required to hold to meet their day-to-day exchanges will depend upon the development of the financial system. Where this system is highly developed and borrowing to finance needed purchases is both easy and economical, business and individuals will be able to facilitate their purchases by holding smaller transactions balances. We can say that, other things being equal, the more highly developed the financial system, the lower the transactions demand for money.

The determinants of the amount of transactions cash balances which we have discussed so far — the community's payments habits, the degree of vertical integration of production, and the development of the financial system — can be considered to change only slowly over time. Therefore, we must look elsewhere to explain variations in the level of transactions balances in the short run. Two determinants listed earlier remain to be considered — the level of income and the rate of interest. Let us assume for the moment that interest rates, along with all the other determinants of the transactions demand for money, except income, remain constant.

In Figure 22-4 the solid lines show an individual receiving $140 at the beginning of each week and spending this income evenly over the week. The broken lines show the same individual after his weekly income has increased to $280 per week. The figure shows that an increase in income is accompanied by an increase in the individual's average money balances (his transactions demand for money). With income of $140 paid on the first day of the week the average transactions balance is $70 while with an increase to $280 also paid at the beginning of the week, the average balance for the week rises to \$140. If we add to these money balances those of business then the total average transactions demand for money is \$140 in the first case and \$280 in the second.

An alternative and more usual way to show the relationship between the total transactions demand for money in a community and changes in the level of income is depicted in Figure 22-5. Here money national income Y is shown on the horizontal axis and the amount of transactions balances demanded L_t on the vertical axis. The transactions demand curve for money kY is linear and slopes up from left to right. By drawing a straight-line curve through the origin we assume that the amount of transactions balances demanded is the same proportion of income no matter what the level of income. What this proportion (expressed by the slope of the line) will be depends upon all the determinants, other than income, of the transactions demand for money. The upward slope of the line indicates the community will want to hold larger balances as income increases. The equation of the demand curve for transactions balances is

$$L_t = kY \quad (1)$$

where L_t is the money supply available for transactions balances, Y the money national income, and k that proportion of national income which the country wishes (or needs) to hold as transactions balances; k is also

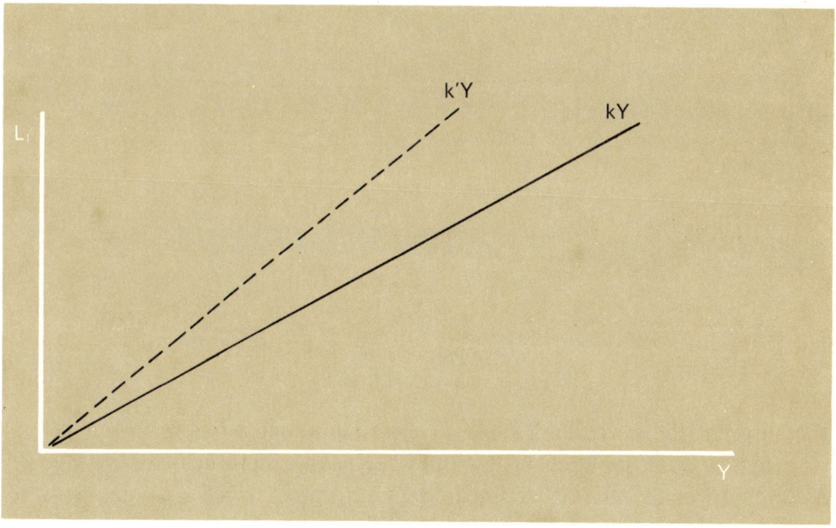

Figure 22-5

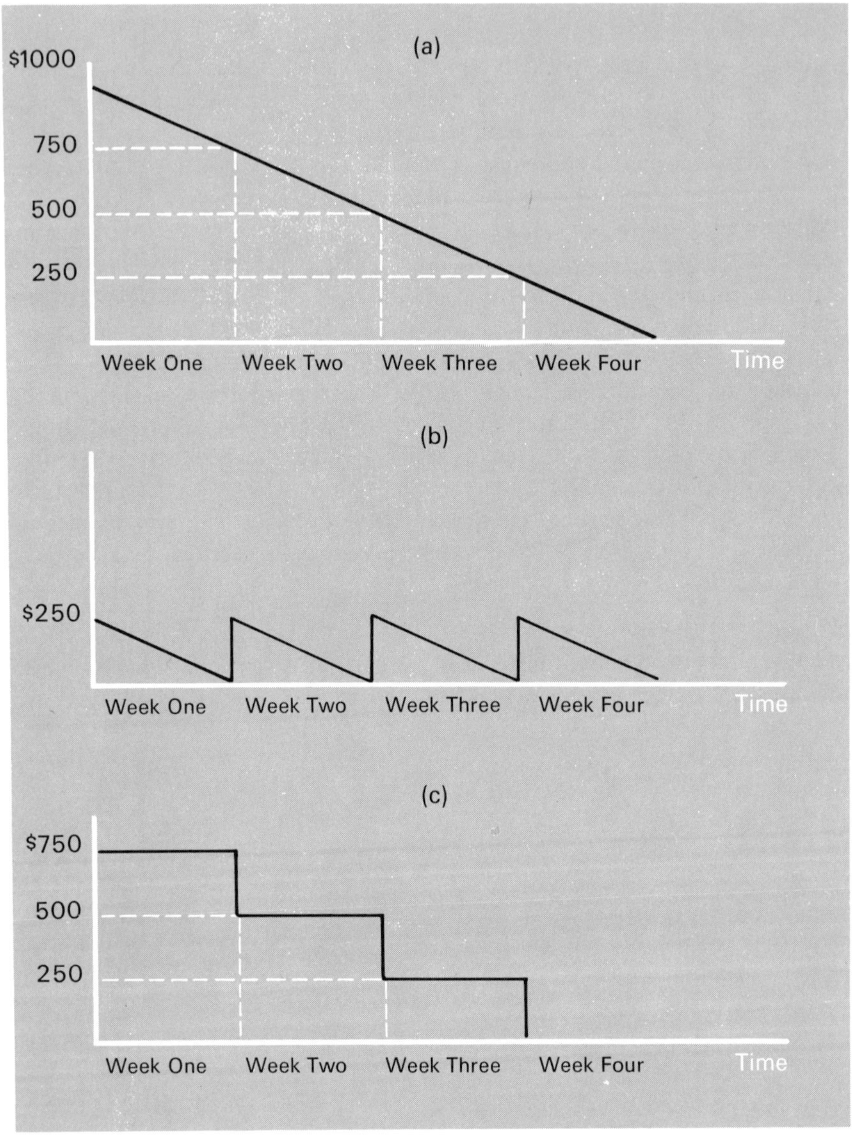

Figure 22-6

the slope of the curve and $k = L_t/Y$. We have met k before in our discussion of the quantity theory of money. It is the reciprocal of the velocity of circulation of money. A linear demand curve which assumes k to remain constant also assumes the same for the velocity of circulation of money. An increase in the velocity as a result, for instance, of a change in payment habits, the vertical integration of business, or a change in the financial system, will cause the demand curve to become flatter; an increase in velocity has occurred if the broken demand curve $(k'Y)$ changes to the solid demand curve (kY).

We now turn to the last on our list of the determinants of the demand for transactions balances — the rate of interest. Economists are still uncertain as to the effect of the rate of interest on the demand for transactions balances. One can make a theoretical case to show why changes in the rate of interest may affect the demand for transactions balances.[1] For example, assume that an individual is paid $1,000 on the first day of each month and spends this income evenly throughout the month so that his saving per month is zero. This is shown in Figure 22-6(a). For convenience, we again assume that the month consists of four weeks. In the middle of the first week, the individual will have spent $125 and will be holding $875 to meet his purchases during the three and a half weeks left in the month. In the middle of the last week he will have spent $875 and will be holding $125 to meet his needs during the remaining half week in the month. The average transactions demand for the individual is $500 for the month as a whole. During the first week alone the individual holds $750 which he does not require, during the second $500, and during the third $250.

If the individual requires $250 in each of the four weeks during the month to meet his purchases of goods and services, he holds $750 which he does not require during the first week, $500 during the second, and $250 during the third. On the first day of the month therefore he can use the $750 which he does not require to purchase an interest-bearing asset. On the first day of each subsequent week he can redeem $250 of his earning assets to meet his weekly requirement. His average cash transactions balances will then be reduced from $500 to $125 for the month as shown in Figure 22-6(b). Part (c) of the figure shows his earning asset holdings during the month, the average of which is $375 for the month.

Whether or not an individual behaves in the manner we have outlined depends upon several factors. The financial system must be sufficiently developed to allow him to buy and sell interest earning assets in the very short run. From the individual's point of view he must weigh the cost of buying and selling and the inconvenience of frequent entry to and exit from the securities market against the net interest he can earn from holding interest-bearing securities. The same is true for business firms. However, the large corporations with millions of dollars not immediately needed for transactions purposes will be more inclined to put money into

[1] See William J. Baumol, "The Transactions Demand for Cash: An Inventory Theoretic Approach", *Quarterly Journal of Economics*, Vol. 66, November, 1952, pp. 545-556; James Tobin, "The Interest-Elasticity of the Transactions Demand for Cash", *Review of Economics and Statistics*, Vol. 38, August, 1956, pp. 241-247.

earning assets if a profit can be realized than will an individual who has only a few hundred dollars. Moreover, the costs involved are lower, and entry to and exit from the securities market is much easier when the amounts involved are substantial. With a given cost of participating in the money and capital markets, switches by the community from idle transactions balances into interest-bearing securities are probably influenced by the rate of interest, particularly at the higher levels.

The relationships among the level of income, the rate of interest, and the transactions demand for money for the economy as a whole are shown in Figure 22-7. Here two transactions demand curves for money are shown at two different levels of income. When the rate of interest is below 5 per cent, the community will not switch from cash to interest-bearing securities because the costs and inconvenience involved are larger than the gains that can be realized. Above 5 per cent some switching will take place and will increase as the interest rate rises to progressively higher levels. Above the 5 per cent level, the transactions demand for money is said to be interest elastic as shown by the backward bending slope of the curve. Thus, given a level of income Y_1 at interest rates be-

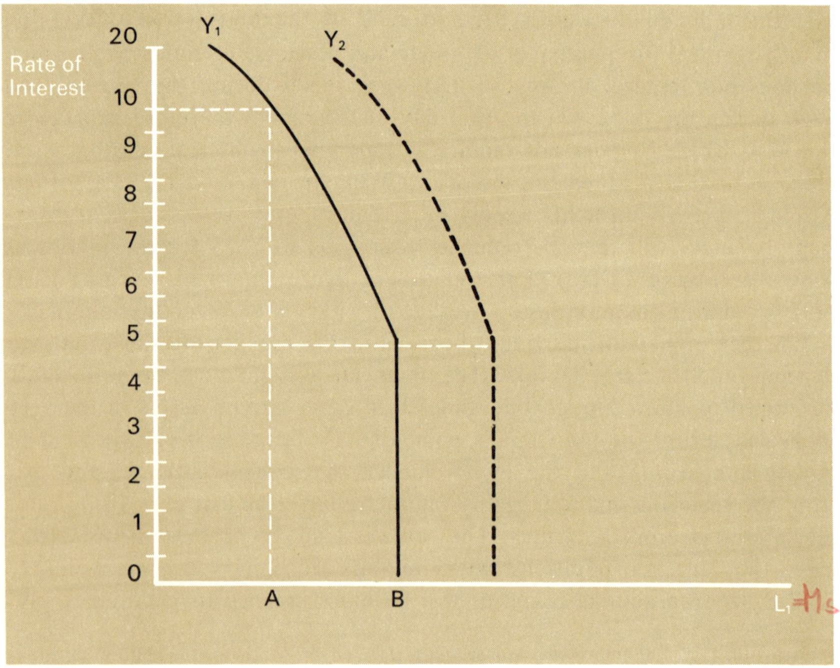

Figure 22-7

low 5 per cent the demand for transactions balances remains at *OB;* at interest rates above 5 per cent it declines. At 10 per cent, for instance, it is *OA*.

When the rate of interest is included as a determinant, the equation for transactions demand for money previously shown is modified and becomes

$$L_1 = l_1(Y,i) \qquad (1a)$$

As before, all the other determinants are not shown explicitly in the equation and are assumed to remain constant.

If transactions balances are directly related to income and inversely related to the rate of interest then the classical and neo-classical assumption of a proportional relationship between average money balances and income is not valid. Moreover the crude quantity theory which assumes a proportional relationship between money and prices is also invalid since k cannot be considered to remain constant.

THE PRECAUTIONARY DEMAND

Persons and businesses hold money in the form of cash as a precaution essentially because of the uncertainty of their future receipts and expenditures. In other words, precautionary balances are held to meet unpredictable increases in expenditures and unpredictable delays in receipts. For example, a business may be confronted with having to pay a higher price for a material necessary to its productive process, or it may find that an important customer to whom it has extended credit has gone bankrupt. To protect itself from such unforeseeable increases in its expenditures or losses in receipts it will hold cash as a **margin of safety.** At the same time a business may hold cash to allow it to take advantage of unexpected bargains in the future which will reduce its costs and increase its profits.

Money in the form of cash may also be held as a margin of safety to reduce what has been described as "the linkage of risks".[2] For example, an individual with very little cash takes a motor trip from Ontario to British Columbia. In Alberta he is arrested for speeding and since he does not have enough cash to pay his fine he is thrown into jail. But his troubles are only beginning. After the humiliating experience of telephoning a friend to send him money he finds that he must remain in Alberta for several days to appear in court. As a result he arrives back at his job several days late and his employer dismisses him. Not only has he lost a

---

[2] For an excellent discussion of the margin of safety motive and the principle of linkage of risks see A. G. Hart and P. B. Kenen, *Money, Debt and Economic Activity*, 3rd ed., Englewood Cliffs, N. J., Prentice-Hall, 1961, pp. 235-238.

few days' pay, but also his job. And so one misfortune leads to another. A business can have the same kind of experience. By holding cash as a margin of safety individuals and businesses are able to weaken the linkage of risks so that one misfortune need not be followed by a host of others. Alternatives to holding cash are the ability to obtain credit or the holding of "near-moneys" which can be readily converted into cash. While credit and "near-moneys" may be substituted for precautionary cash holdings, in the final analysis cash becomes a prerequisite.

Most individuals and firms hold money as a margin of safety in order to maintain a certain financial respectability. In our earlier example, for instance, the individual who had insufficient cash to pay his speeding fine suffered the ignominy of requesting a friend to send money to him. Insofar as the stigma attached to borrowing money has now generally disappeared, individuals and businesses today rely more on their overall wealth holdings rather than on their money holdings to give them desired financial respectability.

Changes in the amount of money held for precautionary purposes are usually considered to depend upon changes in income. One can assume that as an individual's income rises his "obligations" also increase and consequently his need for larger precautionary money balances. Against this assumption is the possibility that at higher incomes it becomes easier to borrow money thus obviating the necessity of holding large money balances. The usual assumption, however, is that changes in precautionary balances are a positive function of the level of income.

The precautionary demand for money may also be expected to vary inversely with the rate of interest. At high rates of interest individuals and businesses may be willing to assume the greater risk of holding a smaller precautionary balance in exchange for the higher interest rate that can be earned by holding interest-bearing assets.

Although the precautionary demand can be formally distinguished from the transactions demand, as we have done above, for analytical purposes the two are now usually considered together. This involves describing only one function called the transactions demand for money which includes the precautionary demand, and relating this function positively to the level of income and to some extent inversely to the rate of interest.

THE SPECULATIVE OR ASSET DEMAND

We have already noted that classical economists assumed that a person would not hold more money than he needed to meet his transactions (including precautionary) requirements. It was considered irrational to hold idle money which could be invested to earn interest. Keynes argued that if an individual expects the rate of interest to rise in the near future, holding idle money balances in excess of those required for transactions (and precautionary) purposes is eminently rational. When individuals hold money rather than bonds they are "speculating" that the rate of interest will rise in the near future and the price of bonds will fall. To understand this proposition and thereby the speculative demand for money we must examine the relationship between security prices and interest rates.

SECURITY PRICES AND INTEREST RATES

Let us consider a government bond on which we can assume there is no credit risk — that is, there is no risk that the interest and principal will not be paid as promised. There is, however, what we call a market risk — the risk that the market rate of interest and therefore the price of the bond may change sometime in the future before the bond falls due. To begin, let us consider a perpetual bond on which the issuer (the borrower) promises to pay to the holder a fixed amount of interest (a coupon payment) with no promise of repaying the principal at a stated period in the future. Although such bonds are now rarely issued, the Canadian government still has perpetual bonds outstanding. They are similar to the Consols issued in the United Kingdom. The only way the holder of a perpetual bond can get cash for it is by selling it to someone else.

Let us assume that the government issues a perpetual bond with a par value of $1,000 and that it promises to pay in perpetuity an amount of interest equal to $50 per year. At the time of issue the market rate of interest — the rate being paid currently on securities with risks similar to our perpetual bond — is 5 per cent. When the market rate is equal to the coupon rate of our perpetual bond, purchasers will be willing to pay the $1,000 par value for the perpetual bond. Now what will happen in the future to the market value of our perpetual if market rates of interest move above or below 5 per cent? This is illustrated in Table 22-1. Sup-

TABLE 22-1

Interest Rates and Bond Prices
(Perpetual Bond)

DATE	Par Value	Coupon Payment	Coupon Rate	Market Rate of Interest	Market Value of Bond
Time of Issue	$1,000.00	$50.00	5 per cent	5 per cent	$1,000.00
Five Years Later	$1,000.00	$50.00	5 per cent	6 per cent	$ 833.33
Ten Years Later	$1,000.00	$50.00	5 per cent	2 per cent	$2,500.00

pose that five years after the bond has been issued the market rate of interest rises from 5 to 6 per cent. If the holder of our perpetual bond wants to sell it, he will be unable to find buyers who will pay him $1,000 because such buyers (lenders) are able to purchase alternative securities which pay a rate of interest equal to 6 per cent. On a $1,000 security the interest would be $60. Since the amount of the interest payment on the perpetual bond is fixed at $50, the only way the holder can find a buyer is to offer it for sale at $833.33. At this price the $50 annual coupon payment is equal to 6 per cent, the current market rate of interest. A rise in the market rate of interest is therefore accompanied by a fall in the price of bonds.

Now suppose that at the end of ten years from the date of issue of our perpetual bond the market rate of interest has fallen from 5 to 2 per cent. The holder of our bond can now expect to receive more than the $1,000 he originally paid. Bond purchasers expect to receive only 2 per cent, or $20 per annum on a $1,000 investment. Our bond holder receiving $50 per annum can now expect to get $2,500 for his bond since $50 represents a 2 per cent return on a $2,500 investment. A fall in the market rate of interest is therefore accompanied by a rise in the price of bonds.

The relationship between the price of a perpetual bond and the market rate of interest is given by the following equation:

$$V = \frac{R}{i} \qquad (1)$$

where V is the current market value of the bond, R the fixed amount of interest paid annually in perpetuity, and i the market rate of interest. In our numerical example we assumed that the government issued a $1,000 perpetual bond promising to pay an annual amount of interest of $50. At the time the market rate of interest was 5 per cent, equal to the coupon rate. Substituting these figures into the equation above, we derive the current market value of the bond.

$$\$1{,}000 = \frac{\$50}{0.05}$$

Whether or not holders of cash will invest their money in such bonds will depend upon their **expectations** about the future market rate of interest. When they expect the future market rate to be 6 per cent they will not want to pay $1,000 but only $50/0.06, or $833.33. If they cannot find bonds on the market at this price that are paying a 6 per cent return, they will be inclined to hold their money idle until such time as the anticipated increase in the rate of interest takes place. Alternatively, if holders of cash expect that the market rate of interest will be 2 per cent sometime in the future they will buy our perpetual bond for $1,000 and hold it rather than cash. If their expectations are correct, then in the future when the market rate has fallen to 2 per cent they will be able to realize a gain by selling the bond for \$50/0.02, or \$2,500. Whether an individual chooses to buy a bond or hold cash depends, therefore, upon his expectations of the future market rate of interest. If he expects the market rate of interest to rise, he will be inclined to speculate and hold cash now in order to purchase bonds in the future when their prices have fallen. Alternatively, if he expects the market rate of interest to fall in the future, he will be inclined to use his cash now to purchase bonds with the hope of realizing a gain if his expectations are correct.

So far we have considered only perpetual bonds which are not redeemed at some specified date in the future. Now let us turn to the more usual case of bonds which have specified redemption dates — conventional bonds. We shall continue to consider government bonds so that we can assume no credit risk but, as before, a market risk. The current value of a bond with given maturity date can be calculated using the following equation:

$$V = \frac{R_1}{(1+i)} + \frac{R_2}{(1+i)^2} + \frac{R_3}{(1+i)^3} + \ldots \frac{R_n}{(1+i)^n} + \frac{A}{(1+i)^n} \qquad (Ia)$$

where i = the market rate of interest

$R_1, R_2, \ldots R_n$ = the number of dollars paid on the bond in years 1 through n

A = principal amount to be paid at maturity in year n

V = current value of the bond.[3]

The same inverse relationship between interest rate and price applies to both conventional bonds with specified maturity dates and perpetual bonds where no maturity date is specified. However, the closer a conventional bond is to its specified maturity date, the less sensitive its price will be to changes in the market interest rate. We saw earlier that the market value of a perpetual paying \$50 interest per year decreases from \$1,000 to \$833.33 with a rise in the market interest rate from 5 to 6 per cent. For a \$1,000 bond paying \$50 interest per year and maturing in ten years, the same rise in the interest rate would reduce market value from

[3] This equation can be reduced to

$$V = R\,\frac{1 - \dfrac{1}{(1+i)^n}}{i} + \frac{A}{(1+i)^n} \qquad (Ib)$$

$1,000 to $926.39. If it were five years from maturity, the value would fall from $1,000 to $957.88, and if it were only one year from maturity it would fall from $1,000 to $990.57.[4] These results are derived by inserting the appropriate figures into equation *(Ia)* and solving.

EXPECTATIONS AND THE RATE OF INTEREST

We have seen that the prices of marketable bonds are subject to change, rising when interest rates fall and falling when interest rates rise. There is, therefore, the possibility of making a capital gain or incurring a capital loss by holding bonds. Keynes assumed that the choice between holding money and holding bonds is determined by individuals' expectations about future changes in the rate of interest, and that individuals hold money because they speculate that interest rates will rise in the future (that future bond prices will be lower).

We can assume that people view the current rate of interest as high or low because they have some **normal range** of interest rates in mind against which the current rate is being compared. Individuals' conceptions as to what is the normal range of interest rates are based on recent experience. If they have become accustomed to interest rates that have varied from 5 to 8 per cent, an increase in the rate to 10 per cent may be looked upon as a temporary aberration and a return to the normal range may be expected. Alternatively, a drop in the rate to 2 per cent may be looked upon as an abnormally low rate with the expectation of an increase to the normal range in the future. Whether the current rate of interest is considered high or low depends upon the generally held view of what is the normal range of interest rates. Although Keynes recognized that a change in the current rate of interest affects one's concept of the normal range of rates, he assumed that a change in the current rate would not ordinarily lead to an equivalent change in expected future rates (what we have referred to as the normal range of rates).

The more the current rate of interest rises above the normal range of rates, the more general the expectations that it will decline and the greater the inducement to shift from money to bonds in order to take advantage of anticipated capital gains. Alternatively, the further the current rate of interest falls below the normal range of rates, the more gen-

---

[4] This assumes that 5 per cent was the coupon rate on both the perpetual bond and the three conventional bonds with varying maturities. As coupon rates on securities customarily vary directly with maturity, a coupon rate of 5 per cent on the perpetual bond might be accompanied by rates of, say, 4, 3 and 2 per cent respectively on the ten-, five- and one-year conventional bonds. These refinements, however, do not destroy our basic proposition that the fall in value resulting from an equal rise in the interest rate on each maturity will be less for the shorter maturity than for the longer.

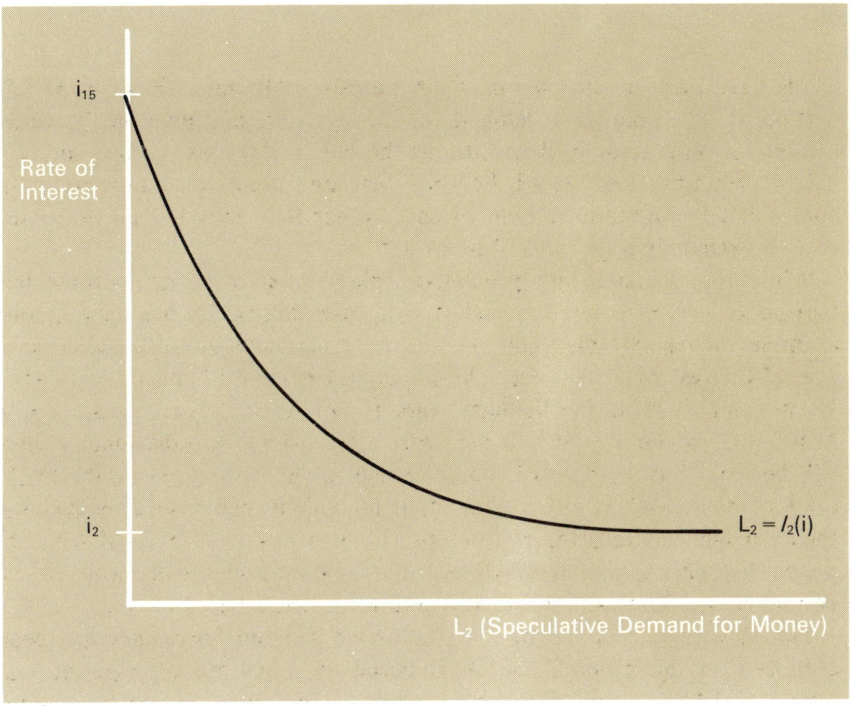

Figure 22-8

eral the expectations that it will rise and the greater the inducement to shift from bonds to money. The latter shift is made to avert expected capital losses and to obtain a "cash position" to purchase bonds when they are expected to be "cheap".

The relationship between the demand for speculative balances and the rate of interest is shown in Figure 22-8 by the speculative demand for money curve. The equation expressing this relationship is

$$L_2 = l_2\,(i) \qquad (2)$$

The speculative demand for money depicted by the curve $l_2(i)$ is drawn assuming individuals to have on the average a fixed concept of the normal range of interest rates. A change in their concept of the normal range of rates would be reflected by a shift in the curve.

The speculative demand for money curve shown in Figure 22-8 shows that given the state of expectations, when the rate of interest reaches 15 per cent individuals consider it to be above its normal range and expect that it can only fall. Individuals will therefore put all their money into bonds and hold zero speculative cash balances. Even if bond prices were to creep lower than 15 per cent they would consider the high rate of interest to be earned as offsetting any capital loss that might result in case bonds have to be cashed before their maturity. Although the extreme left portion of the speculative demand for money curve is drawn on the vertical axis, it may actually lie a little to the left of this axis because individuals distributing their wealth between cash and bonds probably prefer to hold a fixed minimum amount of cash rather than invest it all in bonds, even at extremely high rates of interest.[5]

While the demand for speculative balances curve in its extreme left portion is perfectly interest inelastic at rates above 15 per cent in our example, in its extreme right portion it is perfectly interest elastic at a rate of interest of 2 per cent. The horizontal portion of the curve is what Keynes described as the **liquidity trap.** It implies that there is some rate of interest, in our example 2 per cent, below which no additional money will be lent. Any amount of money which might be created by the banking system as well as any amount that individuals can save after meeting their current demands for consumption is held in speculative balances. At a very low rate individuals will feel that holding bonds will mean almost certain capital loss as interest rates return to their normal range.

The Keynesian analysis of the speculative demand for money has been criticized on the grounds that it is based on a pattern of expectational behaviour which is not necessarily always in operation, and that it cannot explain why an individual might hold speculative money balances and bonds. An individual is assumed to expect either that interest rates will rise in which case he holds only money, or that they will fall in which case he holds only bonds. Keynes assumed that a mass exodus from money into bonds or vice-versa does not occur because different people have different expectations with regard to the future. This view, however, is open to criticism because individuals' expectations may converge if, for example, a low interest rate persists for a sustained period. The fear of capital loss will disappear and the community will hold no idle money balances.

James Tobin has proposed an alternative explanation of the demand for idle money balances independent of the Keynesian one-sided expectational behaviour.[6] Suppose individuals are uncertain about future changes in the rate of interest. While they expect it to change, they consider their chances of capital gain or capital loss on holding bonds to be equal. If they hold money, they neither benefit nor lose with a change in the rate of interest. On the other hand, if they hold bonds, they take on the burden of risk because of their uncertainty of future interest rates.

---

[5] See J. Tobin, "Liquidity Preference as Behaviour Towards Risk", *Review of Economic Studies*, February, 1958, pp. 65-86.

[6] *Ibid.*

Some individuals may be considered "risk takers" and others "risk averters". For the former, risk has positive utility; they are prepared if necessary to give up some interest income from bonds in order to take on more risk. However, they can have more of both interest income and risk by increasing the proportion of bonds to cash. The "risk takers" are assumed to hold bonds in preference to money balances.

For "risk averters", risk has disutility and will be accepted only if interest income provides adequate compensation. The higher the rate of interest, the larger the compensation and therefore the greater the risk they are willing to accept. Moreover, the higher the rate of interest, the larger the proportion of bonds to money that they are willing to hold. The net effect of the behaviour of "risk takers" and "risk averters" is that as interest rates decrease the quantity of idle money increases. Tobin's risk hypothesis explaining a demand for idle money which is sensitive to interest rate change is free of the Keynesian one-sided expectational behaviour and the assumption that expectations will not ultimately converge.

SPECULATIVE DEMAND AND PORTFOLIO SELECTION

Keynes assumed that money is held to meet transactions requirements and as an alternative to holding bonds. However, the choice of assets to be held as a store of value is not restricted to money and bonds but includes a wide assortment of other financial assets and probably also nonfinancial assets. The Keynesian theory of the demand for money can therefore be extended and treated as part of the theory of consumer choice or portfolio selection. This approach, which is now called the portfolio approach, was pioneered by James Tobin of Yale University.[7]

The community can be assumed to want to maintain some optimum distribution among the different assets in which wealth can be held. If we assume a community with given preferences as to the composition of its wealth holdings, then any change in total wealth which disturbs this preference will produce shifts in the amounts of the various assets held. Let us assume an increase in an asset other than money which disturbs the optimum distribution of wealth. In order to retain its desired ratio of money to total assets, the community will want to shift out of other assets into money — the demand for money increases. Alternatively, if the total money supply increases at a faster rate than other wealth holdings,

[7] Tobin, James, "The Theory of Portfolio Selection", in F. H. Hahn and F. P. R. Brechling, *The Theory of Interest Rates*, London, Macmillan, 1965, pp. 3-51.

the community will want to regain its desired ratio of money to total wealth by giving up money for other assets.[8]

Defining the factors which explain the community's propensity to substitute money for other wealth holdings, especially other financial assets, has become the major task of those following the portfolio approach to explain the demand for money. Most of the evidence to date suggests that the relative yields on various financial assets are perhaps the most important explanatory variable of the substitution effect just discussed. Much of the evidence, however, suggests that the community's reaction to changes in yields is relatively slow and that the substitution effect may therefore be an unimportant explanation of the demand for money in the short run. This, however, may change as the size of individual wealth portfolios becomes larger and as the cost of obtaining information and engaging in market transactions falls.

THE TOTAL DEMAND FOR MONEY

We have defined three separate demands for money — the transactions demand, the precautionary demand and the speculative or asset demand. The transactions and precautionary demands have been combined and expressed by the equation $L_1 = kY$. The speculative demand has been expressed by the equation $L_2 = l_2(i)$. Combining these two equations we have an equation describing the total demand for money M_d.

$$M_d = L_1 + L_2 = kY + l_2(i) \qquad (3)$$

If we recognize that the rate of interest also determines the transaction demand, equation *(3)* can be written:

$$M_d = l_1(Y, i) + l_2(i) \qquad (3a)$$

or more generally

$$M_d = l(Y, i) \qquad (3b)$$

Equation *(3b)* can be amended to explicitly include total wealth as a variable and by adding a variable, say X, to represent all the other factors which may influence the demand for money. Our equation for the total demand for money now becomes

$$M_d = L\,(i, Y, W, X) \qquad (3c)$$

Represented by X are such diverse factors as the distribution of income,

---

[8] Substitution will not take place on a one for one basis. For example, assume that the community's wealth is \$15 billion in money and that this is held in the desired ratio of \$5 billion in money and \$10 billion in other assets. If other than money assets change by \$2 billion the desired ratio is regained with a change of only \$1 billion in money holdings.

price expectations, the degree of uncertainty about business forecasts, the community's payments habits, the degree of vertical integration of production, the development of the financial system, and the desired distribution of the various wealth forms. Traditionally, most of these factors have been considered to change only slowly over time or wealth holders' reactions to changes in them have been considered very slow. As a result they have been regarded as playing an insignificant role in determining the demand for money. More recently with the increased attention being given to the portfolio approach, many of these factors are being considered as having more than just a long-term effect on the demand for money.

THE DEMAND FOR MONEY SCHEDULE

Since there is no way to show variations of the five variables included in our demand for money equation *(3c)* in a two dimensional diagram, explicit reference to three variables must be eliminated. Our choice, as indicated in Figure 22-9, is to retain M_d the total demand for money and i the rate of interest. The line labelled LL represents the amount of money that is desired at varying rates of interest assuming the level of income and other things as being given. It slopes downward from left to right

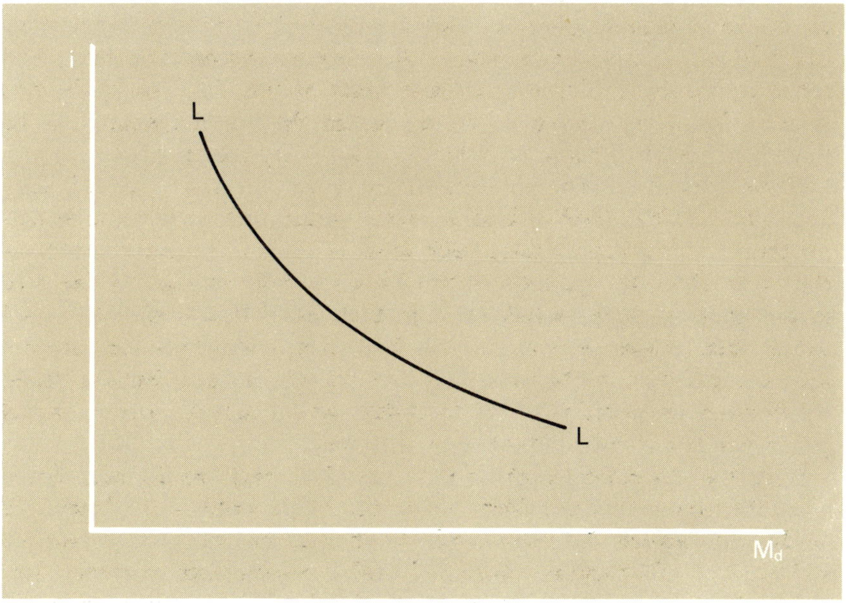

Figure 22-9

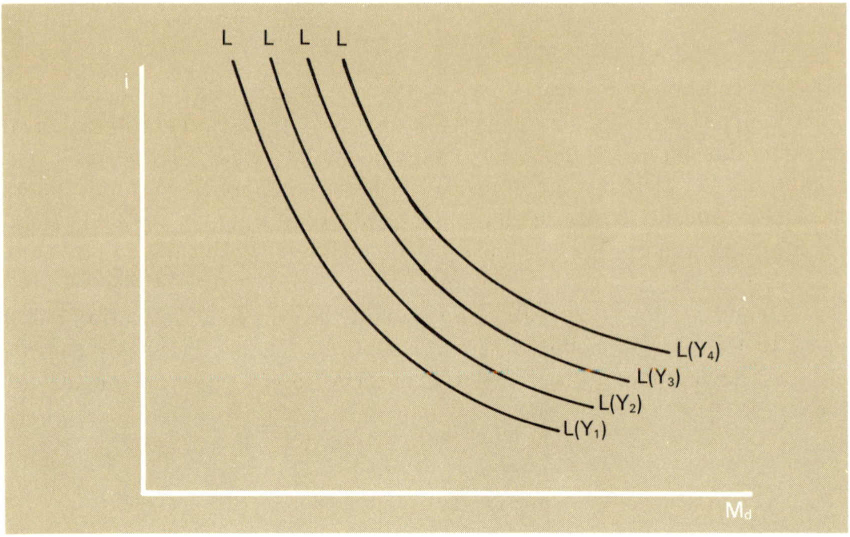

Figure 22-10

indicating an inverse relationship between the demand for money and the rate of interest. If we follow the Keynesian assumption that at very high rates of interest no money is held for speculative purposes, the upper left hand portion of the demand for money curve is perfectly vertical (perfectly interest inelastic). If on the other hand we allow for the Keynesian hypothesis that at some low rate of interest the community will hold all additions to its money idle, the curve becomes perfectly horizontal (infinitely elastic) in its extreme right portion. In drawing the total demand for money curve we have omitted these two assumptions because we consider them to be either invalid or very special cases.

If the level of income increases we can expect to find a new *LL* curve appropriate to this level of income. Thus we can draw a separate demand for money curve representing each level of income as in Figure 22-10. But what about the position of the *LL* curve with changes in the other determinants we have included in our *X* variable? If, for example, people expect their future incomes to rise from past levels they may increase their expenditures in the present by holding less money. Such a change would move the position of the total demand for money curve to the left just as would a decrease in the level of income.

With the development of financial markets and the introduction of what the community considers to be better alternatives for holding its wealth the desired distribution of wealth may change. The community will want to hold these new forms of wealth in preference to money. As a result, other things remaining the same, the demand for money curve will shift to the left. Various other examples can be given to explain the position and shifts of the demand curve for money. As we shall see later, economists have been concerned with the stability of the demand for money curve because, aside from its slope, shifts in the curve have important implications for monetary policy.

A RESTATEMENT OF THE QUANTITY THEORY

Although it is now generally recognized that the demand for money is interest elastic, Milton Friedman of the University of Chicago and a small group of disciples still cling to the quantity theory approach which stresses a close relationship between the quantity of money and the level of income.[9] Friedman maintains that the demand for money is quite responsive to changes in income (an income elasticity of 1.8) and that no interest elasticity of money demand can be shown to exist empirically. Friedman's critics feel that he arrives at his conclusions partly because he defines money much more broadly than other researchers and partly because he uses an unorthodox definition of income. Friedman defines the money supply to include commercial bank time deposits while other researchers prefer to define money more narrowly to include only currency and commercial bank demand deposits. Instead of relating the money supply to the GNP or some other similar national-accounts concepts of income as is more generally done, Friedman uses what he calls **permanent income.** We can think of permanent income as the constant rate of income that can be permanently maintained over an individual's lifetime. It is the total sum that an individual could consume while keeping his wealth intact. It depends upon the individual's initial stock of financial wealth, on the expected stream of his income receipts that are independent of his wealth holdings, and on the rate of return on wealth that is expected to hold over the rest of his lifetime.

Friedman's demand for money equation may be expressed in the following way:

$$\frac{M}{P} = L\left(r, \frac{\triangle P}{P}, Y_r, W, U\right) \qquad (4)$$

where M is the money supply broadly defined and P the price level. The determinants of the demand for money — and here Friedman considers the real demand for money as being the appropriate quantity to be measured — are the real rate of interest on financial assets r, the rate of return on nominal money which is taken to be the rate of change of the

[9] Friedman, Milton, "The Quantity Theory of Money — A Restatement", in Milton Friedman (ed.), *Studies in the Quantity Theory of Money*, Chicago, University of Chicago Press, 1956, pp. 3-21.

price level $\Delta P/P$, real income Y_r, the ratio of non-human capital to human capital W, and tastes U. Friedman's demand for money equation resembles the portfolio approach in that he assumes that money is only one of the many forms in which wealth is held. Besides money, wealth may be held in the form of bonds, equities, commodities and "human capital". However, unlike the portfolio theorists he believes that the rate of interest or the "substitution effect" is secondary to the "income effect" in explaining changes in the demand for money. Moreover, while the portfolio theorists are inclined to conclude that money has no unique qualities as an asset, Friedman considers it a luxury good. He takes the observed decline in the income velocity of money in the United States up to the Second World War as evidence that money is a luxury good and at higher levels of income proportionately more cash balances are demanded.

The modern quantity theory of money as represented by our summary of Friedman's approach attempts to show that there is a predictable relationship between changes in the money stock and changes in the GNP. This concept is based on the assumption that the supply of money is determined independently of the demand for money and that the demand for money is stable relative to its determinants. The demand for money can also be expressed in terms of the income velocity of money which is considered to be stable in relation to its determinants. Stability, however, does not mean that velocity is constant but that it is predictable. Insofar as velocity is predictable the relationship between the demand for money and its determinants is also predictable.

UNSETTLED ISSUES

Although the demand function for money balances has been subject to a great deal of empirical investigation over the last few years, particularly in the United States, a general consensus as to its nature has yet to be reached.[10] In 1962 Harry Johnson cited what he considered to be the more important issues remaining unsettled as "first, what specific collection of assets corresponds most closely to the theoretical concept of money...; second, what the variables are on which the demand for money so defined depends; and third whether the demand for money is sufficiently stable to provide, in conjunction with the quantity of money, a

[10] For a discussion and review of the literature see David M. Jones, *The Demand for Money: A Review of the Empirical Literature*, Staff Economic Studies, Washington, Board of Governors of the Federal Reserve System, 1966.

better explanation of money income and other aggregates than is provided by models around income-expenditure relationships". [11]

What collection of assets corresponds most closely to the theoretical concept of money? Should it be confined to currency and bank demand deposits, or should it include bank saving and time deposits, demand deposits of non-bank financial institutions, fixed-value government bonds or other assets? Many economists still feel that money should be narrowly defined and include only those assets which represent a stock of immediate purchasing power — currency and bank demand deposits. They argue that money's unique characteristic is its means of payment and consider its low transactions costs its distinctive feature. On the other hand, those who choose to define money more broadly look upon it as a financial asset whose distinctive feature is liquidity. This issue therefore is a conceptual one which may not be resolved from empirical investigation.

Many issues in the demand for money remain unsettled because of the statistical problems related to their measurement. This is the case in assessing the relative importance of income and wealth as constraints in the demand for money function. Because they tend to move together over time it is statistically difficult to explain the importance of wealth and income separately.

Direct evidence of the relative stability of the demand for money function — its immunity to unpredictable shifts — is also inconclusive. Much of the evidence to date suggests that the demand for money function has been relatively stable over the long run. No such evidence is available for its short-run stability. For example, curves showing the income velocity of money in Canada for each of the postwar business cycles suggest that the short-run demand for money function has been quite unstable.

Although Friedman has failed to find any role for interest to play in determining the demand for money, subsequent empirical studies appear to show rather conclusively that there is a close relationship between the demand for money and the rate of interest. What interest rate or rates represent the most appropriate measure of the opportunity cost of holding money remains to be settled. The outcome of this issue is important for monetary policy. If short-term rates are more relevant than long-term rates for holding money, a conclusion which has gained support, important implications follow for monetary policy. If investment is more sensitive to long rates than to short, and if the first impact of changes in the money supply is on short rates, support is given to those who argue that

---

[11] Johnson, Harry G., "Monetary Theory and Policy", *American Economic Review*, Vol. 52, June, 1962, pp. 344-345.

monetary policy is ineffective for short run stabilization. How interest rates of various terms are inter-related is still an open question. In a later chapter we shall discuss some of the theories that have been advanced to explain the term structure of interest rates. Also unsettled is the Keynesian concept of a liquidity trap — that the demand for money is perfectly interest elastic at some low rate of interest. While much of the recent empirical evidence fails to lend support to the Keynesian hypothesis, it cannot be considered to discredit it completely.

There are other unanswered questions in the formulation of a demand for money theory. How rapidly do decision units adjust their money balances to changes in market variables? To what extent does the speed of adjustment depend on the variables that cause the disturbance? What differences exist in the demand for money functions for different sectors of the economy?

SELECTED READINGS

Baumol, William J., "The Transactions Demand for Cash: An Inventory Theoretic Approach", *Quarterly Journal of Economics,* Vol. 64, November, 1952, pp. 545-556, reprinted in Richard Thorn (ed.), *Monetary Theory and Policy,* New York, Random House, 1966, pp. 165-177.

Duesenberry, James S., "The Portfolio Approach to the Demand for Money and Other Assets", *Review of Economics and Statistics,* Vol. 45, February, 1963, pp. 9-24, reprinted in Richard S.Thorn (ed.), *Monetary Theory and Policy,* New York, Random House, 1966, pp. 222-247.

Ellis, Howard, "Some Fundamentals in the Theory of Money", *The Quarterly Journal of Economics,* Vol. 52, 1937-1938, pp. 431-471, reprinted in American Economic Association, *Readings in Monetary Theory,* New York, Blakiston Company, 1951, pp. 89-128.

Friedman, Milton, "The Demand for Money: Some Theoretical and Empirical Results", *Journal of Political Economy,* Vol. 67, August, 1959, pp. 327-351, reprinted in Richard S. Thorn (ed.), *Monetary Theory and Policy,* New York, Random House, 1966, pp. 86-117.

Friedman, Milton (ed.), *Studies in the Quantity Theory of Money,* Chicago, University of Chicago Press, 1956.

Gilbert, J. C., "The Demand for Money: The Development of an Economic Concept", *Journal of Political Economy,* Vol. 61, April, 1953, pp. 144-159.

Hansen, Alvin H., *A Guide to Keynes,* New York, McGraw-Hill, 1953.

Hart, A. G., and P. B. Kenen, *Money, Debt and Economic Activity,* 3rd ed., Englewood Cliffs, N.J., Prentice-Hall, 1961, Ch. 13 and 14.

Hicks, Sir John, *Critical Essays in Monetary Theory,* Oxford, Clarendon Press, 1967.

Johnson, Harry G., "Monetary Theory and Policy", *American Economic Review,* Vol. 52, June, 1962, pp. 335-384.

Jones, David M., *The Demand for Money; A Review of the Empirical Literature,* Staff Economic Studies, Washington, Board of Governors of the Federal Reserve System, 1966.

Keynes, J.M., *The General Theory of Employment, Interest and Money,* London, Macmillan, 1936.

Metzler, L.A. "Wealth, Saving and the Rate of Interest", *Journal of Political Economy,* Vol. 59, April, 1951, pp. 93-116.

Modligiana, Franco, "Liquidity Preference and the Theory of Interest and Money", *Econometrica,* Vol. 12, 1944, pp. 45-88, reprinted in American Economic Association, *Readings in Monetary Theory,* New York, Blakiston Company, 1951, pp. 186-239.

Moore, Basil B., *An Introduction to the Theory of Finance,* New York, The Free Press, 1968.

Newlyn, W. T., *Theory of Money,* London, Oxford University Press, 1962, Ch. 4, 5 and 6.

Teigen, Ronald, "The Demand For and Supply of Money" in Warren L. Smith and Ronald L. Teigen, *Readings in Money National Income and Stabilization Policy,* Homewood, Ill., Richard D. Irwin, 1965, pp. 44-76.

Tobin, J., "Liquidity Preference and Monetary Policy", *Review of Economics and Statistics,* Vol. 24, May, 1947, pp. 124-131.

Tobin, J., "The Interest Elasticity of the Transactions Demand for Cash", *Review of Economics and Statistics,* Vol. 38, August, 1956, pp. 241-247.

Tobin, J., "Liquidity Preference as Behaviour Towards Risk", *Review of Economics Studies,* Vol. 25 (2), February, 1958, pp. 65-86, reprinted in Richard S. Thorn (ed.), *Monetary Theory and Policy,* New York, Random House, 1966, pp. 178-203.

Tobin, J., "A Dynamic Aggregate Model", *Journal of Political Economy,* Vol. 63, April, 1955, pp. 103-115, reprinted in Richard S. Thorn (ed.), *Monetary Theory and Policy,* New York, Random House, 1966, pp. 205-221.

Whalon, E. L., "A Cross-Section Study of Business Demand for Cash", *Journal of Finance,* Vol. 20, September, 1965, pp. 423-439.

23

MONEY: SUPPLY AND DEMAND

We can now begin to fit together some of the building blocks which we assembled in previous chapters. In Chapter 18 we defined the supply curve of money as:

$$M_s = f(R, i, r_d, r_t, B, \frac{D_d}{D_t}, c)$$

where R is the reserve base, i the rate of interest, r_d and r_t the reserve requirements for demand and time deposits respectively, B the bank rate, D_d/D_t the ratio of demand to time deposits and c the ratio of currency held outside the banks to total commercial bank deposits. Let us assume that all the variables except the rate of interest are given and that the banking system supplies money as depicted by the money supply curve *MM* in Figure 23-1. As interest rates rise the banking system is prepared to increase the money supply as long as it has excess reserves.

In the last chapter we expressed the equation of the demand for money as:

$$M_d = L\,(i, Y, W, X)$$

where i is the rate of interest, Y the level of income, W wealth, and X all other factors which influence the demand for money. In Figure 23-1 we assume that W and X are given and that the level of income is Y_1. The demand for money curve is $LL(Y_1)$.

Given the level of income Y_1, the money market is in a state of equilibrium where the demand for money schedule $LL(Y_1)$ and the supply of money schedule *MM* intersect. Equilibrium is achieved when the demand for and supply of money is equal to M_3 and the rate of interest is i_1. At i_2, for example, there is an excess supply of money $(M_4 - M_2)$; the banking system is willing to supply an amount equal to M_4 but individuals

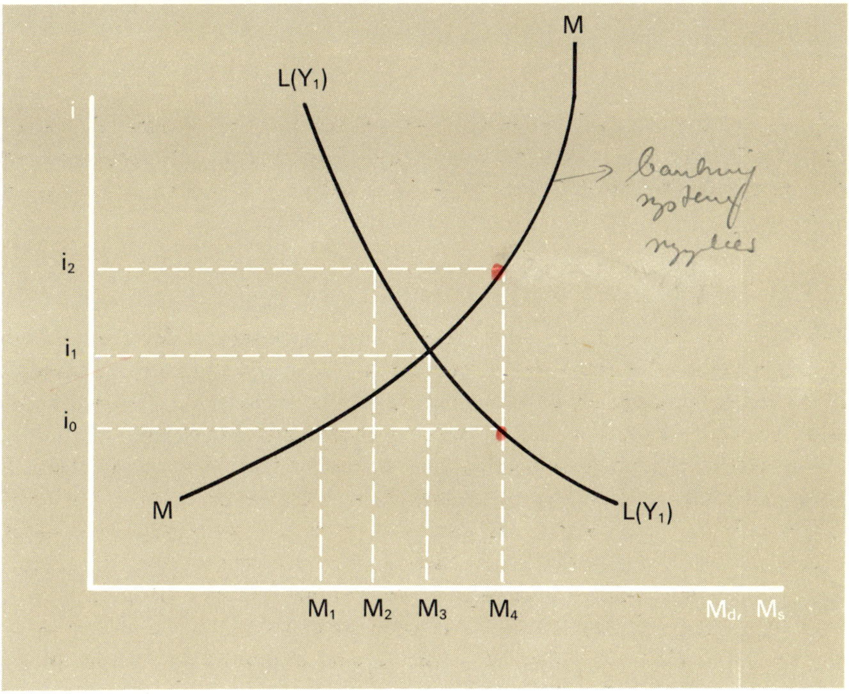

Figure 23-1

want to hold only M_2. Individuals rid themselves of their excess money balances by increasing their demand for bonds. As a result bond prices rise and the rate of interest declines. With a decline in the rate of interest, individuals will want to hold more money. In terms of Figure 23-1 there is a movement down and to the right along the demand for money curve. As the rate of interest declines the banking system becomes less willing to make loans and create money. There is a downward movement and to the left along the supply of money schedule. These downward movements come to a halt when the rate of interest is again equal to i_1 and the demand for money is M_3, equal to the supply of money. We assume here and in the following paragraph that investment expenditures are interest inelastic and that therefore the level of income remains constant.

When the rate of interest is at i_0 there exists an excess demand for money equal to $(M_4 - M_1)$. Let us assume individuals attempt to satisfy this demand by selling bonds. As a result bond prices fall and the rate of interest rises. At higher rates of interest individuals will want to hold smaller money balances; there is a move upward and to the left along the $LL(Y_1)$ curve. Moreover, as interest rates rise the banking system will increase its loans and create money, and so there is a move upward and to the right along the MM schedule. These movements will come to a halt as before when the rate of interest is i_1 and the demand for money is

M_3, equal to the supply of money. Given the level of income Y_1 monetary equilibrium exists only when the rate of interest is i_1 because only at this rate will the excess demand for (or supply of) money be equal to zero.

INCOME AND THE RATE OF INTEREST

We can now proceed one step further and introduce, at least as a first approximation, the relationship between income and the rate of interest. A complete description of the relationship between these two variables will have to wait until still more building blocks are assembled.

We saw in the previous section that given the level of income, there is some particular rate of interest at which the total demand for money will just equal the actual supply of money. The rate of interest that equates the supply of and demand for money is the equilibrium rate of interest. The forces that produce a change in the equilibrium rate of interest also lead to a change in the level of income. For example, as we will show in the following chapter, a decline in the rate of interest may lead to an increase in investment and consumption demands and therefore an expansion in income. Changes in the rate of interest can therefore be assumed to lead to changes in the level of income. This is illustrated in Figure 23-2. Diagram (a) is the same as Figure 23-1 except that this diagram shows a demand for money curve for each of four levels of income. Given the money supply curve *MM* we now have four equilibrium rates of interest i_1, i_2, i_3, i_4, corresponding respectively to the four levels of income Y_1, Y_2, Y_3 and Y_4. In Diagram *(b)* we plot all the combinations of i and Y at which the demand for money is equal to the supply of money: the intersection points of the *MM* and the various *LL* curves. The *LM* curve is simply the locus of all equilibrium combinations of i and Y. Any combination of i and Y that does not lie on this line is one of disequilibrium. At any point to the left of and above the *LM* curve the supply of money exceeds the demand. This excess supply will create pressure for lending and spending that will tend to lower i and raise Y until a combination of i and Y lying on the *LM* curve is attained. For example, if at income level Y_1 the rate of interest is i_2 instead of i_1, the amount of money demanded is M_0 but the amount of money the banking system is willing to create is M_2. The banks will be willing to accept lower rates of interest in order to be able to invest their funds profitably. As interest rates decline borrowers will be willing to increase their investment and consumption expenditures which will tend to raise Y. Thus the combination of i and Y will be reached where the demand for and supply of money are equated. Conversely at any point to the right of and below the *LM* curve the demand for money exceeds the supply. For example, if at income level Y_2 the rate of interest is i_1, instead of i_2, the amount of money demanded is M_3 whereas the amount supplied is only M_1. As a result forces will be set in motion that will tend to raise i and reduce Y.

The position of the LM curve is determined by the same factors which determine the positions of the demand for money and the supply of money curves. Should the monetary authorities increase the monetary base (R in the money supply equation) the MM curve and therefore the LM schedule will shift to the right. At any given rate of interest the amount of money that can be created will have increased and as a result a higher level of expenditures (income) can be maintained. This can be explained in yet another way. If the rate of interest and all the other factors which determine the speculative demand for money remain unchanged, a larger amount of money will now be available for transactions purposes. If the community initially held a desired ratio of transactions balances to income it will want to spend its now excess transactions balances. The spending will be reflected in an increase in income. When the former ratio between transactions balances and income is re-established a new equilibrium level of income is attained.

Now let us assume a shift to the right of the family of LL curves as a result of an increase in W (wealth) or a change in X (all other factors

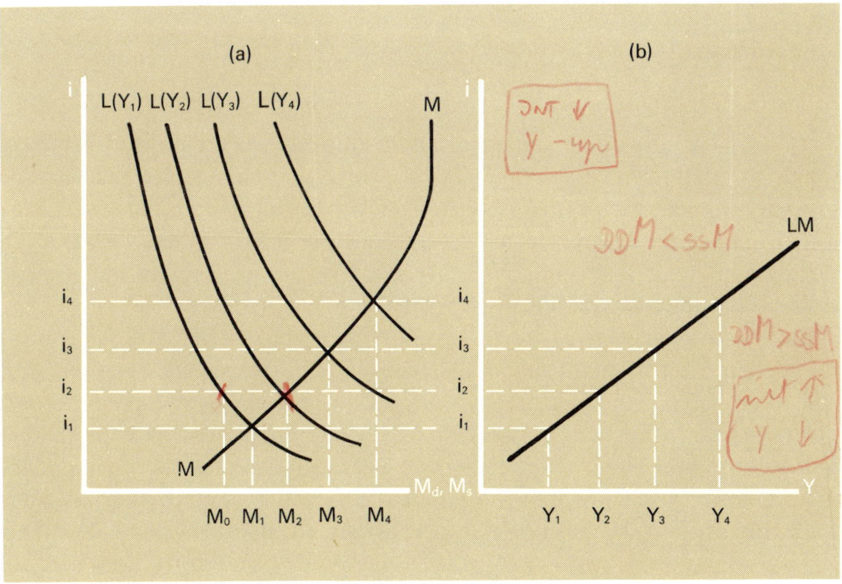

Figure 23-2

except Y and i which determine the demand for money). With a rightward shift of the family of LL curves the LM curve shifts to the left. A given rate of interest can now equate the demand for and supply of money at a lower level of income. With no change in the rate of interest and other things remaining the same, there is no change in the speculative demand for money. The increased desire to hold money as a result of changes in W or X must therefore be satisfied by a reduction in expenditures on goods and services. Consequently income will fall. Assuming no change in the community's desired ratio of transactions balances to income, at a lower level of income there will be a reduction in the amount of transactions balances demanded. Thus a given rate of interest now equates the demand and supply at a lower level of income.

The community may attempt to satisfy its increased desire to hold larger money balances because of a change in W or X by selling bonds. As a result, bond prices decline and the rate of interest increases. Equilibrium in the money market will be re-established at a higher rate of interest but with no change in the level of income.[1] If, on the other hand, the increased desire to hold larger money balances is satisfied by the community's attempt to sell bonds and at the same time by a reduction in the demand for goods, equilibrium in the money market will be attained only after interest rates have increased and the level of income has declined.

PRICE LEVEL AND THE DEMAND FOR AND SUPPLY OF MONEY

So far in our discussion we have not mentioned price changes. We have implicitly assumed that changes in income Y are changes in real income (output), while prices remain constant. Changes in income, however, may also result from changes in the level of prices. When all the resources in the economy are fully employed, for example, an increase in income can come about only as a result of an increase in prices.

So far we have also assumed that the community's demand for money is a demand for nominal money balances. It can be argued, however, that the community values its money holdings in real terms and not in nominal terms. In other words, individuals are not concerned with the actual amounts of money but rather with its purchasing power. When individuals are concerned with only the nominal amount of their money holdings they are said to be suffering under **money illusion.** If they view their

[1] This is a short-run situation where investment expenditures are assumed to be completely interest inelastic.

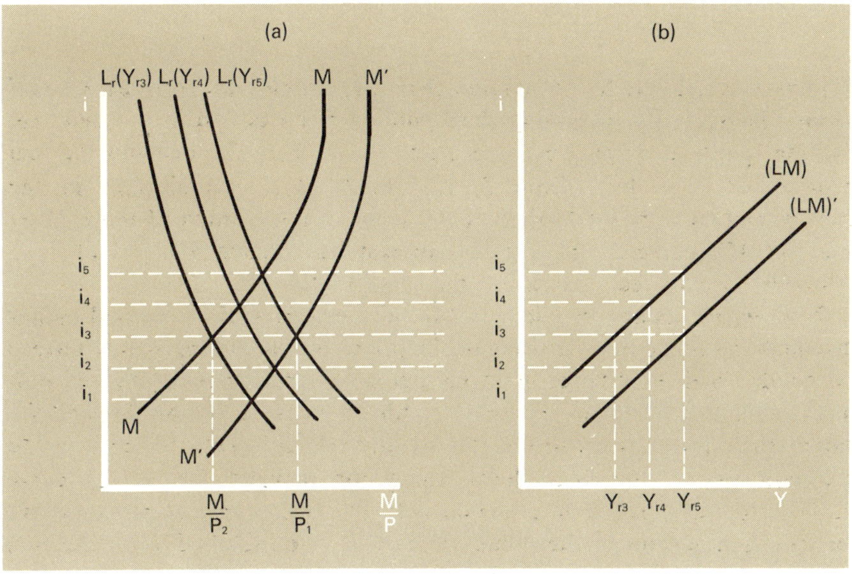

Figure 23-3

money in real terms they are free of money illusion. With money illusion our demand for money equation is

$$M_{dr} = \frac{M}{P} = L(i, Y_r, W_r, X)$$

where M_{dr} is the real demand for money, M the nominal money supply, P the price level, i the rate of interest, Y_r real income, W_r real wealth and X all the other factors which may influence the demand for real money balances.

In Diagram *(a)* of Figure 23-3 we have drawn three real demand for money schedules at real incomes of Y_{r3}, Y_{r4} and Y_{r5} assuming W_r and X remain constant. The supply of money schedule MM records the *nominal* amount of money that the banking system is prepared to create. It is a real money supply schedule only when prices remain constant. If prices change, we have to draw a real money supply schedule for each price level. For example, suppose the money market is in equilibrium when the rate of interest is i_3 and the level of real income is Y_{r3}. Equilibrium occurs at the point where the demand for money curve $L_r(Y_{r3})$ and the money supply curve MM intersect. The price level now falls from P_2 to P_1 as shown by a shift of the MM curve to $M'M'$. With lower prices individuals require less money to meet their transactions needs. Given the interest rate level of i_3 there is an excess supply of real money balances equal to $M/P_2 - M/P_1$. Individuals can rid themselves of this excess in various ways. First, let us assume that they employ all their excess real money balances by increasing their goods purchases and as a result real income (physical output) expands from Y_{r3} to Y_{r5}. The demand for real money balances shifts from $L_r(Y_{r3})$ to $(L_r(Y_{r5})$. Equilibrium in the money market is re-established at the point of intersection of the $L_r(Y_{r5})$ and $M'M'$ curves. The rate of interest has remained invariant at i_3 while the level of real income has increased to Y_{r5}.

Next let us assume that individuals rid themselves of excess real money balances resulting from a decrease in prices by purchasing bonds instead of goods. With no change in goods purchases real income (physical output) remains unchanged. However, with an increase in the demand for bonds their prices rise and the rate of interest falls. This is shown in the diagram by a movement down along the demand for money curve $L_r(Y_{r3})$ to the point of intersection with the real supply of money curve $M'M'$. Equilibrium in the money market is re-established when the rate of interest has fallen to i_1 and the level of real income is Y_{r3}.

Finally, let us assume that individuals rid themselves of excess real money balances by purchasing both bonds and goods. The increase in goods purchases is reflected by a shift in the demand for money curve $L_r(Y_{r3})$ to $L_r(Y_{r4})$. Equilibrium in the money market is re-established when the rate of interest has fallen to i_2 and the level of real income has increased to $L_r(Y_{r4})$.

A decrease in the level of prices and therefore an increase in real money balances creates disturbances in the money market. Equilibrium is re-established after real income has increased with the rate of interest remaining invariant, or after the rate of interest has declined with the level of real income remaining invariant, or after the rate of interest has declined and the level of real income has increased. Alternatively, a rise in the price level may be accompanied by an increase in the rate of interest and a decline in the level of income. This may appear paradoxical because in practice output (real income) and prices tend to move in the same direction. In our analysis we have assumed that after an initial price change no further changes in prices take place as a result of any change in output. The relationship between output and prices is explored in a subsequent chapter.

Our analysis in terms of Diagram (a) of Figure 23-3 is summarized Diagram (b) of the figure. For every different price level there is a different LM schedule; the schedule for consecutively lower price levels is successively further to the right. In the diagram the schedule at price level P_2 is (LM) and at the lower price level P_1 it is $(LM)'$.

SELECTED READINGS

See lists following Chapters 21 and 22.

24 INCOME DETERMINATION

In the last chapter where we developed the *LM* curve we observed that there are various combinations of the rate of interest and the level of income which produce equilibrium in the money market — where the desired amount of money demanded is exactly equal to the actual money supply. In this chapter we shall first discuss the concept of national income and then show how the equilibrium level of income is determined. However, we shall be confronted with a dilemma similar to that in the last chapter. There we found that we could not specify the equilibrium rate of interest without knowing the equilibrium level of income. In this chapter we shall find that we cannot specify the equilibrium level of income without knowing the equilibrium rate of interest. This dilemma will be resolved for us in the following chapter where we observe the simultaneous determination of both the equilibrium level of income and the equilibrium rate of interest.

THE CONCEPT OF NATIONAL INCOME

To understand how the level of income is determined we must first make sure of our concept of national income. In Chapter 20 we introduced the income equation of exchange which we expressed as:

$$MV_y \equiv P_yT_y \equiv Y$$

where M is the total stock of money and V_y its income velocity of circulation, T_y the physical volume of final goods and services currently produced, and P_y the average price of this output. The total money value of output currently produced during a given period is $P_y T_y$ or Y which by definition is equal to MV_y the amount of money paid for total output. In classical and neo-classical economics T_y was assumed to be determined by the economy's resources (factor endowments). Full employment was assumed to be maintained at all times as a result of flexible relative prices including the rate of interest. P_y, on the other hand, was considered to be determined by M, the money stock. This followed from the assumption that the income velocity of money V_y, as well as T_y as previously noted remained relatively constant, at least in the short run. Thus the level of money national income Y was determined by the stock of money which determined P_y and by the amount of real resources which determined T_y. Moreover, by invoking Say's Law of the market it was held that aggregate demand would equal aggregate supply. Because classical and neo-classical economists assumed T_y to remain constant at the full employment level their attention was centred on the determinants of V_y and the relationship between changes in the money stock and the price level. Keynes could not accept the traditional concept that an economy always tended toward full employment. He therefore focused his attention on T_y or more generally P_yT_y which we now know as gross national product or income.

Gross national product or income is viewed or measured in two major ways: as the expenditures for a nation's total output; and as the sum of the shares of gross income accruing to the economic units of a nation and the disposition of this income. The first is usually referred to as the product or expenditure approach and the second as the earnings or income approach. Since both these measures are in terms of money flows they must be given a time dimension. The common practice is to measure these money flows over the period of a year.

The economic system is composed of households, business units, governmental units and foreign units. As we shall see, during any given year their total expenditures must be equal to the total value of all goods and services currently produced. By adding together the total expenditures on final goods and services by these four economic units over a period of a year we derive gross national product. This is summarized by the following equation:

$$Y \equiv C + I + G + (X - M) \qquad (1)$$

Y = gross national income

C = personal consumption expenditures by households for goods and services

I = gross private domestic investment which includes expenditures for new residential and non-residential construction, expenditures for producer's durable equipment such as machinery, and net changes in the size of business inventories

G = government expenditures on goods and services

(X − M) = net imports of goods and services which is the amount of a country's output sold abroad less the value of goods and services imported

Equation *(1)* is a definitional identity — total expenditures are by definition equal to the value of all goods and services currently produced. But is everything that is currently produced currently purchased by someone? The answer to this question is found in the definition of purchases or expenditures. The economist chooses to define these to include both voluntary and unintentional or involuntary purchase of final output shown in equation *(1)* as part of business investment. All goods currently produced, but held as unintentional inventory are considered as purchased by business or as involuntary business investment. By including both voluntary and involuntary purchases, total expenditures are by definition always equal to the total value of final output currently produced.

The *C*, *I* and *G* components in equation *(1)* include not only expenditures on currently produced domestic output of final goods and services but also expenditures on imports. Because of the statistical difficulty of netting out of each of the *C*, *I* and *G* components the amount representing imports the Dominion Bureau of Statistics makes one estimate to include all imports — the *M* component in equation *(1)*. *M* is subtracted from the other components in order to derive the total expenditures on domestic output. Alternatively, one can at least theoretically divide the *C*, *I* and *G* expenditures to show the amount of each devoted to the purchase of domestic output and to the purchase of imports. This is done in equation *(1a)* where the *d* subscript denotes domestic purchases and the *m* subscript foreign purchases.

$$\mathrm{Y} \equiv (\mathrm{C_d} + \mathrm{C_m}) + (\mathrm{I_d} + \mathrm{I_m}) + (\mathrm{G_d} + \mathrm{G_m}) + \mathrm{X} - \mathrm{M} \qquad (1a)$$

Since

$$\mathrm{C_m} + \mathrm{I_m} + \mathrm{G_m} \equiv \mathrm{M} \qquad (1b)$$

equation *(1a)* may be simplified and shown as

$$\mathrm{Y} \equiv \mathrm{C_d} + \mathrm{I_d} + \mathrm{G_d} + \mathrm{X} \qquad (1c)$$

Equation *(1c)* tells us the total expenditures made by the four major economic sectors to purchase domestic production currently produced. This equation expresses the aggregate demand for a nation's output. It may also be viewed as expressing the source of income of the members of a nation, because from each sale of final output a receipt or income is obtained.

Now let us turn to the other approach of deriving gross national income which totals the gross income accruing to the nation's economic units. Income is earned from production in the form of wages, salaries, rents, interest and profits. The economic units to which income accrues are not, however, its final disposers. For example, in addition to earned income, housholds receive transfer receipts in the form of pensions and welfare payments. From these must be subtracted transfer payments made by households, the most important of which represent government taxes. After transfer adjustments households are left with personal disposable income which they can spend or save. Business disposable income is the amount of money income left to businesses after adjustments for transfer receipts and payments including taxes. Business disposable income is usually defined as business saving. It accrues to business firms as a result of the moneys set aside as depreciation and other allowances for declines in the value of capital goods and from undistributed after-tax profits retained by corporations. The income of government consists essentially of taxes with some smaller amounts from the sale of goods and services. Equation *(2)* expresses the total value of output distributed as income to households Y_d, to business S_b, to government G and to foreigners F.

$$Y \equiv Y_d + S_b + G + F \qquad (2)$$

We can now ask ourselves how this income is spent. Total income may be disposed of in five ways: for the consumption of domestic goods and services C_d; the purchase of foreign goods and services M; for household saving S_p; and business saving S_b; and the payment of taxes T. This is summarized by equation *(3)*.

$$Y \equiv C_d + M + S_p + S_b + T \qquad (3)$$

Equation *(3)* shows how the gross national income is used. Insofar as equation *(1c)* can be considered as the nation's aggregate demand for its output, equation *(2)* and therefore equation *(3)* may be considered the country's aggregate supply. This follows from the fact that income is earned from the productive services supplied by factors of production.

Figure 24-1 summarizes what we have been discussing. The top half of the diagram shows the sources of income earned by the production of commodities and services. The bottom half of the diagram shows how income is used.[1] For any past period the sum of the components shown in the top half of the diagram must be equal to the sum of the components in the bottom half of the diagram. Therefore, combining equations *(1c)* and *(3)*

$$C_d + I_d + G_d + X \equiv C_d + S_p + S_b + T + M \qquad (4)$$

Equation *(4)* is an accounting identity, true by definition for any past period. This is what economists call **ex post analysis.** Ex post what a nation

[1] Although it is not shown explicitly in our analysis, the government may also save. If during any period its receipts exceed its expenditures, the government can be said to be saving. If, on the other hand, its expenditures exceed its receipts, it can be said to be dissaving.

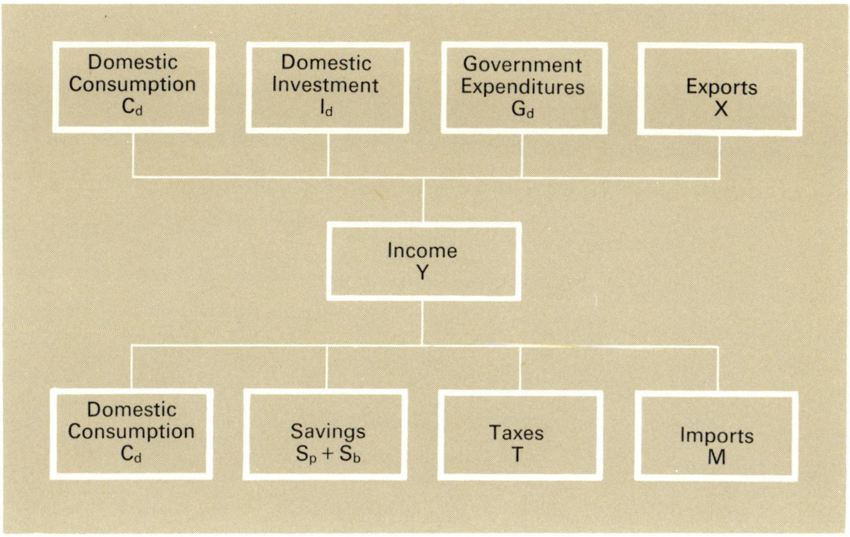

Figure 24-1

produces must be demanded by someone, if not voluntarily then involuntarily. If, however, we consider the components in equation *(4)* not as measures of what has happened, in an *ex post* sense, but as representing planned or desired behaviour, in an **ex ante** sense, our equality holds only in equilibrium. If all plans are realized equilibrium exists and aggregate supply will meet anticipated aggregate demand.

DETERMINING THE LEVEL OF INCOME

The actual level of output or income depends upon the relationship between planned or desired aggregate demand and planned aggregate supply. When the economy produces just enough goods to meet anticipated demand an equilibrium level of income is attained. If during any period more is produced than economic units desire to purchase producers must involuntarily add to their inventories. As a result they will reduce their production and output and income will subsequently decline. Alternatively, if during any period aggregate production falls short of desired demand producers will attempt to satisfy this demand by running down their inventories. Then they will expand production which in turn will increase output and income in the following period. The conditions which lead to stable or equilibrium output or income, and changes therein, can be summarized in terms of equation *(4)* as follows:

1. Condition for stable output and income (equilibrium)

$$C_d + I_d + G_d + X = C_d + S_p + S_b + T + M \qquad (4a)$$

2. Condition for rising output and income

$$C_d + I_d + G_d + X > C_d + S_p + S_b + T + M \qquad (4b)$$

3. Condition for falling output and income

$$C_d + I_d + G_d + X < C_d + S_p + S_b + T + M \qquad (4c)$$

Since C_d is found on both sides of equation *(4)* we can drop it and discuss the determination of the level of income in terms of the following equation:

$$I_d + G_d + X = S_p + S_b + T + M \qquad (5)$$

Equation (5) now tells us that the level of income is determined by plans for I_d, G_d, X, S_p, S_b, T and M. We must now consider the determinants of each of these magnitudes separately after which we can combine them to show how together they determine the level of output or income.

THE DETERMINANTS OF (S_p + S_b + T + M)

Personal Saving and Consumption Demand

Households dispose of their income either by spending it or by saving it. Hence given their level of disposable income a decision to consume less (both domestic and foreign goods and services) is at the same time a decision to save more. Or alternatively a decision to save less is at the same time a decision to consume more. Because of this interrelationship between personal saving and consumption we can consider the determinants of one as being also the determinants of the others.

Disposable Personal Income. Of all the determinants of consumption demand which we shall list, the level of disposable income is dominant. The notion that consumption changes in a predictable way with changes in income was labelled by Keynes the "propensity to consume" and was made the foundation of his theory of income determination. Keynes focused on the **marginal propensity to consume** which is the ratio between changes in consumption and changes in income and which expresses the percentage change in income that would be spent on consumption. It is generally assumed that the marginal propensity to consume has a value of less than unity and that it remains relatively constant, although it is felt that as income reaches higher levels the marginal propensity to consume probably becomes smaller.

We shall assume that consumption is determined essentially by current disposable income but alternative formulations can be made. One can assume that consumption is influenced by the highest income levels attained in (recent) past years. Hence if current income declines consumers will be reluctant to reduce their accustomed living standards, and consumption may fall but by proportionately less than income. Alternatively if income increases consumer expenditures will increase with a lag as consumers have to become accustomed to the possibility of a higher standard of living.[2] Milton Friedman has presented the hypothesis that consumption is based on what consumers regard as their permanent income.[3] Income changes which consumers consider as merely transitory would not be expected to produce changes in consumption. Friedman has found evidence of a much more stable relationship between permanent income and consumption than between current or measured income and consumption.

Consumer Wealth. Most individuals desire to accumulate wealth in the form of physical and financial assets. For example, many individuals wish to own their own homes. To achieve home ownership they will save out of current income and therefore spend a smaller proportion of their income on consumer goods and services. However, as they aquire their homes and other physical goods, they will reverse their spending and saving pattern. Other things being equal, the larger the stock of physical assets held by the public and the newer this stock, the less need for consumers to save to buy more, and the larger their consumption expenditures.

Financial assets in the form of cash, savings deposits, bonds, stocks and certain life insurance policies constitute a community's liquid wealth. Individuals desire liquid wealth to meet contingencies. In order to build up their desired liquid wealth holdings they tend to save more and spend

---

[2] This is what Duesenberry has called the "relative income hypothesis". See J. S. Duesenberry, *Income, Saving and the Theory of Consumer Behaviour*, Cambridge, Mass., Harvard University Press, 1952; F. Modigliani, "Fluctuations in the Savings-Income Ratio: A Problem in Economic Forecasting", in *Studies in Income and Wealth*, Vol. 2, New York, National Bureau of Economic Research, 1949. J. Tobin, "Relative Income. Absolute Income and Savings", in *Money, Trade and Economic Growth, Essays in Honor of John H. Williams*, New York, Macmillan, 1951.

[3] See M. Friedman, *A Theory of the Consumption Function*, New York, National Bureau of Economic Research, 1955; F. Modigliani and R. Brumberg, "Utility Analysis and the Consumption Function — An Interpretation of Cross-Section Data", in K.K. Kurihara (ed.) *Post-Keynesian Economics*, New Brunswick, N.J., Rutgers University Press, 1954; R. Brumberg, "An Approximation to the Aggregate Savings Function", *Economic Journal*, Vol. 66, 1956, pp. 66-72.

less of their disposable income. However, given their level of disposable income, once they hold the desired level of liquid wealth the opposite will be true; they will tend to spend more and save less out of current disposable income. Insofar as individuals have in mind some desired ratio of liquid wealth to disposable income, they may, after an increase in income spend proportionately less until the desired ratio is again attained.

If individuals are not suffering from money illusion, they will view their liquid wealth from the point of view of its real value, its purchasing power, rather than its nominal amount. Thus changes in prices will change individuals' desire for a certain amount of real liquid wealth and will affect their consumption and saving pattern. Let us assume, for example, that there is an increase in the price level. The value of physical assets and stocks usually increases along with the price level. But the value of financial assets such as cash, savings deposits, life insurance policies and government savings bonds, all of which have a fixed nominal value does not change. With an increase in the price level the purchasing power of these liquid assets will tend to decrease. Insofar as individuals are more concerned with the real value of their liquid assets than with their physical assets, an increase in the price level will induce them to reduce their consumption expenditures in order to build back any decline in the real value of their financial assets.

The Rate of Interest. The rate of interest may affect consumption demand directly or only indirectly through its effect on saving. Insofar as consumers borrow to purchase goods and services, credit conditions will influence their consumption demand. When interest rates decline consumers may be induced to borrow and satisfy a consumption demand now rather than wait until later. Although consumers are often unaware of how much interest they are paying when making instalment loans, interest payments affect the size of the monthly payments and hence purchases. During periods when the banks are loaned up and money is scarce some borrowers who are prepared to borrow at existing interest rates are unable to do so because those who were considered better credit risks were given first consideration. When the banks' cash position improves, along with that of other lenders, credit is again made available to borrowers considered to be poorer credit risks. In other words, not only the price of credit but also its availability may affect consumption demand.

In Chapter 22 we observed the relationship between the market rate of interest and bond prices. A change in the market rate of interest is accompanied by a change in the opposite direction in the value of existing bonds. Thus when the rate of interest declines consumers holding a large proportion of their liquid wealth in form of bonds may consider themselves wealthier. As a result they may increase their consumption demand. The opposite, of course, may be the case when market interest rates rise. The wealth effect following a change in the rate of interest is similar to that following a change in the price level discussed earlier.

We have said that the rate of interest may also affect consumption indirectly through its effect on consumer saving. Since interest is paid to savers to compensate them for giving up current consumption, the higher the interest return the more they will be induced to save. If they save more they will of course be able to consume less out of current income. A rise in the rate of interest may, however, also affect saving and consumption in the opposite direction. Some people accumulate financial assets in order to be able to obtain a specific amount of income in the future from the return provided by their financial assets. If the market rate of interest increases it follows that they will require a smaller amount of financial assets to obtain the desired amount of future income. Hence with a rise in the rate of interest they need to save less and are able to consume more of their current income.

Economists believe that in general a rise in the rate of interest tends to increase savings and lower consumption. Alternatively, a decrease in the rate of interest tends to discourage saving and increase consumption. The degree of the relationship between the rate of interest and saving and consumption is, however, still in doubt.

Social Customs and Attitudes Toward Saving. Not so many years ago saving was considered a virtue next to godliness and cleanliness and borrowing for purposes of consumption a sin to be avoided. This attitude has gradually changed and borrowing to consume beyond what is ordinarily allowed by the level of current disposable income has become an important way of life. In large part this has been the result of the introduction of new products, especially consumer durables.

The introduction of government pension schemes as well as the provision of pension plans by business and non-government institutions has also produced significant changes in the community's attitudes toward spending and saving.

The Composition of the Population. For any given aggregate disposable income, the younger the population, the larger the portion spent for consumption purposes. The older the population, generally, the less the need to purchase durable consumer goods, and also the less the need to save.

If the population is relatively young its level of education may also influence its pattern of spending and saving. People with college educations probably save very little because they expect their incomes to rise. Furthermore, professional and business people save less than unskilled workers who have little prospect for increasing their incomes significantly.

Distribution of Income. Keynes observed that the very rich save a larger proportion of their income than the poor. The larger the proportion of income going to high income groups with already high living standards, the less is spent on basic consumption goods, and therefore the greater the tendency to save a large proportion of additional income.

Expectations. If individuals expect prices to rise they may increase their consumpion demand out of current income before the purchasing power of their income declines. If they expect their income to rise in the future, they may also be inclined to spend a larger proportion of their income than they would if they anticipated no change or a fall in income. Moreover, if individuals expect that goods may become scarce in the future, say because they anticipate war, they will spend a larger than usual proportion of their current income to stock up.

The Saving and Consumption Equation

The determinants of saving and consumption which we have listed may be included under four main categories: disposable income Y_d; consumers' wealth *W*; the rate of interest *i*; and all other determinants *U*. From these factors we can formulate two equations, one for personal saving.

$$S_p = f_s (Y_d, i, W, U) \tag{6}$$

and one for personal consumption

$$C_d = f_c (Y_d, i, W, U) \tag{6a}$$

From our previous discussion we can interpret these equations. If *U* remains constant, the rate of saving increases with a rise in disposable income, or a rise in the rate of interest, or a decrease in consumers' wealth. Alternatively, consumption increases with an increase in disposable income, a fall in the rate of interest and an increase in consumers' wealth. The relationship between saving and disposable income as well as saving and the rate of interest is positive while the relationship between saving and consumer wealth is inverse.

In Figure 24-2 we show diagramatically the relationship between saving and income. The vertical axis in the figure measures planned personal saving and the horizontal axis income. Instead of showing saving as a function of disposable income we show it as a function of gross national product, as this will simplify our discussion in its later stages. Insofar as Y_d and *Y* have historically moved in an almost parallel fashion, our use of *Y* rather than Y_d will not distort our overall analysis. The saving function in Figure 24-2 shows the relationship between saving and income assuming that the *i*, *W*, and *U* variables in equation *(6)* remain constant. At a later stage we shall discuss the implications of this assumption.

Figure 24-2

Business Saving

In our earlier discussion of the concept of national income we said that business saving may be considered to be synonomous with the disposable income of business. Business saving is the result of moneys set aside as capital consumption allowances — that is, as depreciation and other allowances for declines in the value of capital goods — and the result of moneys retained by corporations as undistributed after-tax profits. The most important determinant of these two types of business saving is probably the level of income. As the level of income increases or as businesses expect the level to increase they are probably inclined to increase their saving. Other important factors which influence business saving include government taxes, corporate dividend policies and corporate policies with respect to capital consumption allowances. The latter may be either directly or only indirectly affected by government policies.

In equation form business saving is expressed as:

$$S_b = f_b(Y, U_l) \tag{7}$$

where Y is gross national income, and U_l represents all the other factors which we have mentioned as influencing business saving. Assuming U_l to remain constant the relation between business saving and income is shown by the S_bS_b curve in Figure 24-3. The curve is drawn to show that business plan to increase their saving proportionately with every increase in the level of income.

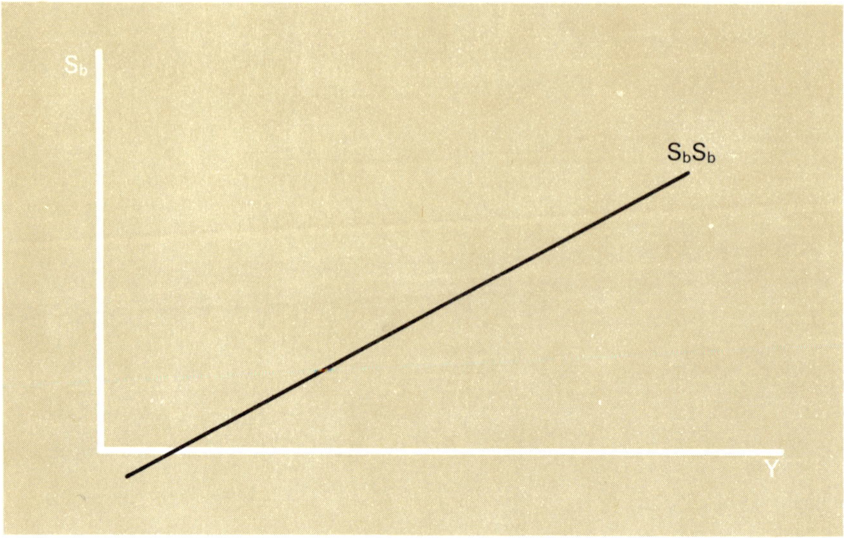

Figure 24-3

Government Taxes

An equation explaining the amount of government tax receipts may be expressed as:

$$T = f_t (Y, Z) \tag{8}$$

where Y is the level of income and Z represents all those factors which influence legislatures in formulating their tax policies. Included in Z are the nation's demands for governmental goods and services, and the government's debt policies. In Figure 24-4 we assume Z to remain constant as given and draw the tax curve TT showing the relationship between tax receipts and the level of gross national product. The curve slopes up from left to right indicating that taxes increase as income increases. For simplicity we have also drawn it to pass through the origin indicating that tax collections are a constant proportion of changes in income. The position of the curve is determined by all those factors represented by Z.

Imports

Goods and services produced by foreigners are imported by households, business and government. In our earlier discussion of household consumption demand we included both the demand for domestic production and the demand for foreign goods and services. Thus, following our earlier discussion we can say that the demand for imports by households is determined by the level of disposable income Y_d (or the level of income

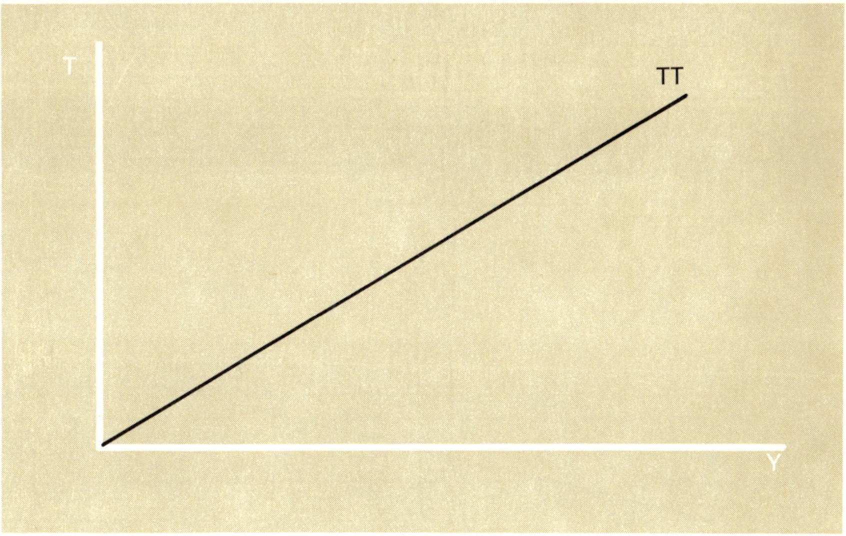

Figure 24-4

Y), the rate of interest *i,* as well as a host of other factors U_2. Similarly, the factors which explain business investment also explain the demand by business for imports. In a subsequent section we shall show that the major determinants of business investment are the rate of interest *i,* the level of income *Y,* and other factors U_3, which include changes in technology, cost expectations and business psychology. The government's demand for imports is more difficult to define but generally may be said to depend upon the availabiltiy of goods and services produced domestically. The price differential between foreign and domestic goods and services influences the demand of all three sectors for imports.

For simplicity we shall assume that the nation's demand for imports is determined by gross national income *Y,* the rate of interest *i,* and all other factors which are represented by U_2. Thus the equation for the demand for imports is

$$M = f_m (Y, i, U_2) \qquad (9)$$

If U_2 remains constant, we may assume that the import rate increases with a rise in gross national product and a decline in the rate of interest.[4] In Figure 24-5 we assume *i* and U_2 to remain constant and draw an im-

4 This relationship between imports and the rate of interest is oversimplified in that it assumes that capital flows are insensitive to interest rate differentials. If Canadian interest rates decline relative to those in other countries we may expect capital outflows. This may lead to a reduction in the value of the Canadian dollar in terms of foreign currencies. The consequent "price effect" may discourage imports into Canada from abroad. Hence in this case, a decline in the rate of interest in Canada may lead to a reduction in imports.

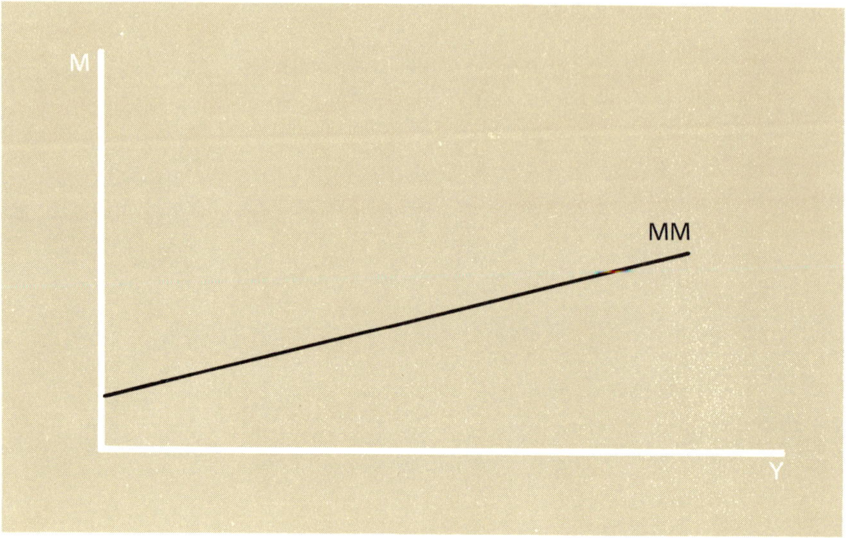

Figure 24-5

port curve MM showing the relationship between total imports and the level of gross national income. The curve does not pass through the origin at o because at zero gross national income some imports may still be bought and paid for from a nation's reserves, either actual or borrowed.

The (S_p + S_b + T + M) Curve

In Figure 24-6 we have drawn separate curves showing the relationship among personal saving, business saving, taxes, imports and gross national income. By adding these curves to each other vertically we derive the total curve $(S_p + S_b + T + M)$. This curve, shown in Figure 24-6 tells us the expected total of S_p, S_b, T and M at various levels of income.

The $(S_p + S_b + T + M)$ curve will shift with changes in the determinants (other than Y) of S_p, S_b, T and M which we noted earlier. Some examples are listed below.

The $S_p S_p$ curve may shift upward for a variety of reasons, such as a rise in the price level which reduces the real value of consumers' wealth holdings, a rise in the interest rate which may also reduce the value of consumers' wealth holdings because of the decline in the market price of their bond holdings, a rise in the interest rate which induces consumers to reduce their purchases on consumer goods and hence to save more, and a change in the community's attitude toward thrift and so on. With an upward shift in the S_pS_p curve the $(S_p + S_b + T + M)$ curve will also shift upward by an equal amount.

A shift in the MM curve will also cause an equal shift in the $(S_p + S_b + T + M)$ curve. Movements in the MM curve may occur as a result of such factors as a change in consumers' real wealth holdings, a change in

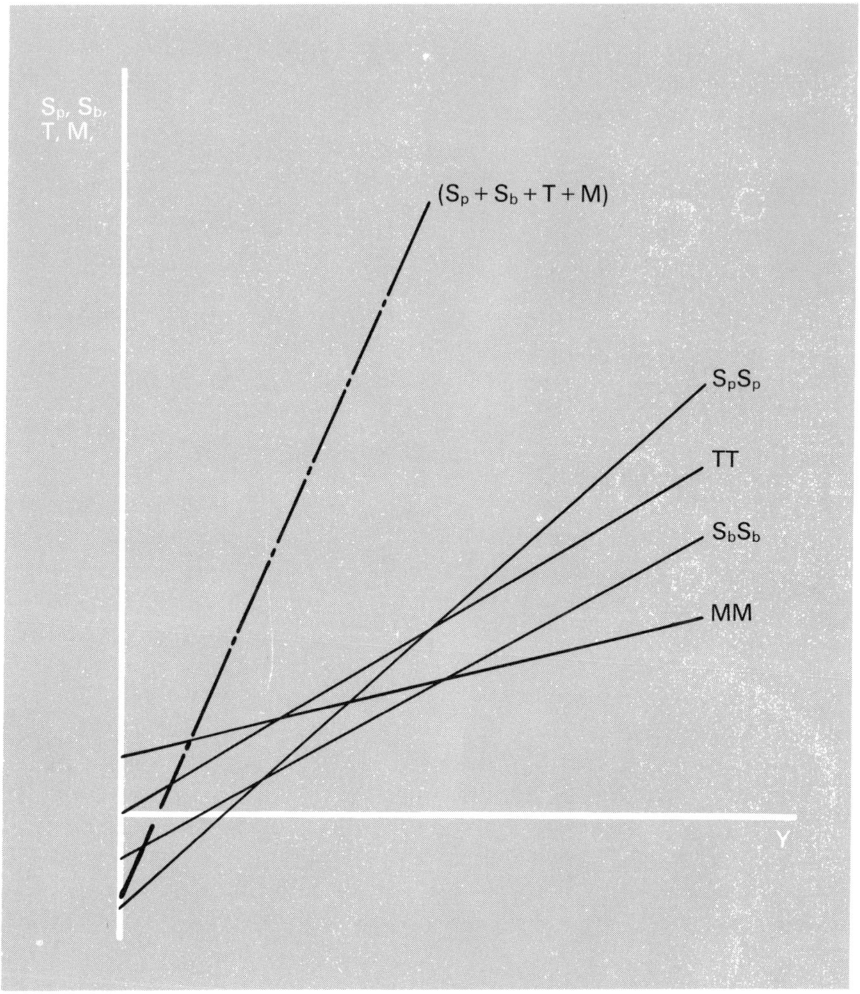

Figure 24-6

the rate of interest, a change in the price differential between domestic and foreign goods, and a change in the community's preference for foreign goods.

A shift in either the S_bS_b or TT curve is not accompanied by a shift of equal amount in the $(S_p + S_b + T + M)$ curve. If business decides to save more at each level of income, the S_bS_b curve shifts upward. If business decides to effect this saving by retaining more dividends, personal disposable income will fall by the amount that business increases its saving. Personal saving will fall but not by the same amount as personal disposable income because the decline in personal disposable income will lead not only to a decline in personal saving but to a decline in consumer demand as well. The amount of the downward shift in the S_pS_p curve following an upward shift in the S_bS_b curve will depend upon the marginal propensity to save. Since this is usually assumed to be less than one the S_pS_p curve will not shift downward by as much as the S_bS_b initially shifted upward. Thus an upward shift in the S_bS_b curve accompanied by a smaller downward shift in the S_pS_p curve will result in an upward shift in the $(S_p + S_p + T + M)$ curve which is less than the initial upward shift in the S_bS_b curve.

If the government increases its tax receipts by an equal amount at each level of oncome this will be reflected by an upward shift in the TT curve. Insofar as an increase in government taxes reduces the disposable income of both business and households an upward shift in the TT curve is accompanied by a downward shift in the S_bS_b and S_pS_p curves. While the S_bS_b curve will shift downward by an amount equal to the reduction in business disposable income, the S_pS_p curve will shift downward as we noted earlier by an amount which is less than the decline in personal disposable income. Therefore, the net effect of an increase in government tax receipts at each level of income is an upward shift in the $(S_b + S_p + T + M)$ curve which is less than the initial upward shift in the TT curve.

As income increases business may decide to increase its saving and government may increase the *tax rate.* In the first case, instead of an upward shift all along the S_bS_b curve, there will be only an upward turn. Similarly, with an increase in the tax rate the TT curve will not shift but only turn upwards. An initial upward turn in the S_bS_b curve will be accompanied by an upward turn in the $(S_p + S_b + T + M)$ curve. But as in our previous analysis this curve will turn upward less sharply than the S_bS_b curve did. This follows from our previous analysis. The same is true for an upward turn in the TT curve following an increase in the tax rate.

Although we have analyzed only an upward shift or turn in the individual curves, a similar analysis follows an initial downward shift or turn in any one of these curves.

THE DETERMINANTS OF (I_d + G_d + X)

Gross Domestic Investment

Gross private domestic investment consists of three main types of investment expenditures — those for plant and equipment, those for residential construction, and those which comprise desired net increases in business inventories. We shall assume that most of the nation's investment is in the form of capital assets such as productive plants and equipment and that the determinants of this type of investment apply in general to other types of investment.

Investment expenditures will be undertaken as long as the *expected* benefits from a proposed investment exceeds its costs. The costs of undertaking an investment are generally considered to be the market rate of interest that has to be paid to provide the funds to acquire a capital asset or to undertake a capital project. Where a firm does not go to the market to borrow the required funds but uses its own funds the costs may be considered in terms of the alternative opportunities foregone — the interest rate sacrificed by using the money itself rather than by lending it to others.

Economists usually analyze the expected benefits from investment in terms of the **marginal efficiency of capital** which is the expected *rate* of return on the original purchase price or cost of a proposed investment calculated over the entire life of the investment. It may be thought of as a rate of discount which when used to discount the expected net returns gives a value equal to the present purchase price or cost of a proposed investment.

A business firm can calculate the marginal efficiency of a capital asset if it knows the cost of acquiring the asset and the expected annual net return after all costs except interest charges from the productive use of the asset. For example, let us assume that P is the cost of the asset and R_1, R_2, R_3, ... R_n the annual expected net returns in each year 1, 2, 3... n. The marginal efficiency of the capital asset r, can be calculated using a standard discount formula.

$$P = \frac{R_1}{(1+r)} + \frac{R_2}{(1+r)^2} + \frac{R_3}{(1+r)^3} \cdots + \frac{R_n}{(1+r)^n}$$

Suppose that a business firm can acquire a capital asset for $4,800 which has a productive life of three years after which time it has no value, not even scrap value. During the first year of its productive life the asset provides the firm with a net return of $1,050, during the second year $882 and during the third year $3,473. When substituting these values into the formula we find that the marginal efficiency of the capital asset is 5 per cent.

$$\$4{,}800 = \frac{\$1{,}050}{(1 + .05)} + \frac{\$882}{(1 + .05)^2} + \frac{\$3{,}473}{(1 + .05)^3}$$

Whether a firm will undertake a proposed investment depends upon the cost of acquiring the funds needed (the market rate of interest) and the expected net rate of return from the investment over its lifetime (the marginal efficiency of capital). Investment expenditures will be pushed to the level at which the marginal efficiency of capital equals the market rate of interest.

Diagram (a) of Figure 24-7 shows a nation's marginal efficiency of capital schedule. The vertical axis of the diagram measures the marginal efficiency of capital (MEC) and the horizontal axis the volume of investment. The *MEC* schedule slopes downward from left to right indicating that MEC varies inversely with the volume of investment. Two reasons explain this relationship. First, each addition to the capital stock increases the existing amount of this stock. As the stock increases each addition will receive more competition from the existing stock which will decrease the expected returns from additions. Second, with an increased amount of investment the marginal cost of producing capital goods may increase. Given the expected net return, any increase in the present cost of a capital asset will decrease its marginal efficiency.

Given the *MEC* curve we still do not know the total amount of invest-

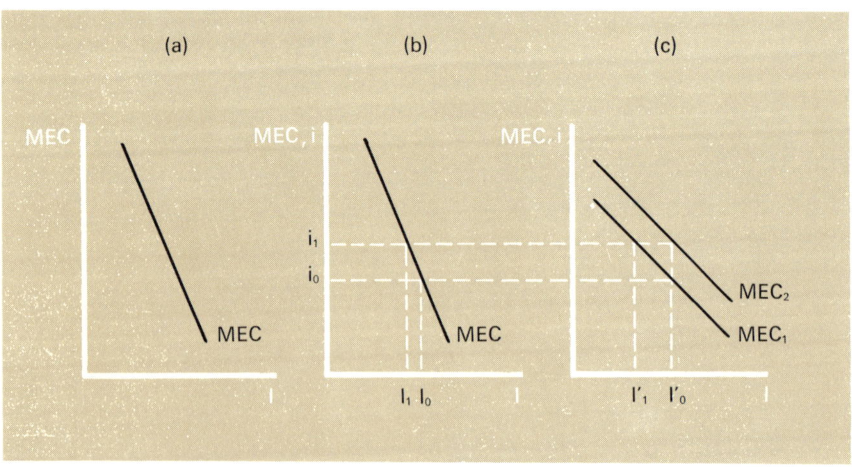

Figure 24-7

ment that the economy will undertake at any given time. To know this we must also know the market rate of interest. We noted earlier that investment will proceed up to the point where the MEC of the last unit of investment is equal to the market rate of interest. This is illustrated in the Diagram (b) of Figure 24-7.

The diagram is similar in every respect to Diagram (a) except that the vertical axis now measures not only the MEC but also the market rate of interest i. The *MEC* curve can now also be considered an investment demand function. When the market rate of interest is i_o the total amount of investment undertaken is I_o. When the rate of interest rises to i_l the level of investment decreases from I_o *to* I_l. Or alternatively, when the rate of interest falls from i_l to i_o the level of investment increases from I_l to I_o.

The sensitivity of investment expenditures to changes in the rate of interest depends upon the slope of the *MEC* curve—that is, the investment function. Although economists generally agree that the investment function slopes downward from left to right, there is considerable disagreement as to how rapidly it falls (how great is its elasticity). If it slopes quite steeply (if it is relatively inelastic) large fluctuations in the rate of interest are required to induce changes in the level of investment. On the other hand if its slope is quite flat (relatively elastic) small fluctuations in the rate of interest produce large changes in the level of investment. These points are illustrated in Diagrams (b) and (c) of Figure 24-7. With a change in the rate of interest from i_o to i_l, in Diagram (b) where the investment function is relatively inelastic the change in the level of investment is only from I_o to I_l, whereas in Diagram (c) where the investment function is relatively elastic the change in the level of investment is from I'_o to I'_l.

Even if we assume that the investment function is elastic, a change in the market rate of interest may leave the level of investment unaltered. This will be the case if a change in the rate of interest is accompanied by a shift in the *MEC* curve. For example in Diagram (c), a rise in the rate of interest from i_o to i_l is accompanied by a shift in the *MEC* curve from MEC_l to MEC_2. As a result the level of investment remains at I'_o where it was before the rate of interest rose. Our example is, of course, the extreme case; shifts in the *MEC* curve need not swamp the effects on investment of interest rate changes. At times the shifts may actually strengthen the effects of a change in the rate of interest on investment.

The height or position of the *MEC* curve and shifts in it may be explained by such factors as the level of income and its expected change, cost expectations, changes in technology and the state of business psychology. This however is not a complete list of the factors which determine the marginal efficiency of capital and therefore the level of investment.

The Level of Income and its Expected Change. The expected gross revenue from a proposed investment depends upon the anticipated sales of its ouput. A businessman has no way of estimating his future sales with certainty. One of his best guides, however, is probably the current level of gross national income and its level in the recent past. If he expects income to increase in the future and if he estimates that the present stock of capital equipment is insufficient to meet the increased demand for output, he will be inclined to expand his capital investments.

Cost Expectations. Earlier we showed that one of the magnitudes required to calculate the marginal efficiency of capital is the expected net return from an investment. Net revenue is calculated by deducting costs from gross revenue. These costs include labour, material and government taxes. If business entrepreneurs expect labour unions to press for higher wages in the future, or the cost of raw materials to increase, or tax rates to rise, they will expect their net return and therefore the marginal efficiency of capital to be lower. As a result, given the cost of obtaining investment funds, they will tend to reduce planned investment expenditures.

Technology. If innovations are being made fairly rapidly, new products are being developed as well as new and more efficient methods of production. The development of new products often provides a need for new plant and equipment to produce the new goods. A new process which permits lower costs of production to one producer often forces his competitors to follow suit, thereby causing a new wave of investment expenditures.

State of Business Psychology. Economic trends are highly unpredictable. Even with the indicators now available, those planning capital investment are left to guess the outcome. Their prognostications will be influenced by the opinions and anticipations of their equally uncertain fellows. As one might expect, waves of optimism and pessimism are the result. Unfortunately much too often during periods of optimism rates of return on future investments are badly overestimated while during periods of pessimism they are badly underestimated.

The Investment Demand Equation

We have said that investment is determined by the market rate of interest and the marginal efficiency of capital and that the latter is determined by among other things gross national income, cost expectations, technology and the state of business psychology. For simplicity we shall show these determinants as i the rate of interest, Y the level of income and U_3 all other factors which determine the demand for investment. In equation form, we have

$$I_d = f_I(i, Y, U_3)$$

From our previous discussion we can say that the relationship between interest and investment is inverse, and the relationship between income and investment, and between investment and all the other factors which we have considered is positive. If we now assume that i and U_3 remain constant as given we can show the relationship between income and investment diagramatically as is done in Figure 24-8. Investment demand I_d is measured on the vertical axis and gross national income Y, on the horizontal axis. The I_dI_d curve is drawn to show that the higher the level of income, the greater the investment demand.

Government Expenditures

The second component in $(I_d + G_d + X)$ is government expenditures, including those made by all three levels of government. While the federal government meets exclusively the costs for national defence, it shares in varying degrees almost all other governmental expenditures with the other

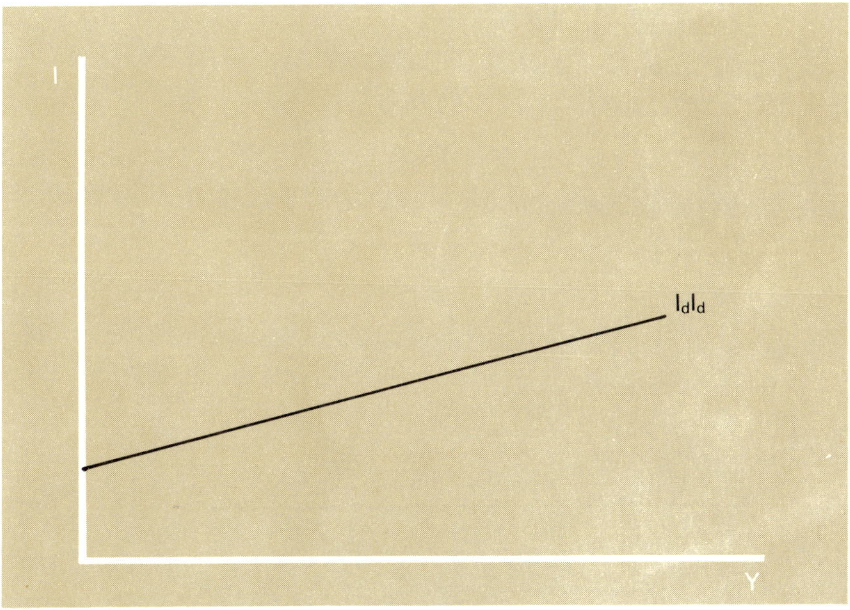

Figure 24-8

levels of government, especially with the provincial governments. Government expenditures are determined by legislative action, a practice which is an inherent part of our democratic system. The determinants of this action are many and varied. We shall represent them by the symbol *Z* and express the equation for government expenditures as

$$G_d = f_g(Z) \tag{11}$$

We use the *Z* symbol because we assumed that the factors which determine the amount of government taxes are the same as those which determine the amount of government expenditures. In Figure 24-9 we have drawn a government expenditure curve. It is drawn parallel to the horizontal axis since we assume that government spending is independent of the level of gross national income. The height or position of the curve depends upon *Z*, the factors which influence legislative action.

Exports

Like government expenditures, the demand for Canadian goods and serv-

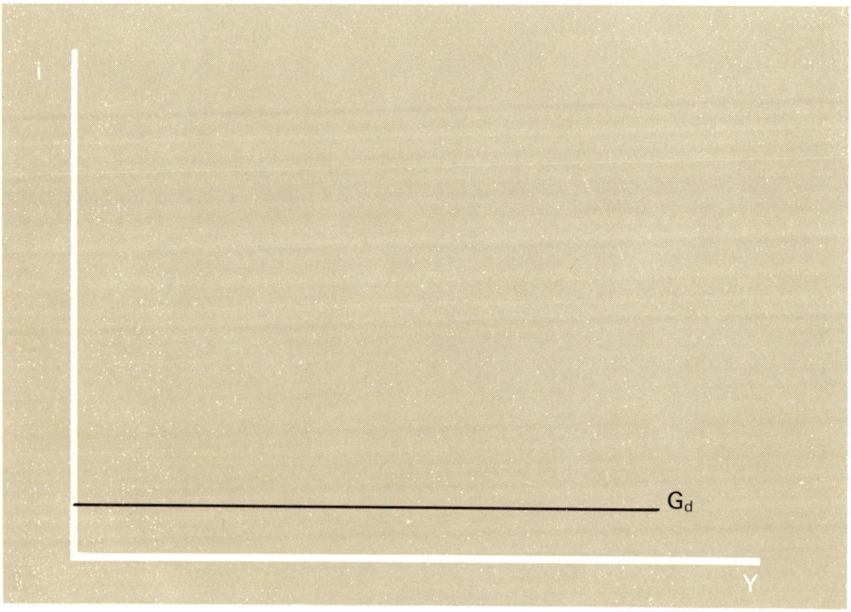

Figure 24-9

Figure 24-10

ices by foreigners, X, is not determined by Canada's gross national income.[5] The demand for its exports depends upon the price differential between Canadian and foreign goods, the preference by foreigners for Canadian goods rather than their own, the requirement by foreigners for Canada's natural resources, the level of foreign incomes, foreign import restrictions and the availability of Canadian dollars or credit to pay for Canadian goods and services. These are only some of the determinants of the demand for Canadian goods by foreigners. If we let F represent all the determinants of exports, the equation for the demand for exports may be written as

$$X = f_x(F) \tag{12}$$

In Figure 24-10 the export expenditure curve is drawn parallel to the horizontal axis indicating that Canadian export expenditures are independent of the level of income in Canada. The height or position of the XX curve depends upon F, the factors which we have considered to influence export demand.

---

5 This is not quite true. Insofar as our exports sales depend upon our imports from foreigners which are determined by our level of income, our exports may indirectly depend upon our level of income.

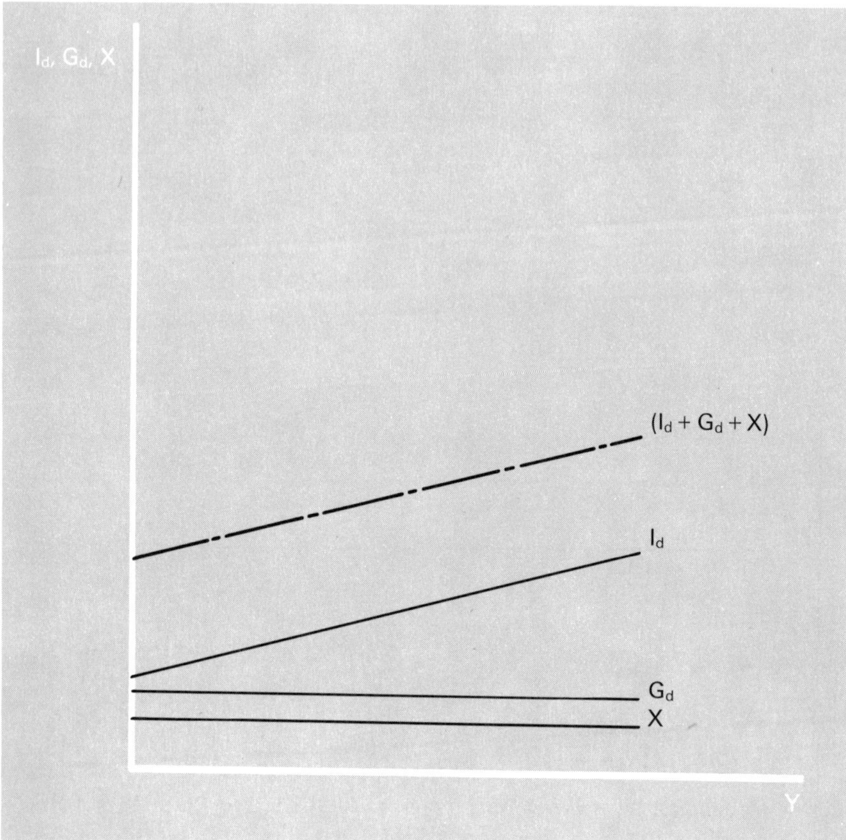

Figure 24-11

The (I_d + G_d + X) Curve

By adding together vertically the individual I_d, G_d and X curves as is done in Figure 24-11, we derive the total $(I_d + G_d + X)$ curve. This curve will shift with a shift of any one of the three curves from which it is derived. Shifts in any one of these three curves result from changes in their determinants which we have listed, other than the level of income.

THE (S_p + S_b + T + M) AND (I_d + G_d + X) CURVES

The level of income is determined, as is shown in Figure 24-12, at the point of intersection of the $(S_p + S_b + T + M)$ and $(I_d + G_d + X)$ curves. Where these two curves intersect the planned expenditures on $(I_d + G_d + X)$ are equated to the planned withdrawals $(S_p + S_b + T + M)$ from the income stream. If the economy is producing at Y_1 instead of Y_o (the point of intersection of the two curves), planned expenditures on $(I_d + G_d + X)$ exceed the planned withdraw-

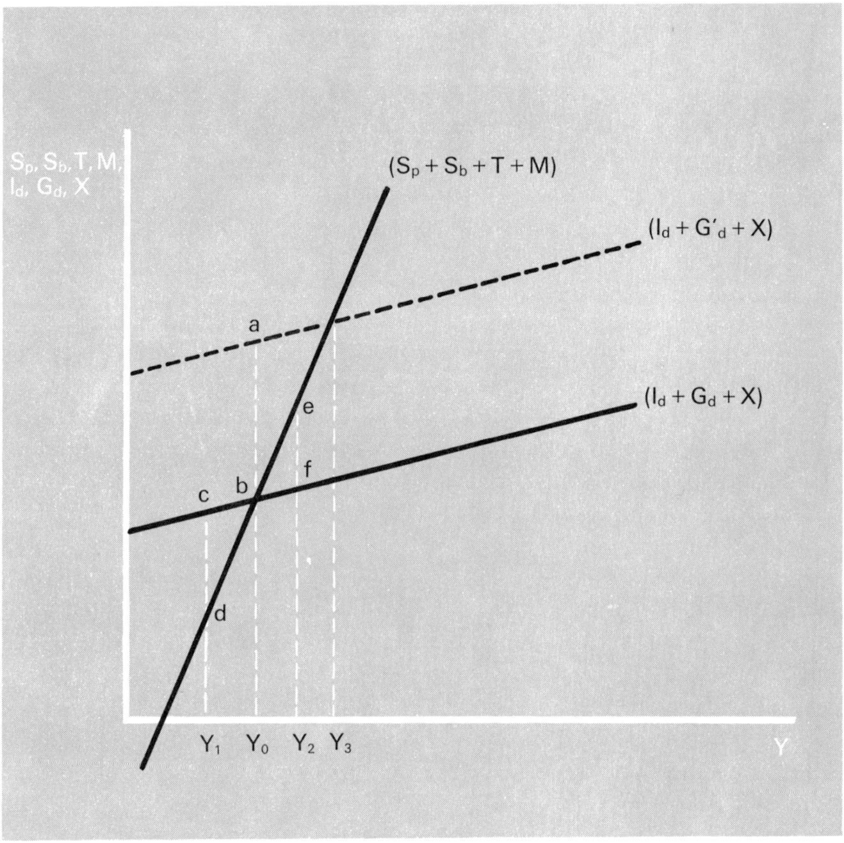

Figure 24-12

als $(S_p + S_b + T + M)$ from the income stream. Since more goods in the amount of *cd* are wanted than are being produced, the demand will be met by running down inventories and business will be induced to expand output. As business increases production, incomes expand and the economy moves toward the equilibrium level of income Y_o.

If, on the other hand, the economy is producing at Y_2, planned withdrawals from the income stream $(S_p + S_b + T + M)$ exceed expenditures on $(I_d + G_d + X)$ by *ef*. Business will now have to accumulate inventories, a process we referred to earlier as involuntary investment. Business will react by reducing its production, incomes will fall, and the economy will move toward the equilibrium level Y_o.

THE INCOME MULTIPLIER AND SHIFTS IN THE CURVES

In the previous section we looked at the determination of income assuming that the $(S_p + S_b + T + M)$ and $(I_d + G_d + X)$ curves remained constant as given. That is to say, we assumed that only the level of income directly determined the separate magnitudes comprising these curves while all other determinants remained constant. We have already noted that if the relationship changes between these magnitudes and their determinants other than the level of income, the curves will shift or turn. Let us suppose that the government increases its expenditures at each level of income, and the $G_d G_d$ curve in Figure 24-11 shifts upward as does the $(I_d + G_d + X)$ curve. The latter curve, as is shown in Figure 24-12, shifts upward by an amount equal to *ab*. As a result income increases from Y_o to Y_3. This increase in income is larger than the autonomous increase in government expenditures shown by the shift equal to *ab* of the $(I_d + G_d + X)$ function. Why does the level of income increase more than the initial autonomous increase in government expenditures? We assumed that before the increase in government expenditures income or output was at its equilibrium level. Total production was voluntarily purchased by the economic units. Under these conditions any increase in government demand must be satisfied by a reduction in inventories. With an unplanned reduction in their inventories businesses will be induced to expand production thus increasing income. But by how much can we expect the level of income to increase? The increase in income will depend upon the total leakages from the income stream. The leakage from each additional dollar of income is shown by the slope of the $(S_p + S_b + T + M)$ curve. The flatter this curve the larger the change in income from a shift of the $(I_d + G_d + X)$ curve: The steeper this curve the smaller the change in income from the shift. The slope of the $(S_p + S_b + T + M)$ curve can be expressed as

$$\frac{\triangle S_p}{\triangle Y} + \frac{\triangle S_b}{\triangle Y} + \frac{\triangle T}{\triangle Y} + \frac{\triangle M}{\triangle Y} \text{ or } \frac{\triangle(S_p + S_b + T + M)}{\triangle Y}$$

Where

$\frac{\triangle S_p}{\triangle Y}$ represents household marginal propensity to save,

$\frac{\triangle S_b}{\triangle Y}$ business marginal propensity to save,

$\frac{\triangle T}{\triangle Y}$ the amount of each additional dollar of income leaked out of the income stream in the form of government taxes, and

$\frac{\triangle M}{\triangle Y}$ the marginal propensity to import.

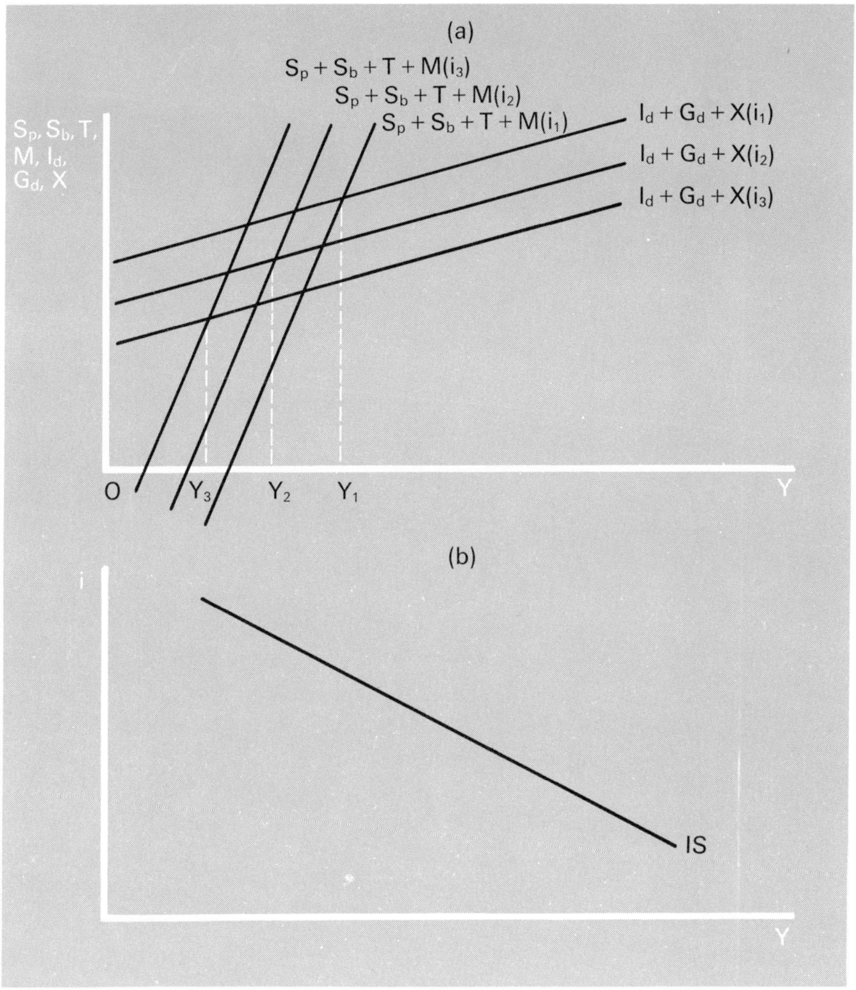

Figure 24-13

The change in income following autonomous change in government expenditures can be shown as

$$\triangle G \bullet \frac{1}{\frac{\triangle S_p}{\triangle Y} + \frac{\triangle S_b}{\triangle Y} + \frac{\triangle T}{\triangle Y} + \frac{\triangle M}{\triangle Y}} = \triangle Y$$

The fraction by which government expenditures must be multiplied to derive the consequent change in income is called the **income multiplier.** The income multiplier — that is the reciprocal of the slope of the (S_p+S_b+T+M) curve — may be used to explain the effect of any shift in either direction of the (I_d+G_d+X) curve. Such shifts, as we have already mentioned, are the result of movements in the I_dI_d, G_dG_d and XX curves.

INTEREST RATE CHANGES AND INCOME DETERMINATION

In the theory of income determination which we have developed so far we have shown that changes in autonomous expenditures produce changes in the level of income by an amount equal to the income multiplier times the changes in these expenditures. This oversimplified explanation assumes that the rate of interest remains constant. The rate of interest can be explicitly included in our theory of income determination insofar as personal saving and domestic investment are a function of interest rate changes. We noted earlier that personal saving varies positively and domestic investment inversely with the rate of interest. Thus for each successively higher rate of interest we can draw successively higher S_pS_p curves and successively lower I_dI_d curves. Moreover for each successively higher rate of interest we can draw successively higher $(S_p + S_b + T + M)$ curves and successively lower $(I_d + G_d + X)$ curves. This is done in Diagram (a) of Figure 24-13 where successively higher rates of interest are shown as i_1, i_2 and i_3. The diagram shows that there is an inverse relationship between the rate of interest and the equilibrium level of income: the higher the rate of interest the lower the equilibrium level of income. This relationship is explained by our assumptions that as interest rates increase the S_pS_p curve and therefore the $(S_p + S_b + T + M)$ curve shift upward while the I_dI_d curve and therefore the $(I_d + G_d + X)$ curve shift downward. Thus, the two curves intersect at a lower level of income.

The relationship between the rate of interest and the level of income is summarized by the *IS* curve in Diagram (b) of Figure 24-13. This curve can be considered to show equilibrium in the commodity market in that planned expenditures for $I_d + G_d + X$ equal planned $S_p + S_b + T + M$ at any point on the curve; the desired total demand for a nation's output is just equal to the production plans of business. At any point to the left of the *IS* curve there exists excess demand which businesses will satisfy by increasing output and therefore income. At any point to the right of the *IS* curve there exists excess supply which will lead to a contraction of output and income.

SELECTED READINGS

Ackley, Gardner, *Macroeconomic Theory*, New York, Macmillan, 1961.

Dernburg, Thomas F., and Duncan M. McDougall, *Macro-Economics*, 2nd ed., New York, McGraw-Hill, 1963.

Dewey, Donald, *Modern Capital Theory*, New York, Columbia University Press, 1965.

Dillard, Dudley, *The Economics of John Maynard Keynes*, New York, Prentice-Hall, 1948.

Duesenberry, James S., *Income, Saving and the Theory of Consumer Behaviour*, Cambridge, Mass., Harvard University Press, 1949.

Duesenberry, James S., *Business Cycles and Economic Growth*, New York, McGraw-Hill, 1958.

Ferber, Robert, "Research on Household Behaviour", *American Economic Review*, Vol. 52, March, 1962, pp. 19-63, reprinted in *Surveys of Economic Theory*, Vol. 3, London, Macmillan, 1967, pp. 114-154.

Hamburger, Michael, "Interest Rates and the Demand for Consumer Durable Goods", *American Economic Review*, Vol. 57, December, 1967, pp. 1131-1153.

Hansen, Alvin H., *A Guide to Keynes*, New York, McGraw-Hill, 1953.

Hansen, Alvin H., *Business Cycles and National Income*, expanded ed., New York, W. W. Norton, 1964, Ch. 11.

Keynes, J. M., *General Theory of Employment, Interest and Money*, New York, Macmillan, 1936, Ch. 8 to 13.

Klein, Lawrence, *A Textbook on Econometrics*, Evanston, Ill., Row Peterson and Company, 1953, Ch. 3.

Kurihara, Kenneth, *Introduction to Keynesian Dynamics*, London, George Allen & Unwin, 1956.

McKenna, Joseph P., *Aggregate Economic Analysis*, rev. ed., New York, Holt, Rinehart and Winston, 1965.

Mueller, M. G. (ed.), *Readings in Macroeconomics*, New York, Holt, Rinehart and Winston, 1966.

Samuelson, Paul, "The Simple Mathematics of Income Determination", in *Income, Employment and Public Policy: Essays in Honor of Alvin Hansen*, New York, McGraw-Hill, 1948.

25 EQUILIBRIUM IN MONEY AND PRODUCT MARKETS

In previous chapters we developed a theory of equilibrium in the money market and a theory of income determination. In Chapter 23 we observed that there are many combinations of the rate of interest and the level of income at which the demand for money is just equal to the actual money supply. We showed these equilibrium combinations of the interest rate and the level of income in terms of the *LM* curve. This curve was drawn to slope upward from left to right to indicate that higher levels of income must be accompanied by higher rates of interest to provide equilibrium in the money market. In Chapter 24 we observed that different rates of interest are associated with different equilibrium levels of income. We showed the combinations between the rate of interest and the equilibrium level of income at which planned $I_d + G_d + X$ is equal to planned $S_p + S_b + T + M$ in terms of the *IS* curve. This curve was drawn to slope downward from left to right to indicate that higher rates of interest must be accompanied by lower levels of income to provide equilibrium in the product market.

In Figure 25-1 the *LM* and *IS* curves are drawn in Diagram (a). The level of income *Y* is shown on the horizontal axis and the rate of interest *i*, on the vertical axis. The point of intersection of these two curves tells us the one combination of the rate of interest and the level of income at which there is equilibrium in both the money market and the product market. Diagrams (b) and (c) show the equilibrium conditions in the product and money market respectively that correspond with overall equilibrium conditions.

Given the *IS* and *LM* curves the equilibrium rate of interest i_e and the equilibrium level of income Y_e are simultaneously determined. Any combination of *i* and *Y* that does not provide simultaneous equilibrium in the money and product markets is accompanied by market forces which will

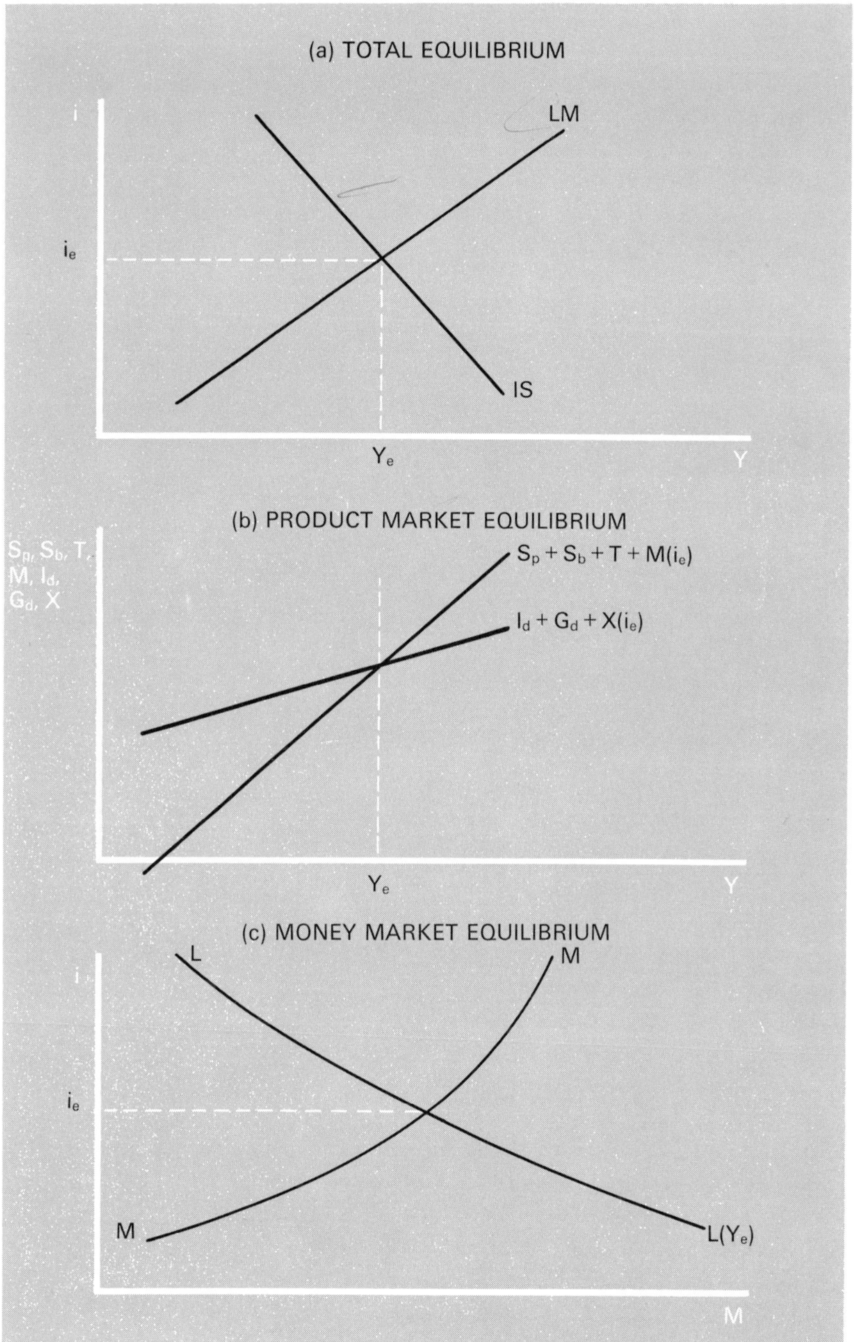
(a) TOTAL EQUILIBRIUM
i
LM
i_e
IS
Y_e
Y
(b) PRODUCT MARKET EQUILIBRIUM
S_p, S_b, T, M, I_d, G_d, X
$S_p + S_b + T + M(i_e)$
$I_d + G_d + X(i_e)$
Y_e
Y
(c) MONEY MARKET EQUILIBRIUM
L
M
i
i_e
M
$L(Y_e)$
M

Figure 25-1

move the economy toward the total equilibrium combination of i_e and Y_e. Let us illustrate this proposition.

We noted in a previous chapter that at any point above and to the left of the *LM* curve the amount of money that the community desires to hold is less than the existing stock of money. Let us call this a state of **excess supply of money.** Let us call any point below and to the right of the *LM* curve a state of **excess demand for money.** In a previous chapter we also noted that at any point below and to the left of the *IS* curve planned $I_d + G_d + X$ is larger than planned $S_p + S_b + T + M$. Let us call this a state of **excess demand in the product market.** Likewise any point above and to the right of the *IS* curve is a state of **excess supply in the product market.** In Figure 25-2 we show possible paths toward equilibrium from selected points of disequilibrium.

Equilibrium in the product market and excess supply in the money market (Point A). Holders of money will attempt to rid themselves of the excess supply by purchasing securities. Security prices then rise and the rate of interest falls. At lower rates of interest, investment is stimulated and income increases.

Thus with income expanding and the rate of interest declining, the economy moves toward equilibrium in both the money and product markets. This is shown in the figure by the path drawn from point *A*.

Excess supply in the product market and excess demand in the money market Point B). The excess supply in the product market tends to reduce income. If the excess demand for money is satisfied by the sale of securities, the consequent rise in the rate of interest will accentuate the decline in income. As income falls less money will be required for transactions purposes and more will be available for speculative purposes. Moreover at higher interest rate levels there will be a smaller demand for speculative balances. While the money market may achieve momentary equilibrium, the decline in the level of income will produce a state of excess supply in the money market. Hence with a decline in the rate of interest and the level of income the economy moves toward equilibrium in both markets. This is shown by path *I* from point *B* in Figure 25-2.

If the initial excess demand in the money market had been satisfied entirely by a reduction in expenditures, the rate of interest would not at first have increased. From the start both the rate of interest and the level of income would have fallen. This would have resulted in a move toward equilibrium from point *B* as is shown in path *II*.

Excess demand in both the product and money markets (Point C). The excess demand in the money market is satisfied by the sale of existing securities. Security prices fall and the rate of interest increases. The ex-

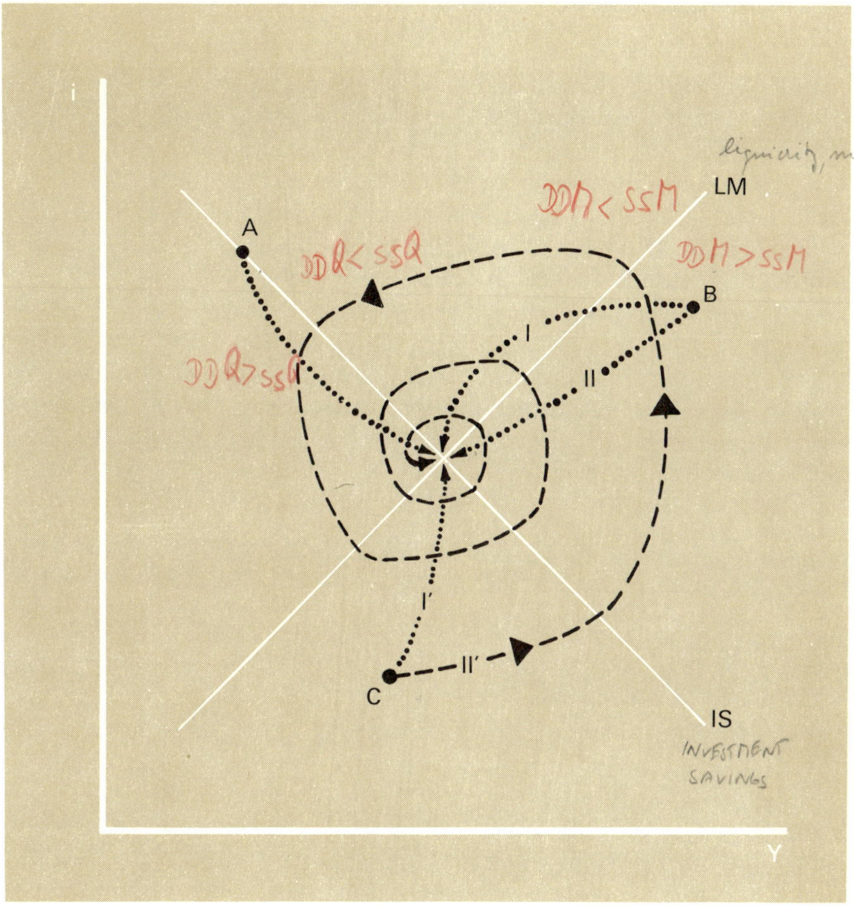

Figure 25-2

cess demand in the commodity market will initially tend to increase income but this will come to a halt as the rate of interest increases. Hence the economy moves toward equilibrium from point *C* as shown by path *I′*.

The speed at which the economy moves toward equilibrium depends upon the time it takes for adjustments in each market. If we assume that there are lags, we can expect a converging "cobweb" path toward equilibrium. This is shown in Figure 25-2 as path *II′* from point C.

MONEY MARKET CHANGES

Disturbances in equilibrium originating in the money market may be shown as shifts in the *LM* curve. Shifts in this curve may be associated with changes in the determinants of the demand for money other than the rate of interest and the level of income and with changes in the determinants of the money supply. For example, if the money supply increases as a result of the central bank increasing the monetary base, with no changes in the demand for money function, the *LM* curve shifts to the right. Also, if the money supply function remains constant and the community decides that at each given level of income and rate of interest it wants to hold smaller money balances, say because of a change in expectations or a change in payments practices, the *LM* curve again shifts to the right.

Before we consider the implications of a shift in the *LM* curve we must review and extend our earlier analysis of the shape of this curve. The shape of the *LM* curve is determined by the shapes of the demand for and the supply of money curves. To begin we shall assume a given monetary base with the banking system fully loaned up. This is shown by the perfectly vertical money supply curve M_s in Diagram (a) of Figure 25-3.

In Chapter 22 we expressed the demand for money in equation form as

$$M_d = kY + l_2(i)$$

where kY is the demand for transactions balances and k is some proportion of the level of income. The speculative demand for money is a function l_2 of the rate of interest. In Diagram (a) we have drawn a total

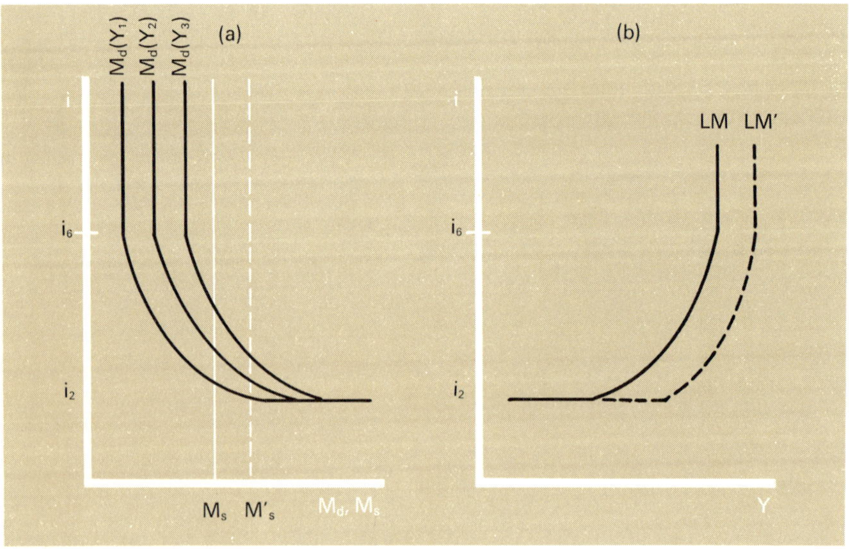

Figure 25-3

demand for money curve at various levels of income to illustrate the behaviour of the community regarding its money balances at the various levels. We assume that the amount of money desired for transactions purposes is a constant proportion of income — that is, that k remains constant. At interest rates above i_6 the left hand portion of the demand for money curve is drawn completely vertical. We assume that when the rate of interest is i_6 or higher, the interest loss from holding speculative money balances is so great and the expected risk of capital loss from a further rise in the interest rate so small that no money is held for speculative purposes. Our assumption is a special case of the more general classical assumption that money serves only as a medium of exchange and is held only for transactions requirements. If, on the other hand, the rate of interest is at i_2 we assume that the interest loss from holding speculative money balances is so low and the risk of capital loss so great that the community desires to increase its speculative balances. The possibility of people hoarding cash when the rate of interest is very low was referred to earlier as the Keynesian liquidity trap. In Diagram (a) the liquidity trap region of the demand for money curve is shown by the horizontal lower right portion of the curve. Between these two extreme cases of the community's demand for money — at interest rates between i_2 and i_6 — the demand for money is inversely related to the rate of interest. At successively higher rates of interest the community is assumed to desire successively smaller amounts of money for speculative purposes.

In Diagram (b) of Figure 25-3 the *LM* curve is derived directly from Diagram (a). It is drawn by plotting the various rates of interest at which the total demand for money is equal to the given money supply at given levels of income. The *LM* curve indicates that when the rate of interest is above i_2 successively higher rates of interest up to i_6 are accompanied by successively higher levels of income. Increases in income make more money available for transactions purposes because as the rate of interest rises from i_2 to i_6 less of the fixed money supply is desired for speculative purposes. However, with a given value of k, larger amounts of money will be fully absorbed for transactions purposes only at higher levels of income. If, for example, an increase in the rate of interest from i_3 to i_4 releases $5 million from speculative balances, and k has a value of .50, the equilibrium level of income will have to increase by $10 million in order for the released money to be completely absorbed for transactions purposes. At interest rates above i_6 when no speculative balances are held, equilibrium in the money market exists only if the total money supply is employed for transactions purposes. Hence with a given money supply of, say, $20 billion and k equal to .50 the equilibrium level of income will be $40 billion when the rate of interest is above 6 per cent. Moreover, the level of income will remain at $40 billion for all levels of interest above i_6 as shown by the vertical portion of the *LM* curve in Diagram (b).

It will be remembered from our earlier discussion of the Keynesian liquidity trap that at some low rate of interest, i_2 in our example, the community has a preference for speculative money balances. Hence, given the money supply, less money is available for transactions purposes; the smaller the amount of money available for transactions purposes, the lower the level of income that can be supported. Therefore, in the liquidity trap lower left region of the *LM* curve, equilibrium in the money market is attained at both a low rate of interest and a low level of income.

Assume that the money supply curve M_s in Diagram (a) shifts to the right to M'_s as a result of an increase in the monetary base due to open market purchases by the central bank. At each rate of interest the community holds the desired amount of speculative balances; therefore, the entire increase in the money supply is available for transactions purposes. If equilibrium is to be re-established in the money market following the increase in the money supply, the level of income will have to rise sufficiently at each given rate of interest for the additional money to be required for transactions purposes. If, for example, the money supply increases by $5 million and *k* has a value of .50, equilibrium in the money market will be re-established when the level of income has increased by $10 million at each rate of interest. This is shown in Diagram (b) by the parallel shift of the *LM* curve to *LM′*.

Given the demand for money curve and given the shift in the *LM* curve following an increase in the money supply, we know the combinations of the rate of interest and the level of income which will allow equilibrium in the money market. Moreover, we know that the combination which allows equilibrium at the same time in both the money and product market must lie somewhere on the *LM* curve. Where it will lie on the *LM* curve depends upon where this curve intersects the *IS* curve. This, in turn, depends upon the position and shape of the *IS* curve.

When we considered the *IS* curve in the last chapter, we found that its shape depends upon shifts in the $(S_p + S_b + T + M)$ and $(I_d + G_d + X)$ curves resulting from a change in the rate of interest. Moreover, we noted that the slope of the *IS* curve also depends upon the slope of the $(S_p + S_b + T + M)$ curve, which we associated with the income multiplier. If both the $((S_p + S_b + T + M)$ and $(I_d + G_d + X)$ curves are unresponsive to changes in the rate of interest, the *IS* curve is perfectly vertical — perfectly interest inelastic. Two such curves are drawn in Diagram (a) of Figure 25-4. Given interest inelastic *IS* curves, any increase in the money supply will leave the level of income unaffected. Furthermore, if the *IS* curve intersects the *LM* curve in its liquidity trap region as does $(IS)_o$ in Diagram (a) the rate of interest will also remain unaf-

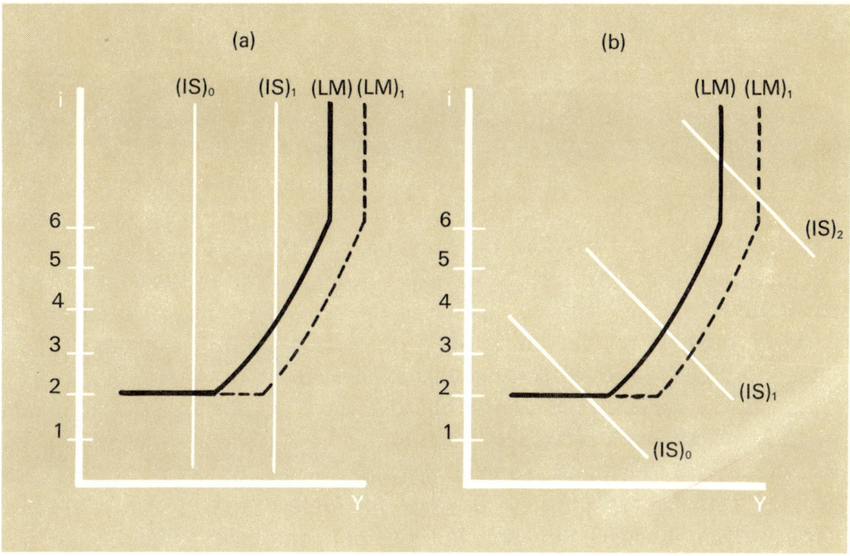

Figure 25-4

fected. If the position of the *IS* curve is to the right of the liquidity trap region as is $(IS)_1$, an increase in the money supply will still leave the level of income unaltered but the rate of interest will be lowered.

Keynes, writing during the midst of the depression of the 1930's, believed that the *IS* curve is interest inelastic because investment was generally unresponsive to changes in the rate of interest. He was therefore very skeptical of the effectiveness of monetary policy in increasing the level of income. Instead of using monetary policy to shift the *LM* curve Keynes suggested that the authorities should attempt to shift the *IS* curve through the use of fiscal policy — changes in government taxes and expenditures, particularly the latter. [1]

It is now generally conceded that except, perhaps, during periods of deep depression both the $(S_p + S_b + T + M)$ and $(I_d + G_d + X)$ curves shift at least a little with changes in the rate of interest. The sensitivity of these curves to the interest rate means that the *IS* curve is not vertical but slopes downward from left to right. The slope of the *IS* curve is also determined by the slopes of the $(I_d + G_d + X)$ and the $(S_p + S_b + T + M)$ curves. The slope of the $(I_d + G_d + X)$ curve, assuming G_d and X to be autonomously determined, expresses the rate of change in investment with respect to a change in income. Earlier we referred to the slope of the $(S_p + S_b + T + M)$ curve in terms of the income multiplier. The flatter the *IS* curve, the larger the multiplier, and the steeper the *IS* curve, the smaller the multiplier.

---

[1] Keynes did not employ the *IS* and *LM* curves in his analysis.

In Diagram (b) of Figure 25-4 we have drawn three *IS* curves, each interest elastic. The $(IS)_0$ curve intersects the *LM* curve in its liquidity trap region. When the interest rate is i_2 the community is assumed to be willing to accommodate an increase in the money supply by selling securities to the central bank and the banking system at current prices. All of the receipts from the sale of securities are added to the community's speculative balances with no change in the rate of interest. Moreover, the level of income remains unaffected since none of the increase in the money supply is used for transactions purposes.

The $(IS)_2$ curve in Diagram (b) intersects the *LM* curve where it is perfectly vertical. In this case the community is willing to accommodate the increase in the money supply by selling securities to the central bank and the banking system only if it receives higher prices for its securities. Therefore, an increase in the money supply must be associated with a decrease in the rate of interest. As long as the rate of interest does not fall below i_6 all of the increase in the money supply will be used for transactions purposes. Income will expand and equilibrium in the money market will be restored when the community again holds the desired proportion of money to income. As long as the rate of interest remains above i_6 the value of k and not the slope of the *IS* curve determines the equilibrium level of income following an increase in the money supply.

The $(IS)_1$ curve in Diagram (b) intersects the *LM* curve where it is neither perfectly vertical nor perfectly horizontal. In this case also, the community is willing to accommodate an increase in the money supply by selling securities to the monetary authorities only if it can sell its securities at higher prices. With an increase in the money supply interest rates fall. But now with a decrease in the rate of interest the community will want to add to its speculative balances. Therefore only part of the increase in the money supply will be available for transactions purposes and to support a higher level of income. For this reason income will not expand by as much as it did at the point of intersection of the $(IS)_2$ and *LM* curves. Moreover, the extent of the increase in income will depend now upon the slope of the *IS* curve. The more interest elastic spending and the larger the multiplier, the larger will be the increase in income following an increase in the money supply.

So far we have assumed that the demand for transactions balances is a constant proportion k of each level of income. Let us now assume first that the demand for transactions balances decreases at each level of income as the rate of interest rises, and second that given the rate of inter-

[2] The first assumption can be shown diagramatically by drawing a different transactions demand for money curve for each rate of interest and the second by drawing transaction demand for money curves which are non-linear instead of linear. We have not drawn such curves here.

est the value of k declines as the level of income rises.[2] When we introduced these assumptions in Chapter 24 we expressed the demand for transactions balances as $l_l\ (Y, i)$. The assumption of an interest elastic demand for transactions balances is shown in Diagram (a) of Figure 25-5 by the absence of the vertical portion of the total demand for money curve and the flatness of the slope of this curve compared to the demand for money curve in Figure 25-4. This is also reflected in the shape of the *LM* curve drawn in Figure 25-5. Moreover the liquidity trap region of this curve is relatively shorter. This region would not be shorter had we assumed, as is probably more realistic, that the transactions demand for money is sensitive to changes in the rate of interest only after the rate of interest has reached relatively high levels. With an interest elastic demand for transactions balances, a change in the money supply will not produce a parallel shift in the *LM* curve; the size of the shift is larger the higher the rate of interest.

The assumption that the value of k declines as the level of income rises implies that at each rate of interest the transactions demand for money increases but at a decreasing rate as the level of income rises. This is indicated in Figure 25-5 by a successively flatter total demand for money curve at each higher level of income, and by the flatness of the *LM* curve.

From our earlier analysis it follows that with a flattening out of the *LM* curve monetary policy is less effective. For example, when the value

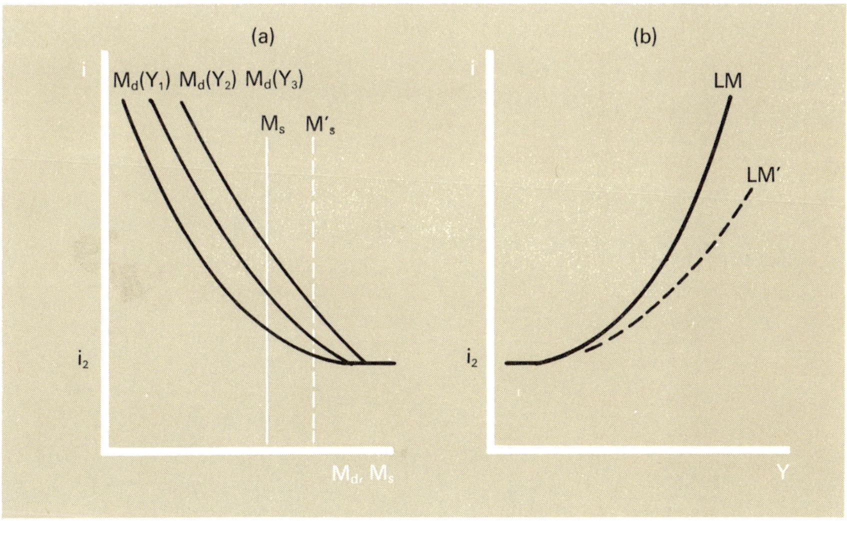

Figure 25-5

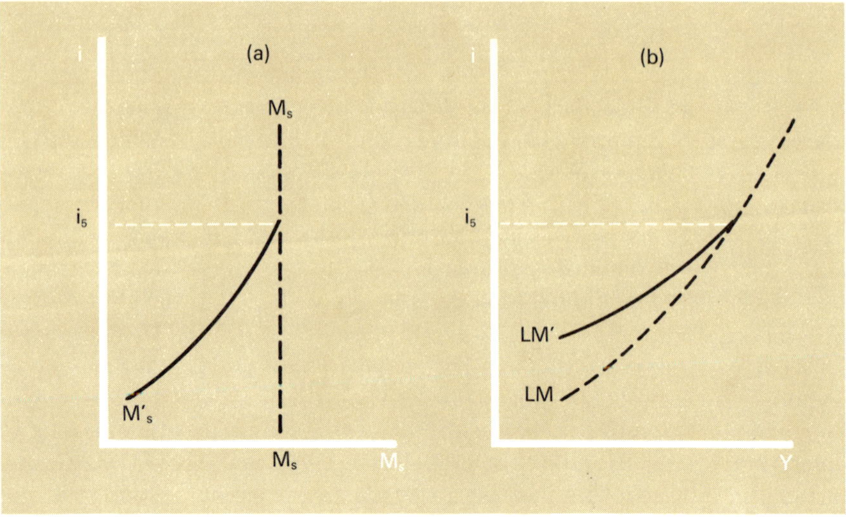

Figure 25-6

of k decreases with an increase in the rate of interest, some of the contractionary effects following a decrease in the money supply will be offset by an increase in the velocity of circulation of money. Moreover, if the value of k decreases as income increases, at higher levels of income larger reductions in the money supply are required to offset the higher velocity of circulation of money.

Our attention has been focused on the demand for money curve assuming a perfectly vertical money supply curve indicating that with a given monetary base the banking system holds no excess reserves. In our discussion of the money supply curve in Chapter 18 we mentioned that at low rates of interest the banking system may be willing to hold excess reserves and that these excess reserves will be used for credit expansion as the rate of interest rises. In Diagram (a) of Figure 25-6 two money supply curves are drawn. The broken-line money supply curve M_s assumes that with a given monetary base the banking system is always fully loaned up. The solid line M'_s curve assumes the same given monetary base but the banking system is fully loaned up only after the rate of interest has risen to i_5. At interest rates above i_5 the two money supply curves are identical.

In Diagram (b) two LM curves are drawn by plotting the various combinations of the rate of interest and the level of income at which equilibrium in the money market exists for each of the two assumed money supply curves in Diagram (a). (The relevant demand curves are not shown in Diagram (a). It will be noted that the solid-line LM curve (given the M'_s curve) is flatter than the broken-line LM curve at interest rates below i_5. The two curves converge and become identical at interest rates above i_5 when, given the monetary base, the banking system is and remains fully loaned up. The flatter *LM* curve to the left of the point of convergence indicates that at each level of income, equilibrium exists at a higher rate of interest than is the case with the broken-line *LM* curve. This happens because the money supply is smaller at rates of interest below i_5 given the M'_s money supply curve than it is given the M_s curve. We can therefore conclude that given the monetary base the shape of the *LM* curve depends upon, among other things, the behaviour of the banking system with respect to excess reserves.

Our analysis has concentrated on adjustments toward equilibrium following an increase in the monetary base. We have observed that the nature of the adjustments depends upon the assumptions one makes regarding the demand for money. Moreover, we have also observed that the adjustments toward equilibrium following an increase in the monetary base depend upon the assumptions one makes regarding the behaviour of the banking system in employing its excess reserves. Our analysis applies only to the short-run since we have assumed that changes in the money supply are not accompanied by shifts in the demand for money curve. In the last chapter we considered a shift in the demand for money curve as result of a change in the price level. This curve may shift also as a result of a change in the community's desire for liquidity.

PRODUCT MARKET CHANGES

Disturbances in equilibrium originating in the product market may be shown as shifts in the *IS* curve. We have seen that shifts in the *IS* curve are associated with changes in the determinants, other than the rate of interest and the level of income, of the $(S_p + S_b + T + M)$ and the $(I_d + G_d + X)$ curves. For simplicity let us assume a shift in the $(I_d + G_d + X)$ curve following legislative action to increase government expenditures on goods and services. These additional expenditures are financed by the sale of government securities to the non-bank public. The $(I_d + G_d + X)$ curve shifts upward by the amount of the change in government expenditures. Now, by how much does the level of income increase? This will depend upon the multiplier and the interest elasticity of the *LM* curve. In Figure 25-7, we have drawn three *IS* curves and their shifts following an increase in government expenditures. Each set of *IS* curves intersects an *LM* curve in each of its three distinct regions.

Where the *IS* curves intersect the *LM* curve in its liquidity trap region, the increase in income is equal to the change in government expenditures times the income multiplier. The full income multiplier is at work. The $(IS)_0$ curve shifts to $(IS)'_0$ and the level of income increases from Y_1 to Y_2.

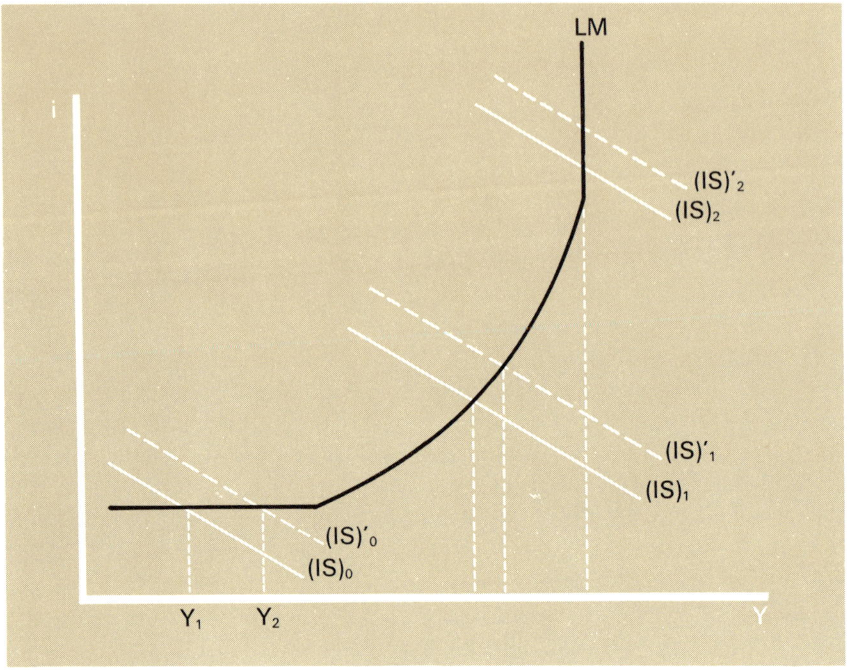

Figure 25-7

At the other extreme, where the *IS* curve intersects the *LM* curve in its interest inelastic section, an increase in government expenditures will have no effect on the equilibrium level of income. The government can borrow to increase its expenditures only by selling its securities at attractively lower prices. Hence, the rate of interest will rise causing private spending to decrease by the amount government spending has increased. Thus there is no change in the equilibrium level of income — only an increase in the equilibrium level of interest — as shown in Figure 25-7 by the movement of the $(IS)_2$ curve to $(IS)'_2$.

Finally, let us consider what is probably the more normal situation where the *IS* curve intersects the *LM* curve as it slopes upward from left to right. As before, government borrowing will result in an increase in the rate of interest. However, the community will then want to reduce its speculative money balances. The money released in this way plus the additional money that the banking system will supply at higher interest rate levels will be added to transactions balances.[3] The increase in transactions balances will support a higher level of income. The new equilibrium

[3] The increase in the money supply is represented by a movement up the *MM* curve and not a shift in this curve. In the case of the shift of the *IS* curve from $(IS)_2$ to $(IS)'_2$, we assumed the banks to have no excess reserves.

level of income will not be equal, however, to the increase in government expenditures times the multiplier. As the interest rate increases, private spending will decrease. For this reason the full effects of the multiplier will not be realized. The shift in the *IS* curve from $(IS)_2$ to $(IS)'_2$ in Figure 25-7 illustrates this situation.[4]

EQUILIBRIUM AND FULL EMPLOYMENT

In our analysis of the *IS* and *LM* curves, we have implicitly assumed that the price level remained constant and that a change in money income was at the same time a change in real income of equal amount. With an economy at less than full employment, one can assume that an increase in income is not accompanied by a rise in prices and can therefore be considered as an increase in real income.

Now let us assume that the economy is at equilibrium at more than full employment. For example, let us suppose that equilibrium occurs at Y_e in Figure 25-8 and that full employment occurs at Y_f. Although given the $(LM)_o$ and $(IS)_o$ curves,[5] Y_e is the equilibrium level of income, this cannot be considered a position of **stable** equilibrium.

Given its resources the economy can produce only an amount of real output equal to Y_f. Hence at Y_e there exists a state of excess demand for *real* goods and services which will tend to drive up prices. As prices rise, the real stock of money decreases as shown by the *LM* curve shifting to the left. The *LM* curve will shift to $(LM)_l$ intersecting the $(IS)_o$ curve at full employment output, Y_f. Alternatively, if the equilibrium level of income is at less than full employment output, with flexible prices downward, the decline in prices will increase the real stock of money. As a consequence the *LM* curve will shift to the right until it intersects the *IS* curve at full employment output. Only at this level of output will the *LM* and *IS* curves intersect at a point of stable equilibrium.

Essential to our argument above is the assumption of price flexibility. The classical economists assumed that if relative prices including the rate of interest were flexible and money was not held as an asset, the economy would always be at full employment equilibrium, at least in the

4 With induced monetary effects the multiplier in a closed economy with no government may be expressed as

$$\frac{1}{1-b} + \frac{l_2 k}{f}$$

where b is the marginal propensity to consume, l_2 the slope of the speculative demand for money curve, k the assumed ratio of transactions balances to income, and f the slope of the investment function.

5 For simplicity, we have drawn the curves in Figure 25-8 linear.

long run. Keynes questioned the assumption that prices were perfectly flexible and showed that equilibrium at full employment was the exception rather than the rule. Some economists in the post-Keynesian tradition have argued that even with complete price flexibility there is no assurance that the economy will achieve equilibrium at full employment output. Their argument is based on the stability and the elasticity of the *IS* curve. For example, in Figure 25-9 the economy is initially at the level of income Y_e which is at less than full employment. If full employment equilibrium is at Y_f, this level of income can be achieved by an increase in the money supply which causes the $(LM)_0$ curve to shift to the position occupied by the $(LM)_1$ curve in the figure. If however the full employment level of income is Y_f, given the position and elasticity of the $(IS)_0$ curve, it is impossible for an *LM* curve to intersect it at this level of income. In this case the full employment level of income cannot be attained through manipulation of the money supply even with flexible prices.

Other economists, notably Don Patinkin, following earlier work by A.C. Pigou, have argued that equilibrium at full employment is possible

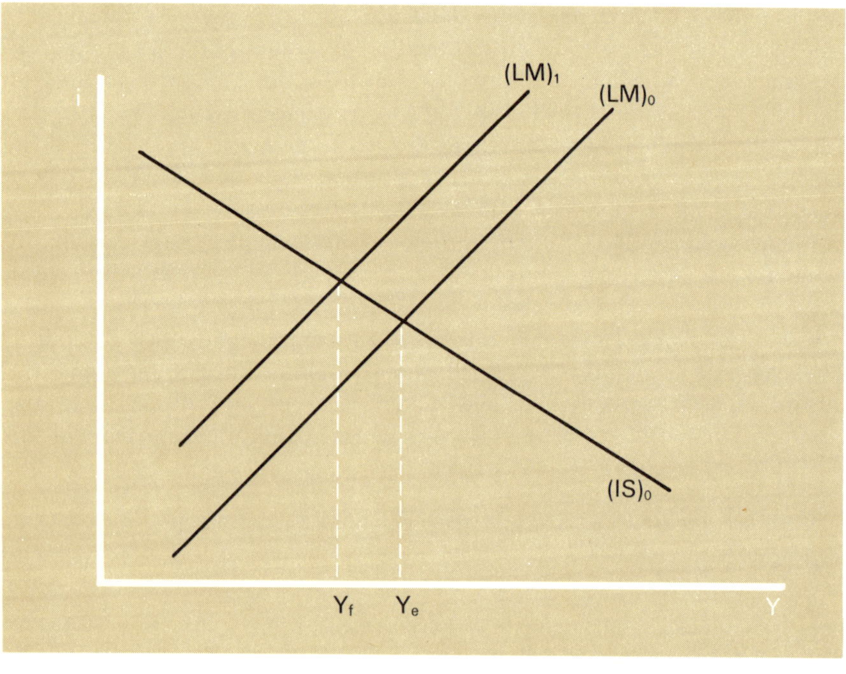

Figure 25-8

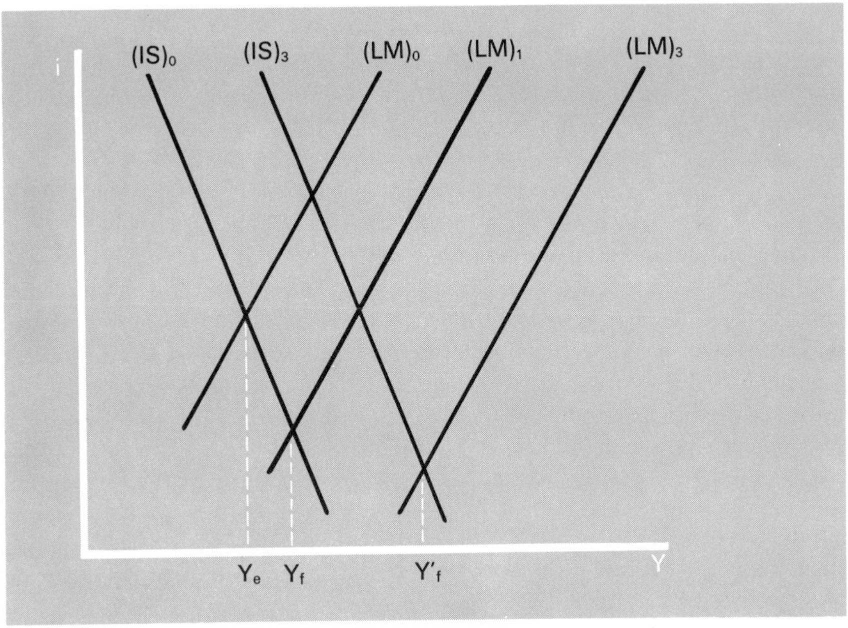

Figure 25-9

via the monetary effect.[6] Patinkin has demonstrated that with a decline in prices not only does the *LM* curve shift rightward but so does the *IS* curve. He argues that with a decline in the price level the real purchasing power of the community's money balances, and therefore its total real wealth, increases. If the community desires to maintain some stable relationship among its expenditures, its real money balances and its real wealth, it will increase its expenditures when its real wealth increases. Thus the *IS* curve shifts to the right with a rise in real wealth associated with a decline in prices. This is now generally referred to as the **real balances** or **real wealth** effect. In Figure 25-9 if the real balances effect is sufficiently strong to shift the $(IS)_o$ curve to $(IS)_3$, full employment equilibrium Y'_f is attained. Even with a smaller shift or no shift at all in the *IS* curve this level of income can be attained if at the same time the *IS* curve becomes more elastic.

In today's world, the assumption of complete price flexibility required for a significant real balances effect is probably only academic. Moreover, if prices fall and the community expects the trend to continue for some time it may reduce rather than increase its expenditures despite the

6 Patinkin, Don, *Money, Interest and Prices*, Evanston, Ill., Row Peterson, 1956, and A.C. Pigou, "Economic Progress in a Stable Environment", *Economica*, 1947.

increase in its real wealth. Under these circumstances the *IS* curve may not shift rightward and the economy may not achieve full employment equilibrium.

A FINAL NOTE

In this chapter, we have presented an equilibrium theory in terms of "Keynesian economics". Keynes himself did not employ the *IS* and *LM* curves; these were first employed by J. R. Hicks and Alvin H. Hansen[7] and have since become the standard tool to show that Keynes did indeed present a "general theory of employment, interest and money". As we have seen, the Keynesian analysis shows how changes in the money supply may affect the level of output and employment through their effect on the interest rate, which in turn affects aggregate demand and thus output and employment. The theory of money and interest is therefore inseparable from the theory of output and employment. Changes in the money market are accompanied by changes in the product market and vice versa; the equilibrium rate of interest and the equilibrium level of income are simultaneously determined.

Keynes developed his theory in response to what he considered an error in classical economics — the classical dichotomy which separated monetary theory from value or price theory. In more recent times, Patinkin has attempted to demonstrate that classical theory can be used to show the interdependence of all sectors within the economy. He shows that the demands for and supplies of commodities depend not only on relative prices but also on the real value of the community's cash balances. Moreover, he believes that there is sufficient evidence to indicate that at least some of the classical writers, or later writers in the classical tradition, recognized the role played by the real balance effect. According to Patinkin, the real balance effect links the money and product market thus eliminating the classical dichotomy.

SELECTED READINGS

See lists following Chapters 22 and 24.

---

[7] Hicks, J.R., "Mr. Keynes and the 'Classics': A Suggested Interpretation", *Econometrica*, Vol. 5, April, 1937, pp. 147-159. Alvin H. Hansen, *A Guide to Keynes*, New York, McGraw-Hill, 1953.

26

THE TERM STRUCTURE OF INTEREST RATES

In our discussion of what determines the rate of interest and in our analysis of the rate of interest and economic activity, we assumed that there was only one rate of interest at any one time. This is an oversimplification since at any given time there are almost as many rates as there are financial assets. In this chapter we shall discuss the various theories which have been put forward to explain differences in interest rates. Our attention will be focused especially on the differences in interest rates as related to the maturity of debt instruments. The differences in rates according to maturity create what's called the term structure or maturity pattern of rates.

RISK AND LIQUIDITY PREFERENCE

Lenders demand a risk premium — that is, they charge a rate of interest — according to their assessment of the credit-worthiness of the borrower. If a borrower has displayed good management and integrity in the past, if he has met all his financial obligations as requested, lenders can count on him to do the same in the future. They will consider him a good credit risk and demand from him only a small risk premium. On the other hand, if the borrower's credit-worthiness is unknown or doubtful lenders will demand a relatively high risk premium. As a rule, the possibility that a borrower may default in meeting his obligation increases with the length of time for which the loan is made. The risk premium demanded on long-term loans is larger, therefore, than that demanded on short-term loans. Differences in interest rates can therefore be explained, at least in part, by differences in credit risks.

Aside from a credit risk there is also the risk of a capital loss and the risk of a loss of income. Let us assume that a lender extends a loan by purchasing a bond that matures in ten years. After five years the lender finds himself short of cash and is required to sell the bond. If interest rates are now generally higher than they were when he purchased the bond, he will not be able to sell it for the original purchase price; he will have to take a capital loss.[1] If, however, interest rates are generally lower, he will be able to make a capital gain.

The lender can attempt to reduce or eliminate the risk of a capital loss by purchasing bonds (extending loans) with short-term rather than long-term maturities. However, he will then be involved in a risk of a different kind. Suppose that he buys a five year bond but finds at the end of the fifth year when it matures that he does not require the money. If during the five years interest rates generally decline, he will now have to be satisfied with a lower rate of interest — a smaller income — if he wants to keep his money in the market. Thus although the lender reduces or eliminates the risk of capital loss by investing short rather than long, he exposes himself to the risk of a loss of income.

The borrower as well as the lender may run the risk of a capital or income loss. If he borrows money for a period shorter than that for which funds are required he exposes himself to the risk of a loss of income. If interest rates are generally higher when he has to renegotiate his loan, he experiences a loss of income. The loss could have been avoided if he had originally borrowed on a term long enough to meet his requirement. By borrowing long he can eliminate the risk of a loss of income (as well as the risk of a gain in income) but he then exposes himself to the risk of a loss (or a gain) of capital. If he borrows long and then finds that he has overestimated his requirement period, he may lose part of his

TABLE 26-1

Income and Capital Risks

Loans	*Lenders*	*Borrowers*
Short-term contracts	Risk of income loss if interest rates fall	Risk of income loss if interest rates rise
Long-term contracts	Risk of capital loss if interest rates rise	Risk of capital loss if interest rates fall

capital by terminating his loan before its maturity. Lenders usually demand a penalty payment for the privilege of terminating a loan before its contractual maturity date. Moreover, in the case of a marketable security, if interest rates have generally increased since the security was sold the borrower can buy back the bond only if he is prepared to pay more for it than he originally received when he sold it. Of course, if interest rates have fallen, he will be able to reap a capital gain.

[1] The relationship between the price of bonds and market rates was discussed in Chapter 22.

Income and capital risks of lenders and borrowers are summarized in Table 26-1. For the lender the capital risk applies only if the term of the loan exceeds the availability of his funds; the income risk applies if the term of the loan falls short of the period for which his funds are available. For the borrower the capital risk applies only if the term of the loan exceeds the period for which the funds are required; the income risk applies if the term of the loan falls short of his requirement period. Capital and income losses or gains are eliminated if the terms of loans are identical with the availability periods of lenders' funds and the borrowers' requirement periods. However, borrowers are usually more certain of the period for which they require funds than are lenders of the period for which their funds may be available. Lenders, therefore, are more likely to underestimate the period of availability than are borrowers to overestimate the period of requirement. As a result there may be preponderance of excess funds available in the short run tending to hold short rates lower than long rates.

The plentiful supply of excess short funds has been explained in terms of individuals' normal preference for liquidity. Individuals are assumed to be risk-averters. Regardless of their expectations about future interest rates they prefer short-term to long-term securities because of their closeness to money. With no positive expectations about future interest rate levels, individuals do not consider the chance of a capital gain as compensation for the chance of an equal loss. Hence they are willing to accept a smaller yield on short-term securities in order to remain close to money.

If lenders prefer short-term to long-term investment, borrowers will be forced to take loans for periods shorter than their requirements. This, as we have seen, exposes them to the risk of a loss of income. Because borrowers demand lower interest rates to compensate them for assuming this risk, short rates tend to be at a discount from long rates. A preference for investing short may create an excess demand for long-term requirements. As a result pressure will be placed on lenders to extend the availability period of their funds. Lenders are then exposed to the risk of capital loss. They may be induced to take the risk if they are provided with adequate compensation in the form of a higher interest rate payment. Thus long rates tend to be at a premium over short rates as shown by Curve II of Figure 26-1.

INSTITUTIONAL FACTORS

Financial institutions as well as non-financial corporations usually consider it prudent to manage their portfolios so that the maturity distribution of their assets and liabilities are similar. That is to say, they hedge their liabilities with assets of equal maturity distributions. We have seen that the liabilities of the chartered banks are primarily demand deposits and time deposits subject to relatively short notice. Moreover the banks prefer to hold cash and secondary reserves in the form of short-term securities against a relatively large proportion of these deposit liabilities. Large business firms who have transaction balances temporarily in excess of their current requirements, but which they may need on short notice to make payments usually desire to avert risk but to increase their earnings by investing in relatively short-term securities. The liabilities of life insurance companies, on the other hand, are of a long-term nature. Therefore they hold most of their assets in the form of long-term investments to avoid the uncertainty of a variable return from constant reinvestment in short-term securities.

If, as has been traditional, the liabilities of the banks dominate the financial markets, their desire for short-term securities influences short-term security prices and yields. Furthermore, the banks' demand for short-term securities may explain why short rates are lower than long rates as shown by Curve II in Figure 26-1. At the same time, however, changes in the maturity structure of the total debt outstanding may explain at least some of the changes in the maturity structure of interest rates.

Other institutional factors which may influence the structure of interest rates are the differences in tax treatment of capital gains and interest returns, and call and other special provisions associated with certain security issues. Since these are all special cases of the more general explanation of the structure of interest rates, we shall not deal with them here.

EXPECTATIONS

Although interest rates of all maturities tend to rise and fall together, causing upward or downward shifts in the term structure of interest rates — the maturity yield curve — such shifts are usually accompanied by changes in the shape of this curve. As interest rates and security prices move up and down, short-term interest rates usually fluctuate over a wider range than long-term interest rates, while long-term security prices tend to fluctuate over a wider range than short-term security prices. Changes in the pattern of interest rates (that is, changes in the shape of the maturity yield curve) have been explained by changes in the community's expectations of future interest rates.

Let us suppose that borrowers and lenders as a whole expect interest rates to rise in the near future. Lenders will tend toward short lending so as to have cash available for the higher yields expected in the future and to avoid the capital and income losses associated with long-term securities during periods of rising rates. Funds will shift to the short end of the

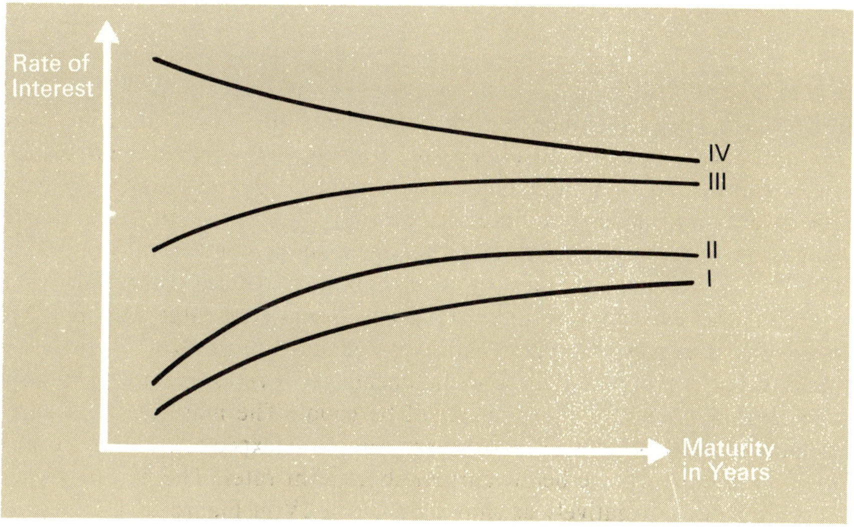

Figure 26-1

market. On the other hand, borrowers will now tend to borrow long to avoid the loss of income associated with higher rates in the future. The demand for funds will shift to the long-end of the market. This behaviour by lenders and borrowers will tend to lower short-term rates relative to long-term rates. The maturity yield curve will become steeper as shown by Curve I of Figure 26-1.

Now let us suppose that borrowers and lenders expect interest rates to fall in the near future. Lenders will sell short-term securities and buy long-term securities in order to increase their opportunities for capital gains. Borrowers will prefer to borrow short in order to reduce their costs in the future should rates indeed fall. These activities will tend to increase short-rates relative to long-rates. The maturity yield curve will become flatter as shown by Curve III in Figure 26-1.

Expectation theorists argue that the maturity choices of lenders and borrowers are determined predominantly by their expectations as to *future short-term rates* and that these choices cause long-term rates to equalize with the average of short-term rates expected in the future.[2] For example, suppose that investors hold identical expectations with complete certainty. The current rate for one-year loans is 3 per cent and is expected to rise to 4 per cent, 5 per cent and 6 per cent respectively for the next three one-year periods. The current rate for a four-year loan

[2] All institutional factors are assumed away, all securities are assumed to be riskless and arbitrage is assumed to be possible without restraint between maturities of different terms.

would be about 4.5 per cent, the average of these rates. At 4.5 per cent interest the investor would be able to get the same return from investing for four years as he could obtain for investing for one year and successively reinvesting in similar one-year contracts over the next three years. Short-term and long-term interest rates are linked by the fact that a long-term loan may be effected either by a single contract of long duration or by a series of periodically renegotiated short-term contracts.

If, as the expectations theorists argue, long-term rates are modified geometric averages of current and expected short-term rates, when future short rates are expected to remain unchanged over some relevant horizon, current long and short rates will be equal. The maturity yield curve is horizontal. However, if short-term rates are expected to fall, current long-term rates will lie below current short-term rates. The maturity yield curve will slope negatively as shown by Curve IV in Figure 26-1.[3]

When market rates rise the community is not necessarily led to believe that future rates will be higher. Individuals' expectations may be determined by what they regard as "normal" or "conventional" rates. During inflationary or boom periods interest rates may rise above levels which are considered normal. Individuals may expect rates to fall in the future to their normal levels. Under these circumstances, as we explained earlier, lenders will tend to invest long and borrowers to borrow short and the maturity yield curve of interest rates will become flatter or negatively sloped. This behaviour on the part of lenders and borrowers has important implications for monetary policy. If during inflationary periods the monetary authorities concentrate on increasing the short rate, a rise in the long rates may not result if the community expects the increase in short rates to be only temporary. Because the long rate of interest is probably a more important determinant of total spending, particularly investment spending, long rates will have to increase if monetary policy is to be effective. The authorities must therefore rely more on a "package deal" which includes fiscal as well as debt management policy in order to change the community's expectations.

Similarly a decline in market rates of interest does not necessarily lead the community to believe that future rates will be lower. If rates decline below what individuals consider normal levels, say during periods of economic recession, they may expect an increase in rates to normal levels in the near future. With the expectation of rising rates, lenders will tend to invest short and borrowers to borrow long. The maturity yield curve will

3 Another maturity yield curve not shown in Figure 26-1 is a humped curve. Such a curve results when short rates are expected to be somewhat higher over the next several years but thereafter are expected to decline again.

become steeper.[4] A monetary policy concentrated on the short end of the market to force down short rates cannot be relied upon to decrease long rates also. The monetary authorities must therefore attempt to influence the long-term market directly by concentrating their purchases in this market, and government policy must be directed toward affecting the community's expectations regarding the course of future interest rate levels.

FLUIDITY: SUBSTITUTION AND ARBITRAGE

The hypotheses presented so far concerning the term structure of interest rates focus on explanations of the differences in rates at any given time. The fluidity hypothesis is based on the assumption that the term structure of interest rates over time has remained relatively constant, and endeavours to explain why. In other words, it attempts to show that changes in short rates are likely to be almost parallel to changes in long rates and vice versa; fluctuations in rates in one maturity range are likely to shift the maturity curve but not to change the shape of the maturity yield curve significantly. The fluidity hypothesis was developed to explain the behaviour of American and British money markets during the 1920's. It is based on the assumption that there is a high degree of substitutability of security instruments for most lenders and borrowers in credit and capital markets, and on the arbitrage activities of professional traders.

Although, as we mentioned earlier, financial institutions tend to concentrate on a specific maturity range of assets to hedge the liabilities in which they specialize, most institutions trade continuously in securities of all maturities. This activity on the part of institutions, and the high degree of substitutability of security instruments assumed for both borrowers and lenders is considered to provide fluidity in financial markets. Fluidity is assumed to provide a link between financial assets of different maturities and to explain the coincidence in direction and timing of movements of different interest rates. Fluidity theorists admit that a lowering of the short rate by the monetary authorities may not be followed by a proportional decline in the long rate during economic depressions when the demand for long-term investment funds is weak or non-existent.

Aside from the activities of financial institutions and, of course, those of the government, fluidity in financial markets may result also from the

---

[4] In our earlier discussion of the demand for speculative money balances we assumed that when interest rates fall but are expected to rise shortly, individuals will prefer to hold money. If potential lenders would rather hold money than invest short, short rates may not decline significantly but the scarcity of funds for long borrowing may accentuate the increase in long rates.

arbitrage activities of professional traders. Arbitrage is the practice of simultaneously purchasing and selling securities of different maturities for profit.

The logical inference from the fluidity theory is that the monetary authorities need not operate in both long and short securities in order to shift the maturity yield curve up or down. If they want to move long-term rates, they need not take the risk of creating disorderly market conditions by operating in the long end of the market. This opinion prevailed among the Federal Reserve authorities in the United States after 1951 when they introduced the "bills-only" policy (abandoned in the early 1960's).

MONETARY POLICY

Where there are relatively perfect credit and capital markets displaying a high degree of fluidity, changes in the Bank rate and central bank open market operations which produce changes in short-term interest rates may be reflected in proportional changes in long-term interest rates. The same may be true even without a high degree of market fluidity if expectations play an important role in linking security markets and if the market expects changes in short-rates to be permanent. If, however, the market expects changes in short rates to be temporary, long rates may move little, if at all, with short rates. For example, the market may expect that the monetary authorities will fail to achieve and maintain a particular level of short-term rates. As a result changes in short rates will not be reflected by changes in long rates. Hence it may be argued that monetary policy which concentrates on the short-end of the market dulls with use if repeated attempts by the monetary authorities to establish a level of interest rates fall short of their goals. Only when monetary policy is used infrequently, and when the community expects that the short rates achieved in the market will be maintained for some time, will this policy be successful in influencing long rates and thereby investment and aggregate demand. Because monetary authorities can never be certain of the community's expectations a good case can be made for the central bank operating in all maturity ranges and at times calling upon debt management and other government policies for assistance.

The importance of central bank flexibility for operating in all maturity ranges is shown by the operations of the Federal Reserve System in the United States in 1961-1962. At that time depressed domestic conditions called for relatively low long-term rates. However, at the same time for international balance of payments purposes high short-term rates were called for. A negatively sloped maturity yield curve was desired. Toward this end the Federal Reserve sold short-term securities to force up short rates and purchased long-term securities to force down long-term rates. The policy proved successful only so long as the market expected that the government's policies would succeed and that long rates would rise in the near future.

SELECTED READINGS

Aschheim, Joseph, *Techniques of Monetary Control*, Baltimore, Johns Hopkins Press, 1961, pp. 55-60.

Axilrod, Stephen H., and Ralph A. Young, "Interest Rates and Monetary Policy", *Federal Reserve Bulletin*, Vol. 48, No. 9, September, 1962, pp. 1110-1137.

Conard, J. W., *An Introduction to the Theory of Interest*, Berkeley, University of California Press, 1959, pp. 287-367.

Conard, J. W., *The Behaviour of Interest Rates*, New York, Columbia University Press, 1966.

Culbertson, John M., "The Term Structure of Interest Rates", *Quarterly Journal of Economics*, Vol. 71, November, 1957, pp. 485-517.

Hicks, J. R., *Value and Capital*, 2nd ed., Oxford, Oxford University Press, 1946, Ch. 11-13.

Lutz, F. A., "The Structure of Interest Rate", *Quarterly Journal of Economics*, Vol. 55, November, 1940, pp. 36-63.

Lutz, F. A., *The Theory of Interest*, Chicago, Aldine, 1968.

Malkiel, Burton Gordon, *The Term Structure of Interest Rates: Expectations and Behaviour Patterns*, Princeton, N.J., Princeton University Press, 1966.

Meiselman, David, *The Term Structure of Interest Rates*, Englewood Cliffs, N.J., Prentice-Hall, 1962.

Michaelsen, J. B., "The Term Structure of Interest Rates: Comment", *Quarterly Journal of Economics*, Vol. 77, 1963, pp. 166-174.

Modigliani, F., "Liquidity Preference and the Theory of Interest and Money", *Econometrica*, January, 1944.

Riefler, W. W., *Money Rates and Money Markets in the United States*, New York and London, Harper and Bros., 1930.

Riefler, W. W., "Open Market Operations in Long-Term Securities", *Federal Reserve Bulletin,* Vol. 44, No. 11, November, 1958, pp. 1260-1274.

Smith, Warren L., *Debt Management in the United States,* Study Paper No. 19 for the Joint Economic Committee; materials prepared in connection with the Study of Employment, Growth, and Price Levels, Eighty-sixth Congress, Second Session, 1960.

Turvey, Ralph, *Interest Rates and Asset Prices,* New York, Macmillan, 1961.

Wannacott, Paul, *The Height, Structure and Significance of Interest Rates,* working paper prepared for the Royal Commission on Banking and Finance, Ottawa, November, 1962.

Wood, John H., "Expectations, Errors and the Term Structure of Interest Rates", *Journal of Political Economy,* Vol. 71, April, 1963, pp. 160-171.

27

THE ROLE AND EFFECTIVENESS OF MONETARY POLICY

The *raison d'être* of monetary policy is to influence the demand for goods and services so as to achieve the objectives of overall economic policy — price stability, a high and stable level of employment, external balance and economic growth. In the previous chapters we considered both traditional and modern monetary theories with only incidental attention to their implications for monetary policy. In this chapter we shall consider specifically the interrelationships between theory and policy. The various theoretical explanations of the monetary mechanism will be reviewed and the policy implications of each of these theoretical positions shown. The explanations of the monetary mechanism are divided into four groups: the credit conditions approach, the quantity of money approach, the liquidity approach, and the availability of money approach. These four approaches are by no means distinct since they have characteristics in common. The differences among the four, as we shall see, are in their foci.

In this chapter we shall also discuss two current issues: the differential effects of monetary policy, and the lags in the effects. Finally, we shall consider the very crucial question which arises from the discussions in the chapter: should the discretionary powers enjoyed by the monetary authorities in most countries be replaced with some automatic rule?

THE CREDIT APPROACH

The credit approach is represented by Keynesian economic theory. The role of money is seen as affecting the demand for goods and services essentially through its prior effect on the rate of interest. The relationship between money and the rate of interest is explained in terms of the community's liquidity preference, or more generally, its demand for money. The demand for money function which expresses the liquidity preference is considered to be independent of the money supply. The demand for money is regarded as a relatively stable function of a limited number of variables, the most important of which is probably the rate of interest. Keynes, himself, believed that the demand for money was normally interest inelastic except during periods of economic recession when he believed it to be completely interest elastic, a phenomenon known as the Keynesian liquidity trap. Modern Keynesians believe that changes in the money supply produce fairly predictable changes in the rate of interest but that the interest rate response depends upon the assumed interest elasticity of the demand for money function. However, the interest elasticity of this function is still an unsettled issue of monetary theory.

So-called Keynesian economists assuming implicitly that under normal conditions the rate of interest is sensitive to changes in the money supply, focus their attention on the relationship between the rate of interest and expenditures. Opinion among them, however, is divided as to the strength of this relationship. Those who take the position that monetary policy is not effective — the so-called "money does not matter" group — believe that expenditures are essentially a function of income and not of the rate of interest. Others, probably the majority of Keynesians, are prepared to admit that expenditures may be somewhat sensitive to the rate of interest.

The pre-war Oxford studies showed that businessmen in Britain were affected to a very limited extent by changes in credit conditions.[1] These studies, which received wide attention, contributed to the early scepticism concerning the effectiveness of monetary policy. In 1956 and 1957 studies by the Oxford Institute of Statistics and by the Association of British Chambers of Commerce and the Federation of British Industries, respectively, confirmed the earlier conclusions that businessmen's reactions to changing credit conditions were only marginal.[2] The Committee on the Working of the Monetary System, the so-called Radcliffe Committee, appointed in 1957 to investigate the British monetary system, noted that " . . . when we confined our questions strictly to the direct effects of interest rate changes in making businessmen alter their decisions to buy and sell goods and services, we were met by general scepticism".[3] Stud-

---

1 Meade, J. E., and P. W. S. Andrews, "Replies to Questions on Effects of Interest Rates", *Oxford Economic Papers*, No. 1, October, 1938; H. D. Henderson, "The Significance of the Rate of Interest", *Oxford Economic Papers*, No. 1, October 1938; P.W.S. Andrews "A Further Inquiry into the Effects of Rates of Interest", *Oxford Economic Papers*, No. 3, February, 1940.

2 For a report of the surveys conducted by the Oxford Institute of Statistics see H. F. Lydall, "The Impact of the Credit Squeeze on Small and Medium-sized Manufacturing Firms", *The Economic Journal*, Vol. 67, September, 1957, pp. 415-431.

3 *Committee on the Working of the Monetary System Report*, London, Her Majesty's Stationery Office, August, 1959, p. 158, paragraph 451.

ies made in the United States both before and after the war discovered similar insensitivity of business decisions to changes in credit conditions. Robert Eisner, for example, after making a survey of business decisions during 1951-1952 and 1954-1955, concluded "that the supply of money capital was not a crucial determinant of capital expenditures" and that "Questions directed at the role of interest rate received almost uniformly negative response".[4]

In Canada, the Porter Commission conducted a mail survey of businesses with follow-up interviews to ascertain the correlation between credit conditions and business investment during three periods of monetary restraint, 1956-1957, 1959-1960 and mid-1962.[5] The Commission's studies explicitly interpreted credit conditions to include both the cost of money (the rate of interest) and the availability of money. Moreover, it explicitly assumed that credit conditions were influenced by both monetary and debt-management policies. The Commission found that credit restraint during the years under review did not affect a significant proportion of businesses because they were able to respond to credit conditions in ways that left their financial arrangements unaffected. The significance of this point had been largely overlooked in the earlier studies in Britain and the United States. In Canada businesses were able to respond to restrictive credit conditions in the following ways:

Borrowing Abroad. Foreign subsidiaries, particularly American, were able to escape credit restraint by receiving funds directly from their foreign parents or indirectly by postponing payment for goods and services received from the parents. Given the high proportion of firms in Canada with foreign affiliation, monetary policy was unable to affect the expenditures of a substantial portion of Canadian industry. Firms which turned to foreign parents and foreign capital markets were prepared to assume the foreign exchange risk inherent in using foreign funds.

Sale and Leaseback Arrangements. This type of arrangement involves the sale of real estate by a corporation which then leases it back for its own use. The Commission found that this method was frequently used to finance retail outlets with foreign funds during periods of credit restraint in Canada.

---

4 Eisner, Robert, *Determinants of Capital Expenditures - An Interview Study*, University of Illinois Bulletin, 1956. See also J. F. Ebersole, "The Influence of Interest Rates upon Entrepreneurial Decisions in Business - A Case Study", *Harvard Business Review*, Autumn Number, 1938.

5 *Report of the Royal Commission on Banking and Finance*, Appendix Vol., Ottawa, Queen's Printer, 1965 and *Report of the Royal Commission on Banking and Finance*, Ch. 21.

Trade Credit. Some corporations were willing to increase the credit they generally extended to their customers. Thus funds from firms with relatively easy access to foreign and domestic capital markets were transferred to those whose source of funds was more restricted.

Commercial Paper Market. Closely associated with the increase in trade credit during postwar periods of credit restraint was the development of a commercial paper market in Canada. When difficult to obtain from usual sources, especially the banks, funds could be borrowed through the use of commercial paper from firms with temporarily excess balances. This type of financing led to the establishment of a commercial paper market. In many cases commercial paper provided funds at rates lower than those offered by the banks. Over the long run, the establishment of a commercial market assisted monetary policy because it kept temporarily idle funds invested thereby preventing the sudden mobilization of funds during periods of credit restriction.

Restricted Dividends. When funds were not readily available a few firms, especially small ones, reduced their dividend payments. In this way they were able to obtain cash to finance capital expenditures without resorting to the market.

Debt and Equity. Although most firms probably prefer to maintain some fixed relationship between their debt and equity financing, the Porter

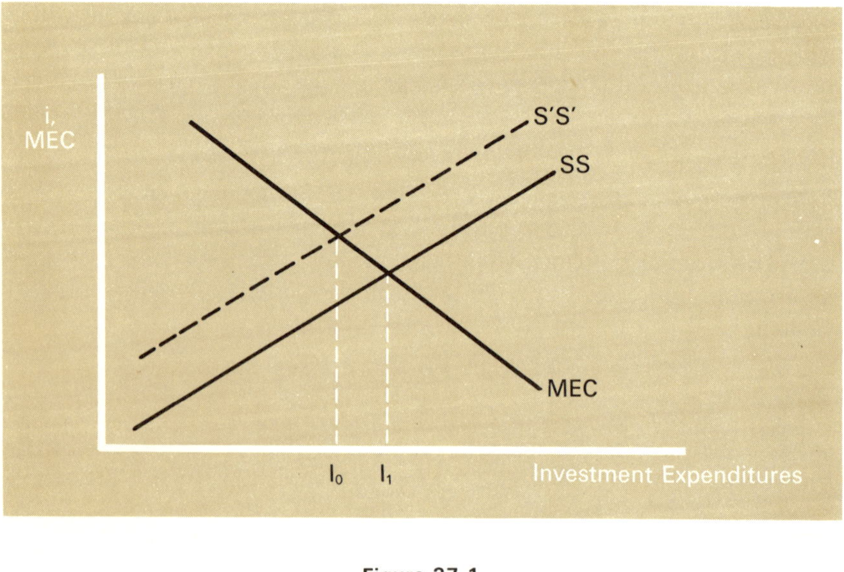

Figure 27-1

Commission found that the high interest rates led some firms to issue equities (shares) as a substitute for borrowed funds (bond issues). Some firms which issued bonds attempted to obtain lower rates by attaching conversion privileges in order to take advantage of the more favourable conditions in the equities market.

While some firms were able to escape restrictive monetary policy through financial adjustments during the periods surveyed by the Commission, other firms did not consider such adjustments necessary, or were unable to make them. But why would firms not deem it necessary to react to conditions of monetary restraint? The motivation of businesses can be explained in terms of our earlier analysis of the demand for investment expenditures. There we explained the demand for investment expenditures in terms of the cost of investment funds (the rate of interest) and the marginal efficiency of capital curve. In Figure 27-1, we show the cost of funds in terms of a supply schedule representing the marginal cost for varying amounts of funds made available to firms during a specified period of time. The curve slopes upward from left to right indicating that firms believe the cost of funds increases as additional amounts are obtained. The demand for investment expenditures is determined by the marginal efficiency of capital represented by the *MEC* curve. With a restrictive monetary policy the supply of funds schedule shifts upward and to the left, from *SS* to *S′S′* in Figure 27-1. With such a shift one would expect the demand for investment funds to decline from I_l to I_o. However, the Porter Commission found that the demand did not always decline because some firms were unaware that a shift in the *SS* curve had taken place. This may have been due in part to the anemic nature of monetary policy which resulted in relatively small and gradual shifts in the curve.

Also some firms were able to use their their own funds previously accumulated (so-called internal funds) to which they did not add the increase in their opportunity cost as market rates increased. In the case of long-term projects, some businesses considered only the long-term cost of borrowing funds. Hence during periods of credit restraint, they were willing to borrow at higher rates on short-term expecting to be able to refinance at lower rates in the future when credit conditions changed. For these firms higher costs of borrowing funds induced them to curtail their investment expenditures only insofar as they expected interest rates to remain high for some time into the future.

Even if businesses are cognizant of an upward shift in the *SS* curve which they cannot escape by making financial adjustments, they may still fail to reduce their investments expenditures. They may regard their *MEC* curve as perfectly interest inelastic or to shift only over time. Much of the evidence collected not only by the Porter Commission but by the earlier studies which we have mentioned, indicates that the *MEC* curve is in fact quite steep. The earlier evidence of inelasticity in the *MEC* curve was an important reason for the sharp reversal in attitude toward monetary policy in the 1930's and 1940's. Most Keynesians — those who use the credit approach to explain the effectiveness of monetary policy — accept the idea of a fairly steep *MEC* curve.

The Porter Commission found that businesses which had a commitment of expenditures under way when credit conditions tightened were reluctant to postpone the completion of investment projects because they felt postponement would affect their expected rate of return — that is, shift the *MEC* curve down and to the left. The same was true for businesses which undertook capital investment programs after credit restraint had been introduced to improve the quality or the amount of their output in order to retain their market position. Some firms estimated their rate of return from undertaking investment expenditures to be extremely high and, consequently, the cost of credit would have had to change substantially more than the monetary authorities were prepared to allow. Still other firms, particularly the larger ones which were continuously undertaking investment projects, did not curtail their investment expenditures during periods of monetary restraint because this implied the underutilization of their engineering and coordinating staffs. Such staffs would have been difficult to replace at a later date and many because of their substantial experience were considered an important asset to the firms.

Even in some of the highly capital-intensive utilities where one would expect changing interest rates to be significant, the Porter Commission found that investment projects were insensitive to the higher cost of funds. Many utility firms placed such high priority on meeting the demands for their services that they went ahead with their expansion plans. The same was true of municipal and provincial governments.

While most studies have been concentrated on the influence of monetary policy on business spending for plant and equipment, Ralph Hawtrey has long held that changing credit conditions exert influence mainly on inventory investment.[6] The evidence from the Commission's work indicates that inventory adjustments in response to changing credit conditions have been quite limited.

The evidence gathered by the Porter Commission was consistent with the general view that a change in credit conditions has to be substantial before a large proportion of the capital expenditures of businesses is affected. As one firm replied to the Commission's survey, "If we were making tea cosies or table napkins, it might be a different matter, but if

---

[6] See R. G. Hawtrey, *Capital and Employment*, London, Longmans, Roberts and Green, 1937; *Currency and Credit*, 4th ed., New York, Longmans, Green, 1950.

a deal we are contemplating would be affected by a 2% change in borrowing costs, we would have no business contemplating it in the first place".[7]

The evidence gathered by the Porter Commission was also consistent with the general view that businesses are largely insensitive to changes in the cost of credit. This, of course, adds grist to the mill of economists who assess the effectiveness of monetary policy in terms of the response of expenditures to a change in the rate of interest. Moreover it also supports their contention that monetary policy should be replaced by fiscal policy. They argue that the most important explanatory variable of changes in gross national product is a change in autonomous expenditures, particularly government expenditures and the export of goods and services.

THE QUANTITY OF MONEY APPROACH

Instead of concentrating on the rate of interest and business expenditures to explain the effectiveness of monetary policy, the quantity approach concentrates on the direct relationship between the quantity of money and consumption. As in the credit approach, the demand for money is regarded as a relatively stable function of a limited number of variables. Here, too, this function is considered to be independent of the supply of money. However, unlike the credit approach which assumes that the channel of influence of a change in the money supply is on credit conditions, the quantity approach assumes the channel of influence is on individual portfolio balances. The quantity approach assumes that individuals have a preference function which describes their holdings of money, financial assets and goods. If the monetary authorities increase the quantity of money, individuals will feel that they hold an excess of money relative to other assets. They will attempt to rid themselves of this excess by exchanging money balances for financial assets (lending) and for goods and services (spending). Over twenty years ago, Harold Somers explained individuals' reactions to an increase in the money supply.[8] He asserted that an individual may dispose of his wealth and income in four ways: by holding cash, by exchanging it for securities, by spending it on consumer goods, and by purchasing productive assets. The combination of these four alternatives which he chooses depends upon his assessment of the

---

7 *Report of the Royal Commission on Banking and Finance*, Appendix Vol., 1965, p. 360.

8 Somers, Harold, "Monetary Theory and the Theory of Interest", *Quarterly Journal of Economics*, 1940-1941, reprinted in *Readings in the Theory of Income Distribution*, Philadelphia, Blakiston Company, 1951, pp. 477-498.

rate of return on each and his assessment of changes in these rates. The return on holding cash is the subjective return of having the satisfaction of immediate purchasing power. Securities provide a rate of return which can be summarized as the rate of return on a standard security. The rate of return on consumption may be expressed as the extra satisfaction expected from consuming now rather than later and the rate of return on a productive asset may be thought of as the marginal efficiency of capital.

If the money supply is increased, the yield on financial assets declines as does the subjective yield on money. (The latter results from the additions to the stock of money in the hands of individuals.) With lower yields on both money and financial assets, individuals will be induced to increase their expenditures on both consumption and production. Whereas the credit approach relies on manipulating the money supply so as to control business investment expenditures by changing the interest rate, the quantity approach attempts to influence individuals' portfolio behaviour by altering the money supply so as to effect changes in a broader range of yields and consequently on a broader range of expenditures, particularly consumer expenditures. Moreover, while a change in the rate of interest is crucial for the effectiveness of monetary policy under the credit approach, the quantity approach requires only a change in the money supply. In the latter case the rate of interest need not change at all. As Friedman and Meiselman have put it, "An increased amount of water may flow through a lake without raising its level more than momentarily."[9]

Those who follow the quantity approach, especially Milton Friedman of the University of Chicago, have attempted to show that there is a direct relationship between money and economic activity and that with few exceptions the direction of causation is from money to economic activity. Moreover they have concluded that monetary policy has been ineffective in the postwar period because the monetary authorities have not used their discretionary powers wisely and because there are long and variable lags in the effects of monetary policy. We shall consider both these contentions in some detail later.

Most of the criticism of the quantity approach has been directed against the assumed stability and elasticity of the demand for money function, and against the assumed independence of the supply of and demand for money. This criticism applies to the credit approach also as it uses these assumptions to explain the relationship between the stock of money and the rate of interest.

---

[9] Friedman, Milton, and David Meiselman, "The Relative Stability of Monetary Velocity and the Investment Multiplier", *Stabilization Policies*, Commission on Money and Credit, Englewood Cliffs, N.J., Prentice-Hall, 1964, p. 221.

In the early years after the Second World War, monetary economists, concerned with the effective operation of monetary policy, saw the large increase in the short-term public debt as a source of strength for monetary policy. They looked to the expanded debt to provide a wider market in which the central bank could carry out its open market operations without creating undue disturbances in the money and credit markets. Unfortunately with the importance that the governments of Britain, the United States and Canada placed upon debt management policies, monetary policy became the servant of debt management rather than its master or partner.

After the mid-fifties, due primarily to the work of John G. Gurley and Edward S. Shaw,[10] the centre of attention of monetary policy shifted to the obligations of the non-bank financial intermediaries. The so-called **Gurley-Shaw thesis** argues that the growth of non-bank financial intermediaries has been accompanied by a qualitative improvement in the liabilities of these institutions. Insofar as these liabilities have become similar to monetary assets they have become close substitutes for money. Not only has this produced downward shifts in the demand for money curve, but it has also made this curve more interest elastic. If the monetary authorities can predict changes in the demand for money curve with some accuracy, such changes need not weaken the effectiveness of monetary policy. However, monetary policy will be rendered ineffective if the monetary authorities have insufficient information about these changes, and if changes in the money supply are offset by changes in the demand for money. As yet there does not appear to be sufficient evidence that the demand for money function has become less stable with the growth of near-money substitutes. On the other hand, as Gurley and Shaw have pointed out, monetary policy should no longer centre its attention on the activities of the commercial or chartered banks exclusively, but should consider also those of the non-bank financial intermediaries. Although Gurley and Shaw have not made specific statements, they have intimated that monetary policy should be more broadly based and the central bank's regulatory powers extended to non-bank financial intermediaries.

THE LIQUIDITY APPROACH

Both the credit and quantity approaches to explaining the effectiveness of monetary policy emphasize the role of changes in the money supply. The credit approach, as we have seen, focuses on changes in expenditures, especially investment expenditures following changes in the rate of inter-

[10] Gurley, John G., and E. S. Shaw, "Financial Aspects of Economic Development", *American Economic Review*, September, 1955, pp. 527-538, and *Money in the Theory of Finance*, Washington, D.C., Brookings Institution, 1960.

est while the quantity approach focuses on the portfolio behaviour of individuals. The liquidity approach as explained by the British Committee on the Working of the Monetary System in its report in 1959 took a different view of the monetary mechanism:

> Though we do not regard the supply of money as an unimportant quantity, we view it as only part of the wider structure of liquidity in the economy. It is the whole liquidity position that is relevant to spending decisions, and our interest in the supply of money is due to its significance in the whole liquidity picture.

The Committee argued that "A decision to spend depends not simply on whether the would-be spender has cash or 'money in the bank', although that maximum liquidity is obviously the most favourable springboard. There is the alternative of raising funds either by selling an asset or by borrowing".[11]

The Committee noted that there are two targets against which changes in interest rates can be aimed in order to alter the level of total demand. First, by bringing about appropriate changes in the rates of interest, monetary authorities can induce a change in the incentive to purchase capital goods. The Radcliffe Committee called this the "interest incentive" effect and was of the opinion that it has very little impact on the decisions of business firms. Second, monetary policy can alter what the Committee called the "general liquidity" of the whole economy. By changing the interest rate, monetary authorities can influence the liquidity conditions of financial institutions, business firms and people in general. The whole structure of interest rates is affected by an interest rate change that alters the liquidity of the various groups of financial institutions, and this in turn affects the liquidity of the whole economy. The Committee felt that the real force of interest rates lay in their effect on this general liquidity.

In the opinion of the Committee a decision to spend depends not simply upon whether the would-be spender has cash or money in the bank, but also on his ability and willingness to raise funds by borrowing or by exchanging his own assets for the more attractive ones issued by financial intermediaries. The ease with which spending units can raise funds depends both upon the composition of the spender's assets and his borrowing capacity, and upon the willingness and ability of financial institutions to lend and thereby finance spending units. The Committee concluded that the crucial factor in every spending decision is not the immediate access to money but the general liquidity of the whole economy. Therefore, to be effective monetary policy must take into consideration this crucial factor.

---

[11] *Committee on the Working of the Monetary System Report*, p. 132, paragraph 389.

In Canada the Porter Commission viewed the monetary mechanism in much the same way as did the British Radcliffe Committee. It explained the influence of monetary policy upon expenditures in terms of changes in credit conditions, a concept which had formed part of the Bank of Canada's brief to the Commission. Credit conditions were defined as "the cost, terms, general availability of credit to borrowers and, consequently, the terms and yields on which savers may invest their funds".[12] The Commission felt that credit conditions influenced spending units' decisions to increase their expenditures by

> reducing their rate of current saving in the form of financial assets, by borrowing, or by disposing of real or financial assets accumulated out of past income . . . Each of these methods of financing involves an impairment of the spender's position compared with what it might otherwise have been. Every spender must continually weigh the attractions and advantages of an increase in spending against the risks, difficulties and disadvantages involved in financing it . . . In short, it is the whole range of credit conditions — i.e. the difficulties, costs, and risks of borrowing, and the attractions of acquiring and holding financial assets — which is the link between financial markets and real expenditures.[13]

The Commission observed that changes in the money supply, especially "massive" changes, may be important determinants of credit conditions, but are by no means the only determinants. Large changes in the quantity of financial assets other than money also influence credit conditions and at times may dominate the influence of changes in the money supply. Other influences on credit conditions mentioned by the Commission include

> changes in underlying public attitudes toward spending and saving, alterations in the profitability of physical investment — whether stemming from technological change or changes in the economic climate at home or abroad — shifts in fundamental investor preferences and expectations, and many other factors.[14]

The Porter Commission defined credit conditions to include the cost and availability of funds to spending units. The influence of the cost of money on expenditures as the Commission described it is synonymous with the Radcliffe Committee's interest incentive effect. The availability of money concept is closely related to the Radcliffe Committee's concept of the general liquidity effect insofar as both focus on the behaviour of

---

12 *Report of the Royal Commission on Banking and Finance*, 1964, p. 423.

13 *Ibid.*, pp. 424-425.

14 *Ibid.*, p. 425.

financial institutions and imperfections in the financial system. As we shall see, the importance of the availability of funds for the effectiveness of monetary policy received wide attention during the early 1950's.

The Radcliffe Committee believed that lending by financial institutions can be indirectly controlled through changes in the level and structure of interest rates. The Committee argued, therefore, that the centre piece of monetary action is the level and structure of interest rates and not the supply of money. However, since it considered highly fluctuating interest rates undesirable, and thought that the lending of financial institutions should not be directly controlled ordinarily, the Committee concluded that greater stress should be placed on fiscal policy as a short-term stabilizer. Monetary policy, on the other hand, should be used to set the tone for longer-run developments,[15] and to control emergency situations when runaway inflation threatens. The Radcliffe Committee discarded any suggestion of liquidity controls to make monetary policy broader in scope "not mainly because of its administrative burdens, but because the further growth of new financial institutions would allow the situation continually to slip from under the grip of the authorities".[16]

While the Radcliffe Committee regarded interest rates as influencing expenditures through liquidity, the Porter Commission believed the impact of changed liquidity to be manifested through changed interest rates. Because of the more direct role given to interest rates by the Porter Commission, it was less reluctant to discard monetary policy as an instrument for economic stabilization and concluded that "in all but the very shortest cyclical fluctuations, the actions of the authorities can play a useful stabilizing role...".[17]

THE AVAILABILITY APPROACH

Following the introduction of Keynesian theory and the early studies which suggested that the interest elasticity of demand for loanable funds was close to zero, monetary policy was largely supplanted by fiscal policy for economic stabilization purposes. In the early 1950's, central bankers, particularly those associated with the Federal Reserve System in the United States, advocated the return to a more flexible use of monetary

---

15 See *Committee on the Working of the Monetary System Report*, paragraphs 511 and 524.

16 *Ibid.*, paragraph 894.

17 *Report of the Royal Commission on Banking and Finance*, 1964, p. 438.

policy. They accepted the view that saving, investment and spending, generally, were insensitive to changes in the rate of interest, but did not believe that this necessarily made monetary policy ineffective. Their defence of a more flexible use of monetary policy was embodied in what is variously known as the "availability doctrine", the "new theory of credit control", the "credit rationing doctrine" and the "Roosa effect".[18]

The basic proposition of the availability doctrine is that monetary policy works much more through restricting the availability of credit than through increasing its costs, and much more through its effects on lenders than its effects on borrowers. According to the theory, in the postwar financial environment government debt had become an important part of the asset holdings of most financial institutions, and small changes in the yields of government securities induced substantial changes in the lending patterns of these institutions. With only a small increase in the yield of government securities, say, as a result of open market purchases by the central bank, instituions were assumed to increase their holdings of such securities at the expense of extending private loans. This was explained by a combination of factors.

First, and probably most important, the availability doctrine assumes that because of imperfections in the money markets, yields on government and private debt do not move in unison. Many institutions, especially banks, were assumed to be slow and reluctant to change their lending rates as market conditions changed. In some cases government legislation imposed ceilings on interest rates and these ceilings remained constant or changed only slowly over time.

Second, it was assumed that the traditionally conservative nature of financial institutions makes them reluctant to take losses by selling government securities to increase the availability of funds for private lending. The increase in the yield of government securities relative to that of private debt makes them more attractive to institutional investors. Moreover, with an increase in the yield and a decrease in the price of government bonds which constitute a large proportion of their assets, institutions will feel that their liquidity position is jeopardized and will switch from private loans to government securities. The margin of unsatisfied borrowers is therefore widened and as institutions are reluctant to raise their own lending rates non-price rationing results. Thus spending is reduced and monetary policy made effective.

---

[18] Much has been written on the availability doctrine. The most complete analysis of it is in Assar Lindbeck, "The 'New' Theory of Credit Control in the United States", *Stockholm Economic Studies*, Pamphlet Series No. 1, 2nd ed., Stockholm, Almquist & Wicksell, 1962.

Critics have pointed out that if imperfections in the money and capital markets increase as a result of restrictive monetary policy, an increasing number of financial investors may sell off some of their government securities, even at capital losses, in order to invest in alternative higher yielding assets. It has also been pointed out that although short-term rates usually rise more than long-term rates during periods of credit restrictions, the prices of short-term securities fall less than the price of long-term securities. Thus the decline in the value of existing portfolios of government securities does not significantly affect institutions which hold substantial amounts of short-term securities.

Finally, the availability doctrine as presented in the early 1950's stressed the psychological effects of a change in monetary policy on both lenders and borrowers. With an increase in interest rates lenders were assumed to expect still higher rates and to postpone part of their supply of credit to take advantage of the expected higher rates in the future. Borrowers on the other hand were assumed to expect a future reversal of the change in the credit markets and therefore to postpone part of their demand to benefit from expected lower rates in the future. The opposite expectations assumed for borrowers and lenders are hard to justify.

Although the availability doctrine has been largely discredited as an important explanation of the effectiveness of monetary policy, it has made an important contribution to monetary theory. It drew attention to what traditional theory had largely neglected — monetary policy may affect aggregate demand by its effects on lenders as well as on spenders. The Porter Commission explicitly included the availability concept in its definition of credit conditions, and the Radcliffe Committee included the same concept implicitly when it considered the whole liquidity of the economy. Moreover, in its assessment of postwar Canadian monetary policy the Porter Commission found that alterations in the availability of funds for residential construction played an important role in determining the activity in this important sector of the economy. A significant part of postwar residential construction was financed under the National Housing Act. Under the act approved lenders made residential mortgage loans guaranteed by the government which also specified the maximum interest lenders could charge. The act placed a ceiling on the interest rate allowed on NHA mortgages which did not fluctuate with market rates. Whenever alternative lending offered attractively higher rates, lenders turned away from NHA loans. As market rates rose fewer funds were available for residential construction and this sector was forced to contract. While the total funds in the economy did not decline, a redirection of the flow of new loanable funds into different types of assets took place. This, in turn, influenced the spending pattern of the economy in a way which assisted monetary policy.

THE DIFFERENTIAL IMPACT

In recent years attention has been turned to the possible discriminatory nature of monetary policy. It has been pointed out that restrictive monetary policy may have a larger impact on firms which

(1) employ a high proportion of borrowed funds in working and fixed capital,
(2) require a high capital-output ratio,
(3) show a low rate of growth and small profit margins,
(4) produce goods and services for sectors which are severely affected by credit conditions,
(5) have no foreign connections,
(6) are relatively small.

The research undertaken for the Porter Commission provides evidence that many firms in Canada which are subsidiaries of foreign corporations have been able to escape restrictive monetary policy by turning to alternative sources of funds in the United States and elsewhere.[19] This has been especially evident in the petroleum and associated industries where there is a high degree of foreign ownership. There is also evidence that firms which depend upon bank credit to finance inventories, many of which are in the textile industry, have been affected more by restrictive monetary policies than firms which rely on their own funds. Moreover, larger firms, which are usually those with high rates of growth and healthy profit margins, have had a bargaining advantage in obtaining funds. This may be explained by the fear of financial institutions of losing the good will of major accounts. Since many of the larger firms are also located in large financial and industrial centres there may also have been some regional discrimination in the allocation of funds during periods of monetary restraint. Firms which are refused accommodation from financial institutions are usually too small to make use of market issues. The Porter Commission concluded that the impact of monetary policy has not been unduly concentrated in particular regions or particular industries. However, it pointed out that expenditures for residential construction were considerably affected by the availability of mortgage funds and of interim construction credit from the chartered banks.

Until November 1966, the maximum rate of interest on National Housing Act mortgage loans was administratively set. After that date it was allowed to fluctuate in relation to changing yields on long-term Gov-

---

[19] See "The Distribution of the Effects of Monetary Policy", in *Report of the Royal Commission on Banking and Finance*, Appendix Vol., 1965, pp. 371-395.

ernment of Canada bonds. During periods of monetary restraint the NHA maximum interest level usually lagged behind that of other alternative long-term investments and institutional lenders turned away from making NHA mortgage loans. Since these loans provided a major source of residential financing, residential construction declined until market conditions changed and financial institutions again switched to NHA loans. At times the government reduced some of the discriminatory impact of monetary policy on residential construction with direct loans made available by the Central Mortgage and Housing Corporation. In 1954 an additional source of NHA financing was opened when the chartered banks were first allowed to make such loans. However, when the ceiling on NHA loans rose above the 6 per cent level the banks were allowed to charge they virtually withdrew from NHA loans.

Monetary policy has also had a differential impact on financial institutions. Because of the legislative restrictions imposed on the banks, many of which were eliminated with the amendments to the Bank Act in 1967, the banks found it difficult to compete effectively with non-bank financial institutions. Among the legislative restrictions which produced inequities were the relatively high reserve requirements for the banks, the 6 per cent interest ceiling on bank loans and the restrictions on the type of investments the banks were allowed to make.

LAGS IN EFFECT

With the more flexible use of monetary policy after the early 1950's economists began to turn their attention to the lags associated with its effectiveness. Three main elements in monetary policy adjustments have been distinguished: the inside lag, the intermediate lag, and the outside lag.

The **inside lag** is the lapse between the time action is needed and the time it is actually taken. This lag has been broken down into two subdivisions: the **recognition lag** between the time that action is needed and the time it is recognized by the monetary authorities, and the **administrative lag** between the time that the need for action is recognized by the authorities and the time they actually take action. In their study for the Porter Commission, Harry Johnson and John Winder[20] found that between

[20] Johnson, Harry G., and John W. Winder, *Lags in the effects of Monetary Policy in Canada*, working paper for the Royal Commission on Banking and Finance, Ottawa, November, 1962. For similar studies in the United States see M. Friedman, "The Supply of Money and Changes in Prices and Output", *The Relationship of Prices to Economic Stability and Growth*, Compendium, Joint Economic Committee, Washington, 1958; Thomas Mayer "The Inflexibility of Monetary Policy", *Review of Economics and Statistics*, November, 1958; A. Ando, E. C. Brown, R. Solow, and J. Kareken, "Lags in Fiscal and Monetary Policy", *Stabilization Policies*, Commission on Money and Credit, Englewood Cliffs, N.J., Prentice-Hall, 1963.

1950 and 1962 the inside lag in Canada averaged six months for changes leading to monetary expansion and eleven and three quarter months for changes leading to monetary contraction.

The **intermediate lag** is the lapse of time between the taking of action by the monetary authorities and the accumulation of some desired total effect on an intermediate target such as a change in interest rates or in bank lending. The length of this lag depends upon the behaviour of the chartered banks and other financial institutions and upon the functioning of financial markets. The Johnson-Winder study found that a relatively small lag existed from 1950 to 1960 in the response of Canadian chartered banks to the cash management of the Bank of Canada. However, it also found an extremely long lag in the adjustment of the long rate of interest to the short rate of interest.

The **outside lag** is the lapse of time between changes in credit conditions and the initial impact on production and employment. This lag can also be divided into two parts: the **decision lag** between changes in credit conditions and changes in spending decisions, and the **production lag** between changes in spending decisions and initial changes in production and employment.

The econometric work carried out for the Porter Commission indicated an average lag of about three months, and on occasion as short as a few weeks, between the availability of funds and construction starts under the National Housing Act. However, in other sectors of the economy the direct effects of monetary policy on expenditures were more difficult to assess. The evidence suggested that a major proportion of the direct effects on employment and output following a change in credit conditions come within a period ranging from a few weeks to six to nine months.

Harry Johnson in summarizing the research he and John Winder conducted for the Porter Commission concluded that "the effect of monetary policy on the Canadian economy is imprecise, slow and variable; there is a relationship present, but it is extremely hazy".[21] He goes on to say that for short run economic stabilization policymakers should keep in mind the following three points:

> The first is to become accustomed to the notion that monetary policy works slowly and imprecisely, and to lower their sights in stabilization policy. The second is to invest resources in improving both knowledge of how monetary policy works, and the technique for using it efficiently. The third is to govern monetary policy primarily with reference to long-run objectives of economic growth, devoting it to the maintenance of a stable long-run monetary environment, and to rely on other instruments — fiscal policy, and possibly direct controls of various kinds — for short-run economic stabilization.[22]

[21] Johnson, Harry G., *The Canadian Quandary*, Toronto, McGraw-Hill, 1963, p. 187.

[22] *Ibid.*

RULES VERSUS AUTHORITY

Controversy over the relationships between the stock of money and the level of output and prices on the one hand, and the control of the money stock on the other, is by no means new. Before the Keynesian revolution when the quantity theory was part of the accepted gospel, controversy centred on how the money stock was to be managed. In the 1920's Irving Fischer proposed a system of "100% money" for the United States.[23] He saw the mismanagement of the credit-creating powers of commercial banks at the root of cyclical disturbances. He blamed the banks for expanding the money supply too quickly during boom years and contracting it too rapidly during recession. He suggested that the commercial banks should hold reserves equal to their deposits. In this way only the central bank could increase the money supply and it would do so by adding to bank reserves. Those who mistrusted the actions not only of the commercial banks but also of the central bank further advocated the return to an automatic system such as the pure gold standard. Under such a system the central bank would not have the discretion to change the reserves of the commercial banks at will but only according to the availability of gold. Such a system had already been tried and abandoned because under it the money supply was determined by mining conditions and not by the economic needs of the society.

Realizing the short-comings of a gold standard system others proposed replacing discretionary actions of the central bank by some sort of "automaticity". One such proposal was made by Benjamin Graham who suggested a commodity reserve dollar.[24] The value of the dollar was to be defined as a specified bundle of representative basic commodities. The government would stand ready to buy and sell this composite group of commodities at a stated price. Insofar as the commodities chosen were to be reasonably representative of prices in general, the government's commitment to buy and sell would stabilize the price level. Moreover, the right combination of money to goods would be automatically maintained. While at first sight Graham's proposal appears attractive it has inherent weaknesses. Two of these are the difficulty of storing perisable goods which would certainly have to be included in the representative bundle, and the depletion of government reserves during lengthy periods of inflation.

During the 1930's, those most critical of allowing governments or their central banks discretionary power assumed that monetary authorities

23 Fischer, Irving, *100% Money*, rev. ed., New York, Adelphi Company, 1963.

24 Graham, Benjamin, *Storage and Stability*, New York, McGraw-Hill, 1937.

were disinclined to increase the money supply. They assumed that a chronic shortage of purchasing power resulted from this unwillingness. The idea of a social credit, expressed by C. H. Douglas, [25] became very popular in Alberta and remnants of it are still to be found in Canada. Douglas proposed the payment of a "National Dividend" to provide the community with the purchasing power necessary to buy the national output. Similar proposals were put forward in the United States by Upton Sinclair and the Townsend Clubs. [26]

Alternatives to the schemes for more automatic expansion of the money supply were the proposals for more automatic increases in the velocity of the circulation of money. One such proposal had been made around the turn of the century by a German, Silvio Gesell. [27] He suggested issuing paper notes or script money which could remain legal tender only if the required monthly stamp were attached to it. Thus the holder of such script money would be induced to rid himself of it before the next period in which he would have to purchase a stamp to keep his money current. A script money scheme was introduced in Alberta in the 1930's but came to a sudden end when the Alberta legislation was declared *ultra vires* by the Supreme Court.

There are few economists today who believe that the most serious problem associated with allowing governments and central banks discretion in manipulating the money supply is their unwillingness to allow it to grow sufficiently over the long-run. Those who want some sort of automatic mechanism are more concerned with the discretionary power allowed central banks to control short-run cyclical fluctuations. Friedman and Shaw [28] in the United States are two of the most ardent advocates of replacing the discretionary powers of the Federal Reserve with a "rule" for its operations. They believe that the authorities should provide maximum freedom for private enterprise, except for such restraints to trade as

25 Douglas C. H., *Credit Power and Democracy*, London, Cecil Palmer, 1920.

26 See for example *Economic Meaning of the Townsend Plan*, Public Policy Pamphlet 20, Chicago, University of Chicago Press, 1936.

27 The work of Gesell was not noticed or was completely forgotten until it was mentioned by Keynes. See *The General Theory of Employment, Interest and Money*, London, Macmillan, 1951, Ch. 23.

28 See Edward S. Shaw, "Money Supply and Stable Economic Growth", in American Assembly, *United States Monetary Policy*, New York, Columbia University Press, 1958, and Milton Friedman's testimony before the Joint Economic Committee, *Employment, Growth and Price Levels*, Hearings, (1959-1960), Part 4, pp. 605-637. Friedman's proposals are elaborated in his *A Program for Monetary Stability*, New York, Fordham University Press, 1960.

the control of monopolies, and should allow the price system to bring about the necessary adjustments.[29]

Friedman points out that forecasting is an art rather than a precise science and therefore actions by the central bank to offset cyclical movements are subject to error. Even if the central bank could correctly recognize turning points and take appropriate action, there are long and variable lags between the time when the authorities take action and when the effects of such action take hold. Hence a restrictive monetary policy to combat inflation will make itself felt later when the economy is already slipping into recession, and conversely, a policy of monetary ease may take effect at a time when inflation is setting in. Shaw's solution to this problem is to stop trying to use monetary policy as a counter-cyclical device and put the monetary system on an "automatic pilot". He has suggested increasing the money supply each year by a constant percentage calculated in terms of the long-run growth needs of the economy — probably about 3 to 4 per cent per year. The money supply would be allowed to increase sufficiently to meet the normal needs of the economy but not enough to permit serious inflation as the schemes proposed in the 1930's would have done.

Friedman has also proposed replacing discretionary policy with a rule whereby the authorities would increase the money supply each year by an amount corresponding to the estimated growth in the nation's productive capacity. A modification to the Shaw-Friedman proposals would be to allow the authorities to use the long-run monetary growth needs of the economy as a norm for monetary policy action and to permit them some discretionary power to vary policy around this norm.

Unfortunately, money will not manage itself, nor is monetary policy a precise science. The central bank "must operate to a considerable extent by the method of successive approximation, constantly adjusting its operations in the light of all the evidence it can get, as it becomes available, about changing economic and financial conditions".[30] Therefore, heavy reliance on monetary policy for short-run stabilization is probably unjus-

---

29 See Henry C. Simons, "Rules versus Authorities in Monetary Policy," *Journal of Political Economy*, 1936.

30 Bank of Canada, *Evidence of the Governor Before the Royal Commission on Banking and Finance*, Ottawa, May, 1964, p. 127.

tifiable. However, this does not mean that discretion should be replaced by rules. As Paul Samuelson has put it:

> In principle, the choice has never been between discretionary and non-discretionary action; for when men set up a definitive mechanism which is to run forever afterward by itself, that involves a single act of discretion which transcends, in both its arrogance and its capacity for potential harm, any repeated acts of foolish discretion that can be imagined.[31]

SELECTED READINGS

American Assembly, Neil H. Jacoby (ed.), *United States Monetary Policy*, rev. ed., New York, Frederick A. Praeger, 1964.

Ando, A., and F. Modigliani, "The Relative Stability of Monetary Velocity and the Investment Multiplier", *American Economic Review*, Vol. 55, September 1965, pp. 693-728.

Brown, E. Cary, *et. al.*, *Stabilization Policies*, a series of research studies for the Commission on Money and Credit, Englewood Cliffs, N. J., Prentice-Hall, 1963.

Cagan, Phillip, "Current Issues in the Theory of Monetary Policy" in Michael J. Brennan (ed.), *Patterns of Market Behaviour: Essays in Honour of Philip Taft*, Providence, Brown University Press, 1965, pp. 135-154.

Cairns, James P., and H. H. Binhammer, *Canadian Banking & Monetary Policy*, Toronto, McGraw-Hill, 1965, Part 2.

Committee on the Working of the Monetary System Report, London, Her Majesty's Stationery Office, August 1959.

Culbertson, J. M., "Intermediaries and Monetary Theory: A Criticism of the Gurley-Shaw Theory", and "Reply", *American Economic Review*, Vol. 48, March 1959, pp. 119-138.

de Leeuw, Frank, and Edward Gramlich, "The Federal Reserve-Mit Econometric Model", Board of Governors of the Federal Reserve System, *Federal Reserve Bulletin*, Vol. 54, January 1968, pp. 11-40.

Economic Council of Canada, *Conference on Stabilization Policies*, Ottawa, Queen's Printer, 1966.

---

31 Samuelson, Paul A., "Reflections on Central Banking", *National Banking Review*, September, 1963, p. 16.

Friedman, Milton, *A Program For Monetary Stability*, New York, Fordham University Press, 1959.

Friedman, Milton, "The Role of Monetary Policy", *American Economic Review*, Vol. 58, March 1968, pp. 1-17.

Gurley, J. G., and E. S. Shaw, "Financial Aspects of Economic Development", *American Economic Review*, Vol. 45, September 1955, pp. 515-538.

Gurley, J. G., and Edward Shaw, "Financial Intermediaries and the Saving-Investment Process, Journal of Finance, Vol. 11, May 1956, pp. 257-276.

Gurley, J. G., and Edward S. Shaw, *Money in a Theory of Finance*, Washington, Brookings Institution, 1960.

Hamburger, M. J., "Interest Rates and the Demand for Consumer Durable Goods", *American Economic Review*, Vol. 57, December 1967, pp. 1131-1153.

Havrilesky, Thomas, "A Test of Monetary Policy Action", *Journal of Political Economy*, Vol. 75, June 1967, pp. 299-304.

Hay, Keith, "Money and Cycles in Post-Confederation Canada", *Journal of Political Economy*, Vol. 75, June 1967, pp. 263-273.

Horwich, George, *Monetary Process and Policy: A Symposium*, Homewood Ill., Richard D. Irwin, 1967.

Johnson, Harry G., *Essays in Monetary Economics*, London, George Allen & Unwin, 1967, Part 2.

Johnson H. G., and W. L. Winder, *Lags in the Effect of Monetary Policy in Canada*, working paper prepared for the Royal Commission on Banking and Finance, Ottawa, Queen's Printer, November 1962.

Kareken, J. H., "Lenders' Preferences, Credit Rationing, and the Effectiveness of Monetary Policy", *Review of Economics and Statistics*, Vol. 39, August 1957, pp. 292-302.

Kareken, J. H., *et. al.*, discussion on "Monetary and Fiscal Policy in a Fully Employed Economy", *Jurnal of Finance*, Vol. 22, May 1967.

Lindbeck, Assar, *A Study in Monetary Analysis*, Stockholm, Almquist & Wicksell, 1963.

Mints, Lloyd W., *Monetary Policy For A Competitive Society*, New York, McGraw-Hill, 1950.

Ritter, Lawrence S., "The Role of Money in Keynesian Theory" in Deanne Carson (ed.), *Banking and Monetary Studies*, Homewood, Ill., Richard D. Irwin, 1963, pp. 134-150.

Report of the Royal Commission on Banking and Finance, Ottawa, Queen's Printer, 1964.

Report of the Royal Commission on Banking and Finance, Appendix Volume, Ottawa, Queen's Printer, 1965.

Saving, Thomas R., "Monetary-Policy Targets and Indicators", *Journal of Political Economy,* Vol. 75, Supplement, August 1967, pp. 446-456.

Scott, Ira O., "The Availability Doctrine: Development and Implications", *Canadian Journal of Economics and Political Science,* Vol. 23, November 1957, pp. 532-539.

Simons, Henry, *Economic Policy for a Free Society,* Chicago, University of Chicago Press, 1948.

Smith, Warren L., "On the Effectiveness of Monetary Policy", *American Economic Review,* Vol. 46, September 1956, pp. 588-606.

Smith, Warren L., and Ronald L. Teigen, *Readings in Money, National Income and Stabilization Policy,* Homewood, Ill., Richard D. Irwin, 1965, Ch. 1.

Tucker, D. P. "Dynamic Income Adjustment to Money-Supply Changes", *American Economic Review,* Vol. 56, June, 1966, pp. 433-449.

Tussig, A. Dale, "Can Monetary Policy Influence The Availability of Credit", *Journal of Finance,* Vol. 21, March 1966, pp. 1-13.

Yeager, Leland B. (ed.), *In Search of a Monetary Constitution,* Cambridge, Mass., Harvard University Press, 1962.

Young, John H., "Credit Conditions and The Bank of Canada", *The Canadian Banker,* Vol. 74, Spring 1967, pp. 198-207.

PART SIX

MONEY AND THE INTERNATIONAL ECONOMY

28 INTERNATIONAL PAYMENTS TRANSACTIONS

So far we have been concerned primarily with the monetary relationships within one country; we have, by and large, assumed a **closed economy** — one with no foreign trade. However, Canada is one of the most open economies in the world. In 1966, for example, the value of exports of goods and services was 22 per cent and the value of imports was 24 per cent of the gross national product. Our trade intercourse with other countries is of great benefit not only to us but also to our trading partners. Through specialization international trade leads to more efficient allocation of resources in the same way as internal trade does. In earlier chapters we pointed out that specialization is facilitated by the presence of a commonly acceptable unit of account and medium of exchange. The absence of an international monetary unit is probably the most important reason why international specialization is not so intensive as that found within most countries, especially industrialized nations.[1] Without a common unit of account international trade is more cumbersome than internal trade and is less willingly undertaken. The degree of possible international specialization, therefore, is limited.

The lack of an international monetary unit introduces a complication into trade between nations. Whereas, in internal trade, transactions are finalized by the exchange of goods for the country's monetary unit, in international trade an additional exchange is required — the money of one country must be exchanged for that of another country. Moreover, the seller of a good in Canada must know not only the price of the good in terms of Canadian dollars, but also the price — that is, the rate of

[1] It can probably be argued that gold serves as an international monetary unit insofar as many of the national monetary units are represented by a fixed weight of gold. Moreover, in the final analysis, gold is still an international medium of exchange in final settlement of debt among countries.

exchange — of Canadian dollars in terms of the currency of foreign countries. One of a nation's prime concerns is that rate at which units of foreign currencies exchange for a unit of domestic currency. This is known as the **foreign exchange rate.** Before we consider the determination of this rate we must know something about the causes of international indebtedness which result in payments to be made between one country and another. Moreover, since payments to be made by one country are to some degree offset by receipts from others, we must also learn how these differences are settled.

BALANCE OF INTERNATIONAL PAYMENTS CONCEPTS

A country's balance of international payments statement is a summary of all economic transactions between its residents (individuals, firms and government) and the rest of the world during a given period of time. It records the money value of the flow of merchandise, services bought and sold, sales and purchases of assets of all kinds and gifts made to or received from the rest of the world. A transaction is included in the balance of payments whether or not it involves a money payment as long as a resident is dealing with someone outside his national boundaries.

Transactions in the balance of payments statement are recorded following the system of double-entry bookkeeping. For every transaction two entries are made: a debit and a credit. Every transaction must affect at least two items in the balance of payments statement, and since assets must be equal to liabilities, debit must be equal to credits in order to balance the statement. Alternatively, since for each debit item there is a corresponding credit item the total balance of payments statement *must always be in balance.* [2] But how does one decide whether a transaction is to be recorded as a credit (with a plus sign) or as a debit (with a minus sign). To begin, one should keep in mind that credits provide a country, say Canada, with claims against foreign resources and debits provide foreigners with claims against Canadian resources. All credit items represent actual or potential sources of foreign exchange and conversely all debit items represent actual or potential uses of foreign exchange. Hence exports of goods and services which *give rise* to receipts of international

---

2 Other accounting procedures generally followed include: (1) valuing items in the balance of payments statement in terms of the monetary unit of the country for which the statement is drawn up, (2) defining residents to include all individuals, corporations, institutions, governments and government agencies ordinarily domiciled in the country, (3) providing for "errors and omissions and unrecorded items" since the balance of payments statement is an *estimate* of the value of transactions and must show a balance between total debits and credits, and (4) constructing the balance of payments statement to account for transactions over either a three-month period or a period of a year.

monetary claims are credits, and imports of goods and services which *give rise* to payments of international monetary claims are debits. Since exports of goods and services are recorded as credits, what constitutes the corresponding debit items in the balance of payments? The debit items are the monetary arrangement by foreigners for the payment of Canadian exports. Foreigners can make payment by turning over their foreign monetary claims, such as American dollar deposits with New York banks, to Canadians.[3] Payment can also be made by foreigners transferring their Canadian monetary claims, such as Canadian dollar deposits with Toronto banks, to Canadians. In the first case Canadians acquire foreign assets; in the second they reduce their liabilities to foreigners. Either way, the transaction is recorded as a debit in the balance of payments statement.

Since imports of goods and services are recorded as debits, what constitutes the corresponding credit items? The credit items are the monetary arrangement by Canadians for the payment for foreign imports. Canadians can make payment by turning over their Canadian monetary claims, such as Canadian dollar deposits with a Toronto bank, to foreigners. Payment can also be made by Canadians transferring their foreign monetary claims, such as their American dollar deposits with New York banks, to foreigners. In the first case Canadians are increasing their liabilities to foreigners; in the second they are giving up assets to foreigners. These monetary transactions are recorded as credits in Canada's balance of payments statement.

The rules for deciding whether an item is a debit or a credit may be summarized as follows:

Debit Entries

A. Goods and services acquired from foreigners
B. Gifts made to foreigners
C. Assets acquired from foreigners
D. Reduction in liabilities to foreigners

Credit Entries

A. Goods and services sold to foreigners
B. Gifts received from foreigners
C. Assets given up to foreigners
D. Increase in liabilities to foreigners

---

[3] Where the foreigners are, say, Americans, the transfer of American dollar deposits would represent the transfer of domestic monetary claims from the American point of view.

Let us consider next international capital flows. When Canadians borrow in a foreign country they sell to foreigners Canadian debt instruments such as Canadian securities. The sale of securities just like the export of goods and services gives rise to receipts of international monetary claims and is therefore recorded as a credit. Canadian borrowing abroad (foreign lending and investing in Canada) is referred to as a **capital inflow.** When Canadians lend abroad they import foreign debt instruments which give rise to international monetary payments. This, as we have already mentioned, is recorded as a debit. Canadian lending and investing in a foreign country is referred to as a **capital outflow.** Capital flows are usually defined as either long- or short-term. Financial claims with an *original* maturity of more than one year, such as bonds, and financial claims that serve as instruments of long-term finance but have no specific maturity, such as equity stocks, are considered long-term capital items.[4] These are usually further subdivided into direct investment and portfolio investment. The distinction made between the two is that direct investment gives the investor managerial control. No ownership is associated with portfolio investment such as bonds. Short-term capital movements consist of the transfer of financial claims with an original maturity of one year or less and of financial claims that act as short-term credit instruments. These, for example demand deposits, need not have specific maturity dates.

CANADA'S BALANCE OF INTERNATIONAL PAYMENTS

Table 28-1 shows Canada's balance of international payments for 1965. The table is divided into three parts: I the Current Account, II the Capital Account and III Balancing Items. Current account items are separated from others because they directly affect the level of national income within a country. For example, exports of goods and services represent an outlet for current production; receipts from their sale as well as from investment income are part of current income. Alternatively, imports of goods and services add to the goods and services available from current domestic production while their payment constitutes leakages from the income circuit. The difference in the value of merchandise exports and imports is referred to as the **balance on merchandise trade.** In 1965 Canada had a credit, or surplus, in its merchandise trade balance with foreigners which gave rise to receipts of international monetary claims. However, the surplus on merchandise trade was more than offset by the debit, or deficit, on the total of other current account items.

[4] Bonds with an original maturity of, say, twenty-five years are long-term instruments at their time of issue. They are no longer long-term securities when they come within one year of maturity.

TABLE 28-1

Canada's Balance of International Payments for 1965
(millions of dollars)

	Credits	Debits	Balance
I. CURRENT ACCOUNT			
A. Merchandise Trade			
Exports	+8,745		
Imports		−8,627	
Balance on merchandise trade			+ 118
B. Other Current Transactions			
Gold production available for export	+ 138		+ 138
Travel	+ 747	− 779	− 32
Interest and dividends	+ 310	−1,071	− 761
Freight and shipping	+ 673	− 755	− 82
Official contributions		− 92	− 92
Inheritances, immigrants' and emigrants' funds	+ 211	− 211	0
All other current receipts and payments	+ 640	−1,012	− 372
Balance on other current transactions			−1,201
Current Account Balance			−1,083
II. CAPITAL ACCOUNT			
A. Long-Term Capital Movements			
Direct investment	+ 405	− 125	+ 280
New issues and redemptions of Canadian securities abroad	+1,209	− 382	+ 827
Trade in outstanding Canadian securities, net		− 219	− 219
Trade in foreign securities, net		− 84	− 84
Government of Canada loans and subscriptions	+ 10	− 14	− 4
Other long-term capital, net		− 87	− 87
Total Long-Term Capital Movements			+ 713
B. Short-Term Capital Movements			
Change in Canadian holdings of foreign bank balances and other short-term funds	+ 138		+ 138
Change in Canadian dollar holdings of foreigners	+ 102		+ 102
Other short-term capital movements	+ 287		+ 287
Total Short-Term Capital Movements			+ 527
Capital Account Balance			+1,240
III. BALANCING ITEMS			
Changes in Official Holdings of Gold and Foreign Exchange			
Change in official holdings of gold and foreign exchange	+ 11		
Change in net International Monetary Fund position		− 168	
Total			− 157
Grand Total, Balance of Payments			0

\+ = Net increase in Canadian liabilities; — = Net increase in Canadian assets

Source: Bank of Canada, Statistical Summary, 1966 Supplement, pp. 150-153.

The compilers of Canada's balance of payments consider gold production available for export as a semi-monetary item and therefore show it separate from merchandise exports. It is shown as a credit because it is considered an item which gives rise to foreign monetary claims or is itself a representative foreign monetary claim by Canada. Travel by foreigners in Canada provides receipts while travel by Canadians outside Canada results in payment of foreign monetary claims. In 1965 Canadians travelling abroad spent more than foreign travellers and tourists spent in Canada.

One of the most important foreign payment requirements for Canada is the payment of interest and dividends on foreign investments in Canada. While Canadians receive similarly derived income from their investments in foreign countries these receipts are relatively small in comparison to the payments made. Although this imbalance has been of concern to many Canadians it must be remembered that foreign investments in Canada which result in our payment of interest and dividends abroad have not only made possible Canada's rapid economic development but have also supplied the country with the means to meet its foreign interest and dividend payments.

The debit balance on account of freight and shipping shows that in 1965, as has been the case over the years, Canadians paid more to foreigners than they received from them for supplying these services. Immigrant and emmigrant remittances to and from Canada usually produce an annual surplus of receipts over payments. However, the table indicates that in 1965 receipts were excactly offset by payments.

All other receipts from current transactions include payment by foreign governments for maintaining diplomatic and military establishments in Canada, personal remittances of a non-commercial nature, miscellaneous income including transfers of income and profits not listed separately elsewhere and income from business services. All other current payments include government transactions such as official representation and military expenditures abroad and membership assessments in international organizations, miscellaneous payments including income and profits not listed in the interest and dividends account, business services and other transactions including payments by subsidiaries in Canada to head offices abroad.

In most of the years since the end of the Second World War, Canada has had an overall debit balance in its current account. Although the balance on merchandise trade has shown a surplus in recent years, this has been more than offset by net payments on other current transactions. Annual deficits in the current account can be carried as long as Canada is able to borrow from foreigners and as long as it has foreign assets to give up to foreigners.

The second broad category of the balance of payments statement, the capital account, shows the long-term and short-term loans Canadians make to or receive from foreigners. Over the years two items have provided the country with its most important source of foreign monetary claims to finance its current account deficits. These have been direct foreign investment in Canada and the net sale to foreigners of new issues (new issues less retirements at maturity) of long-term Canadian securities. Aside from purchasing new issues of Canadian securities foreigners have also invested by purchasing outstanding Canadian stocks and bonds. In recent years however, as was the case in 1965, receipts from foreigners for the purchase of outstanding Canadian securities have been more than offset by payments to foreigners from the resale of such securities to Canadians. While Canadians have repurchased outstanding Canadian securities from foreigners they have also purchased outstanding foreign securities. In 1965, for example, Canadian payments to foreigners for purchase of outstanding foreign securities were larger than receipts from the repurchase of these securities by foreigners.

When the Canadian government makes advances or loans to foreign governments or subscribes to the capital of international organizations, a capital outflow takes place from Canada. If the government makes payment with Canadian currency the government's foreign liabilities increase; if it makes payment with foreign monetary claims its foreign assets (gold and foreign exchange) decrease. The opposite, of course, is true when foreigners make repayments. Other long-term capital movements include transactions in long-term foreign debts and Government of Canada assets, as well as miscellaneous long-term capital items.[5]

Short-term capital movements consist of two main types: changes in holdings by Canadians of foreign bank balances and other short-term funds, and changes in the Canadian dollar asset holdings of foreigners. The latter include Canadian dollar deposits, Canadian government demand liabilities, Treasury bills, commercial paper, and finance company paper obligations. The compilers of the balance of payments account add in another item, "other short-term capital movements", which includes changes in loans and accounts receivable and accounts payable as well as a balancing item representing errors and omissions resulting from differences between direct measurements of current and capital accounts.

During 1965 the overall net capital inflow to Canada was $1,240 million. Of this, $1,083 million was required to offset the current account deficit. The remaining $157 million was added to Canada's international

---

[5] Included here in 1965, for example, was a net payment under the Columbia River Treaty from the United States equivalent to $32 million (Canadian).

monetary reserves. Changes in these reserves, shown in the third and final major category of the balance of payments statement, consist of changes in official holdings of gold and foreign exchange, and changes in Canada's net position with the International Monetary Fund. As is shown in the table, Canada increased its net position with the Fund in 1965 by $168 million. This was accomplished by employing the $157 million that remained from capital inflows after meeting the deficit on current account, and by reducing Canada's official holdings of gold and foreign exchange by $11 million.

The signs used in the balancing account are usually a source of confusion because one is inclined to look upon an increase in Canada's international reserves as a capital inflow that should be recorded as a credit and not as a debit. How does one explain this apparent contradiction? In drawing up the balance of payments statement it has been customary to assume that all payments and receipts are made in Canadian dollars. Hence debit transactions result in dollar payments by Canadians to foreigners, and credit transactions involve dollar receipts by Canadians from foreigners. If now net receipts from foreigners are received in foreign exchange, for balance of payments accounting we assume that this is offset by an import of Canadian dollars and, therefore, shown as a debit item.

EQUILIBRIUM AND DISEQUILIBRIUM IN THE BALANCE OF PAYMENTS

We have seen that the balance of payments statement is based on a double entry system and that by definition each international transaction always includes both a payment and a receipt of equal amount. Can there then be a balance of payments surplus or deficit, and can there be any disequilibrium in the balance of payments? When we speak of a balance of payments surplus or deficit we refer to the balance obtained from the summation of selected items. Which items should be included in such a summation is one of the more controversial questions in balance of payments methodology. Another is whether a surplus or deficit balance derived by this method does in fact reflect any disequilibrium in the balance of payments.

Sometimes, particularly in Europe, a balance of payments surplus or deficit is identified with the balance on current account. Most economists would admit that this concept of surplus or deficit is much too narrow, especially if it is associated with disequilibrium in the balance of payments. For example, a developing country, of necessity, is confronted usually with a deficit on current account. However, since this deficit may be readily financed by the inflow of long-term capital due to profitable investment opportunities, a deficit on current account need not reflect a disequilibrium situation. Hence economists today often speak of the **basic balance** which is derived by combining the balance on current account and the balance on account of long-term capital flows. Historically, Canada's basic balance has usually been a surplus although its balance on current account has been a deficit. Whether such a surplus reflects disequilibrium in Canada's balance of payments depends upon whether such a situation can be maintained into the future.

Another concept of balance employed today is the so-called **overall balance.** It is derived by combining the net balances on current account, long-term capital movements and short-term capital flows. Overall balance is said to be maintained if there is no net change in the country's official holdings of gold and foreign exchange over a period of, say, from five to ten years. This concept of balance or equilibrium is usually also associated with the question of equilibrium in the foreign exchange rate. Table 28-1 shows Canada's overall balance during 1965.

Still another concept of balance divides the main elements in the balance of payments into **autonomous** and **accommodating** transactions. An autonomous transaction is independent of, and not induced by, other transactions in the balance of payments. In contrast, an accommodating transaction is a compensating or financing transaction which takes place in response to an autonomous transaction. For example, imports and exports of goods and services are independently determined by such factors as differences in tastes, income, relative prices and national foreign policies and are therefore autonomous. Long-term capital movements are also determined independently by expectations of profit or other income from productive investments. Unilateral transfers — receipts and payments for which there is no *quid pro quo* — are usually also autonomous transactions. This is the case with unilateral transfers such as the payment and receipt of inheritances and the movement of immigrants' and emigrants' funds. Government contributions for such purposes as relief, economic development projects and military aid are also autonomous unilateral transfers. However, government transfers intended to assist a recipient country to finance autonomous imports are accommodating transfers.

Short-term capital movements may be either autonomous or accommodating. If they take place in response to changes in credit conditions (changes in the availability and cost of credit) they are independent of other items in the balance of payments and therefore autonomous. However, short-term capital movements in the form of changes in bank balances or book accounts are accommodating in that they occur in response to other transactions in the balance of payments. Changes in the country's official holdings of gold and foreign exchange as well as in its net position with the International Monetary Fund are also accommodating transactions.

Now that we have defined autonomous and accommodating transactions and classified the items in the balance of payments as one or the other, we can derive a measure of balance of payments surplus or deficit. A deficit in the balance of payments may be said to occur when payments for autonomous transactions are in excess of receipts from autonomous transactions. A balance of payments surplus may be said to exist when receipts from autonomous transactions are in excess of payments for such transactions. In other words, the balance of payments may be said to be in equilibrium when, over a period of time, the net balance on autonomous items is zero. But why should a net debit or credit on account of autonomous transactions reflect disequilibrium in the balance of payments? Disequilibrium exists only insofar as such net balances are not maintainable. A country is always faced with the uncertainty of the availability of sufficient accommodating finance. Short-term capital movements are usually quite fickle and therefore cannot be depended upon as a stable source of international finance. A country's official holdings of foreign exchange will sooner or later be depleted with continual demands for financing. A country can, of course, obtain compensatory finance from the International Monetary Fund and foreign governments and institutions, but the amounts of such finance are limited. Hence, a deficit on autonomous transactions which cannot be financed for a period of more than, say, five to ten years reflects disequilibrium in the balance of payments. Alternatively, surpluses on autonomous transactions may also indicate disequilibrium for they too may not be maintainable. Under certain conditions, excess receipts from a surplus on autonomous transactions have to be financed by an increase in a country's money supply. The amount of such an increase is limited by the amount of inflation the country is willing to undergo. Even without the dangers of inflation, a surplus country will suffer external disequilibrium for its surplus implies a deficit which is not maintainable in the balance of payments of one or more other countries.

We have defined balance of payments equilibrium in terms of a zero balance on account of autonomous transactions. Equilibrium exists only if the equality between autonomous receipts and expenditures is obtained without trade or other government controls and without the necessity of an undue degree of unemployment or inflation. Today economists prefer to describe an equilibrium situation as having both "external balance" and "internal balance".

SELECTED READINGS

Badger, Donald G., "The Balance of Payments: A Tool of Economic Analysis", *International Monetary Fund Staff Papers*, Vol. 2, No. 1, September 1951, pp. 86-197.

Dominion Bureau of Statistics, *Canada's Balance of International Payments*, issued annually.

Dominion Bureau of Statistics, *The Canadian Balance of International Payments, A Compendium of Statistics from 1946 to 1965*, Ottawa, March 1967.

Høst-Madsen, Poul, "What Does It Really Mean? — A Deficit in the Balance of Payments", *Finance and Development*, Vol. 3, No. 3, September 1966, pp. 171-178.

Kindleberger, Charles P., *International Economics*, Homewood, Ill., Richard D. Irwin, 1963, Ch. 2.

Lederer, Walther, *The Balance of Foreign Transactions: Problems of Definition and Measurement*, Princeton, N.J., Princeton University, International Finance Section, September 1963.

Machlup, Fritz, *International Payments, Debts and Gold*, New York, Charles Scribner's Sons, 1964, Ch. 5.

Slater, David W., *Canada's Balance of International Payments — When is a Deficit a Problem*, Montreal, Canadian Trade Committee, 1964.

Slater, David W., *Perspective on Canada's International Payments*, Ottawa, Economic Council of Canada, December 1965.

29

FOREIGN EXCHANGE

One important difference between international trade and domestic trade is that international trade usually involves two kinds of monetary units. As a rule foreigners who sell goods, services and claims to residents of Canada want to be paid in their own national monetary units just as Canadians selling goods to foreigners want to be paid in Canadian dollars. Canadian exporters, therefore, are involved in a "double sale" and Canadian importers in a "double purchase" when dealing with foreigners. The Canadian exporter must sell not only his goods but also the foreign monetary claims he receives in exchange. Similarly a Canadian importer must first buy the foreign monetary claims which he uses to purchase the desired goods from foreigners.

Foreign monetary claims are called **foreign exchange.** In addition to coin, notes and bank deposits denominated in foreign monetary units, foreign exchange also includes a variety of highly liquid claims denominated in foreign monetary units.[1] Gold available for international payments is a very special kind of foreign exchange and is usually shown as a separate international monetary unit. The same is true for a country's net position with the International Monetary Fund which we shall consider later.

The most important kind of foreign exchange consists of demand deposits in foreign banks, and in branches and agencies of Canadian banks abroad. Canadian banks also maintain chequing accounts with foreign banks with whom they have a "correspondent" relationship. These accounts are usually denominated in the monetary unit of the country of the correspondent bank. As a rule foreign correspondents of Canadian banks reciprocate by maintaining Canadian dollar deposits with them in

[1] Our definition is broader than the traditional one which includes only those foreign monetary claims which serve as a "medium of exchange" such as bank notes and deposits.

Canada. In recent years it has not been unusual for Canadian banks to hold deposits denominated in American dollars with their correspondents in Britain or in continental Europe. These deposits are known as "Euro-Dollars"[2] and are made for investment purposes in addition to facilitating regular customer demands.

FOREIGN EXCHANGE INSTRUMENTS

A Canadian requiring foreign monetary claims to make payment abroad can obtain such claims in several ways. He can go to his bank and purchase foreign exchange in the form of a cable or mail transfer, a bank draft, or a bill of exchange. A cable transfer represents a claim on a foreign bank deposit. It is an order cabled by a Canadian bank to its foreign correspondent, branch or agency instructing it to transfer a deposit to the purchaser of the cable transfer or to a third party. A mail transfer performs the same function but the order is sent by mail.

Sometimes it may be preferable to make a payment abroad directly to a firm or individual without going through a foreign bank. In this situation the Canadian bank sells a **bank draft** on the bank's foreign balances to a customer requiring foreign monetary claims. This is a written order from a Canadian bank instructing its foreign correspondent branch or agency to make a specified payment to a designated payee on presentation of the draft. The Canadian purchaser of the draft mails it to the designated payee abroad who cashes it as he would an ordinary cheque. This is cleared through the regular foreign banking clearing channels and the Canadian bank's foreign bank balances are debited accordingly.

The bill of exchange is the traditional instrument of international commerce. It is best explained by an example of its use. Suppose a Canadian exporter of cheddar cheese receives an order from a British importer whose credit-worthiness is unknown. Before shipping the cheese the Canadian exporter requests a bank letter of credit from the English buyer. If the English buyer were known to the Canadian exporter such a letter would probably not be requested. A **bank letter of credit** is a promise by a bank to honour all orders of payment drawn against the person to whom it is issued, in our case the English cheese importer. The bank letter of credit is sent to the Canadian cheese exporter who upon receipt arranges with a shipping company to transport the cheese to Britain. The

---

[2] See Paul Einzig, *The Euro-Dollar System*, London, Macmillan, 1964; and Alexander K. Swoboda, "The Euro-Dollar Market: An Interpretation", *Essays in International Finance*, No. 64, Princeton, Princeton University Press, February 1968.

cheese is delivered to the shipping company which issues a **bill of lading** to the exporter stating that it has taken custody of the cheese. The Canadian exporter now draws an order for payment of a specified amount of pounds sterling against the English importer; this order is known as a **bill of exchange** or a **trade bill.** The exporter could have drawn the bill against the English bank in which case it is a **banker's bill.** Now suppose the Canadian cheese exporter requires Canadian dollars immediately. He will take the bill of exchange together with the bank letter of credit, the bill of lading and other documents such as insurance certificates to his bank and request it to discount the bill — that is, purchase it at the current rate of exchange. If the bank buys the bill the Canadian exporter will then have Canadian dollars and the bank will have foreign exchange in the form of a bill of exchange. The bank now sends the bill to its foreign correspondent branch or agency in Britain which will probably present it to the importer for acceptance. In accepting the bill the importer writes "Accepted", the date and his signature on the face of the bill. The acceptance or endorsement of the bill is a promise to fulfil its conditions. This converts it into a promissory note on the part of the importer and it is now known as a **trade acceptance.** If the original bill had been a **sight bill** — one which specifies payment upon presentation — the importer would have made payment immediately upon acceptance in return for which he would have received the bill of lading to claim the cheese on its arrival from Canada. The Canadian bank will now hold foreign exchange in Britain in the form of pound notes or pound bank deposits.

If the original bill of exchange had been a **time bill** specifying payment by the importer at the end of, say, sixty or ninety days, the importer would probably have been requested to accept it in return for the bill of lading. However, in this case the English bank would have either held the acceptance on behalf of the Canadian bank until maturity or discounted it in the money market. The choice would have depended upon the instructions the English bank had received from the Canadian bank. An acceptance payable sometime in the future is a credit instrument on which interest is earned. Whether the acceptance is held until maturity or cashed (discounted) will depend upon the interest that can be earned on alternative monetary claims.

There are many variations in the handling of bills of exchange. For example, if an English importer is well known and has an excellent credit rating, a Canadian exporter probably will not request a bank letter of credit but will send the bill of lading and other documents directly to the importer after the bill of exchange has been drawn. In this case the bill of exchange is called a **clean bill.** Or, the Canadian exporter may draw a banker's bill, with or without a letter of credit, on the importer's bank. The bill then becomes a **banker's acceptance.**

THE FOREIGN EXCHANGE MARKET

National monetary claims are exchanged in foreign exchange markets which are extensions of the money markets in world financial centres. Unlike stock markets, the foreign exchange market is not housed in specific places. Whereas, for example, the Toronto stock market is located on the floor of the Toronto Stock Exchange, the foreign exchange market has no such specific home. When the London money market was at its zenith before the First World War, English merchants and bankers met twice a week on the floor of the Royal Exchange in the heart of London to buy and sell bills of exchange. However, after the war the activities of the Royal Exchange came to an end and, as is now the case in every country, the foreign exchange market became a market between banks. Moreover, the bill of exchange, the traditional monetary instrument for making and receiving foreign payments, has been replaced largely by instruments for transferring bank balances between residents and foreigners.

In Canada almost all foreign exchange transactions are handled by the chartered banks. The hub of the foreign exchange market is the head office trading departments of banks in Toronto and Montreal. In its trading departments at head office, each bank first balances sales of foreign exchange against purchases transacted at its many branches. This is known by those working in a bank's trading department as "marrying of". If on any one day purchases exceed sales the bank will add to its net holdings of foreign exchange or offer some for sale in the market, or both. Alternatively, if sales exceed purchases, the bank will have to reduce its net holdings or purchase exchange in the market or both. To make sales or purchases of foreign exchange a bank usually turns to the inter-bank market. Canadian banks do not deal directly with one another but through brokers employed by the Canadian Bankers' Association and located in Toronto and Montreal. This brokerage system initiated in October 1950 is uniquely Canadian and is possible only because of the relatively small number of banks in Canada. In other countries foreign exchange brokers are more numerous and are in business for themselves. They make their living by charging a commission (brokerage) on buying and selling foreign exchange. In Canada the brokers are salaried employees of the Canadian Bankers' Association. They have a direct telephone line to the trading department in each bank's head office. If a bank wants to buy foreign exchange it phones a broker and makes a bid; if it wants to sell it makes an offer. Bids and offers are made for stated amounts at specified prices. When a broker receives a bid or an offer from a bank, without revealing its name, he informs the other banks. He usually telephones first the banks who have indicated that they may be in the market themselves. If he can arrange a deal between buyer and seller he reveals the names of the participants and sends written confirmations to them in the form of "trade slips". The banks arrange for the actual transfer of the money instruments involved. For example, if Bank A sells $100,000 U.S. to Bank B, Bank A will transfer on the following day to Bank B's New York correspondent, branch or agency $100,000 U.S. At the same time Bank A will receive Canadian dollars from Bank B in an amount determined by the rate of exchange at which the American dollars were sold.

When a Canadian bank wishes to change its net foreign exchange position it need not confine its trading activities to the Canadian inter-bank market. The trading departments at the banks' head offices have direct communications with brokers and banks in the main financial centres of the world. In practice, a Canadian bank usually does not have to intitiate bids and offers but only to respond to those that arrive constantly by telephone, telex and cable.

EXCHANGE RATE QUOTATIONS

A foreign exchange rate is a price — the price of the monetary unit of a foreign country. In most countries the price is usually quoted in terms of the number of local currency units required to make one foreign unit. For example, on June 30, 1967, the Swiss franc was quoted in Montreal and Toronto at $0.25 Canadian. From the Swiss point of view $1 Canadian was quoted at 4 francs. On the same day the American dollar was quoted at $1.07968 Canadian which is the same as the Canadian dollar being quoted at $0.92032 U.S. Table 29-1 shows the Canadian dollar equivalent for a selected number of foreign currency units quoted on June 30, 1967.

In Canada it has also been customary to quote the American dollar and the British pound at a premium over, or a discount under, the Canadian dollar. Hence, in the above example when the American dollar was quoted at $1.07968 Canadian it was at a premium above the Canadian dollar of 7⅞ per cent, or alternatively the Canadian dollar was at a discount under the American dollar of 7⅜ per cent.[3]

At any given time one can obtain various rates on foreign exchange depending upon the type of instrument on which the rate is quoted. In Table 29-1 we show cable rates. Other rates include those on mail transfers, sight and time bankers' drafts, and sight and time bills of exchange.

---

3 When the American dollar is at a premium the Canadian dollar is not at the same time at an equivalent discount because of the basis on which the percentages have to be calculated. For example, a 25 per cent premium is equal to a 20 per cent discount since 80 represents a discount of 20 per cent from 100 but 100 represents a premium of 25 per cent over 80.

TABLE 29-1

Selected Foreign Exchange Quotations

June 30, 1967

Country	Unit	Canadian Dollar Equivalent
Australia	Dollar	$1.205
Austria	Schilling	.041891
Brazil	Cruzeiros Novas	.40164
Burma	Kyat	.22593
Denmark	Krone	.15577
Dominican Republic	Peso	1.07968
France	Franc	.22028
Germany (Fed. Republic)	Deutsche Mark	.27073
Ghana	New Cedi	1.50625
Hong Kong	Dollar	.18749
India	Rupee	.14345
Iraq	Dinar	3.01250
Japan	Yen	.00298
Netherlands	Guilder (or Florin)	.29969
Panama Republic	Balboa	1.07968
Portugal	Escudo	.03768
South Africa	Rand	1.50625
Switzerland	Franc	.25013
U.S.S.R. (Russia)	Rouble	1.19845
United Kingdom	Pound	3.01250
United States	Dollar	1.07968
Yugoslavia	Dinar	.08637

Source: Bank of Montreal, Monthly foreign exchange quotations.

The rate quoted on cable transfers is the highest since the selling bank immediately loses foreign exchange equal to the amount specified in the cable. In the case of other instruments the bank retains foreign balances or does not have to hold an amount of foreign currency before the instrument arrives for payment or until the time specified in it. The more time a bank has before an actual transfer of foreign balances is required, the lower the rate quoted on the foreign exchange instrument employed. Rates on bills with identical maturities also vary with the credit standing of the firm or bank on which bills are drawn.

EXCHANGE ARBITRAGE

When restrictions do not hamper the market mechanism competition tends to establish one rate of exchange between two national monetary units at a given time in two separate foreign exchange markets. For example, suppose the Swiss franc trades for $0.25 Canadian in Montreal and because of a sudden large demand for Canadian dollars in Zurich the franc trades there for $0.24937 Canadian. We assume all rates are cable rates. A trader, by purchasing a Swiss franc in Zurich and simultaneously selling it in Montreal can realize one sixteenth of a cent profit on each franc traded. The simultaneous purchase and sale of foreign exchange is known as arbitrage and the person so engaged as an exchange arbitrager. In the above example the purchase and hence the increase in the demand for francs in Zurich will increase the price of francs in terms of Canadian dollars there. Alternatively, in Montreal the sale and therefore the increase in the supply of francs will depress the price of francs in terms of the Canadian dollar there. These two opposite price movements will continue until the price of francs in terms of Canadian dollars is the same in both markets and no profit can be made from arbitrage.

This example involving the simultaneous purchase and sale of only two national monetary units in two markets is referred to as two-point or bilateral arbitrage. Arbitrage activities are also carried out in three or more markets and in three or more national monetary units simultaneously. Such activities in free markets bring about exchange rates of all national monetary units that bear a consistent relationship with one another. For example, let us take the case of three-point or trilateral arbitrage. Suppose that the price of sterling (British pounds) is $3 Canadian and the price of francs (Swiss) $0.25 Canadian in Montreal. We again assume that all rates are cable rates. In Montreal, therefore, £1 exchanges for 12 francs via their respective dollar rates; this is known as the franc-sterling **cross rate.** But now suppose that at the same time it is possible to buy sterling in Paris at a rate of 10 francs while the dollar price of francs in Paris and the dollar price of sterling in London are identical with their prices in New York.[4] An arbitrager can make a profit from this situation by engaging in the following market activities:

(1) buy 100.000 francs in Montreal for $25,000;
(2) simultaneously sell 100.000 francs in Paris for £10,000;
(3) simultaneously sell £10,000 in Montreal for $30,000.

The resulting profit is $5,000 less cable costs. The purchase of francs in Montreal will raise their dollar price, the sale of francs in Paris will raise the franc price of sterling, and the sale of sterling in Montreal will lower its dollar price. When the franc-sterling cross rate in Montreal is identical with the franc price of sterling in Paris, arbitrage will no longer be profitable and, therefore, will cease. In a system of unrestricted exchange markets, arbitrage activities maintain mutually consistent relationships

[4] Normally arbitrage dealers work on much smaller margins than those in the example used here for purposes of illustration.

among the exchange rates of all national monetary units in all markets at any given time.

Exchange arbitrage must not be confused with exchange speculation. The arbitrager is engaged in the simultaneous purchase and sale of foreign exchange at a given time and makes a profit because of the rate differentials in *different markets*. The exchange speculator buys (sells) foreign exchange now for sale (purchase) at a higher (lower) price in the future. He hopes to make his profit by the rate differential at *different times*. Unlike the arbitrager, the speculator takes a position in the market: he changes his net foreign exchange position. If he is a "bull" he will buy now with the hope of selling later at a higher price; if he is a "bear" he will sell now with the hope of buying later at a lower price.

THE FORWARD EXCHANGE MARKET

So far we have assumed that all foreign exchange bought and sold is for immediate delivery. This is called **spot exchange,** and is traded in the **spot exchange market** at the **spot rate.** Foreign exchange may also be bought and sold at an agreed price today for delivery sometime in the future. This is referred to as **forward exchange,** and is traded in the **forward exchange market** at the **forward rate.** The forward exchange market resembles the futures markets found in organized commodity exchanges such as those for wheat and coffee. As we shall see, the primary function of any futures or forward market is to offer protection against the risk of price fluctuations.

The standard forward exchange contracts are for delivery in thirty, sixty, ninety or 180 days. Although longer contracts are negotiated they are uncommon. Forward exchange rates are usually expressed as a discount from or a premium over the spot rate. The Bank of Canada publishes "noon rates" on ninety-day forward discounts or premiums on American dollars and pounds sterling in terms of the Canadian dollar differential between spot and forward rates. In the market it has become common to quote forward rates as a percentage per annum premium or discount to facilitate comparison with interest rate differentials.

The primary function of the forward exchange market is to provide protection against the risk of exchange fluctuations. For example, a Canadian manufacturer sells goods to the United Kingdom for which he will be paid pounds at the end of ninety days. Since he is interested in making profits from manufacturing only he wants to know immediately upon sale the amount of Canadian dollars he will get for the pounds at the end of ninety days. This he can do by entering into a contract with his bank whereby he sells the pounds to the bank immediately for future delivery, at the price agreed upon when the contract is written. In other words, the manufacturer fixes the Canadian dollar price of his sale to the United Kingdom by selling forward pounds to his bank. The manufacturer is said to be **hedging** his foreign exchange risk. Hedging is the sale of any asset, not only foreign exchange, balanced by purchases so that there is no net open position (that is, no price risk) in the market.

When the bank purchases pounds forward from the manufacturer, how is the price it will pay in Canadian dollars determined? Banks, like manufacturers, usually do not want to assume foreign exchange risks. When the bank buys forward exchange it can cover itself, or obviate risk, with a **swap** transaction. A swap is a simultaneous forward purchase and spot sale or a simultaneous forward sale and spot purchase. In our example, at the same time that the bank buys forward pounds from the manufacturer it sells an equal amount of pounds spot. By selling pounds spot the bank reduces its holdings of pounds but at the same time increases its holdings of dollars. If we assume that pounds were invested in ninety-day British Treasury bills yielding 5 per cent and that the bank can earn only 4 per cent by investing the equivalent amount of dollars in ninety-day Canadian Treasury bills it is confronted with a loss. This loss will be charged to the manufacturer as part of the price at which the bank buys pounds forward from him. Hence, if interest rates are higher in foreign than in domestic money markets the price for forward exchange (the forward rate) will tend to be at a discount under the spot exchange rate.

Now let us take the case of a Canadian importer who has to make pound payments at the end of ninety days. He wants to be certain of his Canadian dollar cost when payment is due. He, too, can eliminate the exchange risk by hedging. He buys forward pounds from his bank at an agreed upon rate. The rate at which the bank will sell pounds forward is determined as follows:

1. The sale of forward pounds by a bank is covered by a spot purchase of pounds (a swap).
2. From the spot purchase the bank receives pounds which it invests in London, say, at 5 per cent.
3. With the spot purchase of pounds the bank gives up Canadian dollars invested in Canada, say, at 4 per cent.
4. The bank makes a profit on the interest rate differential and therefore the rate at which it sells forward pounds is a discount under the spot pound rate.

In this example, as in the previous one, interest rates abroad are higher than they are at home. In both examples the higher foreign interest rates result in a gain for the bank. This tends to place the buying and selling rate of forward pounds at a discount under the spot rate. Alternatively, if interest rates are lower at home than abroad the forward rate will tend to be at a premium above the spot rate.

The extent to which international interest rate differentials determine the spread between spot and forward exchange depends upon interest arbitrage and the degree of speculation in the foreign exchange markets. If markets are stable with little or no speculation, the forward spread is determined entirely by **interest arbitrage** which is the transfer of funds from one market to another to take advantage of higher interest rates. Since the prime motive for such transfers are interest rate differentials, funds moved abroad for this purpose are hedged in the forward market. For example, suppose a Canadian investor buys ninety-day British Treasury bills because the rate on these bills is higher than that on equivalent bills in Canada. At the same time that he buys pounds to purchase the British bills he sells pounds forward ninety days for dollars. The pounds he sells forward will be equal to the amount he receives from the British bills when they mature at the end of ninety days. Suppose also that forward pounds are at a discount of 1.5 cents which is .5 per cent of the spot rate or 2 per cent per annum. Thus the investor pays $3 for a pound spot and sells it three months forward for $2.985. In order to realize a gain the British bill rate must exceed the Canadian bill rate by more than this 2 per cent loss on the exchange transaction. Let us assume that the following situation exists:

	Yield %
British Treasury bills	7
Canadian Treasury bills	4
Interest Rate Differential	3
Cost of forward pound cover	2
Net Yield	+1

The flow of funds to Britain as a result of interest arbitrage will continue until the international interest rate differential and the discount on forward exchange (the cost of forward cover) are equal. Interest arbitrage itself will tend to bring this about. The demand for spot pounds for investment in British bills will force up the spot rate while the sale of pounds forward will depress the forward rate. Both these forces will tend to increase the discount on forward pounds. The flow of funds to Britain will also influence interest rates in both Canada and Britain so as to reduce the differential in these rates. Hence all these factors will tend to bring about an interest parity relationship — the equality of the forward discount of foreign exchange and the interest rate differential between countries. [5] This parity relationship is realized only if there are no funds moving from country to country as a result of speculation. For example, during 1962 when foreigners lost confidence in the Canadian dollar and repatriated funds invested in Canada, the spread between the spot and forward rate bore little relationship to the interest rate differentials which existed at that time. Both the American dollar forward and the pound sterling forward moved to premiums over spot that were much higher than the existing interest rate differentials.

SELECTED READINGS

Bank of Canada, *Evidence of the Governor Before the Royal Commission on Banking and Finance,* Ottawa, Bank of Canada, 1964.

Crump, Norman, *The A.B.C. of the Foreign Exchanges,* London, Macmillan, 1963.

Einzig, Paul, *A Textbook on Foreign Exchange,* New York, St. Martin's Press, 1966.

Holmes, Alan R., *The New York Foreign Exchange Market,* New York, Federal Reserve Bank of New York, 1959.

Lall, Sanjaya, "What Does It Really Mean? The Forward Exchange Market", *Finance and Development,* Vol. 4, No. 3, September 1967.

Report of the Royal Commission on Banking and Finance, Ottawa, Queen's Printer, 1964, Ch. 15.

Shepherd, Sidney, *Foreign Exchange in Canada: An Outline,* Toronto, University of Toronto Press, 1958.

[5] The relationship between the spot and forward exchange rate when the interest arbitrage is the prime determinant may be expressed as

$$R_f = R_s \frac{1 + i_d}{1 + i_f}$$

where R_f and R_s are the forward and spot foreign exchange rates respectively and i_d and i_f are the domestic and foreign interest rates respectively.

30 EXCHANGE RATE SYSTEMS AND PAYMENTS ADJUSTMENTS

We noted earlier that the foreign exchange rate is the price of one country's monetary claims in terms of another country's monetary claims. How this price is determined depends upon the exchange rate system that countries adopt. We shall define four such systems: a freely fluctuating exchange rate system; a fixed exchange rate system such as under the gold standard; a managed or pegged exchange rate system; and an exchange control system. In our explanation of each system we shall also analyze how adjustments in the balance of payments take place.

FREELY FLUCTUATING EXCHANGE RATE SYSTEM

In a competitive market with no government intervention the foreign exchange rate (throughout this discussion we refer to the spot rate) is determined by the forces of demand and supply just as is the price of commodities in the commodity markets. The demand for foreign exchange is determined by all the items in a country's balance of payments statement which entail foreign payments. The demand for these items, in turn, is determined by such factors as

- R, the price of foreign exchange (the value of foreign monetary claims in terms of domestic currency)
- P, relative prices at home and abroad
- i, interest rates at home relative to those abroad
- Y, the level of income at home
- X_f, all other factors such as tastes, expectations, wealth (asset holdings), and trade and payments controls

In equation form the demand for foreign exchange D_f can be expressed as

$$D_f = f(R,P,i,Y,X_f) \qquad (1)$$

The relationship between the variables in the equation is shown in Diagram (a) of Figure 30-1. For simplicity we assume that the demand for foreign exchange is a demand for pounds sterling in terms of Canadian dollars. The *DD* curve shows the amount of pounds demanded at various Canadian dollar prices, where pounds are measured on the horizontal axis and dollars on the vertical axis.

The curve slopes downward from left to right indicating that the demand for pounds increases as their dollar price decreases. The position of the curve is determined by the other variables included in the equation which determine the demand for pounds. For example, if *P* increases — that is, if prices in Canada increase relative to those in Britain — imports can be expected to increase and consequently the demand for pounds curve shifts upward. The same is true for an increase in incomes in Canada. If interest rates in Britain increase relative to those in Canada there may be an increase in the demand for pounds for investment in Britain; the demand curve may shift to the right. This is also true if foreigners lose confidence in Canada's political and economic conditions and expect the Canadian dollar to depreciate in the future. Alternatively, if the price and interest rate differentials move in the opposite direction or Canadian incomes decline the demand for pounds curve will shift downward and to the left.

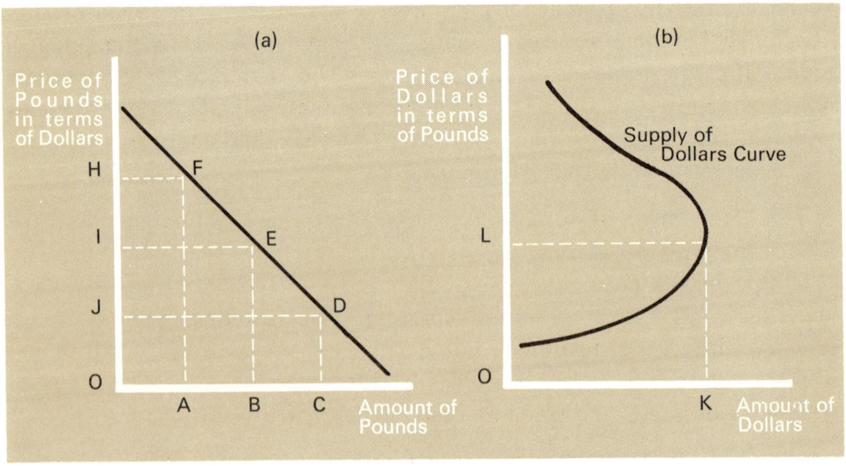

Figure 30-1

We will assume that when Canadians purchase pounds in the exchange market they offer Canadian dollars. Hence the demand for pounds curve, or more generally the demand for foreign exchange, corresponds to an offer of Canadian (domestic) money. It is therefore possible to convert the demand for pounds curve into the supply of dollars curve shown in Diagram (b) of Figure 30-1. When, for example, the price of pounds is $3 and Canadians desire to purchase £1,000 they must be willing to supply $3,000. By multiplying the price of pounds given on the vertical axis in Diagram (a) by the amount (units) of pounds demanded at that price, a corresponding offer of dollars is obtained. Thus, when the exchange rate is *OJ*, the supply of dollars is equal to the product of *OJ* times *OC*, or to the area of the rectangle *OJDC*. Similar rectangles can be drawn for each dollar price of pounds. Note, however, that the areas of these rectangles are different in size. As the price of pounds rises from zero to *OI* the rectangles become progressively larger — the supply of dollars for each pound purchased increases. Moreover, as the price of pounds rises above *OI* the rectangles become progressively smaller — the supply of dollars for each pound purchased decreases. The change in the supply of dollars offered as the price of pounds changes may be explained in terms of the price elasticity of the demand for pounds. The demand for pounds is elastic (larger than one) when the total amount of dollars offered increases with each decline in the price of pounds. The demand for pounds is inelastic (smaller than one) when the total amount of dollars offered decreases with each decline in the price of pounds. The demand for pounds has unit price elasticity when infinitesimally small changes in the price of pounds cause no change in the amount of Canadian dollars offered.

Diagram (b) of Figure 30-1 shows the supply of dollars curve which is derived from the demand for pounds curve in Diagram (a). In Diagram (b) the vertical axis measures the price of dollars in terms of pounds which is the reciprocal of the price of pounds in terms of dollars. (If £1 = $3 then $1 = £.333.) The horizontal axis in Diagram (b) measures the amount of dollars; each distance along this axis corresponds to an area in Diagram (a). For instance, the distance *OK* in Diagram (b) corresponds to the area of rectangle *OIEB* in Diagram (a).

In Diagram (b), when the price of dollars in terms of pounds is less than *OL* (or in Diagram (a), when the price of pounds in terms of dollars is higher than *OI*), the supply curve slopes upward from left to right. With each increase in the price of dollars the amount of dollars offered increases. The elasticity of supply is positive or larger than zero. However, when the price of dollars rises above *OL* (the price of pounds falls below *OI*), the supply curve of dollars bends back upon itself. With each increase in the price of dollars the amount of dollars supplied decreases. The elasticity of supply is negative, or smaller than zero.[1]

In the same way that we derived a supply curve of dollars from a demand curve for pounds we can derive a supply curve of pounds from a foreign demand curve for dollars. Curve *SS* in Figure 30-2 is such a curve. The demand curve for pounds *DD* is a reproduction of the demand curve shown in Diagram (a) of Figure 30-1. In Figure 30-2 we now have a demand and a supply curve for pounds (foreign exchange) and where these two curves intersect the market price of pounds is determined. With a backward bending supply curve this condition may be satisfied at two prices (R_2 and R_3 in Figure 30-2).

In a competitive market free from government intervention only one price can exist at any given time. Suppose that the price of pounds is initially OR_2 where the amount of pounds supplied to and demanded from the market is *OA*. This represents a condition of stable equilibrium in that any deviation from this price, but not above R_3, sets in motion market forces which will reestablish the equilibrium price OR_2. For example, let us assume that such a deviation occurs for reasons other than shifts in the *SS* and *DD* curves, and the price of pounds falls from OR_2 to OR_1. At price OR_1 there is an excess supply of pounds equal to *ab*. With the lower price of pounds in terms of dollars or alternatively the higher price of dollars in terms of pounds, Canadians find British goods cheaper and the British find Canadian goods more expensive. As a result, Canadians buy more in Britain and the British less in Canada. This is reflected in the foreign exchange market by a simultaneous movement upward along the *DD* and *SS* curves until the excess demand for pounds is eliminated and the equilibrium price is re-established at OR_2. Similarly if the price of pounds were to deviate above OR_2 but not above OR_3 market forces would be set in motion which would restore it to OR_2.

A stable foreign exchange rate is attained whenever the supply curve of foreign exchange is negatively sloped or steeper absolutely than the demand curve for foreign exchange.[2]

---

[1] If the elasticity of demand for foreign exchange is η and the corresponding elasticity of supply of domestic currency on the exchange market is ϵ, the following relationships can be shown:

$$\text{when } \eta < 1 \text{ then } \epsilon > 0$$
$$\text{when } \eta = 1 \text{ then } \epsilon = 0$$
$$\text{when } \eta > 1 \text{ then } \epsilon < 0$$

[2] In terms of the previous footnote, the foreign exchange market is stable when $(\epsilon+\eta>0)$

If the definition of the foreign exchange market is restricted to include only the supply of and demand for foreign exchange derived from exports and imports, conditions in the foreign exchange market can be related to conditions in the export and import market (the balance of trade). If the supply elasticities are assumed to be infinite, so that any amount of the exported or imported good would be forthcoming at a given price, the foreign exchange market is stable when the sum of the elasticity of demand for imports at home η_h and

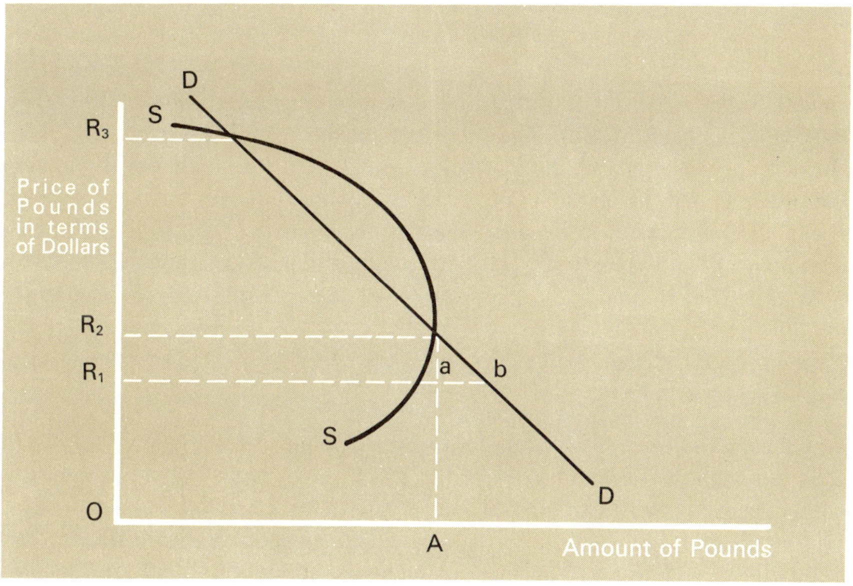

Figure 30-2

Now let us assume that the price of pounds was initially OR_3. In this case any deviation will not set market forces in motioı to bring it back to OR_3. If the rate deviates above OR_3 excess demand exists which will drive the rate higher and farther away from its initial equilibrium.[3] Such a situation may arise if an increase in the rate causes speculators to anticipate further rises. They will increase the quantity of pounds they demand hoping for gain in the future with sales at higher prices. Similarly if the rate deviates below OR_3 it will not return to this level. This too

---

abroad η_f is greater than one, i.e. $\eta_h+\eta_f > 1$. Moreover, assuming initial payments equilibrium and infinite supply elasticities, if the sum of the two demand elasticities is larger than one, the depreciation or devaluation of any one currency relative to the other will improve the balance of trade in the depreciating or devluating country. This is commonly called the Marshall-Lerner condition. If income effects are also introduced into the adjustment mechanism, the sum of the elasticities must be substantially larger than unity. It must be noted, however, that if supply elasticities are relatively low, the Marshall-Lerner condition is sufficient but not necessary for improvement in the balance of trade. Pessimism about the possibility of the Marshall-Lerner condition being realized in practice has led to recommendations against the use of both devaluation and flexible exchange rates to adjust international payments imbalance.

[3] This does not mean that the rate will rise to infinity because one can expect another equilibrium point higher up. The unlikely exception would be an expansion to infinity in the money supply in one of the two countries. If there is an unstable intersection of supply and demand schedules in the foreign exchange market there will be stable intersections on either side of the unstable one. See E. Sohmen, *Flexible Exchange Rates, Theory and Controversy*, Chicago, University of Chicago Press, 1961, pp. 291-292.

may be explained by the destabilizing activities of speculators. When the rate falls speculators anticipate further declines and sell exchange. The already excess supply is increased and the rate driven down still further. Equilibrium will eventually be reached again, but at OR_2. Any rate above OR_3 is unstable because the supply curve is flatter than the demand curve and negatively sloped; the elasticity of supply in the exchange market is smaller in algebraic value than the elasticity of demand.

THE CASE FOR AND AGAINST FREELY FLUCTUATING EXCHANGE RATES

Opponents to freely fluctuating foreign exchange rates maintain that the elasticities of the demand for and the supply of foreign exchange are very small because the elasticities of the demand for imports are small. This pessimistic attitude regarding low elasticities is a much debated issue.

In Figure 30-3 we have drawn an inelastic supply curve *SS* and an inelastic demand curve *DD* for the Canadian dollar on the foreign exchange market. Let us assume that tastes in the United States for Canadian goods change and as a result Americans buy more in Canada; the demand curve for Canadian dollars in the foreign exchange market shifts from *DD* to *D′D′*. This shift causes a large increase in the external value of the Canadian dollar (in terms of the American dollar); from R_1 to R_3. Opponents of freely fluctuating exchange rates argue that such large changes in foreign exchange rates, particularly when they occur frequently, disrupt international trade. With given domestic prices in each country, the exchange rate plays an important role in determining the pattern of international trade. Therefore, large and frequent changes may cause wasteful movements of goods internationally, movements not based on real comparative cost advantages — that is, on the real resources of an economy.

If the demand for foreign exchange is inelastic but the supply of foreign exchange is relatively elastic a shift in the demand curve for foreign exchange will not cause large fluctuations in the foreign exchange rate. In Figure 30-3, given the demand curve *DD* and the supply curve *SS*, with a shift in the demand curve to *D′D′* the foreign exchange rate of the Canadian dollar rises by a relatively small amount from R_1 to R_2.

Opponents of a freely fluctuating exchange rate system also hold that in a purely competitive market destabilizing activity by speculators is the rule rather than the exception. Speculators in foreign exchange are assumed to cause large and possibly cumulative movements in exchange rates. For example, when the price of foreign exchange rises, speculators may expect the rise to continue. They therefore buy foreign exchange causing its price to rise even further. As a result upward movements in the rate may be cumulative. As we have already noted, large fluctuations in exchange rates may lead to a misallocation of economic resources. This may be reflected by a reduction in international trade as a result of traders' reluctance to become involved in the inconvenience and costs of hedging against exchange risks.

One of the chief advantages for a freely fluctuating exchange rate system is that it provides continuous automatic adjustments and eliminates chronic balance of payments deficits and surpluses. For example, in Figure 30-4 Canada's balance of payments is in equilibrium when the external value of the Canadian dollar in terms of the American dollar is R_1. Canada now experiences price inflation while prices in the United States remain relatively stable. As a result Canadians will be induced to buy more in the United States; the supply curve of Canadian dollars on the foreign exchange market shifts to the right from *SS* to *S′S′*. At the same time, Americans will be induced to buy less in Canada; the demand curve for Canadian dollars shifts to the left from *DD* to *D′D′*. Given the new set of demand and supply curves, at the initial exchange rate R_1 for the

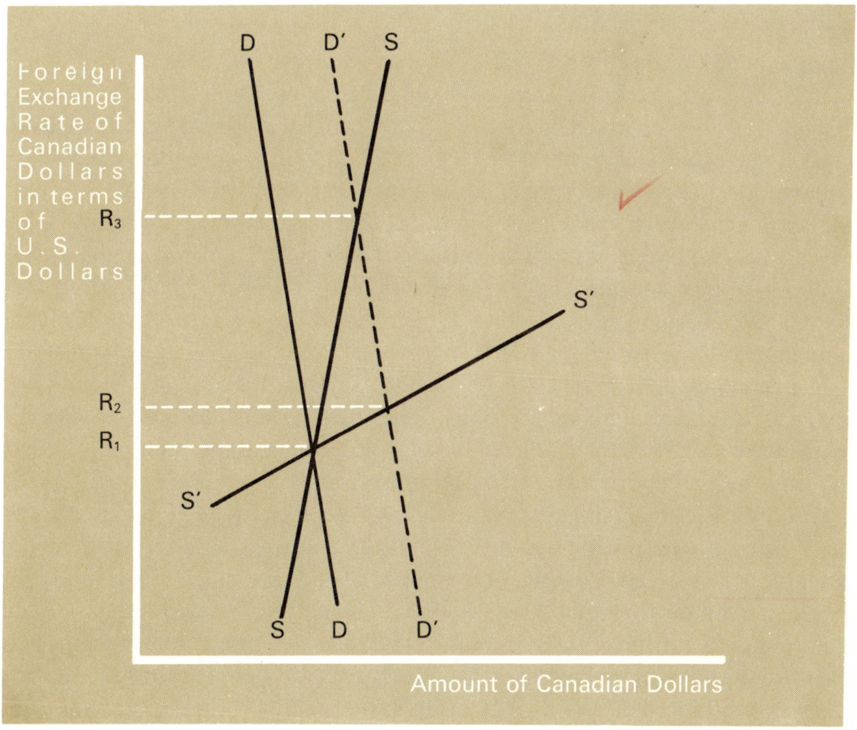

Figure 30-3

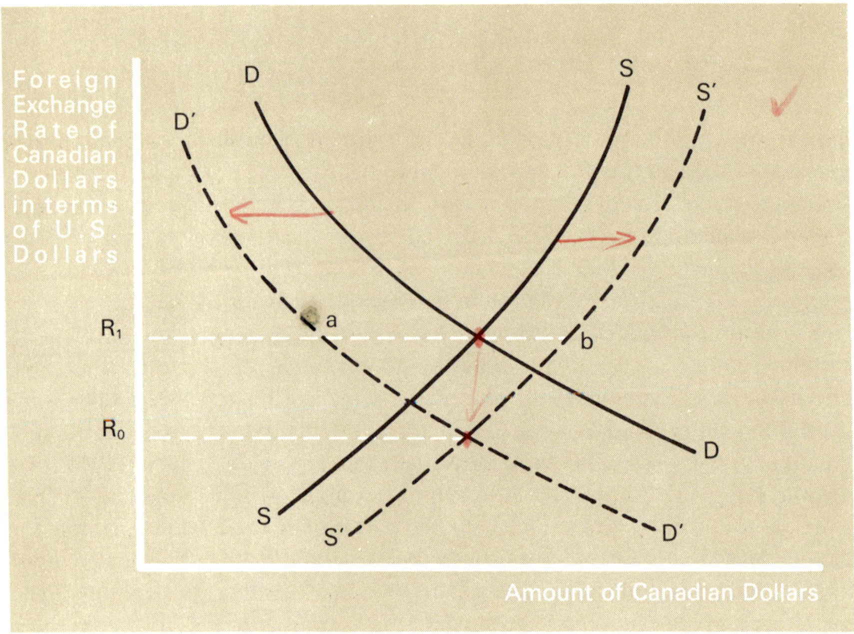

Figure 30-4

Canadian dollar there now exists an excess supply for Canadian dollars equal to *ab* which also reflects a balance of payments deficit. The Canadian dollar is overvalued in terms of the American dollar and in a free market its value will tend to fall. As the external price of the Canadian dollar falls, Canadians will be encouraged to buy less in the United States (a downward movement along the *S′S′* curve) and Americans will be encouraged to buy more in Canada (a downward movement along the *D′D′* curve). Hence market forces are set in motion which will eliminate the Canadian balance of payments deficit and create a new equilibrium foreign exchange value for the Canadian dollar (equal to R_o). Similarly if the demand and supply curves of the Canadian dollar shift so as to produce an undervalued dollar and a surplus in the balance of payments, market forces are set in motion which will eliminate the surplus and establish a new foreign exchange value for the dollar.

Insofar as a freely fluctuating exchange rate system provides a continuous automatic adjustment mechanism to the balance of payments, monetary policy is freed for use for domestic stabilization. For example, assume the authorities initiate a restrictive monetary policy to fight inflation. Consequent higher interest rates will tend to reduce domestic spending. In addition, they will cause an inflow of short-term capital if interest rates in foreign countries do not also move up. The inflow of capital will increase the value of the Canadian dollar on the foreign exchange market which, in turn, will cause imports to rise and exports to fall. Increased imports and decreased exports will tend to push domestic prices down or to depress domestic income or both. Hence, under a freely fluctuating exchange rate system monetary policy can concentrate on domestic stabilization while equilibrium in the balance of payments looks after itself. Moreover, as is shown in our example, the trade balance may reinforce the purely domestic effects of monetary policy.

Although a free exchange rate allows a country much freedom in the use of monetary and fiscal policy for domestic policy purposes there are limits to such freedom. Canada learned this lesson when, after 1957, a tight money policy was continued during a period of severe domestic unemployment. With high interest rates and the consequent inflow of capital the Canadian dollar rose to a level which speculators considered overvalued. The destabilizing speculation which ensued created balance of payments difficulties and an exchange rate crisis in 1962. A freely fluctuating exchange rate allows a wide degree of freedom for the domestic use of monetary and fiscal policy but these policies must be used in ways appropriate for the existing conditions. Canada's experience with a flexible exchange rate system shows that exchange speculation is sensitive to a country's monetary and fiscal policies. When these policies are appropriate, short-term capital movements are generally stabilizing.

Canada's experience with a flexible exchange rate system in the years immediately after 1950 indicates that much of the pessimism concerning elasticities may be unfounded. During these years the foreign exchange rate of the Canadian dollar moved within a rather narrow range. Moreover, the activities of speculators tended for the most part to stabilize rather than destabilize the rate.

FIXED EXCHANGE RATES

The best known system under which exchange rates tend to be constant is the gold standard. Under a gold standard system each government defines its monetary unit in grains or ounces of gold metal and stands prepared to sell gold for its currency and its currency for gold. Since gold represents a common denominator of currency values, a definite pattern of currency values exists among the various countries. For example, at one time the Canadian dollar contained 23.22 grains and the British pound 113.0016 grains of fine gold. The value of the pound in terms of the dollar was

$$\frac{113.0016}{23.22} = \$4.8665.$$

This ratio is known as the gold or **mint par of exchange.** The market rate of exchange could fluctuate freely around mint par within a narrow range determined by the **gold export** and **gold import points.** The exchange rate tended to remain fixed within these gold points because of **gold arbitrage dealings.**

Let us assume, as was generally the case in the pre-1914 period, that all payments between Canada and the United Kingdom were carried out through London. That is, importers in Montreal, Halifax and Toronto bought sterling bills drawn on London while exporters had bills discounted in London. If the supply of bills exactly matched the demand for bills over any given period of time, the pound price was $4.866. But suppose because of a large increase in exports from Britain to Canada the demand for sterling bills exceeded their supply at the given price and the price rose to $4.895. This pound price would be maintained only temporarily because of the profit that could be realized from gold arbitrage. Gold arbitragers would purchase $4.866 worth of gold in Canada and ship it to Britain at a cost of approximately 2.5 cents. There the gold would be sold to the government for £1 sterling which in turn would be sold on the foreign exchange market for $4.895. With the cost of the pound to the arbitrager of $4.891 ($4.866 plus 2.5 cents) and the $4.895 realized from its sale he would make a profit of 0.4 cents on each pound sterling traded. With continuous gold arbitrage and the consequent increase in the supply of pounds on the foreign exchange market, the price of the pound would remain only briefly above its export point which is mint par plus the cost of acquiring and shipping gold.

Next, let us assume because of a large increase in imports to Britain from Canada, the supply of sterling bills exceeded the demand at the given price and the price temporarily fell to $4.80. Gold arbitragers would now buy pounds at the $4.80 price on the exchange market and take them to the British government to be converted into gold. Each pound worth of gold would be shipped to Canada at a cost of 3.9 cents per pound sterling. The gold, in turn, would be sold to the Canadian government for $4.866. The cost to the arbitrager for each pound would be $4.839 ($4.80 plus 3.9 cents) and his receipt from the sale of gold, $4.866. He would realize a profit therefore of 2.7 cents on each pound traded. The demand by the gold arbitragers for pounds in the London exchange market would not allow the price of the pound to remain below its gold import point which is mint par less the costs of acquiring and shipping gold.

Under the gold standard the foreign exchange rate had a fixed upper and lower limit but between these limits, the gold points, the rate was determined by market forces as illustrated in Figure 30-5.

In both diagrams the actual price of the pound in terms of dollars is determined by the market forces between the gold points. At the gold points the elasticity of supply and demand is infinite. With an export surplus in Britain created, say, by a development boom in Canada, the demand curve for pounds shifts to the right from *DD* to *D′D′* in Diagram (a). Up to

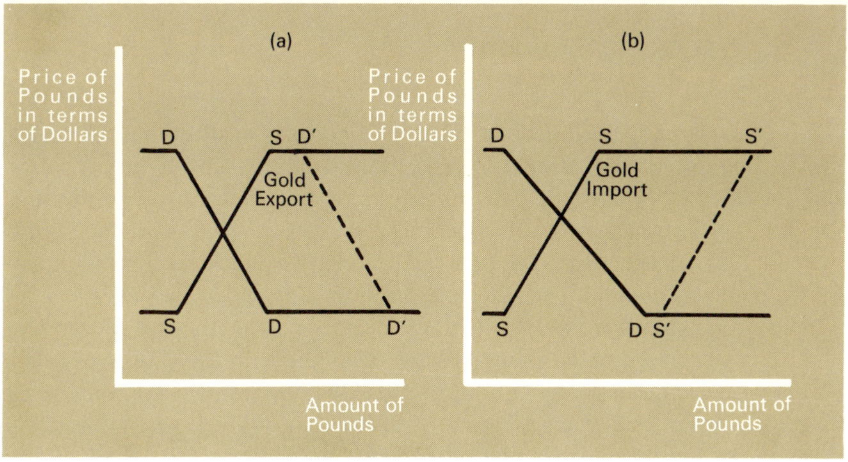

Figure 30-5

the gold points the demand for pounds is satisfied from the supply on the exchange market; above the gold points the excess demand for pounds is satisfied by gold exports to Britain (equal to *SD′*). In Diagram (b), on the other hand, a shift to the right of the supply schedule for pounds from *SS* to *S′S′* created, say, by poor harvests in Britain, will lower the price of pounds to the gold import point. Gold will now leave Britain (equal to DS′).

The early economists assumed that gold flows activated a mechanism which set in motion market forces that automatically adjusted balance of payments disequilibrium thus eliminating the necessity for any further gold flows. They called it the price-specie-flow mechanism.

The Price-Specie-Flow Mechanism

The loss of gold by the deficit country would reduce its money supply and gain of gold by the surplus country would increase its money supply. Central to this theory were the assumptions of full employment and complete price flexibility. The loss of gold and the decrease in the money supply would cause prices to fall in the deficit country. This followed from the assumption of the quantity theory of money which was a cornerstone of the mechanism. On the other hand, with the gain in gold and the increase in the money supply, prices would rise in the surplus country. The price changes in the two countries would lead to an expansion in the deficit country's exports to and a reduction in its imports from the surplus country. Eventually equilibrium in balance of payments would be re-established and the gold flows would halt. In terms of Figure 30-5, price changes in the countries concerned would bring about market forces which would shift the *D′D′* curve in Diagram (a) back to *DD*, and the *S′S′* curve in Diagram (b) back to *SS*.

The price-specie-flow analysis of balance of payments adjustments under gold standard conditions ruled supreme throughout the nineteenth century and during the first third of the twentieth century. The analysis was improved and expanded to take into account institutional developments. The role of fractional reserve banking and central bank policy were included to explain the possible effects of gold movements on the supply of money. It was also shown that if interest rates rose in the deficit country, perhaps with the assistance of a tight monetary policy, an inflow of capital from abroad could replace the gold outflow.

It was not until the 1930's with high unemployment that an alternative to the price-specie-flow mechanism was formulated. In the 1920's dissatisfaction with the mechanism had been expressed by some who considered the price elasticities of the demand for imports too small to produce balance of payments equilibrium. Under conditions of less than full employment, economists began to explain balance of payments adjustments under fixed exchange rates in terms of changes in national income.

INCOME CHANGES AND BALANCE OF PAYMENTS ADJUSTMENTS

Under a freely fluctuating exchange rate system continuous equilibrium in the balance of payments is achieved by relative price changes resulting from movements in foreign exchange rates. Under a fixed exchange rate system adjustments in the balance of payments as explained by the price-specie-flow mechanism come about by relative price changes resulting from movements in national price levels. An important criticism of the price-specie-flow mechanism is its neglect of changes in national income as an explanation of the adjustment process.

To explain the possible role of changes in income in the adjustment process let us assume conditions of less than full employment where price levels in the respective countries remain constant. Let us also assume that the demand for imports, and therefore for foreign exchange, varies directly with the country's national income and that the volume of its exports, and therefore the supply of foreign exchange, varies directly with the incomes of other countries. Under these conditions, as we shall see, a country with a balance of payments deficit at given levels of income both at home and abroad can reduce or eliminate its deficit if incomes at home fall or those abroad rise.

Changes in income affect the balance of payments and vice versa — changes in the balance of payments affect income. We saw earlier that the current account in the balance of payments consist of items which are an integral part of a country's national income. For example, in Chapter 24 we expressed national income with the equation

$$Y = C + I + G + (X - M)$$

Moreover, we defined the equilibrium condition as

$$I_d + G_d + X = S_p + S_b + T + M$$

where exports of goods and services X, like government expenditures G_d and investment expenditures I_d are "injections" into the national income stream. Imports of goods and services M, on the other hand, as well as personal saving S_p business saving S_b and taxes T are "leakages" from the income-expenditure stream. The cu rent account in the international balance of payments is represented by $(X - M)$.

Now let us assume an autonomous increase in exports, (that is, an increase in exports not associated with a change in income) and that as a result the country has a balance of payments surplus. The increase in exports gives rise to an increased demand for materials and capital and to growing demands for the factors of production. National income increases, first by the amount of the initial increase in exports and then by a multiple of the latter amount depending upon the export multiplier. The initial increase in export expenditures will induce a rise in domestic consumption expenditures, and perhaps one in investment expenditures, generating new income. Since import expenditures are a positive function of national income, imports also increase as income rises. But will income, and therefore imports, increase sufficiently to adjust the balance of payments from surplus to equilibrium? The extent to which income increases will depend upon the leakages from the income-expenditure stream. These leakages, saving, taxes and imports, are induced by the increase in income. The size of the leakages depends, therefore, upon the relationship between changes in saving, taxes and imports and changes in income. This relationship is expressed by their respective marginal propensities.

$\frac{\triangle S}{\triangle Y}$ the marginal propensity to save;

$\frac{\triangle T}{\triangle Y}$ the marginal propensity to tax;

$\frac{\triangle M}{\triangle Y}$ the marginal propensity to import.

Given these marginal propensities, the change in income $\triangle Y$ generated by an autonomous change in exports $\triangle X$ is given as follows:

$$\triangle X \times \frac{1}{\frac{\triangle S}{\triangle Y} + \frac{\triangle T}{\triangle Y} + \frac{\triangle M}{\triangle Y}} = \triangle Y$$

The middle term $$\frac{1}{\frac{\triangle S}{\triangle Y} + \frac{\triangle T}{\triangle Y} + \frac{\triangle M}{\triangle Y}}$$

in this equation is known as the **foreign trade multiplier.** The size of the increase in imports as a result of an autonomous change in exports depends upon the magnitude of the increase in income and the marginal propensity to import. There is no assurance that the induced changes in imports will be just sufficient to match the autonomous change in exports. The adjustments may be either too small or too large to restore balance of payments equilibrium. The outcome depends upon the sum of the marginal propensities to save and tax. If the sum of the marginal propensity to save and tax is zero and the sole leakage is through imports the balance of payments will adjust to equilibrium.

An autonomous increase in the exports of one country means an autonomous increase in imports by other countries. The increase in imports will generate a multiple reduction in income in these countries and a subsequent reduction in their imports. This, in turn, may have repercussions in the country which experienced the autonomous increase in exports. The foreign trade multiplier can be modified to include such repercussions.[4]

The monetary effects of balance of payments disequilibrium reinforce the income effects in the adjustment process. The initial expansion in exports increases claims on foreigners and supplies of foreign currencies. As these holdings are converted into domestic currency the money supply increases, interest rates decline and spending and income increase. These conditions induce an increase in imports which then contributes to a reduction of the export surplus.

Although our discussion has been in terms of an autonomous increase in exports leading to an increase in income and imports, a similar analysis explains the reduction in income and imports following an autonomous increase in imports.

MANAGED EXCHANGE RATE SYSTEMS

Managed exchange rate systems imply official intervention in the foreign exchange market where governments or their agencies are prepared to buy and sell foreign exchange to keep the exchange rate at a certain level or within a certain range. In the simplest form of a managed rate system the authorities intervene only to stabilize the rate by moderating the amplitudes of exchange rate fluctuations. In Canada after 1950 when the rate was free the authorities attempted to smooth its fluctuations by "leaning against the wind" from time to time.

The more usual type of managed system, the one under which Canada

[4] See Charles P. Kindleberger, *International Economics*, Homewood, Ill., Richard D. Irwin, 1963, Ch. 10 and Appendix E.

has operated since 1962 and which is now common in most countries of the world, is called a **pegged system.** Under agreement with the International Monetary Fund (IMF) countries using the pegged system define the par value of their monetary unit in terms of a given amount of gold. They are not required to redeem their currencies in gold, but they must maintain their currencies' values within one per cent of the established par. For this purpose they have established **exchange stabilization funds,** also referred to as exchange equalization funds.

Canada's stabilization fund, known as the Exchange Fund Account was established in 1935 with part of the profits from gold revaluation at that time. Until the outbreak of the Second World War most of the responsibility for operating this Account was assumed by the newly created Bank of Canada. Since then the direct responsibility for foreign exchange has been assumed by the government. The Minister of Finance gives instructions to the Bank of Canada which operates the Exchange Fund Account and carries out buying and selling transactions in foreign exchange on behalf of the government. In 1962 the government established the par value of the Canadian dollar at 0.822021 grams of fine gold or 92.5 cents (U.S.) and committed itself to hold the value of the Canadian dollar on the exchange market within the official trading limits of 91.575 cents (U.S.) and 93.425 cents (U.S.).

When the external value of the Canadian dollar tends toward its lower limit the Exchange Fund increases the demand for dollars on the exchange market by purchasing dollars with foreign currencies and gold thereby forcing up the value of the dollar in terms of these currencies. The amount of support that can be given to the dollar in this way depends upon the amount of foreign exchange and gold available to the Exchange Fund Account. Aside from the inventory of gold and foreign exchange which the Account holds, it may also acquire funds by borrowing from the International Monetary Fund and from foreign banks. However, continuous borrowing will dry up this source of foreign exchange. When this happens the Canadian government must negotiate a new lower limit for the dollar with the IMF, impose exchange controls, or use monetary, fiscal or other policies to influence the supply of and demand for the dollar on the exchange market. (In terms of Figure 30-5 the government may use policies that have the effect of shifting the supply curve of foreign exchange to the right and the demand curve for foreign exchange to the left.) For example, monetary policy may be employed to force up interest rates in Canada relative to those abroad in order to attract an inflow of short-term foreign capital and thereby increase the demand for Canadian dollars. If, however, the Canadian economy is depressed at a time when the external value of the dollar is under downward pressure, the authorities will be unwilling to force up interest rates as a means of supporting the dollar. During a period of recession they may also reject the use of fiscal policy to deflate the economy any further in order to reduce imports and expand exports. The government could, however, introduce an export promotion program. If this is unsuccessful, it may become necessary to establish a new support limit for the dollar.

The Canadian dollars accumulated when the Exchange Fund Account sells foreign exchange and gold are credited to the government's account with the Bank of Canada. We saw in Chapter 17 that an increase in the government's balances with the Bank produce monetary contraction. The Bank of Canada usually neutralizes by open market operations the monetary consequences of the operations of the Exchange Fund unless they reinforce the monetary policy objectives the Bank is following at the time. Insofar as the dollars obtained by the Fund are added to the government's overall revenue, they may also influence its budget and debt management operations.

When the external value of the Canadian dollar tends toward its upper limit the Exchange Fund Account increases the supply of dollars on the exchange market by selling Canadian dollars for foreign exchange and gold. These dollars are advanced to the Account by the government which reduces its own balances with the Bank of Canada. Monetary expansion results unless the Bank engages in neutralizing activities. Insofar as the government has to finance advances to the Account out of its budget there are budgetary and debt management implications. The operations of the Exchange Fund Account may at times restrict the government in its use of monetary, fiscal and debt management policies for domestic stabilization purposes.

Purchasing Power Parity

One of the difficulties of both a pegged exchange rate system and a fixed exchange system such as the gold standard is the initial establishment of a par value or mint par for a country's currency. If the par value of a currency is set too high (overvalued) the resulting chronic balance of payments deficits will place a crippling burden on the country's economy. On the other hand, if the par value of a currency is set too low (undervalued), chronic balance of payments surpluses and the accumulation of exchange reserves may result in monetary expansion undesirable for the long run. In the early 1900's Gustav Cassel suggested the purchasing power parity theory for determining the "proper" par value for a country's currency.

The purchasing power parity theory takes several forms. In its crudest version, the absolute form, it states that a freely fluctuating rate of exchange tends to adjust itself to that level where a given currency possesses an equal amount of purchasing power in each of several countries. If, for example, a given amount of domestic commodities sell for \$1 in Canada, the same volume of commodities should sell in Britain for the same number of pounds which a Canadian could buy with \$1. At equilibrium the rate of exchange is the ratio reflecting purchasing power in the countries involved.

The second version of the purchasing power parity theory, the comparative form, is used to determine the present theoretical rate from that which existed in some base period. The base period is one in which the balance of payments was in equilibrium and abnormal conditions were absent. Changes in the exchange rate from the base period are assumed to be reflected in the changes in the price levels in various trading countries. For example, assume prices in Canada and Britain are at 100 in the base period and that \$2 (Canadian) are required to purchase £1 (sterling). If in a subsequent period prices in Canada increase by 100 per cent with no change in Britain, the rate of exchange should reflect this price increase so that \$4 are required to obtain £1. The following formula expresses the comparative purchasing power parity theory:

$$\frac{\text{Index number of prices in one country}}{\text{Index number of prices in second country}} \times \begin{matrix}\text{Rate of} \\ \text{Exchange in} \\ \text{base period} \\ \text{between the} \\ \text{two countries}\end{matrix} = \begin{matrix}\text{Purchasing} \\ \text{power} \\ \text{Parity Rate}\end{matrix}$$

substituting from our example $\frac{200}{100} \times \$2 = \$4 = £$

Because of its shortcomings economists consider the purchasing power parity theory only a rough guide for establishing a new par of exchange following a period of dislocation in the foreign exchange market. One difficulty is the choice of the appropriate index number. Is the wholesale, retail or some type of cost index the appropriate choice? Moreover, what items should be included in the index — the prices of all goods and services or only the prices of items moving in international trade? Another difficulty is that the rate of exchange is also influenced by capital movements which do not necessarily reflect price changes. Furthermore, when prices are used to reflect changes in the exchange rate the effects of structural changes are neglected. For example, a country's currency may be undervalued on the exchange market not so much as a result of price changes, but as a result of the country having developed from an agricultural into an industrial economy. For all these reasons the purchasing power parity theory is not particularly helpful to policy makers in determining an appropriate par value for a currency.

FIXED EXCHANGE RATE SYSTEMS: THE ARGUMENTS

Proponents of fixed exchange rate systems point out that without large fluctuations in foreign exchange rates, international trade and investment can develop in an orderly fashion. Critics note that under fixed exchange rates the only alternative to changing these rates is to adjust domestic prices or incomes, or both, and that this may disturb trade and investment more severely than would fluctuations in exchange rates.

Fixed exchange rates are regarded by their proponents as providing necessary restraints on irresponsible monetary expansion. The gold standard acted as a "gold anchor" or "golden brake". For fear of depleting its gold reserves a country could not inflate its economy faster than other countries. The same is true under a pegged rate system where, in addition to gold, foreign exchange, either owned or borrowed, is part of a country's international monetary reserves. Critics admit that fixed exchange systems guard against irresponsible inflationary policies but claim that they tend to have too great a deflationary bias. The limited availability of gold and other international monetary reserves imposes on countries monetary restraints which tend to depress prices and income. As we shall see in a subsequent chapter, over the last decade or so economists have been concerned with the inadequacy of international reserves and steps have been taken to increase these reserves to avoid deflationary consequences.

The most potent criticism of fixed exchange rate systems is that they do not allow sufficient control over a country's domestic level of employment and prices. A country with inadequate international monetary reserves, chronic payment deficits and rigid domestic prices is forced to deflate its income and reduce employment in order to maintain a given fixed exchange rate and to allow adjustments in its balance of payments to take place. On the other hand, if the same country has price flexibility upward under conditions of full employment, balance of payments surpluses may force it to allow price inflation so that balance of payments adjustments may take place. Hence, under a fixed rate system internal employment and price stability may have to be sacrificed for balance of payments and exchange rate stability. This can be a very high price for a country to pay.

For fixed rate systems to operate smoothly countries must set their rates fairly close to the rate which would be determined by free market forces under normal conditions. As yet no adequate measure has been found to estimate what the equilibrium rate would be in the absence of free markets.

In fixing rates the authorities must resort to trial and error, and successive mistakes may add to exchange market uncertainty. In the postwar period there has been a tendency for countries to live with rates long after they have become inappropriate. When the day of reckoning can no longer be postponed radical internal adjustments must be made.

Severe adjustments are avoided under a flexible rate system where adjustments are allowed to take place continuously. Although under a fixed rate system and with adequate international monetary reserves, countries are allowed time to adjust, experience has shown that periods of grace are usually used to put off until tomorrow what should be done today. Under these circumstances a fixed exchange rate system may actually encourage destabilizing exchange rate speculation.

Another criticism of a fixed exchange rate system is that it transmits the business cycle from one country to another whereas a flexible rate system does not. For example, suppose the United States experiences inflation while Canada successfully maintains price stability. With price inflation in the United States Americans increase their imports from Canada. Under a fixed rate system the consequent increase in Canadian exports will have inflationary effects in Canada. However, under a flexible rate system the increase in American imports (Canadian exports) will depreciate the external value of the American dollar and appreciate that of the Canadian dollar. The changes in the exchange rate will stimulate an increase in American exports (Canadian imports) reversing the initial trade imbalance. Insofar as the effects of inflation in the United States are on the trade balance, the Canadian economy is insulated from American cyclical disturbances. However, if capital flows are induced by exchange rate changes, some cyclical effects may still be transmitted.

EXCHANGE CONTROL SYSTEMS

Exchange restrictions have taken various forms depending upon the desired objectives. In their extreme form they have been employed to regulate all of a country's economic transactions with the rest of the world; this is what is generally implied by exchange control systems. Exchange restrictions, however, whose imposition is only temporary and which affect only a few selected international transactions, need not be incorporated into a comprehensive exchange control system.

Under an exchange control system the government assumes a monopoly of exchange transactions — all foreign exchange required for payment to foreigners must be purchased from the government. Moreover, the government regulates or assumes control of the transfer of monetary and other assets owned or acquired by its residents in foreign countries. The government dictates the prices at which it will buy and sell foreign exchange, as well as the amounts of and the purposes for which foreign exchange is made available. It may set a single price for foreign exchange (usually lower than that determined by free market forces); it may set a selling rate substantially higher than the buying rate; or it may set several rates for a single currency depending upon the nature of the transactions involved. The latter is known as a multiple exchange rate system.

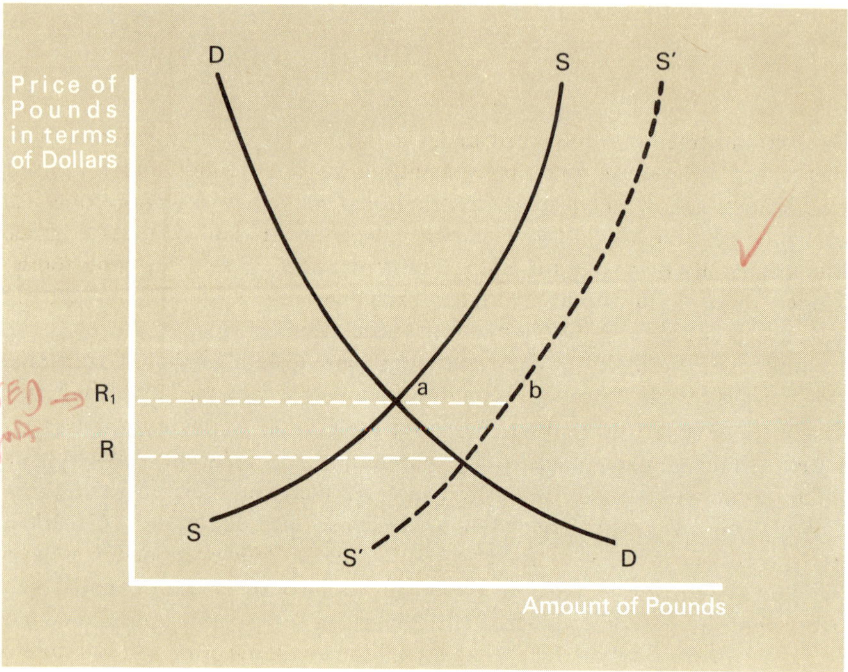

Figure 30-6

Most countries that have resorted to complete exchange control systems ended, even if they did not start, with overvalued currencies. This is a natural phenomenon since controls are almost always imposed to prevent currency depreciation in the face of international payments deficits. Countries in the past have attempted to avoid depreciation because of the consequent adverse shift in the terms of trade — after depreciation imports, as a rule, are more costly per unit of exports. Moreover, countries with a large international indebtedness denominated in foreign currencies have been reluctant to depreciate their own currency because of the extra burden this would impose upon them in meeting their debt obligations.

In Figure 30-6 the normal market forces of supply and demand determine the foreign exchange rate of the pound in terms of dollars at R_1. Suppose that because of political uncertainty or fear of war the British government is afraid of a capital outflow as foreigners repatriate their investments in Britain. To avert depreciation of the pound the government *fixes* the foreign exchange rate of the pound at R_1. If its fears of a capital outflow prove to be correct the supply curve of pounds shifts to the right, say to $S'S'$. At R_1, the fixed dollar price of the pound, there now exists an excess supply of pounds on the foreign exchange market equal to *ab*. If the pound price were not fixed, the excess pounds would drive the pound price down to *R*. Hence at R_1 the pound is overvalued in terms of dollars and the dollars are undervalued in terms of pounds.

Under a pegged rate system, as we saw earlier, the British government would attempt to maintain the pound rate at R_l by purchasing the excess pounds with its foreign exchange reserves. If, instead, it were to impose exchange controls it would interfere directly in the foreign exchange market with measures that would in effect produce desired shifts in the demand and supply curves. For example, it might prevent a shift in the supply curve of pounds from *SS* to *S′S′*. This could be accomplished by not allowing foreigners to repatriate their British investments — by restricting the conversion of pounds into dollars.

The government may also use exchange controls to insure that the available foreign exchange is surrendered to it. In Figure 30-7 the repatriation of foreign investments is shown by a shift in the demand for foreign exchange (dollars) from *DD* to *D′D′*. With the pound price of dollars fixed at R_l' there exists an excess demand for dollars equal to *ef* which will tend to force the exchange value of the dollar up. To prevent this rise and the consequent depreciation of the pound, the British government rations the available amount of foreign exchange (equal to *OE* dollars). As a rule, with exchange rationing those wishing to obtain foreign exchange must procure a licence from the government. Such licencing nearly always implies discrimination among importers, products, services and even countries. Usually, licences are not issued for capital exports and are available only on a limited basis for interest and amortization payments. Importers of "essential" goods and services can usually obtain licences but importers of "non-essentials" cannot. In time of war a further distinction is made between war and non-war materials. A point to keep in mind is that while imports can be restricted with quantitative controls also such as commodity quotas and tariffs, only exchange controls are a sure defence aginst the flight of capital.

With a fixed exchange rate protected by exchange controls a country insulates itself against outside forces and is free to adopt inflationary policies. Inflation tends to convert an initial equilibrium rate into an overvalued rate or to increase any initial degree of overvaluation. Export of goods then becomes more difficult and the consequent decrease in the supply of foreign exchange will have to be met with more severe exchange controls. Almost inevitably exchange controls when practised by more than one country lead to a reduction in trade, barter deals, bilateral trading arrangements and other arrangements which destroy the multilateral nature of international trade.

Multiple exchange rates, first used in Germany in the early thirties, were employed as a device to open export markets when the controlled rate became greatly overvalued. For a variety of other reasons Latin American countries after the Second World War also used multiple exchange rates in one form or another. In its simplest form a multiple exchange rate system has two rates — an official rate (usually overvalued),

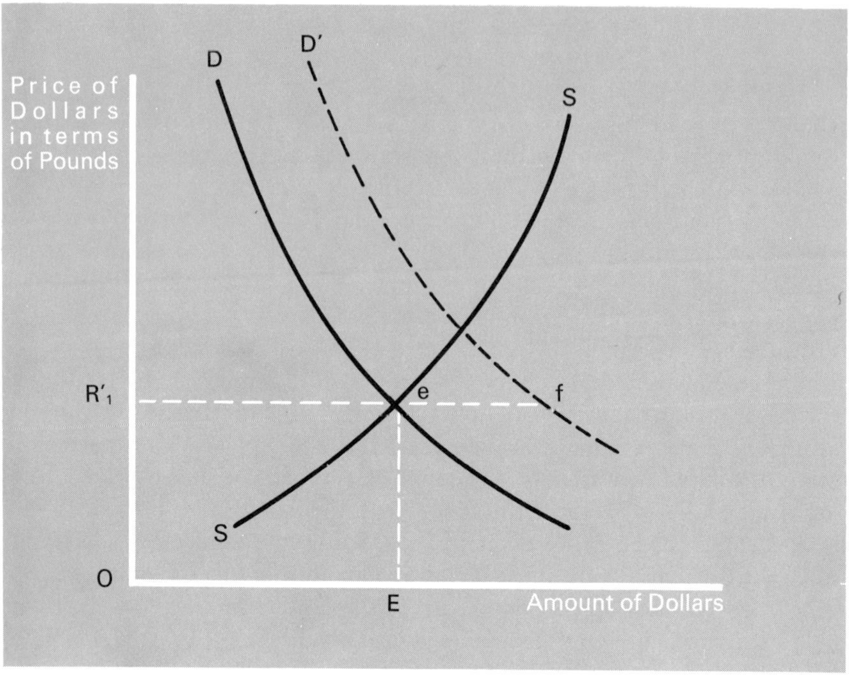

Figure 30-7

and a free rate. If a country has a semi-monopolistic position for some of its export goods, receipt of foreign exchange from the sale of these goods has to be surrendered to the authorities at the official rate. Exporters receive less domestic currency than they would if they could sell their foreign exchange at the lower free rate. Imports of basic necessities are usually permitted at the official rates; importers of such goods and services give up less domestic currency to purchase foreign exchange than they would if they had to buy it in the lower free market. Transactions confined to the free rate usually include exports that need encouragement, non-essential and luxury imports, capital exports and imports, and usually interest and dividend payments. If the free rate depreciates too much the government may attempt to support it or control the transactions allowed at the free rate. However, a controlled free rate usually leads to black markets where foreign exchange is bought and sold illegally.

Although the International Monetary Fund has discouraged the use of multiple exchange rate systems, some of the Latin American and underdeveloped countries still have them. Some of these countries use them as an instrument for accelerating the rate of economic growth. Others, by maintaining a differential between buying and selling rates, use them as a source of government revenue. Most countries are gradually relaxing their direct exchange controls and moving toward a pegged rate system.

SELECTED READINGS

Brown, William A., *The International Gold Standard Reinterpreted 1914-1934,* 2 vols., New York, National Bureau of Economic Research, Inc., 1940.

Caves, R. E., "Flexible Exchange Rates", *American Economic Review,* Vol. 53, May 1963, pp. 120-129.

Ellis, H. S., *Exchange Control in Central Europe,* Cambridge, Mass., Harvard University Press, 1941.

Friedman, Milton, "The Case for Flexible Exchange Rates" in *Essays in Positive Economics,* Chicago, University of Chicago Press, 1953, pp. 157-302.

Gibbons, Alan O., "Foreign Exchange Control in Canada, 1939-51", *Canadian Journal of Economics and Political Science,* Vol. 19, February 1953, pp. 35-54.

Halm, G. N., "Fixed or Flexible Exchange Rates", in *Factors Affecting the United States Balance of Payments,* Compilation of Studies prepared for the Subcommittee on International Exchange and Payments of the Joint Economic Committee, United States Congress, 87th Congress, 2nd Session, 1962.

Machlup, Fritz, *International Trade and the National Income Multiplier,* Philadelphia, Blakiston, 1943.

Machlup, Fritz, *International Payments, Debts and Gold (Collected Essays),* New York, Charles Scribner's Sons, 1968, Part 1.

Meade, James E., *The Balance of Payments,* Parts 3, 4 and 5, Vol. 1, of *The Theory of International Economic Policy,* London, Oxford University Press, 1951.

Meade, J. E., "The Case for Variable Exchange Rates", *Three Banks Review,* September 1955, pp. 3-27.

Mundell, Robert A., "Capital Mobility and Stabilization Policy under Fixed and Flexible Exchange Rates", *Canadian Journal of Economics and Political Science,* Vol. 29, November 1963, pp. 475-485, reprinted in American Economic Association, *Readings in International Economics,* Vol. 11, Homewood Ill., Richard D. Irwin, 1968, pp. 487-499.

Mundell, R. A., "The Monetary Dynamics of International Adjustments under Fixed and Flexible Exchange Rates", *Quarterly Journal of Economics,* Vol. 74, May 1960, pp. 227-257.

Poole, W., "The Stability of the Canadian Flexible Exchange Rate", 1950-1962, *The Canadian Journal of Economics and Political Science,* Vol. 33, May 1967, pp. 205-217.

Scammell, W. M. *International Monetary Policy,* 2nd ed., London, Macmillan, 1961, Ch. 4.

Slater, D. W., "Canadian Foreign Exchange Rates", *The Canadian Banker,* Vol. 69, No. 2, Summer 1962, reprinted in James P. Cairns and H. H. Binhammer, *Canadian Banking and Monetary Policy,* Toronto, McGraw-Hill, 1965.

Sohmen, Egon, *Flexible Exchange Rates, Theory and Controversy,* Chicago, University of Chicago Press, 1961.

Viner, Jacob, *Studies In the Theory of International Trade,* New York, Harper and Brothers, 1937, Parts 6 and 7.

Wonnacott, Paul, *The Canadian Dollar 1948-1962,* Toronto, University of Toronto Press, 1965.

Yeager, Leland B., *International Monetary Relations,* New York, Harper & Row, 1966, Part 1.

31 THE INTERNATIONAL MONETARY SYSTEM BEFORE 1939

THE GOLDEN ERA

In 1821 Great Britain became the first country in modern history to base its monetary unit on only one metal. The Province of Canada adopted gold monometallism in 1853. However, it was not until the 1870's that the major countries of the world abandoned silver and bimetallism for gold. Germany and Sweden turned to gold in 1871, Norway, Denmark and Belgium in 1873, Switzerland, Italy, Greece and France a year later, Holland in 1875 and Uruguay in 1876.

Although the United States went on a *de facto* gold standard in 1879 when specie payment was resumed, it did not formally adopt the gold standard until 1900. By 1914 after some forty countries had accepted the gold standard it became a truly international standard. In most countries acceptance of the gold standard had come to be considered part of the natural order of things and an indication of political and economic maturity.

During most of the thirty-five years from the later 1870's to 1914 the international payments mechanism operated fairly smoothly. Exchange rate fluctuations were relatively small; international movements of capital and trade expanded, and chronic balance of payments disequilibria were avoided. The existence of an international gold standard no doubt played an important role in this stability. However, it was only allowed to play this role because of the particular political and economic conditions and institutional arrangements of the time, and because countries were willing to play according to the rules of the gold standard game.

Except for minor wars peace was maintained during the period essentially because of the military and economic supremacy of Great Britain. Britain was the leading industrial nation and the world's chief trader and financier. It supplied the other countries with the fruits of its industrial expansion in return for food and raw materials. Surpluses and deficits in

Britain's balance of payments were absorbed by the free movement of gold and capital which induced balance of payments adjustments. Money supply changes were sensitive to gold and capital movements; changes in incomes and prices were sensitive to variations in the money supply; and international trade in goods and services was sensitive to changes in income and prices. All this was the result of institutional arrangements and behaviour for which Great Britain assumed the major responsibility.

Most of the world trade, even when it did not originate in or was not destined for Great Britain, was financed through Britain. Sterling bills and deposits served as the principal medium of international payments. Trading credit to finance imports or exports was generally obtained in London. The most important institutional arrangement for the smooth functioning of the gold standard was probably the London money market. It was the financial nerve centre of the world. If at any given time an excess supply of bills were drawn on London, their discount rate would tend to rise. When crisis threatened, other interest rates in the London money market usually moved in the same direction as the discount rate on bills, assisted by the Bank of England. With higher interest rates in London, foreign exporters were inclined to hold sterling bills to maturity and short-term capital would tend to flow to London. Hence countries with balance of payments surpluses financed such surpluses with relatively small gold imports and large short-term capital exports. Alternatively, deficit countries escaped exhaustion of their gold stock with an inflow of short-term capital. An outflow of capital from a surplus country had the same result as an inflow of gold; the money supply would increase as would prices and money income. The country's exports declined while its imports increased and balance of payments equilibrium was restored. At the same time that these adjustments were taking place in the surplus country, opposite adjustments were taking place in the deficit country. With an outflow of gold and an inflow of capital, its money supply declined as did prices and money income. This stimulated an increase in exports and a decrease in imports leading to balance of payments equilibrium.

Three important institutional arrangements are implied in the above adjustment process: a financial nerve centre; flexible prices, wages and money income; and unrestricted trade. Furthermore, during this era the authorities in the respective countries played by the rules of the gold standard game. The most important of these rules was that balance of payments or external equilibrium had to receive preference over domestic or internal equilibrium. This implied that the monetary authorities would allow or even assist the required monetary changes to take place following gold and short-term capital flows. Moreover, if price inflation or unemployment resulted, these were sacrifices which had to be endured.

THE END OF AN ERA

The war in 1914 marked the beginning of the piecemeal dismantling of the international gold standard. At first, most countries made a valiant attempt to hang on to at least the outward symbols of the gold standard. For example, in Britain no restrictions were placed on gold export until 1919, and the Bank of England's legal obligation to buy and sell all gold offered to it at the official price remained in effect until much later. However, after 1914 redemption of bank notes in gold and the export of gold were virtually prevented by appeals to patriotism. Moreover, by pegging the dollar/sterling rate (at about $4.77 U.S.) and by making illegal the purchase and sale of gold at a premium, gold export was made unprofitable. Furthermore wartime shipping risks discouraged gold movements. On the continent there was a general tendency to suspend redemption in gold coin and to place embargoes on gold exports. However, gold importing and official obligations to buy gold at fixed prices remained legal. The exceptions to this general rule were the Scandinavian countries, particularly Sweden, which restricted the flow of gold into their monetary systems as an anti-inflationary measure. On the North American continent, Canada suspended gold convertibility of Dominion notes and bank notes in 1914; in the United States gold exports became subject to official licence in 1917. During the war, the restrictions on free convertibility of currencies and on gold movements broke the former link among national price systems. Prices in the different countries were free to move independently. Varying degrees of inflation ensued as most countries depended upon monetary expansion to finance their war requirements.

THE RETURN TO GOLD

After the war, almost everyone considered a return to the international gold standard as the natural course of events; to do otherwise would have been sacrilege. The United States with comparatively little wartime inflation discontinued controls over gold exports and returned to the full gold standard in June 1919. However, its relatively high tariff barriers and its insistence on debt repayment by wartime allies and of reparations by Germany made it difficult for other countries to follow the American lead immediately. In 1918 the Cunliffe Committee in Britain recommended the removal of all restrictions "without delay" to allow the traditional gold standard adjustment mechanism to function again. By 1920 Britain had relaxed most of her controls on the import and export of capital and the pound fluctuated freely without government intervention. Finally in 1925, after Britain had received an American loan of $300 million, the Chancellor of the Exchequer, Winston Churchill, announced that gold export would again be allowed. However, to economize on gold and yet have the benefits of the gold standard the Bank of England was permitted to purchase gold only in bars valued at around $8,300. Hence a return to gold by Britain meant a gold bullion standard. The pound was convertible at its prewar parity of $4.866 making it overvalued by about 10 per cent. This made Britain's period of readjustment rather painful. High interest rates became the chief weapon against gold outflows. However, high interest rates and trade depression led to business stagnation and chronic unemployment. At times the pound received some support from inflows of capital seeking refuge from still weaker continental currencies, and from central bank deposits as other countries adopted gold exchange standards.

In France, with government deficits, inflationary finance, and recurrent political crises, the franc was not stabilized until mid-1926. Two years later the gold content of the franc was redefined at the prevailing exchange rate and the gold bullion standard was adopted. The new par value for the franc left it undervalued.

By 1929 most countries were back on the gold standard. Some countries, like France, chose new parities that undervalued their currencies. Other countries, like Britain, returned to prewar parities which overvalued their currencies and necessitated painful adjustments. Still other countries, such as Austria, Hungary, Poland, Germany and Russia, adopted new currency units after hyperinflation had destroyed their old currencies. Most of the parities chosen did not adequately reflect the different degrees of inflation in the various countries, a fact which led to the disintegration of the international monetary system.

THE FALL FROM GOLD

We noted earlier that the apparent success of the prewar gold standard depended upon existing institutional arrangements and behaviour. Of prime importance was the London money market. London set the pattern of interest rates, which with relative political and economic stability, induced appropriate stabilizing capital movements. After the war, London was no longer the financial nerve centre of the world, competing now with New York and Paris. With more than one major financial centre, international clearing became more complex and less efficient. Moreover, as a result of the recommendations of the Genoa conference in 1922, many countries linked their currencies not directly with gold but rather with gold-standard currencies. Thus they held a large proportion of their reserves in the form of bank accounts and liquid securities in the main financial centres of gold-standard countries. This practice created a large amount of "ballast capital" which tended to shift with each change of wind. Such shifts took place in response to erratic changes in interest rates, a loss of confidence in currencies resulting from economic and political instability, and at times as a result of irrational behaviour by central bankers. Attempts to liquidate foreign exchange holdings played an important role in the collapse of 1931. The uneven distribution of gold among the nations of the world and the pyramiding of claims on a relatively narrow gold base produced an international monetary system unable to cope with sudden and large shifts from one currency to another and from currencies to gold.

Another reason why the traditional gold standard balance of payments adjustments no longer operated was the reluctance by most countries to follow the rules of the gold game. One of the prime defectors was the United States. During most of the 1920's the United States sterilized gold flows, preventing them from producing appropriate changes in its domestic money supply. In the early 1920's it made loans for relief, rehabilitation and to stabilize European currencies. While these charitable acts compensated for the United States' inappropriate gold sterilization activities, much of their usefulness in stabilizing currency and adjusting balance of payments was negated by American insistence on repayment of war loans and reparations. After mid-1920 when official loans and credits came to an end private lending took their place. Unfortunately, a large proportion of the loans made in the American capital markets were for unproductive commercial purposes which ultimately aggravated rather than assisted the balance of payments difficulties of recipient countries.

France was another major defector from the rules of the gold game. The Bank of France, because it was not allowed to conduct open market operations, was unable to reinforce gold movements. Britain, on the other hand, was one of the few countries which almost consistently responded to gold flows with appropriate domestic money and credit changes.

Even if all countries had desisted from gold sterilization and allowed appropriate domestic money and credit changes to take place, there remained other stumbling blocks to smooth adjustment. The concentration of business enterprise and government support programs prevented downward price flexibility. Governments also introduced social legislation to prevent excessive declines in money incomes. At the same time, when changes in prices and money incomes did occur, international trade could not fully respond due to trade restrictions. In 1921, for example, Britain inaugurated the Key Industries Duties. The United States replaced her low Underwood Tariff of 1913 with the high Fordney-McCumber Tariff in 1922.

Inappropriate parities which left currencies either undervalued or overvalued, large international balances which moved erratically in response to economic and political instability, the insensitivity of monetary systems to changes in reserves, the unsympathetic movement of prices and incomes to the balance of international payments, and restrictions to the free movement of international trade, all resulted in a very fragile international monetary system. This system was unable to withstand the disturbances created by economic depression and financial panic.

Symptoms of economic decline first appeared in the primary producing countries. These countries had expanded their production to meet the demands created by wartime dislocations. After the war various support programs encouraged them to maintain and expand production after producers, cut off by war, had been rehabilitated. The result was overproduction and a downward drift in primary goods prices. Aside from the deflationary pressures of overproduction, there existed an inherent deflationary bias in the international monetary system itself. This was the result of the uneven distribution of the world gold stock. The United States in the early 1920's and France in the late 1920's had a disproportionately large share of the world's gold stock. As a result, other countries had only small gold holdings and were reluctant to expand their money supplies as fast as they otherwise might have. On the other hand, countries with ample gold stocks were reluctant to pursue inflationary policies which would have relieved the strains on other nations.

After 1927, Australia, the Dutch East Indies, Germany, Finland, Brazil, Poland, Argentina and Canada experienced economic recession. But world wide depressionary forces did not become serious until after the downturn of industrial activity in the United States in July 1929 and the stock market crash in October of that year. American lending abroad virtually ceased and the repatriation of funds from abroad began. During the following year the United States government introduced the Smoot-Hawley Tariff which increased tariff rates on both agricultural and industrial goods. Other countries responded by imposing tariff barriers or increasing the height of existing barriers. Some went a step further and imposed trade embargoes. By 1931 there was still hope that the depression had taken its course and recovery was on its way. However, the events following a financial crisis in Austria shattered any such hopes.

In May 1931 the insolvency became known of the Credit-Anstalt, one of the most influential and largest banks in Austria. This led to the withdrawal of foreign short-term credits which did not subside even after foreign loans were made to Austria. Subsequently, a standstill agreement was made by the Credit-Anstalt's chief creditors and President Hoover of the United States proposed a one-year moratorium on all government war debts and reparations. The plight of Austria raised doubts about the solvency of banks in Hungary, Rumania and Germany. Foreign central banks came to Germany's assistance by discounting the equivalent of $100 million Reichsbank bills. This proved inadequate and a further flight from marks to foreign exchange ensued, particularly after the failure of the Darmstädter und National Bank. To preserve its gold and foreign exchange, a temporary stock exchange and bank holiday was declared and exchange controls were introduced. A standstill agreement reached in August immobilized for six months funds owned by Germans to foreign banks. About $70 million in British short-term assets were frozen and the liquidity panic spread to England. An outflow of capital from London had been under way since mid-year. Indeed, in its report the Committee on Finance and Industry (the so-called Macmillan Committee) had already warned of the vulnerability of sterling. Advances of $650 million by American and French banks in August were quickly exhausted and the reserves of the Bank of England continued to decline. When no more foreign assistance was forthcoming and devaluation seemed inevitable, the Bank of France gave orders to sell £6 million. This final blow pushed Britain off the gold standard. On September 21, 1931, Parliament passed legislation suspending the Bank of England's obligation to sell gold. During the first week the pound, whose previous mint par had been $4.87, fluctuated between about $4.30 and $3.40. The depreciation cost the Bank of France an amount equal to seven times its capital. The Netherlands Bank also lost heavily. The decline in the external value of sterling was soon moderated by domestic credit restraints, temporary exchange controls, and by the adoption in November 1931 of a general tariff. In 1932 the Exchange Equilization Fund was established to smooth out excessive short-run rate fluctuations and the pound became in effect pegged. In the same year at a conference in Ottawa final arrangements were made to promote greater economic unity within the British Empire through a system of trade preferences — the so-called Imperial Preferences. To stop further trade discrimination, the League of Nations was requested, at a conference in Lausanne in the summer of 1932, to call another conference and prepare studies on the problems of trade discrimination and exchange instability.

In 1929, Uruguay, Argentina and Brazil left the gold standard and in the following year they were joined by Australia, New Zealand and Venezuela. The move from gold was accelerated after Britain's departure. Canada was among the first to follow in September 1931. Many countries which had strong trade and financial ties with Great Britain pegged their currencies to pound sterling in order to retain their traditional trading markets. This marked the beginning of the so-called **sterling area.** These countries held the major part of their international reserves in the form of sterling deposits and other liquid assets in London which served as their clearing centre.

After the formation of the sterling area only five countries still remained on the gold standard — the United States, France, Switzerland,

Belgium and the Netherlands. Germany, the Balkan countries and Latin American countries adopted exchange control systems.

After Britain left the gold standard attention was focused on the United States where deflation was growing worse. To stop the exodus of gold the Federal Reserve increased its rediscount rate. This in turn increased the deflationary tendencies and encouraged the further hoarding of gold. The Federal Reserve was unable to offset the deflationary forces by open market purchases. It was required to back its notes dollar for dollar with gold and commercial paper discounted by borrowing member banks. Under conditions of economic depression member bank borrowing declined and Federal Reserve holdings of commercial paper decreased. Therefore, more gold had to be used as collateral, but the amount available was dwindling as a result of external and internal drains. In February 1932, the Glass-Steagall Act permitted the Federal Reserve to use government securities as collateral for its notes and it immediately began to purchase such securities. However, by this time many banks were in no position to increase the availability of credit. Loans from the Reconstruction Finance Corporation, established by Congress early in the year kept many banks and other business from failing. By mid-year there were signs of a business revival. Unfortunately, the Central Republic Trust Company of Chicago became vulnerable to runs and in the following year when the Union Guardian Trust Company of Detroit failed, financial panic broke out. On Febrruary 14, 1933, the Governor of Michigan declared an eight-day state wide bank holiday. By March every state in the Union had declared banking holidays and bank deposits were generally no longer redeemable. Soon after Franklin D. Roosevelt became President he declared a four-day nation-wide bank holiday. On March 9, 1933 Congress passed the Emergency Banking Act which affirmed the President's power to regulate or prohibit transactions in gold or foreign exchange as well as the hoarding of gold. This was followed on April 18 by an announcement that the government would issue no further gold export licences. With the embargo on gold exports the United States left the gold standard. The American dollar, free to fluctuate, immediately depreciated. However, since the embargo on gold was considered to be temporary and because the American balance of payments position was relatively strong, the initial depreciation of the dollar on the foreign market was relatively small.

In June 1933 representatives of sixty-four countries met in London, ostensibly to find a way back to gold. The conference floundered because agreement could not be reached on which should come first, a reconstituted gold standard or the lowering of trade barriers. Moreover, as one observer has put it, the "delegates wandered around in a fog trying to learn by remote control what Mr. Roosevelt was currently thinking. The whole conference fell to pieces".[1]

Unlike Great Britain, the United States had not been forced off the gold standard. In large part it had deliberately gone off because of the mistaken belief by many that an increase in the price of gold would cause domestic prices to rise — a principle of the commodity theory of money. Toward this end the government adopted a gold buying program under the authority given to the President in the Thomas Amendment to the Agricultural Adjustment Act passed in May 1933. The price of gold was gradually bid up and at the end of January 1934 the Gold Reserve Act fixed it at $35 an ounce. Before the departure from the gold standard it had been fixed at $20.67 an ounce. The Gold Reserve Act also transferred the gold stock of the Federal Reserve System to the Treasury in exchange for gold certificates. Furthermore, with the profits from gold revaluation, the Exchange Stabilization Fund was established. In effect the United States adopted a limited gold-bullion standard. The government would buy all gold offered to it at $35 an ounce but would redeem dollars in gold only for foreign central banks and governments.

With the United States gold price settled and the American dollar devalued and stabilized, American capital which had fled abroad during the protracted depreciation of the dollar in 1933-1934 was gradually repatriated. Moreover, gold flowed into the United States as a result of its export surplus and the attraction of high gold prices for foreign gold producers. Thus began the "golden avalanche"[2] which continued until checked by foreign restrictions during the Second World War. During the latter part of the 1930's much of the gold coming into the United States was seeking refuge from impending war conditions.

After the American dollar was devalued the British Equalization Account kept the pound/dollar rate in the neighbourhood of $5.00 and most of the sterling area countries followed Britain's move. Canada, whose dollar had fallen relative to the American dollar in 1931-1932 came back to a dollar-for-dollar exchange rate. The gold bloc countries, finding it increasingly difficult to defend the gold parities of their currencies, one by one devalued and aligned their currencies with the American dollar. Among the last to sever itself from gold was France which did so in September 1936.

The announcement of the devaluation of the franc was accompanied by the announcement of the Tripartite Monetary Agreement. France, Britain and the United States, later joined by Belgium, Holland and Switzerland, agreed to maintain convertibility of their currencies at their pegged

1 Quoted in B. M. Anderson, *Economics and Public Welfare*, New York, Van Nostrand, 1949, p. 331.

2 Graham, F. D., and C. R. Whittlesey, *Golden Avalanche*, Princeton, N. J., Princeton University Press, 1939.

rates. Furthermore, all countries were urged to do the same to avoid further competitive exchange depreciation, and were exhorted to start relaxing trade restrictions and exchange controls. The initial devaluation of the franc was not enough and further devaluation took place in May 1938. In effect France became a member of the sterling bloc because it then stabilized the franc in terms of pound sterling at a rate of 179 francs to the pound.

Hence, in 1938 tranquility was almost restored to the foreign exchange markets. Sterling was pegged to the American dollar and the currencies of most other countries, directly or indirectly, were pegged to either sterling or the dollar. The exceptions to this arrangement were those countries, notably Germany and the Balkan countries, which had exchange control systems.

SELECTED READINGS

Bloomfield, Arthur, *Monetary Policy Under the International Gold Standard, 1880-1914*, New York, Federal Reserve Bank of New York, 1959.

Cassel, Gustav, *Money and Foreign Exchange After 1914*, London, Constable, 1922.

Cassel, Gustav, *The Downfall of the Gold Standard*, Oxford, Clarendon Press, 1936.

Condliffe, J. B., *The Commerce of Nations*, New York, W. W. Norton, 1950.

Ellsworth, P. T., *The International Economy*, New York, Macmillan Company, 1950, Ch. 16, 17 and 18.

Graham, Frank D., and C. R. Whittlesey, *Golden Avalanche*, Princeton, N.J., Princeton University Press, 1939.

Hawtrey, Ralph G., *The Gold Standard in Theory and Practice*, 5th ed., New York, Longmans, Green, 1947.

Keynes, John Maynard, *The Economic Consequences of the Peace*, New York, Harcourt Brace and World, 1920.

League of Nations, *International Currency Experiences:Lessons of the Interwar Period*, Geneva, 1944.

League of Nations, *Commercial Policy in the Interwar Period: International Proposals and National Policies*, Geneva, 1942.

Ropke, Wilhelm, *International Economic Disintegration*, London, William Hodge, 1942.

Yeager, Leland B., *International Monetary Relations*, New York, Harper & Row, 1966, Part II.

Young, John Parke, *Inter-war Currency Lessons*, New York, Monetary Standard Inquiry, 1944.

32

THE INTERNATIONAL MONETARY SYSTEM SINCE 1945

The Second World War shattered any hopes there might have been after the Tripartite Agreement of 1936 for consolidating the international monetary system and for a return to multilateral trade. Most countries pegged their currencies to either sterling or the American dollar while the pound was rigidly pegged to the American dollar at $4.03. The sterling area which before the war had consisted of a rather loose arrangement became a cohesive monetary union held together by an elaborate system of controls. Canada was one of the countries which pegged its currency to the American dollar.

During the years preceding the war, Canada had a net current account deficit with the United States which, as long as sterling was convertible, could be financed with her net current account surplus with the sterling area. However, with the advent of war, sterling was no longer convertible. To protect Canadian foreign exchange reserves, especially the reserves of American dollars, the Canadian government introduced foreign exchange controls which were administered by the newly established Foreign Exchange Control Board. At the same time the Canadian dollar was depreciated by about 10 per cent *vis-à-vis* the American dollar and pegged at this level. Because Canada was one of Britain's chief suppliers of essential goods and services, Canadian sterling surpluses expanded. As a temporary measure the Canadian government provided dollars to Britain by repatriating direct debt held there. Later a large part of the accumulated sterling balances in London were converted into interest-free loans and gifts. Although Canada's sterling balances grew, the shortage of American dollars became acute with the import of essential materials from the United States. The Hyde Park Agreement in April 1941 provided for some integration of war production between Canada and the United States in an attempt to increase Canada's net earnings of American dollars.

As had not been done during the First World War, most countries introduced price controls and rationing to prevent excessive inflation. Moreover, taxation rather than inflationary finance was the more common source of war finance. As a result, compared to the situation after the earlier war, price distortions among the major nations were relatively small at the end of the Second World War.[1] An effort was also made to avoid creating a morass of interallied war debt like that which had plagued many countries during the interwar period. Starting in 1941, under its Lend-Lease program, the United States supplied war materials with settlement to be worked out after the war. Eventually thirty-eight countries were included under this program. By the end of 1946 the United States had supplied goods and services amounting to almost $50 billion and had, in turn, received about $8 billion in reverse lend-lease.

RECONSTRUCTION AND DEVELOPMENT

Before the end of the war plans were made to meet the immediate post-war problems of European reconstruction. The long-range problem of providing institutional arrangements for an efficient and stable mechanism of international payments and for the development of world trade and production were also pressing matters.

Physical destruction was far greater during the Second World War than during the First. An enormous reconstruction program was called for. Even before hostilities ended, large grants for relief had been made either directly by Canada and the United States or indirectly through the United Nations Relief and Rehabilitation Administration. By 1947, realizing that Europe needed a much larger and more coordinated program of assistance, the American Secretary of State, George Marshall, called for massive American assistance with European cooperation. European countries immediately responded by forming the Committee of European Economic Cooperation which formulated a program of recovery that extended from 1948 to 1951. In 1948 the United States established the Economic Cooperation Administration (ECA) with an initial appropriation of $4 billion. At the same time seventeen European countries formed the Organization for European Economic Cooperation (OEC) to establish priorities and administer the American aid program which became known as the Marshall Plan. By the end of 1951 nearly $13 billion had been spent under the plan. Aid was given in the form of goods and services which were sold by recipient countries to their residents for local

[1] Four countries experienced hyperinflation either during or immediately after the war — Hungary, China, Rumania and Greece.

currencies known as "counterpart funds". Five per cent of these funds was allocated to the use of the United States, essentially to meet administrative costs, and the remaining 95 per cent was spent mostly on public investment projects. Insofar as counterpart funds were held idle from time to time they served to check inflation.

Institutional arrangements to provide for the mechanism of international payments and the development of world trade and production took form at the Bretton Woods Conference held in New Hampshire in July 1944. The centre piece of the postwar international monetary system was to be the newly established International Monetary Fund. Its purposes as outlined in the Articles of Agreement are listed below. Its sister institution, the International Bank for Reconstruction and Development, was to concentrate on the tasks implied by its name. However, the role envisaged for it in promoting the flow of long-term development capital soon fell far short of the needs. As a result two further institutions were established, the International Finance Corporation and the International Development Association. More recently these have been joined by regional development banks.

THE INTERNATIONAL MONETARY FUND

At the Bretton Woods conference in 1944 two proposals were considered for the creation of an international monetary institution — the British Keynes Plan and the American White Plan. The Keynes Plan proposed the establishment of an international body to be known as the Clearing Union which would create an international means of payment called **bancor.** Both the gold value of bancor as well as the bancor value of national currencies would be fixed. Each member country's central bank would accept payment from other central banks by the transfer of bancor to its credit in the books of the Clearing Union. Countries with balance of payments deficits could obtain bancor by using automatic overdraft facilities with the Union. The total amount of each central bank's overdrafts would be limited in advance to a specified amount of its country's average trade turnover (exports plus imports). To further discourage the irresponsible use of overdrafts, taxes would be levied on both debtor and creditor accounts in excess of specified amounts. Creditor accounts were also to be taxed so that creditors would assume at least some of the responsibility for overall balance of payments adjustments.

The Keynes Plan was abandoned by and large for the American White Plan which proposed an International Stabilization Fund very similar to the International Monetary Fund agreed upon at the Bretton Woods Conference.

Purposes

The Articles of Agreement of the International Monetary Fund set forth the Fund's purposes as follows:

(1) To promote international monetary cooperation through a permanent institution which provides the machinery for consultation and collaboration on international monetary problems;

(2) To facilitate the expansion and balanced growth of international trade, and to contribute thereby to the promotion and maintenance of high levels of employment and real income and to the development of the productive resources of all members as primary objectives of economic policy;

(3) To promote exchange stability, to maintain orderly exchange arrangements among members, and to avoid competitive exchange depreciation;

(4) To assist in the establishment of a multilateral system of payments in respect of current transactions between members, and in the elimination of foreign exchange restrictions which hamper the growth of world trade;

(5) To give confidence to members by making the Fund's resources available to them under adequate safeguards, thus providing them with the opportunity to correct maladjustments in their balance of payments without resorting to measures destructive of national and international prosperity;

(6) In accordance with the above, to shorten the duration and lessen the degree of disequilibrium in the international balance of payments of members.

Structure and Organization

The Fund is an autonomous organization affiliated with the United Nations. Its members are national governments of which there were thirty-five at the outset and 106 in 1967. The chief non-member countries are Russia, Communist China, Poland, Czechoslovakia, Hungary, Rumania, Switzerland and Cuba. Russia signed the Bretton Woods Agreement but did not ratify it. Poland withdrew in 1950 over a dispute concerning policy, and Czechoslovakia was expelled in 1954 for failure to provide information. Cuba withdrew in 1964.

Each member country is allotted a quota which is the basis for its subscription to the capital of the Fund, its voting power, and its capacity to use the Fund's resources. A country's quota is roughly proportioned to its share of world trade.

The governing body of the Fund is its Board of Governors. Each nation appoints a governor who has 250 votes plus one additional vote for each $100,000 of his country's quota. A country receives one additional vote for each $100,000 of its national currency sold by the Fund and loses one vote with each $100,000 of foreign currency it purchases from the Fund. Since the Board of Governors meets only once a year most of its authority is delegated to a Board of Executive Directors. Each of the five nations with the largest quotas appoints one director. During 1966-1967 an additional fifteen directors were elected by the other nations. Each appointed director may cast a number of votes equal to the number of votes possessed by his country while each elected director may cast a number of votes equal to the number of votes possessed by the countries which elected him.

Financial Resources

The financial resources of the Fund consist of a pool of national currencies and gold contributed by the member countries. Each country is allotted a quota related to its importance in world economic activity. When a country becomes a member of the Fund it has to pay in gold an amount equal to 10 per cent of its net official holdings of gold and United States dollars, or an amount in gold equal to 25 per cent of its quota, whichever is less. The remainder of its quota is paid in domestic currency. If a country depreciates its currency it must replenish the Fund's holdings so that the gold value will be maintained. If, on the other hand, the par value of a nation's currency appreciates, the Fund returns a commensurate part of the currency. The initial quotas in 1947 were equal to $7.7 billion (U.S.).

In 1958 concern over the adequacy of the Fund's resources led to a general increase in quotas of 50 per cent with additional increases levied against Canada, West Germany and Japan, in view of their position in world trade and recent relative economic growth, and for a group of members whose quotas were each less than $20 million. These increases raised the total of all quotas to $15 billion by 1961. A second general increase of 25 per cent, with special increases for sixteen members including Canada, was approved in 1965. This brought the total amount of quotas to $21 billion. Canada's quota as of April 30, 1967 was $740 million (U.S.).

In 1962 another step was taken to strengthen the Fund's resources, and to increase its ability to cope with relatively serious disturbances among the major industrial countries. The Fund entered into a four-year agreement, renewed for a further four years in 1966, with ten industrial countries — Belgium, Canada, France, Germany, Italy, Japan, the Netherlands, Sweden, the United Kingdom and the United States. Under the agreement, known as the General Arrangements to Borrow, these ten countries stand ready to lend their currencies to the Fund where additional resources are required to meet emergency situations. Currencies are to be made available to the Fund to meet the needs of the ten participating countries after concurrence has been received from all the ten countries and the Fund. The total amount of these supplementary resources is the equivalent of $6 billion of which Canada's share is $200 million.

Par Values

One of the main objectives in establishing the Fund was to provide for exchange stability. Toward this end each member country, in consultation with the Fund, is supposed to declare a par value of its currency in relation to the gold content of the United States dollar in 1944. As yet not all countries have made such a declaration but most of these maintain *de facto* parities. The par values chosen by the initial members in 1946 were the exchange rates then in effect. Realizing that countries would probably have difficulty in maintaining these parities, exchange controls were allowed during a transition period.

Each country is required to prevent the external value of its currency from fluctuating more than one per cent above or below its declared par value. However, the Fund recognizes that structural changes in the world economy may make some parities unrealistic. When structural changes do occur and create "fundamental disequilibrium" in a country's balance of payments it may propose to the Fund a change in the par value of its currency. The Fund may not object if the proposed change is less than 10 per cent away from the initial parity. A country making a change of more than 10 per cent without the approval of the Fund may have its Fund privileges withdrawn and may even be expelled.

The Fund's Articles of Agreement do not define fundamental disequilibrium. In practice it has been interpreted to mean chronic disequilibrium in a country's balance of payments that cannot be corrected by means other than excessive domestic deflation or restrictive import barriers.

Foreign Exchange Transactions

The principal operating function of the Fund is to provide financial assistance to members to enable them to maintain the declared values of their currencies without having to resort to excessive deflation, restrictive trade barriers or exchange controls. Assistance may take the form either of a **drawing,** repayable within three to five years, which immediately supplies foreign exchange to a country, or a **stand-by** arrangement assuring a member the right to draw a predetermined amount of foreign exchange any time within a six to twelve month period.

Drawing Rights

When a country experiences balance of payments deficits it usually uses its own reserves to bridge the gap before requesting direct assistance from the Fund. If necessary, it may acquire additional reserves by drawing on the Fund. In drawing on the Fund a member country purchases the currencies of other members from the Fund in exchange for its own currency. Such transactions may be considered as equivalent to borrowing. There are limits to the amount of drawings a member country is allowed. These limits are defined in terms of the amount of a member's currency that the Fund accumulates by selling to it other members' currencies. Two basic rules apply: drawings of foreign currencies by a member within any twelve-month period may not cause the Fund's holdings of the member's currency to increase by more than 25 per cent of the member's quota; its total accumulated drawings must not cause the Fund's holdings to exceed 200 per cent of the member's quota. However, the 25 per cent limit has been waived in many instances and waivers have been granted to countries to exceed the maximum 200 per cent limit.

We mentioned earlier that as a rule a country's quota payments to the Fund are made up of a 25 per cent payment in gold and a 75 per cent payment in the member's own currency. The first drawing by a member which increases the Fund's holdings of a member's currency to 100 per cent of its quota is viewed as borrowing back the gold originally subscribed. Hence the first drawing equal to 25 per cent of a member's quota is called **gold tranche.** Members are given the overwhelming benefit of the doubt in requests for drawings within the gold tranche; such drawings are virtually automatic. Requests for drawings amounting to the second 25 per cent of a member's quota (which increase the Fund's currency holdings of the member above 100 per cent but not above 125 per cent of quota), the so-called **first credit tranche,** are liberally permitted. A member has only to demonstrate that he is making reasonable effort to deal with the difficulties producing the balance of payments deficits. Drawings beyond the first 50 per cent of a country's quota require "substantial justification".

When a member's currency is drawn by another country, the member whose currency is drawn acquires an addition to its credit position or a reduction in its liability in the Fund. If a drawing by other countries reduces the Fund's holdings of a member country's currency below 75 per cent of its quota the member acquires a **super gold tranche** which it can draw at will.

Drawings from the Fund are intended primarily to tide member countries over temporary balance of payments and exchange rate difficulties. Hence members are expected to repay the Fund fairly rapidly — within three to five years. By the end of each financial year of the Fund, a member must repurchase with gold or convertible currencies one half of any increase during the year in the Fund's holdings of its currency in excess of an amount equal to 75 per cent of its quota. The repurchase requirement does not apply when the country's own monetary reserves outside the Fund are less than the amount of its quota and when the

Fund's holdings of the member's currency are below 75 per cent of its quota. Moreover, the amount required to be repurchased is reduced by one half the amount of a decrease in the member's own monetary reserves during the year or increased by one half the amount of an increase in the member's reserves unless the member's reserves are still below its quota. These provisions are intended to ensure that no member will ordinarily finance more than one half of any balance of payments deficit by drawing on the Fund or increase its monetary reserves by adding drawings from the Fund to its foreign exchange reserves.

Regardless of the foreign currencies originally drawn from the Fund, a country must repurchase its own currency with either gold or convertible currencies. Moreover, the Fund is not allowed to accept repayments in currencies of which its holdings exceed 75 per cent of the respective countries' quotas. After the beginning of 1964 the Fund's holdings of American dollars rose above 75 per cent of the United States' quota and repayment by members had to be made either in other acceptable currencies or in gold. To facilitate repayment by countries which customarily hold their foreign exchange reserves in the form of dollars, the American authorities drew convertible currencies (mainly European currencies or Canadian dollars) from the Fund and sold them for dollars to members wishing to make Fund repayments.

To encourage countries to repay loans from the Fund as soon as possible and at the same time to discourage abuses of the drawing privileges the Fund levies interest and service charges payable in gold on its sales of foreign exchange. These charges increase according to the size of the Fund's holdings of the borrowing country's currency in excess of its quota and according to the duration of this excess.

Stand-By Arrangements

In 1952 the Fund instituted what are termed stand-by arrangements. Through these a member receives a commitment from the Fund to draw up to a stated amount from the Fund within a period of six months to a year. Stand-by arrangements have been granted by the Fund in order to maintain confidence in currencies under pressure usually as a result of international emergencies, to provide additional resources during seasonal difficulties, to support programs intended to stabilize economies and to provide backing for currency or exchange reforms.

Compensatory Financing of Export Fluctuations

In 1963 the Fund introduced the compensatory financing facility to assist primary producing countries which experience temporary shortfalls in their export earnings through circumstances largely beyond their control.

As first established, the facility allowed members special drawings up to 25 per cent of their quota even if this would bring their drawings above the normal limit of 200 per cent of quota. In 1966 the range of compensatory financing was extended to 50 per cent of quota. However, except in the case of shortfalls in export earnings resulting from disasters or major emergencies, outstanding compensatory drawings may not increase by more than 25 per cent of quota in any twelve-month period. Moreover, requests for drawings which would increase outstanding compensatory drawings beyond 25 per cent of a member's quota are met only if the Fund is satisfied that the member has been cooperating with it to find appropriate solutions for its balance of payments difficulties. Since 1966 compensatory drawings do not affect the nature of the Fund's policy criteria applied to members' subsequent requests for ordinary drawings.

Scarce Currencies

The planners of the Fund foresaw the possibility that member countries' requests to draw a particular currency could exceed the Fund's capacity to supply it. They approached this problem from the point of view that such a disequilibrium in international payments is two-sided and that its removal is the joint responsibility of both surplus and deficit countries. If the Fund has insufficient resources to meet drawings it can require countries to sell their currencies to it for gold or *request* countries to lend currencies to it. In 1964, for example, the Fund sold gold for currencies required to meet drawings made by the United Kingdom. When a single country's currency becomes scarce the Fund can issue a report, prepared in consultation with the member whose currency is scarce, setting forth the cause of the scarcity and making recommendations to correct the situation. If all else fails, the Fund shall formally declare the currency scarce and ration its residual supply with regard to the needs of the member and to the general international economic situation. Once having declared a currency scarce, the Fund may also authorize member countries to impose temporary restrictions on dealings in the scarce currency.

Other Fund Activities

As important as its financial activities is the Fund's role in providing facilities for consultation among member governments. Its influence on members is pervasive and continual. It may warn countries that their policies will lead to balance of payments difficulties. It can apply moral suasion on governments to promote sound and orthodox financial policies. It has also used its influence toward the elimination of exchange controls and trade liberalization.

INTERNATIONAL BANK FOR RECONSTRUCTION AND DEVELOPMENT

The International Monetary Fund's sister institution, also founded at the Bretton Woods Conference in 1944, is the International Bank for Reconstruction and Development, known as the World Bank. It has had two offspring, the International Finance Corporation and the International Development Association. The three together are known as the World Bank Group.

At Bretton Woods the postwar planners realized that one of the major causes of international payments difficulties in the interwar period was the unreliability and erratic nature of long-term private lending. They also realized that international medium and long-term loans would be a prerequisite for postwar reconstruction. Hence they founded the World Bank to assist first in the reconstruction and then in the development of member countries by facilitating the investment of capital for productive purposes. They saw the main role of the Bank as that of providing the leaven for private long-term lending. This role would require the Bank to make its own loans to support and promote private channels of international investment and not to replace them.

Structure and Organization

Initially only countries that were members of the Fund could be members of the Bank but this restriction has been relaxed. The Bank, like the Fund, is an autonomous organization affiliated with the United Nations. It is owned by the member governments who subscribe to its capital. Subscriptions are allotted to member countries much the same as quotas are allotted to Fund members. Moreover, a member's voting power is based on the amount of its subscription in terms of the shares held.

The authorized capital stock of the Bank was initially $10 billion divided into 100,000 shares with a par value of $100,000 each. The capital subscription of each member is divided into three parts. Two per cent of each subscription is payable in gold or United States dollars, which may be used freely by the Bank in any of its operations. Eighteen per cent of each subscription is payable in the currency of the subscribing member. These funds may be lent only with the consent of the member whose currency it is proposed to lend. The remaining 80 per cent of each subscription constitutes a guarantee fund that may be called for payment by members only when such funds are required to meet obligations of the Bank for funds borrowed or loans guaranteed by it.

In 1959 the authorized capital stock of the Bank was increased from $10 billion to $21 billion. Since the purpose of the capital increase was to raise the Bank's guarantee resources, subscription payment by members was not required. While all countries doubled their capital subscriptions, some, including Canada, made special increases in their subscriptions over and above the 100 per cent general increase. In order to preserve parity of treatment among members so that each member would pay the same amount per share, the extra increase by these countries involved the payment of one per cent in gold or dollars and 9 per cent in the currency of the member. Since the general and special increases, the actual proportion of subscriptions paid in has declined to 10 per cent with 90 per cent remaining on call.

In view of the fact that the authorized capital of $21 billion had been almost entirely subscribed, and as there were a number of new countries wishing to join and existing members wishing to increase their subscriptions, the authorized capital was increased to $22 billion in 1963. A similar situation developed in 1965 at which time the authorized capital was increased to $24 billion. As of June 30, 1967, $22.8 billion was subscribed, $740 million by Canada. By far the largest subscriber was the United States with $6.3 billion. This represented 25 per cent of the total votes compared to 3.2 per cent for Canada.

Resources

The immediate resources of the Bank after its establishment consisted of the members' subscription payments of gold and United States dollars. The local currency portion of their subscriptions was to be made available from members when they could afford to export capital. Over $2 billion of this portion was paid in at the end of the Bank's fiscal year in 1967 and approximately $1.7 billion of it was made available for lending. The major source of funds for lending has been borrowing by the Bank. On June 30, 1967, for example, the funded debt of the Bank was a little over $3 billion of which some $76 million consisted of bonds sold in Canada. Also available for lending is the portion of the Bank's net earnings which is not allocated to special reserves to meet the obligations of the Bank on its borrowings and guarantees. The Bank has also obtained funds for relending by selling portions of loans and from principle repayments.

Bank Lending

The Bank may make loans only to member governments or to private organizations when such loans are guaranteed by their respective member governments. Loans range from fifteen to twenty-five years and the rate of interest charged is the rate which the Bank has to pay in the market to borrow, to which is added 1 ¼ per cent for a loss reserve and for administrative expenses. Loans are usually for specific projects and for productive purposes. The Bank's funds are to be used to finance the foreign exchange expenditures directly connected with the project for which the loan is made and not for local currency disbursements which are the responsibility of the member. However, where the local currency requirement has been insufficient the Bank has at times allowed its loans to assist in meeting these requirements. The Bank's loans may not be tied; borrowers are free to use the proceeds to make purchases in any member country as well as in Switzerland, in recognition of that country's cooperation in financial matters.

Before the Bank makes or guarantees a loan it must be satisfied that the prospective borrower cannot obtain the necessary funds upon reasonable terms elsewhere. Moreover, it must be satisfied that the investment project for which the loan is made will assist in the orderly development of a country with adequate prospects for repayment.

During its first two years the Bank concentrated its loans on European reconstruction. Since then loans have been made essentially to the "less developed" countries and have been concentrated in public utilities, particularly power and transportation facilities.

Other Bank Activities

The Bank performs an important service to its member countries by providing technical assistance, including giving engineering advice on problems of specific projects, helping in the organization of domestic development banks and conducting surveys of a country's needs and resources.

INTERNATIONAL FINANCE CORPORATION

The International Finance Corporation (IFC) was created in 1956 as an affiliate of the World Bank in a further attempt to promote private investment in the less developed countries of the world. The IFC supplements the activities of the Bank in two major ways: it provides financial assistance directly to private enterprise without government guarantees, and it provides "venture capital". It does not have to apply the strict standards required by the Bank when making loans, and it can buy the shares of private corporations as long as this does not involve it in their direct management.

The IFC has a modest authorized capital of $110 million, of which $99.9 million was subscribed and paid in by the eighty-eight member countries at the end of June 1967. Canada's subscription amounted to $3.6 million. Subscriptions are proportional to those in the Bank and must be paid in gold or United States dollars at the time membership is granted. Membership is restricted to World Bank members. Although the IFC may be considered an autonomous organization, it shares offices with the Bank, and the Board of Governors and the executive directors of the two organizations are the same.

Although the IFC can raise funds in the open market it has relied on its share capital and reserves, which at the end of June 1967 amounted to $134.6 million. Since 1966 it has been allowed to borrow from the World Bank and by the end of June 1967 IFC had borrowed $100 million from the Bank. The IFC prefers to employ its relatively small capital as a revolving fund to help firms to become established or sufficiently mature to attract private funds. The success of the IFC in mobilizing private capital is reflected by the way private enterprise has been willing to participate with it in investment projects. Its success is also reflected in its ability to revolve its funds by selling the securities of companies which have been developed or expanded. In recent years it has played an important role in providing capital for the establishment of development finance companies.

INTERNATIONAL DEVELOPMENT ASSOCIATION

In 1960 the International Development Association (IDA) was created as the second affiliate of the Bank to fill yet another gap. It provides long-term development loans on more flexible terms than those available from the Bank and the IFC. The IDA makes loans for purposes "of high developmental priority in the light of the needs of the area or areas concerned and, except in special circumstances...for specific projects". But the projects financed need not be "revenue-producing or directly productive". The IDA may grant loans without interest, with long maturities and extend long periods of grace before repayment begins. Moreover, repayment can be made in the currency of the borrowing member whether or not it is convertible. This is an important provision because under it the IDA can provide funds to countries whose balance of payments prospects do not justify them incurring or continuing to incur external debt repayable in gold or foreign exchange. Loans granted by the IDA have been for a period of fifty years with no interest. A service charge of three quarters of one per cent per annum is charged to meet the Association's administrative costs. No repayment is required for the first ten years, one per cent is repaid annually during the next ten years, and 3 per cent per year thereafter until the loan is repaid. Loans by the IDA have been concentrated in the area of "social overheads" — schools, roads, agricultural and sanitation projects.

The resources of the IDA are supplied by its members who must also be members of the World Bank. For purposes of allocating subscriptions countries are divided into two groups. Part I members include the industrial countries whose total subscription has to be paid in gold and convertible currencies. At the end of June 1957 the eighteen countries included in this group had contributed $1.5 billion. Canada had contributed $79.5 million, 5.22 per cent of the toal. Part II members are the less developed countries. They are required to pay only 10 per cent of their subscriptions in gold or convertible currencies. At the end of June 1967, seventy-nine Part II countries had contributed $25 million. The other 90 per cent of their subscription is payable in national currencies and can be used only with the consent of the country concerned. From this 90 per cent a total of $18 million had been released by the end of June 1967. In recent years the funds available to the IDA from its members has been supplemented by loans from the Bank.

OTHER INTERNATIONAL INVESTMENT AGENCIES

There are a variety of other sources of international investment capital for development and mutual economic assistance or for purposes of mutual security. In the United States the Export-Import Bank was established in 1934 to promote and finance trade with Russia. Although its main function is to provide credit to facilitate American exports it has granted loans to foreign governments and foreign business enterprises and financial institutions. For example, it granted a loan to Canada during its exchange crisis in 1962. It has a capital stock of $1 billion provided by the American Treasury.

The International Cooperation Administration (ICA), an agency of the United States Department of State, grants loans to foreign governments and their agencies. These loans are part of the American Mutual Security Program and are granted to "friendly" nations for defence purposes which include economic development projects. The Development Loan Fund (DLF) established in 1957 is another source of development capital provided by the United States.

The Canadian government is a participant in the Columbo Plan and as such provides assistance to nations in Southeast Asia. Assistance is usually provided in the form of goods and services rather than direct financial capital.

An Arab Financial Institution for Economic Development was set up in 1959, the Inter-American Development Bank in 1960, the African Development Bank in 1964 and the Asian Development Bank in 1965. In addition to these banks the European Common Market countries have established the European Investment Bank to aid their less advanced regions.

THE DOLLAR SHORTAGE

Despite the aid received after the war by European countries, their needs for goods and services from North America, first for reconstruction and then for military purposes to thwart the spread of communism, left them with a chronic dollar shortage. Added to their overall requirement for dollars was their inability to earn them. In part this was due to the overvalued parities European countries had established with the International Monetary Fund. Once established, the Fund was reluctant to approve currency depreciation and was unwilling to lend its resources. Since the Fund could not begin to cope with the foreign exchange problems associated with European reconstruction it retired into relative obscurity until the early 1950's. European countries drifted toward tighter exchange controls and bilateral payment agreements.

Under the Anglo-American Financial Agreement in 1946 the United States came to the assistance of Britain by giving her credits of $3.7 billion. Canada added another $1.2 billion. The agreement was of benefit to Canada which was also caught in a dollar shortage. Part of the American dollars supplied to Britain was to settle British import surpluses with Canada, thus providing Canada with United States dollars to meet its import surplus with the United States. Unfortunately, the Americans insisted that their advances to Britain be conditional upon the pound becoming convertible during 1947. Britain met her commitment in July, but immediately lost $1 billion worth of gold as foreigners took the opportunity to rid themselves of pounds accumulated as a result of credit extended during the war. Convertibility had to be abandoned in August.

France devalued the franc before registering its official parity with the International Monetary Fund in 1946. Two years later the franc was devalued further when France adopted a complex system of multiple exchange rates. A general round of devaluation came in 1949 when Britain, with little or no consultation with the International Monetary Fund, announced a 30 per cent devaluation of the pound from $4.03 (U.S.) to $2.80 (U.S.). Twenty-three countries followed the British move within one week and seven more followed later.

Canada was among the countries to follow Britain's move. In 1946 Canada had declared a par value with the Fund at parity with the American dollar. The Canadian dollar was appreciated at the time from its wartime level in order to reduce the inflationary price movements resulting from the early abandonment of price controls in the United States. However, in 1947 with continuing inflation and with the large drawing down of loans extended to foreigners, Canada's foreign exchange reserves declined precariously. The Canadian government responded by borrowing $300 million from the Export-Import Bank in Washington and imposing temporary exchange controls and restrictions. After the 1949 devaluation of sterling Canada was again forced to protect the dollar. The dollar was depreciated in terms of the United States dollar by about 9.1 per cent. During the following year with rumours of revaluation and a large inflow of speculative capital, Canada too flouted the intent of the Fund and, adopting a free exchange rate, abandoned a par for its dollar.

EUROPEAN PAYMENTS UNION

One way to alleviate the dollar shortage was to revive trade within Europe and thereby make European countries less dependent on supplies from North America. Intra-European trade was hampered by the inconvertibility of currencies. Any one country with a balance of payments surplus with another country could not use that country's currency to purchase goods and services from another European country. Large surpluses accumulated in some currencies and large deficits in others could not be offset against each other. This encouraged bilateral payments agreements which were usually accompanied by bilateral trade agreements discriminating in favour of certain imports from bilateral partners and against similar goods obtainable more cheaply elsewhere.

A major step toward currency convertibility and multilateral trade was taken in 1951 with the establishment of the European Payments Union (EPU).[2] The EPU comprised seventeen European countries and, with British membership, overlapped with the sterling area. It functioned as a European clearing house very similar to the Clearing Union proposal of Keynes. At the end of every month, each member country reported its net debit or credit position *vis-à-vis* the other member countries to the Bank for International Settlements in Switzerland which acted as the agent for the EPU. The Bank consolidated each member's debts and claims into an overall net debt to or claim on the Union. Each member was allotted a quota which served as the basis for settlement with the Union. Surplus countries agreed to accumulate credits with the Union up to a certain proportion of their quotas after which they could demand gold or United States dollars from it. These credits could be used to make purchases from any member country and thereby removed much of former trade discrimination. Deficit countries were allowed to accumulate debt with the Union up to a certain proportion of their quotas beyond which complete settlement in gold or United States dollars was required. Under the original arrangements the Union could be called upon to pay out more gold and dollars to creditors than it received from

2 The EPU was preceded by a more modest move to convertibility with the First Agreement on Multilateral Monetary Compensation signed in 1947 and by the Agreements for Intra-European Payments and Compensations signed in 1948 and 1949.

debtors. To meet this possibility the United States provided it with a $350 million fund of working capital. The Union paid interest to creditors and collected interest from debtors which increased with the duration of their debt.

As both intra-continental and inter-continental trade in Europe expanded, member countries were able to settle a larger proportion of their debts with the Union in gold and American dollars. The Union gradually reduced debtor countries' access to credit with it and required debtor countries to pay a larger fraction of their debts to it in gold or United States dollars.

In December 1958 the EPU was terminated when most of its members made their currencies externally convertible. It was replaced by the European Monetary Agreement which, through a European Fund of $600 million, provides short-term loans of up to two years to aid members in balance of payments difficulties. The EPU has been described as a miniature International Monetary Fund, and its success has suggested that regional clearing unions might be an excellent supplement to the operations of the International Monetary Fund.

DOLLAR SHORTAGE TO DOLLAR GLUT

During the 1950's world trade gradually began to flourish again. A high rate of domestic saving and foreign aid allowed a high rate of productive investment in Europe. As Europe rebuilt its productive capacity new technology and more efficient productive methods were introduced. This, together with a moderate increase in prices, made it a keen competitor in world markets. What was considered a chronic dollar shortage soon became a dollar glut. American aid for economic development and American military commitments throughout the world combined with the accessibility of the American capital market created a pervasive flow of dollars into every nook and cranny of world commerce. Not only did the American dollar become the chief trading currency, a position long held by pound sterling, it also became an important foreign reserve asset. Foreigners were induced to hold their accumulation of foreign exchange in dollar assets because New York provided a much greater variety of savings outlets than any other financial centre. Moreover, there was always the inducement for foreign governments and central banks to hold dollars because the American Treasury was willing to convert them into gold at a fixed price.

The American dollar ascended in importance as an international currency, eclipsing the pound sterling. Next to the American dollar, sterling is still the most important trading currency. However, its role as an international reserve asset is confined by and large to the sterling area countries. These countries still have close trading ties with the United Kingdom and keep substantial reserve balances in London. But these balances have tended to decline rather than increase.

Even allowing for the decrease in foreign sterling holdings, sterling and American dollars remain the most important trading currencies and countries hold a larger proportion of these currencies than any others as reserve assets. For this reason we speak of a **key currency system.** However, with the ascendency of American dollars the system has become a **gold-dollar exchange standard.** When sterling reigned there was a **gold-sterling exchange standard.**

PROBLEMS OF THE INTERNATIONAL MONETARY SYSTEM

By the early 1960's general concern focused on the weakness of the gold-dollar exchange system that had evolved. Concern was centred on three major problems: the confidence problem, the liquidity problem, and the adjustment problem. The confidence problem arises from the fact that use of the United States dollar as an international reserve currency is conditional on the American government's willingness and ability to convert the dollar into gold for central bank holders. Any large-scale attempt to convert dollars into gold that would threaten the exhaustion of the American gold stock would precipitate a collapse of confidence in the dollar and a scramble for non-existent gold. This would not only wipe out international liquidity but would plunge the international monetary system into chaos.

The liquidity problem relates to the composition and adequacy of international reserves (see Figure 32-1). The two main components of a country's international reserves are its **owned reserves** and its **unconditional drawing rights** with the International Monetary Fund. Owned reserves consist principally of gold, United States dollars and sterling. However, with the small annual additions to the gold stock and a general turning away from sterling, the major increase in owned reserves depends upon an increase in the foreign liabilities of the United States. Until 1957 foreigners easily added to their dollar reserves as American dollars flowed abroad in abundance. However, as their dollar reserves grew foreigners desired some balanced proportion between gold and dollars. As they converted dollars into gold the United States became concerned with the vulnerability of its gold stock especially as American law required a 25 per cent gold cover for Federal Reserve Credit (notes and deposits).[3] It responded with measures to correct its overall balance of payments deficits. While these measures were designed to bolster confidence in the dollar and halt any further

[3] In January 1968 the President of the United States requested Congress to drop this requirement, a request which Congress granted.

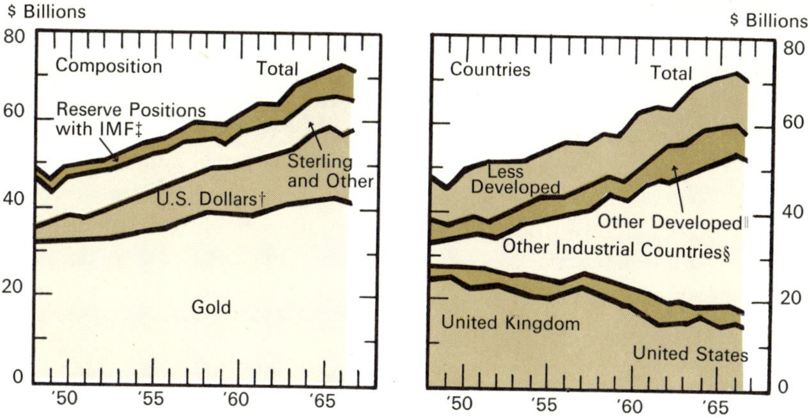

Figure 32-1 Monetary Reserves of Governments and Central Banks*
(End of year, except date for 1967, which are for June)

*Excluding the USSR, other eastern European countries, mainland China, etc. †Including special nonmarketable Treasury bonds sold to foreign governments and central banks and time certificates of deposit with maturity of more than one year and various minor nonmarketable U.S. liabilities held by foreign official agencies. ‡Amounts that can be drawn "essentially automatically" from the IMF, corresponding to members' gold subscriptions *plus* amounts of their currencies sold by the Fund to other members (net) *plus* outstanding lendings to the Fund. §Austria, Belgium, Canada, Denmark, France, Germany (Fed. Rep.), Italy, Japan, the Netherlands, Norway, Sweden, Switzerland. ‖Other European countries, Australia, New Zealand and South Africa.

attempts to convert large dollar holdings into gold they also tended to reduce the supply of dollars accumulated as owned reserves. International liquidity was then curtailed.

The amount of international liquidity in the form of unconditional drawing rights with the International Monetary Fund depends upon the resources of the Fund. These were augmented with increases in quotas in 1961 and 1965 and with the General Agreement to Borrow in 1962. However, even after allowing for the increase in Fund drawing rights, any attempt by the United States to correct its overall balance of payments deficits poses the possibility that international reserves cannot expand sufficiently to support the steady expansion of international trade and payments. This implies that the present system has an inherently deflationary bias on the world economy.

The third problem of the present international system, the adjustment problem, is closely associated with the confidence and liquidity problems. Under a system of fixed exchange rates international reserves are held to enable a country to maintain the declared value of its currency. Without a sufficient amount of international reserves to meet balance of payments disequilibrium three main adjustment processes can be used — trade and exchange restrictions, devaluation, and domestic price and income changes. Under the Bretton Woods agreements trade and exchange restrictions are supposed to be ruled out and devaluation confined to situations of "fundamental disequilibrium".

A country may have a temporary balance of payments disequilibrium due to a sudden outflow of capital. Outflows may result from a sudden loss of confidence in a country's currency due to political instability, or from a change in interest rate differentials between countries. If the country's reserves appear to be inadequate, speculators will move in and intensify the capital outflow. The country may be forced to resort to domestic deflationary policies. Governments, however, are reluctant to take such action because they are committed to economic objectives of price stability, a high level of employment and economic growth. For this reason increased international reserves have been advocated. With sufficient reserves to cushion flights of capital the domestic economy can be reasonably immune to sudden changes in the world economy. Moreover, if a nation's costs and prices are out of line a sufficient amount of reserves will allow it reasonable time to adjust without jeopardizing its long-run economic objectives. On the other hand, it has been argued that with too much international liquidity countries may be reluctant to take adequate domestic measures to correct balance of payments deficits, increasing their difficulties when the day of reckoning finally dawns.

STRENGTHENING THE SYSTEM

As the fragility of the evolving international monetary system has become apparent, steps have been take to strengthen it. Many of these have been concerned with the vulnerability of the system to sudden capital flows, and to the outflow of gold from the United States. Some of the more important modifications to the system are outlined below.

Increasing IMF Resources

We mentioned earlier that the Fund's resources have been increased with two general increases in member quotas and with special increases in the quotas of some members. The total resources of the Fund have also increased with the addition of new members and the General Agreement to Borrow. The Fund, on the other hand, has become more willing to make its resources available to members. A notable addition to the Fund facilities to cope with flights of "hot capital" has been its use of stand-by arrangements. A $500 million stand-by credit extended to the United States in July 1963 emphasized the availability of the Fund's resources for defence of the dollar. A drawing of $1,000 million from the Fund by the United Kingdom in 1964 was an indication that the Fund had come of age. Another extremely significant Fund transaction has been the sale of gold by it in return for United States government securities carrying a gold-value guarantee. This has enabled the United States to replenish its gold stock.

Reciprocal Currency Arrangements

Central bankers have come to recognize the need for joint action by monetary authorities in countries with balance of payments surpluses as well as those with deficits. In 1961 Germany revalued the mark upward by 5 per cent and the Netherlands revalued the guilder by a similar amount. This revaluation was an act of government cooperation insofar as two surplus countries recognized their role in achieving overall balance of payments equilibrium in the world economy. The smallness of these revaluations suggested a possible repetition. When a heavy movement of capital took place from London to Frankfurt and Amsterdam, the continental central banks brought and held sterling under an arrangement worked out in Basle, Switzerland at the Bank for International Settlements. With central banks buying sterling as fast as speculators sold it, speculation of further revaluation soon subsided.

The Basle agreements set the pattern for central bank cooperation in the form of swap or reciprocal currency agreements. In 1962, for example, when a large outflow of capital from Canada occurred the Bank of Canada and the Federal Reserve in the United States entered into a swap agreement. To obtain additional reserves for the Canadian government the Bank of Canada bought spot United States dollars from the Federal Reserve. At the same time it sold United States dollars forward to the Federal Reserve. The consequent spot purchase of Canadian dollars in the market showed Canada's determination not to devalue the dollar any further. Speculation against the Canadian dollar declined and as American dollars flowed back, the forward commitment to the Federal Reserve was met.

Gold Pool

The three most important markets in which gold is freely sold are Londin, Zurich and Paris. A few smaller free gold markets operate throughout the world. In Toronto, for example, a market exists for the sale and purchase of gold. However, most of the gold that is traded in free markets flows through the London gold market, reopened in 1954. It is here that speculation against the dollar is reflected by a rise in the price of gold.

In October 1961 speculation on the possible devaluation of the American dollar caused the price of gold in the London money market to shoot up briefly to over $40 an ounce. To catch gold speculators at their game the Federal Reserve System in the United States began feeding gold to the London market through the intermediation of the Bank of England. Later European central banks joined the Bank of England in an arrangement which became known as the gold pool to stabilize the price of gold.

Until March 1968 the central banks participating in the pool provided gold for sale when necessary to prevent speculators from driving the price abnormally high. They also coordinated their own gold purchases to stabilize price fluctuations of gold. Until early 1968 the transactions by the pool members in the London gold market were fairly successful in stabilizing the price of gold and in reducing speculation against the future gold price of the United States dollar. The operations of the pool prevented an extreme rise in the price of gold during the Cuban crisis in October 1962 and during the sterling crisis at the end of 1964 which followed the French government's announced intention to convert into gold part of its reserves held in dollars. However, with further speculative attacks on the pound in 1967 resulting from the United Kingdom's difficulties in resolving its chronic balance of payments problems, the gold pool found it increasingly difficult to stabilize the price of gold. Although the pool succeeded in maintaining the established price of gold following the devaluation of the pound in November 1967, gold speculation continued and reached unprecedented postwar proportions early in March 1968. With heavy foreign expenditures by the United States to carry on the war in Vietnam and with the reluctance of Congress to adopt the restrictive fiscal measures recommended by the President, fear spread that the United States would soon be unable to continue to convert dollars into gold for foreign governments at $35 an ounce. On March 15 when the stampede for gold reached crisis proportions, the United Kingdom in response to a request from the United States closed the London gold market. Following a meeting in Washington of the governors of the central banks participating in the gold pool and the Managing Director of the International Monetary Fund, a new policy on gold was announced. In order to conserve the stock of monetary gold, the governors agreed to stop supplying gold from monetary reserves to the London gold market or any other gold market. They also agreed to continue to sell gold at $35 an ounce to monetary authorities as long as this gold would not be used to replace gold stocks sold in private markets.

The immediate effect of the new two-price gold system was that the price on the Paris market rose from the official price of $35 an ounce to about $45. The price quickly fell back when speculators realized that the gold pool's decision also implied that the support floor for gold in the free markets had been removed. The price of gold fell again to about $38 an ounce when the London gold market reopened in April.

The two-price gold system was considered an interim measure which, with the announcement of appropriate fiscal measures by the leading countries of the world, would restore confidence in the international monetary system and allow time for major reforms to the system to be instituted.

Special United States Dollar Bonds

In 1962, to protect itself from a sudden sale of dollars for gold the American government started selling special medium-term bonds to foreign central banks. They are known as "Roosa bonds" after the Under Secretary of the Treasury Robert Roosa who was instrumental in introducing them. Some of these bonds are denominated in United States dollars and thus fund American dollar holdings of the purchasers. In other words, foreign central banks give up their immediate claim on gold when they give up dollars for bonds. Other bonds are denominated in foreign currency and as such their sale supplies the United States with foreign currencies to meet its international debts. To induce foreign central banks to purchase Roosa bonds attractive interest rates are offered. Although these bonds are generally non-convertible, some issues have carried the privilege of conversion into ninety-day certificates if the holder needed dollars or gold due to a heavy drain on his reserves.

Central Bank Dealings in Forward Exchange

One way to halt an outflow of capital resulting from speculation or interest arbitrage is for central banks to operate in the forward exchange market. This method of halting capital movements was recommended by Keynes in the 1920's and has been used by the Federal Reserve in the United States since 1962. When speculators are selling dollars for foreign exchange, the Federal Reserve sells forward foreign currencies (buys forward United States dollars). With a fall in the forward price of foreign currencies (a rise in the forward price of the dollar) speculators may be convinced that they will be unable to sell foreign currencies spot at a profit in the future and so they will stop using their dollar holdings to buy it spot now. If a capital outflow is the result of interest arbitrage, Federal Reserve purchases of American dollars forward increasing the forward rate will tend to offset any gains from interest rate differentials and to stop capital outflows on this account.

Further Control of Dollar Speculation

To further eliminate doubts as to the potential strength of the American dollar and thereby to stop the flow of gold out of the United States various steps have been taken by the American government to correct its large overall balance of payments deficits. It has requested other countries to share more in providing economic aid to underdeveloped countries and to assume a larger proportion of foreign military expenditures. In an attempt to stop the outflow of capital it has introduced measures to adjust American interest rates with those in other countries. In 1961 the Federal Reserve introduced what has been called "Operation Twist". It directed its open market operations toward keeping up short-term interest rates to deter capital outflows while holding down long-term interest rates to aid domestic economic growth. In 1962 Congress suspended the interest rate ceilings on time deposits held by foreign and international monetary authorities. To discourage the outflow of dollars resulting from foreign borrowing in the United States an interest equalization tax was imposed in 1965 on the foreign sale of securities in the United States. Specified "less developed" countries were excluded from this tax as was Canada. However, the exclusion of Canada was made conditional on it not allowing its official reserve holdings to amount to more than approximately $2,700 million. This proved to be an expensive price for Canada to pay because the use of monetary policy to control subsequent inflationary tendencies was restricted for fear that higher interest rates would attract an inflow of foreign capital and expand Canadian reserves beyond the agreed level. The interest equalization tax, still in effect at the end of 1967, added about one percentage point to the effective annual interest rate paid by foreign borrowers in the United States. The introduction of the tax was accompanied by guidelines setting out a voluntary program for banks and financial institutions to limit their credit and loans to foreigners, and to repatriate some of their liquid holdings abroad. Guidelines were also issued to industrial corporations suggesting how they could assist in reversing the United States balance of payments deficits.

PROPOSALS FOR REFORMING THE IMF

THE TRIFFIN PLAN

Robert Triffin of Yale University has proposed a plan that would in effect convert the International Monetary Fund into an international central bank — a central banks' bank.[4]

His plan calls for countries to gradually exchange all of their gold and foreign exchange holdings for deposits with the Fund. Fund deposits would pay interest, have a guaranteed gold value, and be readily convertible into national currencies. Moreover, they would be accepted by all countries in payment of their international obligations. The Fund would still continue to lend to countries in need of foreign exchange, but since all such loans would result in additional Fund deposits for the borrowing country, the Fund would create deposits in a manner similar to the lending activity of a commercial bank. Insofar as Triffin would allow the

[4] Triffin, Robert, *Gold and the Dollar Crisis*, Yale University Press, New Haven, Conn., 1960.

Fund to create deposits by open market operations in the financial centres of member countries, the new role of the Fund has been compared more closely to that of a central bank rather than a commercial bank. A primary function of the proposed credit-creating institution is to provide capital to countries that are capital poor. The Fund would expand its loans and investments by purchasing the securities of the International Bank for Reconstruction and Development or the securities of the underdeveloped countries. To prevent the creation of deposits by the Fund from assuming inflationary proportions, Triffin would limit their growth to perhaps 3 to 5 per cent per year. The major objection to the idea of an international institution with reserve-creating powers is the absence as yet of the degree of international political and economic integration it implies.

MULTIPLE KEY CURRENCY SYSTEM

It has been proposed that countries should hold international reserves not only in gold and United States dollars or sterling but also in a number of other currencies, say, the German mark, French franc and Swiss franc. Under this scheme growth in international reserves would depend not only on the payments deficits of the United States but on the aggregate deficits of all key-currency countries with the rest of the world. The plan requires the accumulation of other countries' currencies when they are in deficit — that is, when their currencies are weak. However, it is doubtful if other countries would add a weak currency to their reserve assets. To overcome this difficulty it has been suggested that the International Monetary Fund serve as an intermediary for the holding of currencies.

The proposal has also been made that the ten or so major currency countries deposit an agreed amount of their currencies with the Fund, receiving its deposit asset in the form of "reserve units". A unit would be equivalent to a dollar, but would actually consist of ten or so currencies in proportion to the deposits of each. Hence it has been referred to as a collective reserve unit, a composite reserve unit, or simply a CRU. The proportion that each currency contributes to the value of the unit depends upon the official dollar exchange rate of the currency. If, for example, the German mark is worth 25 cents, a German deposit of 4 billion marks with the Fund would be equivalent to $1 billion. If total deposits were $10 billion, the mark portion of each reserve unit would be equivalent to 10 cents.

The value of the Fund's currency holdings would be guaranteed against devaluation by the country issuing the currency. The amount of its own currency a country would deposit with the Fund would be agreed upon in advance. It is assumed that international reserves in the form of CRU's would increase because countries would be more willing to hold a claim on the Fund than to hold the currency of any one country.

RETURN TO GOLD

Various proposals have been put forward that would tie the international monetary system closer to gold. One, associated most closely with Roy Harrod of Oxford University, calls for an increase in the price of gold.[5] It is argued that this would enlarge the dollar value of the present stock, stimulate gold production and bring gold out of hoards, thereby providing sufficient gold for international monetary reserve assets. However, increasing the dollar price of gold means devaluating the dollar. This probably would cause a loss of confidence in the dollar making it unacceptable to countries as a reserve asset. Unless the lost dollars were replaced by gold from increased production and hoards, international liquidity would be drastically reduced. There is little evidence to suggest that the increase in gold available for reserve purposes would be sufficient to meet future liquidity requirements.

COMBINING AID WITH REFORM

Plans have been put forward which would kill two birds with one stone — expand international liquidity, and provide aid to the less developed countries. The more famous of these is the **Stamp Plan.** Sir Maxwell Stamp suggested that the International Monetary Fund issue certificates to be distributed to the less developed countries. These certificates would be accepted by the industrial countries in payment for exports and would be held by them as reserves. The certificates need not be made redeemable in gold if all Fund members would accept them in payment.

A more sweeping proposal to combine aid with an increase in international liquidity is incorporated in plans for a commodity reserve standard. This plan would give assistance to the less developed countries by stabilizing the prices of primary products, their major exports. Hart, Kaldor and Tinbergen, for example, would allow the Fund or some new organization to draw up a list of specified goods in specified amounts which would form a commodity reserve unit.[6] When the market price of the aggregate unit fell below its normal price, the Fund would purchase all commodities (actually warehouse receipts) in the unit in the specified proportions. Insofar as purchases would be made at a "declared value" the average world price of the bundle of commodities in the unit would

---

[5] Harrod, Roy, *Reforming the World's Money*, New York, St. Martin's Press, 1965, Ch. 3. See also Jacques Rueff and Fred Horsch, *The Role and Rule of Gold: An Argument*, Essays in International Finance, No. 47, Princeton University, June 1965.

[6] Hart, Albert G., Nicholas Kaldor, Jan Tinbergen, *The Case for an International Commodity Reserve Currency*, a memorandum submitted to the United Nations Conference on Trade and Development, Geneva, March 28 to June 15, 1964.

be stabilized. The Fund would make payment by creating deposits (reserves). Hence aid in the form of price stabilization would be combined with a means of increasing international liquidity.

FLEXIBLE EXCHANGE RATES

A flexible international exchange rate system would remove the international liquidity and adjustment problems. If this is the case why do we remain with a fixed rate system? The overriding reason is probably the belief that such a system invites destabilizing speculation. Canada's experience with a flexible exchange rate from 1950 to 1962 indicates that this may be a misconception. Fluctuations in the external value of the Canadian dollar during this period were smaller than the devaluations required in most of the major currencies in the postwar world. The Canadian experiment has shown that in the long run flexible rates are preferable to fixed rates. To convince the international community of this fact, George Halm has suggested a widening of the present range in which the International Monetary Fund allows national currencies to fluctuate.[7] After the first widening of possible exchange flexibility, further widening could follow in stages until ultimately complete exchange rate flexibility is achieved.

A NEW ROLE FOR THE IMF

In 1967 at the annual meetings of the International Monetary Fund held in Rio de Janeiro, the Board of Governors agreed on a proposal to establish a new facility "to meet the need, as and when it arises, for a supplement to existing reserve assets".[8] The proposal, subject to ratification by Fund members' respective governments, provides a means for creating Special Drawing Rights (SDR's) in the Fund which participating countries would accept as reserves and use in international settlements.

The plan does not specify the criteria according to which SDR's should be provided, but it is understood that the general criterion must be a widely recognized need to supplement existing international reserve assets. It has been assumed that there will be a consultative procedure for any decision on reserve creation. According to the plan, the managing director of the Fund, having satisfied himself that there is a need to sup-

---

[7] Halm, George, *The "Band" Proposal: The Limits of Permissible Exchange Rate Variations*, Princeton University, International Finance Section, Department of Economics, 1965.

[8] International Monetary Fund, *Summary Proceedings, Annual Meetings 1967*, Washington, D.C., September 1967, pp. 271-279; David W. Slater, "Special Drawing Rights — A New International Monetary Era", *The Canadian Banker*, Vol. 74, Winter 1967, pp. 6-18.

plement international monetary reserves, will undertake consultations to determine whether there is sufficient support among the participants for the creation of SDR's in the amount he proposes. After receiving the approval of the Fund's executive directors, the managing director will make an official proposal to the Board of Governors. To become effective, any such proposal must be approved by an 85 per cent majority of the voting power of the participants.

The amount of SDR's to be created is determined for a basic period initially set at five years; subsequent periods may be longer or shorter. The 1967 proposal does not specify the amount of SDR's to be created during any basic period or the rate at which they are to be allocated during a period. These decisions are made on the basis of a collective judgment of *global* reserve needs and therefore depend upon the growth of other international reserve assets. Any allocation of SDR's is made to all participating members in proportion to their Fund quotas. Allocations of SDR's take the form of book entries in a special drawing account of the International Monetary Fund. At any time during a basic period it is possible to increase or decrease the rate at which SDR's are created for the remainder of the period or to adopt a new basic period with a different rate of creation. A decision to reduce the rate of issue for the remainder of a current basic period can be taken by a simple majority of the voting power of the participating countries. However, a decision to increase the rate of issue requires an 85 per cent majority vote as does a decision to change or introduce a new basic period. The traditional fear of the central banker concerning overissue is reflected in this mechanism which makes it easier to slow down than to speed up the rate of growth of SDR's.

A participating country is expected to use SDR's allocated to it "only for balance of payments needs or in light of developments in its total reserves and not for the sole purpose of changing the composition of its reserves". The user of SDR's acquires currencies, not out of resources held by the Fund, but directly from other participating countries or indirectly through the intermediation of the Fund.[9] Members are expected to purchase convertible currencies from countries with sufficiently strong balance of payments and reserve positions. A country such as the United States whose currency is held as an international reserve asset may also use SDR's to purchase balances of its own currency held by another country if the latter agrees. In practice, when a country uses SDR's to purchase convertible currencies its SDR holdings in the **special drawing account** with the Fund are reduced and those of other countries from

---

[9] SDR's are transferred by debiting the SDR account of the user and crediting the SDR account of the receiver, with the receiver paying convertible currency to the user.

whom the currencies are purchased increase in the aggregate by an equivalent amount.

SDR's are not to be used for the sole purpose of changing the composition of a country's international reserves. In other words, they are not to be used by a country to build up its foreign currency balances or gold holdings. Although the use of SDR's is not subject to prior challenge, the Fund may make representations to any participant who transgresses the spirit of the arrangement, and may transfer SDR's to that country to restore its SDR holdings.

The use of SDR's does not entail repayment according to a fixed schedule as is the case with the Fund's ordinary resources. However, countries that use SDR's may incur an obligation to restore (or reconstitute) their position to some extent, depending upon the amount and duration of their use. The 1967 proposals contain two principles for reconstitution of drawings made during the first basic period. Participants must pay due regard to the desirability of pursuing over time a balanced relationship between their holdings of SDR's and other reserves. Furthermore, a participating country's average net use of SDR's over the first basic period (taking into account both use below and holdings above its net cumulative allocation) must not exceed 70 per cent of its average cumulative allocation. In other words, a country's average holdings of SDR's over the first period are to be 30 per cent of its average allocation. If, for example, a country has been obliged to utilize all its allocation of SDR's in the early part of the basic period it can reconstitute its average holdings by minimizing the use of SDR's during the remaining part of the period. The reconstitution provisions imply that countries are not to regard their entire allocations of SDR's over time as representing unconditional liquidity. Moreover, the provisions are designed to encourage participating countries not to finance large and persistent payments deficits by the exclusive reliance on SDR's. The reconstitution provisions are less onerous than the repayment (repurchase) provisions applicable for drawings on the Fund's general account. It will be remembered that such drawings must be completely liquidated within three to five years either directly through repayment by debtor countries or indirectly by other members' drawings on the Fund of the debtor's currency.

Near-universal participation will be encouraged, and each participant is committed to accept the initial allocation of SDR's. However, a country may decline any further allotment by opting out although inducements are provided to discourage this. SDR's carry a gold-value guarantee (equal to 0.888671 grams of fine gold), earn a moderate rate of interest, and have an extraordinarily high and easy convertibility into general claims on the Fund. (They are not redeemable in gold.) Moreover, every participating country is obliged to provide its currency in exchange for

SDR's freely until its holdings of SDR's are equal to three times the amount of its cumulative allocations. That is to say, if a country's initial allocation were $100 million and it used no part of this allocation, its acceptance obligation would be $200 million. If a country had transferred all of its initial allocation to other countries, its initial acceptance obligation would be $300 million. A country may, if it so desires, hold SDR's in excess of its acceptance obligation.[10]

The SDR scheme is intended to provide systematic and regular additions to international reserves. Unlike the International Monetary Fund mechanism adopted at Bretton Woods, this scheme is designed to provide permanent additions to international reserves. SDR's are deliberately managed by the nations of the world acting together. Approval of the new scheme and the participation by the major countries of the world will create an unprecedented degree of international cooperation. Moreover, for the first time the international community will control reserves, instead of reserves controlling the community.

SELECTED READINGS

Aufricht, Hans, *The International Monetary Fund: Legal Aspects, Structure, Functions, 1945-63,* New York, Frederick A. Praeger, 1964.

Fellner, William, *et. al., Maintaining and Restoring Balance in International Payments,* Princeton, N.J., Princeton University Press, 1966.

Grubel, Herbert G. (ed.), *World Monetary Reform, Plans and Issues,* Stanford, Calif., Stanford University Press, 1963.

Hansen, Alvin H., *The Dollar and the International Monetary System,* New York, McGraw-Hill, 1965.

Harris, Seymour (ed.), *The Dollar in Crisis,* New York, Harcourt, Brace & World, 1961.

Harrod, Roy, *The Dollar,* New York, Harcourt, Brace, 1954.

Harrod, Roy, *Reforming the World's Money,* New York, St. Martin's Press, 1965.

International Bank for Reconstruction and Development, *Annual Reports,* Washington, D.C.

International Finance Corporation, *Annual Reports,* Washington, D.C.

International Monetary Fund, *Annual Reports* and *Summary Proceedings Annual Meetings,* Washington, D.C.

10 A moderate rate of interest is paid on a country's holdings of SDR's in excess of its cumulative allocations.

Lary, Hal B., *Problems of the United States as World Trader and Banker,* New York, National Bureau of Economic Research, 1963.

MacDougall, Donald, *The World Dollar Problem,* New York, St. Martin's Press, 1958.

Machlup, Fritz, *Plans for Reform of the International Monetary System,* rev. ed., Princeton University, International Finance Section, 1964, reprinted with few additions in Machlup, Fritz, *International Payments, Debts and Gold: Collected Essays,* New York, Charles Scribner's Sons, 1964, Part 4.

Machlup, Fritz, and Burton G. Malkiel (eds.), *International Monetary Arrangements: The Problem of Choice,* Princeton, N.J., Princeton University Press, 1964.

Mikesell, Raymond F., *Public International Lending for Development,* New York, Random House, 1966.

Roosa, Robert V., *Monetary Reform for the World Economy,* New York, Harper & Row, 1965.

Scammell, W.M., *International Monetary Policy,* 2nd ed., New York, St. Martin's Press, 1961.

Slater, David W., "Special Drawing Rights — A New International Monetary Era", *The Canadian Banker,* Vol. 74, Winter 1967, pp. 6-18.

Tew, Brian, *International Monetary Co-operation 1945-65,* 8th ed., London, Hutchinson University Library, 1965.

The Bank of Nova Scotia, "Monthly Review", Toronto, October 1967.

Triffin, Robert, *Europe and the Money Muddle,* New Haven, Conn., Yale University Press, 1957.

Triffin, Robert, *Gold and the Dollar Crisis,* rev. ed., New Haven, Conn., Yale University Press, 1964.

Triffin, Robert, *The World Money Maze,* New Haven, Conn., Yale University Press, 1966.

33

MONETARY POLICY IN CANADA: A REVIEW

EARLY PREFERENCE FOR CHEAP MONEY

The Bank of Canada was born in the midst of the economic depression of the 1930's. Demands for a coordinated easy money policy had been made for a long time in Western Canada and were carried to the House of Commons in Ottawa by J.S. Woodsworth, the leader of the new political party, the Co-operative Commonwealth Federation. The government, cognizant of the chartered banks' opposition to a central bank and itself not convinced of the necessity or possible role of such a bank, appointed the Royal Commission on Banking and Currency (the Macmillan Commission) to provide the answers. The Commission recommended the establishment of a central bank, but cautioned that it "could not cure all the economic ills of Canada" and it "would not be a source of unlimited credit for all borrowers on all occasions".

The establishment of a central bank did not satisfy the demands of another new political group in western Canada, the Social Credit party, which was swept into power in Alberta in 1935. Social Creditors following the dogma of Major C. H. Douglas saw economic stagnation as a way of life as long as orthodox institutions were allowed to maintain the chronic shortage of purchasing power. The Social Credit government of Alberta issued its own money, "stamp script". It was intended to increase the money supply in two ways. First, it was an addition to the existing stock, and second, the stamps which had to be attached to it to make it current increased the velocity of circulating money. This experiment with easy money came to an end in 1937 when the federal government (later confirmed by the Supreme Court of Canada) disallowed provincial legislation on matters which came under federal jurisdiction.

In the few years between its establishment and the Second World War, the Bank of Canada followed a policy of monetary expansion. Its open market operations were relatively small since it was able to provide the banking system with necessary reserves through its purchases of gold and foreign exchange. Moreover, it received substantial assistance in expanding the reserves of the chartered banks from the government's policy of building up its deposits with the chartered banks.

WARTIME MONETARY POLICY

During the first few years of the war monetary expansion was accelerated in a deliberate attempt to induce the economy to move as quickly as possible toward full capacity output. The government increased the money supply by borrowing directly from the banking system. By mid-1941 the economy had reached full capacity output and the government turned from the banking system to the general public as its chief supplier of funds. It tapped the general public through the sale of securities and by introducing new taxes and increasing existing taxes. To further control inflationary tendencies, price ceilings were imposed as were controls and rationing of supplies. Manpower controls were implemented and directives issued.

The prime role of the Bank of Canada throughout the war was to facilitate the sale of government securities. This required it to expand the reserves of the banks to allow them to make the necessary loans to the government and to the public. The public depended upon temporary accommodation from the banks for its bond purchases. To ensure that the public would always remain receptive to the sale of government securities, the Bank of Canada also assumed the responsibility for maintaining orderly conditions in the securities market. This implied maintaining bond prices at an average level that would instill public confidence and at the same time allow the government to borrow at attractive rates. That the Bank was successful in its task is reflected in the amount of government securities taken up by the general public. Of all new funds required by the government during the war, approximately 85 per cent was supplied by the non-bank public and the remainder by the banking system.

During the early part of the war the Bank of Canada provided the government with funds through the direct purchase of government securities. Throughout the war, however, it relied on its open market operations to provide the banks with reserves to allow them to purchase government securities and to make loans to the government and the public. Government loans from the banks took the form of non-marketable deposit certificates which the government sold to them in an attempt to control their liquidity position. The Bank of Canada also provided temporary finance to the government from time to time by accumulating foreign exchange. However, in most cases the potential effects of the Bank's foreign exchange purchases on the reserves of the chartered banks were offset by the switching of government deposits from the chartered banks to the Bank of Canada and by the Bank's open market operations.

POSTWAR EASY MONEY POLICY

The Bank of Canada announced its intention to continue an easy money policy after the war early in 1944 when it reduced the Bank rate and supplied the banks with more reserves than they had ever had before. The Bank's policy was part of the overall government policy presented in the White paper on Employment and Income in April 1945. In the White Paper the government committed itself to "the maintenance of a high and stable level of employment and income" and, following the new Keynesian dogma, fiscal policy was to be the main technique for its accomplishment. To assure that there would be enough purchasing power available to maintain a level of full employment a comprehensive social welfare program was initiated which included family allowances, liberal veterans' benefits and housing legislation.

The expansionary programs introduced by the government, even before the end of the war, were based on two historical memories — the Great Depression and the reconversion depression following the First World War. That depression did not follow as anticipated was in large part the result of government policies. The transition from a wartime to peacetime economy took place much more quickly and smoothly than expected. A significant proportion of the demand for war materials was replaced by the demand for goods and services required for European aid and reconstruction. Purchasing power was provided to the European nations by the liberal credits and aid supplied by the Canadian and American governments.

Domestic demand for goods and services also increased. An unprecedented proportion of the war had been financed through the sale of government securities. After the war the government viewed maintaining the price of bonds as a moral obligation so that they could be sold without loss by their holders. To keep faith with millions of investors, government accounts and the Bank of Canada were active purchasers of bonds in the market. Having deprived itself of many goods and services during the war, the public used its increased liquidity to satisfy its demands. With domestic demands added to foreign demands for Canadian production, prices moved up. Most of the government's policies to resist inflationary tendencies were accidental rather than planned. The only exception was the revaluation of the Canadian dollar in 1946 to insulate the Canadian economy from the increase in prices in the United States following the early abandonment of price controls there. However, any anti-inflationary effects the government's unplanned budgetary surpluses may have had were more than offset by its debt management program. Employing budgetary surpluses to redeem government debt not only returned cash to the public but maintained its liquidity by supporting bond prices.

Somewhat belatedly the Bank of Canada attempted to control chartered bank expansion with moral suasion. In 1947 it suggested to the banks that they scrutinize closely the inventories and receivables of their customers before granting loans. Early in the following year it told the banks that financing capital development with bank credit was undesirable.

Beginning in 1948 yields on Canadian bonds were allowed to rise sharply. This resulted from the government's inability to support bond prices at their existing levels rather than from any intention to allow higher interest rates to dampen inflationary tendencies. During the latter part of 1947 after the large drawing down of foreign loans and the sharp decline in foreign exchange reserves, the government introduced temporary direct import controls, special taxes and exchange restrictions on foreign travel expenditure. The sale of foreign exchange had provided the government with additional funds to support the bond market. However, now faced with the task of building back these reserves and the possibility of smaller budgetary surpluses, the government's ability to support bond prices at their high levels appeared doubtful. The Bank of Canada's ability to provide further support was also restricted by its statutory provision prohibiting it from holding securities of more than two years to maturity in excess of 50 per cent of its note and deposit liability. By the end of 1947 this limit had been reached. In early 1948 the Bank and the government were obliged to abandon their policies of rigidly pegging bond prices. The resulting higher interest rates, however, were no longer required to dampen the inflationary tendencies which had exhausted themselves by late 1948. From this time until late 1949 Canada experienced its first pause in the postwar upward spiral of prices.

RETURN TO MONETARY ORTHODOXY

After a brief pause inflationary tendencies returned at the oubreak of the Korean War to plague the Canadian authorities. Canadians remembering previous wartime shortages hurried to fill their larders. Added to this demand for goods and services was that by the government for defence. An attempt to deal with these demand pressures and the consequent upward movement in prices had to be deferred until a foreign exchange crisis was settled.

In 1949 following the realignment and devaluation of sterling and most European currencies, the Canadian dollar was devalued in terms of the United States dollar by about 9.1 per cent. At the time, the Minister of Finance pointed out that he was not at all sure that the new rate was the proper one for the Canadian dollar and that a subsequent change might have to be made. As a result of an investment boom in Canada and rumours of possible revaluation of the Canadian dollar, speculators bought Canadian dollars in flood proportions during 1950. The consequent large increase in foreign exchange was purchased by the Bank of Canada and by the government's foreign exchange fund account with cash available from the federal Treasury and from the special sale of deposit certificates to the chartered banks. Because the Bank offset only part of its foreign exchange purchases by open market operations, the cash reserves of the banks were allowed to expand. Finally, to prevent any further inflationary consequences of its attempts to hold the external value of the dollar, the government freed the Canadian dollar to seek its own level.

With the exchange rate problem settled, the authorities set out to make a deliberate attempt to control inflation. In October, under the Consumer Credit Act the government issued an order-in-council restricting consumer credit purchases. The Bank of Canada announced a policy of restriction with an increase in the Bank rate from 1½ per cent to 2 per cent. This was supported by a reduction in the net cash reserves provided to the chartered banks. Thus, by late 1950 the Bank of Canada had followed the lead of Western Europe and the United States and had returned to monetary orthodoxy, controlling inflation with monetary measures along a broad front.

In 1951 the Bank of Canada supplemented its quantitative controls which had reduced the cash reserves of the banks with qualitative controls which restricted their lending. In February, the banks agreed to a "credit ceiling" by refraining from buying corporate securities of more than one year to maturity and from extending term loans. In addition the banks agreed to impose margin requirements of at least 50 per cent on loans on corporation stock, to increase margin requirements on instalment finance paper, and to tighten lending practices on commercial and personal loans. The life insurance companies also announced an anti-inflationary investment policy which may have been prompted by central bank moral suasion.[1] In both 1950 and 1951 monetary policy was assisted in fighting inflation by the government's fiscal policy which included an increase in taxes and deferred depreciation allowances.

The return to monetary orthodoxy after 1950 proved fairly successful. Until almost the end of 1953 the economy operated at full employment with relatively little inflation.

[1] The Bank of Canada also requested the stock exchanges to impose more severe margin requirements.

ECONOMIC CONTRACTION

By late 1953 the Korean war boom came to an end and from then to mid-1954 the country suffered its first real postwar recession. Reduced defence expenditures were accompanied by a series of set-backs, including a slackening demand for consumer durables, decreased expenditures on business inventories, machinery and equipment, increased competition in export markets and lower farm income resulting from poor crops and marketing and delivery difficulties. The Bank of Canada was slow to recognize the change in economic conditions and when it finally initiated monetary expansion after 1954, recovery was already well underway. The same was true of the government's fiscal policy; in both its 1952 and 1953 fiscal years it had a budgetary surplus while in the following two years, with economic recovery well under way, it had budget deficits.

ECONOMIC RECOVERY AND EXPANSION

Economic recovery began in late 1954 with increased expenditures on residential construction following lower interest rates and the availability of mortgage money. The 1954 revisions to the Bank Act allowed the banks to make National Housing Act mortgage loans and after only a brief period of reluctance the banks became major suppliers of mortgage funds. The revisions to the Bank Act also changed the statutory calculation of the banks' required reserves which were increased from 5 per cent to 8 per cent. Paradoxically, however, this did not lead to contraction by the banks. Although the banks had been legally required to maintain cash reserves equal to 5 per cent of their deposits, they actually held 10 per cent. Now with the increase in the legal ratio they decided to work toward the new 8 per cent ratio. This was prompted by the development of the money market initiated by the Bank of Canada and by the revisions to the Bank Act which allowed the banks to calculate their minimum required cash reserves on an average monthly basis rather than on an average daily basis.

During 1955 the economy was rapidly approaching full employment and the dangers of inflation were again present. Although the Bank of Canada contracted the reserve base of the banks through its open market operations, the banks were able to expand their loans by running down their Treasury bills and day-to-day loans. Moreover, for the first time, both the chartered banks and the approved money market dealers took substantial advances from the Bank of Canada. The Bank responded by increasing the Bank rate in August and again in October and November. Late in the year it also used moral suasion on the banks to prevent them from making further commitments for "term" lending. The banks also responded to moral suasion by agreeing to maintain a minimum liquid asset ratio of 15 per cent by the end of May 1956. The intent of this new ratio was to prevent them from further switching from money market assets to loans and to render them more sensitive to official measures of monetary restraint.

During 1956 the Bank continued its restrictive monetary policy. The Bank rate was again raised on three separate occasions. It now appeared that the Bank rate was becoming a cost, not merely a psychological, factor in the market as the banks adjusted their own rates in line with it after making public reference to the changes made by the Bank of Canada. Since the Bank rate became an important factor in influencing market rates it is difficult to explain why the Bank abandoned the fixed Bank rate for a floating rate in November 1956. One explanation is that it wished to avoid being blamed by the public for rising interest rates. Moral suasion was again used in 1956 but this time not only on the banks but also on non-bank institutions. However, only the banks responded to the Bank of Canada's request for voluntary credit restraint by agreeing to restrict credit provided to instalment finance companies.

During 1955 and 1956 monetary policy proved generally successful. Interest rates were allowed to increase and the money supply was held relatively stable. On the other hand, both wholesale and consumer prices showed remarkably small increases. During 1956 monetary policy was assisted by a large government budget surplus.

THE MONEY MUDDLE

During 1957 the Canadian economy was showing signs of weakness as its export markets softened. Early the following year, although the rate of unemployment was very high, there were indications that recovery was in sight. However, any recovery that there might have been proved abortive and the economy settled into a general state of stagnation. Throughout 1957 the Bank continued its policy of restraint and only after a loud public outcry did it begin to expand chartered bank cash reserves in the following year; the Bank's timing was probably off by as much as six months. When the Bank finally leaned towards expansion its policy was probably dictated more by government debt management than by its acceptance that easier monetary conditions were appropriate.

In the first part of 1958 considerable uncertainty had developed in the securities market. Adding to this uncertainty was the large requirement for government financing and the large amount of Victory Bonds which were approaching maturity. In order to allay the uncertainties in the securities market and also partly as an anti-inflationary measure, the government embarked on a program to convert its maturing debt into long-term issues. With the conversion program between July and September, the average maturity of the public's holdings of government debt increased from eight years to almost fifteen years. In order to facilitate such a large conversion the Bank of Canada embarked on a temporary expansionary policy. However, soon thereafter it withdrew support and interest rates rose to higher levels. Higher interest rates in Canada drove corporations, provinces and municipalities to the American capital markets and the consequent inflow of foreign capital moved the external value of the Canadian dollar higher. This only added to the difficulties Canadian exporters already faced with weakening international markets.

During 1959 and through the first half of the following year, the Bank of Canada continued to restrict the money supply. The money market now came to play an important role in mobilizing the remaining available cash. For example, the developing commercial paper market made available temporarily excess corporate funds to firms requiring short-term credit. The increase in the velocity of circulation of money that resulted as well as the sale of securities by the banks made further expansion possible.

The annual average unemployment rate exceeded 7 per cent in 1958 and it did not fall below 6 per cent until after 1962. Under these circumstances the Bank's reversion to monetary restraint after mid-1958 came under severe attack as being inappropriate during a period of high unemployment and as contributing to the capital inflow, an overvalued dollar and difficulties experienced by Canadian exporters. In August 1959 the Minister of Finance showed his concern over rising interest rates when he intervened in the Treasury bill auction by refusing bids "involving too high interest rates". However, James Coyne, then Governor of the Bank of Canada, vigorously defended the Bank's policy of restraint with an unprecedented number of public speeches. Toward the end of 1959 the Prime Minister and the Minister of Finance attempted to answer the Bank's critics by criticizing the chartered banks for not allocating credit equitably, and particularly for not looking after the needs of the small borrower — a criticism which was totally unjustified.

By 1960 it became apparent that the Bank's concern with inflation rather than with unemployment and slow economic growth was in conflict with the government's policy. Throughout 1960 and early 1961 the economy was again in a cyclical downturn. The Bank responded with only a mildly expansionary policy. Late in December the government, again somewhat belatedly, introduced a special budget which focused on the structural characteristics of the unemployment problem and foreign ownership and control of Canadian industry. The conflict between the Governor of the Bank and the government should have been resolved by the Governor's resignation, a move Coyne resisted even after requested to do so by the government in May 1961. The government now took a definite stand: it announced an expansionary fiscal policy and presented a bill to the House of Commons declaring vacant the position of the Governor of the Bank of Canada. Although the Commons passed the bill, it was defeated in the Senate. Coyne, feeling vindicated, then resigned. The Senate defeated the bill, not because of the monetary policy of the Bank, but because the government had sought Coyne's resignation over a disagreement with a decision of the Bank's Board of Directors to raise his pension on retirement.

On July 24, 1961, the Board of Directors of the Bank of Canada announced the appointment of Louis Rasminsky as Governor of the Bank. On the same day both he and the Minister of Finance issued statements setting forth the future relationship between the Bank and the government. The basic principle of this relationship is that the government has the ultimate responsibility for monetary policy, and a Governor of the Bank must either agree or resign.

FOREIGN EXCHANGE CRISIS 1962

After the Canadian dollar was set free in 1950 and the forces of demand and supply allowed to determine its value in the foreign exchange market, it moved upward and remained at a premium *vis-à-vis* its American counterpart. At first, this was primarily the result of the large inflow of foreign capital for investment in our natural resources. When this slowed down after the mid-1950's, the Canadian dollar continued to be at a premium due to the capital inflow from provincial, municipal and corporate borrowing in the United States to escape tight monetary conditions at home. Insofar as the high external value of the Canadian dollar discouraged Canadian exports and made foreign goods cheaper it added to the increasing difficulties of unemployment that were widely prevalent.

The publication in 1956 of the first comprehensive report on Canada's international investment position and the report of the Royal Commission on Canada's Economic Prospects opened up for public debate the question on the degree to which Canada was "peddling its birthright and mortgaging its future". In their election campaign in 1957 and again in 1958, the Conservatives took up this theme and followed a strong nationalistic line promising to reduce Canada's deficits on the current account of the balance of payments and its dependence on foreign capital. In the Speech from the Throne in November 1960, the Conservatives made good their promises when announcing that many of the existing incentives to foreign investment in Canada would be removed. In June of the following year the Minister of Finance further announced that steps would be taken not only to lower interest rates to make securities markets more hospitable for domestic financing, but also to employ the resources of the Exchange Fund Account to bring the dollar to a "substantial discount from the U.S. dollar and within a range appropriate to Canada's changing circumstances". These changes constituted an admission by the government that the external value of the Canadian dollar had been held excessively high by a tight monetary policy which had driven Canadian borrowers to foreign capital markets.

During 1961, and particularly after the appointment of Louis Rasminsky as the new Governor of the Bank of Canada, an expansionary monetary policy was initiated and interest rates moved to lower levels. This together with government intervention in the foreign exchange market caused the external value of the dollar to fall. However, with no clear indication of the level at which the government was prepared to stabilize the Canadian dollar chaotic conditions on the foreign exchange market ensued. It now became apparent that foreigners had lost confidence in the management of Canada's financial and economic affairs. The "Coyne Affair" mentioned earlier, foreign apprehensions over nationalistic sentiments particularly after the nationalization of the British Columbia Electric Company in August, and the unsettled political climate all contributed to the loss of confidence. Foreign capital now began to leave the country. The government attempted to decrease or halt the downward movement of the dollar on the foreign exchange market with support provided by the sale of foreign exchange. Finally, on May 2, 1962 in order to stabilize the dollar it established a par value for it with the International Monetary Fund at 92.5 cents U.S. A brief respite occurred, but with the election of a minority government in Canada, the outflow of foreign capital continued. On June 24 the Prime Minister declared an exchange emergency and announced that the government would defend the declared par value of the dollar. Within a few days foreign credits totalling the equivalent of $1,050 million (U.S.) were extended to Canada. These were composed of a drawing equal to $300 million (U.S.) from the International Monetary Fund (comprised of the equivalent of $100 million in pounds sterling, $80 million in German marks, $80 million in French francs, $20 million in Belgian francs and $20 million in Netherlands guilders), a line of credit of $400 million (U.S.) from the Export-Import Bank in Washington, a reciprocal currency arrangement in the amount of $250 million (U.S.) between the Bank of Canada and the Federal Reserve System in the United States and a comparable arrangement with the Bank of England in the amount of $100 million (U.S.). To provide further support to the dollar the government introduced an austerity program to reduce its budget deficits, imposed temporary import taxes on certain non-essential imports and restricted Canadian tourist expenditures abroad. The Bank of Canada again fixed the Bank rate and set it at 6 per cent. By September the crisis was over and the Bank gradually reduced the Bank rate.

BANK OF CANADA IN AN OPEN ECONOMY

By September 1962, confidence in Canada's foreign exchange position had been sufficiently restored to permit the easing of monetary policy thereby providing support for the economic expansion which had begun early in 1961. However, with a fixed exchange rate, the use of monetary policy for domestic stabilization purposes was subject to its prior use to defend the external value of the dollar. If the external value of the Canadian dollar was to be maintained foreign exchange reserves would have to be insulated against destabilizing capital flows and against the measures taken in the United States to deal with is own balance of payments problems.

The return flow of foreign capital soon after the exchange crisis enabled the Bank to reduce the Bank rate in stages and allow interest rates to fall to lower levels, a move that was desirable insofar as there remained a high rate of unemployment and much unused industrial capacity. However, in the months that followed, the Bank's policy of monetary ease had to be interrupted frequently by external events. The first such interruption came in October 1962, with the Cuban crisis. The Bank purchased $111 million of short- and long-term bonds for cash in three days, of which $73 million were bought in one day. The second came in the following year when the United States announced the introduction of new measures to solve its own balance of payments problems. In July the President made public draft legislation for the imposition of an Interest Equalization Tax which would make borrowing in the United States more expensive for foreigners. Canada immediately sought and was granted an exemption on new issues of Canadian securities on condition that the proceeds of borrowing in the United States would not be added to Canada's official holdings of foreign exchange reserves. The original target for official reserves was the June 30, 1963 figure of approximately $2,700 million. Later, after Canada had repaid its 1962 borrowing from the International Monetary Fund it was agreed that any net creditor position which Canada had with the IMF should be regarded as part of official Canadian reserves for the purpose of the agreement with the United States. Although the agreement placed an upper limit on Canadian interest rates relative to those in the United States, no difficulties arose for monetary policy at the time because easy credit conditions were still appropriate for the Canadian economy. In the period following the exchange crisis until after 1964, except for the brief interruptions already noted, the Bank was able to frame its policies on the basis of a firm foreign exchange position. Canada's foreign exchange reserves had increased as a result of large wheat sales to the Soviet Union and the exceptional rise in merchandise exports due to relative price stability at home and buoyant markets abroad.

A major external event affecting the Bank's policy was the American guidelines program announced in February 1965 to encourage the repatriation to the United States of short-term financial assets held in foreign countries by American corporations. Because the ensuing short-term capital withdrawals by Americans were offset by a simultaneous inflow of banking funds from overseas (itself an indirect consequence of the guidelines), Canada's reserve position remained relatively unaffected.

More serious consequences for Canadian monetary policy followed the new American guidelines policy announced in December 1965. Guidelines were established for the purchase of long-term foreign securities by American non-bank institutions and for direct investment abroad. Canada obtained an exemption on non-bank security purchases upon agreeing to reduce the target figure for foreign reserves from $2,700 million (U.S.) fixed in 1963, to $2,600 million (U.S.), and to aim at achieving a new lower level by the end of 1966. The latter commitment was honoured in May 1966 when the gold payment to the International Monetary Fund made as part of Canada's increased subscription to the Fund was considered as a reduction of the target level for reserves to $2,550 million (U.S.).

During 1964 as the slack in the economy was being used up the Bank of Canada started to manage the cash reserves of the chartered banks so as to reduce their liquidity. A further tightening of credit conditions was allowed in 1965. The Bank rate was increased in December and again in March 1966 when the Bank's restraining influence was supplemented by fiscal policy. However, both monetary and fiscal restraint were too late and too weak.[2] The Bank's reluctance to allow interest rates to rise much earlier and much higher is probably explained by external factors. A higher interest rate differential between Canada and the United States would have produced capital inflows which would have made it difficult for Canada to maintain the foreign reserve targets agreed upon with the United States. Under the circumstances, fiscal policy could have been used more vigorously to control demand pressures.

Beginning in the latter months of 1966 there were indications that the Canadian economy, like that of the United States, had entered a period of economic adjustment. Expenditures were beginning to moderate on consumer durables, on business investments in plant and equipment and on business inventories. Interest rates fell, a move welcomed by the Bank of Canada which provided the banking system with relatively generous cash reserves. Moreover, on January 30 the Bank rate was reduced from

---

2 In his 1966 annual report the Governor of the Bank, displaying a remarkable degree of frankness, admitted that the Bank might have shifted much earlier toward restraining the growth of demand.

5¼ to 5 per cent with a further reduction to 4½ per cent on April 7, 1967. However, before mid-year interest rates moved sharply upward, a movement resisted by the Bank of Canada because of domestic considerations and the need to avoid excessive foreign capital flows. The rise in interest rates reflected the community's expectations of a return to inflationary conditions and the prospective increase in demand for funds by all levels of government. With the inflationary psychosis which ensued business and financial institutions rebuilt their liquidity positions so as not to be caught short of the funds which they expected to require in the future. The increased liquidity preference more than offset any downward pressures on interest rates that might have resulted from the Bank of Canada's expansion of the monetary base. Another important influence on rising interest rates was the new competitive spirit among the chartered banks following the revisions to the Bank Act. By the autumn of 1967 their competition for short-term corporate funds had become so aggressive in terms of rates offered that the Governor of the Bank of Canada deemed it necessary to caution them that their activities "appeared to be uneconomic". On September 27 the Bank of Canada, after slowing down expansion of the banking system, increased the Bank rate to 5 per cent.

In the closing months of 1967 and the first months of 1968 external developments again came to play a decisive role in the policies followed by the Bank of Canada. In November 1967 after sterling had been devalued confidence in the stability of the world structure of exchange rates weakened. The Bank of Canada increased the Bank rate by one percentage point to 6 per cent on November 20 following discount rate increases by the Bank of England (by 1½ per cent to 8 per cent) and the Federal Reserve in the United States (by one half of one per cent to 4½ per cent). To relieve speculation on the American dollar Canada sold $100 million worth of gold to the United States and the Bank of Canada requested the banks and other financial intermediaries to refrain from extending credit on the purchase of gold and from facilitating the forward purchase of gold.

In January 1968 the United States announced a stringent new program to strengthen the measures in effect since 1965 to correct its balance of payments difficulties. The new program called for mandatory limits on direct investment abroad by American firms, further reductions in foreign credits held by American banks and financial institutions, restrictions on foreign travel by citizens of the United States, a reduction in some government expenditures overseas and measures to increase exports. Although the new program did not restrict Canada's access to the United States bond market it created apprehension that direct American investment in Canada and the balance of short-term capital flows between the two countries might be adversely affected. These apprehensions along with the still unsettled exchange conditions following the devaluation of the pound caused the Canadian dollar to come under severe selling pressure on foreign exchange markets. To defend the Canadian dollar the Bank of Canada increased the Bank rate effective January 21 by one percentage point to 7 per cent. At the same time the chartered banks agreed to discourage the use of bank credit by foreign subsidiaries endeavouring to transfer abnormal amounts of funds abroad or to replace funds normally obtained from parent companies. The United States Treasury issued a statement emphasizing that "the United States balance-of-payments program does not call for and is not intended to have the effect of causing abnormal transfers of earnings or withdrawals of capital by United States companies having investments in Canada". Although the foreign exchange markets continued to be uncertain, heavy selling of Canadian dollars subsided after these measures were taken.

In order to replenish its exchange reserves Canada used its foreign credit facilities. In January the Bank of Canada drew $250 million under its $750 million currency swap arrangement with the Federal Reserve in the United States. In February the Canadian government made a $426 million drawing from the International Monetary Fund. This consisted of $241 million in credit that Canada had in the past extended to other countries through the Fund and the $185 million equivalent to its gold subscription to the Fund.

As market uncertainties continued early in March, the government announced a new series of fiscal measures designed to restrain domestic demand and reinforce the defence of the Canadian dollar. On March 14, when the London gold market closed, the Minister of Finance asked the banks and other dealers to suspend trading in gold also. Gold trading was allowed to resume on April 3. The Governor of the Bank of Canada in agreement with the Minister of Finance requested the chartered banks and other financial intermediaries to discontinue swapped deposit transactions for the time being. Such transactions tend to put upward pressure on the spot Canadian dollar and downward pressure on the future Canadian dollar in the foreign exchange market. Without these pressures, corporations with forward commitments in American dollars are encouraged to wait for the conversion of Canadian dollars into American dollars and speculators are discouraged from speculating against the Canadian dollar. Moreover, insofar as swapped deposit transactions link Canadian short-term interest rates with rates in the Euro-Dollar market, a break in this link tends to insulate short-term interest rates in Canada from short-term rates in Europe. To show its determination to maintain the declared value of the dollar the government bolstered the country's international credit lines with $900 million in new facilities made available by the United States Export-Import Bank, the German Federal Bank, the Bank of Italy and the Bank for International Settlements in Basel, Switzerland.

The Bank of Canada displayed a remarkable degree of flexibility after 1962 in dealing with the problems of an open economy. The same can be said for some aspects of government debt management. The technique developed after 1962 of building up foreign exchange reserves by selling government bonds (denominated in American dollars) in the United States and of repatriating these bonds when the reserves tended to exceed target levels, gave substantial assistance to monetary policy. The direct purchase of American government bonds also served to stabilize reserves. Fiscal policy, on the other hand, has remained an inflexible tool for stabilization purposes in an open economy, and will probably continue to be inflexible as long as its use remains tempered by political expediency.

SELECTED READINGS

Binhammer, H. H., "Canada's Foreign Exchange Problems: A Review", *Kyklos,* Vol. 17, Nov. 4, 1964, reprinted in John J. Deutsch, *et. al., The Canadian Economy: Selected Readings,* rev. ed., Toronto, Macmillan, 1965.

Bank of Canada, *Annual Report of the Governor to the Minister of Finance,* various issues.

Brewis, T. N., *et. al.,* (eds.), *Canadian Economic Policy,* rev. ed., Toronto, Macmillan, 1965.

Cairns, James P., and H. H. Binhammer, *Canadian Banking and Monetary Policy,* Toronto, McGraw-Hill, 1965.

Canadian Trade Committee, *Canadian Economic Policy Since the War,* Montreal, 1966.

Economic Council of Canada, *Economic Goals for Canada to 1970,* Ottawa, December 1964.

McIvor, R. Craig, *Canadian Monetary, Banking and Fiscal Development,* Toronto, Macmillan Company of Canada Limited, 1961.

Senate of Canada, *Reports of the Special Committee of the Senate on Manpower and Employment,* Ottawa, Queen's Printer, Ottawa, 1961.

INDEX